PSYCHOLOGY OF READING

PSYCHOLOGY OF READING

Second Edition

Keith Rayner
University of California, San Diego

Alexander Pollatsek
University of Massachusetts, Amherst

Jane Ashby
Central Michigan University

Charles Clifton, Jr.
University of Massachusetts, Amherst

Ψ Psychology Press
Taylor & Francis Group
NEW YORK AND LONDON

First published 2012
by Psychology Press
711 Third Avenue, New York, NY 10017

Simultaneously published in the UK
by Psychology Press
27 Church Road, Hove, East Sussex BN3 2FA
www.psypress.com

Psychology Press is an imprint of the Taylor & Francis Group, an informa business

Library of Congress Cataloging in Publication Data
A catalog record for this book is available from the Library of Congress

British Library Cataloguing in Publication Data

A catalogue record for this book is available from the British Library

ISBN: 978-1-84872-943-8 (hbk)
ISBN: 978-1-84872-975-9 (pbk)

Cover design: Aubergine Design
Typeset in Sabon
by RefineCatch Ltd, Bungay, Suffolk, UK

Printed and bound in the United States of America on acid-free paper.

CONTENTS

PREFACE

Reading is a highly complex skill that is prerequisite to success in many societies where a great deal of information is communicated in written form. Therefore it is important to investigate this essential behavior. In the past 40 years a great deal has been learned about the reading process from research by cognitive psychologists. This book is our attempt to summarize that work and to put it into a coherent framework. For the most part, our emphasis is on the process of reading. We are most interested in how readers go about extracting information from the printed page and comprehending the text. We will not be as concerned about the product of reading (or what people remember from what they have read). Nor will we be centrally concerned with issues about how to teach children to read. Each of these issues is addressed in the book (the products of reading in Chapters 8 and 9, and learning to read in Chapters 10 and 11), but the major focus is on the moment-to-moment processes that a reader engages in during reading.

We have written this book for advanced undergraduates and beginning-level graduate students in psychology, although we would hope that our colleagues in cognitive psychology who are interested in the process of reading will find the work useful to them. We suspect that faculty and students in Schools of Education may not find the book consistent with some of their beliefs, but we would hope that they find our point of view interesting and even persuasive. We have tried to write the text so that it is accessible to students who do not have a background in psychology. The book is divided into four sections. In Section I we provide an overview of some relevant background information that should be particularly important to readers who do not have a background in cognitive psychology. In this first section we present an analysis of writing systems and also discuss how readers recognize words. Section II deals with the work of the eyes during reading. In this section we provide basic background information on eye movements during reading, and on the important topic of how words are processed during reading. In Section III our focus changes and we investigate how readers put words together to comprehend sentences and texts. This section contains chapters on inner speech, sentence parsing, and discourse processing. Section IV deals with learning to read, various types of reading disability, and individual differences in reading (including speed reading).

We have written this book so that the instructor need not cover all of it in a course. Chapters 3 through 5 form the core of the book and subsequent chapters presuppose having read them. Chapter 1, however, can be omitted or skimmed by students who have had an undergraduate course in cognitive psychology, and Chapter 2 can be omitted or skimmed by students with a background in linguistics. Chapter 6 provides a discussion of a model of eye movement control in reading (the E-Z Reader model) and might be viewed as somewhat technical and detailed for some readers. However, we think that for the reader interested in fully understanding our position it is important reading. Chapters 7, 8, and 9 provide essential reading on important aspects of skilled reading. Chapters 10 and 11 examine issues in reading development, Chapter 12 deals with dyslexia and reading disabilities, and Chapter 13 deals with individual differences in reading (including speed reading). Each of these sets of chapters forms a separate unit, any of which could be omitted without disturbing continuity. Chapter 14 provides a brief overview and summation of the book.

This book is a revised and updated version of Rayner and Pollatsek (1989), which was titled *The Psychology of Reading*. Many key points from the original version of the book have survived in this new version. Obviously one big difference is that two new authors have been added. All of the authors of the present work have read, commented, and added their voice to all of the chapters in the book. However, in terms of initial drafts of the chapters, the assignments were as follows:

KR: Chapters 1, 4, 7, 13, 14
AP: Chapters 2, 3, 5, 6
JA: Chapters 10, 11, 12
CC: Chapters 7, 8, 9, 14

We thank Paul Dukes, our editor at Psychology Press, for his enthusiasm and encouragement to write this book, and Mandy Collison, for her hard work and efficient handling of the production process. We also greatly appreciate the comments that we received from reviewers. Steven Frisson, Simon Liversedge, and Ed O'Brien reviewed the entire manuscript, and various sections of the book were reviewed by Denis Drieghe, Barbara Foorman, Catherine McBride-Chang, Manuel Perea, Erik Reichle, Tessa Warren, and Jinmian Yang. Likewise, comments by James Juola and Paul van den Broeck, who reviewed the entire earlier version, and by Morton Anne Gernsbacher, Simon Garrod, and Chuck Perfetti, who reviewed some sections of the earlier version, are also greatly appreciated.

We hope that the citations throughout this book point to the intellectual debt we owe to other researchers. If some references are overlooked we can only say that, like any authors, we had to pick and choose exactly what we would cite throughout the book. It will be obvious that we rely heavily on our own work in many instances and we apologize to colleagues if some of their work is not discussed. We also owe a debt of gratitude to many colleagues, graduate students, and post-doctoral fellows who have worked with us, mainly at the University of Massachusetts but also more recently at the University of California, San Diego. Their constant intellectual stimulation has always been central in our work.

The National Institute of Child Health and Human Development, the National Science Foundation, and Microsoft have been very generous in supporting our research on reading and we are pleased to acknowledge their support.

Finally, we owe a particular debt of gratitude to our families, and dedicate this book to them.

ABOUT THE AUTHORS

Keith Rayner is the Atkinson Professor of Psychology at the University of California, San Diego, and Emeritus Distinguished University Professor at the University of Massachusetts. He has published widely on topics related to reading, eye movements, and language processing.

Alexander Pollatsek is Emeritus Professor of Psychology and Research Professor at the University of Massachusetts Amherst. His primary research interests are in reading, word recognition, scene perception, and driving behavior. He has published widely in each area.

Jane Ashby is an Assistant Professor of Psychology at Central Michigan University. Her primary interests are in skilled reading, phonological processing, dyslexia, and reading development.

Charles Clifton, Jr. is Emeritus Professor of Psychology and Research Professor at the University of Massachusetts Amherst. He is primarily interested in psycholinguistics and has published numerous papers dealing with linguistic processing, parsing, and syntactic ambiguity.

PART I

Background Information

In the first three chapters of this book we present some information that will be necessary for you to understand many of the points we will stress in later chapters. In Chapter 1 some key concepts from cognitive psychology are introduced that will be used throughout the book. Cognitive psychology is the branch of experimental psychology that is concerned with how the mind functions and is structured, and in the past 40 years many cognitive psychologists have been very interested in studying how the mind works during reading. In Chapter 1 we introduce many of the basic conceptual tools that cognitive psychologists use when they study mental processes in general, and reading in particular.

Chapter 2 gives an overview of different writing systems that have been used or are in use throughout the world. As in Chapter 1, we also use Chapter 2 to introduce some key concepts from linguistics and psychology. Since the rest of the book will be dealing with the processes that result when readers attempt to decipher the marks on the page, it is essential we have some knowledge of the nature of the stimulus that is the starting point for all those processes. In addition, it is important to discuss the central characteristics of different writing systems, partly to gain some insight into written English and partly because people have misconceptions about many writing systems.

Note that we used the term *processes* a few times in the preceding sentences. This book is primarily about how the mind processes information during reading—we will have virtually nothing to say about motivational and emotional issues during reading. Our focus in this book is on the reading process when it is going well: for skilled readers who are motivated to read, either intrinsically or extrinsically. We assume that such skilled and motivated reading characterizes much of reading and, as you will see, it is enough of a challenge to explain it. However, beginning reading and certain kinds of reading disabilities will be the focus of Part IV.

Chapter 3 is one of the most important chapters in the book because there we first discuss how words are identified. In this chapter we describe some of the work cognitive psychologists have done to understand how isolated words are perceived, recognized, and understood. Some researchers are critical of this work, and suggest that identifying words in isolation is quite different from normal fluent reading. The position that we adopt (and which we will justify at various points throughout the book) is that skilled reading involves a number of component processes, and these component processes can be studied. That is not to say we believe that reading is merely identifying individual words and stringing the meaning of the words together; the process of comprehending text is much more complex than that. However, a moment's reflection should make it clear that, for reading to proceed at all efficiently, we must be able to recognize and understand the meaning of most (if not all) of the individual words that we encounter. In later sections of this book we explore the processes of recognizing words and understanding sentences in normal reading. The background information we present in this first section of this book will help you understand the complex information-processing activities that occur when you read and understand text.

1

INTRODUCTION AND PRELIMINARY INFORMATION

Reading is a complex skill that is pretty much taken for granted by those who can do it. About 35 years ago (when cognitive psychologists first became interested in studying reading) one of the authors, then a graduate student, got into an elevator in the Engineering Department at a famous university in the northeastern part of the United States with a copy of Smith's book *Understanding Reading* (1971) under his arm. A bright young freshman engineering student, upon seeing the book, was quick to remark: "Oh, *reading*; I learned how to do that 15 years ago." That remark is pretty consistent with most people's attitudes about reading. Those who can do it take it for granted. Yet it is an extremely complicated process that is sometimes difficult to learn (particularly in comparison to the ease with which children learn to speak). And illiterate adults find attempts to learn to read agonizingly frustrating.

Anyone reading this book is likely to be familiar with 30,000 or more words and can generally recognize most of them within a fraction of a second. A skilled reader can do this despite the fact that letters that make up the words are often printed in different type fonts. In the case of hand-written letters a reader can still read and comprehend despite rather dramatic differences in style and legibility. In being able to read and identify words in spite of all this variability, a skilled reader is able to perform a feat that is well beyond the capability of the most powerful computer programs available today. But this is not all. Skilled readers can identify words that have different meanings in different contexts. Consider the use of the word *boxer* in the following two sentences:

John knew the boxer was angry when he started barking at him. (1.1)

John knew the boxer was angry when he started yelling at him. (1.2)

These two sentences are identical except for a single word which disambiguates the appropriate meaning of the word *boxer*. The most common meaning for *boxer* is a dog. Since dogs bark and people don't, *boxer* in sentence 1.1 clearly refers to a dog. Likewise, in sentence 1.2 the fact that the *boxer* is yelling leads us to believe that the sentence is referring to a person. If you are very observant, you may have noticed that there are actually two ambiguities in sentences 1.1 and 1.2. Not only is the word *boxer* ambiguous, the pronoun *he* is also ambiguous. Most of the time, in sentences like 1.1 and 1.2, we associate the pronoun with the most recent antecedent. But if the sentence read

The boxer scared John when he started yelling at him.   (1.3)

we would most likely associate the pronoun with *John*. Yet notice even here that it is not completely clear who *he* is. If we replace the word *scared* with the word *attacked* we would probably understand the sentence quite differently.

The point of this discussion is that we can easily understand the meaning of these different sentences despite the fact that individual words have more than one meaning and pronouns can refer to more than one referent. Coupled with this fact is the observation that we can easily understand puns, idioms, and metaphors. For example:

John thought the billboard was a wart on the landscape.   (1.4)

Here none of us would believe that the literal meaning of the word *wart* was intended. We quite easily understand the sentence to mean that the billboard was ugly and spoiled the scene. And, just as we can easily comprehend the metaphor in sentence 1.4, so the idiomatic nature of

John hit the nail on the head with his answer.   (1.5)

presents a difficulty only for non-native readers of English who attempt a literal interpretation of the sentence and find it nonsensical. Thus, skilled readers are very good at combining the meanings of individual words to derive the meaning of sentences and paragraphs and short passages and books. Readers can draw inferences by relying on what they already know to help understand text, and from reading words they can form images of scenes and appreciate poetry.

We have been arguing that the feats of a skilled reader are truly impressive. Very powerful computers cannot do what a skilled reader can do; such machines (or more specifically the programs that run on them), despite tremendous memory capacity, would fail on many of the tasks we have mentioned that a skilled reader handles almost effortlessly. How do skilled readers accomplish this complex task? And how is the skill acquired? These are the central questions of this book. For the most part we will focus on the skilled reader in attempting to explain the process of reading. Our primary rationale is that we must understand the skill itself before we can understand how it is acquired, and our primary orientation in this book is a cognitive psychology/information-processing point of view (i.e., understanding the component mechanisms underlying reading). In the remainder of this chapter we attempt to place the rest of the book into perspective. We will do this by first discussing how researchers have historically viewed reading. Then we will present an overview of the human information-processing system, discussing what types of processing mechanisms may be involved in reading. First, however, we briefly discuss our perspective of reading—that of a cognitive psychologist.

What is cognitive psychology?

Cognitive psychology is the branch of experimental psychology that studies how the mind works. Cognitive psychologists are interested in a wide range of mental activities from attention to memory to language to learning concepts to decision making. Within the cognitive psychologist's toolbox there are a number of tools that are used to try and investigate the topic of interest. Foremost among these tools are what are now generally referred to as *behavioral experiments*; this term is usually used in contrast to *brain-imaging studies*. In behavioral experiments people (referred to as participants) are asked to perform some kind of task. The amount of time that it takes them to complete the task (or respond to a stimulus), and the response they actually make (and its accuracy), are typically measured. We will discuss various types of response time tasks relevant for reading in Chapter 3, but at this point we only want to alert you to the general technique. In brain-imaging studies, which have become very popular in the last 20 years or so, participants are asked to perform some type of task while correlates of neural activity in their brains are measured. The third main tool used by cognitive psychologists is that of producing computer simulations of the issue of interest. As we will see, a number of *models* or computer simulations that are relevant to understanding reading have appeared within the last few years.

We will extensively discuss behavioral techniques and the results of computational modeling throughout the book, but will briefly introduce brain-imaging techniques here (for a good overview, see Dehaene, 2009). Currently, two general types of measurement of brain activity are employed. Two of these techniques, positron emission tomography (PET) and functional magnetic resonance imaging (fMRI), are good at localizing where in the brain certain activities occur, but their temporal resolution is not very precise. They both measure the hemodynamic response, the increase in blood flow to active neurons in the brain. This response occurs over an approximate span of 6 seconds, varying across individuals. As we will see later, many of the important processes involved in reading occur within 250 milliseconds (or one quarter of a second), well beyond the temporal resolution of fMRI and other blood-flow-based brain-imaging techniques. Still, such studies have contributed valuable information about the location of the neural circuits involved in reading and are beginning to examine the neural bases of reading disorders, such as dyslexia (see Frost et al., 2009, for a review). Other neurophysiological measures have a millisecond temporal resolution fine enough for studying reading processes. Electroencephalography (EEG) measures changes in electrical potentials at the scalp that result when large networks of neurons prepare to fire in response to a stimulus. These event-related potentials (ERPs) reflect brain activity from the start of a task (e.g., word recognition), providing a continuous, online measure of the time course of cognitive processes as they unfold. Arguably the most complex brain-imaging technology is magnetoencephalography (MEG), which measures the magnetic consequences of electrical activity in the brain to offer not only fine-grained temporal resolution, but also high spatial resolution, which enables the localization of neural activity to particular areas in the brain. MEG studies have contributed novel findings about the location and time course of brain activity during word reading (see Halderman, Ashby, & Perfetti, in press, for a review). However, the highly sophisticated data acquisition and modeling techniques that MEG requires necessarily limit its use. As informative as these methods are, most of what is known about the complex processes involved in reading has been discovered in carefully controlled behavioral experiments. Thus, most of the research we discuss in this book is behavioral research.

Historical overview of reading research

The roots of cognitive psychology can be traced to the establishment of Wundt's laboratory in Leipzig in 1879. Workers in Wundt's laboratory were keenly interested in questions related to memory, perception, and action. Shortly thereafter there was considerable interest in the process of reading, which reached its apex with the publication of Huey's (1908) *The Psychology and Pedagogy of Reading*. A perusal of the chapters in the first part of his book (the part dealing with the psychology of reading) will reveal that the chapters bear a remarkable similarity to the topics covered in the present volume and most other modern books dealing with the psychology of reading. Huey and his contemporaries were interested in eye movements in reading, the nature of the perceptual span (how much information can be perceived during a fixation of the eye), word recognition processes, inner speech, reading comprehension, and reading rate. Huey's marvelously cogent and concise description of his findings and those of his contemporaries prior to 1908 is still a joy to read. Many of the basic facts we know about eye movements during reading were discovered by Huey and contemporaries using cumbersome and seemingly archaic techniques in comparison to the sophisticated devices currently available to record eye movements during reading. Yet their discoveries have stood the test of time and have held up when replicated using more accurate recording systems. A contemporary of Huey, the French oculist, Emile Javal, first noted that during reading our eyes do not move smoothly across the page as our phenomenological impressions would imply. Rather our eyes make a series of jumps (or *saccades* in French) along the line. Between the jumps the eyes remain relatively still, for about a quarter of a second, in what is referred to as a *fixation*.

In order to study how much information can be perceived in a single eye fixation, the tachistoscope was devised. The t-scope (as it is often called) is a device that allows an experimenter to control how much information is presented to a participant, as well as the duration of the exposure. The t-scope is now largely a historical relic, as it has been supplanted by high-speed computers with millisecond control. However, by varying the amount of information available in the t-scope and by presenting it for a brief duration (to preclude any eye movement), early researchers hoped to infer the size of the *perceptual span* or the area of effective vision during a fixation. Huey's book also describes classic experiments by Cattell (1886) and by Erdmann and Dodge (1898) on word recognition and two full chapters in the book are devoted to the role of inner speech in reading. Huey's lucid observations on inner speech and word recognition processes have largely stood the test of time.

Work related to the cognitive processes involved in reading continued for a few years after the publication of Huey's book. However, serious work by psychologists on the reading process pretty much came to a halt a few years after 1913. In that year the behaviorist revolution in experimental psychology began. According to behaviorist doctrine, the only things worthy of study by experimental psychologists were activities that could be seen, observed, and measured. Since cognitive processes involved in skilled reading cannot be observed and directly measured, interest in reading waned. To be sure, some well-known investigations of eye movements during reading by Buswell and Tinker were carried out between 1920 and 1960, but for the most part their work dealt with purely peripheral components of reading. That is, eye movements can be seen and directly measured, and were by Buswell and Tinker, but attempts to relate the activity of the eye to activity of the mind were virtually non-existent.

In essence, work on the cognitive processes associated with reading came to a standstill in the 1920s and did not begin again until the 1960s. Small wonder then that when Huey's book was republished in 1968 it seemed so relevant! We hadn't learned a whole lot more about the cognitive processes involved in reading in the 60 years between the initial publication of the work and the second appearance of the book. In addition to the work on eye movements during reading by researchers such as Buswell and Tinker, some work on reading did continue during the interval in question. But most of this work was conducted in Schools of Education where the primary focus is generally on more applied aspects of reading. Thus there was work on the most appropriate method to teach reading, and many of the standardized reading tests still in existence today were developed during that period. However, work on the mental processes associated with reading was almost non-existent.

Today many psychologists are interested in reading. Why did this change take place? The primary reason appears to have been the failure of behaviorism to account for language processing in any reasonable way. The promise of behaviorism was always that if psychologists could understand the laws of learning and behavior in simple tasks (like knee jerks and eye blinks), those laws would be generalizable to more complex tasks like language processing. In 1957, B. F. Skinner decided it was high time that the behaviorists produced on this promise, and he published *Verbal Behavior*, which was an account of language from a behaviorist viewpoint. The linguist Noam Chomsky (1959) wrote a scathing review not only of the book, but of behaviorism in general. In essence, Chomsky argued that behaviorist principles could not account for language learning or language processes in general. Around that same time, he also published *Syntactic Structures* (1957), which was a radical departure from traditional linguistic theory. In that work he suggested that the study of language and the mind are intimately related, and he presented an elegant theory of grammar. Many psychologists, disillusioned with behaviorism, became very interested in the relationship between Chomsky's theories of language and work on cognitive processes was underway after a hiatus of over 40 years.

A number of other factors contributed to the re-emergence of the study of cognitive processes around 1960. However, they are beyond the scope of our current discussion. Out of the burgeoning interest in language processes in general, interest in the reading process began once again around 1970. Since the mid-1960s numerous scholarly journals dealing with cognitive processes and human experimental psychology have been founded and nearly every issue of these journals contains at least one article related to reading. In addition, a number of textbooks dealing with reading appeared starting around 1985. Clearly there is now considerable interest among cognitive psychologists in studying reading.

Cognitive psychologists studying reading approach the issue from slightly different perspectives. Some have a background rooted in perception research and see the study of word recognition, for example, as a means to study perceptual processes or pattern recognition using well-defined stimuli. Others approach the study of reading with a background in memory processes and verbal learning theory, or a background in linguistics. They tend to approach the study of reading by examining comprehension processes. Still others are interested in reading in and of itself because they believe, as Huey pointed out over 100 years ago, that to understand what the mind does during reading would be "the acme of a psychologist's achievements, since it would be to describe very many of the most intricate workings of the human mind, as well as to unravel the tangled story of the most remarkable specific performance that civilization has learned" (Huey, 1908, p. 6).

It is our contention that this diversity of interests and backgrounds is healthy and can easily be accommodated within the information-processing approach because it views reading as a highly complex process relying on a number of sub-processes. Thus it is unlikely that there will be a single insight that will answer all of the questions about a complex skill like reading. Rather, breakthroughs will come from researchers working on different sub-components of the reading process. This is not to say that all of the information obtained by cognitive psychologists will not need to be put together, for it will. Rather, it provides a clear justification for examining different component processes of a complex skill.

Critics of the information-processing approach often argue that attempts to isolate component processes of reading result in tasks very unlike real reading. For example, to study word recognition processes cognitive psychologists often present a word for a very brief duration (say 50 milliseconds, one-twentieth of a second). A participant in such an experiment may be asked to pronounce the word or make some type of decision about it (Is it a word? Does it belong to a certain category of things? Is it larger than a breadbox?). In making decisions about the word, participants push one button for a *yes* response and another for a *no* response. Admittedly these tasks are unlike reading. Yet, to respond appropriately, participants may well be using the same processing mechanisms that they use during reading. Perhaps an analogy will help. Suppose we're interested in studying walking. If we study the motor responses that people make when they take two steps, critics may say "But that's not walking. When you walk you go a long way." True, but are the motor responses different when you take two steps? Not completely! What cognitive psychologists strive to do is set up experiments in which the same processing mechanisms are used in the task derived as in reading—sometimes more successfully than others. In the chapters in this book, as with our prior book, we will place the greatest weight on those kinds of experiments that most closely match the task of reading.

It is important to point out that the primary methodology of the cognitive psychologist is empirical experimentation. Theories and models of processes such as reading are also critically important because they help to formulate the kinds of research questions to be asked. But the ultimate test is always an experiment in which contrasting theoretical positions are tested against each other. Sometimes research is undertaken purely for information-gathering purposes (so as to form the groundwork for a model or theory). The point is that what we will take as evidence is not simply somebody or other's idea or intuition, but data obtained in well-controlled experiments. With these points in mind we now turn to a description of the human information-processing system.

Overview of the human information-processing system

In this section we will present an overview of the traditional view of the human information-processing system. We provide a stage analysis, but we caution you that not all cognitive psychologists would agree with the notion of distinct stages. Indeed, the best way to describe the human information-processing system has always been somewhat controversial (for some alternative perspectives see Anderson, 1976; Broadbent, 1984; Craik & Lockhart, 1972; McClelland & Rumelhart, 1986; Rumelhart & McClelland, 1986). The type of model that we will present consists of three distinct stages of processing (sensory store, short-term memory, and long-term memory) in a more or less passive system. We focus on phenomena and analyses that have stood the test of time, and overlook many current debates in cognitive psychology, since our primary intention is to give the flavor of the information-processing approach and to introduce terminology that virtually all cognitive psychologists use (modern textbooks, such as Eysenck & Keane, 2010, provide current overviews). In addition, some of the controversy over details is peripheral to understanding reading.

Figure 1.1 shows an example of a typical stage model of the human information-processing system. It consists of three stages, and each stage has distinct functions and characteristics. However, prior to discussing such a system, we must discuss something about the initial sensory registration of printed words by the eyes and subsequent pattern recognition processes.

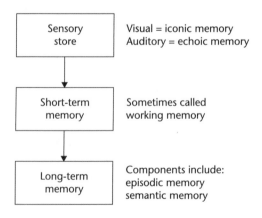

FIGURE 1.1   A simple overview of the human information-processing system

The retina and visual acuity

Vision depends on a pair of specialized organs (the eyes) whose neural receptors can be thought of as being a part of the brain that has extended outside of the cortex. Patterns of light falling on the sensory neurons in the retina result in the sensation of seeing. When you look at a page of text (like the one you are currently reading), you are not able to see all of the words on the page equally well. This is because of *acuity limitations*. In terms of acuity, a horizontal line of text falling on the retina can be divided into three regions: foveal, parafoveal, and peripheral. The foveal area subtends about 2 degrees of visual angle around your fixation point (the specific location that your eyes are centered on); the parafoveal area subtends about 10 degrees of visual angle around fixation (5 degrees to the left and right beyond the fixation point); the peripheral area includes everything on the line of text beyond the parafoveal region. Acuity is greatest in the center of vision (the fovea) and drops off markedly in the parafovea and even more so in the periphery. This is because of the anatomical structure of the retina.

The retina is composed of two types of receptors called *rods* and *cones*. The fovea consists almost entirely of cones. With increasing distance from the fovea, the density of cones decreases and the density of rods increases. Thus the peripheral region of the retina is composed entirely of rods. The parafovea contains a mixture of rods and cones. These two types of receptors serve dramatically different functions. The cones are specialized for processing detail and for acuity. In addition to permitting fine discrimination of detail, cones also serve in the discrimination of wavelengths or hue. The rods, on the other hand, are specialized for detecting movement and permit discrimination of brightness or shades of gray. The rods are particularly important for night vision; when you enter a dark room, at first you feel as if you cannot see anything. However, after a short while (unless the room is totally dark) your rods adapt and you can see.

The most important point to be gleaned from the description of rods and cones is that the acuity necessary for discriminating fine detail (as is necessary in reading) is available only in the center of vision. A simple experiment can demonstrate this quite clearly. If a word or letter string briefly appeared on a video monitor of a computer, and you were asked to say what word (or letters) appeared there, your accuracy in doing so would decrease as the stimulus was presented further from your point of fixation. In the experiment the stimulus is presented briefly enough (about 150 milliseconds or less) that it is virtually impossible for you to move your eyes to look directly at it. Figure 1.2 shows how performance in such a task would depend on how close to

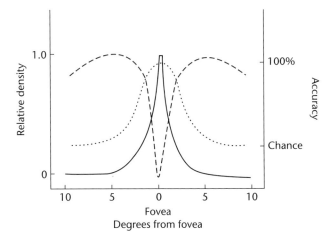

FIGURE 1.2 Relative density of cones (solid line) and rods (dashed line) across the visual field. Dotted line shows the accuracy of identifying a target word exposed briefly to the right or left of fixation

fixation the stimulus was presented. We have also plotted on the figure the relative distribution of rods and cones in the retina. Note that the accuracy function in our experiment is very similar to the distribution of cones in the retina. The purpose of this demonstration is to convince you that, in order to discriminate the fine details of letters and words as we read, we must move our eyes so as to place the fovea over that part of the text which we want to read.

Pattern recognition processes

After we move our eyes so as to place the fovea on the word or words that we want to read, pattern recognition begins. Actually the pattern recognition process for a word may have begun on the prior fixation when the word was in parafoveal vision, as we shall see in Chapter 4. What we are concerned with in this section is how the brain goes about recognizing the letters and words which must be processed for us to read. To take a simple example, how do we recognize the printed letter "A"? Two major theories of pattern recognition have been proposed (for a recent discussion see Grainger, Rey, & Dufau, 2008). The first, *template matching theory*, suggests that we have stored in our brains a representation of every pattern that we can recognize. Thus we recognize the letter A by comparing the pattern of excitation from the cells in the retina to a template stored in memory. If there is a match between representation and the stimulus, the letter A is perceived.

While template matching theory works quite well in computer pattern recognition devices that read letters and digits in highly constrained contexts, such as the digits that specify the code number on your checking account checks, it is well known (Crowder, 1982; Neisser, 1967) that such a system would fail to recognize instances of the letter A that were slightly deviant with respect to shape, size, or orientation, as Figure 1.3 shows. The major problem for the theory in its most rigid form is that it suggests we have a template for every variation of every pattern we are

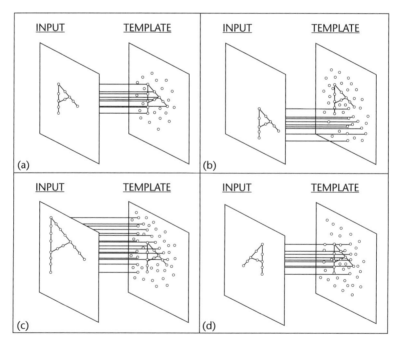

FIGURE 1.3 Illustration of the difficulties with a simple template-matching system for character recognition. (After Neisser, 1967.)

able to recognize. The simple pattern for the letter A, for example, can appear (as we mentioned earlier) in a number of different type fonts and handwriting variations. Yet we are able to recognize it quite easily. It seems unwieldy to think that we have so many patterns stored in our head.

One way to make the template matching theory more workable is to assume that, before comparisons of new input to a stored comparison take place, the input is "cleaned up" or normalized. The normalization process would separate essential information in the stimulus from most non-essential information. For example, variations in size could be taken care of before comparisons to a template occurred by transforming all images to a standard size. Accounting for variations in orientation prior to the matching process also seems quite reasonable. It is somewhat harder to understand how the normalization process would fill in missing gaps and eliminate fuzzy squiggles (as in handwriting) that are irrelevant to recognizing the pattern as the letter A.

While the normalization process gives plausibility to the template matching theory, the second theory, *feature detection theory*, is more parsimonious in accounting for how the pattern recognition process deals with such variation, and is generally considered to be a more viable account. The starting point for feature detection theory is the idea that there are many common elements for letters (consisting of horizontal, vertical, oblique, and curved lines) and that we analyze these component elements in recognizing a pattern. The letters C and G and the letters O and Q, for example, have a great deal of similarity and featural overlap. The distinguishing feature between the C and G is the horizontal line that is present in the G, but not in the C. The distinguishing feature between the O and Q is the oblique line present in the Q, but absent in the O. According to feature detection theory, when a letter is analyzed the first step is to prepare a list of its features and this list is compared with the list stored in memory. This process then is *analytical* in that we put together the different elements of the pattern until recognition occurs. Template matching theory, on the other hand, is more of a *holistic* process. As we implied above, the feature detection theory is considerably less cumbersome since the analytic processes would rely on a small number of features that are common to all type fonts (the distinguishing feature for C versus G remains invariant over different type fonts and handwriting styles), rather than having a different template for each style of print.

What type of evidence is there for feature detection theory? Three types are consistent with the theory: (1) physiological data from animals, (2) stabilized image research, and (3) visual search data. The best-known physiological evidence in favor of feature detection theory comes from work by Hubel and Wiesel (1962) on the visual system of the cat. Via electrical recordings, Hubel and Wiesel were able to examine the rate of firing of individual cells in the visual system as a function of what the cat was looking at. The most important finding from their work for our purposes is that they demonstrated that cortical cells in the visual system fired differentially depending on the stimulus. Cells that were specifically responsive to different visual shapes—line, edge, and slit detectors, as well as more complex detectors—were all discovered. It is easy to generalize from these results (although it should be done cautiously) and suggest that there are likewise feature detectors in humans specialized for firing when the various horizontal, vertical, oblique, and curved lines making up the letters of our alphabet fall in front of our eyes.

In a stabilized image experiment an image can be kept at the same place on the retina (via some rather sophisticated technology), so that to whatever extent the eyes move, the stimulus moves a corresponding amount in the same direction. Even when we are asked to hold our eyes very still, there is a slight movement or tremor of the eyes (called *nystagmus*). The stabilized image technique, however, keeps the stimulus on the same retinal location. Apparently, nystagmus is important for perception because under these conditions perception gradually blanks out so that the observer no longer sees the stimulus. If light remains in the same place on the retina, the cells in that location become fatigued and stop firing, and perception of the stimulus ceases. Movement of a stimulus or movement of the eyes will place a stimulus at a new location on the retina, resulting in new neural firing. What is interesting is that when the image is stabilized, perception does not blank out instantaneously. Rather, it is gradual. Coherent parts, including lines sharing the same orientation, disappear at the same time, as depicted in Figure 1.4. But the manner in which the stimulus fades is inconsistent with a template theory, and provides evidence for the importance of features at various levels of abstraction.

The third line of evidence for feature detection theory is the work on visual search originated by Neisser (1967). Figure 1.5 shows sample stimuli in the task. Participants are asked to find the target letter Z. It turns out that the letter Z is much easier to find (participants are over twice as

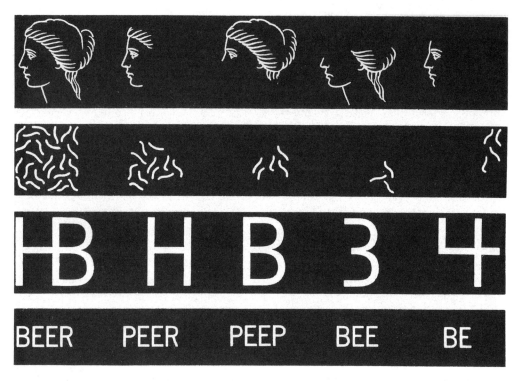

FIGURE 1.4 Perceptual fragmentation in "stopped images." The figures on the left are stimulus patterns; the others are typical products of fragmentation. (From Pritchard 1961.)

STANDARD CONDITION TARGET = Z	NONCONFUSABLE CONDITION TARGET = Z	CONFUSABLE CONDITION TARGET = Z
RYVMKF	CBSOGS	VMWNMW
PTHSHG	UBSQQQ	WYLKWV
GTVCBH	BQOUDG	XMWLLY
HUIRYD	SCDOBC	YXZWZL
KIREGD	CZOQUS	NMWYMN
GBZTBN	DUBCCD	YNLXLI
POLKRF	DOQUCB	MNWXMH
FTIEWR	CCOQOU	LYXWLT
...	...	...

FIGURE 1.5 Neisser's visual search task. A display is exposed and the subject must scan vertically, from top to bottom, until finding a target site. Time to reach the target is recorded as a function of the position of the target

fast) in the middle column than in either of the other columns. The reason, of course, is that the distractor letters in the middle column are all letters that are quite dissimilar to the target and do not share many features with it. Template matching theory would suggest that there should be no difference between the columns since the number of matches that must be made would be equivalent in each. However, feature detection theory can account for the result since virtually the same set of feature detector cells would be firing when the distractors are confusable whether or not the target letter was present. On the other hand, when the target is embedded in dissimilar letters, the cells that fire for the letter Z will only fire when the target is present.

While there are criticisms of feature detection as a theory of object perception in general, it provides a reasonably satisfactory model of how letters and words are processed. One issue that we have not discussed, which will become relevant in a later chapter, is whether pattern recognition processes occur in a *serial* or *parallel* manner. If information is analyzed serially, the pattern recognition processes occur one at a time. Thus, in Neisser's visual search task, feature analysis would occur for one letter and when it was complete would begin on the next and so on. If information is analyzed in parallel, the sensory information from various spatial locations is analyzed simultaneously. Thus, within acuity limits, all of the letters in each row in Figure 1.5 would be analyzed at once. The experiments on word identification that we will discuss in Chapter 3 also argue for parallel processing of letters within words. However, we will argue that serial processing is also important and occurs frequently in reading. Indeed, we will argue that words are identified serially as we read. In particular, we don't process the meaning of word $n+1$ (the word to the right of fixation) until we have processed the meaning of word n (the currently fixated word).

In this section we have argued that the pattern recognition processes that operate on print can best be conceptualized in terms of feature-analytic processes. We return now to a more detailed examination of the information-processing system depicted in Figure 1.1.

The sensory store

The lowest level in the information-processing system is generally referred to as the sensory store. For auditory information, the store is referred to as *echoic memory* (for a discussion see Cowan, 1984). For visual information, the store is referred to as *iconic memory*. Iconic memory is considered to be a temporary and transient memory store in which much of the information physically available in the stimulus is still available after the display has gone off.

In one of the most widely cited experiments in cognitive psychology, Sperling (1960) demonstrated the existence of a visual sensory store. He presented participants with three rows of four letters each for a brief duration (say 50 milliseconds or one-twentieth of a second). In a control condition participants were instructed to report as many of the letters as possible, and the average number of letters reported was 4.5. In the experimental conditions Sperling used a partial report technique in which he cued participants as to which row they should report. Thus if, after the display went off, participants heard a high-pitch tone they were to report the top row, a medium tone the middle row, and a low pitch the bottom row. The tone was presented at various delays after the disappearance of the letters from the screen. Sometimes the tone occurred simultaneously with the offset of the letters and sometimes it occurred up to a second after the letters disappeared.

Sperling's reasoning was that if we have an iconic memory (although he did not call it such), we should be able to use the cue to "read out" the letters from the cued row. If the tone actually occurred prior to the onset of the letters, then we would be able to use that information to focus on the relevant row. Sperling's question was whether or not we can use the cue to examine information after it has physically disappeared from before our eyes. If so, then we must have an iconic memory in which all or most of the information present in the stimulus is still available. In fact, what Sperling found was that participants could report on average 3.3 letters from the row that was signaled. Since the participants had no way of knowing beforehand which row was going to be signaled, it must be the case that participants could get roughly 3.3 letters from each of the rows, which means that they must have had approximately 10 letters available in their memory system.

Keep in mind that when participants in the control condition were asked to report as many letters from the display as they could, they averaged 4.5 letters. How do we account for the discrepancy between the cued partial report trials and the whole report condition? If we assume that iconic memory has a large capacity (say 10 letters from a 3 × 4 array) for a very short duration (perhaps a quarter of a second), and that the rate at which people can "read out" letters is slow (say 3 to 5 letters in a quarter of a second), then the discrepancy can be explained. If the letters are taken from the whole display, performance is limited by the "read out" process. On the other hand, if the tone cues the participants that only one row is relevant, then the participant has time to "read out" most of that row.

Since Sperling's demonstration there have been literally hundreds of experiments investigating the characteristics of iconic memory. This research has revealed that the primary characteristics of iconic memory are that (1) it has a large capacity, (2) it has a duration of roughly a quarter of a second, (3) it is pre-categorical (it stores physical form, not meaningful objects), (4) it is interfered with by new information, and (5) the "read out" rate is relatively slow.

The status and function of iconic memory have been highly debatable for some time (see Coltheart, 1980; Haber, 1983; Turvey, 1977). Some workers in the field have argued that it is an epiphenomenon of the highly sterile and controlled experimental laboratory; after all, when does a stimulus appear before our eyes for a fraction of a second only to disappear completely? Such individuals tend to argue that iconic memory, like our appendix, has no functional utility. Others would argue that all biological mechanisms are adaptive and just because we do not know for certain what function the icon serves, does not mean that it does not have a role in processing.

With respect to reading, it is not at all clear what function iconic memory might serve. Clearly, participants in iconic memory experiments are not reading in the sense that we would normally think of reading. In reading, the stimulus does not disappear from in front of our eyes after only a brief exposure (unless perhaps we try reading in a lightning storm or we are participants in "disap-pearing text" experiments, which we will describe in Chapters 4 and 5). At one time it was thought that something like an iconic memory might play a role in integrating visual information across the eye movements we make during reading. We will discuss that idea in Chapter 4, but to anticipate that discussion slightly the available evidence argues against such a conclusion. Indeed, the fact that we make eye movements so frequently is a problem for the utility of iconic memory in reading. Recall that the duration of iconic memory is roughly a quarter of a second, which is about the rate at which we make eye movements in reading. Given that information in iconic memory is disrupted by new information, and that eye movements occur at the rate they do, plus the fact that the information we want to read is available to us continuously (we can always look back with our eyes), it does not seem that iconic memory plays any role in reading.

At this point you may be asking yourself: If iconic memory plays no role in reading, why was it discussed in such detail? Indeed, why was it discussed at all? There are two reasons why we troubled to present the details of iconic memory. First, our primary purpose in this section is to present an overview of the human information-processing system. Earlier information-processing models of the reading process (Gough, 1972; Mackworth, 1972; Massaro, 1975; Mitchell, 1982) utilized the concept of iconic memory as the initial stage of registration of visual information during reading. Recall that we argued that at this point we are not so concerned about the extent to which the different stages are accurate and useful in understanding reading; they are presented more to give you a flavor for the approach. This brings us to our second reason for discussing iconic memory in such detail: the notion of *buffers* (or temporary storage units) in information processing turns out to be highly useful. Actually, the icon is little more than a buffer in which information is held for some later processing activity. The short life of the icon in fact suggests that the visual features of the print are of little use once the eyes are no longer looking at them. As we shall see later, the notion of a buffer has been very useful in various types of research related to the reading process. Hopefully, by discussing iconic memory in such detail, you will have a sense for how such a concept may be useful in designing experiments and theorizing about reading.

To summarize, iconic memory is the initial stage in an information-processing model. It is highly transient, but with a large capacity. We have also argued that its usefulness for understanding reading is limited since the stimulus is always available to us in reading. However, the concept of a buffer-like store has been very useful in experiments related to the reading process.

Short-term memory

According to the standard view of the information-processing system, the transient nature of iconic memory requires us to get information registered by the sense organs into a more permanent representation. The structure that contains this representation is *short-term memory* (or STM). Considerable information is lost before it can be transferred to STM because the "read out" rate from iconic memory is quite slow. However, a certain amount of information is transferred to STM. But STM has problems of its own. First, and most importantly, it has a limited capacity. The capacity of STM is about seven plus or minus two items (Miller, 1956). Notice that we said *items*, not letters, words, or digits. Indeed, we can learn to short-circuit to some extent the limited capacity of short-term memory by various types of *chunking strategies*. If we say the number 967835241 to you, and ask you to recall it in the same order that it was presented, then if you treat each individual digit as an item you will have a difficult time recalling it. Quite simply, for most people, STM will be overloaded. However, if you treat the number as three 3-digit numbers (967-835-241), then you will most likely be able to recall the number with 100% accuracy. Another way that we deal with the capacity limitation of STM is via a process called *rehearsal*. When you look up a telephone number in the phone book, you often find yourself repeating (rehearsing) it over and over to yourself (often silently, but sometimes aloud) so that you won't forget it. Such a strategy is another way to hold information in STM.

Notice also that we said you often repeat the number over to yourself silently. For a long time it was considered that STM was exclusively an acoustic store. That is, even information coming in the visual modality was assumed to be recoded into acoustic or auditory information. The reason for this was that the kinds of errors that participants make in recalling information in STM tended to be related acoustically, not visually, to the information actually presented. We now know that there are visual and semantic codes in STM. Still, for linguistic stimuli, short-term memory is primarily acoustic, as evidenced by the fact that we try and remember phone numbers from the telephone book by rehearsing them subvocally. This aspect of short-term memory turns out to be particularly important for understanding the role of subvocal or inner speech in reading.

The fact that we engage in various strategies (some of them unconscious) to short circuit the limited capacity of STM has led some workers to talk about a *working memory* (Baddeley & Hitch, 1974) rather than a passive store. That is, short-term memory can be considered a flexible workspace whose limited capacity can be allocated to either storage or processing. Information in STM can remain there as long as it is being worked on. Working memory, in the sense of a flexible workspace for processing, is also heavily involved in reading. Words are integrated in this memory, and as we shall see later, comprehension processes are initiated here.

To summarize, short-term memory has a limited capacity. However, we can hold items there for long periods of time via rehearsal. We also develop efficient strategies for dealing with the limited capacity. STM is also primarily acoustic in nature. Whereas iconic memory was argued to have limited usefulness in understanding reading processes, the characteristics of short-term memory may be important in understanding inner speech in reading and comprehension processes.

Long-term memory

The rate at which we can set up programs to transfer information from STM to *long-term memory* (or LTM) is relatively slow in relation to the rate at which new information enters STM, Because of this, considerable information is lost. However, it is generally believed that once information enters LTM it is stored there permanently. Patients under a local anesthetic whose brain is electrically stimulated can remember things they long since thought they had forgotten, and even relive memories of events that occurred a long while in the past (Penfield & Roberts, 1959). Information in LTM is not organized in a haphazard fashion. Indeed, LTM is highly organized and much of the material that we cannot retrieve has been mislaid, not lost. Thus the major problem with LTM is getting the appropriate retrieval key to access information stored there. This is not surprising given the vast amount of new information we process and store in LTM each day. In addition there is evidence that the new information we learn interferes with our ability to retrieve previously stored information. Likewise, information already stored in LTM can interfere with retrieving newly learned information.

Many cognitive psychologists find it useful to distinguish two types of long-term memory: *episodic memory* and *semantic memory* (Tulving, 1972). Episodic memory is the memory for sequences of events in your life. Semantic memory, which is more important for understanding reading, contains the general knowledge you have. A part of semantic memory that is important for reading is the *lexicon* (which is like a dictionary in your head). The lexicon, which like LTM itself is highly organized, contains the meanings of the 30,000 or more words that you know. The goal of most reading is to understand something new and to store the gist of it in LTM. In order to do so involves processing the meanings of the words we know, or accessing our lexicon in LTM. Further, to understand idioms, metaphors, and the like, we have to use general world knowledge that we have stored there. And, when authors are a bit vague, we must make inferences based on what we already know to understand their point.

Selection of information

An issue relating to the conceptual framework that we have presented is how information is selected to be passed on to the next stage of processing. In vision, of course, the eyes are a major device for selection. You point your eyes at those stimuli you want to process and turn your back on those you want to ignore (metaphorically speaking!). However, as we discussed earlier, this overt selection process is not all-or-none: while stimuli seen in extrafoveal vision are processed less well than those in foveal vision, they are processed.

However, pointing the eyes is not the only selectional mechanism in vision. In our discussion of Sperling's experiments we tacitly assumed that there was a selection process which could help "read out" the appropriate row of letters. A great deal of research has documented the reality of such a covert mechanism of spatial attention. In essence, human and animal participants can respond to visual stimuli more quickly and accurately if they are cued as to where in extrafoveal vision these stimuli will be, even when they do not move their eyes (Posner, 1980). Furthermore, the locus of this attentional system in the brain is becoming increasingly well understood. We will return to these selectional issues in the context of reading in Chapters 4 through 6.

In contrast to the above attentional mechanisms, the processes by which information is selected to go to LTM (or is made more retrievable from LTM) are less well understood. Clearly, factors such as your motivation to remember the material, the length of time it is in STM, and the meaningfulness of the material all affect how well you will remember it later. We will touch on these issues again when we discuss comprehension of discourse in Chapter 9.

The concept of processing stages

An assumption of the model we have outlined above is that there are discrete processing stages. That is, it is assumed that information is processed in one stage, and only when that processing is completed is the information shipped on to the next stage. This assumption underlies a great deal of cognitive psychology because processing will be much easier to study if it can be broken down into simpler components.

Sternberg (1969) proposed a widely used test to determine whether such a stage notion is valid. The test assumes that the dependent variable used to study mental processing is response time, or the time between the presentation of a stimulus and the time to execute a response. We can best explain the idea with an example from Sternberg's experiment. He used a memory search task in which participants were initially given a *memory set* (1 to 6 digits) to hold in memory, and then they had to indicate if a *probe* digit (which was presented visually) was in the memory set. His finding was that the time to determine whether the probe digit matched one of the items in the memory set increased linearly as the memory set got bigger. In fact, the time increased by about 40 milliseconds with each additional memory set item, suggesting that it took participants 40 milliseconds to compare each additional memory item with the probe.

Thus a measurable search process appears to be occurring in STM. What would happen if the probe digit was presented in "visual noise" (i.e., embedded in a lot of random dots so that it was harder to see)? If we view the process of identifying the digit as a stage prior to searching STM, then the digit should take longer to identify when presented in noise, but the rate of search in STM should be unaffected since the identification stage would be complete regardless of whether the digit was "clean" or "noisy." In contrast, if identification and search are not discrete stages so that visual noise is still part of the item being compared to the memory set items, one would expect that the search time per item would increase. In fact, Sternberg obtained the former result—overall times increased with a "noisy" probe digit but memory search times did not—and concluded that identification of the digit was a stage prior to STM search. The basic logic of this experiment has been used widely in cognitive psychology. It will serve us as a useful guide at several points in the book (although we must note that it has not gone unchallenged; see Townsend, 1976)

The reality of information-processing models

If this is your first exposure to information processing, you may be asking yourself to what extent the different structures presented in the model have been localized in the brain. The answer is that, for the most part, they haven't. Neurophysiologists working on brain functions have found chemical changes in the brains of animals during learning stages that could correspond to STM functions. In addition, studies of brain localization have revealed different functions of different parts of the cortex (especially language functions). However, there is not likely to be an anatomical division between STM and LTM. Nor have we localized the lexicon in the cortex, although recent brain-imaging studies have identified areas of the brain that seem to be specialized for language processing (Bornkessel-Schlesewsky & Friederici, 2007).

In fact, the concept of the *mind* is a rather abstract entity. We think of it as the executor responsible for cognitive activity, which presumably can be ultimately explained in terms of the structure and function of the brain. The task of the cognitive psychologist is to learn how the mind is structured and functions. If it were possible, perhaps an ideal way to study reading would be to open up a reader's brain and observe what kinds of activities and changes occurred during reading. But we cannot do this. Furthermore, as we noted earlier, some brain-imaging techniques currently available are relatively slow with respect to moment-to-moment processes, and those that do provide real-time information about brain processes often suggest that these processes occur too slowly to actually be the basis of behavioral phenomena (Sereno & Rayner, 2003). Thus cognitive psychologists are forced to infer characteristics of how the mind works in skilled cognitive tasks like reading on the basis of various types of evidence that we can accumulate. In a sense then, a cognitive psychologist is like a detective searching for clues to how the mind works. The type of structures presented in Figure 1.1 and elsewhere in this book serve as a convenient way of hypothesizing about how the mind works and then summarizing what we know. Throughout this book we will present evidence accumulated by cognitive psychologists about how the mind works in reading and we will frequently use the convention of presenting information-processing flow diagrams such as that presented in Figure 1.1 to summarize what we know. But it would be a mistake to think of these structures as necessarily mapping directly onto parts of the brain.

Brain function and reading

In the previous section we differentiated between the brain and the mind. While much of our focus will be on how the mind works in reading, we also know that there are specific brain functions related to reading. In this section, we briefly review some of them.

Information registered on the retina is transmitted to the visual cortex. The cerebral cortex of humans is divided into two hemispheres that have different, but complementary, functions. Some functions are bilaterally represented in the brain. For example, there is a visual area at the back of both of the hemispheres. However some areas, particularly associated with language processing, seem to be localized almost exclusively in only one hemisphere. For most people, regions of the left hemisphere are responsible for language processing. Regions of the right hemisphere, on the other hand, are specialized for non-verbal, spatial processing. In some left-handed people the functions of the two hemispheres of the brain may be reversed. The two hemispheres are connected by a bundle of nerve fibers called the corpus callosum.

We know about the different functions of the two hemispheres from three types of evidence. First, experiments on normal participants often take advantage of the fact that information seen in the left half of the left visual field of either eye arrives initially in the right hemisphere, and things seen in the right half of the visual field arrive initially in the left hemisphere. Material presented to the center of vision is simultaneously available to both hemispheres of the brain. With respect to the left and right ears the same pattern holds as for the presentation of information to the left or right of fixation in the visual field; information presented to the right ear goes primarily to the left hemisphere and information presented to the left ear goes primarily to the right hemisphere. From experiments in which stimuli are briefly presented in the left or right visual field (or left or right ear), we know that words are processed more efficiently when presented in the right visual field (implying left hemisphere processing), whereas faces and pictures are processed more efficiently when presented in the left visual field. From such experiments it is often argued that the left hemisphere operates in a serial and analytic fashion, whereas the right hemisphere operates in a parallel and holistic fashion, although there is no compelling reason for this conclusion.

The second way in which we know about the functions of the two hemispheres is from research on brain-damaged patients who have one of the two hemispheres missing (from birth or due to brain injury) or from "split-brain" patients whose corpus callosum has been severed as a treatment for epilepsy. With respect to language the basic evidence is that, if certain regions of the left hemisphere are damaged, in most people language functions are impaired, while right hemispheric damage does not produce language impairment. For the "split-brain" patients the evidence is that linguistic information that is put into the left hemisphere is processed normally, whereas there is little comprehension of linguistic information put into the right hemisphere. Recently a great deal about the reading process has been learned by examination of patients with brain damage (and known lesion sites). In Chapter 11 we will review the evidence obtained from such patients.

Finally, experiments using brain-imaging techniques (such as PET, fMRI, and MEG) have yielded evidence regarding areas of the brain involved in language processing. We will omit the details of the physiology, such as the location of language-specific sites; the interested reader should consult Frost et al., 2009; Pugh et al., 1996.

What is reading?

In this chapter so far we have presented preliminary information necessary to understand how cognitive psychologists think about reading. This brings us to a critical question. What do we mean by reading? It is obvious that, to many people, reading is an all-encompassing activity that can take on different forms. For example, when you look at a map to tell you how to get from one place to another, are you reading? When you proofread a paper for typographical mistakes, are you reading? When you look at a computer program to find your programming error, are you reading? When you scan a newspaper for the latest results of the stock market, are you reading? We will take a conservative view here that none of these activities is what we have in mind as reading. It is also obviously the case that when you read a novel on a 5-hour airplane trip you may at times be reading slightly differently than when you read this book: 4 hours into your trip you find that you are only half-way through the book so you start skipping over sections of the book that seem redundant, looking only for relevant and new information so that you can finish it before reaching your destination. You would have a rather difficult time understanding a textbook if you read in such a fashion, yet we can generally read most novels in that way and still end up understanding the story. In our chapter on speed reading we will discuss skimming and the adjustments the reader makes under such conditions. However, apart from that chapter, we will focus on the rather careful type of skilled reading that occurs when you read to comprehend, as when you read a textbook or newspaper article or a narrative in which you do not skim parts of the text. Our focus will also be largely on silent reading. While it is clearly the case that beginning readers spend more time reading aloud than silently, for the most part most people spend far more time reading silently than reading aloud.

It would be easy at this point to get into a lengthy argument about what is and is not reading. We do not wish to do so. Hopefully, it is clear what we have in mind by reading. If forced to provide a definition of reading, we would probably say something like: *reading is the ability to extract visual information from the page and comprehend the meaning of the text*. By focusing on the careful reading of a newspaper article, for example, we do not wish to imply that the other activities that we mentioned are not interesting. Our bias is that activities such as proofreading and skimming probably involve strategies and processes that are different from normal silent reading. Occasionally we will examine such tasks. However, our central concern is how people read during normal silent reading.

This brings us to a second critical question. What is the best way to study reading? The answer to the question is that it depends on which aspect of the reading process you are interested in studying. We mentioned earlier that cognitive psychologists interested in word recognition generally present isolated words to people on a video monitor and ask them to make some kind of judgment about or response to that word. We shall discuss such tasks in detail in Chapter 3. Other researchers interested in the role of inner speech in reading have devised clever techniques to determine its role in understanding written language. If researchers are interested in how much of the text the reader comprehended, then they would want to examine how well readers can answer questions about the content of the text. Techniques used to study inner speech and comprehension will be discussed in Chapters 7 through 9.

If the goal is to study the cognitive processes that occur during normal silent reading of text on a moment-to-moment basis, then any technique that has readers do something different, such as naming words in isolation or reading text out loud, may significantly distort the component process in silent reading one wishes to study, such as word identification or the role of acoustic codes in reading. While it is plausible that the components of reading do not change radically from task to task, there is no guarantee of it. Thus the relevance of any technique is an open question if we do not know how the processes work during silent reading of text.

This brings us to our favored technique for studying cognitive processes during actual silent reading—eye movement recording. Recording of eye movements has a long history in experimental psychology, as should be clear from an earlier section of this chapter. In the last 30 years eye movement data have been widely used to infer moment-to-moment cognitive processes during reading (Rayner, 1978a, 1998, 2009). It is now fairly clear that where readers look, and how long they look there, provides valuable information about the mental processes associated with understanding a given word or set of words (Rayner, 1978a, 1998, 2009). Eye movement recording can be accomplished in a variety of ways, but often involves shining a beam of invisible (infrared) light onto the eye that is reflected back from the cornea or retina to a sensing device, or using an infrared camera to form an image of the pupil whose location is determined by a computer. With this methodology readers are free to look at any part of the text for as long as they wish. As mentioned above, the technique also has a great deal of ecological validity in that participants in eye movement experiments are actually engaged in the task we wish to study, namely reading.

This is not to say that eye movement recording is free from criticism. In order to unconfound movements of the eyes from movements of the head, it has often been necessary to stabilize the head. This is often done via the use of a bitebar (which consists of dental compound that is very soft when a participant initially bites into it, but then quickly hardens to provide a dental impression that keeps the head still). In other cases forehead and chin rests are used and participants generally read from a display placed directly in front of them. Some critics have suggested that the rigid constraints on head movement, plus the fact that in reading outside of the eye movement laboratory we often look down at the text (rather than straight ahead), will lead to different reading strategies. It has even been suggested that the mere fact that our eye movements are being recorded will make us conscious of them and lead us to do something different when we read under such circumstances. Our impression is that these concerns are all ill-founded. Indeed, Tinker (1939) demonstrated quite some time ago that the reading rate of participants when asked to sit in a soft easy chair and read a book chapter did not differ from the reading rate obtained in the eye movement laboratory. Furthermore, recent advances in eye movement technology have made it possible to record eye movements without stabilizing the head in any way (although generally greater precision is available when the head is stabilized).

All of the authors of this book have been participants in experiments using eye movement recordings. Our firm impressions are that reading in the eye movement laboratory is virtually the same as reading outside of it, and it is definitely our sense and intuition that this latter technique provides a much better approximation of reading itself than any other technique. But we do not want to argue that eye movement recording is the only way to study skilled reading. Many of the techniques that will be mentioned throughout this book provide useful information and the best type of evidence would be converging data in which information obtained from a number of the techniques converge on the same answer to a given question. Our intention is to use converging evidence from a number of sources to understand reading, but the data that will receive the greatest emphasis from us will be those that are obtained while the participant is silently reading connected text, rather than simply being engaged in one of the clever tasks cognitive psychologists have devised.

Models of reading

While there are many facts about reading that have been learned by cognitive psychologists (and our emphasis in this book will be to rely on the facts that have been learned), many people find cognitive psychology somewhat frustrating because there is often conflicting evidence on a single issue. There are many reasons why this may be the case, including the fact that our experiments are sometimes not very good. But another reason is that cognitive psychologists often have different models or theories of how some mental process works. What are models and theories? Let's borrow from Carr (1982) in defining these two concepts. A theory is a set of principles (assumptions or rules or laws) that together constitute a verbal or mathematical description of an interesting phenomenon, and an explanation of how or why the phenomenon happens. A theory defines the important characteristics of a phenomenon that are then included in a model of the phenomenon. A model represents a description of the major working parts of a real-life process (such as reading). The description captures the most important characteristics of each part's operation, although it might leave out large amounts of detail. Currently there are a number of models of the reading process that (in our opinion) vary in the extent to which they capture important aspects of the skill (Rayner & Reichle, 2010; Reichle, 2012).

We shall not attempt to describe the various models of reading here (see Chapter 14). Rather, let us simply characterize them as being primarily (1) *bottom-up*, (2) *top-down*, or (3) *interactive* models. Incidentally, these three types of models are characteristic not only of the reading process, but also of descriptions of most of the tasks and phenomena that cognitive psychologists typically investigate. Some books on reading (Just & Carpenter, 1987; Smith, 1971) begin by presenting their audience with a model of reading and then interpreting relevant evidence within the framework of that model. Other books (Crowder, 1982; Crowder & Wagner, 1992; Downing & Leong, 1982; Gibson & Levin, 1975) manage to avoid presenting a model of reading altogether and present only the facts as interpreted by the authors (in some cases the rationale is that a single model cannot capture the complexities of reading or the varieties of types of reading). Still other books (Mitchell, 1982; Perfetti, 1985; Rayner & Pollatsek, 1989; Taylor & Taylor, 1983) present evidence first and then, on the basis of the evidence, describe a model of the reading process. In general our strategy will be to present you with the facts as we see them. Our bias is that there is a danger in presenting the model first and then fitting the facts to the model because such a strategy often makes it sound as if we know more than we really do. We also suspect that researchers often become committed to a particular model of the reading process and then the model itself becomes more important than the data that are collected. However, as will be clear in Chapter 6, we will rely very heavily on a model of eye movement control in reading that we developed, and will use it as a convenient way of presenting some critical issues to you.

We feel that most models are little more than general frameworks for understanding research on reading that provide some biases on which aspects of reading are really important. Our discussion of models below will indicate many of our biases and provide the "bare bones" of a general framework. This framework will acquire more detail as we progress though the book. In the final chapter, Chapter 14, we will briefly try to summarize the framework that has evolved throughout the book.

In bottom-up models (Gough, 1972), most information flows in a passive manner through the human information-processing system. The major idea is that this flow of information is very fast and that knowledge we have stored in memory has little impact on how the processing takes place. In contrast, proponents of top-down models (Goodman, 1970; Smith, 1971) feel that the passive flow of information through the processing system is relatively slow because there are numerous bottlenecks (places where the architecture of the system forces us to slow down). Accordingly, to short-circuit these bottlenecks these models stress that we rely heavily on information stored in memory (general information that we have about the world) to help speed up our processing. The primary way in which readers short-circuit the information-processing bottlenecks is to formulate hypotheses about what they will next read. This view of reading, often referred to as the *hypothesis testing model* of reading, was once very popular. However, a great deal of evidence now suggests that the visual processing of text is actually very fast and the extent to which readers engage in hypothesis testing or guessing behaviors seems to play a minimal role in the process of reading. We will return to this issue at various points throughout the chapters that follow. For now, let us simply point out that we believe a bottom-up view of reading more accurately characterizes much of the available evidence. Having said this, we hasten to point out that we do not think top-down processes play no role in reading. They clearly do. Perhaps our model of the reading process can best be described as a bottom-up model in which the reader gets some help from top-down processes.

We have told you briefly what bottom-up and top-down models are, but we have not yet mentioned interactive models. Interactive models (Just & Carpenter, 1980; McClelland, 1986; Rumelhart, 1977) allow for all sorts of communications between top-down and bottom-up processes. These types of models have become very popular in the last 30 years. Proponents of these models claim that such models are very good in accounting for the data on reading processes. Critics of these models argue that, while they may be able to account for lots of data, they are very unconstrained and hence do not predict in advance very well what the outcome of any particular experiment might be. In contrast, the major virtue of most bottom-up models is that they are very good at making clear predictions about performance measures.

The view of reading that we will be presenting to you will largely be a bottom-up view, but with some influences from top-down processes. Notice that we have used the word *process* a number of times in this discussion. Elsewhere in this book we will make a distinction between the *process* of reading and the *product* of reading. The product of reading is the information that gets stored away in memory; it is what gets comprehended during reading. The major emphasis in this book is on the process, rather than the product, of reading (although the latter will be discussed in Chapters 8 and 9) because, from our point of view, the most important thing to understand about reading is the process. This is a bias that not everyone would agree with. For example, educators would undoubtedly argue that knowing the best way to teach children to read is more important than understanding the process of skilled reading. While we appreciate their opinion, our sense is that if we can understand the process of skilled reading, we may well be able to provide useful information to educators about the end product of what they are trying to teach (Rayner, Foorman, Perfetti, Pesetsky, & Seidenberg, 2001, 2002). In essence, we believe that understanding the end product (skilled reading) should provide firm conclusions about how to instruct novices to become skilled in the task. Hopefully our discussion in Chapters 10 and 11 will highlight some of the ways that we believe research has made clear how children should be instructed to learn to read.

Some cognitive psychologists who study the product of reading would also want to argue with us concerning our bias toward understanding the process of reading. To their way of thinking, what people remember from what they read may be more important than how they go about the process of reading. However, our response to such a point is that understanding the process by which some mental structure is created almost logically entails understanding that structure. In contrast, understanding what gets stored in memory may not reveal much about the processes that created the structure. Thus understanding what is in memory as a result of reading discourse may not be unique to reading—essentially the same structures may be created when people listen to discourse. We are not saying that understanding the product of reading and how that product gets remembered is not important. It's just that reading is a remarkable skill that must be understood quite apart from issues like general comprehension skills and intelligence.

2

WRITING SYSTEMS

Perhaps the place to start our detailed discussion of reading is at the beginning of the reading process: the printed (or written) page. A careful analysis of the information contained in the squiggles on the page will help in understanding the task that confronts the reader. In the course of this analysis we will introduce several linguistic concepts relating to both spoken and written language that are necessary for a meaningful discussion of reading. A general discussion of writing systems will also help to put the task of reading English in a broader context.

Before plunging into a discussion of writing systems we might hazard a definition of what writing is. At first blush the exercise seems silly, since we all know what writing means. One definition is that writing "is the 'fixing' of spoken language in a permanent or semi-permanent form" (Diringer, 1962, p. 13). It seems that such a definition is too broad, since we wouldn't want to count a tape or phonograph recording of speech as writing, even though it may serve roughly the same function as a written transcript. Somehow we feel that writing implies that the record is to be perceived by the eyes. What about Braille? Most people would call that a writing system, so that the eyes aren't necessary. Will any code do? For example, is listening to Morse code reading? We doubt that most people would accept that. So, inherent in writing is some sort of spatially arranged message that is usually perceived by the eyes, but could be perceived by a tactile sense. (While reading systems for blind people, such as Braille, are certainly writing systems, they fall largely beyond the scope of this book since the perceptual system for encoding the message is so different than in ordinary reading.)

The major problem in defining writing comes in trying to determine whether we agree with the requirement that writing "fixes" speech, and if so, what we mean by it. Some people might find that requirement too restrictive, and deem as writing any visual message that conveys meaning. That definition seems too loose, since most people would probably not call a painting such as the "Mona Lisa" writing, but would reserve the term writing for graphic displays that are understood as a code for a spoken message. There is disagreement, however, about how literal a transcription of the spoken word the graphic display has to be, in order to count as writing.

Consider the following communication: there is a picture of Christopher Columbus followed by a picture of three ships followed by 80 suns followed by a picture of an island, etc. Most people in our culture would probably be able to deduce that these pictures stood for a narrative about Columbus (or some explorer) sailing across the ocean, taking many days to do so, discovering land, etc. Is such a representation writing? This appears to be a borderline case: some people would classify it as writing and others wouldn't. To those who would accept it as writing, the necessary features are that there is an ordered sequence of written symbols from which the gist of a spoken message could be obtained. However, others who use the term more restrictively would require that the sequence of symbols gives a word for word translation of the spoken message. As we will see, virtually all modern writing systems, and most of those in the past that have survived, satisfy the more restrictive definition, so that most writing systems are designed to give verbatim representations of spoken language. Whether the process of reading does in fact involve such a decoding into spoken language or a more direct translation into meaning is a subject of much controversy that we will discuss in later chapters.

Although the code for speech provided by most writing systems is word-for-word, it is not complete. Even though some inflection and phrasing is captured by punctuation, much of the inflection and stress in speech is lost, so that the precise meaning of a written message may be unclear (e.g., was Mr. X's comment in the novel meant to be sarcastic or not?). To get a feeling of how much detail is lost, think of how difficult it is to read a line from a play as it would be said by the character speaking the line. In addition, although it is convenient to think of writing as a system for transcribing the spoken language, there is an important sense in which this is not true. That is, typical spoken language is much less orderly than written language. Not only does it contain many things like /um/s and /ah/s, /I mean/s,[1] but it contains repetitions and omissions. This is not only true of casual and colloquial speech, but even of relatively formal speech such as lectures that are not merely being read. Thus, in some sense, writing is a transcription of an idealization of the spoken language.

A good case can be made for the claim that the word is an extremely fundamental unit in language. That is, a message is likely to be basically intelligible (i.e., some subtleties may be lost) as long as the identity of the words and their order remain. Thus, if a writing system can transcribe words accurately, it is likely to be adequate. In fact, the emphasis in all writing systems actually in use is to represent words accurately and most writing systems generally don't bother to represent aspects of speech like the stress on words. Thus the focus in this chapter is on how writing systems represent words.

Possible principles of representation

Logographic

If one is trying to devise a code in which the reader can decipher every word, one possible system is to have a visual symbol represent each word. Thus you can have a picture of a dog represent a dog, a picture of a foot represent a foot, etc. This system is sometimes called a *logography* (Gelb, 1963). In order for the system to be practical, the pictures would have to be fairly schematic so that people other than talented artists could write and also so that the task of writing did not take a ridiculous amount of time. (Some systems of writing, such as hieroglyphics, used what were probably deliberately complex symbols; the purpose of such symbols was to represent religious messages, and the reading and writing of such symbols was often restricted to a priestly caste and considered a magical ability.)

Such a pictorial system runs into problems. The first is one of discrimination: a core vocabulary in the spoken language is at least 2000 words and it is hard to draw that many discriminable pictures. Second, pictures work well for concrete nouns, but less well for other parts of speech. If one uses a picture to represent a verb such as *standing* with a picture of a man standing, the chances are that it will be hard to discriminate that from the symbol to represent *man*. Often, logographic systems use the same symbol to represent two such words and rely on context to allow the reader to determine which meaning is intended. Similarly, abstract nouns can be represented by pictures, such as representing *day* by a picture of the sun. There are some abstract nouns such as *democracy* and *vacuum* that would try the ingenuity of the symbol designer, and most function words (i.e., articles, prepositions, pronouns, and conjunctions) are virtually impossible to represent pictorially.

One solution to the problem of representing abstract concepts with pictures is to allow some words to be represented by arbitrary symbols, such as our use of numerals to represent numbers or our use of % and & to represent the words *percent* and *and*. However, extensive use of such arbitrary symbols would probably tax the reader's (and writer's) memory. A second solution is to relax the principle of one picture per word and allow more than one picture to represent a word. For example, one could represent *god* by two symbols: a picture of a man and a picture of stars. One could represent *sun* by a picture of a sun, but represent *day* by a picture of a sun followed by a picture of a clock to signify that the word is a unit of time. One could represent *ran* by a picture of a man running followed by a picture of a clock to represent past tense, etc. (This solution would still have trouble with words like *of* and *but*, however.)

This latter solution involves analyzing words into component units of meaning such as RAN = action of running + past tense, or DAY = unit of time measured by the sun. Thus, the 100,000 or so words in a language may be built out of a more manageable-sized set of atoms of meaning (perhaps a thousand or so). Linguists use the term *morpheme* to denote certain subword units of meaning. However, these units of meaning may not be separable units in either the spoken or written forms of the language. They often are. For example, *boys* contains the morpheme *boy* and *s* signifies the plural morpheme. However, even though *ran* could similarly be considered to contain the morphemes *run* and "past tense", they are obviously not represented in a simple way in the written word *ran*. In contrast, the obscure and idiosyncratic analysis of DAY above is not a morphemic decomposition. Even so, the question of whether a word can be broken down into component morphemes, and what the appropriate decompositions are, is sometimes controversial. This suggests that words are *the* natural unit in the language rather than the morpheme. However, the definition of word in the spoken language is also not without its problems. The problem is illustrated by the fact that there is no principled reason why *basketball* is written without a space and *tennis ball* is written with one. Defining words to be sequences of letters that are written without intervening spaces would thus be unsatisfactory since there would be no principled way of knowing whether something was a word or not. In addition, most compound words started out as two words and evolved through frequency of usage to being written without a space. Some linguists (e.g., Selkirk, 1982) have attempted a more principled definition of a word such that some compounds written with a space (e.g., *punch card*) are words.

Giving a detailed argument for the necessity of both words and morphemes as linguistic units would be beyond the scope of this discussion. However, even a superficial analysis suggests that neither is the more natural. In two-syllable words, such as *footstool* or *bending*, the morpheme is the basic unit in the speech stream (where each morpheme corresponds to a syllable, in this case) and the decision to call those two syllables a word is based on relatively abstract criteria on which reasonable people may disagree. In contrast, in our previous example of *ran*, the natural unit in the speech stream is the word, and the morphemes (*run* and past tense) are the more abstract units. The fact that most logographic systems use symbols to represent both words and morphemes is testimony to the reality of both units of analysis. Before going on, we should mention one strength of a logographic system: there is no need to know the spoken language in order to decipher it. As long as one knows what the symbols mean, one can decode the meaning of the written language. Indeed, variations of the Chinese writing system are used to code different languages (e.g., Mandarin and Cantonese) that are not mutually intelligible.

Syllabic

One way out of the difficulties posed by a logographic system is to relax the requirement that a picture has to be related to the meaning of a word or of a word part. For example, we might find it hard to come up with a symbol for the word *label*, so we might represent it with the symbol for lay (such as a picture of a person lying down) and the picture for bell. That is, we now allow the picture for bell to stand for the sound /bell/ regardless of whether that sound is related to the meaning of the word *bell*. This procedure of using meaningful pictures to sound out words is sometimes known as the *rebus principle* and most readers of this book have probably encountered it in puzzles, comic books, or newspapers. It is of course not necessary that the sound units represented by pictures are single syllables. In fact, in many writing systems there are some such pictures for single syllables and some for two-syllable units (Gelb, 1963).

If one goes to a system where a character stands for a unit of sound, then the question naturally arises as to whether one needs to make the character look like something meaningful. If a character is to represent the sound /lay/ regardless of its meaning, why bother with a picture that represents one of its meanings? Why not just have an arbitrary symbol (which could be much easier to draw) stand for the syllable /lay/? The answer depends somewhat on the number of syllables (or possibly longer units) that one needs to represent. How many syllables are there in the language? Consider a language like English: there are roughly 25 consonant sounds and 10 vowel sounds. Syllables are possible with a consonant vowel (CV) such as /ba/ or /lay/, a VC such as /ad/ or a CVC such as /bat/. If one restricted oneself to CVCs, there would be roughly $25 \times 10 \times 25$ or 6250 syllables if all combinations were possible. Not all are, but a reasonable fraction are, so that in most languages there are a thousand or so syllables. On the other hand some languages, such as Japanese, have only about 100 syllables, since the syllables are mostly of one form (in Japanese, they are all CVs except for one exception).

If one needed to represent only 100 or so syllables by symbols, then using arbitrary characters to represent them seems feasible, but if there are ten times that many syllables, it does not. One solution would be to use 100 or so syllable signs, but use one sign to represent several syllables. For example, one sign could stand for /ba/, /bi/, and /bu/, or one sign could stand for /du/ and /tu/. (We have already taken advantage of this in our *label* example, since the second syllable's pronunciation is only approximately that of *bell*.) In such a system, there would clearly be times where there are ambiguities, and two distinct words would have the same written form. If the way the symbols are chosen is reasonably clever, then the number of ambiguous words might not be excessive and the ambiguities that occur might usually be disambiguated by the context. Of course, even in the spoken language, there are words that sound the same that have to be similarly disambiguated, such as *bank*, which has several meanings including a financial institution or the edge of a river.

A second solution to the problem of having fewer symbols than syllables is to bend what the symbols stand for. For example, one might represent the syllable *bam* by two signs, one representing *ba* and the second *am*. One could even go further and represent *clam* by symbols for *cl*, *la*, and *am*. Real languages have tended to use both of these solutions, once they decided not to bother with creating symbols that were pictorial. The second solution, however, stretches the principle of a symbol per syllable, since the symbols often stand for smaller units. In fact, as we will see, the distinction between languages based on the syllable and alphabetic languages is often fuzzy.

Phonemic

We all know that English letters represent smaller units in spoken language than the syllable. While the syllable needed no formal definition for the preceding section to make sense, this smaller unit, the *phoneme*, is not nearly as self-evident. One might think at first that a phoneme is the smallest unit that one could say in isolation. However, there are some phonemes (the "stopped consonants": /b/, /p/, /d/, /t/, /g/, and /k/) which cannot be said alone. They need some vowel sound either before or after them to be uttered. Nevertheless, the idea of phonemes being the smallest sound unit in the speech stream is essentially correct. (However, the idea that a letter represents a phoneme is an extreme simplification of the *alphabetic principle*. We will elaborate on that point in detail below.)

There is a somewhat fussy distinction that we need to make. Not all distinguishable speech sounds in the language are distinct phonemes, only those that the language cares about. For example, the /k/ sound in /keep/ and /cool/ are different: if you pay attention to where your tongue is when you make the two /k/ sounds, you will note that it is in a different place, and in fact the sound coming out of your mouth is different in the two cases. (The difference will also be clear if you hold your hand in front of your mouth when saying the two words.) These distinguishable speech sounds are known as *allophones*. We could represent the /k/ sound in *keep* by *k* and the /k/ sound in *cool* by @. The reason that we don't use two symbols to represent the two sounds (and most English speakers are unaware of the distinction until it is pointed out to them) is that the distinction never needs to be made in English. That is, there are never two words that differ only by this distinction: English never has two words only differing by that sound and so we do not need a letter @ to distinguish *keep* and @*eep*. Thus the phoneme is a category: all the allophones that are not distinguished by the language are in the same phoneme. This categorization changes from language to language. Some languages do distinguish the two *k* sounds above and so these sounds are separate phonemes in those languages (and represented by different letters). Conversely, /l/ and /r/ are not separate phonemes in Japanese.

The great advantage of representing phonemes over representing larger units is that there is a smaller number of them. There are fewer than 100 phonemes used in all human languages and a typical language such as English employs about 40 of them (see Figure 2.1). The limit to the number of phonemes is probably a combination of the limit on the different positions the mouth can assume while talking and a limit to the fineness of discrimination possible when perceiving a rapid and continuous message such as typical speech.

Several comments are in order. The first is that a majority of phonemes are consonants. This fact is reflected by the English alphabet, which contains 21 symbols for consonants and 5 symbols for vowels. The second is that the relation between alphabetic symbols and phonemes is not simple. Some phonemes are represented by more than one letter, such as *sh, ch,* and *th,* even though the phonemes are not combinations of the component sounds (e.g., /sh/ is not /s/ + /h/). On the other hand, certain letters represent combinations of phonemes. For example, in English, *j* is usually pronounced /d/ + /zh/ and *x* as /k/ + /s/. Second, as should be obvious to any English speaker, letters can represent more than one phoneme. While English may be extreme in this respect, it is true in most alphabetic languages, particularly in the case of vowels.

Thus, while the ideal of the alphabet is to represent each phoneme by a letter, the correspondence is usually not straightforward. There are several possible reasons for this. The first is economy: since there are usually fewer letters than phonemes in a language it may be easier to have some ambiguities in the representation of the sound than to use a larger set of symbols, which would necessitate finer visual discriminations and also probably slow down the reading and writing processes. Second, there is the matter of variation in the speech signal, both between speakers and in different contexts for the same individual. These differences are most obvious with vowels. Between individuals there are substantial differences in how vowels are pronounced (most notably with different dialects) and the inventors of alphabets may have decided that they wanted to ignore many of those differences (e.g., *i* is pronounced like /aye/ in some dialects of English but like /ah/ in others). Third, words are

CONSONANTS		VOWELS		COMBINATIONS AND DIPHTHONGS	
Symbol	Example	Symbol	Example	Symbol	Example
p	*pill*	i	*seat*	j	*jar*
b	*bill*	I	*sit*	M	*where*
d	*done*	ɛ	*set*	ay	*bite*
t	*ton*	e	*bait*	æw	*about*
g	*gale*	æ	*sat*	ɔy	*toy*
k	*kale*	u	*boot*		
m	*mail*	U	*put*		
n	*nail*	ʌ	*but*		
ŋ	*ring*	O	*coat*		
s	*sing*	ɔ	*caught*		
z	*zing*	a	*cot*		
f	*fat*	ə	*sofa*		
v	*vat*	ɨ	*marry*		
θ	*thin*				
ð	*then*				
š	*shin*				
ž	*measure*				
č	*chin*				
l	*late*				
r	*rate*				
y	*yet*				
w	*wet*				
h	*hit*				

FIGURE 2.1 The standard phonetic symbols used to represent sounds in English. The consonants and vowels listed are clearly basic phonemes, while the sounds represented in the last column could be viewed as combinations of phonemes. Throughout the book, however, we will represent sound in a more informal way, using diagonal slashes together with a (hopefully) unambiguous pronunciation to indicate the sound intended (e.g., /dawg/ to represent the sound of "dog")

pronounced differently in different contexts (e.g., *the* is pronounced /thuh/ or /thee/ depending on whether the word following it has an initial consonant or vowel sound). Fourth, and perhaps most important, the makers of alphabets may not have really understood what phonemes are. The type of analysis needed to uncover the basic phonemes of a language requires a high level of awareness of the sound actually coming out of the speaker's mouth. This requires the very difficult task of ignoring the meaning of the speech (as in the *thuh–thee* example above).

We need to define one more term before proceeding. If languages usually represent more than one phoneme by a letter, then it would make sense to represent similar phonemes with the same letter. One system invented by linguists to characterize differences among phonemes is *distinctive features*. Distinctive features can perhaps be best explained by an example. The *stop consonants* [/b/, /p/, /d/, /t/, (hard) /g/, and /k/] all share the distinctive feature of *stopping*: they are all produced by the mouth briefly cutting off the flow of air. They are distinguished from each other by two other distinctive features, *voicing* and *place of articulation*. Voicing refers to whether the vocal cords vibrate during the consonantal sound or not: the vocal cords vibrate for the voiced consonants, /b/, /d/, and /g/, but not for the voiceless ones, /p/, /t/, and /k/ (place your hand on your voice box while pronouncing the six sounds to confirm this). Place of articulation refers to where the sound is cut off: /b/ and /p/ are cut off in the front of the mouth, /d/ and /t/ in the middle, and /g/ and /k/ in the back.

The basic idea, of course, is that the distinctive features capture the structure of phonemes. If two phonemes share many distinctive features, they are similar. In general the economies of representation in alphabetic languages can be explained by distinctive features (especially with respect to vowels). Long and short vowels, which differ by only one distinctive feature, are commonly represented by a single letter. Similarly, *th* in English may stand for one of two phonemes (as in *this* and *thin*) that differ only by voicing. Other economies seem more arbitrary, however, such as hard and soft *g*, which are quite different phonemes.

You may have wondered whether a writing system could be based on distinctive features. If a set of distinctive features defines a phoneme, then in principle one could represent language by using a set of symbols for the set of distinctive features. One reason why most languages do not represent distinctive features may be that such an enterprise calls for even more careful analysis of language than a phonemic representation, and it is not clear that a really satisfactory set of distinctive features exists for vowels. A second reason that writing systems usually stop at the phoneme may be that not too much economy will be achieved by a distinctive feature representation over a phonemic representation, since the number of symbols required for a phonemic representation (about 25–40) does not seem to place much of a burden on the reader. However, there is a writing system, Hangul (part of the written Korean language), in which distinctive features are important. We will discuss Hangul later in the chapter.

To summarize, the last widely used principle for writing is to attempt to represent each phoneme of the spoken language by a written symbol that we call a letter. While there are a few languages (e.g., Finnish) where this principle is closely approximated, most alphabetic languages only roughly approximate it. We have speculated a bit on why this is so, and will come back to the issue several times later in the chapter when we discuss specific writing systems.

The fact that alphabetic languages only loosely use the alphabetic principle—representing a phoneme by a letter—brings us perhaps to the most important point about writing systems in general. We have seen that there are several units that writing systems could use as the basis for representation: word, morpheme, syllable, subsyllable (e.g., consonant-vowel combinations), phoneme, or even distinctive feature. In principle one could construct a writing system in which only one of the units was represented. In practice, however, no writing system is completely pure and many are complex mixtures.

A brief history of writing

Inventions of writing

No one knows when humans acquired the power of speech, but it is generally assumed that spoken language of some sort evolved at least 100,000 years ago and perhaps much earlier than that. *Homo erectus* (e.g., Java Man and Peking Man), whose brain was not much different from ours, appeared at least 1,000,000 years ago. It is generally agreed that the ability to speak was the result of an evolutionary change in the brain. Certain areas of the human brain associated with speech are markedly larger than in other ape brains. Furthermore, in most humans there is lateral asymmetry in the control of speech functions: certain areas of the left cerebral cortex are specialized for language, suggesting a unique genetic programming. While there are some hints of such asymmetry in chimpanzees, the differences between humans and other apes appear to be essentially qualitative.

In contrast, writing is a relatively recent activity of humans. Moreover, the ability to read and write was not produced by a biological change but by a cultural change. The essential prerequisite for being able to read and write, for a human capable of spoken language, is to belong to a literate culture. However, as reading involves other abilities, such as visual perception, it may tax language abilities more heavily than spoken language, and in general (and in contrast to spoken language), it must be explicitly taught. (We will discuss these issues more fully in Chapters 10–12.)

Writing is arguably the most important invention in human history. The opportunity for human knowledge to build on other knowledge is severely limited without the medium of writing. Not only does writing allow a permanence to human thought, but writing also allows a complexity and scope to human expression that seems barely possible without it. The first great knowledge explosion in Egypt, the Near East, India, China, and Greece is clearly due, in large part, to the invention of writing.

The earliest known artifacts that could be considered writing by the loosest definition are the famous and extraordinarily beautiful cave paintings in southern France and northern Spain, which are about 20,000 years old. The pictures, mostly of animals but with some human figures, possibly tell some sort of story, but may merely be pictures with expressive, magical, or religious purpose. Other assorted pictures have been found antedating the rise of the great civilizations of the Near East, but the earliest artifacts that are clearly writing date from about only 5500 years ago in Mesopotamia.

Why did writing develop so late? (We can conjecture that there are cultural reasons: the society had to be rich enough to allow some people the leisure time to develop a writing system, and also allow sufficient numbers of people to have the leisure time to learn it. Moreover, there had to be things that seemed worth writing down. The first civilizations that exploited large-scale irrigation agriculture seem obvious places where there was sufficient leisure (at least among the ruling class) to create the opportunity to write. However, it is not clear exactly how writing evolved in these cultures. The oldest writing of anything that appears to resemble sentences (found in what is now Iraq), appeared to be for the unromantic purpose of recording business transactions, while the earliest writing found in other cultures was for different purposes (e.g., descriptions of the exploits of kings). However, we have no guarantee that the artifacts that we have are representative of the writings of the civilization. Moreover, we have only a few clues about the immediate precursors of these writings and the significance of these clues is far from clear (see Gelb, 1963).

Sumerian and cuneiform

The oldest Sumerian writings, dating from about 3500 BC, have not been fully decoded. They appear to be pictographic, and are perhaps as primitive a writing system as the Christopher Columbus example at the beginning of this chapter. The writing system developed quite rapidly, however (at least from our distant perspective). Other artifacts that are only slightly later not only use a single conventional symbol such as a sun to represent *sun, time,* and *day,* but also use the symbol for an arrow (pronounced /ti/) to represent not only *arrow,* but also *life,* which was also pronounced /ti/ (Diringer, 1962; Gelb, 1963). Thus, quite early in the history of language, a complete reliance on symbols to represent meaning pictorially was abandoned; at least some symbols represented a particular sound.

At around 3200 BC, another important development occurred. Since clay was an easily obtainable material in the region, more and more of the writing was done on clay. Apparently to speed the writing process, the symbols were pressed into the wet clay with a short stylus (rather than scratched). This meant that the symbols were composed of short line segments rather than the smooth curves that would be natural for pictorial representations. A typical symbol would be made by about three to ten line segments, and so would be an extremely stylized version of the pictorial symbol that it evolved from. (If the examples of symbols such as those in Figure 2.2 are representative, it is doubtful that someone not versed in the writing system could guess the meaning of more than 10% of the symbols.) Because there was uneven pressure applied to the tool when making the

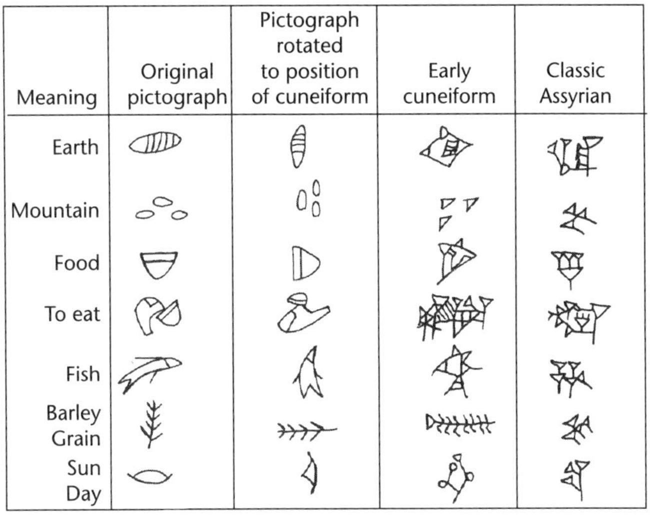

FIGURE 2.2 Examples of the evolution from pictographic symbols to the more abstract cuneiform writing of Classic Assyrian. Adapted from Diringer (1962) with permission of Thames and Hudson (London)

line segments, they were wedge-shaped (i.e., thicker at one end than the other). This feature was captured by the name of the writing system, *cuneiform*, which means wedge-shaped.

Thus, in only about 300 years, the writing system had evolved from a primitive picture writing system that could probably only transmit the gist of a message to a fairly stylized system in which symbols represented meanings in a relatively abstract way and in which there was some reliance on the principle that a symbol represents a sound rather than a meaning. We will see that this story is universal: complete reliance on pictures to represent meaning is usually a brief stage, which soon develops into a system that uses symbols to represent sounds as well as meanings. As we have hinted in the first section of this chapter, these changes make sense. Drawing recognizable pictures for each word in the language is clearly impossible. The use of several pictures to represent a word meaning helps, but is cumbersome enough that the writers and readers will quickly think of other solutions. These solutions involve making the symbols more schematic and/or not tied to meaning.

It appears that at first the Sumerians used the same symbol to stand for several words related in meaning or several words with identical pronunciation, and hoped that the correct meaning would be deduced from context, much as English-speaking readers would know that *chest* meant a box rather than a part of the body when reading *He put the jewels in the chest*. Two methods were developed in the writing system, however, to help in deciphering the symbols. One was the use of *determinatives* (Diringer, 1962), which were non-pronounced symbols that indicated the word class (e.g., bird, country, number, plural noun). The second system was to introduce a pronunciation hint. Thus, if a symbol could stand for several words related in meaning but having different sounds (such as sun, day, time), one might follow that symbol with a second symbol, called a *phonetic complement* (e.g., a symbol standing for the syllable /ime/). As a result, the two syllables together would be interpreted as "word which means something like sun and sounds like /ime/, so it must be *time*." These two additions to the writing system were fairly universally used in writing systems that used symbols to stand for the meanings of words (and still are used in Chinese).

The cuneiform system of writing was adopted by several groups speaking different languages. The Akkadians (aka the Babylonians and Assyrians), whose language spread throughout the Middle

East, adopted the cuneiform system around 2500 BC. By around 1700 BC the writing appeared to be relatively codified with around 600–700 symbols. About half the symbols stood for meanings and the other half stood for sounds. There is some disagreement among scholars (cf. Diringer, 1962; Gelb, 1963) as to whether all the sound representations were syllabic or whether some stood for phonemes as well. Cuneiform writing also spread to other groups; to the Elamites at around 2500 BC and much later (around 500 BC) to the Persians. In the Elamite system there were only about 100 symbols, most standing for syllables, and in the Persian system there were only 41 symbols, all of which stood for syllables.

Cuneiform, like all of the ancient writing languages, was a complete mystery until about 200 years ago. The fact that it was adopted by the Persians was fortunate from our standpoint since Persian is an Indo-European language related to our own. Even so, it first had to be deduced that the characters in the Persian cuneiform writing stood for syllables, before the syllables were decoded. The decoding of the Persian writing system took about 80 years and was the key to fairly rapid progress in deciphering the Babylonian writing system and then the other forms of cuneiform including the original Sumerian writing system. Few of the ancient languages have been fully decoded, however.

Egyptian

The original Egyptian writing, *hieroglyphic* writing (meaning holy carving) is almost as old as the Sumerian, dating from about 3000 BC. It is not known whether the Egyptian writing system was in some way derived from the Sumerian or invented independently. Almost from the earliest examples of the writing, there is a strong reliance on representing sound. There were symbols that stood for meanings (logographs), symbols that stood for sounds (single or double syllables), symbols that were phonetic complements (giving a clue to the pronunciation of a word), and determinatives (giving the category of the word).

The name hieroglyphic was given by later people, since the writing was mostly used for holy or monumental writing and it was usually written on stone (at least in the collection of artifacts). However, it was sometimes written for other purposes and on materials such as wood and papyrus. The symbols were very elaborate and beautiful (see Figure 2.2), but not well suited for mundane purposes such as business transactions. Hence a second system called *hieratic* writing developed, starting only a little later than hieroglyphic writing. It was more or less a cursive form of hieroglyphics written with a brush-pen. The characters, however, were somewhat simplified and (as in cuneiform) the forms became less and less related to the meanings they represented. Many of the symbols were joined, as in our cursive writing. A third version (also cursive), called *demotic* writing (i.e., writing of the people) appeared about 700 BC. It employed even simpler and more abstract versions of the symbols.

It was possible to decipher the ancient Egyptian writings because public decrees from this later period were often written in hieroglyphics, demotics, and Greek (which had become the dominant language in the area). The hieroglyphic writing was probably used to emphasize the sacred nature of the decree. A piece of such a document, the famed Rosetta Stone (see Figure 2.3), discovered in 1799, helped in the deciphering of both ancient scripts using the Greek as a key. (The last stage of the ancient Egyptian language, Coptic, was known to the decipherers.)

Chinese

The earliest Chinese writings are significantly more recent than those of the Near East, dating from about 1500 BC. The forms are sufficiently different from modern Chinese that originally the writings could not be understood by later scholars. Even today the writings have not been completely

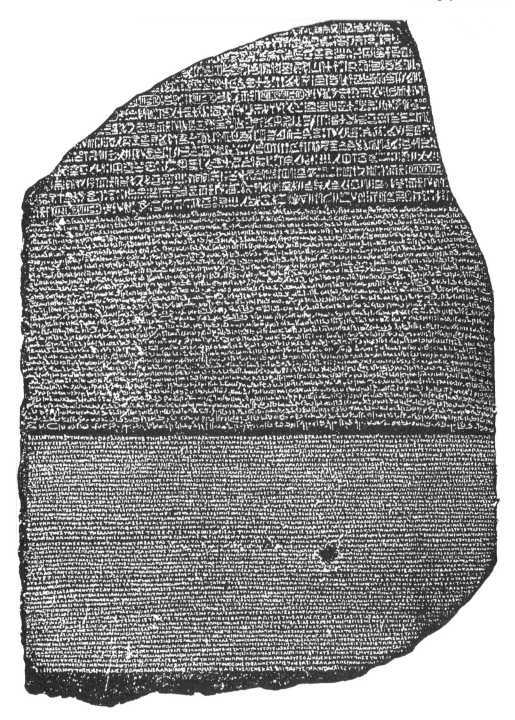

FIGURE 2.3   Photograph of the Rosetta Stone, the key to deciphering hieroglyphic and hieratic writing. The top is written in hieroglyphic, the middle in hieratic, and the bottom in Greek

deciphered, although there is no dispute about the meanings of about a quarter of the symbols. One interesting feature is that at least some of the symbols represent sound (as phonetic complements). This has led experts to believe either (a) that these artifacts are not the beginning of the writing system, and that there are older, more pictorial, writings that are lost or undiscovered, or (b) that the writing system was an adaptation of the writing from the Near East. At present there is no good evidence to choose between those possibilities.

Over time, the form of the symbols changed (especially with the invention of the brush in the third century BC and paper in the second century AD), but the structure of the written language has changed little since the oldest writings. (The form has also changed little since AD 100.) We will return to discuss Chinese later in the chapter. Two points are worth emphasizing, however: (1) The characters in Chinese, while having their origins in pictures, are often abstract, and not obviously identifiable to someone who hasn't been taught the meaning. (2) The system is not merely one in which there is a symbol per word (or morpheme); sound is represented in the system as well.

Other original writing systems

Ancient writings have been discovered in the Indus valley (now in Pakistan) that are dated somewhere between 2500 and 3000 BC. There is no indication that the writing system was borrowed from any other. However, no writings have been found in the area between 2500 and 1000 BC, so that it is hard to know what the significance of the early writings is in the history of writing. The symbols are pictographic, but since it has not been decoded, little has been discovered about the writing system. (As there are about 300 symbols it is unlikely that the principle is completely syllabic.)

The writings of the great civilizations of the new world, especially the Mayan and Aztec, are the subject of great controversy, largely because they have also been barely deciphered. The fact they have not been seems to be largely the result of racism or culturalism. Variants of the languages represented are spoken today and people continued to write in the Mayan script (for example) until about 200 years ago. However, the Spanish had no interest in the native culture and even went to great lengths to destroy much of the writing.

Enough was preserved by the Spanish to know the Mayan symbols for units of time. Thus the meaning of some of the texts, which were calendars, is clear. These calendars are extraordinarily accurate in determining the length of the year. However, so little of the written language has been decoded that there is little certainty about the writing system. For example, Diringer (1962) claims that the Mayan and Aztec written languages were essentially in the same stage as the second stages of Egyptian and Sumerian languages (i.e., containing some syllabic signs), whereas Gelb (1963) views them as systems more primitive than "true writing" (roughly at about the level of the previous Christopher Columbus example).

The development of the alphabet

Most of us have been taught in school that the alphabet was invented only once and it was invented by the Phoenicians. This teaching is essentially true, since all alphabetic writing systems can be traced to the Phoenicians. However, there is controversy about whether the Phoenician system is a true alphabetic system, since it did not represent vowel sounds; the first writing system that is unambiguously alphabetic, in the sense of attempting to represent each phoneme with a letter, is the Greek.

The alphabet was not the inspiration of one person, but rather a gradual development. As we have seen, almost the earliest writing systems employed some kind of sound principle, and by

2000 both the Egyptian and cuneiform writing systems had developed many symbols to represent syllables. As we hinted in the introduction, the difference between a *syllabary* (a writing system based on the syllable) and an alphabet (a writing system based on the phoneme) is not that clear.

All known syllabaries contain about 100 or so symbols. (It is not clear whether this is a practical limitation imposed on the writer or reader.) Since the Near Eastern spoken languages contained far more syllables than that, symbols had to represent more than one syllable. The two standard principles for grouping syllables were discussed earlier. The first was to use a symbol to stand for a set of syllables that shared the same consonant sounds. For example, there would be one symbol for /bat/, /bit/, /bet/, /but/, /bot/, /boot/, etc., or one syllable for /ta/, /ti/, /tu/, /toe/, etc. The second system was that the syllables represented by the same symbol would share a vowel sound and have different (but similar) consonant sounds. For example, one symbol would stand for /tak/ and /tag/ and /taq/ (q stands for a related consonant sound not present in English). In Babylonian cuneiform writing, both systems of multiple representation were used, although the second principle (preserving the vowel sound and making the consonant sound ambiguous) predominates. However, in the Egyptian system the first principle was universally used. The cuneiform system also represented some syllables by joining two symbols: so that /ral/ would be the symbol for /ra/ plus the symbol for /al/.

In retrospect, we can see elements of the alphabet in both systems of writing. In the Egyptian system a symbol that represented all syllables that were /t/ plus a vowel is quite close to representing the phoneme /t/. In addition, the representation of a single syllable in cuneiform by two syllables indicates that units smaller than the syllable were being represented in the writing system. However, as indicated earlier, syllabic representation was only one principle in both the cuneiform and Egyptian writing systems; there were also characters to represent meaning as well. There were several other such writing systems in the Near East at this time (2000 to 1000 BC).

The first system that appears to have completely dispensed with both logographic signs and symbols that represented more than a single consonant appeared in Phoenicia (modern Lebanon and Syria) about 1300 BC. This system had roughly 25 to 30 symbols, each one corresponding to a consonantal sound. As indicated above, there is controversy among scholars about whether the Phoenician system (and related systems) should be called alphabetic or syllabary. The details of this controversy need not concern us, since the essential character of the system is clear: (a) all the symbols represented consonantal sounds which could be combined into a syllable containing more than one consonant; (b) vowel sounds were only occasionally represented, so that representation of the phonetic principle in the writing system was incomplete.

While the Phoenician writings are the oldest that have been discovered, there are similar, roughly contemporaneous, writings in various other Semitic languages (e.g., the ancient Hebrew of the Torah) that were spoken in the same general geographical region. The similarity of the writing systems makes it clear that there was extensive contact among the people of the area. It is not at all unlikely that a new discovery could indicate that some other group invented the system before the Phoenicians. The Phoenicians, however, were the first great sailors and traders, and were instrumental in exporting the system to the rest of the world. All known alphabetic systems appear to be derived from this system.

The alphabetic principle thus seems to have evolved in two stages: first the consonants were represented and later (with the Greeks) the vowels were represented. Why is this so? One possibility is that this progression was inevitable since most of the information in discourse is carried by the consonants, s ths phrs sggsts. However, there are indications that this development also had its roots in the particular language. Remember that the Egyptian system also did not represent vowel sounds (as contrasted with the Babylonian cuneiform). The ancient Egyptian language and Semitic languages shared the feature that, for a large number of words, the consonants represent the basic meaning and the vowels indicate the form. Thus the sequence of consonants in Hebrew and Arabic, /k/, /t/, and /b/ (which we might indicate by /k*t*b/) indicates something about writing that can appear in many forms (e.g., in Hebrew, /katab/ means *he wrote*, /kaytib/ means *writer*, /kit/ means *book*). While other languages sometimes use this principle (e.g., *ring, rang, rung* in English), it is much more fundamental in these languages. Thus, in these languages, it is not merely that the meaning of the message can be deciphered from a representation of the consonants, but that the essence of the meaning is often represented by the consonants.

The fact that the alphabetic principle was not independently invented again suggests that this two-stage development, if not absolutely necessary, made the creation of an alphabetic system much easier. One possibility is that potential inventors of an alphabetic system in other language systems felt that they would have to represent all the aspects of the sound (including accent and stress) and found such a task overwhelming. A second possibility is that these spoken Semitic languages, in which the structure of the form is represented directly in the structure of the underlying meaning—consonants represent the base meanings and vowels the grammatical form—helped the writers of that language to be more analytic about the sounds of the language and thus to be more aware of the phonemic units. As we will see in Chapters 10 and 11, the concept of a phoneme is relatively abstract and certainly not obvious to children or other people learning to read.

There is much uncertainty about the parentage of these Semitic alphabets. The fact that vowels are not represented suggests that they were derived from the Egyptian system, which had about the same number of symbols to represent syllables of the form consonant-vowel (CV). However, neither the names nor forms of the symbols are clearly related to the Egyptian (or any other system), so there is no clear consensus among scholars about the evolution from a mixed logo-graphic syllabic system to the consonantal system of the Phoenicians and others.

In contrast to the uncertainty about the parentage of the Phoenician writing system, the story of its subsequent evolution is reasonably clear. The Greeks adapted the Phoenician symbols for their language. However, there were some symbols left over which did not correspond to letters in the Greek language; these were used for the vowels. What is somewhat less clear is whether the representation of vowels evolved gradually (many of the symbols used for vowels represented soft, and hence somewhat vowel-like, consonant sounds in the Semitic languages), or whether some scribe had a blinding flash of insight about vowels and then used the leftover symbols to represent them.

All of the European writing systems are derived from the Greek alphabet. New letters have been invented to represent sounds not represented in the Greek alphabet and the visual forms have changed a bit. However, the basic system is virtually the same as it was over 2000 years ago. The two modern European writing systems of importance besides the Greek are the Roman alphabet, used in English and most western European countries, and the Cyrillic alphabet, used in eastern European countries where the Russian Orthodox religion was predominant. (Serbo-Croatian, the most common language in what used to be Yugoslavia, is today written in both alphabets.)

The other major writing systems that are alphabetic derive from the Semitic scripts (such as Phoenician and Hebrew) through the Aramaic language, which became the dominant language in the Near East by around 500 . The Semitic writing systems were increasingly used to represent the spoken language, and replaced cuneiform. The Aramaic script (which was only slightly changed from the Hebrew script) was in turn adapted to represent both the Arabic language and the languages of India. These scripts, in turn, were widely disseminated throughout much of southern Asia to places as far as the Philippine Islands and to much of northern Africa. Many of these systems that are more directly based on the Semitic writing system (most notably modern Hebrew and Arabic) still incompletely represent vowels. While there are characters to represent some vowels, the vowel symbol is often omitted and sometimes marked by a diacritical mark, a mark above or below an adjoining consonant. In this sense, many of these scripts are not fully alphabetic.

Some comments about progress

Throughout this section we have discussed the evolution of writing systems. In fact, for much of the world, writing has started out with picture writing, moved to a form of sound representation (usually syllabic) and then moved to an alphabetic system. In fact, no culture has moved the opposite way: i.e., abandoned a syllabic system for a pictographic one or abandoned an alphabetic system for a syllabic one. Thus, in an evolutionary sense, the alphabet is "fittest": it has won out where it has competed. While some of the use of alphabetic systems can certainly be traced to armed conquest (most notably those of Christianity and Islam), many adoptions of the alphabet cannot (for example Turkish adoption of a Roman alphabet in the twentieth century). This suggests that there may be some sense in which an alphabetic writing system is better (at least for those spoken languages that have adopted the alphabetic system).

However, such a conclusion must be tempered with two observations. The first is that it is not clear exactly why it is better. For example, there is no good evidence that alphabetic languages can be read faster than non-alphabetic languages such as Chinese. While there is some suggestion that alphabetic languages are easier to learn to read than Chinese, the data are largely anecdotal, and there are other non-alphabetic writing systems, such as Japanese, which appear to present no problem in mastering reading. Thus the superiority of alphabetic systems may be more related to the technology of writing and printing. Writing of non-alphabetic languages may take longer (Taylor, 1981), printing of non-alphabetic languages is definitely harder, and dictionaries of alphabetic languages are definitely easier to construct and use.

The second observation is that the alphabetic system may be fittest for languages that have adopted the system, but may be less fit for languages that have not. Thus non-alphabetic writing systems in use today may not be anachronisms, but may serve to represent those spoken languages as well as an alphabetic system could. We will briefly consider a few representative non-alphabetic contemporary writing systems (together with a few alphabetic ones) to illustrate the variety of writing systems in use today.

Some current writing systems

Logography: Chinese

The Chinese writing system (and variants of it) is the only important logographic system in common use today. Hence it is worth discussing in some detail. However, as we shall see, the common view of the Chinese writing system as picture writing is a gross oversimplification. There is also confusion about the number of characters one would need in a language like Chinese. A language like English has 100,000 or more words, so it is sometimes assumed that Chinese needs that many characters. However, the number of words is fewer in Chinese, since many of our words are inflected forms (e.g., *word-words, bring-brings-brought*), whereas Chinese does not use inflections. A more important reason why hundreds of thousands of characters are not needed in Chinese is that a character represents a morpheme (which is also a syllable) rather than a word. For example, Beijing, which means north capital, is represented by two characters, one for north /bei/ and one for capital /jing/. While a traditional complete dictionary (the K'anghsi dictionary of 1716) has 40,000 characters (more recent dictionaries have up to 80,000 characters), a dictionary of about 8000 characters suffices for most purposes (Martin, 1972). Elementary school children in China are reported to learn about 3500 characters, which enables them to read newspapers and books fluently. This sounds as if it would be hard, and it is. In the last century Chinese schools shifted to initially teaching children to read using Pinyin, an alphabetic version of Chinese, and then introducing the traditional logographic system. This system was developed for the official language of China (Mandarin) which virtually all educated Chinese learn at some point in their schooling.

One important feature of the two dominant Chinese spoken languages (Mandarin and Cantonese) should be mentioned: they are tonal. That is, a vowel sound can be spoken with several pitch contours (e.g., rising, falling, rising-falling) which change the basic meaning of the syllable. (In English, such changes would only convey pragmatic information such as focus.) Thus there are many more syllables in Chinese than in a non-tonal language. This makes it unlikely that a workable syllabary (with arbitrary characters) is feasible for Chinese. However, the number of syllables is still much smaller than the number of morphemes (and characters) so there is homophony in Chinese (as in most written languages).

Characters have usually been classified into six types (Taylor, 1981). In the first type, *pictographs*, the character is a representation of an object. However, this representation is often highly stylized (see Figure 2.4). For example, the character for *sun* (which was originally represented as a circle

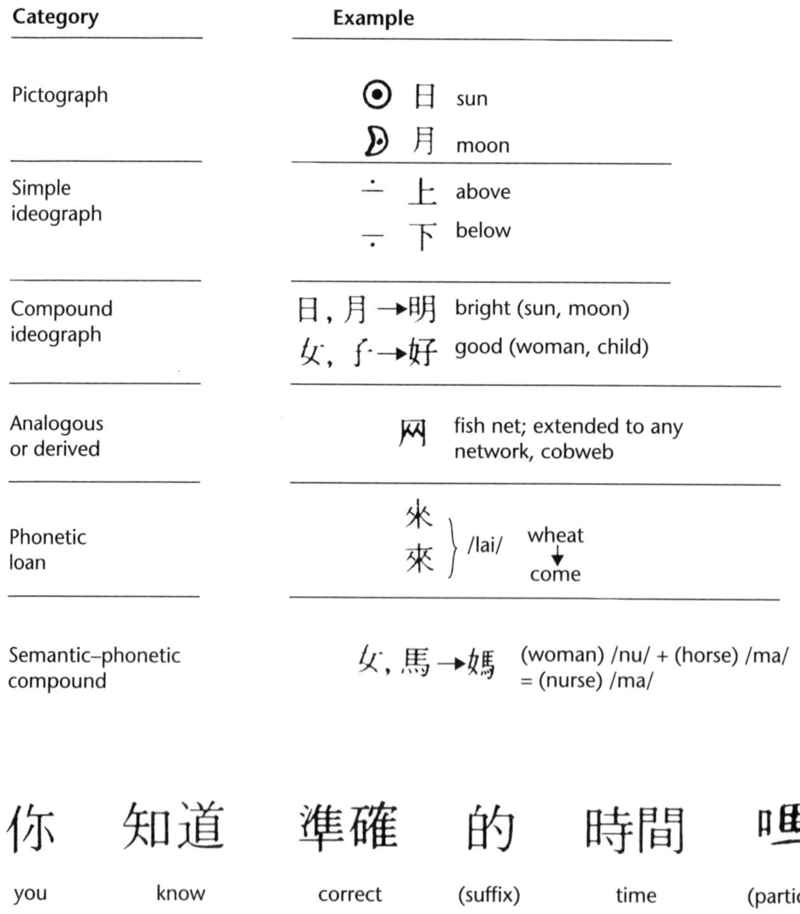

Category	Example	
Pictograph	⊙ 日	sun
	☽ 月	moon
Simple ideograph	⸪ 上	above
	⸫ 下	below
Compound ideograph	日, 月 →明	bright (sun, moon)
	女, 子 →好	good (woman, child)
Analogous or derived	网	fish net; extended to any network, cobweb
Phonetic loan	来 來 } /lai/	wheat ↓ come
Semantic–phonetic compound	女, 馬 →媽	(woman) /nu/ + (horse) /ma/ = (nurse) /ma/

你　知道　準確　的　時間　嗎

you　know　correct　(suffix)　time　(particle)

FIGURE 2.4 (Top) Six categories of Chinese characters. (Bottom) An example of a Chinese sentence. (From Taylor, 1981, with permission of Academic Press.)

with a dot in the center) is now represented as a rectangle with a horizontal line through it. In the second type, *simple ideographs*, the character represents the idea. For example, the characters for *above* and *below* show a line with something above and below it, respectively, or *middle* is represented by a quadrilateral with a vertical line through the middle. In *compound ideographs*, the character is composed of two or more simple pictographs or ideographs. For example, *bright* is composed of the characters for sun and moon, and *good* by the characters for woman and child. In *phonetic loans*, words from other languages are spelled with Chinese characters using the rebus principle. A fourth category, *analogous*, uses characters in a roughly metaphorical way, such as the character for a fish net is used to describe networks. In the last type, *semantic-phonetic compounds*, the character is composed of two *radicals*, one which represents the approximate meaning and the other the approximate sound. Thus *nurse* (pronounced /ma/) is written as *woman* (pronounced /nu/) plus *horse* (pronounced /ma/). The basic idea is that the character means "woman that sounds like /ma/". (The phonetic complement often is only similar in pronunciation to the syllable.) The radicals that constitute complex characters are sometimes written adjacently but compressed, and sometimes in quite complex and overlapping spatial arrangements.

The above classification scheme makes clear that the characters are not the smallest unit, since many characters are composed of radicals. Some of these basic building blocks, called *semantic radicals* (such as the character for *woman* in the nurse example above), have a special status. The dictionaries arrange characters according to their semantic radicals, and all the words in the K'anghsi dictionary can be organized by 214 radicals.

The key, therefore, to learning what seems like a bewildering number of characters is not so much that they are pictures, but that they are structured. One estimate is that only about 5% of the characters are simple ideographs or pictographs, and about 90% are semantic–phonetic compounds (Alleton, 1970, cited in Martin, 1972). (The simple characters are encountered more than 5% of the time, however, since they tend to represent common words.) Thus, to summarize, Chinese is not picture writing: many of the characters are highly stylized and not really pictures of the morphemes, and a principle of sound coding is involved in representing much of the language.

Syllabaries: Japanese and Korean

The Japanese and Korean writing systems are interesting because they make extensive use of syllabaries, and in fact either could be written totally within the respective syllabary system and be comprehensible. However, both systems are hybrids, and also use characters derived from the Chinese writing system, even though neither spoken language is similar to Chinese (or each other). Let us consider the two in turn.

Japanese

The Japanese language has little relation to Chinese except that there are some vocabulary items in Japanese of Chinese origin. In addition to profound differences in both vocabulary and linguistic structure, a marked surface difference between the languages is that Japanese is not tonal. In fact there are only about 100 syllables in Japanese (fewer than in most Western languages) since there are no consonant clusters and almost all the syllables are of the form consonant-vowel (the only consonant that can end a syllable is a nasal, which appears as /n/ or /m/ depending on context). One obvious consequence of a language with a small number of syllables is that if all morphemes are represented by single syllables, there would be an unacceptable number of homophones. Therefore it should come as no surprise that in Japanese, morphemes are often more than one syllable, and most words are polysyllabic. (Because of the simple syllabic structure in Japanese, however, there are still a large number of homophones.) Thus, in an attempt to borrow the Chinese writing system to represent Japanese, one could either create a system that consistently uses a character to represent a morpheme or one that consistently uses a character to represent a syllable, but one would have to abandon the Chinese system of representing both simultaneously. In fact, as we shall see, the Japanese written language is a mixture of systems embodying the two principles.

The Japanese system that in fact evolved is a mixture of two different systems (see Figure 2.5). In the first system, called *Kanji*, the symbols are a subset of the Chinese characters, and have the same meanings as in Chinese. (Thus one character represents a morpheme.) Kanji is used to represent the roots of content words (i.e., nouns, verbs, adjectives, and adverbs). The system is complicated in that a character can have several different readings (i.e., pronunciations). Some of the

Sound	Katakana	Kanji	Hiragana	Add (")	Sound: voiced	Add (°)	Semi voiced	
ha	ハ	八波	は	ば	ba	ぱ	pa	⎫
hi	ヒ	比	ひ	び	bi	ぴ	pi	
f,hu	フ	不	ふ	ぶ	bu	ぷ	pu	take both (") & (°)
he	ヘ	彡部	へ	べ	be	ぺ	pe	
ho	ホ	保	ほ	ぼ	bo	ぽ	po	⎭
ka	カ	加	か	が	ga			⎫
ki	キ	幾	き	ぎ	gi			
ku	ク	久	く	ぐ	gu			take only (")
ke	ケ	介計	け	げ	ge			
ko	コ	己	こ	ご	go			⎭
na	ナ	奈	な					⎫
ni	ニ	仁	に					
nu	ヌ	奴	ぬ					take neither (") nor (°)
ne	ネ	祢	ね					
no	ノ	乃	の					⎭

鶏肉とベーコンは 1.5cm の角に切る。

chicken   BACON   cube   cut

FIGURE 2.5 (Top) Katakana and Hiragana symbols. (Bottom) An example of a Japanese sentence taken from a cookbook illustrating use of Kanji, both types of Kana and Roman characters as well. (From Taylor, 1981, with permission of Academic Press.)

readings are related to the original Chinese pronunciations (*On* readings) and others to Japanese roots (*Kun* readings). However, there can be more than one reading of each type so that there are often five or so readings for a single Kanji character. (The meanings of all the readings are related, however.) The number of Kanji characters is smaller than in Chinese: there are 1850 official characters and about 1000 unofficial ones in common use.

The second system, called *Kana*, uses characters that are simplifications of Chinese characters. The Kana characters form a syllabary: one character represents a syllable. (Actually, the sound unit that is represented by these characters, the *mora*, is slightly smaller than a syllable.) There are 46 basic Kana characters together with two diacritical markings (″ and °). The diacritical markings change the features of the consonant sound (e.g., whether it is pronounced /ha/, /ba/ or /pa/). Since, as mentioned earlier, Japanese has a relatively small number of syllables, the approximately 100 Kana symbols are capable of representing any syllable in the language. Hence Japanese could in principle be written using only Kana. However, the system is a hybrid. The roots of content words are represented by the Kanji, with two different forms of Kana serving two different purposes. One form, *Katakana* (kata = fragment; kana = borrowed name) is used to represent loan words from other languages (such as *baseball*). The other, *Hiragana* (hiri = cursive; gana = borrowed name), is used to represent grammatical prefixes and suffixes, function words, and some content words. The Hiragana characters are basically cursive versions of the Katakana characters, although for a few pairs there is little resemblance between them. (In English, too, script and printed forms sometimes also differ markedly, as with capital A and capital Q.)

One estimate (Taylor, 1981) is that 65% of the characters in normal text are Hiragana, 30% are Kanji, 4% are Katakana, and 1% are Arabic numerals and Roman letters. However, it seems that a greater part of the meaning is conveyed by the Kanji than that estimate represents. At first blush it might appear that such a hybrid system would be very hard to read. However, reading rates in Japanese (see Chapter 4) are comparable to those in English. Furthermore, literacy rates in Japanese are among the highest in the world, suggesting that learning the Japanese writing system presents no more difficulty than an alphabetic one (perhaps less). One interesting aspect of Japanese reading instruction is that children are started out on the Kana (Hiragana) symbols and only introduced to the Kanji symbols gradually. The lower rates reported on reading problems in Japanese have suggested to some people (e.g., Rozin & Gleitman, 1977) that using a syllabary might be the best way to introduce children to reading, even in cultures with alphabetic languages.

Korean

The Korean written language is, in basic outline, like the Japanese system. In South Korea 1300 Chinese characters represent the roots of most content words (as with Kanji) and a sound-based system, called *Hangul* (meaning great letters), represents the rest (as with Kana). (North Korea, however, has totally eliminated the Chinese characters.) Hangul is worth discussing briefly because of a unique feature. It does not merely represent syllables by arbitrary characters; instead, it is composed of components that represent phonemes and articulatory features. There are five basic consonant symbols that indicate the shape of part of the mouth when making the articulation (e.g., an L-shaped symbol represents the shape of the point of the tongue when it makes an /n/). The 19 consonant symbols are derived from these basic symbols by adding strokes to represent distinctive feature changes. A long horizontal or vertical bar together with a short bar or two represents a vowel sound. The system is a syllabary, however, in that the symbols for the phonemes are not linearly arrayed as in a standard alphabetic language but packaged into blocks which represent syllables. (There are rules which dictate the relative positions of the phoneme symbols.) Hangul syllable characters look, to the Western eye, roughly like Chinese characters, although they are less curved (see Figure 2.6).

ㄱ /g/ : the root of the tongue as it closes the throat passage and touches the soft palate.

ㄴ /n/ : the shape of the point of the tongue as it touches the ridge behind the teeth.

ㅅ /s/ : upper (╱) and lower (╲) tooth get together.

ㆆ /h/ : unobstructed throat passage in producing /o/ is joined by two strokes.

ㅁ /m/ : the shape of the closed mouth.

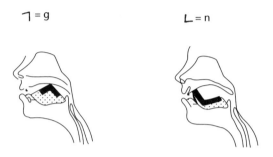

Position	Articulation manner					
	Basic symbols					Doubled
	Continuant	(Add)	Stop	(Add)	Aspirated	Lateral	Tense
Velar			ㄱ	⁻	ㅋ		ㄲ
Lingual	ㄴ	⁻	ㄷ	⁻	ㅌ	ㄹ	ㄸ
Bilabial	ㅁ	’’	ㅂ	’’	ㅳ → ㅍ		ㅃ
Sibilant	ㅅ	⁻	ㅈ	˙	ㅊ		ㅉ, ㅆ
Glottal	ㅇ			⁻	ㆆ		

Complexity level	Linearly arranged C V C C	Packaged in block	Syllable	Morpheme (native)
I	ㅏ	아	V/a/	suffix; ah
I	ㄷ ㅏ	다	CV/da/	all
II	ㅏㄹ	말	VC/al/	egg
II	ㄷ ㅏㄹ	달	CVC/dal/	moon
III	ㄷ ㅏㄹ ㄱ	닭	CVCC/dalg/	hen

FIGURE 2.6 (Top) Illustration of how Hangul represents the articulation of five basic consonants. (Middle) Illustration of how basic Hangul consonant symbols are added to produce other consonant symbols. (Bottom) Illustration of the packaging of Hangul syllable blocks in three complexity levels. (From Taylor, 1981, with permission from Plenum Press and Academic Press.)

Thus Hangul is unique in that it is, at the same time, an alphabetic system and a syllabary. A simple syllabary would have probably been unworkable in Korean, since it has a few thousand syllables (in contrast to the 100 or so syllables of Japanese). It was invented relatively recently (in the fifteenth century) under the direction of the emperor. As in Japanese, literacy is high and reading problems are low (although such data are often unreliable) suggesting that Hangul is a good writing system. The scholars who created it decided on the system after studying various alphabetic systems. Whether it represents an improvement over standard alphabetic systems is unclear.

English and other alphabetic systems

There are many alphabetic systems with interesting features. We will focus on English since it is the language of this book as well as being the most widely used alphabetic language. Most readers of English know only too well that the representation of sound by the alphabet is only approximate. However, only some of the ways in which it falls short are sheer perversity. Let us consider what the options are for alphabetic languages.

Spanish, a widely used alphabetic language, is quite regular in its spelling rules. One indication of the commitment in Spanish to a close relation of spelling to sound is the fact that *ch, ll, ñ,* and *rr* are called letters. In the case of *ch, ll,* and *rr,* this means that the combination is not merely a blend of the other two: *ch* is pronounced approximately as in English, *ll* as either /ly/ or /y/ depending on the dialect, and *rr* as a more trilled sound than the single *r*. A few consonants have more than one sound (e.g., *c* is either hard or soft as in English and *g* is either hard /g/ or /h/). However, the rules are totally regular: soft before *e* or *i*, hard before everything else. The vowels each have a long and a short sound, and fairly simple rules allow one to determine which. Combined vowels indicate certain soft consonant sounds. For example, ue is pronounced /way/ which is approximately how the two component vowel sounds /oo/ and /ay/ would be pronounced if done quickly. *U,* however, has other functions as well. First, it always appears after *q* (as in English) and it has a special function after *g*. When it appears after a *g* and before an *e* or *i* it is not pronounced, but merely indicates that the *g* is hard as in *guerra* (and an umlaut over the *u* is needed to indicate that the *u* is to be actually pronounced as in *vergüenza*). In addition there are rules that indicate where stress is to be placed, and if a word violates the rule an accent is placed on the vowel of the stressed syllable.

Thus, while Spanish is phonetic in the sense that one can sound out a Spanish word reliably knowing the rules, the rules one applies are more complex than the simplest alphabetic procedure of a single letter representing a single phoneme. Moreover, misspelling an unknown word in Spanish is possible, since more than one letter can stand for a single sound (e.g., *s* and *c* can both represent /s/ in many dialects and *g* and *j* can both represent /h/). However, there is a language (Finnish) in which the principle of one letter for each phoneme is even more closely approximated. In Finnish there is one letter for each consonant sound (and vice versa) and a reasonably literal representation of vowel sounds (although vowel sounds undergo subtle transformations in various contexts). While the simplicity of the structure of the spelling rules in Finnish is fairly rare, there are several other languages (e.g., Italian, Serbo-Croatian, Hungarian) in which the relation between spelling and sound is about as simple as Spanish. This raises the obvious question of why English spelling is so complex if other languages can manage with simpler spelling systems.

There are essentially four components to the answer. The first is that much of the apparent irregularity of English is not really irregularity, but applications of rules similar to the ones discussed so far. For example, *c* and *g* are hard or soft depending on the vowel following it, certain clusters of letters are really single letters such as *ch, sh, th*, and *ph*, and (similar to the *u* following a *g* in Spanish which is not pronounced but changes the pronunciation of the *g*) silent *e* lengthens the vowel sound preceding it.

The second component is historical. Spelling of English was codified relatively early for European languages and it was codified at a time when the pronunciation was changing. Indeed, it is worth noting that in English, as in most alphabetic languages, spelling of words used to be quite idiosyncratic, so that the spelling of words could differ quite a bit from book to book (although all spellings would be an attempt to capture the sound, but perhaps in different dialects). Thus, at one time, *bough, rough, through*, and *though* all had the same final consonant sound. The spoken language changed, but the written language was frozen to reflect the sounds at an earlier time. In addition, since English is a composite of Germanic and Romance languages, different spelling systems come into play. One example is the pronunciation of *g*. Since *g* is always hard in Germanic languages, there are many exceptions of Germanic origin (e.g., *girl, gift*) to the "g soft before e and i" rule (which comes from the Romance languages). In addition, there are certain eccentricities, such as replacing *i* with *y* at the ends of words that reflect scribal practice (*y* was thought to look nicer at the end of words).

The third component is that the structure of English spelling is different from that of Spanish and Finnish in that (in many cases) the spelling is meant to indicate the morphemic structure of the word rather than the pronunciation. Thus the spelling of *vineyard* indicates that it has something to do with vines at the expense of representing the pronunciation of the *i* as long instead of short. Two general examples of this principle are pluralization—*s* represents the plural regardless of whether it is pronounced /s/ (*tops*) or /z/ (*bins*)—and past tense: *ed* represents the past regardless of whether it is pronounced /ed/ (*related*), /t/ (*based*), or /d/ (*spelled*). Another general example is with derived words such as *courageous* or *rotation*. In English, pairs such as *courage-courageous* are spelled similarly, even though the vowel sounds in the stem change and the consonant sounds change in pairs such as *rotate-rotation*. In contrast to English, a language like Spanish will conceal the morphological relation between words to indicate the correct pronunciation. Thus, as a rule, morphemically related words in English are spelled alike to indicate their related meaning, while in a phonetically based language like Spanish, representing morphemic relationships is secondary to representing the sound.

There have been some claims that the system in English is close to optimal in reflecting the underlying morphological structure by a system of subtle rules (Chomsky & Halle, 1968). While the claim may be justified in certain limited sets of vocabulary, there are too many inconsistencies in its application to take the claim seriously. In sets like *pin-pinning, pine-pining* the spelling somewhat obscures the morphemic relationship in order to preserve the sound rules (long *e* before a single medial consonant or final e; short e before a double medial consonant or final consonant). Other examples that are similar to the usual Spanish procedure are *picnic-picnicking, panic-panicking*. Moreover, derivations do not always preserve the spelling of the morpheme as in *pronounce-pronunciation*.

The fourth way in which English spelling is designed to represent meaning apart from sound is different spelling for homophones such as *their-there, cite-site*. Here the written language is making a distinction that the spoken language does not. Of course, using different spellings for homophones is not limited to English: it is common in logographic languages such as Chinese and the Kanji system in Japanese and in many alphabetic languages. While it is rarer in languages such as Spanish, it does occur (e.g., *sí* meaning *yes* is written with an accent over the *i* to distinguish it from *si* meaning *if*).

Alphabetic languages are sometimes classified as having a "shallow" or "deep" orthography depending on whether the rules of spelling merely represent the sound (as in Spanish) or the morphemic structure as well (as in English), respectively. The above discussion indicates that the distinction is not absolute, however, since most alphabetic languages embody both principles to some extent. However, there are things in alphabetic writing systems (especially English) that are idiosyncratic and make little sense (e.g., writing the past tense of the verb *lead* as *led* but writing the metal as *lead*).

Some general comments about writing systems

Direction of writing

Writers of English are so used to the direction of writing being left-to-right that they forget a left-to-right order is by no means universal. In fact, languages have used almost all conceivable systems to order print on the page. English and other contemporary European languages that use alphabets are all written from left to right with the order of the lines of print going from top to bottom. In contrast, Hebrew, Arabic, and other Semitic languages are written from right to left, but with the lines of print also going from top to bottom. In Chinese the traditional organization of print was in columns, with a column being read from top to bottom and the columns read from right to left. However, in mainland China a horizontal system now predominates, with the direction of print going from left to right. Japanese can be written vertically or horizontally in either order (although the left-to-right order is far more prevalent). Historically, languages have been written in various directions. The Egyptian writing was originally vertical, but later was right-to-left, while cunciform was left-to-right. The early alphabetic writings in both Greek and Roman, while always in rows, were by no means uniform as to direction, going from left to right, right to left, or using a more creative solution, called *boustrephedon*: one line of writing would be from left to right with the next right to left, with the direction of the characters reversed! (Boustrephedon means "as the ox plows".)

What is one to make of all this non-uniformity? It clearly suggests that the direction of print is relatively arbitrary, although there do appear to be two constraints. First, in going vertically (either within a line or between lines), the direction is virtually always top-to-bottom, suggesting that there is something natural about the top being the starting place. Second, for alphabetic languages, the print is always organized in rows rather than columns. The organization of writing into rows rather than columns makes sense from what is known of visual perception, since there is better acuity further out from the center of fixation in the horizontal direction than in the vertical direction. Thus, if it is important to see a great deal of text along the line, row organization would be preferred over column organization. The fact that Chinese used vertical organization of the lines of text suggests that it is not important (or possible) to see a great deal of text at one time in Chinese.

It is surprising that left-to-right is not a more preferred order for writing, since when writing right-handed (as over 90% of most populations do) the hand can assume a more natural position and not smear what has been written if it is written in ink. However, two factors may explain why right-to-left is used as much as it is. The first is that writing systems may have evolved when the standard writing might not have been with ink but rather with such non-smearable methods such as carving on stone or wood. (The fact that cuneiform was left-to-right may not have been an accident, since it was written in wet clay, where the smearing might have been a problem.) The second is that the order may have been codified in a writing system, and then other writing systems derived from it may have adopted the same order. Thus the Semitic languages may have copied the Egyptian order and the Japanese and Korean the Chinese order.

It would be hard to determine experimentally whether the order of the print matters to the reader. Comparing across languages (such as comparing reading speed in Hebrew and English) would be of little value since there are many differences between the two languages besides the order of print (but see Albert, 1975). Since Chinese has been written in both a vertical and horizontal format, it would seem to offer the best opportunity to study the effect of the writing system independent of language differences. However, a study by Shen (1927) found a difference in favor of the vertical system, whereas a more modern study (Sun, Morita, & Stark, 1985) found a big difference in the opposite direction. The difference between the findings probably reflects the fact that the vertical format predominated 80 years ago (and thus the readers had much more experience with it), while the horizontal format predominates in mainland China today.

More generally, if we compare across two different sets of readers to test whether differences in the writing systems matter, it is hard to eliminate linguistic and/or cultural differences in the comparison. If we compare within individuals, it is hard to be sure that the familiarity with the writing systems is equated. Thus we are unlikely to get a definitive answer to the question of whether the order of print matters. The fact that languages have used different orders and there appears to be no gross difference in reading speeds in readers of different languages suggests that there is no optimal order. The only exception may be that alphabetic languages work better in rows than columns because visual acuity is better in the horizontal direction. (However, since all alphabetic languages have a common source, the reason that they are all horizontally organized may merely be historical.)

Punctuation and spacing

In English and most other alphabetic languages, word boundaries are indicated by spaces,[2] sentence boundaries by periods, and clause and many phrase boundaries by commas, parentheses, semicolons, and other punctuation markers, but morpheme boundaries are only occasionally marked by hyphens. In contrast, in most logographic languages morpheme boundaries are clearly marked while, as indicated earlier, word boundaries are not. Further, in many languages, sentences are marked (e.g., by a small circle but no space between two adjacent characters) and punctuation marks analogous to commas are also used. In Japanese, because of the mixing of the logographic and syllabic characters, words and morphemes are both marked pretty well. A content word might be marked by more than one Kanji character, but then its wordness would be indicated because the surrounding characters would be Kana (which look quite different). On the other hand, the morphemic structure of a word is revealed not only by the series of Kanji characters, but inflections are marked by a Kana symbol adjacent to the Kanji root. It is still the case in Japanese that word boundaries are not consistently marked. The written languages derived from Chinese originally did not use punctuation either, so that morphemes were the only consistently marked unit. However, punctuation to indicate phrases and other larger units is now fairly commonly used, and in some of these written languages spaces are used to indicate word boundaries.

We should emphasize, however, that the system of punctuation in alphabetic languages is not straightforward. For example, as any writer knows, the rules for the use of commas are not codified in English. Commas do not mark all phrase boundaries (presumably only those where the speaker takes a relatively long pause) and furthermore indicate other things as well (such as enumeration). Moreover, it is clear that no system of punctuation makes any serious attempt to indicate how what is written should sound. For example, as indicated above, there is rarely any consistent marking of where there would be pauses; in addition, writing systems rarely indicate where the pitch or volume of the spoken utterance would rise and fall.

Another aspect of syntax that is usually only haphazardly marked in writing is the part of speech of a word. In Japanese, content words and function words are indicated by the Kanji–Kana distinction (although content words are written in Kana as well). In English we indicate proper nouns (and their adjectival forms) by capitalization while in German all nouns are capitalized.

The above discussion makes clear that writing systems have been mainly designed to ensure that the written language has been captured at the level of the word or morpheme. Some higher-order units, such as sentences, are fairly consistently marked now in most writing systems, but much of the higher-order structure of the spoken language is not consistently indicated.

Is there a best system of writing?

The answer obviously depends on what you mean by best. The history of writing suggests a clear evolutionary trend. Cultures started out with picture writing in which the symbols were arranged as if in a picture, rather than in a definite sequence. These systems evolved to a logographic system, which in turn evolved to syllabic systems and finally to alphabetic systems. While not all cultures have evolved to alphabetic systems, the order seems fixed: there are no recorded instances where a culture has moved backwards in the sequence. Such an evolutionary argument suggests that alphabets are fitter (in the Darwinian sense) than syllabaries, which in turn are fitter than logo-graphic systems. However, if we are to take the evolutionary argument seriously, we have to remember that fitness is always defined in terms of the ecological niche of the organism (or culture).

There are many dimensions on which one can evaluate a writing system. For example, one advantage of a logographic system is that the same writing system can be used to represent different languages or dialects, as opposed to a sound-based system. (The distinction between a language and a dialect is not clear: one common definition is that a language is a dialect with an army.) Historically, the Chinese writing system was used to represent a large number of different languages that were not mutually intelligible. The phonetic complements would be useful if the morphemes were pronounced roughly in the same way (as in French, Spanish, and Italian). On the other hand, a logography is much harder to codify (dictionaries are much harder to organize and use) and to produce (writing Chinese appears to be much slower than writing alphabetic languages and printing it is far more difficult). Thus a major selective pressure for the evolution away from logog-raphies may have been to make writing and printing easier. The fact that China now uses an alphabetic system (Pinying) to help people to learn to read suggests that logographies may be harder to learn. The advantage of alphabetic systems over syllabaries appears to be that, for many languages, the number of symbols needed to represent each syllable unambiguously is too great for either the writer or reader (or both). However, for a language like Japanese, it is not clear that an alphabetic system would be an improvement over Kana, since the number of syllables is so small.

There is little in the above discussion to suggest that a major contributor to the evolution of the alphabet was the ease of reading. The only possible exception is the evolution to the alphabet from the Middle-Eastern syllabic systems, which ambiguously marked syllables and perhaps had an unacceptably high level of ambiguity for the reader. That is, the ambiguity in syllabic systems is not likely to be a problem for a writer, so that it is unlikely the introduction of an alphabetic system was driven by pressure to make writing easier.

The evolutionary argument suggests that each writing system has evolved to be fittest in its own particular niche and that no existing writing system is better at representing its spoken language than any other. Languages like Spanish may have shallow orthographies because the relationship between the morpheme and the sound is more transparent than in English, which may need a deeper orthography. Certainly there is no reliable evidence that there are any marked differences between writing systems, either in how rapidly they can be read by skilled readers or how easily they can be learned by beginning readers. (We will touch on these issues later in the book.) On the other hand, one should not blindly accept each writing system in use to be optimal to represent that spoken language. There are undoubtedly many aspects of each written language that represent the debris of history and tradition that are irrelevant to current writers and readers. In addition, ecological niches change. For example, the advantages of the Chinese system over an alphabetic system may have outweighed the disadvantages several hundred years ago in their culture. However, now, when many more people are literate, the ease of printing, typing, and doing word-processing an alphabetic language may outweigh the disadvantages (and the large effort needed to convert from one system to the other) and may cause a transformation in the Chinese writing system.

Notes

1 Throughout the book we will adopt the convention of enclosing a spoken utterance with "/" marks. There is a more formal system for indicating pronunciation illustrated in Figure 2.1 using symbols that more accurately indicate what the sound of the utterance actually is; however, for our purposes, using the stan-dard alphabet will be adequate.

2 Thai is an exception, as it uses an alphabetic orthography with no spaces between words.

3
WORD PERCEPTION I: SOME BASIC ISSUES AND METHODS

The question of how words are identified is clearly central to understanding reading. It has also been a major focus of research in cognitive psychology for the last 40 years. Much has been learned—not only facts, but also a greater awareness of what the issues really are. However, there are still some areas where our ability to both ask and answer questions is limited.

While laypeople undoubtedly differ in how they believe that word identification occurs and what its place is in the total process of reading, let us attempt a sketch of one commonsense view that emphasizes learning to read in order to raise some questions and to indicate where the discussion will lead. Many people think that the question of how children learn to read their native language is central to understanding the reading process, including skilled reading. As we hope to show in this chapter, a naive version of this developmental perspective gives a misleading picture of skilled reading. However, we would like to present such a perspective to raise some important questions about reading. Some of them will be largely resolved in this chapter, but many will recur throughout the book.

When one starts out from a developmental perspective it appears that recognizing the printed word is the central problem of reading. Presumably the 6-year-old child has a reasonably well-developed system for understanding spoken language, and the major thing to be learned is how to plug the squiggles that are on the page into that system. This suggests that if children can learn to access the words of the spoken language from the written representation, then they should be able to understand the written representation of age-appropriate text. This suggests one central question about reading: Is word recognition all that needs to be learned?

If one looks at the beginning reader, this process of trying to identify written words is extremely effortful, and in fact some children fail to learn to do it fluently. In contrast, their processing of more complex speech than the simple texts they are attempting to read appears to be relatively effortless and biologically programmed (in the sense that all people without significant brain damage appear to be able to comprehend spoken language well). While the adult (or even older child) can decode words with far less effort than the beginning reader, it might seem from this perspective that the processing of words is the bottleneck in the reading process: the major "unnatural" and effortful step that has to be grafted onto an almost reflexive language-understanding system designed by evolution (Dehaene & Cohen, 2007). This leads to a second general question: Is identifying words effortful and the rest of the reading process automatic?

In addition to suggesting that word processing is effortful and the rest of the reading process is automatic, this view also suggests that identifying words (especially with an alphabetic writing system) is largely a process of going from the letters to the appropriate sounds. While the last chapter has made clear that the relationship in most alphabetic systems is more complex than going from individual letters to individual units of sound, it would appear that if the beginning reader has the general idea of the alphabetic principle, he or she can go from the print to a sound, and for most words the sound will be close enough to that in the spoken language to be able to access the correct meaning. This leads to a third question: Are words identified by accessing the sound and then the meaning?

If we think of the translation from letters to sound, we might think that reading is a letter-by-letter process (albeit fast). That is, the letters in a word might be processed serially (i.e., one at a time) from left to right (in Indo-European languages) in order to identify a word. This view is also concordant with the usual introspection that one's attention seems to sweep across the page smoothly from left to right. This leads to a fourth question: Are letters in words processed serially or are words processed as wholes?

Clearly, as readers become more proficient in reading they become more fluent at identifying words. What exactly has been learned? A fifth question is: Do skilled readers learn to apply something like the rules of spelling in a fluent way or do they learn specific associations between visual patterns and the sound and/or meaning of the word? There is an obviously important sixth question that we will defer to later chapters, as this chapter discusses the large literature on the encoding of isolated words: Does context radically affect the process of word identification? However, we think that the evidence from later chapters indicates that, although context does affect initial encoding processes, the process of word encoding is not radically different in isolation and when reading text. Thus the studies discussed in this chapter are quite relevant to understanding the reading process. In fact, as you may have guessed, most of the picture of reading presented above that we have identified with the naive layperson is incorrect for the skilled reader. (While the reading process is far less well understood for beginning readers, much of it may be incorrect for them as well.) In fact, much of what we know about word identification in skilled readers can be summarized by the following statements. (While not all reading researchers would agree with them, most would.)

1. Word recognition in skilled readers is generally straightforward and takes something like a quarter of a second per word. In contrast, higher-order processes such as constructing the correct syntactic structure, relating word meanings, and fitting the text into what the reader understands about the world are usually the problem when reading is difficult.
2. Word recognition is not merely converting letters to sounds and then sounds to meaning. However, converting letters to sound does play a role in the identification of words. In addition, conversion to sound does play a part in the reading process after word identification— among other things, it aids short-term memory.
3. Words are not processed serially letter-by-letter. The letters in common short words appear to be processed in parallel (i.e., at the same time), although words are not learned as visual templates or "gestalts". Longer words often do not appear to be processed all at once; however they are also not processed letter-by-letter.
4. Words are processed pretty much the same way in isolation as in text. While context affects the speed of processing words a bit, its effects are often surprisingly small.

(What is known about the other two questions—what people learn when they learn to read and whether they use rules of spelling in reading—is not easily summarized in a sentence or two. The latter will be discussed in the present chapter and the former in Chapters 10 and 11.)

The fourth point has important methodological implications, because it justifies the use of experiments in which words in isolation are identified to illuminate how words are processed in reading. Although we will briefly allude in this chapter to how words are processed in context, we need to provide quite a bit of information about eye movements (in Chapter 4) in order to discuss how words are actually processed in context. Thus identification of isolated words will be our focus in this chapter, and we will focus on the core issues that the research on words in isolation has been most successful in answering (points 1–3 above). Isolated words were the focus of most of the earlier experiments on word recognition because it is more difficult to study how words are processed while reading text (both because it requires more sophisticated equipment and because the experimenter has far less control over the situation).

Since context does have some effects on word encoding, however, findings with isolated words cannot be assumed to be perfect indicators of how the word identification process operates in reading text. As a result, a discussion of how words are processed in sentence context will be delayed until Chapter 5. This discussion will also return to many of the core issues discussed in the present chapter to indicate how our knowledge of word identification has progressed since this classic research with words in isolation and we will suggest at various points in the chapter how the conclusions from this research may be an oversimplification.

How long does it take to identify a word?

Before going on to discuss the questions raised earlier in some detail, perhaps the best way to introduce the issues and familiarize you with the techniques used to get at those issues is to ask the naive question of how long it takes to identify a word.

Response time methods

Let's start with something simple. We present a participant with a word on a visual display and measure how long it takes the participant to say the word aloud. If we can precisely control when the presentation of the word began and can precisely measure when the participant first starts making the response, we would have a measure of something relevant. But is this measure the time to identify a word? What prevents us from concluding that it is?

First, we have measured the time it takes for something to emerge from the participant's mouth. What we are interested in, however, is the time that it took for the participant's brain to achieve a state that we call "identification." After the participant has identified the word, several other processes must take place for a response to occur: (a) the participant must decide what response is called for in the experiment—in this case it is saying the name of the word; (b) the participant must retrieve the motor program for executing the response; (c) the command must be sent down nerve pathways to the mouth; (d) the muscles of the mouth and throat must execute the command. All of those processes take time. Thus the time we have measured is the time it takes to identify the word plus some excess baggage that we might want to simplify and call "decision time" and "response execution time." This problem, however, is clearly not unique to the naming task we have selected; it would be true of any response to a word that is presented.

In fact, it takes practiced participants about 400–500 ms to name common words (or, more precisely, to get the beginning of the word out of their mouths). Thus we might feel that such an experiment would at least allow us to say that people identify a word in less than 400–500 ms. However, there is another basic problem facing us: Exactly what do we mean by "identifying a word"? In reading, the important thing is getting to the meaning of the word. But when someone has named a word, does he or she necessarily know its meaning? The answer is clearly "no." We can name words that we do not know the meaning of, and there are people with some kinds of brain damage who can name many words and nonwords, but appear to have no idea of the meaning of what they are reading (see Chapter 12). Thus getting to the name of a word in memory does not necessarily mean that its meaning has been accessed. Although both of these events may occur at roughly the same time for normal people (i.e., when they name a word, they know the meaning of it), it is by no means a foregone conclusion that getting to the name implies getting to the meaning. In fact, one of the central questions of word processing is how those two events—accessing the name of a word and accessing the meaning of a word—are related.

Perhaps there is a better task for getting at whether the person has accessed the meaning of a word. Let's try a categorization task, such as asking the participant to judge whether the word is an animal or not. We would then be pretty certain that the participant has accessed the word's meaning. However, to achieve that goal we may have paid a high price. The naming task is a relatively easy and effortless one. Although there is a decision stage, the decision of executing the vocal response /dawg/ when we see *dog* seems natural, relatively quick, and relatively constant across words. However, the categorization task seems less so. In judging whether a word is an animal, participants are relatively slow to respond "yes" to *starfish* and relatively slow to respond "no" to *bacteria* or even to *rose*, but quite quick to respond "no" to *stone*. It is clear that the decision stage in the categorization task is much more intrusive: participants need to do mental work after they have identified the meaning of the word in order to decide if it is in the appropriate category. In spite of all this, participants can usually make these category decisions for relatively common instances within about 700 ms, so that we can be quite sure that the meaning of a word is identified within that time.

Is there no other, simpler task that allows us to be sure that the participant has processed the meaning but doesn't involve an extensive decision stage afterwards? Unfortunately, no one has been clever enough to come up with one. One task that is widely used to measure the time to identify a word is *lexical decision*. In the lexical decision task the participant is shown a letter string and asked to decide if it is a word or not. (Obviously, nonwords such as *mard* are used as well.) This task is simpler (and faster) than the categorization task. Indeed, response times in a lexical decision experiment are only slightly slower (about 500 ms) than response times in a naming experiment. Moreover, we know that participants must, in some sense, have identified the word when they respond "word." However, we can't be at all sure that participants know its meaning at the moment that they respond "word." (Responses in a lexical decision task are almost always finger presses: one key is pressed for "word" and another key is pressed for "nonword.")

Brief presentation methods

Perhaps methods that time the response are not the best way to assess word-encoding time. Instead one can time the presentation of the stimulus. If we flash a word briefly on the screen (say for 60 ms), and if the participant can still identify it (e.g., name it and give a synonym), would that mean that it only took the participant 60 ms to identify a word? (Note that the response time is often not measured in such experiments; the time pressure is primarily produced by the brief exposure.) There are several problems with making that conclusion. The first is that even though the stimulus is only physically present for 60 ms, the visual representation lasts longer than 60 ms. This is the phenomenon of iconic memory discussed in Chapter 1. The data on iconic memory suggest that the visual image would last for at least about 250 ms, although it would be fading over that interval.

Can we defeat iconic persistence? A procedure designed to do that is *masking*. After the presentation of the stimulus, a pattern mask, usually consisting of bits and pieces of letters or letter-like forms, is presented in the same location. That is, the participant sees the word for 60 ms followed immediately by the mask. Subjectively the word looks like it disappears when the mask comes on. In spite of this, participants, with a little practice that gets them used to this mildly bizarre situation, can identify words if they are exposed for about 60 ms (Adams, 1979).

Does this demonstrate that it takes about 60 ms to identify a word? Well, it does seem to demonstrate that it takes at least that long, since you need a 60-ms dose of visual information to do it. However, masking is a complex phenomenon which is still far from understood. Even though the stimulus looks as though it disappears after the mask comes on, the information is likely to be somewhere in the brain and available for further processing. Indeed a likely possibility is that, after 60 ms or so, the visual information from the masked stimulus is transferred to some kind of visual short-term buffer memory store where the mask cannot disrupt it so that the word identification processes can still operate on the information; however, information in this buffer may not always lead to conscious perception.

Even if we didn't posit such a short-term store, however, these data would not be compelling evidence that word identification took as little as 60 ms. That is, we must keep in mind that 60 ms is only the time the stimulus is on before the mask appears. However, that doesn't mean that only 60 ms have elapsed between when the stimulus has come on and when the mask (in some fashion or other) tells the brain to let go of the first stimulus. We know it takes some time for the nerve impulses to travel from the eye, through the optic nerve, and into those regions of the brain that identify visual stimuli. These regions that subserve object recognition are in areas known as secondary visual cortex (Petersen, Fox, Posner, Mintun, & Raichle, 1988). The data indicate that this neural transmission time takes about 80–100 ms. To pick a simple number, let's say that it takes about 100 ms. Thus the word presented is moving up the visual pathways to the pattern recognition system and the mask is following it 60 ms later. If the mask takes as long as the stimulus to get to those centers and interrupt processing of the stimulus, then the mask will arrive there 160 ms after the stimulus was presented. That is, the brain might only process the stimulus for 60 ms, but the total time elapsed between when the word appears and when the brain is forced by the mask to stop processing it would be 160 ms. Thus, if one accepts all of these assumptions, these brief presentation methods would indicate that word processing takes at least about 160 ms (even if we assume that the information completely disappears when the mask reaches the appropriate brain areas). More recent work (Cohen et al., 2000), using a combination of functional magnetic resonance imaging (fMRI) and evoked potential techniques, indicates that there is a brain area in the left hemisphere (the fusiform gyrus) that may be specialized in the identification of visual words and that the timing of this area being activated is consistent with the other estimates of word identification in this section (180–200 ms).

Estimates from reading text

Perhaps we are making it all too complicated and artificial. Why don't we examine real reading? The typical college student reads at about 300 words per minute or 5 words per second. That means that words in text are, on average, processed in about a fifth of a second or 200 ms. There are several problems with using this as an estimate of word-encoding time, however. The first is that there is time used up in reading that has little to do with word identification. Reading can be slowed down for difficult text (and text can be difficult even without unusual words) to about half that speed. Thus it is clear that reading is more than word identification. On the other hand, we can't be sure that the reader is really identifying every word. He or she may guess at individual words or even phrases, and it is very difficult to test for whether all the words in the text have been identified.

In spite of all the problems being raised, we do seem to be converging on an estimate of word identification time. The reaction time studies demonstrated that word identification probably takes less than 400 ms, the experiments with brief presentations demonstrated that it takes at least 160 ms, and the estimate from reading suggests a number something like 200 ms. (We will discuss more careful analyses of reading using eye movement data later.)

Physiological methods

Perhaps we are wasting time with indirect methods. What about examining the brain itself to see when a word is recognized? The first problem is clearly that we have to study humans to study reading, and ethics prevent us from opening the skull to answer our question. Even if we could, we wouldn't know how to recognize word identification in the brain. We don't know for sure where it takes place and we also don't know whether we are looking for a pattern of increased electrical activity, decreased electrical activity, or some other, subtler, change of state in the brain.

While there are several methods that can be used for studying human brain states without surgery, at present only one method—event-related potentials (ERPs)—is adequate for studying the time course of the processing of incoming stimuli. This method uses electrodes held against the scalp and measures relatively gross electrical activity in the brain. The method is very imprecise for determining where the electrical activity is coming from. The signal is also very "noisy," so that the records from many trials have to be averaged in order to draw any conclusions. These records of electrical activity have certain relatively well-defined peaks that occur at certain approximate times after the stimulus is presented (although there is dispute about whether these peaks really are the same across tasks and participants). If we forget about these disputes for the moment, there are several peaks of interest (Kutas & Hillyard, 1980; Van Petten & Kutas, 1987). Earlier research indicated that there is a peak at 50–100 ms after the onset of the word, but it appears to be associated more with the detection that "something has happened" rather than identification of a particular stimulus. Another peak commonly found in the ERP record occurs at about 300–400 ms after the onset of the word and appears to be the one that corresponds to making a decision about which response to select. Thus neither of these peaks appears to be plausibly related to the time to identify a word. A plausible estimate comes from an experiment by Sereno, Rayner, and Posner (1998), in which they compared the ERPs to low-frequency (rare) and high-frequency (common) words. As Figure 3.1 indicates, there is a larger negative component to low-frequency words at just under 150 ms (note, negative is plotted down in this figure, which is not always the case in ERP research papers) as well as a larger positive component to low-frequency words at about 300 ms. The earlier component suggests that word identification may take place in about 150 ms, which is consistent with the other estimates we discussed.

What, then, can we conclude from all the above methods? We are certain that 700 ms (categorization reaction time) is much too slow for an estimate of the time to access the meaning of a printed word. We are pretty sure, but not certain, that 400–600 ms (naming time or lexical decision time) is too slow for an estimate. We are also pretty sure that 60 ms is too fast for an estimate and that something like 150 ms is about right, although we shouldn't be too surprised if word identification could take place in as little as 100 ms or as much as 200–250 ms after the word is first sensed by the eye.

Before going back to the questions raised at the beginning of the chapter, let us conclude this introduction by considering the question of whether the speed of identifying a word is influenced by the frequency of the word in the language. The frequency of the word is usually measured by taking some corpus of text that is assumed to be representative and actually counting the number of times that a particular word appears. The frequency count for American English that was standard for many of the earlier studies is Francis and Kučera (1982); however, there are new corpora with much larger databases such as the HAL corpus of the English Lexicon project (Balota et al., 2007) for American English and the CELEX corpus for British English (Baayen, Piepenbrock, & Gulikers, 1995). (See also Brysbaert & New, 2009.) To give you some feel for frequency counts, words such as *irk, jade, cove, vane*, and *prod* have counts of about 2–5 instances per million words counted, whereas words like *cat, coat, greet*, and *square* all have frequencies greater than 30 per million.

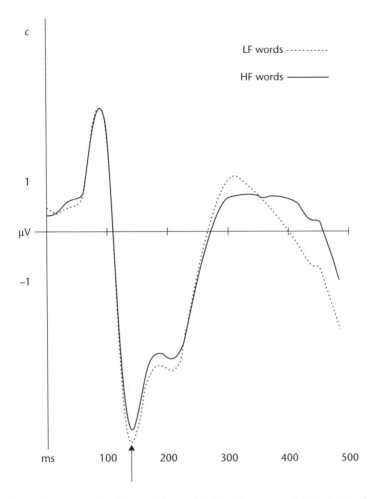

c

LF words ···········

HF words ————

1

μV

−1

ms   100   200   300   400   500

FIGURE 3.1   Illustrative event-related potentials (ERPs) from Sereno et al. (1998). The figure shows the ERP responses to high- and low-frequency words. The arrow indicates the point of early increased negativity to low-frequency words

The difference in lexical decision time between a high-frequency word such as *coat* and a low-frequency word such as *cove* is about 100 ms; however, the difference in naming times is considerably less: about 30 ms (Balota & Chumbley, 1984). Clearly, at least one of these differences cannot be an estimate of how much longer it takes to identify a low-frequency word than to identify a high-frequency word. In reading, the difference in fixation time (i.e., the time the reader looks at a word) between high- and low-frequency words is also something like 30 ms (Inhoff & Rayner, 1986). Thus 30 ms seems like a better estimate of the effect of frequency on the time to identify a word. It should be pointed out that high-frequency words tend to be short and low-frequency words tend to be longer; however, the frequency effects reported above were obtained when the high- and low-frequency words are equated for the number of letters.

Let us now return to the questions raised at the beginning of the chapter. Our discussion of the time it took to access a word had several goals in mind. First, we wanted to demonstrate how questions have to be sharpened in order to be answerable. For example, terms like *word identification* are not precise enough. Second, we wanted to introduce the experimental tools that we have available for answering questions about word processing. Third, we wanted to carry through an argument fully enough to see what sorts of answers we usually have. Each technique has its own problems, but if enough techniques appear to converge on a common answer, we can have a reasonable degree of confidence in our conclusion. (Sometimes we are lucky; sometimes we are not: techniques may converge on an answer or they may not.) Fourth, we wanted to supply one piece of data that suggests words in isolation are not processed dramatically differently than words in text: the times we estimated for word identification are not radically different in the two cases. (Rest assured that we will return to document this assertion fully later in the chapter and in Chapter 5.)

Is word processing automatic?

The claim was made earlier that, perhaps contrary to intuition, the identification of the meaning of a printed word was a relatively straightforward process, and the part of reading that was using up most of the effort required to read was likely to be the higher-order processes: those processes that put the meanings of words together so that sentence structure can be grasped and the meaning of sentences and paragraphs can be understood, and possibly those that indicate the intention and tone of the author.

Although there are claims that word identification is not only straightforward but also automatic, the claim of automaticity is a bit of an overstatement. Nonetheless, the basic point will be seen to be valid: for the skilled reader, identifying the meanings of words is a rapid process and is generally not the usual bottleneck in reading. This issue is important, since it shapes one's overall model of the reading process. For example, some models of reading that have been influential in teaching reading view word identification as the hard and unnatural step, and therefore assume that readers depend heavily on context to identify words (e.g., Goodman, 1970; Smith, 1971). On the other hand, if identifying words is relatively automatic, context is likely not to be crucial in determining how quickly and accurately words are identified.

You may be getting impatient by now and wondering what on earth we mean by *automatic*. To the layperson, the word "automatic" connotes something that is rapid, involuntary, and effortless. We will adopt Posner and Snyder's (1975) three criteria for automaticity that formalize this intuition: (a) that the person may be unaware of the process; (b) that the execution of the process is not under the conscious control of the participant—that is, that the participant's intention to perform the task may be irrelevant to whether it is done; (c) that the process takes no processing capacity— that is, that it uses no resources that other mental operations might also use. These criteria are offered as a tentative definition in order to structure discussion. However it may be too much to ask of word identification to satisfy all three criteria. The criteria may be too strict: perhaps no process (with the possible exception of some reflexes) satisfies all three criteria.

Is identification of words unconscious?

How could we possibly identify the meaning of a word and be unaware of it? Consider the following experimental situation. A word is flashed briefly and is followed by a pattern mask, as described above, but the word is exposed for only about 20 ms before the pattern mask appears (remember, something like a 50–60-ms exposure is needed for the participant to be able to identify a four- to six-letter word 100% of the time). If the experimental situation is arranged carefully— the pattern is an effective mask, and the word and mask are about the same brightness—people will say that they couldn't see the word, and will not be able to perform above chance when asked to report whether or not a word was presented prior to the mask, but the meaning of the word will be identified.

How could we test whether a word has been processed if the reader is unaware of its meaning? We need a subtler test than asking the person to report the word. Let us assume that *dog* is the word that was flashed briefly. One possibility is to present two words a short time afterward that can be clearly seen (let's say *dog* and *boy*) and ask the participant to choose which of the two was the briefly exposed word. Participants are also at chance level on this test of recognition memory, so that we still have no evidence that participants have identified the word (Balota, 1983).

So experimenters needed to be even more devious, which necessitates explaining an experimental procedure known as semantic priming (Meyer & Schvaneveldt, 1971). For the moment we will forget about brief exposures. In a priming experiment the experimenter shows two words in sequence: the prime and then the target. The sequence might be the words *dog* and *cat*. The experimenter is primarily interested in how quickly the second word, the target, is processed. In particular, is *cat* processed any more rapidly when a related word such as *dog* precedes it than when an unrelated word such as *fan* precedes it? If we measure the response time to judge that *cat* is a word (the lexical decision task), participants will usually be about 30–50 ms faster to respond "yes" when *dog* is the prime for *cat* than when *fan* (an unrelated word) is. A similar, but somewhat smaller, effect can be obtained when the participant names the target. The precise interpretation of the semantic priming effect described above is still debated. However, for our present purposes the important point is that the effect demonstrates that the meaning of the prime has been processed, as the speed of processing the target is dependent on the meaning of the prime.

Now let's return to our situation where *dog* is flashed for approximately 20 ms followed by a mask. Instead of asking participants what they saw, we ask them to make a lexical decision on another letter string about 500 ms later. Amazingly enough, participants will be faster to judge that *cat* is a word when preceded by *dog* than when preceded by *fan*, even though they have no awareness of seeing the priming word. Thus the meaning of the priming word has been identified, because the time to judge the target is influenced by whether the prime is related to it in meaning, even though the participant is unaware of identifying the prime. While this phenomenon of unconscious priming is somewhat controversial, it has been replicated many times (e.g., Allport, 1977; Marcel, 1983; Balota, 1983; Fowler, Wolford, Slade, & Tassinary, 1981; Carr, McCauley, Sperber, & Parmelee, 1982). Moreover, the size of the semantic priming effect is often unaffected by whether the participant can identify the target stimulus or not (e.g., Balota, 1983; Carr et al., 1982; Van den Bussche, Van den Noortgate, & Reynvoet, 2009).

We have been a bit vague about what *awareness* means, and this has been a subject of controversy. The standard criterion is that the participant is at chance level if asked to say the word. However, one experimenter (Marcel, 1983) reported semantic priming even when the participant was no better than chance at distinguishing between whether a priming stimulus preceded the mask or nothing preceded the mask. While not all researchers are convinced that semantic priming can be obtained even when the participant is totally unaware that a stimulus was present (Cheesman & Merikle, 1984; Holender, 1986), it is clear that the meaning of a word can be "looked up" by its visual representation without the conscious experience of perceiving the word. Thus the identification of the meaning of visual words is automatic according to the first criterion outlined above.

Is intention to process a word important?

In some sense, the experiments discussed above may have already made the point: the word's meaning is processed even though the participant is unaware of that fact. However, since the participant is trying to do well in the experiment and trying to see everything as well as possible, perhaps he or she is intending to process the stimulus (even if unaware of having processed it) and this intention is important for the meaning being extracted. Would participants extract the meaning in the above semantic priming experiments even if they were not trying to process the prime? We don't know for sure, since the experiment has not been carefully done. However, there is clear evidence that the meaning of a word is extracted when the participant is trying hard not to process it. The standard experiment that demonstrates this is one in which participants see a word printed in colored ink and are supposed to name the color of the ink. If a participant sees a color name (e.g., *red*) printed in green ink, the time to say "green" is very slow. This interference, called the Stroop effect (Stroop, 1935), is a large effect—participants are usually about 200 ms slower to say "green" to *red* written in green ink than to a simple green color patch—and it only decreases a bit with extended practice (Dyer, 1973). Participants know that the word name is interfering, but they can't avoid processing it! (See MacLeod, 1991, for a comprehensive review of research on the Stroop effect.) A similar effect is obtained when participants see the word *cat* in the middle of a line drawing of a dog and attempt to name the line drawing (e.g., Rayner & Posnansky, 1978).

Although these phenomena tell us that something about the word is processed when one is trying to ignore it, we don't know for sure that it is its meaning rather than the name of the word. One way to test for whether the meaning of the word has been accessed is to compare the condition when the word in green ink is a competing color word such as *red* with a condition when it is an unrelated word such as *ant*. In fact, while both words interfere with saying "green" (compared to when a green color patch is presented), the interference effect is substantially greater for *red* than for *ant* (Keele, 1972). Thus it appears that the interference has two components: (1) because unrelated words interfere, there is competition between the name of the word and the name of the ink; (2) because color names interfere more, the meaning of the word competes with the meaning of the color. A second finding that reinforces this conclusion is that an associate of a competing color name such as *blood* interferes with saying "green" more than an unrelated word such as *ant* does (Dyer, 1973).

However, there appears to be a sense in which word encoding is not completely automatic. That is, in virtually all of the studies we have cited above the word is in the same spatial location as the information participants are supposed to be processing. Thus it appears that one's spatial attention is focused on the word. There is evidence that this focus of spatial attention is necessary to identify a word. For example, Besner, Risko, and Sklair (2005) used a priming paradigm in which there were two strings of alphanumeric characters presented, one above the other, and equidistant from where the person was supposed to fixate. For both the prime stimulus and the target stimulus, one of the strings was a word and the other was a sequence of digits. (This was a repetition priming paradigm; the prime word was identical to the target word except that one was in lower case and the other in upper case.) When the position of the target (i.e., whether it was going to be in the upper or lower string of symbols) was cued just before the presentation of the prime, there was a substantial priming effect when the prime was in the same location as the target, whereas when the prime was in the other location there was no priming effect. Thus it appears that the cue caused attention to be moved to the target location, and when the prime was not in that location, it was not processed. In contrast, when the cue did not give any information as to where the target was, there was priming both when the prime and target were in the same location and when they were in different locations. Thus the priming did not depend on whether the prime and target were in the same location, but whether the prime location was attended to.

To summarize, the Stroop effect demonstrates that both the name and meaning of a word are processed by skilled readers even when they are trying hard not to process them. So identifying a word appears to be automatic both in the sense that it may go on without awareness and also that it goes on even when the person is trying not to do it. However, the last study cited indicates that spatial attention needs to be directed to a word to be processed. Hence intention to process the word seems not to be the critical variable as to whether a word is processed or not, but instead whether spatial attention is directed to the word's location. (We will see more evidence for this when we discuss word identification in reading in Chapter 5.)

Does word identification take processing capacity?

Before plunging ahead to answer this question, we need to discuss briefly what one means by processing capacity and how one would test for it. In our discussion of cognitive psychology in Chapter 1 we touched on the concept of limited capacity. Most theories of cognition assume (either explicitly or tacitly) that many cognitive acts need some sort of attentive process and that there is a finite amount of this attention which limits how much information can be processed at a time. Some processes, such as the normal control of breathing, are assumed not to need any attentional processing, while others, such as the processing of discourse, are assumed to need attentional processing, since it is very difficult to process two conversations at once.

The basic test for whether a process requires attentional capacity seems simple: if a process can be performed at the same time as another process and not interfere with it, then it can be assumed not to require attention, whereas if it interferes in some way with the performance of the other task, then the process probably uses some attentional capacity. For example, if it were true that one could multiply two-digit numbers in one's head as rapidly while driving a car as while sitting in an easy-chair, then one would want to conclude that neither driving nor mental arithmetic (or both) takes any (limited) capacity. On the other hand, if the mental arithmetic slowed down during driving or more errors were made, then one would conclude that both tasks were using a pool of limited capacity or resources. Put simply, the test of limited capacity is usually whether two things can be done at the same time as well as one.

We will assume that a good demonstration that a process does not require capacity is if it does not slow down or interfere with other processes. However, it is not necessarily the case that interference is due to limited resources being shared. To see this, let us return to the Stroop task. We found that it took longer to say "green" to *red* printed in green ink than to say "green" to a green color patch. Does that mean that processing the form, *red*, and the color, green, each used processing resources? This conclusion seems unlikely: the interference is different when the word was *red* than when it was *ant*, and it is not clear why it should take more resources to identify *red* than to identify *ant*. Moreover, if the participant sees *green* in green ink, then the naming time is even faster than for the color patch (Hintzman, Carre, Eskridge, Owens, Shaff, & Sparks, 1972). Thus interference between two tasks is not necessarily the result of competition for attentional resources. Indeed, a reasonable explanation of the Stroop effect is that both the color and form of the printed word are identified without needing any capacity, but after both are processed, they produce responses which compete with each other.

We could be more confident that processing a word took no limited capacity if we could demonstrate that two printed words could be processed as quickly as one. We could test this if we had a task that presents the same response requirements when two words are presented as when one word is presented, so that difference between the two conditions (if observed) could be ascribed to the greater difficulty of identifying two words. (Naming clearly won't work.) One task that has been employed is visual search. The participant is presented with one or more words and asked to determine whether (for example) there is an animal name present (Karlin & Bower, 1976; Reichle, Vanyukov, Laurent, & Warren, 2008). Thus the response—a key press to indicate yes or no—is identical regardless of the number of words. The data indicate that the response time to make a category decision (e.g., whether the name of an animal is in the visual display) is longer the more words there are in the display (about 200 ms extra per additional word). So it appears that processing words does take capacity.

However, the process that takes capacity may not be the identification of the meaning of the words; it may be the subsequent step needed to decide whether a word is in the experimentally specified category. Can we determine which is true? There is a similar experiment involving letters and digits. The participant is presented with from one to six characters and asked to indicate whether a digit is present. In this task there is little increase in the time to detect a digit when there are five letters present than if there are none (Egeth, Jonides, & Wall, 1972). Thus it appears that participants can process the meaning of six characters, and furthermore categorize them as letters and digits, as rapidly as they can process one. Hence categorization per se does not necessarily take capacity. However, the categorization of characters as letters and digits may be more automatic than the categorization of words.

Unfortunately there is no clear solution here at present, so let's try to remember what we know. First, if we look at the Stroop data we know that the meaning of the word is processed along with its color and, as far as we can tell, accessing the meaning of the word does not take away resources from processing the color (or vice versa). If we look at the search data we get the opposite picture: categorizing two words takes more time than categorizing one, so that some process associated with categorizing words appears to take resources. Thus, although it appears to take between 100 and 200 ms to identify a word, we don't know how much (if any) of this processing time takes limited central processes and thus takes time away from other processes that are required in reading, such as constructing the syntactic structure of a sentence, constructing the meaning of the sentence, or whether a statement is literal or metaphoric.

How does the processing of words relate to the processing of letters?

Physically, the description of a word (especially a printed word) in English seems obvious. If a 2-year-old child gave you a book and asked you what a word was, your task would be quite simple. You would explain that the words were the physical entities between the spaces, and you could go on to explain that the letters were the little units inside words that were separated by the smaller spaces. (The task of explaining what letters are would be substantially more difficult with hand-writing.) In contrast, a syllable, which is not physically marked in any clear way, would be much harder to explain by pointing to the text.

All of the above underscores what may seem obvious; words are units of meaning, and thus the people who devised most alphabetic writing systems thought it was important to delineate them in order to decipher the sequence of letters. Although it also may seem obvious that letters must be natural units in the perception of words, this is not necessarily the case—especially for skilled readers. That is, the process of word recognition for skilled readers is so fast and automatic that it is possible the process of letter identification may be bypassed. For example, Smith (1971) claimed that skilled readers identify English words pretty much the same way they identify a picture: they recognize the word as a visual pattern through its visual features, and the fact that it is composed of letters is irrelevant to the perception of a word. The position at the other extreme also has its adherents (e.g., Gough, 1972). Gough claimed that letters are used to recognize words, and that the reader reads a word letter-by-letter serially from left to right and encodes the word as the sequence of letters. Although this view has been criticized as being unfeasible because it would be too slow, data that we present in the next section indicate that letters can be scanned at about 10 ms per letter (Sperling, 1963); thus the typical reading rate of 300 words per minute is consistent with such a scanning process.

We think the data are now quite clear that the truth is between these two extremes. That is, we think it is clear that words are processed through their component letters, but that the letters are not processed sequentially, but in parallel. This is not likely to be true for longer words, but even there the letters are almost certainly not processed one at a time but in two or three clumps. The remainder of this section will first describe two experiments with shorter words (usually four to five letters) that we believe clearly rule out these extreme views. Then we will outline a relatively simple model of word processing that is consistent with these two experiments. The framework of this model will also help us to frame other important issues in word perception such as whether the sound of the word plays a role in accessing its meaning.

Letters in words are not processed sequentially

An obvious consequence of the assumption that letters are processed serially in order to perceive a word is that a single letter should be processed more quickly than a word. Sperling (1963), as noted above, provided an estimate that random letters are processed serially at the rate of 10 ms per letter. He found (roughly) that if an array of unrelated letters was exposed for 10 ms (followed by a pattern mask) one letter could be reported. However, given a 20-ms exposure, two letters could be reported, given a 30-ms exposure, three letters could be reported, and given a 40-ms exposure, four letters could be reported. (Not many more than four letters could be reported even with longer exposure durations, as short-term memory limitations came into play.)

If letters in words were also processed serially, what would one predict for the time to identify a word? As words are not composed of unrelated letters, one might expect that processing a four-letter word would require less time than processing all four letters of an unrelated letter string. For example, if the first letter of the word was a *t*, then the reader might expect the second letter to be an *h* or an *e*, and if it were, processing time for the second letter could be shortened by this expectation. However, and this is the important point, the serial letter-by-letter model of word processing predicts that it should take longer to process words than individual letters, because processing the letters after the first letter will take some time, even if each of these letters is processed more rapidly than the first.

More than 125 years ago Cattell (1886) tested this prediction by briefly exposing either a word or a letter and asking people to report what they saw. In fact, people were better able to report the word than the letter! His experiment has several flaws, however. First, there was no mask presented after the words or letters, so that although the words and letters physically disappeared, the iconic representation (see Chapter 1) of the stimuli undoubtedly remained. Thus there may not have been much time pressure in encoding the visual information, and the errors observed may have been largely failures of short-term memory. Second, there was no control for guessing. People may not have actually seen all of the letters of a word but could have been able to guess fairly well from seeing a part of a word what the whole word was.

These factors would not explain why words were reported more accurately than letters, however. The first merely states that the icon may have lasted long enough to allow adequate time for both words and letters to be encoded. The second argues again why there may not have been much of a difference between words and letters. To explain why words were actually better than letters, another factor is required. The one generally posited is that words are more memorable than letters. First, the words used in these experiments were usually concrete nouns that should be more meaningful than letters. Second, if one is in an experiment with many trials, the words are changed from trial to trial, whereas letters would have to be repeated. It could become very confusing to keep track of which letters were seen on which trials.

Cattell's experiment lay dormant until the cognitive psychology revolution of the 1960s, when Reicher (1969) replicated the experiment, attempting to remove possible artifacts (see also Johnston, 1978; Johnston & McClelland, 1974; Wheeler, 1970). First, he used a pattern mask to control the effective stimulus presentation time. Second, he changed the task to eliminate guessing as an explanation and to minimize the effect of memory. He presented a target stimulus: either a word such as *WORD*, a letter such as *D*, or a scrambled version of the word such as *ORWD*. (The letters were all upper case.) The target stimulus was followed by the pattern mask and two probe letters, one above the critical letter of the target word and the other below it (see Figure 3.2). In this example the probe letters would be D and K, and they would appear above and below where the D had been in WORD, ORWD, or D. The letters were chosen so that either would spell a word when combined with the other letters of the display (in this case WORD or WORK). Thus knowing or assuming that the target stimulus was a word would not allow the person to perform above chance (50% correct) in the experiment.

Reicher found that the critical letter in the target word was reported more accurately than the same letter in isolation. He also found that the letter in isolation was reported with about the same accuracy as the letter in the nonword (e.g., ORWD). Thus Cattell's phenomenon appears to be real: letters in words are actually identified more accurately than letters in isolation. The phenomenon forces one of two conclusions. If the errors in the experiment are due to limited encoding time forced by the mask, then the serial model cannot be correct, since it should take longer to encode four letters than one. If the serial model is to be salvaged, one would have to argue that the mask did not really impose perceptual difficulties and that the differences in the experiment were due to errors in short-term memory. While subsequent experiments have demonstrated that memory (in some sense) plays a part in the word superiority effect (Mezrich, 1973; Hawkins, Reicher, Rogers, & Peterson, 1976), there are several reasons to believe that Reicher's result is perceptual. First, the exposure duration is critical: if the target stimulus is exposed for 80 ms before the mask appears, then performance is about 100% even for the four-letter nonwords (Adams, 1979). Thus short-term memory, in some simple sense, cannot be the limiting factor in these experiments. Second, the phenomenon that is probably most devastating for the serial model is that the D in the random string of letters ORWD is identified as accurately as the D in isolation. Since this condition should pose memory difficulties at least as great as the isolated letter condition, it would appear that there is no way the serial model could explain why the target letters are reported equally accurately in the two conditions.

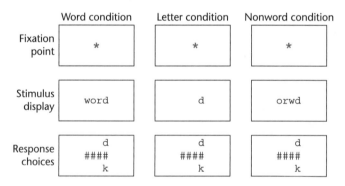

FIGURE 3.2 Sample displays from the experiment by Reicher (1969)

Words are not visual templates

Reicher's experiment rules out the hypothesis that letters in words are processed serially, but what does it establish? One possibility is that skilled readers develop special templates for words, and that words and letters are actually processed by different systems that have nothing to do with each other (with the word system operating more rapidly). (A variant of this view is that a word is defined by a set of visual features.) However, we will argue (not just to be perverse) that any theory that ignores the component letters is almost certainly wrong, and that versions of a parallel letter-encoding model can in fact explain the word superiority effect. Indeed, a clear piece of evidence indicating that a template model is not the explanation for the word superiority effect is that there is also a pseudoword superiority effect! Letters in *pseudowords* (pronounceable nonwords) like *MARD* are processed more accurately than letters in isolation (Baron & Thurston, 1973; Hawkins et al., 1976). In fact, although letters in words are processed slightly more accurately than letters in pseudowords in most experiments, there are several experiments in which there is no difference between the two (e.g., Baron & Thurston, 1973; but see Carr, Davidson, & Hawkins, 1978).

To get a sense of what is wrong with the visual template model, consider what it would mean to say that the perception of a word did not go through the perception of its component letters. It would mean that there is some sort of visual template of the word *dog* that would be compared against all visual patterns and, if they were sufficiently similar to the visual template, then the visual pattern would be recognized as *dog*. Alternatively, as indicated above, one could posit that there are collections of visual features that define each word. However, we can recognize *dog* if it is written as *dog* and *DOG*, and in innumerable different typefaces (including some fairly strange ones used on computer screens).

Perhaps the clearest demonstration of the ability to identify words even when the surface form is novel involves the use of text written in AlTeRnAtInG cAsE sUch aS tHiS (Smith, Lott, & Cronnell, 1969). Given a little practice, readers can read it as fast as normal text when the sizes of all the letters are equated, and only a little slower than normal when the text looks like the above. Smith et al.'s result could be criticized because measuring reading rate may not be a sufficiently sensitive measure of processing difficulties; if the text is easy enough, people may be able to guess words and letters in the alternating case condition well enough to get by. In contrast, there is some evidence for a cost due to alternating case in lexical decision experiments. The original experiment examining this issue (Coltheart & Freeman, 1974) observed only a 12-ms slowing to "word" decisions for alternating case words than for words written in lower case. However, more recent experiments (e.g., Perea & Rosa, 2002) have observed substantially greater effects. The problem in interpreting these experiments is whether the slowing of the response is due to slowing the actual word identification time or merely to cautiously slowing the response because the word looks strange.

How would either of these versions of whole-word theories attempt to explain these results? A template theory seems totally helpless, since most people clearly have not encountered words in that form before. Smith, who espoused the feature theory, argued that the features for recognizing words are independent of the case of the letters. This seems pretty far-fetched, as it is hard to see what features certain upper and lower case letters such as A and a, R and r, or D and d have in common. The fact that the case of the letters appears to be largely irrelevant to the perception of words has led to the widespread acceptance that word identification proceeds largely through case- and font-independent *abstract letter identities* (Besner, Coltheart, & Davelaar, 1984; Coltheart, 1981; Evett & Humphreys, 1981; Rayner, McConkie, & Zola, 1980). It also leads to the conclusion that word shape is not an important cue for word identification (for corroborating evidence see Paap, Newsome, & Noel, 1984).

A relatively simple model of word perception

Let us briefly assess the argument so far. The experiments in word recognition described earlier appear to rule out the hypothesis that letters in words (or even in short nonwords) are processed serially. Second, it appears unlikely that the rapid perception of words is due to a visual template or set of features for each word (there will be more evidence below against template theories). This appears to leave as the only contending hypothesis the idea that letters in words are processed in parallel and the encoding of a word goes through the component abstract letters. (See Figure 3.3 for a schematic version of such a model.) However, since words are perceived better than either individual letters or strings of unrelated letters, one needs to say more than that letters are processed in parallel. That is, in some way, the encoding of letters in words must be mutually facilitative.

Let us start out with a proof by blatant assertion: there are computer simulations of such a parallel encoding model that in fact can predict the word superiority effect. The initial ones were by McClelland and Rumelhart (1981), Paap, Newsome, McDonald, and Schvaneveldt (1982), and Rumelhart and McClelland (1982). While we make no claims that this type of model must be the way that the brain perceives words, such a mechanism is at least plausible and is reasonably consistent with what we know about word perception. (However, it will need to be complicated, as we will discuss later.) We will try to give you a feeling for how these models work, but if the following is not clear either you will have to take our word for the fact that they can explain these data or you will have to consult the originals. We will concentrate on the Paap et al. model, since it is somewhat easier to see how it works.

As can be seen in Figure 3.3, working upwards from the bottom of the diagram, at the first stage of analysis there are visual features such as horizontal lines, edges, corners, etc. These feed into letter detectors at the second level of analysis and the letter detectors, in turn, feed into word detec-

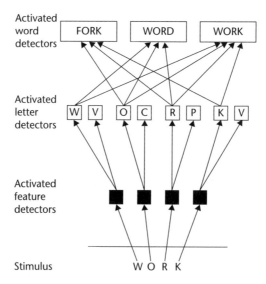

FIGURE 3.3 Schematic diagram of a model of word identification in which component letters are processed in parallel. There are three stages: feature detectors, letter detectors, and word detectors. Note, however, that at the letter detector and word detector stages, more than one detector is activated by the input. For example, at the letter level, the "W" in the stimulus not only activates the "W" detector, but also the "V" detector. (It might also activate other letter detectors as well, but less strongly as they are less visually similar to a "W.") However, what the diagram does not indicate is that the excitation is usually not equal, so that the "W" detector would almost always be more strongly excited by the letter "W" than the "V" detector would. A similar logic occurs at the word level. Another way in which the diagram is oversimplified is that only excitatory connections are shown. However, in most models there would be inhibitory connections as well. Thus, the presence of the letter "K" in the final position would inhibit the "WORD" detector

tors. (To simplify things we have left out another level which would distinguish between case- and font-dependent letter detectors for A, a, α, and **a**, which would all feed into a single abstract "A" detector.) The detectors work in pretty much the way that individual neurons (nerve cells) work: if there is enough activity in the neurons that provide input to a particular neuron, that neuron will become active. Thus, an *A* would be recognized in a given location if the features that constitute one of these representations of an *A* (such as horizontal lines, slanted lines, acute angle pointing up) are excited by the visual input. (Novel typefaces would presumably be learned either by creating new detectors for each of the letters or by modifying the features of one of the old detectors to be able to recognize the new ones as well.)

An important aspect of these models is that the activation of a detector is not all-or-none. If four features of a capital *A* are active, then the *A* detector is more active than if three features are, which in turn would produce more *A* detector activity than when only two *A* features are active. The same applies at the word level. The *dog* detector would not need activity from each of the *d, o,* and *g* detectors to start its activity: there would be some activity in the *dog* detector given any activity in the component letters, and the more activity in the component letters, the more activity in the *dog* detector. These earlier models also assumed that the word detector knows the exact spatial position of the component letters; otherwise it couldn't tell *dog* from *god*. Especially for longer words, this assumption seems unrealistic (e.g., that the reader would automatically encode that *o* was the seventh letter of *detectors*). We will return to this issue later and discuss some more recent work that probes the issue of letter order carefully. However, for the moment, let us assume that letter position is encoded perfectly.

Back to the word superiority effect! Recall that the participant is presented with a briefly presented word or letter followed by a mask, and errors are made. Thus not all the visual features have been adequately processed. For the purposes of the argument, let us assume that a particular exposure duration sets the level of visual information so that each letter detector is only excited to 50% of its maximum level. However, it is reasonable that the word detector could be excited to a higher level (let's say 80% of its maximum level). How? Because of the redundancy of words: only a small fraction of the possible combinations of letters are words in the language. Thus even a hint of *d, o,* and *g* may make the stimulus much more likely to be *dog* than any other word. In the Paap et al. model, letters are identified by reading off either the letter detector activation directly, or by reading off the word detector activation. Thus, since letters in isolation would have to be identified solely on the basis of letter detector activity while letters in words can be identified either on the basis of word detector activity or letter detector activity, letters in words will be identified more accurately than letters in isolation, even though the letter detection level comes before the word detection level.

The McClelland and Rumelhart (1981) interactive activation (IA) model and its many successors (e.g., Coltheart, Rastle, Perry, Langdon, & Ziegler, 2001; Grainger & Jacobs, 1996) work slightly differently in that the activation from the word-level detectors feeds back to the letter-level detectors. These models thus appear to be quite different, as there is no such explicit feedback in the Paap et al. model. However, functionally, the Paap et al. model has feedback in the sense that the explicit identification of letters is partly due to reading off the word detectors (e.g., "I identified the stimulus as *dog*, so the third letter must be a *g*").

The above is a sketch of how these models explain the word superiority effect. We have glossed over complexities, the major one being how the decision is actually made on what letter is actually in a given spatial position. The decision is complex since it must pay attention to activity at both the letter and word detector levels, and it must also sort out competing activity (e.g., if a D is present, the *D* detector would be active, but so would the *O* and *P* detectors, since those letters share visual features with *D*). Although you might still find it hard to see how a letter in the word can be identified better than a letter in isolation even when guessing has been controlled for, the Paap et al. and McClelland and Rumelhart models both make good quantitative predictions about the size of the difference in accuracy between identification of letters in words and letters in isolation.

There is a point that must be emphasized: the data we have been discussing are the percentage of correct identifications given a forced choice between two letters. As the model makes clear (see Figure 3.3) letter identification is only indirectly related to either the activation of words or the activation of letters. In general, any task that humans perform will only be indirectly related to a fundamental psychological process. Moreover, so far neither we nor Paap et al. have committed ourselves to what in the model would correspond to perception of a word or perception of a letter. The simplest possibility is that the word (or letters) is perceived if the excitation in a particular detector exceeds a certain threshold—let's say 75% of the maximum possible excitation. That assumption leads to what may sound like an absurd prediction, namely that a word could be perceived before its component letters are perceived. However, the prediction might not be absurd. First, misspellings of words are sometimes (incorrectly) identified as the correctly spelled word and the reader is unaware of the misspelling (Ehrlich & Rayner, 1981); hence, these "words" are, in some sense, perceived before their component letters. Similarly, words can be misperceived (i.e., perceived as other words). Perhaps more strikingly, one can often be aware that a letter string such as *diffrence* is a misspelling, but take a while to discover what is wrong. These examples all suggest that the perception of words and letters are somewhat independent processes.

You may have thought that we glossed over the pseudoword superiority effect because it would be impossible for these models to explain it. However, the Paap et al. model was in fact constructed largely to explain the pseudoword superiority effect. Our exposition of the models so far cannot explain how letters in pseudowords are identified almost as accurately as letters in words. However, if one mechanism is added, then they can. (As we will see, a similar mechanism will be used to explain how a pseudoword is pronounced.) The mechanism is as follows. When a letter string appears, it not only excites the lexical entry that is identical to it, but "neighbors" of it as well. Thus, if the stimulus is *WORK*, it not only excites the lexical entry *work*, but it also excites *word, wore, fork*, and other lexical entries that are orthographically similar to it (see Figure 3.4). The question of how "similarity" is defined is complex: the similarity of the stimulus and the word detector would undoubtedly depend on the number of letters that they had in common in the same positions and the visual similarity of the letters that differed, and might also depend on the position of the difference (e.g., a difference between the stimulus and the lexical entry in the first letter position might be more important than a difference in a later position). However similarity is defined—let us assume (for simplicity) that it merely depends on the number of letters in common—the excitation would be greater, the more similar the letter string was to the lexical entry. The word *WORK* would be identified correctly since the excitation would be greatest for *work*.

What if the stimulus is *MARD*? Even though it has no lexical entry, it has neighbors like *card, ward, mark, mare, maid*, etc., and each of these entries would be excited to an appreciable degree (Figure 3.4). To explain how a letter is detected we need to make another assumption, namely that the person can read letters off the lexical entries at each letter position. In the above example most of the excited lexical entries would "vote" for *m* in the first position, *a* in the second position, *r* in the third position and *d* in the fourth position, so that the letters of the pseudoword *MARD* could be read off of the word detectors. (The "read off" process would be in parallel, though.) In the model, letters in real words are read off of the word detectors in the same sort of way, so that there is some "noise" from the wrong votes of neighbors. However, it is still probably difficult to believe that this process would in fact lead to almost as accurate letter identification for pseudowords as for real words, so you will have to take our word that the model does in fact predict such a result. (As

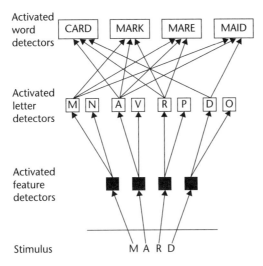

FIGURE 3.4 The same mechanism as in Figure 3.3 in the process of identifying a pseudoword. As in Figure 3.3, only some of the activated letter and word detectors are shown. What is also not shown in the model is an additional stage that would "poll" the activated word detectors to find the most popular letters at each letter position (see text). There are more complex versions of this model, in which there are "letter cluster detectors" as well (e.g., a detector for MA in the initial position). As subsequent discussion will indicate, these additional detectors are needed in order to account for all of the phenomena involving pseudowords

indicated above, the McClelland and Rumelhart model has a slightly different metaphor—feedback from the word detectors to the letter detectors—which is equivalent to the process of reading the letters off of the word detectors described above.)

This parallel letter model, if suitably modified, thus has a lot more flexibility and power than it appeared to at first. A point that should be emphasized is that while there are no subword units in the model other than letters, the process of reading the letters off of the word detectors is analytic: the polling of the word detectors is letter-by-letter. This point will become even more important when we consider how words (and pseudowords) are pronounced.

The role of near misses in word identification

The discussion above has indicated that word identification is more than a simple pipeline where a word is recognized if and only if the appropriate letters appear in the appropriate position. Later we will discuss one clear counter-example to that: a word is sometimes misidentified as its homophone (e.g., *meet* is misidentified as *meat*). However, before discussing the role of sound in the encoding of words, there are two lines of research that get at aspects of uncertainty in identification at the orthographic level. The first, which seems to follow from the above models, is that the existence of orthographically similar words affects the identification of a printed word. The second is how errors in letter order affect the encoding of words.

The first question has been investigated extensively by asking whether the presence of orthographic neighbors has an effect on encoding time or accuracy for a word, and if so, whether the effect is inhibitory or facilitative. Earlier, we used the notion of an *orthographic neighbor*, classically defined as a letter string of equal length to a target word but with one letter substituted (e.g., *ward* is an orthographic neighbor of *wand*). Recently there has been research (e.g., Davis, 2010; Davis,

Perea, & Acha, 2009) showing that this is too restrictive a view of "neighbor" and that one should consider other types of neighbors such as deletion neighbors (e.g., *wad*) or addition neighbors (e.g., *waned*). However, we will restrict our discussion to the classic (substitution) definition of "neighbor", as the same general points apply.

The questions that research on word neighbors has primarily focused on are (a) the effect of the number of word neighbors on identification time and accuracy and (b) the effect of the frequency of these word neighbors on identification time and accuracy. Your first reaction may be that it is obvious that the effect of having more neighbors and higher-frequency neighbors would have to be inhibitory. That is, if a printed word activates not only the lexical entry of the actual word, but also the lexical entries of similar words such as neighbors (as in the models we have discussed), then the presence of these neighbors would appear to lengthen the verification stage in order to determine which of these activated entries is the printed word. However, the process may not be that simple: if a word has many neighbors, then there might be active feedback to the letters that they and the actual printed word have in common that could facilitate processing of the word.

Of course, both interference and facilitation may be occurring, and the pattern of data could be quite complex. This is one reason why a distinction has been made between neighbors that are higher frequency than the target word and neighbors that are lower frequency. At one extreme, if a word has many neighbors but they are all lower frequency than the target word, one might expect that facilitation effects would come to the fore. That is, having all these neighbors might maximize the chance that the letter detection process is facilitated but minimize competition in a verification stage. In contrast, having a single neighbor that is higher frequency may mainly cause interference in the word-encoding process.

The effect of word neighbors was originally studied largely using the lexical decision task. Thus the comparison would be between lexical decision times to two words that were matched on variables such as word frequency and length but which differed in their neighborhood characteristics. The findings are quite consistent with what the discussion so far has led you to expect. That is, the standard finding is that when two words differ on the number of neighbors (often with the number of higher-frequency neighbors controlled), lexical decision times are shorter for the words with more neighbors, whereas increasing the number of higher-frequency neighbors usually has an inhibitory effect on lexical decision time (e.g., Andrews, 1989, 1992; Carreiras, Perea, & Grainger, 1997; Grainger, 1990; Grainger & Jacobs, 1996; Grainger & Segui, 1990; Huntsman & Lima, 1996; Johnson & Pugh, 1994; Perea & Pollatsek, 1998).

The related issue is what the effect is of having all the correct letters of a word, but not necessarily in the correct order. As we said earlier, it seemed that assuming that each letter position was encoded perfectly was unrealistic, especially for longer words. Indeed, a widely circulated statement on the Internet several years ago claimed that resarceh at Cmabrigde Uinervtisy fuond that sentences in whcih lettres weer transpsoed (or jubmled up), as in the setnence you are now raeding, were as easy to read as normal text. In fact, there was no such research (see http://www.mrc-cbu.cam.ac.uk/people/matt.davis/Cmabrigde/), but the example makes it clear that one can make sense out of such text, although at some cost in time and effort (Rayner, White, Johnson, & Liversedge, 2006). At a deeper level, the example indicates that the presence of the correct letters in the wrong location is not irrelevant to word identification and thus that the "slot coding" assumption of the models we have discussed (i.e., that the visual information about the identity of each letter that appears goes only into the appropriate letter position slot) may need to be modified. At present there have been two types of models that have attempted to explain how letters out of order can be processed.

The first type, an absolute coding model, is a variant of the model that we assumed earlier. This type of model assumes that each letter is given an absolute position value, but that there is perceptual uncertainty in the coding (Gómez, Ratcliff, & Perea, 2008). Thus, for the *m* in *experiment,* it would be most likely coded as position seven, but it would be reasonably likely to be coded as position six and eight and positions five and nine some of the time. In addition, in such a model one might think of the coding either as having absolute values as above or possibly with respect to their distances from the beginning or the end of the word.

The second type of model, a relative coding model, attempts to solve the problem differently. That is, instead of coding letter positions absolutely, such models posit that order information comes from encoding short sequences of letter positions (e.g., Mozcr, 1983; Seidenberg & McClelland, 1989). One possibility is that all adjacent bigrams in a word are coded. Thus *dog* would be coded as *[space]d, do, og*, and *g[space]*, and *experiment* would be coded as *[space]e, ex, xp*, etc. This seems plausible, as it does not seem to be unreasonable that the relative order of pairs of letters could be preserved almost without error. There are of course other possible schemes. One would involve longer units such as trigrams. A second coding scheme that has been proposed is open bigram pairs (Whitney, 2001). For example, the open bigram pair *p–m* would encode the information that *p* is before *m* in *experiment*.

One phenomenon that has been explored to determine the role of letter position in encoding words is the effect of transposed letters (TL) on word encoding. The typical kinds of transposed letters that have been studied are adjacent to each other (e.g., *clam* vs. *calm*). A major motivation for studying these transpositions is that a model in which letter position is coded absolutely, the fact that the "right" letter is in the "wrong" position should be irrelevant. That is, *calm* is two letters different from *clam*, and if anything should be more orthographically different from *clam* than *cram* is.

One way transposed letters have been studied is analogous to those looking at the effects of having a neighbor—but in this case, the neighbor is one that differs in two transposed letters, such as *clam* as a neighbor for *calm* or vice versa. Words with such neighbors are compared to ones without such transposed neighbors with all other characteristics of the words, such as frequency and length, controlled. The typical finding is that the response latency was longer and error rates were higher for words like *clam* than the control words for both lexical decision and naming (e.g., Andrews, 1997; Chambers, 1979).

Such effects show that transposed letter neighbors cause interference, but do not conclusively demonstrate that the effect is necessarily due to the right letters being in the wrong position. That is, the same interference effects might be observed with neighbors that differ in having two replacement letters (e.g., *talk* and *tick*). To investigate this question, the standard paradigm is to compare performance in some way between a TL condition when two letters of a word are transposed and a replacement letter (RL) condition where the same two letters are replaced by different letters. One way that this comparison has been made is in a lexical decision task focusing on responses to nonwords. For example, is it harder to decide that *jugde* (a TL neighbor of *judge*) is a nonword than *jupte* (a RL control)? The data are clear in both English and Spanish: both the correct "no" response times to the TL nonwords are longer than to the RL controls and the error rates for the TL nonwords are also higher (Andrews, 1996; Chambers, 1979; O'Connor & Forster, 1981; Perea, Rosa, & Gómez, 2005).

Such studies definitely indicate that the assumption that letters are coded perfectly in specific channels determined by their letter position is incorrect, even for relatively short words. However, they are also problematic for a model that posits that words are coded through bigrams and trigrams. Using the example above, both *jugde* and *jupte* have the same number of bigrams mismatching judge: for *jugde, ug, gd*, and *de* mismatch, and for *jupte, up, pt*, and *te* mismatch. Thus, although such schemes do a good job of encoding word order, they appear to do a bit too good a job, in that they also seem to be intolerant of letter transpositions. In contrast, these results are reasonably consistent with a model that posits that order information is coded with random location error such as

Gómez, Ratcliff, and Perea (2008). They also appear to be consistent with a coding scheme that includes open bigrams, such as the SERIOL model (Grainger & Whitney, 2004; Whitney, 2001; Whitney & Cornelissen, 2008), because the number of shared open bigrams would be higher for *jugde–judge* than for *jupte–judge* (e.g., *u–g* and *u–d*).

Another type of paradigm that has been used to study transposed letters is one in which a TL neighbor is compared to a RL control as a prime in the masked priming paradigm of Forster and Davis (1984). In this paradigm (see Figure 3.5) the prime is, in some sense, in the middle of a sandwich: it is preceded by a forward mask (typically a row of ######) and then followed by the target which also masks it. All the stimuli are presented in the same location and the duration of the prime is usually about 40–60 ms. This duration is selected so that there are effects of the prime but participants are rarely aware of the identity of the prime. Another feature of the paradigm is that primes are usually in lower case and the targets are in upper case so that visual overlap between prime and target is minimized.

The advantage of this masked priming paradigm over the one just discussed is that one can examine the TL effects on the processing of words rather than on nonwords. More specifically, will the correct letters in the wrong position be of value during the early stages of word processing? The answer is clearly "yes." There are longer response times for RL prime–target pairs (e.g., *jupbe–JUDGE*) than for TL pairs (e.g., *jugde–JUDGE*) in a lexical decision task (also see Andrews, 1996; Christianson, Johnson, & Rayner, 2005; Perea & Carreiras, 2006; Perea & Lupker, 2003, 2004; Schoonbaert & Grainger, 2004). Most of the experiments cited here employed the lexical decision task, but some employed naming or semantic categorization.

These transposed letter effects thus indicate that there is uncertainty in how letter position is encoded such that letters help to activate a word even if they are in the wrong place (but not too far from the correct location). They clearly rule out a model that posits that letter information only comes in coded by a precise location code. They also rule out models that attempt to explain coding solely through assuming that the coding is done through adjacent letter combinations such as bigrams. In contrast, a result that is difficult for such an absolute position model with error to explain is that there are also TL effects from non-adjacent transposed letters. For example, Perea and Lupker (2004) and Lupker, Perea, and Davis (2008) found significant masked priming effects for spaced consonant transpositions in Spanish and English (e.g., *relovution* was a better prime for *REVOLUTION* than *retosution*).

```
#####     Premask

jugde     Prime

JUDGE     Target
```

FIGURE 3.5 An example of Forster and Davis's masked priming paradigm with a transposed letter (TL) prime. Typically, the premask would appear for something like 500 ms (although the timing of the premask is not critical) and the prime would appear for something like 40–60 ms. The target would then appear until the participant responds. Usually the prime and target are in different cases (as here) to minimize physical overlap between them. See text for the other priming conditions; the other primes would also be in lower case

Related to the latter transposed-letter experiments, there is a strange pattern of results with respect to differences between vowels and consonants. That is, it is clear that the identity of consonants plays a more important role in identifying a word than do vowels. For example, given the sequence of letters *c-s-n-* (where the dashes stand for missing letters), one is much more likely to figure out that the word intended is *casino* than if given the sequence *−a-i-o*. There are also masked priming studies indicating that if the prime and target mismatch on consonants, there is less priming than if the prime and target mismatch on vowels (e.g., Carreiras, Duñabeitia, & Molinaro, 2009). However, there is an opposite vowel-consonant difference when it comes to location. For example, it is harder to make a nonword judgment to CANISO than to CINASO (Lupker et al., 2008; Perea & Lupker, 2004). This implies that the position of vowels is more crucial to word recognition than the position of consonants. This is also borne out by masked priming experiments where, unlike the TL priming effect for transposed consonants cited in the above paragraph, there is no TL priming effect for transposed vowels (e.g., *reluvotion* was no better a prime for REVOLUTION than was *relavition*). The explanation for this difference between the relative importance of vowels and consonants in location and identity coding is far from clear. One possibility is that the consonants activate the word detectors earlier, and as long as there are not too many words having the same consonants (holding the position of the first consonant constant),[1] the word detector is sufficiently activated so that the location of the consonants is largely ignored and then the location of the vowels is important in the final stages of identifying the word.

To summarize, we are far from understanding how letter position is coded in visual word identification. We do know that the idea that each letter position is a separate channel and the letter information comes to that channel without error is wrong. We also know that even though coding adjacent ordered bigrams of a word is a clever way to code letter position, it cannot explain TL effects. Possibly a combination of assuming random error in coding position together with looser units like open bigrams or unordered bigrams will turn out to be a viable model. Such a model, however, cannot be too indulgent with respect to error because people can distinguish between correct spellings and incorrect spellings. Another point that is probably worth making is that all of these experiments tacitly assumed that the coding is occurring at the orthographic level, as orthography was confounded with phonology in most experiments. That is, because the order of the phonemes is basically the same as the order of the letters, it is not completely clear whether many of the order effects are occurring at the orthographic level or the phonological level. However, there is evidence that, when phonology is controlled, there are still significant orthographic effects. For example, in Spanish, *cholocate–CHOCOLATE* vs. *chodonate–CHOCOLATE* produces the same TL effects as *racidal–RADICAL* vs. *ramibal–RADICAL* despite the change of phonology of the *c* in RADICAL (Perea & Carreiras, 2006).

The role of sound in the encoding of words

We will assume for the rest of the book that the Paap et al. And McClelland and Rumelhart models give an essentially correct picture of the relationship between word and letter identification: the letters in a word are processed in parallel and lead to identification of the word. (Again, this may not be true for longer words; see Chapter 5.) But is the access even to shorter words that simple? In the models presented so far, each word is represented as a unit as in a mental visual *lexicon* or dictionary, and access to each *lexical entry* or word detector in the lexicon is by a direct visual route in which the only subword units are letters or letter sequences. In such a model, all other information about the word, such as its meaning, pronunciation, etymology, is available only when the lexical entry has been accessed (just as the information about the pronunciation and meaning of *work* is found when the reader gets to the entry for *work* in a real dictionary). This raises the question of whether it is really true that the sound of the word is irrelevant to getting to the meaning, even though it is accessed at essentially the same time.

One of the most contentious issues in word perception is the relationship between getting to the sound of a word and getting to its meaning. Although there is a reasonable consensus that the commonly held view that skilled readers go directly from print to meaning without going to the sound of a word is false, there is considerable disagreement in the field as to (a) how important a role sound coding plays and (b) how to conceptualize the relationship between sound coding and orthographic coding. Part of the reason for the disagreement is that different experimental paradigms give quite different pictures of the role of sound coding; thus there is a related disagreement about the relevance of various paradigms to the issue.

Let's start with a paradigm that argues for a very central role for phonological coding in identifying words: the semantic categorization task mentioned earlier. Meyer and Gutschera (1975) compared the ease of rejecting pseudomembers of a category to that of non-members. For example, if *fruit* is the category, *pair* is a pseudomember (i.e., a homophone of a member) and *rock* is a non-member. They found that participants made more errors with pseudomembers (i.e., falsely classified them as members of the category) and were slower to respond when they were correct. Unfortunately, in the Meyer and Gutschera experiment, the pseudomembers also had more letters in common with members, so that it is not clear whether this result was due to visual similarity or because the pseudomembers were homophones of a category member. This was remedied by Van Orden (1987) who controlled for visual similarity (in terms of number of letters the two words had in common). The effect is surprisingly large: pseudomembers that differed from members by only one letter (e.g., *meet*) were falsely classified as members of the category (e.g., *food*) about 30% of the time, while non-members that also differed by one letter from members (e.g., *melt*) were classified as members only about 5% of the time. Since the words were visible for 500 ms, people were misclassifying words a quarter of the time when they were clearly visible! Moreover, when correct *no* responses were made to the pseudomembers of the category in this task, response times were also much slower than to non-members.

We think this work with homophones clearly indicates that phonological codes are relevant and important in accessing the meanings of words. However, there is considerable controversy about how early the sound codes are activated to produce this interference with making a correct decision. In addition, there is considerable disagreement about the mechanism by which sound codes (we'll refer to them as phonological codes from now on) are activated. Before going on, we need to make a terminological distinction that will help subsequent discussion. We will use *homophones* to refer to two words that are pronounced identically but have different spellings (such as *hare–hair*) and different meanings, and *homographs* to refer to two words that are spelled identically (e.g., *port–port*) but have two different meanings (a harbor and a type of wine). A homograph can have two different pronunciations (e.g., the fish *bass* vs. the musical instrument *bass*). If the pronunciations are the same, we have a *homonym*.

Two possible routes to sound

These semantic classification experiments indicate that the phonological code activated by a letter string is involved in getting to its meaning. But how is this sound code activated? For a word like *hair* it could be simply that the lexical entry is activated by the letter string and this in turn activates a stored phonological representation. Thus it is possible that the interference effect described above occurs simply because the phonological code is activated before the meaning of *hair* is activated, and that phonological code activates a lexical entry for *hare* which activates the meaning "animal." The story for how the sound code is activated for *sute* must be different, however, as there is no lexical entry for this letter string. Instead the sound must be constructed (somehow) from the visual information. This distinction between getting to the phonological codes for words and nonwords has led to the hypothesis that there are two distinct routes for getting to the phonological code: one called addressed phonology, in which the phonological code is simply "looked up" at a memory "address," and the other called assembled phonology, in which the phonological code is assembled or constructed at the time when the visual stimulus is presented (Coltheart, Davelaar, Jonasson, & Besner, 1977). Furthermore, according to some versions of such a dual-route hypothesis (e.g., Coltheart et al., 2001), the assembly process is through a set of rules. Most of the literature (and most of the controversy) has centered on the following two issues: (a) whether there are two distinct and independent routes and (b) whether the assembly process for nonwords works through spelling-to-sound rules or in some other way.

One piece of evidence for the existence of two distinct routes is that there are people with brain damage who seem to have selective damage for either the addressed route or the assembled route to phonology. Patients termed surface dyslexic can come up with a pronunciation for virtually all words and nonwords (although understanding little); however, they mispronounce many irregular words by regularizing them, such as pronouncing *island* as /izland/ (e.g., Marshall & Newcombe, 1973). Their problem appears to be that the assembled phonology system is intact while the direct system is damaged. (The addressed phonology system in these patients is not completely damaged, however, since not all irregular words are regularized.) On the other hand, people with phonological dyslexia pronounce most words correctly, but are virtually unable to pronounce nonwords (Coltheart, 1981). Their problem appears to be that the addressed phonology system is relatively intact but their assembled phonology system is almost completely damaged. The proponents of a single-system view argue that since the data from these patients are more complicated than the presentation above, this is not conclusive evidence for two systems. For most people including ourselves, however, the evidence is conclusive enough that the burden of proof is on the single-system theorists to show why the two-system theory is wrong. (We will discuss the dyslexia data again in more depth in Chapter 12.)

This seems to be evidence for there being two distinct systems. However, it is (a) far from clear how such an assembly process would work (especially in a language with as many irregularities as in English) and (b) far from clear that the above data imply that the two systems work independently in the normal reader. One hypothesis for how the assembly process would work is through spelling-to-sound rules (Coltheart, 1978; Coltheart et al., 2001). The term "rule," however, does not necessarily mean that the application of these rules is a conscious process; indeed, given the speed with which nonwords can be pronounced (about half a second), conscious application of rules seems quite implausible. A full discussion of this controversy could easily take a whole chapter, and furthermore we don't think there is any clear consensus, so we will present what we see to be the relevant issues and the most interesting data. The task that is most commonly employed is to present a word or nonword and ask someone to name it as rapidly as possible.

Pronouncing words and nonwords

Although the phonological code for words for normal readers could logically be obtained solely through addressed phonology, the data indicate otherwise. One of the areas of greatest interest is comparing the pronunciation of *irregular* and *regular* words. This is because the pronunciation of irregular words (e.g., *one, two, choir, women*) must, in some sense, be looked up in memory locations, whereas the pronunciation of regular words such as *tree* does not need to be looked up. Instead, their pronunciations can also be obtained through assembly, just as the pronunciation of *mard* is obtained through some assembly process. On this view, the correct pronunciation of regular words could be either looked up or assembled, whereas the correct pronunciation of an irregular word has to be looked up.

If we assume this analysis to be correct, what would we predict about the difficulty and/or speed of pronouncing regular words, irregular words, and pseudowords? Although the assumptions so far would not make any predictions about the relative ease of pronouncing irregular words and pseudowords, we might expect that irregular words would be pronounced more quickly, because it seems plausible that the addressed phonology process (where the pronunciation is stored in the lexicon) would be faster than the assembled route. In fact it does take somewhat longer to pronounce pseudowords than words. However, it is still a relatively rapid process; the difference between the time to pronounce words and pseudowords is 200 ms for unpracticed people but appreciably less for practiced people (Baron & Strawson, 1976). This efficient processing of pseudowords should not be surprising; the organism should be equipped to deal with all plausible stimuli almost as efficiently as ones actually encountered before.

What about regular versus irregular words? The above analysis indicates that regular words would be pronounced more rapidly if we assume that the time courses of the assembled and addressed phonology processes have appreciable overlap. There are two possible mechanisms for this. First, the pronunciation of irregular words such as *one* could be slowed down by conflict; that is, the addressed phonology system generates the pronunciation /won/, the rule system generates the pronunciation /own/, and there would be conflict between the two analogous to that in the Stroop paradigm discussed earlier. Second, the pronunciation of regular words could be speeded up by having two independent mechanisms generate the same pronunciation, and thus the response would be strengthened relative to responses which had only one mechanism feed into them.

In fact, a reliable finding (Baron & Strawson, 1976; Seidenberg, Waters, Barnes, & Tanenhaus, 1984) is that regular words are pronounced more rapidly than irregular words. However, there is little difference in naming time between regular and irregular words if they are frequent in the language, whereas there are clear differences between the two if they are less frequent in the language (Seidenberg et al., 1984a). That makes sense in terms of a dual mechanism explanation. The assembled mechanism should be little influenced by the frequency in the language since it is based on "rules." However, the addressed route should be faster for high-frequency words than for low-frequency words. Thus, for high-frequency words, the addressed route may be fast enough to make the indirect route largely irrelevant, at least for this pronunciation task. For lower-frequency words, the two routes are of more comparable speed; thus low-frequency regular words should be pronounced more quickly than low-frequency irregular words since there are two ways to access their phonological code.

Although the above discussion of these data was couched in terms of a dual-route theory, we think the explanation of these data in terms of other theories would ultimately be quite similar, although the conflict for irregular words would be at a somewhat different level. What, then, is there disagreement about? We think it largely centers on whether it is plausible that (a) there are really rules for the pronunciation of English words and (b) they can be applied within a few hundred milliseconds. Nonetheless, nonwords have to be pronounced somehow and they can be pronounced fairly rapidly. If the phonological code for them is not assembled by rules, then how is it assembled?

A major reason that the antagonists of a rule-governed system are unhappy with postulating such a system is that it is far from clear how to specify the rules of pronouncing English. For example, is the word *dumb* regular or irregular? If it is regular, many of the rules would have to be fairly context specific (e.g., "*b* is silent after *m*"). If one didn't allow such rules, then the pronunciation of *b* would be independent of context, and the silent *b* in *dumb*, *numb*, and *thumb* would be irregular, which doesn't seem right. We probably also need such contextual rules in our system to handle certain common things, such as the ubiquitous "silent e" which is not itself pronounced but lengthens the sound of the previous vowel (e.g., *fate* vs. *fat*). However, how do the rules deal with *comb, combing*, and *combine*? We could call either *combing* or *combine* irregular, although this seems intuitively unsatisfactory. On the other hand, if we stay within a rule framework we now have to postulate more complex rules: the *b* in *combing* is silent because it is part of the syllable (or morpheme) *comb*, whereas the *b* in *combine* is pronounced because it is in a different syllable than the *m*. (The rule for knowing that the *m* and *b* are in different syllables would presumably involve morphemic knowledge—knowing that *ing* in *combing* is a suffix and that *com* in *combine* is a prefix. However, the task of figuring out that *com* is a prefix is made more difficult by the fact that *bine* isn't a word.) For longer words, there are also difficult questions about how to construct general rules for assigning stress to syllables without creating tons of irregular words. Coltheart et al. (2001), however, have a working model that incorporates a rule system and does a satisfactory job.

The critics of a rule system propose that a lexical system looking quite a bit like that of Paap et al. can handle the pronunciation of both words and nonwords. We will see how it works. First, consider a nonword such as *mard*. It excites a neighborhood of lexical entries as before, such as *ward, card, mart, mark, maid, mare*. Each of these lexical entries, in turn, excites the pronunciation of that word. The pronunciation of *mard* is then generated by polling each unit of sound (phoneme) in turn. Thus most of the neighbors vote for an /m/ sound in the first position, an /ah/ sound in the second, etc. Thus, according to the model, the apparently rule-governed behavior of generating pronunciations to novel strings is not due to abstract rules but to making a computation on knowledge contained in the lexicon (Brooks, 1977). This type of model has been termed an *analogical model* since the pronunciation of the novel string is generated by something like an analogy with known words. We are not completely happy with the term since it does not really capture the type of computation done on the lexicon to derive a pronunciation. However, for lack of a better term, we will refer to these models as analogical models.

This is a clever system for producing rule-like behavior, but (a) is there evidence for it and (b) does it really work? The strongest evidence for such a model is that there appear to be lexical influences on the pronunciation of nonwords (Glushko, 1979). That is, a nonword such as *bint*, which has word neighbors that are inconsistent in their pronunciation (e.g., *pint, hint, mint*) takes longer to pronounce than one such as *tade* whose word neighbors are consistent. Glushko also found similar effects with words. Words whose pronunciation is regular but which have irregular neighbors (e.g., *gave* which has *have* as a neighbor) also take longer to pronounce than those who have no irregular neighbors (e.g., *coat*). However, proponents of a rule system could argue that these effects are produced by differential strengths of rules: rules that are consistently applied are stronger than those that are not.

The problem with the simple analogical system described above, however, is that it doesn't really work. One difficulty is that nonwords such as *joov* are easy to pronounce in spite of the fact that they have no near neighboring words (Coltheart, 1981): there is no word beginning with *joo* and none ending in *oov*. To generate a pronunciation for *joov* with such a model, one has to postulate that words such as *groove* and *join* are neighbors, but this stretches the idea of neighbor quite a bit. In addition, the analogical mechanism would have to be quite clever in knowing how to line up the appropriate elements so that the extra phoneme in *groove* is taken care of. There would be similar problems in pronouncing longer nonwords that have virtually no word neighbors such as *mardtork* or *brillig*. Accordingly, the analogical model proposed by Glushko was complicated by expanding the lexicon to include bits and pieces of words. In his model virtually all subsets of words were in the lexicon (e.g., the lexicon would include *wor…, wo…, …ork, w…, …rk*, etc. in addition to *work*), and all of these units would have pronunciations attached. When a word or nonword appears, all of these units (both the word and subword units) are activated and a pronunciation is computed from all of these units.

As you have probably surmised, such a model seems pretty close to a rule model. It is not too different to say that the *a* in *mardtork* is pronounced /ah/ because of a rule indicating that *a* followed by *r* is pronounced that way and to say that there are lots of ...*ar*... entries excited in the mental lexicon which dictate the pronunciation /ahr/. Given that any test of either the rule or analogue view is a test of a specific implementation of that view, it is hard to determine (a) which general metaphor is better or (b) whether they are just two different metaphors for thinking about "rules." In any case, it is clear that the way that the human figures out the pronunciation of a new nonword is a very complex computation.

Although we think most people would find something like the analogical system more satisfying than one in which complex rules are stored but may not be open to consciousness (sometimes even after reflection), we think there is a thought experiment that indicates that a rule system can rapidly generate phonological codes. First, we should mention that most of the controversy about spelling-to-sound translation has used English in the experiments, and English is probably the worst case in terms of the regularity and complexity of the spelling system. In contrast there are many languages, such as Spanish, for which there is a simple spelling-to-sound rule system. Moreover, if a monolingual English speaker was given an explanation of the (quite simple) spelling-to-sound rules in Spanish, it seems likely that with a little practice (and having very few Spanish words in one's mental lexicon to make analogies with) he or she could pronounce Spanish words reasonably rapidly (albeit with an accent).

To the best of our knowledge, such an experiment has not been done. However, if the results came out as we predicted, it would appear that a rule system is capable of getting to the phonological code of a letter string quite rapidly. As indicated above, one way an analogue system could possibly explain such results would be to posit subword units (e.g., syllables) that were the intermediaries between the visual letter string and the phonological code. However, it would again seem that the analogical hypothesis and the rule hypothesis were pretty similar, and perhaps the main difference between the two views is whether the process is all going on at once or sequentially through the word, as Coltheart's rule system is posited to do. One phenomenon that Coltheart et al. (2001) use to argue for a sequential model is that the difference between regular and irregular words in naming latency is largest when the irregularity is in the initial location of the word. However, it doesn't seem difficult for a parallel model to account for this by giving greater weight to initial letters. In addition, it is not clear that degree of irregularity is controlled in comparing initial and non-initial letters.

We have taken a long detour here that focused on how nonwords are pronounced. However, the more important issue in reading is how the phonological codes of real words are accessed. As you might have suspected, the models for dealing with this question get even more complex. At one extreme is a single-system model, in which something like the analogue system described above produces the pronunciation for words as well (Glushko, 1981; Humphreys & Evett, 1985). In such a single-system view, when a word such as *one* is encountered, the lexical entry for *one*, all its parts, and all its neighbors' parts are excited and the pronunciation is based on the phonological codes excited by all that input. In order for this view to account for the fact that *one* is pronounced correctly almost all the time, the excitation of the item's lexical entry would have to be much stronger than the excitations of its neighbors in order for the conflicting pronunciations of the neighbors to only slow down—but not overrule—the pronunciation offered by the lexical entry of *one*. Keep in mind that, in the single system, the direct connection between a stimulus and its own lexical entry has no special status: it is only stronger than all the others.

Such a single-system view seems problematic for several reasons. First of all, it would seem difficult to explain why instructions could change the output. If asked to pronounce *have*, someone would say /hahve/, but if asked to pronounce it according to the rules of English they could easily switch and say /hayve/. It is not clear how, in a single-system view, instructions would change what is said. Similarly, such a single-system view has a difficult time explaining the acquired dyslexia data we presented above, which seem to argue that assembled or addressed phonology can be selectively knocked out by brain damage. The alternative explanation of these data usually offered by proponents of a single system is that it is the size of the mental units that generate phonological codes which are disabled that distinguishes between the surface dyslexic and phonological dyslexic patients: disabling bigger units leads to behavior like surface dyslexia and disabling smaller units leads to behavior like phonological dyslexia. However, such an explanation seems quite close to positing two systems in which the big units produce addressed phonology and the small units produce assembled phonology.

The other major issue is the independence of the systems. In Coltheart's system, the addressed and assembled phonology systems work completely independently even in normal humans. They each produce a phonological code, and only at the end does the organism get to choose. Presumably, in the normal case, the fastest route produces the pronunciation. (This kind of model is sometimes known as a "horse-race" model: the fastest route or "horse" wins.) This, as indicated above, gives a nice explanation of the regularity data. That is, there is little or no regularity effect for high-frequency words (presumably because the addressed route is virtually always fastest) but for lower-frequency words the assembled route wins some of the time, which will be a benefit for regular words. However, there is a facet of the model that should not go unnoticed. It argues that, for most words within our sight vocabulary, the fact that the alphabet was invented largely to capture the sound of words is virtually irrelevant. In a language such as English that has so many irregular words it almost seems to argue that the main function of the rule system is to interfere with identifying words. Since we find this aspect of the horse-race model slightly troubling, we think a more interactive dual-access model such as the cooperative access model (Carr & Pollatsek, 1985) is more satisfactory.

Such an interactive model is similar to many of the single-system models; however, it does posit that there are two distinct systems: an assembled phonology system and an addressed phonology system. In such a model the assembly system not only activates /own/ when *one* is presented, it also activates a set of phonological codes that are similar in sound, such as /on/ and /cone/. The addressed route also activates a set of candidates exactly as in Paap et al. together with their associated phonological codes. The lexical entry that gets the most summed activation from the two systems is then identified as the word. Thus the two systems cooperate in exciting lexical entries in the visual and sound neighborhoods of the word rather than each sending forth a single lexical candidate or "horse." This means that the assembly system adds activation to the correct entry beyond what would come from the addressed system for regular words and thus should facilitate lexical access. Moreover, as we indicated above, most other alphabetic languages are reasonably regular and one would expect the involvement of the two systems to be facilitative almost all the time. It seems unlikely to us that readers of English would use a qualitatively different system.

Although there would be some inhibition produced by irregular words due to increased competition between the sound codes, most irregular words in English are not that irregular and most of the ones studied in the regularity effect experiments merely have one irregular sound—usually a vowel (e.g., *pint*). Even in the case of more irregular words such as *one*, although the rules would completely miss the initial /w/ sound, they would correctly predict that the final consonant sound was /n/ and would get a reasonable approximation to the vowel sound. This may be one reason why the regularity effect is as small as it is. The regularity effect might only get a clear test if the language included wildly irregular words (such as if *droon* were a word and it was pronounced /step/). In fact there appears to be a clear difference in naming times for wildly irregular words such as *choir* and regular words (Baron & Strawson, 1976; Seidenberg et al., 1984a). Thus some of the inconsistency between experiments on the regularity effect may be because some experiments used only the mildly irregular words and got negligible effects as a result. In fact, Seidenberg et al. (1984a) reported large differences between what they dubbed "strange words" (such as *choir*) and regular words, and smaller differences between normal irregular words such as *pint* and regular words. They claimed that the large effect obtained with strange words was not only due to their unusual pronunciation, but also to their unusual orthographic structure (many are loan words from other languages).

Perhaps it seems counter-intuitive to posit a model in which one adds a noisier and error-prone channel (the assembled phonology channel) to an error-free channel (the addressed channel) for getting at the sounds of words. However, we think there is clear evidence from the processing of spoken language that such a cooperative access type of process goes on. That is, when we comprehend speech (as people did almost all of the time before cell phones) there are two routes to comprehending what is said: the sound of the speech and the visual information about the position of the mouth (primarily the lips). Both clearly convey information, since (a) we can comprehend speech when we cannot see the speaker and (b) some deaf people can make reasonable sense out of speech just from reading the lips. Moreover, we have the clear impression that looking at the speaker helps in the comprehension of the speech. Yet it is clear that reading the lips alone is inadequate for fully understanding speech (certain differences in the speech signal are not reflected in the external appearance of the face and mouth). Indeed, there is evidence that lip information is integrated with the sound information in processing speech. McGurk and MacDonald (1976) have shown that if people see a videotape of a mouth saying /ga/ while simultaneously hearing /ba/ on the soundtrack, they will sometimes perceive the sound as /da/. This makes sense in terms of a cooperative computation model, since /da/ is similar to both /ga/ and /ba/, and as a neighbor of both /da/ may get more total excitation from the two channels (sound and visual) than either /ga/ or /ba/ does.

In sum, although some researchers might not agree with us, we think that the models of how one accesses the phonological codes of words are not all that different. All argue for some sort of assembled process being relevant to accessing the phonological codes of real words as well as pseudowords. Where they differ is in the details of the assembly process and how distinct this process is from an addressed process. However, before returning to the issue of the relation between accessing the sound and the meaning of a word, we want to document that assembled phonology is critically involved in the identification even of high-frequency words, because the data indicating that there is little or no regularity effect for high-frequency words in the pronunciation task may have suggested the opposite.

The clearest evidence indicating that phonological coding is relevant for accessing higher-frequency words comes from priming paradigms. We will just mention one (that was done in Spanish) using the Forster and Davis (1984) masked priming paradigm we introduced when discussing the transposed letter effects. This experiment capitalized on a feature of Spanish that is similar to that of English: the vowel after a *c* influences the pronunciation of the *c* (Pollatsek, Perea & Carreiras, 2005). In Spanish if the *c* is followed by an *a, o,* or *u*, the sound is like a /k/ (just as in English), and in Castillian Spanish if the *c* is followed by an *e* or *i*, the sound is /th/ (in English and Latin American Spanish, it would be /s/). The question is, for a target like CANAL (which is a high-frequency word in Spanish), whether one gets different priming effects from *conal* and *cinal* (which are both pseudowords). That is, both primes are different from the target in the second letter position, but *cinal* differs from CANAL by two phonemes whereas *conal* differs from it by only one phoneme. The answer is that there was a bigger priming effect (i.e., a shorter lexical decision time) for *conal* as the prime than for *cinal*. In a control condition where the vowel does not change the pronunciation of the first consonant (*ponel* and *pinel* as primes for PANEL) there was no difference between the priming conditions, indicating that the difference above was not due to *i* and *A* being less similar than *o* and *A*. As we will see when we get to Chapter 5, similar early phonological effects are observed when people read text silently.

The role of assembled phonology in getting to the meaning of words

So far we have been asking whether people get to the sound of a word before they get to its meaning and, if so, how they get to that sound. Figure 3.6, which summarizes our discussion of the previous section, indicates that both the direct lexical and rule/analogy systems are active in determining how a string of letters is pronounced. We now consider the related question of what systems are involved when printed words access the lexicon and meaning. The central question of this section is raised by arrow 2 in the figure: Does the rule/analogy system succeed in generating a pronunciation of a word in time for the sound generated to aid in lexical access? According to one extreme view (Gough, 1972) the rule system generating the phonological code is the only route by which lexical access occurs. (This cannot be true, however, since readers would be unable to discriminate *there* from *their*.) However, perhaps the most common view today is the opposite extreme: virtually all access to meaning is by the direct visual route, with the route going through rules (or analogies) to sound and then to the lexical entry playing a minor role, if any, in the access of word meanings. That position is reasonable, but is not the only one possible. Let us consider the evidence.

One body of research that has examined whether the rule/analogy system is involved in the access of meaning employs the lexical decision paradigm. One question is whether the time to

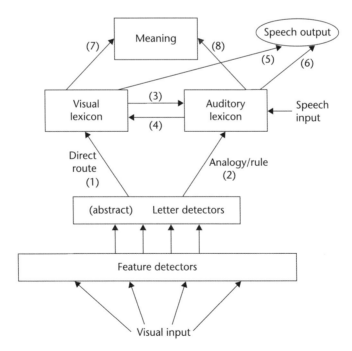

FIGURE 3.6   A model of word recognition. Encoding of meaning would involve cooperative use of paths 1–7 and 2–8. Lexical decision would involve paths 1 and 2–4, although signals from the auditory lexicon would interfere with certain responses (as with pseudohomophones). Naming words would primarily involve routes 1–5 and 2–6, while naming pseudowords would primarily involve route 2–6. The analogy/rule route would include letter cluster detectors (or some equivalent) not shown in Figure 3.5

correctly judge a regularly spelled word to be a word is less than that for an irregularly spelled word. The data on this regularity effect have not been consistent: some studies have found a regularity effect (e.g., Bauer & Stanovich, 1980; Parkin, 1982) and others have not (e.g., Coltheart et al., 1977).

A second question is whether correct "no" responses to *pseudohomophones* (i.e., nonwords such as *phocks* which have the same pronunciation as a real word) are longer than for other nonwords that are not pseudohomophones. The pseudohomophone effect, in contrast, has been obtained quite consistently (Coltheart et al., 1977; Rubenstein, Lewis, & Rubenstein, 1971) although there are some failures to find it (Dennis, Besner, & Davelaar, 1985). However, the relevance of the pseudohomophone effect has been questioned, on two grounds. The first is that, although the pseudohomophone effect establishes that the rule/analogy system is involved in generating a phonological code that is involved in deciding whether a nonword is indeed a nonword, it does not establish that the system is involved in the lexical access of real words (Coltheart et al., 1977). Second, there are claims that the pseudohomophone effect may be an artifact: pseudohomophones may look more like real words than other pseudowords. The second criticism, however, can be countered since it has been shown that deep dyslexic patients (similar to the phonological dyslexic patients discussed previously) who appear to have a grossly impaired rule/analogy system do not show the pseudohomophone effect (Patterson & Marcel, 1977).

A clear demonstration of an effect of sound-based codes on lexical decision times for words comes from a priming experiment by Meyer, Schvaneveldt, and Ruddy (1974). They showed that the time to decide whether *touch* was a word was slowed down when preceded by a word such as *couch*, which induces an incorrect expectation about the pronunciation, compared to when *touch* was preceded by an unrelated word. (If a word such as *bribe* is preceded by a rhyming word such as *tribe*, there is a small facilitation effect compared to when *bribe* is preceded by an unrelated word.)

However, the above experiments involve the lexical decision task, and it is far from clear that deciding that a string of letters is a word implies that the meaning of the word has been accessed. Moreover, the lexical decision task may involve certain checking strategies, such as going through the sound code after entering the lexicon, that are specific to the task and are irrelevant to accessing the meaning of the word (Balota & Chumbley, 1984, 1985; Chumbley & Balota, 1984; Seidenberg, Waters, Sanders, & Langer, 1984). Thus it would be nice to have some more direct evidence for phonological involvement in the access of the meaning of a word.

One possibility would be to demonstrate a *touch–couch* effect on reaction time in a categorization task (i.e., to decide whether a visually displayed word is a member of a semantic category such as *furniture*). The problem with this task is that categorization time depends on factors other than the time to access the word, such as how good an exemplar of the category a word is (e.g., it is easier to judge *robin* to be a bird than to judge *turkey* to be a bird). These variables are thus likely to overpower the relatively small effect found by Meyer et al. (1974). In fact, although there is a hint of the biasing effect in the categorization task, it is fairly weak (McMahon, 1976).

Another result that indicates that assembled phonology is involved in getting to the meanings of words involves the use of homophones in the semantic categorization task described earlier. Although the basic finding (e.g., that it's hard to reject *meet* as a food) clearly implicates that phonological access is involved in getting to a word's meaning, it doesn't necessarily implicate a rule/analogy system. That is, *meet* could activate its lexical entry by the direct visual route, which in turn would activate the sound of the word, which then would activate *meat*. While such a sequential process is possible, it is not at all clear why it would cause so much interference, since it would take two extra steps for *meet* to access the meaning of *meat* than for it to access the meaning of *meet*.

Two follow-up experiments, however, provide clearer evidence for an assembled phonology route to meaning. First, Van Orden, Johnston, and Hale (1987) found virtually the same-sized interference effect when pseudohomophones were employed in a categorization task (e.g., *sute* is classified as an item of clothing) as when homophones were (e.g., *hair* is classified as an animal). Thus the meaning of *suit* must have been accessed by assembled phonology. Another experiment by Lesch and Pollatsek (1998), using a similar paradigm, indicates that this is true for real words as well. They used a semantic relatedness judgment task (i.e., decide whether the two words on the screen are semantically related) and found slower *no* responses and more errors on false homophone pairs such as *pillow–bead* than on control pairs. That is, *bead* could be considered as a false homophone of *bed* because *bead* could be pronounced /bed/ analogously to *head* being pronounced /hed/. Although the effects in this latter experiment were less dramatic than those in the categorization tasks above, they clearly indicate that phonological coding other than a direct look-up route is involved in getting to the meaning of a word. (We will return to this issue in Chapter 5.)

Processing simple and complex words

Most of the literature on the identification of words that we have discussed has used short (three- to six-letter) words. The word superiority effect experiments (and simulations) have virtually all used four-letter words. The regularity literature we have just discussed employs a somewhat wider range of words, but a majority of them are still six to seven letters or fewer and have only one morpheme (unit of meaning). Moreover, almost all the words used were nouns with a sprinkling of verbs and adjectives. Thus our picture of word identification is incomplete. In this section we introduce two additional kinds of words. First, we briefly discuss function words (prepositions, conjunctions, articles, and pronouns); there is some evidence that they may be processed differently than the types of words we have discussed so far. We then discuss what is known about the processing of complex words. Since the bulk of the research on word identification is not in these areas, however, our picture will remain sketchy.

Function words

Psycholinguists often make a distinction between function words, which include prepositions, conjunctions, articles, and pronouns, and content words, which include nouns, verbs, and adjectives. Although there is fairly general agreement that the two classes of words may be psychologically different, there is some uncertainty about the precise boundary between the two (e.g., most people don't know where to put adverbs). One way in which function and content words appear to be different is that function words are a closed class; that is, there are a relatively small number of them in the language (roughly a few hundred) and that is all. In contrast, content words are an open class: the number of nouns, verbs, and adjectives are not only large, but not bounded, with new ones being invented each day. Another way they appear to differ is that most content words mean something in a way that function words do not: a content word such as *tree* means something in isolation, but *and* means little in isolation. One possible test of meaningfulness would be whether an isolated word could be a meaningful utterance: one could envisage the noun *dog*, the verb *climb*, or the adjective *red* or even the abstract noun *democracy* being uttered in isolation to express something, but not the function word *of*. (Locational prepositions such as *above* and pronouns, however, seem to be about as meaningful as content words.) Most function words seem to have meaning primarily as joiners of content words: they are the glue that holds sentences together. Function words are also among the most frequent words in the language (*the* is the most frequent word in English).

Much of the data suggesting that function words are special comes from the neuropsychological literature. Perhaps the most striking finding is that there are people with brain damage whose ability to read aloud and comprehend content words is virtually intact, but whose ability to read aloud and comprehend function words is markedly impaired (Coltheart, Patterson, & Marshall,

1980). This pattern of deficits occurs for many of the phonemic dyslexic patients described earlier. It also occurs for many patients with aphasia (i.e., general language problems), especially for a class of aphasia known as Broca's aphasia. Patients with Broca's aphasia usually have difficulty uttering function words in spontaneous speech as well, so that their speech is telegrammatic. Phenomena such as these suggest that function words may be represented in a lexicon separate from content words.

Complex (multimorphemic) words

We mentioned above that there is no limit to the number of content words in a language. In fact, one of the striking aspects of human language is the generativeness of words. One way that new words are generated is to describe new places, concepts, technological inventions, etc. However, new words are also generated in profusion from old words. If a word is something set off by spaces, there are languages in which new (compound) words are created every minute. For example, in German, one can say "the cameoverfordinnerlastTuesdaynight man." While English is not so extreme, new compound words such as *headroom* are probably being constructed each day.

The question that we would like to raise here is whether the lexical access model proposed so far is really adequate to explain the full spectrum of words. One reason to believe that the parallel letter-processing models we have considered so far may be inadequate for recognizing all words is that it may be unreasonable that all words whose meaning you know are actually stored in the lexicon. As mentioned earlier in the chapter, there are books that have tabulated the frequency of usage of English words (taken from a corpus of text such as magazine articles or books). There are many words that do not seem at all strange (e.g., *abusive, creases, ponder, thinning*) that have a frequency of usage of 1 part in 1 million. Even if one assumes that high school students have each read something like 4000 pages of text a year for 10 years, and if a typical page has about 500 words on it, they have only read something like $4000 \times 10 \times 500$ or 20,000,000 words in their life. Thus they have probably seen words in the 1 per million category only an average of 20 times in their lives. However, due to statistical fluctuation, the chances are pretty good that there are many of these words in this category that they have never seen. Moreover, there are many forms of a lot of words. For the words listed above, are you confident that you have seen them in the past tense (if they are verbs) or the plural (if they are nouns)? Yet you would likely be able to recognize those words easily if you encountered them. Moreover, there are various forms of words (e.g., *character, characteristic, characteristics, characteristically*, etc.). It thus seems reasonable that not all of these forms are actually stored, but instead are constructed from a base form and some sort of rule.

Even if all words are actually stored in a mental lexicon, however, there might be good reasons to have a more complex access procedure than a single-stage parallel look-up. First of all, there might be a limit to how many letters can be accessed in parallel by the visual system. Thus there may be some sort of sequential access for longer words, whereby they are accessed a part at a time. Since short words appear to be processed in parallel, the most plausible size for the units of sequential access would appear to be larger than a single letter and perhaps on the order of 4–6 letters. A second reason for a sequential access process is that it might aid in understanding the word. That is, almost any linguistic analysis would indicate that the meaning of the word *ended* is (*end* + past tense). If lexical access were in two stages, the meaning might be understood as a part of the access process rather than requiring an additional step.

An influential model of a two-stage access process for polymorphemic words was proposed by Taft and Forster (1975, 1976) and modified subsequently (Taft, 1979, 1985, 1986). In the original version, with which we are still most comfortable, the first stage of lexical access is accessing a root morpheme. The way the root morpheme is defined is somewhat different for two types of polymorphemic words. The first type, affixed words, have a stem and prefixes and suffixes (e.g., *ending*, *include*, *selective*, *undoing*). For these words the root morpheme (underlined in the examples) is simply the stem to which the prefixes and suffixes are added. The second type, compound words, such as *headstand* and *toadstool*, are made up of two essentially equal morphemes (both of which are usually words). Taft and Forster defined the root morpheme of all of these polymorphemic words (including compound words) to be the first morpheme except for prefixed words. This definition goes against more linguistically motivated definitions (e.g., Selkirk, 1982) since, for most compound words in English, the second morpheme is conceptually the root: a headstand is a type of stand and a footstool is a type of stool. However, Taft and Forster wanted a model in which the reader could rely on the orthography and would not need deep linguistic knowledge.

To this end, Taft (1979, 1985, 1986) proposed that accessing a polymorphemic word was a two-step process in which accessing the unit he dubbed the *BOSS* (Basic Orthographic Syllabic Structure—roughly speaking, an index to the root morpheme) was the first step. This unit was defined by an orthographic principle which (roughly) takes as many consonants as possible following the first vowel of the word. You may wonder how this system would deal with prefixed words, since the first morpheme in such words is the prefix, which is not the root morpheme. Taft (1981) developed a special process (prefix stripping) to deal with prefixed words. He hypothesized that if a word started with something that could be a prefix, the system assumed that it was in fact a prefix, stripped it off, and then located the root morpheme (e.g., *re* would be stripped off *rejuvenate*, and then the word looked up under the root which would be *juvenate* or some part of it). In the case of a pseudoprefixed word, he hypothesized that *re* would be stripped from *repertoire*, the lexical entry *pertoire* searched for; and only when not located would the lexical entry *repertoire* be searched for. He found that lexical decision times were faster for prefixed words than pseudoprefixed words; however, the difference was only about 30 ms, not plausibly the time to strip the prefix, search, and then search again. What seems more plausible is that access is going on in parallel—with Taft's decomposition route being faster than the direct route. However, we should note that Taft's more recent model (2006) is much more complex, involving morphemic decomposition at several processing stages.

According to the Taft and Forster (1975) model, all classes of complex words are accessed by the same basic process: (a) initial access is to the root morpheme (via the BOSS); (b) subsequently the actual word is accessed. A file drawer metaphor might help to explain the idea (Forster, 1976). Initial access of the root morpheme gives you access to a file drawer which contains all the words containing the root morpheme. For example, if you saw *ending*, your first stage of processing would land you in a file drawer containing all the words having *end* as the root morpheme such as *ended*, *ending*, *endplay*, *endgame*. Your search for *ending* would then be restricted to these items. We should note that Taft and Forster's model does not deal with identifying the meaning of a morphemically complex word that you have not seen before. These would have to be identified by a different, constructive process.

Perhaps the experiment that gives the best feeling for Taft and Forster's model is one in which participants made lexical decisions on prefixed words. Taft (1979) coded the words for both the surface frequency (the frequency of the compound word itself) and for the root morpheme frequency (the sum of the frequency of all words containing the root morpheme). If access of complex words were merely a look-up of each word in a separate lexical entry, then one would expect the surface frequency to predict lexical decision time. In fact Taft found that lexical decision time was affected by the frequency of the root morpheme even when the surface frequency was controlled. However, Taft also got an effect of surface frequency when root morpheme frequency was controlled. Bradley (1979) carried out a similar experiment using suffixed words and also generally found that lexical decision times were a function of root morpheme frequency.

The explanation for these results seems pretty straightforward. If the first stage of lexical decision time is accessing the root morpheme (or file drawer), then the frequency of the root morpheme should be a major determiner of lexical access time. How does surface frequency come into play in Taft and Forster's model? Search through the file drawer is a sequential process, in which what matters is the relative frequency of the entries in the drawer (i.e., how far down the list is the entry you are searching for). Thus the lower the surface frequency, the lower the word should be in the file drawer. However, how far down it is in the file drawer would depend not only on the surface frequency of the word, but also on the frequency of the other items in the file. Thus it is hard to predict how far down a word should be just from its surface frequency, except to say that it should usually be farther down.

One problem with the lexical decision task for studying complex words is that the pattern of data changes quite a bit depending on the choice of nonwords. Unfortunately, however, none of the other standard laboratory tasks is well suited for studying complex words. For example, naming latency (i.e., the time to begin the pronunciation of a word) suffers from the problem that people may begin pronouncing complex words well before they have completely accessed them. Categorization tasks tend to be difficult, since many polymorphemic words are either difficult to categorize or the categorization may depend only on the root morpheme. Perhaps the best task to employ would be to measure the time to finish saying the word. However, it is technically much more difficult to measure the offset of a spoken word than the onset (since it is usually more gradual) and thus this technique has not been used.

A more promising approach for studying the role of morphemes has emerged using the masked priming of Forster and Davis (1984) discussed earlier. This is because the target word is held constant and thus problems concerning the difficulty of judging the lexicality of the target are held constant. (In addition, as the participant is not aware of the prime, any artifacts due to decision processes are minimized, if not eliminated.) Typically, the paradigm involves presenting a morphemically complex word (e.g., *CLEANER*) as the prime and the root morpheme (e.g., *clean*) as the target. This is contrasted with the priming effect obtained from a prime–target pair with similar letter overlap but no morphemic relationship (e.g., *BROTHEL–broth*). A major finding of this literature is that there has been significantly greater priming from the morphologically related primes (Feldman, 2000; Pastizzo & Feldman, 2002; Rastle, Davis, & New, 2004), indicating that morphemes enter into the word identification process at a fairly early stage. However, an experiment by Rastle, Davis, and New (2004) indicates that part of the effect is due to the end of the word being a suffix rather than that the prime and target are morphologically related. In their experiment the prime was either a word that had an ending that could be (but wasn't) a suffix (e.g., *CORNER*) or one whose ending couldn't be a suffix (e.g., *BROTHEL*). Rastle et al. found significantly greater priming from *CORNER* to *corn* than from *BROTHEL* to *broth*, indicating that suffixes (or even possible suffixes) are extracted as units early in word processing.

We will leave the discussion of complex words for now and return to it in Chapter 5, as much has been learned about these words in reading experiments using eye movement measures. However, we think the experiments discussed above do make clear that the models we used in the first part of the chapter are likely to be inadequate for polymorphemic words and that a more complex model is needed that involves identifying at least some of the component morphemes and putting them together in some fashion.

Cross-language studies of word perception

Throughout the second half of this chapter we have focused on two major issues. The first was how letters within words are processed; we have argued that letters within shorter words are processed in parallel, and presented a model of how letter recognition and word identification relate to each other. The second is the role that sound plays in word perception, and we have argued that there are two routes to the lexicon, one that goes directly from the printed letters to the lexicon (a direct route) and one that involves initially transforming the printed letters into a sound representation and accessing the lexicon via the sound representation (an indirect route). We have also indicated that longer words that have more than one morpheme are perceived in a more complex way in which at least some of the morphemes are distinct units. This raises the question: To what extent are the conclusions that we have reached generalizable to languages other than English?

First, with respect to the issue of how letter processing relates to word processing, we suspect that what we have said holds true for any alphabetic system. With logographic systems such as Chinese the issue is a moot point because the printed characters represent morphemes rather than something like a phoneme. With writing systems that involve something like syllabaries (e.g., Japanese Kana), although we know of no direct evidence on the issue, we suspect that the relationship between the characters and words is similar to the relationship between letters and words in an alphabetic system.

The second issue, the role of sound representations in accessing the lexicon, is more interesting and has been studied rather extensively (Henderson, 1982, 1984; Hung & Tzeng, 1981). Numerous studies have been conducted to (1) compare word perception in alphabetic systems with shallow orthographies (i.e., those with a close correspondence between letters and phonemes) like Serbo-Croatian (Feldman & Turvey, 1983; Katz & Feldman, 1983; Lukatela, Papadic, Ognjenovic, & Turvey, 1980; Lukatela, Savic, Gligorijevic, & Turvey, 1978; Turvey, Feldman, & Lukatela, 1984) with alphabetic systems with deep orthographies (i.e., those in which morphemic properties are more directly related by the writing system) like English, (2) compare syllabaries to English (Besner & Hildebrandt, 1987; Morton & Sasanuma, 1984), and (3) compare logographic systems to English (Tzeng, Hung, & Wang, 1977). In addition there has been some interest in comparing Hebrew (where critical information used in converting to the sound representation is not explicitly contained in the print) to English (Bentin, Bargai, & Katz, 1984; Navon & Shimron, 1981).

There is evidence, however, indicating that morphology may play a more central role in word identification in some languages than it does in Indo-European languages. Much of the evidence comes from Semitic languages (e.g., Arabic and Hebrew). As indicated in Chapter 2, a fundamental difference between these languages and languages such as English is that the root morpheme is a sequence of consonants (usually three) and the other morpheme (called the *word pattern*) is neither a prefix nor a suffix, but an infix. Thus there is no simple orthographic procedure (such as that proposed by Taft and Forster) for dividing the word into root morpheme and word pattern. This suggests that identifying the root morpheme may be a more basic part of the word identification process in these languages than in English. One piece of evidence for this comes from work with transposed letters. Velan and Frost (2009) found that, when two letters of a root morpheme in Hebrew were transposed, there was a much larger cost on lexical decision time than for a similar transposition in English. Similarly, Perea, abu Mallouh, and Carreiras (2010) and Velan and Frost (2009) found a much larger cost when TL primes were used in Arabic and Hebrew, respectively, than the cost for such primes in Indo-European languages. It is plausible that morphemes may play a more direct role in languages like Chinese (where morphemes are directly represented in the orthography); however this has not yet been tested.

Our impression is that the results of the studies mentioned above (and others) lead to the conclusion that the specific orthography may alter the extent to which a reader relies on one route or the other, but that the results are consistent with the hypothesis that cross-culturally there are two routes to the lexicon. The work done on Serbo-Croatian has led some investigators (Turvey et al., 1984) to argue that accessing the lexicon via the sound representation is not an optional strategy for readers of that language. However, there is reason to suspect that readers of that language can also access the lexicon via the direct route (Besner & Hildebrandt, 1987; Seidenberg, in press). The regularity of the grapheme–phoneme correspondence in a shallow orthography like Serbo-Croatian may simply lead readers to rely more heavily on the route through sound to the lexicon. Likewise, ideographic systems (like the Japanese Kanji) might lead to a heavier reliance on the direct visual route than English (Morton & Sasanuma, 1984). It has been suggested (Morton & Sasanuma, 1984) that syllabic systems (like the Japanese Kana) have to be translated into a phonological code before lexical access is possible. However, Besner and Hildebrandt (1987) showed that Japanese loan words written in Kana (Katakana) were named faster than nonwords, indicating that access to the phonology did not always proceed directly from print to sound without reference to the lexicon. Finally, studies with Hebrew readers (Bentin et al., 1984; Navon & Shimron, 1981) have shown that, although the direct route is very important in lexical access, the phonological route is used by these readers even though Hebrew orthography is more imprecise than English as a code for the phonological representation.

In summary, we think that while different writing systems may influence readers to rely more heavily on one route than the other, the present evidence suggests that both routes are used in all languages. Once readers have acquired the ability to decipher the written symbols, reading may be a relatively culture-free cognitive activity (Gibson & Levin, 1975; Hung & Tzeng, 1981) in the sense that the writing system may have little effect on the process of reading. Thus we believe that the points we will stress in the remainder of this book are generally true cross-culturally (we will point out in Chapters 4 and 5 how properties of the writing system influence eye movements). Of course, differences in cultures and the structures of languages may have profound influences on how people comprehend both spoken and written discourse. Such concerns, however, are largely beyond the scope of the current book.

A final issue

There is a current controversy about modeling word encoding that we need to mention, as the reader will undoubtedly come across it in any follow-up reading in the current literature. We have waited until the end of the chapter to discuss it because we are not sure whether a newer class of distributed parallel processing models are fundamentally different from the parallel models we have discussed earlier, or whether they just reflect a different modeling style.

These newer models (including Harm & Seidenberg, 2004; Plaut, McClelland, Seidenberg, & Patterson, 1996; sometimes called triangle models because they posit interacting effects of orthography, phonology, and meaning) are instances of parallel distributed processing (PDP) models. They attempt to "go down" a level of processing and model word recognition at the level of individual neurons or collections of neurons; however, in these models the way in which neural processing is modeled is quite idealized and simplified. A major motivation for such models is that they want to get away from the idea that there are lexical entries, as posited by the models that we have used to guide thinking in this chapter. The models we have discussed are sometimes called "localist" models, in that they claim that discrete "nodes" corresponding to letters and words are activated. In contrast, PDP models are "distributed," in that they contain only low-level detectors that are (idealized) neurons or collections of neurons. These detectors respond to stimuli in a graded fashion, and patterns of activated detectors represent individual words and letters. For example, a detector in the orthographic processing system might respond quite strongly to DOG and reasonably strongly to DOT and DOC, but actually might respond even more strongly to something else that is not a word. The detectors in the phonological and semantic systems would likewise not be tuned to a specific sound or meaning, but would be coding something about the sound or meaning. The response system would attempt to construct a response from the firing pattern of all of these hundreds or thousands of detectors.

On the one hand, distributed models are attractive, as it is extremely unlikely that there is a single neuron or collection of neurons in the brain that corresponds to the lexical entry of *DOG*. On the other hand, the brain does decide at some point that the word on the printed page was *dog*. Moreover, at our current level of knowledge it isn't clear that distributed models are really distinguishable from the localist word-processing models that we introduced earlier, or whether they are fundamentally equivalent but are using a different conceptualization in which lexical access has been pushed back a level.

Most experimental attempts to distinguish between the types of models rely on making quite specific assumptions about the details. Indeed we suspect, as suggested above, that the two types of models may be logically equivalent, but are just at different levels of explanation. As a result, because we feel that phenomena are easier to think of in terms of the models we introduced earlier, we have focused on them. Perhaps at some future time it will become clearer whether the additional assumptions that allow these two classes of models to explain data will be much more natural in one framework than the other. One way in which PDP models may be superior is that they may give a more coherent explanation of how people learn to read words better, as they do not rely on positing visual word detectors. Another resolution might be the development of models that combine the best features of the models that have been developed in the distributed and the localist traditions (e.g., Perry, Ziegler, & Zorzi, 2007). However, at the present time we think the reader will find the types of models we have discussed earlier to be better heuristic devices for thinking about the reading process in skilled readers[2].

Summary and conclusions

At the beginning of the chapter we raised several questions about the processing of words. Some of them have turned out to have simpler answers than others. One question that was raised was whether word processing was an automatic process or whether identifying words was a major part of the mental effort that went into reading. We saw that words in isolation (at least relatively common and short words) could be identified without awareness and without intention, a seemingly automatic process. While it was far from clear that the activity involves no mental effort—indeed it appears to take about 200–250 ms to identify a word—the process of identifying words appears to be a relatively small part of the difficulties skilled readers may have when reading text. We will discuss the effects of context on word identification in detail in subsequent chapters. The data from this chapter, however, allow us to make an educated guess as to what the answer will be: since accessing the meaning of words is such an automatic and easy process when words are seen in isolation, we would not expect context to speed up processing very much. We also would be surprised if identifying words in text would be performed in a substantially different way than words in isolation. That is, it would seem wasteful to have two different word recognition mechanisms, each of which is so rapid and accurate. The answer to the second question—whether letters within a word are processed in parallel or in series—is related to the above: letters in words (at least short words) appear to be processed in parallel. Although parallel processing is often identified with automatic processing, the data we reviewed indicated that identifying words is likely to use central processing capacity.

The rest of our discussion did not yield any simple answers. In fact, the data make clear that the identification of words is a very complex process: much more so than one would have supposed at the outset. Sound encoding appears to play some part in accessing the meaning of words in fluent reading; however, there is substantial disagreement about what the role is. In some views, largely based on the small regularity effect which appears only for low-frequency words, it is very minor (e.g., Seidenberg et al., 1984a). However, there are data that lead to a different conclusion. First, even high-frequency words may be biased by sound codes (Pollatsek et al., 2005) and words (or even pseudowords) can be misclassified as their homophones (Van Orden, 1987). A major problem in deciding on the role of sound in word encoding is that irregularities in most languages are minor, so that it is not clear whether it is reasonable to expect a large regularity effect. There is no simple resolution to the problem. The position we have taken is that the data are consistent with a cooperative computation model wherein entries in the lexicon are excited by both the direct visual route and the indirect rule-to-sound route, with the recognized word being the entry that has accrued the most combined excitation. That is, we see the sound system as heavily involved in lexical access. At present, however, reasonable people can hold almost diametrically opposite views on the subject. The common ground for all positions is that direct visual access is important and that sound encoding plays some part.

There is also evidence that morphemically complex words are probably looked up in two stages, possibly with the help of morphemic rules (e.g., Taft, 1985; Taft & Forster, 1976). Thus word encoding appears to involve three systems: the direct visual route, a spelling-to-sound route, and a morphemic decomposition route—that is, a direct route and two more constructive processes. Since most of the evidence that word processing is automatic comes from the study of relatively short, frequent words (i.e., those for which the direct route could predominate), it is possible that word processing is not so automatic for words whose access relies more heavily on the more constructive routes.

We should emphasize that this chapter has for the most part dealt with a relatively narrow window of word perception: we have discussed (a) skilled readers (b) of English (c) reading isolated printed words. However, our brief discussion of cross-cultural studies led us to conclude that the points we stressed were generally true for other writing systems. We have focused on English, since it has been studied far more intensively than any other language. We have not discussed handwriting, since there are few studies on recognition of handwriting. It is possible that the perception of handwriting operates differently from print. First, since handwriting is often quite messy, sentential context may be more important in deciphering it than print. Second, since letters are not transparent visual units as in print, more constructive processes may be needed in addition to automatic letter detection.

Let us close with some comments on the relevance of the study of skilled readers to the process of learning to read. First, the better we understand the word identification process in skilled readers, the better we understand what the *goal* of reading instruction should be. However, even a perfect understanding of the skilled reader may say little about the beginning reader. At one extreme, the adult reader may be exactly like the beginning reader but do everything much more quickly and in a much more automated way. At the other extreme, the beginning processes may be a crutch to get over some hurdle, so that skilled reading may involve totally different processes than that of beginning reading. Thus there may be little in the processes of skilled reading that indicates how the reader acquired those skills. We will discuss these issues in depth in Chapters 10 and 11. The point we wish to close with here is that much of the research and many of the issues in learning to read have been framed by the research on skilled reading of words that we have discussed in this chapter.

Notes

1 In all of the above experiments the location of the initial consonant was preserved.
2 In addition to the models discussed in this chapter, other models dealing with various aspects of word perception have been proposed. These include the Bayesian Reader (Norris, 2006), the SOLAR model (Davis, 2010), the SERIOL model (Whitney, 2001), the Multiple Read Out model (Grainger & Jacobs, 1996), and the Overlap model (Gomez, Ratcliff, & Perea, 2008).

PART II

Skilled Reading of Text

In reading text we do much more than identify words. However, identification of words is clearly an important first step in comprehending text—as the eyes move across the printed page, presumably words are first identified and then glued together into larger structures such as phrases, sentences, and paragraphs. From these larger structures we are able to comprehend the text we are reading. We are able to infer the gist of the text or certain relationships, and store this information in memory. The central task in reading research is to understand how all this is accomplished by the reader. If we are really to understand the process of reading, we would like to know the details of this cognitive activity from moment to moment. For example, if a sentence such as "The man bit the dog" is read, we would like to know when and how each word was identified, when and how the reader identified the man as the actor and the dog as the recipient of the action, and when and how the reader realized that the sentence was grammatically correct but mildly absurd.

A central tenet of this book is that the record of how the eyes move during silent reading of text is by far the best way to study the process of reading. Other methods are useful (such as the single word methods described in Part I), but usually disturb the process of reading so much that one is never sure whether the conclusions drawn from them would generalize to normal silent reading. Since eye movements can be measured relatively unobtrusively when someone is silently reading text, they allow us to study real reading. In addition to being unobtrusive, the eye movement record does allow us quite a bit of insight into the cognitive processes of reading (as we hope the next several chapters will document). However, understanding the relationship of eye movements to cognitive processes in reading requires mastering some technical detail.

The plan of the next three chapters is as follows. In Chapters 4 and 5 we discuss how visual information is extracted from the printed page. Chapter 4 presents some basic facts about eye movements and discusses what information is extracted from the page on a single glance or fixation. Chapter 5 continues the discussion by examining the flow of information when the eyes move across the page during the skilled act of silent reading. More specifically, we try to determine to what extent cognitive events control eye movements, and attempt to relate the acquisition of the information from the printed page to the movements of the eyes. Since these two chapters focus on extraction of visual information, they naturally focus on the identification of words. Chapter 6 presents an implemented computational model of the control of eye movements in reading. This model allows us to integrate many of the facts that were presented in earlier chapters and to explore how they interact in determining when and where the eyes move in normal reading.

4

THE WORK OF THE EYES

When we read we have the impression that our eyes (and mind) sweep continuously across the text except for a few places in which we encounter difficulty, and at those points we pause to consider what we have just read or regress (go back) to reread earlier material. However, that impression is an illusion. First, the progress of the eyes across the page is not continuous. The eyes come to rest for periods that are usually between 150 and 500 ms; these periods when the eye is close to immobile are called fixations. Between the fixations are periods during which the eyes are moving rapidly. These eye movements are called saccades after the French word for jump. Saccades are ballistic movements (i.e., once they start, they cannot be altered). When we read our eyes generally move forward about seven to nine character spaces with each saccade. The duration of a saccade in reading varies with the distance moved, with a typical saccade taking about 20–35 ms. Since, for all practical purposes, no visual information is extracted from the printed page during saccades because of saccadic suppression (Matin, 1974), all visual information is extracted during fixations. The pattern of information extraction during reading is thus a bit like seeing a slide show. You see a slide for about a quarter of a second, there is a brief off time, and then a new slide of a different view of the page appears for about a quarter of a second. This pattern of fixations and saccades is not unique to reading. The perception of any static display (i.e., a picture or a scene) proceeds the same way, although the pattern and timing of fixations differs from that in reading (Rayner, Li, Williams, Cave, & Well, 2007). An exception is when the eyes track a moving target (i.e., a pursuit movement). In this case the eyes move relatively smoothly (and much slower than during saccades) and useful visual information is extracted during the eye movement.

The second way in which our subjective impression is an illusion is that the eyes do not move forward through the text as relentlessly as we think. While most saccades in reading move forwards, about 10–15% move backwards and are termed regressive saccades (or regressions for short). Think of regressions this way: since we make about four to five saccades per second, we make a regression about once every 2 seconds. This makes it likely that we are generally unaware of most regressions. While we are probably aware of some regressions that reflect major confusion, requiring us to go back a considerable distance in the text to straighten things out, we are likely to be unaware of most regressions which are quite short, only going back a few characters (to the preceding word or two).

Another type of eye movement in reading is the return sweep when the eyes move from near the end of one line to near the beginning of the next. Although return sweeps are right-to-left movements they are not counted as regressions, since they are moving the reader forward through the text. Return sweeps are actually quite complicated as they often start five to seven character spaces from the end of a line and they generally end on about the third to seventh character space of the next line. Return sweeps often fall short of their goal and there is often an additional short right-to-left saccade after the large return sweep. However, the leftmost fixation is still sometimes on the second word of the line. Thus most of the time about 80% of the line falls between the extreme fixations on it. (Later we will explain why readers may often fail to fixate the beginning and end words of lines.) The small saccades following return sweeps are probably corrections for errors in aiming the eyes; it is difficult to execute a long saccade perfectly, with the eyes usually undershooting the target position. Since the details of such motor execution are peripheral to our concerns here, most of the interest in eye movement records is on what the eyes do on the middle four-fifths of the line. Of course, if one wants to get global measures of reading such as the overall reading speed, return sweeps must be counted as well.

Another point about the general properties of eye movements during reading is that the two eyes are not always perfectly aligned on the same position in a word. For a long time it was assumed that the two eyes typically land on the same letter in a word, or that they were perfectly aligned. However, while on over 50% of the fixations the two eyes are aligned on the same letter, they are on different letters quite often and sometimes the two eyes are even crossed (Liversedge, Rayner, White, Findlay, & McSorley, 2006; Liversedge, White, Findlay, & Rayner, 2006). While this is an important fact about the characteristics of eye movements during reading, it is also the case that how long the eyes remain in place isn't dramatically affected by whether or not the two eyes are on the same letter (Juhasz, Liversedge, White, & Rayner, 2006; for a complete review see Kirkby, Webster, Blythe, & Liversedge, 2008).

In this chapter, and throughout the rest of this book, our focus will be on eye movements during silent reading. However, we need to point out that there are both similarities and differences between the eye movements readers make in silent and oral reading. Much of what we know about eye movements during oral reading stems from seminal work reported by Buswell (1922), but there have been some recent investigations of eye movements during oral reading (Inhoff, Solomon, Radach, & Seymour, 2011; Laubrock & Kliegl, 2011) using much better and more accurate eye-tracking systems than Buswell had available. Nevertheless, most of Buswell's findings have held up rather well. What are the differences between silent and oral reading? The average fixation duration in oral reading is about 50 ms longer than in silent reading, the average saccade length is shorter overall, and there are more regressions. All of these findings are undoubtedly related to the fact that readers don't want their eyes to get too far ahead of their voice. Thus there are places in the eye movement record where the reader is obviously keeping the eyes in a holding pattern so that this doesn't happen. The eye–voice span, the distance the eyes are ahead of the voice, is generally the focus of research on eye movements during oral reading. The main finding is that the eyes are typically about two words ahead of the voice, and if the eyes get too far ahead readers (unconsciously) slow down the eyes' movements so as to not get too far ahead.

To summarize, the eyes move forward (about seven to nine character spaces on average) in reading, but not relentlessly so. They pause for periods of approximately 200–250 ms, and move backward about 10–15% of the time. In this chapter we will discuss in considerable detail much of the cognitive processing during all this activity and its relation to the ongoing pattern of eye movements. This topic is interesting in itself, as it is at the core of understanding visual cognition in reading and visual cognition more generally. In addition, understanding the details of the work of the eyes in reading is an invaluable tool for understanding the process of reading. We claim, in fact, that eye movements are by far the best tool to understand the process of normal silent reading (which undoubtedly accounts for well over 90% of the reading adults do).

In Chapter 1 we discussed alternative methods for studying reading of text (as opposed to individual words). The current chapter deals with how visual information is extracted from text. Thus we will focus on what useful information readers extract during fixations and on how the eyes are guided through text. Necessary to understanding both topics is some basic information about eye movements in reading. These data will be far more meaningful, however, if we make them concrete by examining an example of an eye movement record. Before we do, it is important to note that readers' eye movements are very much influenced by the lexical properties of the fixated words. So, for example, how long readers look at a word is strongly influenced by factors like word frequency. We will document these findings in more detail later, but for now it is important to keep in mind that factors like how frequent the word is in the English language has a large impact on how long the eyes remain on any given word.

Basic characteristics of eye movements

Figure 4.1 shows part of a page of text with a record of a reader's eye movements superimposed on the text. The average saccade length is about 8.5 characters, but the range is 1 character to 18 characters. The average fixation duration is 218 ms, but the range is 66 to 416 ms.

Notice that, for the most part, words are fixated only once. However, *enough* is fixated twice and *pain* and *least* are not fixated at all. Since a fixation lands on or near almost all words, it appears that a major purpose of eye movements is to bring all words close to the fovea, the region in the center of vision that is best for processing fine detail (see Chapter 1). However, what is causing the variability? Why are some words not fixated while others are fixated twice? Is this just miscalculation of the eye movements as in return sweeps, or does it reflect something deeper?

Similarly, why do fixation durations differ? Does a long fixation time on a word indicate that the reader is taking more time processing the fixated word, or are these variations in fixation time random? Assuming that fixation times are not random (which indeed they are not), what fixation time do we use to index the processing time for a word? If there is a single fixation on a word, there is little choice: we simply measure the fixation duration on the word (this is typically referred to as single fixation duration). However, consider the case of *brainstorm* in Figure 4.1. There are a number of possible candidates to measure processing time here. The first is the duration of the first fixation (first fixation duration) which is 277 ms. The second is gaze duration, which is the total fixation time on the word before the eye moves off (or 277 ms + 120 ms = 397 ms). (This measure assumes that the second fixation was needed to finish processing the fixated word.) Another possibility is the total viewing time, which includes later fixations on the word that are the result of regressive saccades. In the case of *brainstorm* the total viewing time would be 576 ms. (This measure assumes that the regression was made in order to continue processing the word in some way, although sometimes it means that the reader needed to verify that the original encoding of the word was correct.) Two other frequently used measures are single fixation duration (when only a single fixation is made on a word, as in the case of *sweet* and *reward*) and go-past time (sometimes called regression path duration: the amount of time that it takes the reader to move forward in the text, including regressions back to prior text as in fixations 41–44 in Figure 4.1).

Variation of reading measures

The record in Figure 4.1 is typical of adult readers. Figure 4.2 shows the distributions of fixation times and saccade lengths from a large corpus of data from adult readers. As can be seen in

Roadside joggers endure sweat, pain and angry drivers in the name of

1	2		3	4		5	6	7	8
286	221		246	277		266	233	216	188

fitness. A healthy body may seem reward enough for most people. However,

9	10	12	13	11	14	15	16	17	18	19
301	177	196	175	244	302	112	177	266	188	199

for all those who question the payoff, some recent research on physical

21	20	22	23	24	25	26	27
216	212	179	109	266	245	188	205

activity and creativity has provided some surprisingly good news. Regular

29	28	30	31	32	33	34	35	36	37
201	66	201	188	203	220	217	288	212	75

bouts of aerobic exercise may also help spark a brainstorm of creative

38	39	42	40	43	41	44	45	46	47	48
312	260	271	188	350	215	221	266	277	120	219
									50	
									179	

thinking. At least, this is the conclusion that was reached in a study that

49	51	52	53	54	57	55	56	60	59
266	213	210	216	416	200	177	113	206	220
						58			
						218			

FIGURE 4.1 An excerpt from a passage of text with fixation sequence and fixation durations indicated

Figure 4.2, both the average saccade size and average fixation duration of our little segment (and the variability as well) are reasonably in agreement with the larger aggregation of data.

Text differences

The averages and distributions in Figure 4.2 should not be regarded as numbers engraved in stone: reading measures such as reading rate, mean fixation duration, mean saccade length, and percent of regressive fixations vary from text to text. Table 4.1 shows some of the variability for adults reading text on various topics, with more difficult text requiring longer fixations, smaller saccades, more regressions, and hence a slower reading rate.

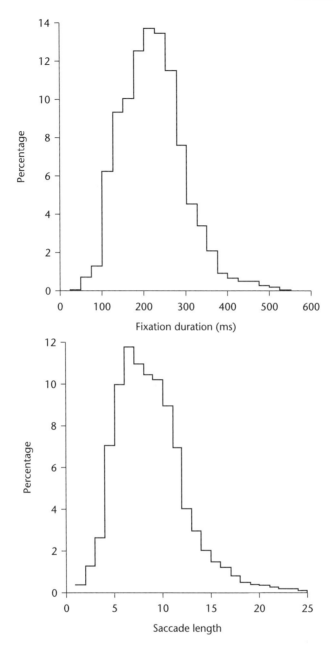

FIGURE 4.2   Frequency distribution of fixation duration (upper graph) and saccade length (lower graph) for eight college-age readers. Return sweeps of the eye have been excluded from the distribution. Short fixations following the return sweep, which are followed by corrective saccades, have also been excluded

Typographic differences

Is the pattern of eye movements dependent on typographic features, such as letter size, type of font, length of line? Tinker (1963, 1965) studied this question in some detail for English (see Morrison & Inhoff, 1981, for a review of this work). His data are complex, but the following brief summary

TABLE 4.1 Variability in adults reading different types of text

Topic	Fixation duration[a]	Saccade length[b]	Regressions (%)[c]	WPM
Light fiction	202	9.2	3	365
Newspaper article	209	8.3	6	321
History	222	8.3	4	313
Psychology	216	8.1	11	308
English literature	220	7.9	10	305
Economics	233	7.0	11	268
Mathematics	254	7.3	18	243
Physics	261	6.9	17	238
Biology	264	6.8	18	233
M	231	7.8	11	288

Mean fixation duration, mean saccade length, proportion of fixations that were regressions, and words per minute reading time (WPM) for 10 good college-age readers reading different types of text.

[a] In ms.

[b] In character spaces (4 character spaces = 1° of visual angle).

[c] Percentage of total fixations that were regressions.

captures the essence. First, the type of font made a minor difference, although all of the fonts that Tinker studied were (subjectively) relatively easy to read. There are some fonts that appear to be pathologically difficult (such as the elaborate script used in German known as "fractur"), and these slow the reading process appreciably. Indeed, a recent experiment in which a standard font (Times New Roman) was compared with a more difficult font (Old English) revealed that the more difficult-to-encode font led to more and longer fixations, shorter saccades, and more regressions (Rayner, Reichle, Stroud, Williams, & Pollatsek, 2006). Slattery and Rayner (2010) also found that clearer text (in which the letters were in sharper focus) led to faster reading than when the text was not as clear.

Second, it is difficult to make inferences about how the size of the characters influenced reading speed from Tinker's data since the size of a character and the number of characters per line were confounded in most of the studies: there were more characters per line when the print was smaller (Morrison & Inhoff, 1981). However, Tinker varied line length (keeping the size of the characters constant) in one study, and the differences he observed for differing size of characters appear to be explained by line-length effects. He found that there was an optimal line size of approximately 52 characters. This optimality is parsimoniously explained by a trade-off between two opposing factors. If the line is too long, return sweeps become increasingly difficult to execute and readers may wind up on the wrong line. On the other hand, as we will shortly see, readers can extract information from more than one word on a line during a fixation. If lines are too short, readers will not be able to take full advantage of the fact that they can extract information from more than one word per fixation. The optimal line length thus appears to be the best compromise between these opposing design considerations. We should remark, however, that all these effects are relatively minor, so that the fundamental conclusion to be drawn from the work on typography is that reading appears to proceed at about the same rate if the type font, size, and length of line employed are at all reasonable.

Viewing distance effects

In reading, the average saccade is about seven to nine letter spaces long, or about 2 degrees of visual angle at a normal reading distance. However, the value of seven to nine letter spaces appears to be more fundamental in that the average saccade size is seven to nine letter spaces regardless of the retinal size of the text (as long as the letters are not too big or too small). Thus, for example, regardless of whether a given text is 36 cm or 72 cm from the eyes, the average saccade length is still about eight letters even though eight letters subtends twice the visual angle at 36 cm as it does at 72 cm (Morrison & Rayner, 1981; O'Regan, 1983). This fact suggests that the visibility of the text is relatively invariant to absolute size over an extended range of distances. As a result, data on saccade length are typically expressed in letter spaces, which appears to be the natural metric in reading rather than degrees of visual angle. A recent clever manipulation (discussed in more detail later) has shown that when letters outside the center of vision are larger on each fixation (thereby compensating in some sense for the poorer acuity with letters outside the center of vision), how far the eyes move is still driven by number of characters (Miellet, O'Donnell, & Sereno, 2009).

The fact that the distance of the text (and hence the absolute size of the letters) makes little difference in saccade size is probably due to a trade-off between two factors: (a) when the text is nearer, the letters are bigger and easier to see; however, (b) when the text is nearer, a given letter will be further from the center of fixation, hence harder to see (see Chapter 1). Of course, there are limits; the text will be impossible to read if a mile away or against your face.

Orthographic differences

A question related to typographic differences is whether the writing system influences the process of reading. The information we presented in this chapter so far concerning eye movements is based on data collected from readers of English. Do the characteristics of eye movements change when people read text which uses other writing systems?

The answer to this question is clearly "yes" as experiments that have examined the patterns of eye movements of Chinese and Japanese readers have demonstrated. However, a major problem with comparing saccade sizes in English with either of these languages is what to use as the unit of measurement. The previous section implied that the letter (or letter space) is the fundamental unit of measurement for English. However, there are no letters per se in either Chinese or Japanese: the characters stand for syllables and/or morphemes (see Chapter 2). If one measures by characters (i.e., a letter is a character), then eye movements of Chinese and Japanese readers tend to be much smaller than eye movements of readers of English. Chinese readers move their eyes about two characters on average (Shen, 1927; Stern, 1978; Wang, 1935). (Remember that a character is a morpheme rather than a word, so that this is less than two words.) Readers of Japanese text, which is made up of morphemic characters (Kanji) and syllabic characters (Kana), move their eyes about three and a half characters (Ikeda & Saida, 1978). This again is less than three and a half words, since it often takes several characters to make a word. Since the average saccade in English is about seven to nine characters (about a word and a half), it appears that the average saccade length is if anything a bit less in English than in Chinese and Japanese if one equates for number of words or morphemes.

Readers of Hebrew also have smaller saccades (about five and a half characters on average) than readers of English (Pollatsek, Bolozky, Well & Rayner, 1981). Hebrew differs structurally and orthographically from English in some important ways. First, as discussed in Chapter 2, not all vowels are represented orthographically in Hebrew. In addition, many function words in Hebrew are clitic, meaning they are attached like prefixes or suffixes to content words. The net effect of these differences is that Hebrew sentences normally contain fewer words and fewer letters than their English counterparts. In short, although Hebrew is basically an alphabetic system, the information is also more densely packed than in English.

The average saccade lengths of Chinese, Japanese, and Hebrew readers suggest that the informational density of the text determines how far the eyes move in each saccade. This finding seems consistent with the fact that, for readers of English, as the text becomes more difficult (and hence the informational density is greater), saccade length decreases. However, it is an open question whether the differences in informational density across languages are best thought of in terms of the density of the meaning or the amount of visual information per character (measured perhaps by the number of strokes or lines in the character). For Hebrew the characters seem of approximately equal complexity to English, so the differences between Hebrew and English are more likely to be explained by differences in the amount of meaning per character. However, the Chinese and Japanese writing systems are so different from English that it is hard to say which type of informational density is operating to produce the differences in reading. We suspect that both the visual and semantic factors are contributing.

Fixation durations for readers of Japanese, Chinese, and Hebrew are fairly similar to those of readers of English. Despite the fact that reading in these languages is slower when measured superficially, reading rates, when measured in terms of amount of meaning extracted per unit time, seem to be equivalent. In fact, when the reading rate in Hebrew was based on the number of words in the English translations of the Hebrew sentences, the average reading rate for the Israeli and English speaking participants was nearly identical (Pollatsek et al., 1981).

One final dimension of orthographies is the direction in which the characters proceed. As we pointed out in Chapter 2, there were no clear conclusions that could be drawn about the effect of the direction of print on the eye movements or the efficiency of reading. In general, the results were consistent with the hypothesis that differences in the direction of print do not matter and that all differences observed in reading speed were due to the more familiar orthography being read more easily (Shen, 1927; Sun et al, 1985). A similar conclusion follows from laboratory experiments which manipulated the direction of print. Tinker (1955), for example, found that readers of English initially read vertically arranged English 50% slower than horizontally arranged text. However, with 4 weeks of practice their reading speed was only 22% slower than for the horizontal text. In a number of experiments, Kolers (1972) likewise showed that, with practice, readers of English can read text arranged in a right-to-left fashion fairly well. Children learning to read can also read from right to left as easily as they read left to right (Clay, 1979). While relatively short amounts of practice in the laboratory did not abolish differences in the arrangement of text (Kolers, 1972), they also suggest that differences between arrangements of print, if they exist, are likely to be quite small. There is some physiological reason to believe that a horizontal arrangement in any language may be better: visual acuity falls off faster in the vertical direction than the horizontal direction. However, given that no direction of text is preferred over any other suggests that this physiological fact may have a relatively small effect on reading speed.

A few comments about saccades and fixations

At the beginning of this chapter we claimed that reading was a slide show in which the eyes remained in place for a certain period of time (the fixation) and then moved quickly with no visual information extracted during the move (the saccade). While these claims are essentially true, they are slight oversimplifications. We will briefly discuss the complexities, so that we can set the record straight. However, for the remainder of the chapter and book these complexities are so insignificant that we can safely deal with the slide show metaphor.

Saccades

First let us consider the assertion we made that no visual information is extracted during a saccade. You can demonstrate for yourself that little is perceived during saccades by looking in a mirror and trying to watch your eyes move. You will not see them do so. This reduced perceptibility of stimulation during saccades was discovered over 100 years ago (Dodge, 1900; Holt, 1903).

Why don't we see anything during the saccade? First, the eyes are moving so fast during a saccade that the image "painted" on the eyes by a fixed stimulus would be largely a smear and thus highly unintelligible. However, we are not aware of any smear. Thus there must be some mechanism suppressing the largely useless information that is "painted" on the retina during the saccade. One putative mechanism is central anesthesia. That is, it is possible that when the brain knows that the eyes are making (or about to make) a saccade, it sends out a signal to the visual system to ignore (or attenuate) all input from the eyes until the saccade is over. There is in fact evidence (Matin, 1974) that the thresholds for stimuli shown during or even a bit before a saccade begins and after it ends are raised (with the effect much more pronounced for stimuli presented during a saccade). This increased threshold before and after the saccade is not of much importance for reading since the letters seen in text are far above threshold. Thus it is not clear whether these relatively small threshold effects would mean that the ability to extract information from the text would be altered significantly. (That is, it might be like the difference between reading with a 60-watt bulb and reading with a 150-watt bulb.) However, the threshold effects are more likely to be significant with the moving eye, where the contrast between the light and dark parts of the smear would be far less.

For many years central anesthesia was accepted as the main mechanism by which information during saccades was suppressed. However, more recent experiments indicate that a different mechanism explains at least part of the suppression. It can be demonstrated that under certain (unnatural) circumstances, visual input during the saccade can be perceived (Uttal & Smith, 1968): when the room is totally dark prior to and after the saccade, and a pattern is presented only during the saccade, a smeared image of the pattern is perceived (Campbell & Wurtz, 1978). Since the blur is thus seen if no visual stimulation precedes or follows it, the implication is that the information available prior to and after the saccade during normal vision masks the perception of any information acquired during the saccade. This phenomenon has been related to laboratory phenomena of masking such as those used in subliminal priming experiments (see Chapter 3). In sum, while we can't say for sure that absolutely no visual information is extracted during saccades in reading, the evidence indicates that if visual information gets in during a saccade, it is of little practical importance. Indeed, Wolverton and Zola (1983) replaced the text with a mask during each saccade as people read and it was not perceived nor did it affect reading in any way.

Definition of fixations

Our claim that the eyes are immobile during a fixation is a bit of an oversimplification. As indicated in Chapter 1, very small rapid movements, called tremor or nystagmus, go on constantly to help the nerve cells in the retina to keep firing. However, these are so small as to be of little practical importance in studying normal reading. There are also somewhat larger movements called microsaccades and drifts. While the reasons for these movements are not completely clear, it appears that the eyes occasionally drift (i.e., make a small and rather slow movement) due to less than perfect control of the oculomotor system by the nervous system. When this happens, there is often a small (one character or less) microsaccade (i.e., a much more rapid small movement) to bring the eyes back to where they were. Some of the drift is also actually vergence between the two eyes, serving to reduce fixation disparity between the eyes.

Many experimenters assume that these small movements are "noise" and adopt scoring procedures in which these small movements are ignored. For example, some scoring procedures take successive fixations that are separated by a character or less and lump them together as a single fixation. Some microsaccades may be under cognitive control (like other saccades) and thus some experimenters believe that microsaccades should be treated no differently from other saccades. Another alternative is a more sophisticated pooling procedure in which fixations are pooled if the intervening saccade is a character or less and at least one of the fixations is short (100 ms or less).

Most eye movement data in reading have been adjusted using some sort of procedure that pools some fixations and ignores at least some small drifts and microsaccades. In some cases the eye movement recording system is not sensitive enough to detect these small movements, so such movements are automatically ignored. Others with more sensitive equipment decide on some sort of criterion for pooling. Since drifts and microsaccades are relatively uninteresting aspects of the eye movement record for reading, and since there is enough complexity in the data without worrying about them, our subsequent discussion will ignore them for the most part.

Summary

We have summarized the basic facts about eye movements in reading. The eyes move about four or five times per second and jump an average of about seven to nine letter spaces each time they move for readers of English. However, the eyes move back about 10–15% of the time and there is large variability in both the extent of the forward motion and the amount of time they stay in a fixation. Since virtually all the information is extracted during the fixations, the interest in fixations is on how their duration reflects the processing of information during the fixation. Since saccades exist to move the eyes to another fixation, the interest in saccades is the extent to which the direction and size of the saccade reflect what is being processed.

The perceptual span

Since the eyes move four to five times a second during reading, it seems reasonable to assume that they move to new locations on the page because the amount of information that can be extracted from a given fixation is limited. However, some advocates of techniques for increasing reading speed claim that many of our eye movements are not necessary and that large amounts of information can be extracted from a single glance (see Chapter 13). Thus, if we are to understand which view is true—whether eye movements are a central functional part of the reading process or just a bad habit picked up from old-fashioned reading methods—we have to discover how much information from the printed page is obtained from an individual fixation during silent reading of text. As we will see, the constant movement of the eyes is not a bad habit: the region from which we can obtain useful information during each eye fixation is relatively small.

One reason why some people may believe a large amount of information can be extracted from a single fixation is that it often seems to us that we can see many words on the page at the same time. However, this is an illusion. Many of the words are seen on a fixation only in the sense that the reader knows that some word-like object is in a given location. The brain takes the details extracted from each location and integrates them somehow into a perception that the detail from a wide area is seen on each fixation. We discuss this integration process in the next section.

In this section we will briefly describe various attempts to determine the size of the effective visual field (or perceptual span) on a fixation in reading. We will first review tachistoscopic techniques, then techniques based on eye movements, and conclude the section by discussing the technologically more sophisticated gaze-contingent moving-window technique.

Fixed-eye techniques

The tachistoscope (t-scope), which we introduced in Chapter 1, was designed in part to determine how much useful information could be acquired during an eye fixation in reading. Psychologists hoped to measure the perceptual span by asking participants to report all they could see when a sentence was exposed briefly, say 100–200 ms. Since such an exposure duration is brief enough to preclude the possibility of an eye movement during the presentation, the technique measures how much information can be reported from a single fixation. Thus, to some extent, the technique simulates a single fixation in reading.

An experiment by Marcel (1974) serves to illustrate the logic of the method and its attendant problems. Marcel had participants read a short fragment of a passage in a t-scope. When they reached the final word of the fragment, they read it aloud. The pronunciation of this word caused the text to disappear, and 100 ms later some more words were presented for 200 ms, just to the right of where the pronounced word had been. The participants' task was to report as many words from the second set as possible. This second set of words was not actually text, but a sequence of words that varied in how closely they approximated normal English. When the sequence of words was essentially random, participants were able to report just over two words (or roughly 13 character spaces), while when the sequences were close to normal English, they reported three or four words (18 to 26 character spaces). Since the stimuli in this last condition are most like normal text, perhaps three to four words provides a good estimate of the perceptual span in reading.

There are three potential problems with this type of research. First, the delay between the offset of the passage fragment and the onset of the target words is quite different from anything encountered during normal reading. The delay is usually about 600 ms (about 500 ms to begin pronunciation of the last word of the first fragment plus the 100 ms experimental delay). Second, eye positions were not monitored so that the experimenter did not know where the participants' eyes really were. The third and greatest problem, however, is that the experimenter has no control over the extent to which the participant is consciously guessing. In Marcel's experiment, for example, since the participants attempted to report what had been seen, there was little control over the speed of the response. Thus better performance on the sequences that closely approximated English may have been because the participant could guess which words were likely to follow from the constraints of the text (possibly aided by partial information obtained from the stimulus). In contrast, the use of random sequences gets around the guessing problem but may disrupt the normal reading situation.

Another tachistoscopic technique that has been frequently used to make inferences about the perceptual span in reading (Feinberg, 1949) involves asking a participant to fixate some point and then identify stimuli (words or letters) presented at various distances from fixation so briefly that no eye movement can occur. On the basis of the results from such experiments (see Figure 4.3), estimates of the perceptual span have generally been in the range of two or three words, or about 10–20 characters (Feinberg, 1949; Woodworth, 1938).

A strength of the latter method is that, by the use of isolated words in the visual field, one can limit the guessing problem and get a better estimate of whether the word can be identified on the basis of the available visual information. The method has its problems, however. As we discussed in Chapter 1, Sperling (1960) demonstrated that we are able to see much more than we can retain and later report. Thus, what participants report from a brief word or letter presentation can not be taken as a complete specification of what they actually saw. Even if the verbal report coincided with what the participant saw, there is no particular reason to believe that the estimate of the perceptual span obtained from either type of tachistoscopic presentation discussed here actually coincides with that of a fixation in reading. A second problem is that the responses are not timed. Thus one

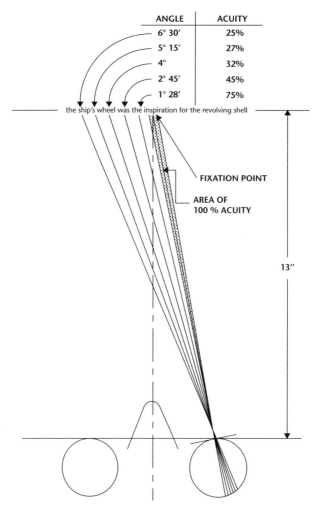

FIGURE 4.3 Example of how the perceptual span is estimated from tachistoscopic acuity data. (From Taylor, 1965.)

discovers whether the word can be identified on the basis of the available visual information but not whether it can be identified as quickly as it needs to be in normal reading.

Even if all the guessing problems could be removed, there might be a real difference between the perceptual span in silent reading and in t-scope presentation of words or sentences. The perceptual span in reading could be larger either because the contextual constraint in text allows a reader to identify words with less visual information than in t-scope presentations, or because the requirement to hold the eyes still interferes with normal perception. On the other hand, the perceptual span in reading could be smaller because the rapid sequence of fixations and the complexity of the surrounding stimulus pattern may lead to "tunnel vision" (Mackworth, 1965).

Primitive window techniques

A somewhat different technique involving experimental control of what is seen on a given fixation is to present text but to limit the amount that is visible to a reader at a given moment.

Poulton (1962) had participants read aloud from text over which a mask containing a "window" was passed. Only the text in the window could be seen. Thus the text was immobile and the window passed over it, allowing only a certain amount to be seen at once. The speed and size of the window varied systematically on different trials and readers' eye movements were recorded. Newman (1966) and Bouma and de Voogd (1974) reversed the procedure by having the participants hold fixation and the text moved on a screen from right to left. The size of the window was manipulated by varying the number of letters on the screen at any moment.

These experiments typically found that smaller windows create greater disruptions in reading than larger windows. These techniques, however, are suspect since they disrupt normal reading: the reader's natural eye movements were inhibited (in the latter case, fixation had to be maintained; in the former, the reader had to follow the moving window); in neither situation could the reader re-examine text (via regressions); in addition, these particular experiments suffered because the participants were required to read the text orally.

Estimates based on reading where natural eye movements are allowed

The techniques mentioned so far seem to be unsatisfactory. They involve tasks that disrupt the normal reading situation. In addition, they provide rather discrepant estimates of the size of the perceptual span with the estimated size ranging from one or two to four words. It would clearly be better if one could estimate the perceptual span directly from normal silent reading.

One simple technique for estimating the perceptual span from natural reading is measuring the average number of words per fixation. That is, one simply records eye movements during reading and divides the number of words read by the number of fixations used to read those words (Taylor, 1965). Using such a technique Taylor estimated the perceptual span for skilled readers to be 1.11 words. While this method is simple and unobtrusive, it is unfortunately based on the assumption that the perceptual spans on successive fixations do not overlap. In other words, it assumes that a given word or letter is never processed on more than one fixation. As we shall see, this assumption is false.

Gaze-contingent display change techniques

The gaze-contingent moving-window technique introduced by McConkie and Rayner (1975) uses the idea of the moving-window techniques discussed before—to manipulate what is seen on a given fixation—but does so in the task of normal silent reading, where the participants can move their eyes wherever and whenever they wish. This is accomplished by presenting the text on a video monitor and making display changes in this text as the participant is moving his or her eyes. This research relies on sophisticated eye-tracking equipment interfaced with a computer, which is also interfaced with the video monitor. The position of the reader's eye is sampled every millisecond by the computer and changes in the text are made contingent upon the location of the eye. Because this type of research has been very influential for our understanding of skilled reading and has provided clear answers concerning the size of the perceptual span, we will describe it in some detail (for further review see Rayner, 1978a, 1998, 2009).

In the prototypical moving-window experiment a version of mutilated text (in which every letter from the original text is replaced by another letter) is initially displayed on the video monitor. However, when the reader fixates on the text the display is immediately modified by the replacement of letters within a certain region around the fixation point with the corresponding letters from the original text. This creates an experimentally defined window region of normal text for the reader to see on that fixation. When the reader makes an eye movement the text in the window area returns to this unreadable form and a new window of normal text is created at the location of the new fixation. Thus, wherever the reader looks, there is a window of normal text to read in a background of mutilated text. Table 4.2 shows a line of text and four successive fixations for one reader under moving-window conditions.[1] (Because of the sophistication of the equipment, the display changes can be made in about 5–10 ms; this change is rapid enough that the reader does not see the changes that are taking place.)

The basic assumption in this research is that when the window becomes smaller than the reader's perceptual span, reading will be disrupted. By varying the size and location of the window region, the experimenter can determine what area of the text the reader is actually extracting useful information from on a fixation. By varying the type of information in the background area, the experimenter can maintain or destroy various types of information that may be potentially useful during reading and thus be more analytical about the type of information that a reader is extracting from a region of the visual field.

In the original moving-window experiment McConkie and Rayner (1975) had participants read text when the window was 13, 17, 21, 25, 31, 37, 45, or 100 character spaces in width. A window size of 17 meant that the reader had normal text for the letter directly fixated and for 8 letter spaces on either side as shown in Table 4.3. (With a window size of 100, the entire line was

TABLE 4.2 An example of a moving window

Fixation number	Example
1	Xxxxhology means persxxxxxxx xxxxxxxxx xxxx xxxx xxxxxxx. Xxxx xx x
	*
2	Xxxxxxxxxx xxxxs personality diaxxxxxx xxxx xxxx xxxxxxx. Xxxx xx x
	*
3	Xxxxxxxxxx xxxxx xxxxxxxxxxx xiagnosis from hanx xxxxxxx. Xxxx xx x
	*
4	Xxxxxxxxxx xxxxx xxxxxxxxxxx xxxxxxxxx xxom hand writing. Xxxx xx x
	*

The asterisk represents the location of fixation on four successive fixations.

TABLE 4.3 An example of a line of text and the various text patterns derived from it

Text	Graphology means personality diagnosis from hand writing. This is a
XS	Xxxxxxxxxx xxxxx xxxxonality diagnosis xxxx xxxx xxxxxxx. Xxxx xx x
XF	XXXXXXXXXXXXXXXXXXXXXonality diagnosisXXXXXXXXXXXXXXXXXXXXXXXXXXXXXXX
VS	Cnojkaiazp wsorc jsnconality diagnosis tnaw kori mnlflra. Ykle le o
VF	Cnojkaiaqpawsorcajsnconality diagnosisatnawakoriamnlflrqaaaYklealeao
DS	Hbfxwysyvo tifdl xiblonality diagnosis abyt wfdn hbemedv. Awel el f
DF	Hbfxwysyvoatifdlaxiblonality diagnosisaabytawfdnahbemedvaaaAwelaelaf

On each line a window of size 17 is shown, assuming the reader is fixating the letter *d* in *diagnosis*.
XS = Letters replaeced with Xs—spaces preserved.
XF = Letters replaced with Xs—spaces filled.
VS = Letters replaced with similar letters—spaces preserved.
VF = Letters replaced with similar letters—spaces filled.
DS = Letters replaced with dissimilar letters—spaces preserved.
DF = Letters replaced with dissimilar letters—spaces filled.

almost always present.) The participants also read with the six different types of text mutilations shown in Table 4.3. The texts were 500-word passages and the participants were told that they would answer questions afterwards that would test their comprehension of the passages.

McConkie and Rayner found that reducing the size of the window had a substantial effect on reading speed as reflected in various measures of eye movement behavior, increasing reading time by as much as 60%, but had no effect on readers' ability to answer questions about the text. Rayner and Bertera (1979) subsequently used window sizes ranging from 1 letter space to 29 letter spaces. With windows as small as 7 letter spaces, readers can usually see little more than one word at a time. This reduces their reading speed to about 60% of their normal reading speed. However, they can still read with normal comprehension. Rayner and Bertera found no effect on comprehension unless the window was reduced to only one character (in which case readers are literally reading letter-by-letter).

The first question that McConkie and Rayner asked was how large the window had to be made in order for readers to be able to read normally (i.e., at both normal speed and comprehension). The answer was 31 letter spaces or 15 letter spaces to each side of fixation. When the window was reduced to less than that, reading rate was reduced. In other words, the experiment indicates that the perceptual span extends to something like 15 letter spaces from the fixation point. This finding has been subsequently replicated by a number of studies with the extent of the span to the right of fixation being 14–15 letter spaces (DenBuurman, Boersema, & Gerrissen, 1981; Rayner & Bertera, 1979; Rayner, Castelhano, & Yang, 2009a; Rayner, Inhoff, Morrison, Slowiaczek, & Bertera, 1981). Interestingly, Miellet et al. (2009) also replicated the basic findings concerning the perceptual span when they used a novel gaze-contingent paradigm in which the letters outside of the center of vision were larger on each fixation (see Figure 4.4). Their results basically demonstrate that acuity

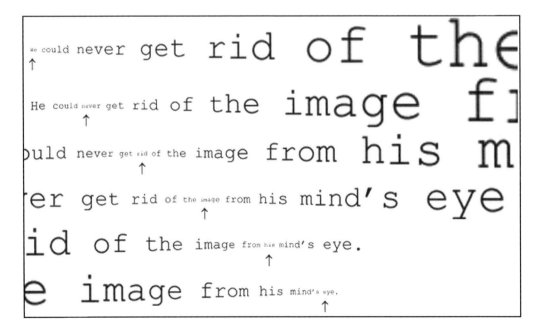

FIGURE 4.4   Graphical depiction of the parafoveal magnification (PM) paradigm, from Miellet et al., 2009. The location of each fixation is indicated with an arrow and the corresponding display for that fixation is represented. Consecutive lines represent the chronological order of fixations

limitations, while important, are not the main factor influencing the size of the perceptual span. Thus, readers appear to extract some sort of useful information out to about 14–15 letter spaces to the right of fixation (see below for why only information to the right of fixation is mainly relevant) but extract no useful information beyond that. But what kind of information is it? Do they extract the meaning of words out that far, or only some information about the component letters, or do they merely extract some information about where words begin and end that might be useful in knowing where to place the next fixation?

One way to attack the question of how far from fixation different kinds of information can be extracted is by experimentally manipulating the information that is outside the window of normal text. McConkie and Rayner investigated the perceptual span for word boundary information by comparing two kinds of altered displays outside the window. In one, all letters in words were replaced by Xs but the spaces between words were preserved, while in the other, the spaces were replaced by Xs as well. By comparing performance in these two background conditions one can tell how far from fixation the presence of spaces makes a difference. When the window size was 25 characters or fewer (12 or fewer letter spaces to the right of fixation), reading was faster when spaces were present among the Xs in the background than when they were not. On the other hand, when the window size was 31 or greater (15 or more letter spaces to the right), there was no difference between the background conditions. Thus it appears that readers use the information of where spaces are out to about 15 character positions from fixation, probably to help guide their eye movements into that region.

McConkie and Rayner also attempted to determine how far from fixation information about the shapes of letters and words is extracted. They compared backgrounds in which the letters were visually similar to the letters in the text (having the same pattern of ascenders and descenders) with backgrounds in which the letters were visually dissimilar (see Table 4.3). The same logic applies here, if there is a difference between these two background conditions at a certain window size, then some information about the shapes of letters and/or words is being extracted beyond the end of the window. Their data indicated that letter shape information was not extracted as far out as word boundary information, since there were differences between these two background conditions only for windows up to 21 letter spaces (10 to the right). It is worth noting that the "window of consciousness" for letter information is significantly smaller than that, extending little beyond the fixated word. If the fixated word is preserved, and the background vaguely resembles normal text (e.g., spaces are left between the words and all letters in the background are replaced by similar letters), the reader is rarely aware of seeing anything other than normal text (even those who know that it isn't normal). However, they are often aware that they are reading slowly and that something is holding them back.

Further studies have greatly increased our understanding of the perceptual span (see Rayner, 1998, 2009). We should point out that single sentences were employed in many of these experiments, since it is technically difficult to make display changes rapidly and not have a lot of flicker in the text display. Fortunately these sentence-reading experiments have closely replicated those using passages of text, so that we can be reasonably confident that the data from the sentence-reading experiments is a good approximation to what would be obtained under more natural reading conditions.

Another question is whether the perceptual span is symmetric. In the original McConkie and Rayner experiments, the distance that normal text was extended was the same on both sides of fixation so that it was not possible to test whether readers extract more information from one side of fixation than the other. To test the symmetry of the perceptual span, McConkie and Rayner (1976a) independently varied the left and right boundaries of the window of normal text and found that when the window extended 4 letter spaces to the left of fixation and 14 to the right, reading was virtually as fast as when the window extended 14 letter spaces in each direction. In contrast, when the window extended 14 letter spaces to the left of fixation and 4 to the right, reading was markedly impaired. Thus, for readers of English, the perceptual span is asymmetric, with information from the right of fixation being used much further out.

Rayner, Well, and Pollatsek (1980) and Rayner, Well, Pollatsek, and Bertera (1982) further extended the work on the size of the perceptual span. Their major finding was that the left and right boundaries of the perceptual span are somewhat differently constituted. They compared conditions in which the window was experimentally defined by the number of visible letters with conditions in which the window was experimentally defined by the number of visible words. They found that the major determiner of the left boundary is the beginning of the currently fixated word. That is, when the left boundary of the window was manipulated, the speed of reading could be predicted by knowing whether the currently fixated word was visible: beyond ensuring that the beginning of the fixated word was visible, the number of letters to the left of fixation had virtually no effect. On the other hand, the right boundary of the perceptual span does not appear to depend on word boundaries. When the window to the right of fixation was varied, the major determinant of reading speed was the number of letters visible: given that a certain number of letters were visible, it made little difference whether whole words were preserved or whether a word was partially visible (even the fixated word). For example, the reading rate was the same when the right boundary of the window was three letters to the right of the fixated letter as when the right boundary was defined to be the end of the fixated word, in spite of the fact that, in the former case, the fixated word was not entirely visible about a third of the time. The fact that reading speed did not appear to depend on whether the right boundary of the window maintains the integrity of words (see Table 4.4) suggests that readers acquire information about parts of words from parafoveal vision.

Rayner et al. (1982) reported more detailed evidence about the partial word information that readers obtain from parafoveal vision. They asked participants to read when (1) only the fixated word was visible and all other letters to the right of fixation were replaced by another letter, (2) the fixated word and the word to the right of fixation were visible and all other letters were replaced by another letter, or (3) the fixated word was visible and partial information about the word to the right of fixation was visible. In the third condition one, two, or three letters of the word to the right of fixation were visible (see Table 4.4). When the first three letters in the word to the right

TABLE 4.4 Examples of conditions in the Rayner et al. (1982) study and reading rates associated with them in words per minute

Window size		Sentence	Reading rate
1W	(3.7)	An experiment xxx xxxxxxxxx xx xxx xxx	212 wpm
2W	(9.6)	An experiment was xxxxxxxxx xx xxx xxx	309 wpm
3W	(15.0)	An experiment was conducted xx xxx xxx	339 wpm
3L		An experimxxx xxx xxxxxxxxx xx xxx xxx	207 wpm
9L		An experiment wax xxxxxxxxx xx xxx xxx	308 wpm
15L		An experiment was condxxxxx xx xxx xxx	340 wpm

In the W conditions word integrity is preserved, while in the L conditions the right boundary is determined by the number of letters visible. The values in parentheses are the average number of letters visible in the W conditions. In all cases, the fixated letter is the second *e* in *experiment*.

of fixation were visible and the other letters were replaced by visually similar letters, reading rate was not much different from when the entire word to the right of fixation was visible. This result indicates that partial word information is utilized during reading and that an individual word may be processed on more than one fixation. These experiments also indicated that letter information was obtained at least nine letter spaces from fixation (see also Underwood & McConkie, 1985).

The moving-window technique demonstrates that information beyond 14–15 letter spaces to the right of fixation is of little use in normal reading. One possible reason for this is that the reader is busy enough processing the information that is closer to fixation, so that he or she has little use for any more information. One variation of the moving-window technique, the moving-mask technique (Rayner & Bertera, 1979), demonstrates that parafoveal information is of little value even when you need to have it because foveal information is not available. The moving-mask technique is the inverse of the moving-window technique: the normal text is displayed outside of the center of vision and a visual mask moves in synchrony with the eyes, making it impossible for the reader to obtain useful information foveally (Rayner & Bertera, 1979; Rayner et al., 1981). Thus, foveal vision is completely masked (see Table 4.5), and an artificial scotoma of the retina is created. (There are people who have such scotomas due either to retinal damage or to brain damage and they have great difficulty reading.)

Rayner and Bertera (1979) found that when foveal vision (i.e., the central seven letters around the fixation point) was masked, reading was still possible from parafoveal vision but at a rate of only 12 words per minute (see also Fine & Rubin, 1999; Rayner et al., 1981). When foveal vision and part of parafoveal vision (i.e., the central 11–17 letter spaces around the fixation point) were masked, reading was almost impossible. Readers in the experiments knew that there were words (or at least knew there were strings of letters) outside of the center of vision, but could not tell what they were. They were more likely to be able to identify short function words like *the, and*, and *a*, particularly when they were at the beginning or end of the line. The errors that readers made when foveal and parafoveal vision were masked indicated that they were obtaining information about the beginning letters (and sometimes ending letters) of words in parafoveal vision, as well as letter shapes and word length information, and trying to construct coherent sentences out of the information available. For example, the sentence *The pretty bracelet attracted much attention* was read as *The priest brought much ammunition* and *The banner waved above the stone monument* as *The banker watched the snow mountain*. There was also no indication that the gist of the sentences was comprehended if the words were not identified.

Let us briefly recap what we know about the span of perception during reading so far. We know that it is limited, and the limitation on the right side appears to be chiefly due to limitations in perception: even when foveal information is eliminated, readers still extract little useful information about letters and words beyond about 14–15 letter spaces. On the left side, information is extracted from a smaller area, generally including at most the word currently fixated on (although see Binder, Pollatsek, & Rayner, 1999, for a discussion of situations in which readers may attend to words to the left of fixation). Furthermore, research using the gaze-contingent moving-window

TABLE 4.5   An example of a moving mask of seven letters

```
An exXXXXXXX was conducted in the lab.
       *
An experiXXXXXXX conducted in the lab.
          *
An experimenXXXXXXXnducted in the lab.
             *
```

The asterisk marks the location of fixation on three successive fixations.

paradigm (Pollatsek, Raney, LaGasse, & Rayner, 1993) demonstrated that readers do not obtain useful information below the currently fixated line. Thus readers appear to limit their attention to words on the line currently being read. Pollatsek et al. also found that if the task was changed to a visual search task (where participants had to find specific target words in paragraphs), then participants can obtain useful information below the currently fixated line.

Reading skill also influences the size of the perceptual span, since beginning readers (Häikiö, Bertram, Hyönä, & Niemi, 2009; Rayner, 1986) and dyslexic readers (Rayner, Murphy, Henderson, & Pollatsek, 1989) have smaller spans than more skilled readers. Presumably, difficulty encoding the fixated word leads to smaller spans for both beginning and dyslexic readers. Older readers read more slowly than younger college-age readers (Laubrock, Kliegl, & Engbert, 2006; Rayner, Reichle et al., 2006) and their perceptual span seems to be slightly smaller and less asymmetrical than younger readers (Rayner, Castelhano, & Yang, 2009a).

The perceptual span in other writing systems

Before going on to explore what information is extracted from the right of fixation, let us briefly discuss what is known about the perceptual span in other orthographies. Within the alphabetic writing system, moving-window experiments have been done in Dutch (DenBuurman et al., 1981), Finnish (Häikiö et al., 2009), and French (O'Regan, 1980), with identical results to those in English.

Moving-window experiments have also been conducted with Chinese, Japanese, and Hebrew readers. Not only does the writing system affect eye movement characteristics, it also influences the size of the perceptual span. As noted in Chapter 2, the writing system that is the most different from English is Chinese. Research using the moving-window technique has demonstrated that for readers of Chinese (which is now typically read from left to right in mainland China), the perceptual span extends from one character to the left of fixation to two to three characters to the right (Chen & Tang, 1998; Inhoff & Liu, 1998). Obviously this is much smaller than the perceptual span in English if one uses the character as the unit. However, as we noted earlier, Chinese characters are not the same as English letters, and when one considers that most Chinese words are made up of two characters (although there are also many one-character words, and some three- to four-character words), then the amount of information being processed on each fixation, when measured in terms of words, is probably not that different from English.

Ikeda and Saida (1978) used the moving-window technique to study Japanese readers. (Remember, Japanese is a hybrid language consisting of morphemic characters, Kanji, and syllabic characters, Kana.) They found that the perceptual span extended about six characters to the right of fixation. Thus, for the Japanese writing system, the perceptual span is considerably smaller than for English if one equates a Japanese character with a letter. The perceptual span is even shorter when ideographic characters are used. Osaka (1987) used the moving-window technique and found that the perceptual span for Japanese readers is smaller when the text consists primarily of logographic Kanji characters than when it consists primarily of syllabic Kana characters. However, Japanese text is considerably more dense than English, leading to the observation that more information is processed per fixation. Thus, while it is hard to compare across languages (since the perceptual span in English seems to be defined mainly in terms of letters), it appears that the perceptual span is roughly two to three words (the fixated word and generally two words to the right of fixation) in the writing systems that have been examined.

With Hebrew text, Pollatsek et al. (1981) found that, for native Israeli readers reading Hebrew, their perceptual span was asymmetric to the left of fixation, whereas when these same readers read English, their perceptual span was asymmetric to the right of fixation. Thus the asymmetry of the window is not "hard-wired." Not only does it vary from language to language, but bilingual readers can alter the area from which they extract information when they switch from language to language. The major difference between Hebrew and English, of course, is that Hebrew is read from right to left. That means that the dominant pattern of eye movements is the opposite in the two languages. An important implication is that readers concentrate their attention on the material that is in the direction where they are about to move their eyes.

The perceptual span in Braille

As long as we are talking about other writing systems, it might be of some interest to digress for a moment to discuss what is known about how tactual information is "read" by the blind. The most common system for alphabetic languages is known as Braille (after its inventor's name). In Braille a 3 × 2 matrix of raised dots represents a letter; dots thus can potentially appear in any one of six locations, and the pattern of present and absent dots defines the letter. The arrangement of the letters is from left to right as on a printed page with spaces between the words. For many Braille readers the size of the perceptual span is one letter (Bertelson, Mousty & D'Alimonte, 1985b). They read with one finger, one letter at a time. Braille readers also typically don't skip words, and maintain physical contact with the page even on return sweeps (although they move more quickly on the sweeps than when they read a line of text).

Some Braille readers use the right index finger to read and the left index finger mainly as a place marker to help them find the appropriate line on the return sweep (Bertelson et al., 1985b; Mousty & Bertelson, 1985). This enables them to increase their reading speed by almost 30% over when they read with only one finger. Other Braille readers (the most skilled), however, appear to use both index fingers to extract information. Some will keep their two index fingers adjacent to each other (on adjacent letters) while they read the entire text. However, a more typical pattern is to move the two in synchrony on adjacent letters in the middle of a line, but then continue moving the right index finger to the end of the line while moving the left one to the beginning of the next line and start reading the next line at the same time that they are reading the end of the previous one (Bertelson et al., 1985b). The right index finger usually rejoins the left on the next line after a word or two is read by the left. The perceptual span of these most skilled Braille readers thus appears to be two letters, at least some of the time, since they can read more than 30% faster with two fingers than with one. However, the details of what is happening are somewhat unclear. Since using the left index finger as a place marker provides appreciable benefit in itself, it is hard to know exactly how much benefit is actually a result of extracting information from both fingers simultaneously. Using this two-hand method, however, the best Braille readers can read about 100–140 words per minute (Bertelson et al., 1985b).

What is a reader doing on a fixation?

We are closing in a bit on what information the reader is extracting on a fixation. The information to the left of the fixated word in English (or to the right in Hebrew) seems to be largely irrelevant because the reader is not attending to it. The moving-window and mask experiments suggest that information further than about 14–15 character spaces to the right of fixation is not used because of acuity and capacity limitations in processing text. However, we still need to discuss how the information from the fixation point to the right-hand boundary of the perceptual span is used. Rayner et al.'s (1982) experiment cited earlier makes it clear that more than the fixated word is processed. When the window only included the fixated word, participants read at only about 200 words per minute in contrast to about 330 words per minute when there was no window. The simplest conceptual model to handle that fact would be that readers make sure to encode the fixated word on each fixation but that on some fixations they may also encode another word or two. However, other data from Rayner et al. (1982) indicated that reality is more complex. Since readers were not particularly bothered by incomplete words—in fact, the major variable affecting reading speed was the number of letters available to the right of fixation—readers must be doing something more complex than extracting words as visual units (see also Chapters 3 and 5).

One possibility is that words are encoded only a limited distance from fixation, but that letter information is extracted further out. This conclusion emerged from a study by Rayner (1975b) which used another type of gaze-contingent technique (the boundary technique). We will discuss this study in some detail because the technique it introduced has been used rather extensively since the original study to examine how far away from fixation different types of information are obtained and how information is combined across saccades (for reviews see Rayner, 1998, 2009). In this technique the experimenter attempts to determine what kinds of information are acquired from a particular word location in a paragraph (called the critical word location or CWL) when readers fixate different distances from it. This is accomplished by changing the contents of the CWL when a saccade crosses an invisible boundary location. The logic of the method is that if a certain aspect of the stimulus in the CWL has been encoded in the parafovea and then changed when the word is fixated, some disruption of normal reading would be expected. In particular, we might anticipate a longer-than-normal fixation after the change had been made, since the reader would have to resolve the conflict in the information obtained from the two fixations. The advantage of the boundary technique over the moving-window technique is that more precise control over parafoveal information is possible since one word is selected for manipulation. In addition, since the region of abnormal text is small, normal reading is even more closely approximated. In Rayner's experiment the stimulus in the critical word location when it was fixated (the target word) was always a word that fit into the text. However, the stimulus in the CWL before the boundary had been crossed was sometimes a word and sometimes a nonword (see Figure 4.5 to get an idea of the possibilities).

Rayner was able to observe a large number of instances on which the reader's eyes fixated different distances to the left of the CWL on the fixation prior to the stimulus change and then directly on the CWL after the change. It was assumed that if the reader's fixation was sufficiently far to the left of the CWL no information would be acquired from that region. If this were the case, the reader would then fail to notice any of the different types of display changes. (We use the

I.   The old captain put the chovt on the . . .
                                       1   B
II.   The old captain put the chart on the . . .
                                       B   2

Key: B—Location of the boundary which triggers a change in the display.
                1—Location of the last fixation prior to crossing the boundary.
                2—Location of the first fixation after crossing the boundary.

Alternatives in target location for base word *chart*:
    chart—identical word (W-Ident)
    chest—word with similar shape and letters (W-SL)
    ebovf—nonword with similar shape (N-S)
    chovt—nonword with similar shape and letters (N-SL)
    chyft—nonword with similar letters (N-L)

FIGURE 4.5   Boundary study: An example of the type of display change that occurred in Rayner's boundary experiment

words *notice* and *detect* to mean that there is some effect on the eye behavior of the reader, rather than that the reader is consciously aware of these changes; in fact, in such experiments readers are typically not aware of the changes.) On the other hand, if the fixation were closer to the CWL the reader might obtain some information, perhaps word-shape or letter information or even meaning, and if the stimulus change caused a change in that type of information a longer fixation would result. However, if the stimulus change were of a type which did not cause a change in the type of information the reader had acquired, no change would be detected, and no disruption of reading would occur.

Since some of the initially displayed stimuli in the CWLs were nonwords, this raises an interesting question: How near to the CWL did the reader's eyes have to be before the nonwordness of the letter string in the CWL affected reading? One way to examine this was to examine the fixation prior to the display change, grouped according to how far they were from the CWL, and calculate the average fixation duration at each distance. Rayner found that the existence of a nonword in the CWL did not affect the fixation duration unless the CWL was no more than three letter positions to the right of the fixation point. If the CWL began four or more letter positions to the right of the fixation point, the wordness of its temporary occupant had no effect on the length of this fixation.

The durations of fixations on the CWL immediately after the display change were also examined, classified according to (1) the type of display change that had occurred and (2) the location of the previous fixation. These data are shown in Figure 4.6. Reading was unaffected by any stimulus change if the fixation prior to crossing the boundary was more than 12 letter spaces to the left of the CWL. If the previous fixation was 7 to 12 letter spaces to the left of the CWL, readers did pick up information about the shape of the word or its component letters and information about the identity of the extreme letters of the stimulus in the CWL, since if either of these changed when the boundary was crossed, the fixation on the target word was increased. In contrast, if the initially displayed stimulus had the same word shape and the extreme letters were the same as the target word, very little disruption was noted. Finally, the fixation on the target word was affected by the wordness of the preview when the preview was as much as six characters away from

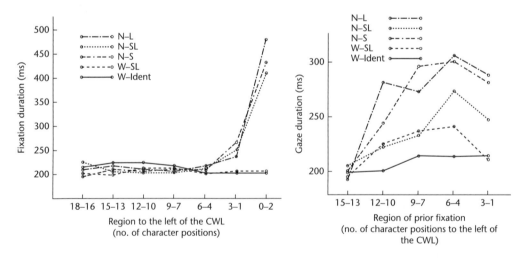

FIGURE 4.6 Data from Rayner's study. Panel on the left shows fixation time of last fixation prior to crossing the boundary; panel on the right shows gaze duration on target word after crossing the boundary. In our example, the base word is *chart* and previews of *chart, chest, ebovf, chovt,* and *chyft* represent the W-Ident, W-SL, N-S, N-SL, and N-L conditions, respectively

fixation. Thus this measure appears to be a more sensitive measure of whether lexical information was extracted than the duration of the prior fixation.

Rayner's results were originally interpreted as evidence that word shape information is obtained from parafoveal words that the reader cannot identify. However, subsequent research (to be discussed soon) has demonstrated that when word shape effects emerge, it is really because words that begin with the same letters and share the same overall shape (as in Rayner's study) have many letter features in common. Rayner's results also suggest that the meanings of words to the right of fixation are not extracted very far from the point of fixation, since the reader appears to be unaware that a nonword was present if it started further than three to six letter spaces from it. This conclusion is reinforced by a study (McConkie & Hogaboam, 1985) in which participants were reading silently with their eye movements monitored. At certain places in the text the screen went blank and participants were asked to report the last word that they had read. There is a guessing problem here, since the participant may be able to figure out a word not actually seen on the basis of prior context. Nonetheless, the results are consistent with the boundary studies reviewed in this section. McConkie and Hogaboam found (see Figure 4.7) that the word readers reported most frequently was the word that they had last fixated on, although the word to the right of fixation was sometimes reported. However, words to the left of the fixated word or two or more to the right of the fixated word were rarely reported.

More on preview benefit

The experiment by Rayner was the first to examine the nature of preview benefit in reading: when readers have a valid preview of a word prior to fixating it, they spend less time on it than when

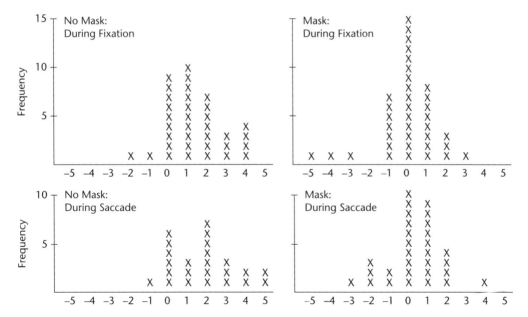

FIGURE 4.7   Frequency distribution of the location of the last read word with respect to the location of the last fixation on which text was present. 0 represents the last word fixated and 1 represents the word to its right. In the Mask conditions (right panels), a mask came on when the text went off, while in the No Mask condition (left panels), the text just went blank. Distance is measured in word units, without regard for word length

they don't have a valid preview of the word. Two additional points are important to understand with respect to preview benefit. First, Henderson and Ferreira (1990) used the boundary technique and manipulated foveal processing difficulty while also varying the availability of parafoveal information. They found that difficult foveal processing led to the reader obtaining no parafoveal preview from the word to the right of fixation. These results suggest that the amount of information processed on a fixation is somewhat variable and can be influenced by factors such as the length of the currently fixated word and the difficulty associated with processing the fixated word (see also Kennison & Clifton, 1995; Rayner, 1986; White, Rayner, & Liversedge, 2005a). Second, readers typically obtain preview benefit from the word that they are going to move to next (McDonald, 2006). Thus, while they generally obtain preview benefit from word n+1, they do not obtain preview benefit from word n+2 (Angele & Rayner, 2011; Angele, Slattery, Wang, Kliegl, & Rayner, 2008; Kliegl, Risse, & Laubrock, 2007; Rayner, Juhasz, & Brown, 2007). Interestingly, a study with Chinese indicated that Chinese readers are more likely to obtain preview benefit from word n+2 than are English readers (Yang, Wang, Xu, & Rayner, 2009). Furthermore it appears that, unlike readers of English (see below), Chinese readers obtain semantic preview benefit from words not yet fixated (Yan, Richter, Shu, & Kliegl, 2009; Yang, Wang, Tong, & Rayner, 2011). Both effects probably have to do with the fact that word n+1 and word n+2 are typically closer to the fixation point in Chinese than English.

Word skipping

Another index of how far to the right of fixation words can be identified is word skipping. Word length has the largest influence on word skipping: short words are reliably skipped more than longer words (Brysbaert, Drieghe, & Vitu, 2003; Rayner, Slattery, Drieghe, & Liversedge, 2011). Thus three-letter words are skipped about 67% of the time, whereas seven- to eight-letter words are fixated most of the time (Rayner & McConkie, 1976). Since, as indicated before, the area to the left of the fixated word is largely ignored by the reader, if a word is skipped it either must have been identified before it is skipped or the reader simply has made a guess as to what the word is without having seen it. Since word skipping is a ubiquitous part of the eye movement record, identification of the word to the right of fixation is reasonably common if guessing does not account for most of the skipping. At times words can be skipped from reasonably long distances. In a later boundary experiment by Balota, Pollatsek, and Rayner (1985; see also Drieghe, Rayner, & Pollatsek, 2005; Pollatsek, Rayner, & Balota, 1986), it was found that the CWL was occasionally skipped (although less than 1% of the time) when the prior fixation was greater than nine character spaces from the beginning of the CWL. Thus it appears that the meaning of a word in the parafovea can sometimes be extracted fairly far from fixation, although this is not usually the case even with highly predictable words.

In the Balota et al. (1985) experiment the target word was highly predictable from the prior sentence context. Skipping occurred much less frequently when a word other than that predicted by the context was in the CWL, so that skipping in the experiment was not merely due to readers guessing that the stimulus in the CWL was the predicted word. Balota et al.'s experiment differed from the original Rayner experiment as the target word was not highly predictable from the prior sentence context in the latter. This difference suggests that variables such as the predictability of a word can influence how far out from fixation words can be encoded and meaning extracted. We will discuss effects of word predictability in more detail in the next chapter.

In the previous two sections, much of our discussion was driven by some well-known experiments that were first reported nearly 40 years ago. We focused on them because in many respects they forged new ground in our understanding of skilled reading. Furthermore, the results have largely stood the test of time: the basic McConkie and Rayner studies with the moving window have been replicated numerous times and for several alphabetic writing systems.

To summarize, the perceptual span is limited, extending from the beginning of the currently fixated word to about 15 character spaces to the right of fixation. The area within which word identification takes place is even more limited. Readers can sometimes identify the word to the right of the fixated word (and sometimes may identify two words to the right of fixation, particularly when the fixated word and the next two are short words). In fact, as we mentioned earlier, readers often do not fixate either the first or last word of a line in text. Apparently, the last word of a line is often fully processed in the parafovea. It is somewhat harder to understand why the first word of a line is sometimes not fixated. One possible explanation is that the first fixation on a line is approached by a (leftward) return sweep. If a reader's perceptual span mirrors the direction of eye movements (as with the Israeli readers discussed earlier), it could be that covert attention shifts leftward on the first fixation so that the span includes the word to the left of the fixated word on those occasions.

While readers can identify words that they do not fixate, for most content words often no word beyond the fixated word is fully identified (cf., Kliegl, 2007; Kliegl, Nuthmann, & Engbert, 2006). Since we have seen that preserving some letters in a parafoveal word aids reading, it appears that partial information about a word can be encoded on one fixation and used to aid identification of the word on the subsequent fixation. We now turn to a discussion of what we know about how information is integrated across fixations.

Integration of information across eye movements

Several converging pieces of data from the last section suggested that some words are processed partially on one fixation and then finished on the succeeding fixation. Another indicant that words are processed on more than one fixation is the fact that the perceptual span is about double the average size of a saccade for readers of English. This comparison is not completely fair, however, since the perceptual span is not an average: it is measuring the maximum distance that information can be extracted. Nonetheless, the discrepancy between the perceptual span and the size of the average saccade reinforces the conclusion that the eyes are moving to an area of text that has been processed to some extent.

Integration of information across saccades is by no means a conscious process, since we are generally not aware of our eye movements. Each eye movement changes the pattern of light on the retina, and yet we perceive a stable, coherent image of the words we are looking at. We never have the feeling of having stimulus input for a quarter of a second or so followed by a break in input due to the saccade. The research on saccadic suppression we discussed earlier explains why you don't see "junk" between the slides. However, we don't have a detailed understanding of why the gaps between fixations are not noticed. Somehow the brain is able to smooth out the discrete inputs from each eye fixation and create a feeling of a continuous coherent perceptual world.

If information about a word is obtained on two successive fixations, the first when the word is in the parafovea and the second when it is in the fovea, and if the integration process is useful in reading, the parafoveal preview of the word should facilitate later foveal processing of the word. We shall thus discuss integration of information across fixations largely in terms of such facilitation. It has been known since as early as Dodge (1906) that parafoveal previews facilitate later identification. However that facilitation, in itself, is not necessarily evidence for integration across saccades, since the word may have been fully identified in the parafovea. What is needed to document integration across saccades is to make the parafoveal preview and foveal target stimuli similar but not identical, and to determine whether there is still facilitation from the preview.

An experimental technique requiring participants to name isolated words (originated by Rayner, 1978b) has produced a lot of information about integration across fixations (Balota & Rayner, 1983; McClelland & O'Regan, 1981; Rayner, McConkie, & Ehrlich, 1978; Rayner, McConkie, & Zola, 1980). It is a miniaturization of the boundary technique. Participants are asked to fixate on a central fixation point, and when a letter string appears in parafoveal vision, they are to make an eye movement to it. During the saccade the initially displayed stimulus is replaced by a *target* word which they are to name as fast as possible. The parafoveal stimulus is thus visible for the approximately 200 ms from when the parafoveal letter string appears until the eye movement begins. In spite of the fact that it is visible for such an extended time, participants are almost never aware of the identity of the parafoveal word and are rarely even aware that there has been any change! Thus they have no trouble deciding which word to name.

Figure 4.8 shows the basic pattern of results from the experiments. If the stimuli presented on fixation n and fixation n+1 are identical, there is facilitation in naming the target word (compared to when a row of asterisks or unrelated letters are initially presented parafoveally). More important is the fact that facilitation occurs even if the parafoveal preview only has some letters in common with the target word. As one would predict from the perceptual span experiments, the amount of facilitation depends on how far into the parafovea the stimulus occurs. That is, there is more facilitation when the initial stimulus is 1 degree from fixation than when it is at 3 degrees and hardly any facilitation at 5 degrees (i.e., 15 letter spaces) from fixation. Thus the results indicate that participants can use partial parafoveal information about a word to aid their recognition of that word when it is later fixated, but only when the preview is less than 15 letter spaces from fixation.

The fact that *chest* in the parafovea facilitates the later identification of *chart* implies that some information extracted from *chest* was useful in the later identification of *chart*. Indeed, it is pretty

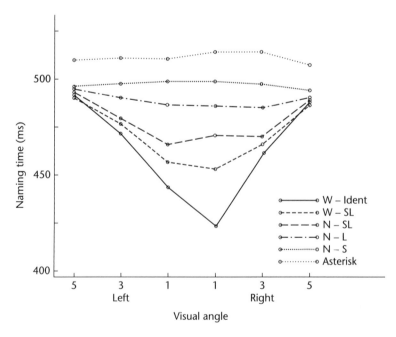

FIGURE 4.8 Mean naming time as a function of initially displayed alternative and visual angle. In our example, the base word is *chart* and previews of *chart*, *chest*, *ebovf*, *chovt*, and *chyft* represent the W-Ident, W-SL, N-S, N-SL, and N-L conditions, respectively. The asterisk preview was a row of asterisks

clear that *chest* and *chart* are orthographically similar, and this mere fact does provide some facilitation (Williams, Perea, Pollatsek, & Rayner, 2006). However, the deeper issue is: Why does the fact that two words are orthographically similar yield preview benefit? In the research literature five potential sources of facilitation have been examined in detail: (1) some of the visual features of *chest* are stored and aid later identification of *chart*; (2) some aspect of the meaning of *chest* has been encoded by the parafoveal preview of *chart* which facilitates later identification (although that seems improbable in this particular example); (3) some sort of sound codes (e.g., phonemes or syllables) activated by *chest* (perhaps the initial /ch/) aid later identification of the word *chart*; (4) some of the letters are identified and these abstract letter identities (not the letter forms) are what are facilitating; and (5) the lexical entry of *chart* is partially activated by the parafoveal preview of *chest* which aids in the later identification of *chart*. The distinction we wish to draw between 1 and 4 is that the information about letters is in a visual form in 1, but a more abstract form in 4. The distinction we wish to draw between 2 and 5 is that in 2, some aspect of the word's meaning as well as its identity is activated in the parafovea. Of course, these hypotheses are not mutually exclusive, as facilitation could have more than one source. As we will see the evidence points at present to a relatively simple answer: there is no evidence for either of the first two mechanisms being operative, so that, by a process of elimination, 3, 4, and 5 appear to be the sources of integration. We will discuss the evidence against the first two in turn.

Is visual information integrated across eye movements?

The idea that detailed visual information is integrated across eye movements may seem the most plausible, since it corresponds to our intuitions that we see a single seamless world when visual information from two fixations is brought together into a single representation of the visual world (McConkie & Rayner, 1976b). That is, readers may obtain gross featural information from parafoveal vision during a fixation and store it in a temporary visual buffer, an integrative visual buffer. The visual information stored in the buffer would then be used as a base to which new information is added when the region (previously in parafoveal vision) is fixated. The alignment of the information from the two fixations would presumably be based on (a) knowledge about how far the eyes moved and (b) the commonality of the patterns from the two fixations. Of course, all this computation would generally be unconscious, since we are usually not aware of moving our eyes. The integrative visual buffer in reading can be thought of as being like iconic memory (see Chapter 1), except that information is preserved in the visual buffer across eye movements.

While this view of information integration is perhaps the most intuitively appealing of the alternatives, the evidence against it is quite strong. First, Rayner et al. (1978) showed that proper alignment was not necessary in order to obtain the results shown in Figure 4.8. Recall that alignment or justification of two successive images in the buffer should be based on keeping track of how far the eyes moved. However, Rayner et al. found that the same pattern of results was obtained in an experiment in which the stimulus pattern rather than the participants' eyes moved. That is, an initially presented stimulus appeared in parafoveal vision and, after a period of time approximating the sum of the saccadic latency and saccade duration (about 200 ms), the target word to be named appeared foveally and the parafoveal stimulus simultaneously disappeared. Notice that the sequence of events on the retina is the same as when the eyes move to a parafoveal stimulus: an initial stimulus impinges on the parafoveal retina followed by a stimulus in foveal vision. In one condition, however, an eye movement intervenes between two retinal events while in the other condition the eye movement is simulated by moving the stimulus rather than the eyes. If keeping track of how far the eyes move is important for the integration process, performance should be much worse in the no eye movement condition than in the standard eye movement condition. However, Rayner et al. found no major differences between these two conditions.

More damaging to the integrative visual buffer notion were two experiments which directly tested whether visual features could be integrated. The first demonstrated that changes in the visual form of the information had no effect if the meaning was not altered (Rayner, McConkie, & Zola, 1980). Rayner et al. found that changing the case of a word between the preview and target (e.g., *CASE* changed to *case*) had no effect on how long it took to name the word, even though there were still clear facilitating effects from parafoveal previews. The second tested integration of visual information in a different way. O'Regan and Levy-Schoen (1983) presented half of the features of each letter of a word on one fixation and the other half on the subsequent fixation. (Both stimuli were in the same spatial location.) Participants in this condition were rarely ever able to identify the target word. In contrast, when the two halves were presented in the same spatial location one after the other in quick succession, participants readily identified the target word. Thus the visual information that can be integrated within a fixation cannot be integrated when a saccade intervenes.

At this point you may well be saying to yourself that all of the experiments we have described in this section do not really involve participants in the task of reading. Perhaps, as we have pointed out before, the tasks used in these experiments encourage a strategy that is different from what normally happens when we read. However, it turns out to be the case that a number of experiments in which participants are actually reading (see below) yield results consistent with the conclusions we have reached from the experiments described up to this point.

The question of whether integration is dependent on keeping track of how far the eyes move has been tested in the reading situation as well. In these experiments (McConkie, Zola, & Wolverton, 1980; O'Regan, 1981) participants were reading text, and at selected points the entire line of text was shifted to the left or right during the saccade. In the normal state of perception, the distance that the image has moved from fixation to fixation is determined by the distance that the eyes moved. If the alignment of the visual information obtained on two successive fixations is dependent on this calculation of how far the eyes have moved, then considerable disruption should be produced when the text is shifted. Even if it is shifted only a few characters there should be massive disruption, since the letter information in the two images will conflict in all locations. Since small corrective saccades sometimes occurred after the shift, the shift was possibly sometimes registered in the brain (if not in consciousness). However, these eye movements could have been because the eyes landed on a position other than intended rather than the shift actually being registered in the brain. Nonetheless, shifting the text two or three character positions resulted in no conscious awareness of the shift and produced negligible effects on reading speed and comprehension.

Similarly, the issue of whether integration occurs by integrating the visual forms on two successive fixations was tested by McConkie and Zola (1979). They had participants read passages printed in AlTeRnAtInG cAsE, and changed the case of every letter during certain saccades, so that successive visual images would not be similar. Thus *cAsE* on fixation n would appear as *CaSe* on fixation n+1 and *cAsE* on n+2. These changes were not noticed by readers and they had virtually no effect on comprehension or on reading speed (for a more recent demonstration see Slattery, Angele, & Rayner, 2011). In addition, the basic finding that partial information facilitates naming of the fixated word (e.g., *chest* facilitates naming of *chart*) parallels the finding described in the previous section (Rayner et al., 1982) that reading was faster when the first two to three letters of the word to the right of fixation were visible than when they were altered.

In summary, the basic findings that emerged from the parafoveal naming experiments have been corroborated in experiments involving silent reading. The two experimental situations thus provide convergent validity for the conclusions, combining the ecological validity of the reading situation with the more tightly controlled naming experiments in which the response is transparently tied to word identification.

Partial encoding of meaning

There are two different ways in which one might think the reader extracts partial meaning from a word. The first is that the whole word is processed, but only dimly. That is, the activation from the physical stimulation does not lead to identification of the word, but may lead to a vague idea of the meaning of the word. Perhaps a semantic feature is activated. The second way is that a specific meaningful segment of the word, a morpheme, is identified. We consider each of these possibilities in turn.

Semantic preprocessing

As we look around the world we feel we have a vague idea of what things seen only in the parafovea and periphery are. For example, if we are not directly looking at a dog we may be aware that it is an animal, and have a vague idea of its size, but may not be able to make a precise identification of it. Moreover, there is evidence in picture perception that there are possibly unconscious influences of such partial meaning on processing. For example, in picture perception, the eyes quickly move to regions judged to be informative (Antes, 1974; Mackworth & Morandi, 1967) or semantically anomalous (Becker, Pashler, & Lubin, 2007; Loftus & Mackworth, 1978; Rayner, Castelhano, & Yang, 2009a; cf., Henderson, Weeks, & Hollingworth, 1999). These phenomena suggest that something similar may be going on in reading.

However, it is important to point out that there are rather substantial differences in the stimulus pattern between text and a picture (Loftus, 1983; McConkie & Rayner, 1976b). With text the pattern is rather homogenous, made up of letters and spaces, and it is likely that lateral masking of words and letters (by adjacent words and letters) is much greater in text. A single distinctive and informative feature of an object in a picture may convey meaning in a way that no single visual feature of a word does. It may well be these distinctive features that allow for rough semantic classifications of objects and guide the movement of the eye in picture perception.

Another reason that semantic preprocessing seems like an attractive explanation for parafoveal preview effects is because of the unconscious priming experiments described in Chapter 3 (e.g., Allport, 1977; Balota, 1983; Marcel, 1983). In these experiments words are briefly presented followed by masks in the fovea. If conditions are set up right, the participant will be unable to identify the word, but the speed in identifying a semantically related word that follows will be increased. Marcel (1978) suggested on the basis of the foveal priming studies that meaning is simultaneously available from a number of places on a page. For example, Marcel noted that if you turn the page of a book and are reading the top line, something at the bottom of the page may catch your eye. He further argued that this is only possible if its meaning has been analyzed independently of where attention is. A key assumption in this inference is that a brief foveal presentation of a word is analogous to a word in parafoveal vision during reading.

The analogy may be misleading. Although a briefly presented foveal word and a parafoveal word are both visually degraded, they are degraded in different ways. Brief foveal words are degraded by their duration and by backward masking; parafoveal words in text are degraded by acuity and lateral masking. In reading normal text these acuity and lateral masking considerations make it difficult to identify words at increasing distances from the fixation point. The phenomenon of foveal masking is still poorly understood; however, it appears that there is some sense in which the stimulus is fully identified, but something about the mask dissociates it from awareness and direct access. On the other hand, it seems implausible that partial semantic access can occur from vague information about a word such as global shape, length, or knowing a letter or two. One possible explanation for the phenomenon that Marcel described—something at the bottom of the page catching your eye when you turn the page—is that when you begin to move your eyes to bring them to the top of the page you may make a short fixation near the bottom of the page. Thus this phenomenon may be explained by something similar to the foveal masking experiments rather than by semantic preprocessing in the parafovea or periphery.

In reading there is no clear evidence supporting semantic preprocessing. One attempt to demonstrate semantic preprocessing uses a variant of the semantic priming technique described in the previous chapter. A semantically ambiguous word such as *bank* is presented in the fovea and one of two words that could disambiguate the word, *river* or *money*, is presented in the parafovea. Both words are presented briefly and the participant is tested on which meaning he or she associates with the foveal word, *bank*. If participants perform at above chance levels in choosing the meaning suggested by the parafoveal word, then it implies that the meaning of the parafoveal word has been processed.

In fact, participants perform above chance. However, we already know that parafoveal words can be identified from our previous discussion of skipping. The key question is whether partial meaning can be processed. The way this has been examined (Bradshaw, 1974; Inhoff, 1982; Inhoff & Rayner, 1980; Underwood, 1980, 1981), is to test both for which sense of *bank* the participant selects and to test whether the parafoveal word has been identified. If participants can select the appropriate meaning at above chance levels, even when the parafoveal word has not been consciously identified, one would have evidence that semantic preprocessing has taken place. Unfortunately the results from these experiments are not completely consistent. Some have found above chance performance and others have not. However, even in those that obtained above chance performance, it was not much above chance. In addition, the experiments that obtained above chance performance are difficult to evaluate as certain factors (such as eye location, guessing, and readout from iconic memory) were not controlled. In sum, there is little clear evidence for semantic preprocessing from these experiments (see also Rayner & Morris, 1992).

Rayner, Balota, and Pollatsek (1986) provided a more direct test of semantic preprocessing in reading using the boundary technique described earlier. The stimulus that appeared in the target location before the base word (*song*) was fixated was either a visually similar nonword (*sorp*), a semantically associated word (*tune*), or an orthographically and semantically different control word (*door*). While the visually similar preview facilitated processing of the base word relative to the control condition (fixation time on the base word was reduced), there was no difference between the conditions employing semantically related and unrelated parafoveal previews. That is, there was no evidence for semantic priming in these conditions. In contrast, the pairs of related words presented sequentially in the fovea produced the usual semantic priming effect when the second word was named. More recently, other attempts to determine if there is semantic preview benefit using the boundary paradigm (Altarriba, Kambe, Pollatsek, & Rayner, 2001; Hyönä & Häikiö, 2005) have likewise failed to find evidence in favor of such benefit in reading. Interestingly, while there is little evidence for semantic preview benefit in English, there is some evidence for semantic preview benefit in Chinese (Yan, Richter, Shu, & Kliegl, 2009; Yang, Wang, Tong, & Rayner, 2011) and German (Hohenstein, Laubrock, & Kliegl, 2010). Whether the latter studies are due to characteristics of the writing system remains to be determined: Chinese maps more directly to meaning than does English and in German the target words (all nouns) have a capital letter at the beginning of the word.

Identification of morphemes

We appear to be down to four possibilities for integration of information across saccades in reading: the entire lexical entry is activated, sound codes are activated, a meaningful subunit (a morpheme) is activated, or merely some of the letters are activated. Before discussing the involvement of morphemes we need to review more details of the parafoveal preview experiments.

Rayner, McConkie, & Zola (1980) demonstrated that significant facilitation was produced when the first two or three letters were constant across the two fixations (e.g., *chest–chart*). No facilitation was obtained when only the first letter was constant across fixations nor was there facilitation when all letters were the same except the first letter (e.g., *board–hoard*). Thus it appears that encoding the beginning letters of the word is crucial to obtaining parafoveal facilitation. Interestingly, Inhoff (1987) found this was true when readers had to read from right to left so that the parafoveal preview was to the left of fixation and thus the beginning letters were furthest from fixation. He also found that when practiced participants read text from right to left, a preview of the beginning three letters of a six-letter word provided facilitation in reading. Of course, when reading from right to left the beginning letters are further away from fixation so it is not just that the beginning letters of the word to the right of fixation are close to the current fixation point; there is something important about those letters. The pattern from moving-window experiments in which only the first part of word n+1 was exposed also indicates that the information from the first two or three letters of a word provides much of the parafoveal benefit, particularly if the remainder of the word consists of letters that are visually similar to the real letters of the word; if the remaining letters are not visually similar, readers do not read as well as when the entire word n+1 is present (Inhoff, 1989a; Lima & Inhoff, 1985; Rayner et al., 1982). While the first few letters of a parafoveal word provide significant preview benefit, studies using transposed letters (e.g., switching the letters *st* to *ts*) have indicated that readers do get some useful information from the letters at the ends of words, particularly shorter words (Johnson, Perea, & Rayner, 2007).

Since information from the first two to three letters of a word appears to provide much of the preview benefit, the logical place to look for extraction of a morpheme from a parafoveal word is at the beginning. Moreover, it also suggests that it would help to look for relatively short morphemes. Lima (1987) hypothesized that the beginning letters may facilitate, at least in part, because they aid in identifying the initial morpheme of a word. She tested her hypothesis using prefixed words, since most of the prefixes in common use have from one to three letters and because prefixes form a small set of highly familiar word-initial letter patterns. In particular she wanted to determine whether there was any evidence that "prefix stripping" (see Chapter 3) could begin before a word is fixated. Words with prefixes (such as *mistrust*) were compared with pseudoprefixed words (such as *mistress*). The stimuli were matched on number of syllables, word length, and word frequency and a sentence frame was prepared into which either of the words would fit (*The teenager's abrupt/absurd answer . . .*). In Lima's experiments the boundary technique was used. Prior to the display change, the CWL contained the letters common to the two words plus random letters or Xs (*abnsbl* or *abxxxx*) or simply a string of random letters or Xs (*kmnsbl* or *xxxxxx*). When the reader's saccade crossed the boundary, the word *abrupt* or *absurd* (depending on the condition) was displayed at the CWL.

Lima found that participants looked at the target word for less time when the initial letters of the target word were present than when they were not. She also found, as mentioned in Chapter 3, that prefixed words were fixated for a shorter amount of time than pseudoprefixed words. However, the benefit of the parafoveal preview was the same for prefixed and pseudopre-fixed words. There are two possibilities for this equality. If one assumes that prefix stripping is the first step of the only route to identification of both kinds of words (which then has to be followed by a second access in the case of pseudoprefixed words), then prefix stripping in the parafovea is tenable: the parafoveal preview would start off the identical first stage of word identification (prefix stripping) in the two cases. However, we argued in Chapter 3 that it is more plausible to assume that access of pseudoprefixed words can go on directly as well as having to go through the false start of prefix stripping. If this is the case one would expect greater parafoveal benefit for prefixed words, since access of them would be aided by identifying the initial morpheme as well as the first three letters. Since the parafoveal benefit did not differ between prefixed and pseudoprefixed words, we have some evidence that morphemes are not extracted in the parafovea. Furthermore, in a replication and extension of Lima's study, Kambe (2004) likewise obtained no evidence for morphological preview benefit in English. Interestingly, in Hebrew (in which it can be argued that morphemes play a more central role in word processing), experiments using the boundary technique have obtained evidence of morphological preview benefit (Deutsch, Frost, Peleg, Pollatsek, & Rayner, 2003; Deutsch, Frost, Pollatsek, & Rayner, 2000, 2005).

An experiment employing compound words provided additional evidence against morphemic units in parafoveal information extraction in English. Inhoff (1989b) employed six-letter compound words such as *cowboy*. As with Lima's experiment, he employed preview conditions in which the whole word *cowboy*, the first morpheme *cowxxx*, or no letter information *xxxxxx*, was present in the parafovea. Inhoff employed two controls: pseudocompound words such as *carpet*, where the first three letters were also a word but not a morphemic subunit, and monosyllabic words such as *priest*. He found the same preview benefit in all three cases, indicating that neither the first morpheme nor the first syllable was a significant unit in integration across saccades. Inhoff's results appear to contradict those of Lima and Pollatsek (1983). Lima and Pollatsek found that a preview of the first morpheme speeded lexical decision more than a preview of the beginning letters when they did not form a morpheme. However, the morpheme preview in the Lima and Pollatsek experiment was foveal and thus the integration was not across two fixations.

Sound codes

Let us next consider the possibility that the reader is extracting some sound-based code from the parafoveal stimulus such as the initial phonemes or the first syllable of the word. This possibility seems particularly appealing since many of the studies that we have described with individual words required participants to name the word that is present on the second fixation. Perhaps information acquired from the parafoveal word permits the participant to begin to form the speech musculature properly for saying the word. This would reduce the time needed to initiate an utterance when the target word occurs in the fovea following the eye movement.

There is now good evidence that sound codes are used to integrate information across eye movements and are part of the benefit readers obtain from preview information. For example, Pollatsek, Lesch, Morris, and Rayner (1992) found that sound codes are used in integrating information across saccades. A homophone of a target word (*beech* as a preview for *beach*) presented as a preview in the parafovea facilitated processing of the target word seen on the next fixation more than a preview with a non-homophone matched in orthographic similarity (*bench*) to the target word. Because the orthographic similarity of the preview to the target also plays a part in the facilitative effect of the preview, however, codes other than phonological codes (such as abstract letter codes) are preserved across saccades. Further evidence for the role of phonological coding in integrating information across saccades will be presented in Chapter 5.

Letters vs. words

The evidence available thus suggests that parafoveal previews help in two ways (Blanchard, Pollatsek, & Rayner, 1989). First, the word in the parafovea may be fully identified (and perhaps skipped). Second, it may only be partially activated, with this partial activation speeding later identification of a word. We have reviewed rather convincing evidence that visual codes do not play any significant role in partial identification of words. The evidence also indicates that semantic preprocessing plays no role, at least in English. Furthermore, there is no evidence for the involvement of morphemes in integration across saccades in English. However, there is strong positive evidence for the involvement of sound codes.

How is information integrated across saccades? As we argued earlier, one possibility is that several letters may be identified which speeds later identification of the word. Let us briefly sketch how the process may work. Suppose the reader is fixated seven character spaces to the left of the beginning of the word *changes* (as in Fixation 1 in Figure 4.5). The reader may be able to unambiguously identify the first letter (*c*) and make some preliminary identification of the next few letters. The letters *b* and *h* share many features in common, as do the letters *c, a, e*, and *o*. It seems likely that after the reader has identified the *c* that knowledge of orthography would rule out *b* as the second letter. Similarly, the *c* can be eliminated as the third letter and orthography further constrains *a* as the most likely third letter. Thus, preliminary letter identification of the letters *cha* would occur on fixation *n*. Alternatively it may be the case that the threshold for letter identification is not reached until fixation n+1. In this case, preliminary letter identification for the beginning letters of the parafoveal word begins on fixation *n*, but is incomplete. Information based partly on visual features and partly on orthographic rules would begin accumulating for the beginning letters of the parafoveal word, but identification would not take place until after the eye movement.

We should like to emphasize that preliminary letter identification, as described above, involves abstract letter identities. Thus incomplete activation of letters would have to be of the form "this letter is likely to be a b" rather than in the form of visual features, since changing case (and hence visual features) made no difference in the amount of facilitation. This also reinforces a point made in Chapter 3 on word recognition. The fact that changing the case of words from fixation to fixation does not interfere with reading strongly argues that word shape is not an important cue used in recognizing words. When word shape is found to have an effect (as with some of the parafoveal priming studies) the effect is likely to be merely a by-product of letter features. That is, when two words have the same shape, it follows that the component letters share more distinctive features.

An interesting question is whether activation of letters (primarily but not exclusively beginning letters) produces partial activation of a word. Possible models for such partial activation by Paap et al. (1982) and Rumelhart and McClelland (1982) were discussed in Chapter 3. In these models, letters in letter strings not only activate the letter detectors but a neighborhood of word detectors. Thus, *chest* in the parafovea could excite a neighborhood of lexical entries that are similar to it (e.g., *chest, chart, chalk*) and such subthreshold activation is what produces the facilitation of the later identification of *chart*. If one made suitable assumptions that beginning letters were weighted more heavily than end letters in determining the pattern of activation, the pattern of parafoveal facilitation could be explained.

One piece of data that suggests the facilitation is in terms of partially activated word detectors rather than fully activated letter detectors is the absence of certain kinds of errors in the parafoveal naming experiments. Some of these experiments (Rayner, McConkie, & Zola, 1980) were set up with pairs such as *train* in the parafovea followed by *clash* in the fovea. If the first two letters *tr* of the parafoveal string are fully identified on some trials and then integrated with the information from the foveal string, one might expect the participant to identify the string as *trash*. However, such errors did not occur. That is consistent with viewing facilitation as due to partial activation of a neighborhood of lexical entries. While *trash* would get reasonable excitation from the stimulus *train*, it would get little further excitation from *clash*, since the mismatch in the first letters would be weighted heavily.

That is not to say that the lack of "illusory conjunctions" rules out the possibility that parafoveal facilitation can be due to letter identification. What it does rule out is a model in which some letters are fully identified in the parafovea and then those letter positions are ignored when in the fovea. There is thus no strong evidence one way or the other about whether parafoveal facilitation works through the partial activation of lexical entries or the activation of component letters. We will thus assume that both are possible.

The control of eye movements during reading

In the previous sections we discussed some basic facts about eye movements. We then examined the amount of information that was extracted from a fixation and how this information was combined across fixations. The two major conclusions that emerged are that the reader can process somewhat more than the fixated word on a fixation and that some words are processed on more than one fixation. However, our picture of eye movements is incomplete; we have said little about the time-course of what is happening from fixation to fixation during reading. When we discussed basic facts of eye movements, we indicated, for example, that the reading rate, average fixation duration, and average saccade length all varied with different kinds of texts. Yet we said little about how the differences in the text change these variables. That is, for more difficult text we know that the reading rate slows down, the average fixation duration increases, the average saccade size decreases, and the number of regressions increase. However, we have not discussed what, on a given fixation, causes the fixation to be longer, the following saccade shorter, or a regression to be made. Similarly we know how much information is acquired on a fixation, but we have only touched upon the time course of the acquisition of this information.

In this section we will discuss in some detail how eye movements are controlled in reading. We do so for two reasons. First, eye movements are an important part of the reading process and it is important to understand all components of reading. Second, we believe that eye movement data are very important for making inferences about cognitive processes in reading. Indeed, in subsequent chapters we will rely heavily on eye movement data in trying to understand various processes that occur in reading.

The issues of eye movement control and the time course of extraction of information from the text are closely related, since the amount of cognitive control possible in reading is dependent on the speed of information extraction. We know that the average fixation in reading is about 225 ms. If it took only 50–60 ms to encode the fixated word, then there would be plenty of time to program and execute an eye movement conditional on the encoding of the word being completed. On the other hand, if it took about 225 ms to encode a word on a fixation, cognitive control of eye movements would slow down reading, assuming that programming and executing an eye movement takes appreciable time. That is, if one waited until the word were encoded to program an eye movement to move to the next word, the average fixation duration in reading would be the 225 ms encoding time plus the time it took to program and execute the eye movement to the next word (on the order of 125–175 ms). Thus the average fixation duration in reading would be at least 350 ms, or a lot longer than it actually is.

If the encoding time for the fixated word were 225 ms, one would need to program the eye movement in anticipation of encoding the word in order to achieve fixation durations as short as 225 ms. One possible strategy would be to program an eye movement at a fixed time after the beginning of a fixation, selecting that time so that most words would be encoded before the eye moved. If this time were judiciously selected, few regressions would be needed to go back to words that were not fully encoded, and reading could proceed with the average fixation being around 225 ms. In other words, if words can be encoded quickly, cognitive control of eye movements makes sense. On the other hand, if words can't be encoded quickly, then it might be better to put the eyes on "automatic pilot." In either case, however, a procedure would be needed to interrupt the forward flow when something has not been understood, so that a regression can be made.

At this juncture let us define a few terms that we will use in describing control of the eyes. At one extreme is the automatic pilot version of eye control, which we will call *global control*. By global control we mean a model of eye movement control in which the eyes are programmed at the beginning of a chunk of text to move forward at a predetermined rate: on each fixation, the signal to move the eye is made at a prespecified time after the beginning of the fixation and the saccade length is also prespecified. To account for variability in fixation times and saccade lengths, such a model would have to posit that there is random variability, both in the time to execute the eye movements and in how far the eyes actually move. Such a model would, as we mentioned, need an additional system that could interrupt and cause a regression to be made.

At the other extreme is *direct control*. Direct control means that the signal to move the eyes is the identification of the currently fixated word. It also means that the decision of where to move the eyes is based on visual information extracted from the currently fixated word. An intermediate position is that eye movements are under cognitive control (i.e., directed by information recently extracted in the text) but not necessarily by information extracted on the current fixation. In other words, direct control is the extreme case of cognitive control.

A particularly strong form of direct control is that assumed by the immediacy hypothesis (Just & Carpenter, 1980). The immediacy hypothesis is that the eyes do not move on until all processing of the fixated word is completed. By "all processing" Just and Carpenter meant not only lexical access of the word, but integrating it into the meaning of the sentence, paragraph, etc. as well. If the immediacy hypothesis were true, then examining the eye movement record to infer cognitive processes would be easy, since fixation time on a word would index all the processing time associated with that word. At the other extreme, if global control were true, individual fixations would reveal only the rate that was preset for the passage of text, and thus little about the process of reading.

As we shall see, it appears that most eye movement control is direct and it is possible that most eye movements in reading may be under cognitive control. That is, it appears that the movement of the eyes is largely predictable from the text currently fixated, although the relationship is somewhat more complex than Just and Carpenter hoped it was. Thus, while the eye movement record is a very valuable tool for inferring the cognitive processes of reading, it has to be interpreted very carefully.

Evidence for cognitive control

We would have a complete account of eye movements (and probably of the process of reading) if on each fixation we could account for why the fixation duration was as long as it was, and why the saccade following it moved the eyes to the particular location where they landed. Our present state of knowledge is more modest. We do know many variables that influence both the length of fixations and the direction (and size) of saccades, and we can make reasonable guesses about what underlying processes are likely to modulate the behavior of the eyes. We shall begin this section by briefly reviewing the evidence that there is some cognitive control of eye movements.

One of the reasons for starting off with such a modest agenda is that at one time (the 1960s and early 1970s) the possibility that there was any cognitive control of eye movements was viewed with some skepticism. There were three arguments underlying this skepticism. The first was that several studies examined eye movement records from silent reading and attempted to correlate the length of fixations and saccade sizes with certain aspects of the text (see Morton, 1964). These studies failed to find any significant relationship between the eye movement record and the text. The second was that several studies demonstrated that the length of a fixation was uncorrelated with either the length of the following saccade or the length of the following fixation (see Andriessen & deVoogd, 1973). This lack of correlation suggested to some that the variability in both measures was random and hence the eyes were under global control. The third was that the time to encode a word was believed to be relatively slow (at least 200 ms) and so direct control was viewed as implausible (see Bouma & deVoogd, 1974). Moreover, without direct control, indirect cognitive control would be of little value. What good would the information from a word or two back be in telling the reader how long to fixate the current word or where to move next?

The last plausibility argument, of course, is quite weak, since the time to identify a word is likely to be shorter than 200 ms (see Chapter 3). But what of the first two pieces of data? The lack of correlation between the eye movement record and the text being read has not agreed with most subsequent reports. The earlier findings are probably due to (a) relatively inaccurate eye recording instruments and (b) relatively small data sets being analyzed. The advent of more accurate eye-tracking equipment, and the use of computers that enabled large amounts of data to be analyzed, have led to the discovery of interesting relationships between the text and the pattern of the eye movements (which we will discuss shortly). In contrast, the lack of correlation of fixation duration with saccade length and between successive fixation durations has been subsequently reported several times and with relatively large data sets (McConkie & Zola, 1984; Rayner & McConkie, 1976), so it is likely to be a fact about reading. However, it does not necessarily mean that the pattern of eye movements is random. Subsequent research has demonstrated that in more local situations (when text is difficult, for example) long fixations can be preceded by and followed by short saccades, and when the text is not particularly difficult longer saccades lead to longer fixations (Kliegl et al., 2006).

Basically, there is no strong reason to expect successive saccades to be positively correlated within a given text. While certain passages may be difficult and cause all fixations on them to be relatively long, there are also reasons to expect successive fixation durations to be negatively corre-lated (most notably the high probability that a long content word will be followed by a short func-tion word and vice versa). Hence, overall, the positive and negative dependencies could very well sum to an approximately zero correlation. The independence of fixation duration with saccade length is more interesting. It raises the possibility that the decisions of where to move the eyes and when to move the eyes might be made independently (Rayner & McConkie, 1976). For example, some mechanism might aim the next eye movement towards the third letter of the next word, and then a later mechanism (such as identification of the fixated word) might trigger the actual deci-sion to move the eye. Accordingly, we will review evidence that these decisions are under separate cognitive control.

Control of saccade length

There is a considerable body of data that shows a close relationship between the number of letters in a word and where the reader fixates. First, Rayner and McConkie (1976) computed the prob-ability of a fixation landing on words of different lengths and the probability of fixating on a letter within a word of a given length. They found that as word length increased, the probability of fixating the word increased. This finding is not particularly interesting, since it is consistent with global control: even a random sequence of fixations would produce more fixations on long words. However, a random sequence of eye movements would also imply that the probability of fixating on a letter would be independent of its position in a word or on the length of the word that contained it. Rayner and McConkie found that any single letter in a four- to seven-letter word was more likely to be fixated than one in a shorter or longer word. As we will see, letters in short words tend to be fixated less often because short words tend to be skipped, and individual letters in long words probably tend to be fixated less often than those in middle-length words because there is more redundancy in the long words. In addition, the location of a fixation in a word is not random; there is a preferred viewing location in words that is between the beginning and middle letters of the word (McConkie & Zola, 1984; O'Regan, 1981; Rayner, 1979; Rayner, Fischer, & Pollatsek, 1998). Moreover, the eyes tend to not land on the period or the spaces at the end of a sentence (Rayner, 1975b). In addition, readers are less likely to fixate on spaces between words than on letters in words.

The above analyses are in terms of the position of fixations. Another index of cognitive control is the length of saccades. First, the word to the right of fixation has been shown to influence the length of the saccade. The eye tends to jump further when a long word is to the right of fixation than when a shorter word is there (O'Regan, 1975, 1979; Rayner, 1979). In addition, the size of a saccade is sensitive to manipulations in the text. Moving-window experiments have demonstrated that saccade length decreases when window size is less than 15 character spaces to the right of fixation (when the spaces between words outside of the window are filled).

The above data show that the movement of the eyes is sensitive to the length of words. Thus the eyes appear to be guided by a computation based on the boundaries of a word (delineated by spaces). The fact that the eyes tend to jump over blank regions indicates that such geometric computations are at least part of the story. More direct evidence for such control comes from an experiment by Morris, Rayner, and Pollatsek (1990). (We will use the notation that the fixated word is word n, the next word in the text is word n+1, the prior word is word n−1, etc.) In one condition, the only useful information to the right of the fixated word was the spaces delimiting word n+1 (all the letters to the right of word n were converted to Xs). In spite of the fact that word n+1 was all Xs before it was fixated, readers made a longer saccade off word n, the longer word n+1 was. Thus word length, per se, had an effect on the size of the saccade.

Further evidence that word length information has a major effect comes from two other sources. First, when the spaces between words are eliminated, so *thatwordsinsentencesruntogether* (as in the prior string of words), reading slows down by about 40%. Part of the problem is that word recognition is hampered, but another big part of the problem is that the space information (or word length information about upcoming words) is gone and this leads to much shorter saccades (Perea & Acha, 2009; Rayner et al., 1998). Second, experiments in which gaze-contingent changes are made during reading have demonstrated that if the word length of an upcoming region changes during a saccade, so that *backhand* becomes *back and* or vice versa, the eyes move further when *backhand* was in the parafovea than when *back and* was (Juhasz, White, Liversedge, & Rayner, 2008; White, Rayner, & Liversedge, 2005b).

However, the length of a word is confounded with its frequency in the language (shorter words tend to be more common). Thus some of the word length effects in natural reading may not be due to where the word boundaries are but to the processing of the letters in between. One clear demonstration of the effect of word length is in studies of when words are skipped. While shorter words are skipped more than longer words, several studies have shown that words tend to be skipped if they are frequent or otherwise easier to process even when length is controlled. For example, *the* is skipped more than other three-letter words (O'Regan, 1979, 1980), high-frequency words are skipped more than length-matched low-frequency words (Rayner, Sereno, & Raney, 1996), and words that are predictable from the prior sentence context are skipped more as well (Balota et al., 1985; Drieghe, Rayner, & Pollatsek, 2005; Ehrlich & Rayner, 1981; Rayner & Well, 1996). In addition, the direction of eye movements is under cognitive control. Readers are much more likely to make a regression when the word fixated is one indicating that the previous analysis of the sentence was invalid (Frazier & Rayner, 1982; Rayner & Frazier, 1987). (We mention these predictability and sentential effects now to make our case for cognitive control, but will defer a discussion of them to later chapters.)

Control of fixation duration

We have seen that the decision of where to move is controlled both by low-level visual information, such as the position of spaces, and by higher-level variables such as the meaning of the text. The next few chapters will discuss in detail a variety of factors that control when we move our eyes.

Words that are infrequently used in the language require longer fixations than frequently used words. This finding was first reported in the 1980s in experiments in which word length was controlled (Inhoff & Rayner, 1986; Rayner & Duffy, 1986). Word length needed to be controlled since there is a natural confounding of word length and word frequency; infrequently used words tend to be longer than frequently used words (Kliegl, Olson, & Davidson, 1982). The finding of a word frequency effect is extremely robust (with too many studies to cite here; for review see Rayner, 1998, 2009). Second, fixation durations tend to be shorter on words that are predictable from the prior sentential context than on less predictable words (Balota et al., 1985; Drieghe et al., 2005; Ehrlich & Rayner, 1981; Rayner & Well, 1996; Zola, 1984). Third, lexically ambiguous words (words with two or more meanings like *bank*) will sometimes result in longer fixation times than words with a single meaning (Duffy, Morris, & Rayner, 1988; Rayner, Cook, Juhasz, & Frazier, 2006; Rayner & Duffy, 1986; Rayner, Pacht, & Duffy, 1994). Fourth, fixation times on a word are also influenced by a host of other variables including age of acquisition (Juhasz & Rayner, 2003, 2006) and familiarity (Williams & Morris, 2004) even when word frequency is controlled. Fifth, gaze durations are influenced by a variety of factors involving inference and semantic interpretation, including such things as the difficulty of identifying the antecedent of an anaphor (like a pronoun, or a noun phrase that refers back to a previously mentioned entity) (Duffy & Rayner, 1990; Ehrlich & Rayner, 1983; Schustack, Ehrlich, & Rayner, 1987). Sixth, in sentences containing syntactic ambiguities, fixation duration can increase when readers reach a disambiguating word in the sentence (Frazier & Rayner, 1982). Finally, gaze durations are longer at the ends of both clauses and sentences than within the clauses and sentences (Hirotani, Frazier, & Rayner, 2006; Just & Carpenter, 1980; Rayner, Kambe, & Duffy, 2000; Rayner, Sereno, Morris, Schmauder, & Clifton, 1989).

This list hardly includes all the factors that influence fixation durations (for more information see Rayner, 1998, 2009, and the next few chapters of this book). However, in the remainder of this section we will focus on how the identification of words and of lower-level information, such as the location of word boundaries, expressed in the eye-movement record. While other factors are important, factors that influence word recognition in isolation (such as length and frequency) have the largest, most consistent, and most easily manipulated effects on gaze duration (e.g., Blanchard, 1985; Just & Carpenter, 1980; Kliegl et al., 1982). Thus we can get a reasonably clear picture of eye guidance even if we ignore higher-level factors. We begin by considering the question of how directly eye movements are controlled by the properties of the word currently being fixated.

Evidence for direct control

At first blush it might appear that the fact that fixations on a frequent word (*church*) are shorter than on a less-frequent word (*mosque*) would be evidence for direct control. However, it is possible that the shorter average fixation time on *church* is due to those instances when it was fully identified in the parafovea on the prior fixation. In fact, a moment's reflection will lead you to realize that, in reading normal text, one can never be certain on what fixation a given piece of visual information was extracted, so that evidence of direct control can never be gotten from a completely natural reading situation. Thus we have to turn to techniques in which the text is displayed contingent on eye movements.

Direct control of saccades

Rayner and Pollatsek (1981) provided the first airtight evidence for direct control of saccades. They used a variant of the moving-window technique in which the window size varied randomly from fixation to fixation. They found that the length of a saccade following a fixation increased markedly as the size of the window of normal text on that fixation increased from 9 to 17 to 33 characters. Since the variation in window size was totally unpredictable, the variation in saccade length must have been influenced by the text actually seen on that fixation. Rayner and Pollatsek (1981) also examined whether the length of the saccade following fixation n was influenced by the size of the window on fixation n−1. In fact, saccades following fixation n were longer the bigger the window on fixation n−1 was, indicating that there is delayed control of saccade length as well as direct control.

Direct control of fixation duration

In order to test for direct control of fixation duration in reading, Rayner and Pollatsek (1981) presented a visual mask at the end of each saccade that effectively delayed the onset of the text. The rationale of the experiment was that if fixation duration is dependent on information encoded on the current fixation, then delaying the onset of the text should increase fixation duration by an amount related to the text delay. To ensure that the fixation duration depended on the text delay on the current fixation, they varied the delay interval randomly from fixation to fixation. There was clear support for direct control: the fixation duration increased as the delay of text increased from fixation to fixation. (However, the delay on fixation n−1 had no effect on the duration of fixation n.)

A stronger test of direct control is whether the fixation duration increases by an amount equal to the text delay. If we assume that the signal to move the eye is the identification of the fixated word, then one would expect that delaying the text by 200 ms should delay the fixation duration by 200 ms as well. The data of Rayner and Pollatsek's study are not consistent on this point. In one experiment in which the delay was constant from fixation to fixation, the fixation duration increased by the delay interval (for relatively small delay intervals). However, in the random delay experiment cited above, the fixation duration increased by a smaller amount than the delay interval. In a later experiment (Morrison, 1984), both fixed and random delay conditions resulted in smaller increases in the fixation delay than the text delay. Thus it appears that the eyes do not always wait for the currently fixated word to be fully processed in order to move on.

A more striking confirmation of indirect control was the finding that when there were long delays (200 ms or more), readers sometimes moved their eyes even before the text appeared. If you think carefully about it, these anticipatory saccades are counterproductive. That is, if the reader had fixated for 190 ms (in the 200 ms fixed delay condition) and then an eye movement occurred, text would not be presented for another 200 ms. Such eye movements thus appeared to be the result of some automatic process independent of reading. When these anticipatory saccades were removed from the data for the long fixation durations, the average increase in fixation duration was approximately equal to the text delay. This analysis suggested to Rayner and Pollatsek that fixation durations may be produced by a mixture of direct control and global control: on some fixations the signal to move the eye is some foveal processing event (such as the identification of the fixated word), while on others the fixation ends due to an anticipatory saccade (i.e., one that is programmed independently of encoding operations during reading). For shorter delay intervals anticipatory saccades would be hard to identify, and thus the imperfect relation between text delay and fixation duration could be because those fixations are also a mixture of direct control and anticipatory saccades. A careful analysis of anticipatory saccades (Morrison, 1984) indicated, however, that they were not unrelated to the ongoing text and that they were best thought of as being programmed on the previous fixation. However, Rayner and Pollatsek's basic idea that fixation durations are a mixture of direct control and more indirect control may be correct.

Another interesting finding emerged from the Rayner and Pollatsek experiments. The manipulation of window size had very little effect on fixation duration and the manipulation of text delay had no effect on saccade length when anticipatory saccades were removed. This suggested, first of all, that the two decisions (when to move and where to move) were made independently. It also suggested what the main contributors to those decisions were. When the smallest window size (nine letter spaces or four spaces to the right of the fixated letter) was employed in the Rayner and Pollatsek experiments, fixation durations increased somewhat. However, there was no difference in fixation times when the larger two windows (17 and 33 letter spaces) were employed. In the latter two conditions, but not the smallest, the fixated word was visible most of the time. Thus it appears that, if the fixated word is visible, there are relatively small effects of window size on fixation time (the bulk of the moving-window studies are consistent with this). Since text delay markedly affected fixation duration, it does seem as though fixation duration is mainly controlled by some event connected with encoding of the fixated word and is little affected by parafoveal information. On the other hand, since the size of the window had a clear effect on saccade length, it appears that parafoveal information has a major effect on the decision of where to move the eyes.

What information is involved in direct control?

Let us briefly summarize what we have established. First, we argued that the movement of the eyes is sensitive to the text being read, both to low-level information such as the length of words (and presence of spaces between words) and to higher-order variables such as the frequency of a word in the language or the predictability of a word from sentence context. Thus the eyes are under cognitive control. Second, in the last section we demonstrated that the movement of the eyes is under some direct control, since very dramatic changes, such as delaying the onset of the text after the beginning of a fixation and restricting the size of the window (with a homogenous field of Xs outside the window), affected the fixation duration and saccade size, respectively. However, the latter demonstration is quite crude, since it shows that initially presenting visual "garbage" in the fovea (a homogenous field) will delay fixation and presenting visual garbage in the parafovea will shorten saccades. We need more subtle experiments to tell us what information is actually driving the eye during reading.

Saccade length

First, let us consider saccade length. Pollatsek and Rayner (1982) attempted to be more diagnostic about the role of word boundaries. In their study the only information that was manipulated from fixation to fixation was the spaces between words (i.e., the letters in words were intact). They found that when the space between word n+1 and word n+2 was filled in, saccade length was smaller. Moreover, they found that if the space was filled in 50 ms after the fixation began, there was no effect on saccade length or any other measure of reading. That is, filling in this space was effective only during the first 50 ms. Their conclusion was that the location of the space to the right of word n+1 was used to help compute where word n+1 was, and hence where to direct the next eye movement. An alternative possibility is that the presence of the space filler may have interfered with the identification of words n+1 and n+2. Pollatsek and Rayner attempted to mini-mize this possibility by employing a noise character (which was quite visually dissimilar to letters) as a space filler in some conditions. Hence the space filler should have rarely been encoded as a letter and hence should itself rarely abet incorrect word identification. However, the space filler may have made letters near it harder to identify by lateral inhibitory mechanisms (see Chapter 1), so that we cannot really be sure that the effect is on word boundaries.

A more direct test by Morris et al. (1990) was to release the blank spaces between words in a homogenous field at varying time delays (see Figure 4.9). Since there were no letters to identify in the parafovea, any effect of introducing the space would have to be in providing word boundary information. They found that the introduction of spaces produced longer saccades, and further-more that their introduction had little effect if it occurred after 50 ms.

We know that the saccade is guided by more than word boundary information, since word n+1 is skipped more often when it is frequent in the language or predictable. However, such an effect need not be direct. The first experiment documenting the direct control of letter information was by McConkie, Underwood, Zola, and Wolverton (1985). Their design was similar to that of Rayner and Pollatsek in that they randomly varied window size from fixation to fixation. However, there were two differences. First, on most fixations there was no window (the whole line of text was presented), but on those fixations on which a window was employed, the window size and location (i.e., whether the left or right boundary was farther from fixation) were varied. Second, they preserved all spaces, with all letters outside the text being replaced by random letters. They found that fixations on which there was a window produced shorter saccades, indicating that the

Full Parafoveal Mask (Control)
They help migratingxxxxxxxxxxxxxxxxxxxxxxxx.   (beginning of fixation)
                    *
They help migratingxxxxxxxxxxxxxxxxxxxxxxxx.   (after X ms)
                    *
They help migrating toadsxxxxxxxxxxxxxxxxxx.   (beginning of next fixation)
                         *

Releasing Both Spaces
They help migratingxxxxxxxxxxxxxxxxxxxxxxxx.   (beginning of fixation)
                  *
They help migrating xxxxx xxxxxxxxxxxxxxxx.   (after X ms)
                  *
They help migrating toadsxxxxxxxxxxxxxxxxxx.   (beginning of next fixation)
                        *

Releasing First Space
They help migratingxxxxxxxxxxxxxxxxxxxxxxxx.   (beginning of fixation)
                  *
They help migrating xxxxxxxxxxxxxxxxxxxxxx.   (after X ms)
                  *
They help migrating toadsxxxxxxxxxxxxxxxxxx.   (beginning of next fixation)
                        *

FIGURE 4.9 Some conditions in the Morris et al. (1990) experiment. If the space information is not released after about 50 ms, it has virtually no effect. (Asterisk indicates fixation point.)

particular letters presented on a fixation influenced the size of the saccade. Since the boundary of the window was only four letters to the right of the fixated letter, it is possible that letter information in the parafovea as well as the fovea was influencing the size of a saccade.

Thus it appears that saccade size is under direct control of various types of information: word boundary information extracted from the parafovea early in the fixation and by letter information. It may be that letter information in the parafovea influences saccade size chiefly by determining whether or not the parafoveal word is fully identified and skipped.

Fixation durations

Rayner and Pollatsek's (1981) data, discussed previously, suggested that fixation duration is controlled by identification of the fixated word. However, the increase in fixation duration caused by delaying the text could be caused by waiting for anything text-like to appear rather than waiting for anything as complex as the identification of the word.

As we showed in Chapter 3, the frequency of a word in the language strongly influences word identification time. Thus, if word frequency also influences fixation time in reading, then it is assumed that the signal to move the eye (at least some of the time) is the encoding of the fixated word. To ensure that the fixated word is in fact encoded only when it is fixated, however, the reader has to be denied a preview of it. Inhoff and Rayner (1986) varied the frequency of selected target words (equating the number of letters), and in one condition participants had no parafoveal preview. The results were complex. When there was no preview, word frequency had no effect on the duration of the first fixation on the target word but did have an effect on the gaze duration. That is, the speed of encoding a word (without a parafoveal preview) did not appear to influence the decision of when to move the eye after the first fixation. However, since gaze duration reflects the probability that a word is fixated twice, the speed of encoding a word in this condition appeared to affect the decision of where to make the next fixation. The story was different when readers did have a normal preview. In that case, both first fixation and gaze duration were affected by the frequency of the fixated word.

The most parsimonious explanation of these data is that encoding of a word, if fast enough, can influence the decision of when the eye moves. Thus, when there is a parafoveal preview to speed word identification, the frequency of the word can affect the first fixation duration. In contrast, if encoding is a little slower, it still may influence where the eye goes (specifically, whether the word is refixated or not). Thus, without a parafoveal preview to speed word identification, the frequency of the word can still affect the number of fixations on a word. These data suggest that part of the skill of reading is using parafoveal information to encode words rapidly enough so that the encoding of these words can efficiently program the next eye movement.

Perhaps the strongest evidence for direct control of eye movements in reading comes from disappearing text experiments (Ishida & Ikeda, 1989; Liversedge, Rayner, White, Vergilino-Perez, Findlay, & Kentridge, 2004; Rayner et al., 1981; Rayner, Liversedge, & White, 2006; Rayner, Liversedge, White, & Vergilino-Perez, 2003; Rayner, Yang, Castelhano, & Liversedge, 2011) in which the text is masked or simply disappears at a certain time in each fixation. We discuss these experiments more in Chapter 5, but describe one striking result here. Reading proceeds quite normally if the reader gets to see the text for 50–60 ms before it disappears (or before the mask comes on; it doesn't make much difference to the results if the text is masked or disappears). This does not mean that words can be identified in 50–60 ms, but it does mean that readers are able to encode all of the visual information they need from the text in this time frame. What is more interesting, and very strong support for the notion of direct control, is that how long the eyes remain in place is very much influenced by the frequency of the fixated word: if the word is a low-frequency word, the eyes remain in place longer than if it is a high-frequency word. So, even though the word is no longer there, how long the eyes remain on that location is determined by the frequency of the disappearing word. This is very striking evidence in support of direct control and the idea that lexical processing drives the eyes through the text.

Finally, the contrast between eye movements during normal reading versus mindless reading (Reichle, Reineberg, & Schooler, 2010) and visual search through text (Rayner & Fischer, 1996; Rayner & Raney, 1996) provides very compelling evidence that decisions about when to move the eyes are under direct (cognitive) control in reading, but not during mindless reading or visual search (see Chapter 13). Specifically, when participants search through a passage of text for a target word, the word frequency effect disappears. Likewise, when participants lapse into a mindless reading state (where they keep moving their eyes across the text but report not processing the meaning), the word frequency effect disappears. Both demonstrations are highly consistent with the view that in reading there is a tight link between the eyes and lexical/cognitive processing.

Summary

In this chapter we have discussed some basic features of eye movements during reading. Primary among them was the fact that readers fixate a majority of words in text. The bulk of the chapter was spent in determining exactly what could be processed on a fixation. The amount of information that can be processed on a fixation was shown to be the fixated word plus some additional information to the right of it. We suggested a simple view that might explain this fact, namely that on some fixations one word was processed, on some fixations two words, and possibly on some fixations three words are processed. However, it appears that the story is more complicated than this, since parts of words appear to be extracted which aid identification of those words on later fixations. Thus the task of identifying what is processed on a fixation in reading is not simple. However, the fact that the information extracted from a fixation is limited means that there is an excellent chance that the pattern of eye movements will be able to tell us quite a bit about the cognitive activities underlying reading. Indeed, in the last part of the chapter we discussed what is known about how the eyes are controlled in reading and we demonstrated that the decision about where to move the eyes next and when to move the eyes are both strongly influenced via cognitive processing.

Note

1 In all of the gaze-contingent studies (i.e., moving window, moving mask, and boundary paradigms) fixed width fonts are used so that letters don't "jump" around when a display change is made.

5

WORD PERCEPTION II

Word identification in text

In Chapter 3 we introduced methods for studying isolated words and some basic issues in how printed words are encoded. From the research we discussed, several conclusions emerged: (1) encoding of shorter words occurs through a process in which the letters are processed in parallel; (2) conversion to sound is definitely involved in accessing the meaning of a word for skilled readers, although there is some controversy about how important or universal that involvement is; (3) for longer words (especially those with more than one morpheme) this parallel processing is likely to break down and such words are likely to be processed in more than one chunk; (4) word encoding is relatively automatic. (We will have more to say about the last issue later in this chapter when we discuss whether more than one word is processed at a time.) We also asserted in Chapter 3 that the conclusions drawn from those studies were largely true when words were in sentence context. Thus it would seem like a good place to start this chapter by documenting that most, if not all, of these conclusions have been borne out with eye movement data before plunging into the newer questions that have become the focus of much of the word-processing literature in the last 20 years.

In this chapter we will first revisit some basic questions that we have touched on in prior chapters regarding eye movements. Then we will discuss whether letters in a word are processed in parallel or in series and whether sound coding is crucially involved in accessing the meaning of a word. These discussions will be followed by reviews of: (a) how meaning is extracted from the text (focusing on the processing of lexically ambiguous words), (b) serial versus parallel processing of multiple words during reading, and (c) morphological processing especially as related to long words. We end the chapter by discussing how contextual information is used in reading to facilitate word identification.

Basic questions revisited

Some of the relevant data have already been presented in Chapter 4, but before we go over these and other eye movement data, we first need to clarify how eye movement data can answer questions about how words are recognized. Indeed, one reason why it took considerable time for researchers to consider eye movement data as relevant for answering questions about word identification was that it was thought to be implausible that anything like fixation time on a word could reflect how long it took to process a word.

The argument for being skeptical that eye movement measures are useful indices of ongoing cognitive processes in reading goes like this. First, given that eye movements to simple stimuli (like a sudden onset of a light) take something like 150–175 ms to execute (e.g., Becker & Jurgens, 1979; Rayner, Slowiaczek, Clifton, & Bertera, 1983), and the data indicate that it takes about 60–75 ms for this kind of simple stimulus to be registered in the visual processing areas in the brain, it follows that the time to decide to make and execute an eye movement is at least something like 75–90 ms. Second, as we argued in Chapter 3, it takes about 175–200 ms to identify a word. Thus, given that a typical fixation duration in reading is between 200 and 300 ms, it would appear to be unlikely that identifying a word could be rapid enough to influence most eye movements in reading.

The last part of Chapter 4 indicated, however, that this argument cannot be right because variables such as the frequency of a word can influence fixation time on that word. It also indicated that one of the flaws in the argument is the assumption that the processing of a word begins only when it is first fixated. That is, the data from window and boundary experiments indicate that the encoding of many (if not most) words begins when they are immediately to the right of the word being fixated. There are arguments that we will present later indicating that it is indeed plausible that eye movement measures—notably fixation time measures on a word (such as gaze duration) and the probability that a word is skipped—can reflect ongoing cognitive processing. However, for now we will just reassert that this is almost a necessary consequence of the data presented in Chapter 4. More specifically, we will present a model in Chapter 6 in which words are processed sequentially (i.e., word by word) that explains how such immediate effects on eye behavior can occur in reading. In this model the signal to move the eyes to the next word is reaching a level of encoding of the fixated word. The time to reach this encoding level is sensitive to various aspects of word encoding such as the frequency of the word, its predictability from the prior text, and whether the word has more than one meaning.

The measure that appears to be most appropriate as an index of something like initial encoding time for a word is gaze duration. As indicated in Chapter 4, gaze duration is the sum of the fixation durations on a word between when it is first fixated and when the eyes move to another word. (More precisely, this measure only counts first-pass fixations; that is, if a word is initially skipped on a trial, the data from that trial are not used in estimating the gaze duration in that condition.) Although we will focus on gaze duration in this chapter, we should make clear that we are not claiming that any single measure that one can extract from the eye movement data can be viewed as "the time to access the lexicon" or the "time to access the meaning of a word." This is because, as indicated in Chapter 4, even though there is quite a bit of evidence for direct control in programming eye movements, there is substantial evidence that not all effects of processing a word are accounted for by fixation times on that word. For example, there is substantial evidence that the frequency of a word also affects fixation time on the next word. Such delayed effects are often called "spillover effects" (Rayner & Duffy, 1986). This indicates that the difficulty of encoding a word has effects that are not reflected in gaze duration on that word. However, as we will argue, these spillover effects are fairly minor and in many cases it isn't unreasonable to think of gaze duration as a pretty good approximation of initial word encoding time. Another measure that we will mention fairly frequently is first fixation duration. This plausibly is even an earlier measure of cognitive activity as it reflects the decision of when to move the eyes after first fixating a word. In contrast, gaze duration depends on (a) the duration of the first fixation, (b) the probability that the word is refixated, and (c) the duration of the second fixation. (For the shorter monomorphemic words that we will discuss in this first section, words are rarely fixated more than twice.)

Two of the major issues discussed in Chapter 3 were whether sound coding is crucially involved in accessing the meaning of a word and whether letters in a word are processed in parallel or in series. The second issue is complex, because it is intertwined with the issues of processing words on more than one fixation and whether more than one word is processed at a time. Hence we will deal with the sound coding issue first.

How early is phonological information from words extracted in reading text?

In Chapter 3 we concluded from the research on isolated words that there was general agreement that sound codes were involved in the access of word meaning, but that there was some disagreement as to how important this sound coding is. On the one hand, the finding that *meet* was wrongly classified as a food on a significant fraction of the trials indicated an important role of sound coding in accessing meaning, but on the other hand, the fact that the regularity effect (i.e., the difference in lexical decision time between regularly and irregularly spelled words) was small indicated that sound coding might have a marginal effect, largely limited to low-frequency words. The eye movement data, however, indicate a very central role for phonological coding when people read text. Among other things, these data indicate that phonological coding starts to occur even before a word is fixated.

Convincing data come from the use of the boundary technique, which was discussed in Chapter 4. To remind you, in this technique the relation of the preview to the target word is manipulated (see Figure 5.1). Chapter 4 introduced one set of experiments (Pollatsek, Lesch, Morris, & Rayner, 1992), in which homophones of target words were used as previews and compared to orthographic control previews (e.g., *beech–beach* vs. *bench–beach*). Fixation times (both first fixation durations and gaze durations) on the target words were shorter when the preview was a homophone, which indicates that phonological codes are being extracted from words even before they are fixated (see also Henderson, Dixon, Petersen, Twilley, & Ferreira, 1995). Another display change technique, fast priming (Sereno & Rayner, 1992), indicates that phonological coding also occurs early within a fixation (Lee, Binder, Kim, Pollatsek, & Rayner, 1999; Lee, Rayner, & Pollatsek, 1999; Rayner, Sereno, Lesch, & Pollatsek, 1995). In this paradigm (see Figure 5.2), the preview is a string of letters unrelated to the target word. When the reader's saccade crosses the boundary this preview is replaced by a prime, which is displayed for something like 35 ms, and is in turn replaced by the target word. Thus the sequence of events in the fast priming technique is similar to that in the masked priming paradigm of Forster and Davis (1984) discussed in Chapter 3—except that the eyes are moving freely. (That is, in both paradigms, the sequence of events in the target word location is a meaningless initial stimulus followed by a prime and then a target.) As with the preview

Fixation n

<pre>
            * |
The generous man gave every sent to charity.
</pre>

Fixation n+1

<pre>
                     | *
The generous man gave every cent to charity.
</pre>

FIGURE 5.1 Illustration of the boundary technique. The vertical line above the space between *every* and *sent* represents the boundary (which is invisible to the participant). On all fixations before crossing the boundary, the text in the example would be as on the first line. During the saccade that crosses the boundary, the text in the target word changes from the preview word to the target (*sent* and *cent*, respectively, in the illustration). Other previews used were *cent* (identical), *rent* (orthographic control for the homophone), and *rack* (a visually dissimilar control)

Fixation n

```
       *        |
The generous man gave every dlri to charity.
```

First 50 ms on Fixation n+1

```
                |  *
The generous man gave every sent to charity.
```

After the first 50 ms on Fixation n+1

```
                |  *
The generous man gave every cent to charity.
```

FIGURE 5.2   Illustration of the fast priming technique. The vertical line above the space between *every* and *cent* represents the boundary (which is invisible to the participant). On all fixations before crossing the boundary, the text in the example would be as on the first line. During the saccade that crosses the boundary, the text in the target word changes from the nonsense string of random letters to the prime (*dlri* and *sent*, respectively, in the illustration). Then, on the initial fixation on the target word location, the prime *sent* changes to the target *cent* after the prime duration interval. Other primes used were *cent* (identical), *rent* (orthographic control for the homophone), and *rack* (a visually dissimilar control)

manipulation above, when a homophonic fast prime (*sent*) appears before the target word *cent*, fixation durations on the word are shorter than when the fast prime is an orthographic control word (*rent*).

These experiments thus indicate that phonological coding is occurring quite early in the processing of a word. We should also point out that, in both paradigms, the reader is unaware of the content of the preview or prime. Indeed, as indicated in Chapter 4, readers are rarely, if ever, aware of display changes across saccades. In the fast priming technique the reader is aware that something has happened when the display change is made, but is rarely aware of what the prime was.

An obvious question is whether this early extraction of phonological information is restricted to alphabetic languages. This was first tested by Pollatsek, Tan, and Rayner (2000), who employed the naming version of the boundary paradigm (discussed in Chapter 4). In this experiment there was a single Chinese character in the parafovea, and when the participant made a saccade to fixate the character, display changes were made in some conditions. (The participant's task was to name the character.) As with the experiments above, the key comparison was between when the preview was a homophone of the target character and when the preview was a non-homophone that was as visually similar to the target as the homophone was. As with the experiments above, there was a clear advantage when the preview was a homophone. Pollatsek et al. (1992) observed a similar advantage in English for homophones over visual controls in this naming version of the boundary paradigm.

Later experiments tested whether this homophonic effect in Chinese generalized to reading sentences. The findings were generally consistent with the naming experiment, indicating that phonological codes are extracted early in Chinese, but the details were somewhat variable. For example, Liu, Inhoff, Ye, and Wu (2002) found that the beneficial effects from a homophonic character only appeared when the characters were refixated. However, there were reliable effects on the target word when the preview character and its *radical* (a sub-character unit) were both homo-phonic to the target character (Tsai, Lee, Tzeng, Hung, & Yen, 2004). We should mention that one difficulty is evaluating whether effects are early or late in Chinese. That is, Chinese is written without spaces between words; as a result, it is hard to know exactly how saccades are targeted in Chinese (for discussion see Li, Liu, & Rayner, 2011; Yan, Kliegl, Richter, Nuthmann, & Shu, 2010). Thus the variability in finding clear preview effects on fixation time on the target word may just be because there is a greater disconnect in Chinese than in alphabetic languages between where the eyes are fixating and the current focus of spatial attention.

In Chapter 3 we introduced the distinction between addressed and assembled phonology. Although the above experiments all indicate that phonological coding is occurring early in reading text, none specifically addresses the question of whether any of this early coding is assembled (i.e., constructed from the sequence of letters rather than just by a look-up process from the lexicon). One paradigm for examining the role of assembled phonology is the (phonological) regularity effect (see Chapter 3). Inhoff and Topolski (1994) and Sereno and Rayner (2000) found that phonologically irregular words such as *pint* were fixated longer than phonologically regular words such as *dark*. This phonological regularity effect occurred early in the eye movement record, as it was observed on first fixation duration in both studies. In Sereno and Rayner (2000) there was not only a regularity effect on gaze duration, but also an interaction between regularity and word frequency, with a larger effect of regularity for low-frequency words. This is the same pattern as discussed in Chapter 3 with the lexical decision task (e.g., Seidenberg, Waters, Barnes, & Tanenhaus, 1984) and was a key motivation for a model of phonological coding that posited a race between addressed and assembled routes to phonology. Also, the finding indicating that regularity effects are small for higher-frequency words is consistent with the type of interactive dual-route model that we were arguing for in Chapter 3.

Identifying effective primes is another way to study assembled phonology. The masked priming experiment (Pollatsek, Perea, & Carreiras, 2005) discussed in Chapter 3 (where *conal* primed *CANAL* better than *cinal* did) indicates that such assembled phonological processing occurs early in processing isolated words. This particular manipulation has not yet been tried with sentences. However, a very similar manipulation in a boundary study by Ashby, Treiman, Kessler, and Rayner (2006) indicated that assembled phonology is involved in extracting information from previews. Target words were preceded by nonword previews whose final consonant made the preview's vowel either congruent or incongruent with the vowel phoneme in the target. For example, the target word *rack* was preceded either by the congruent nonword preview *raff* or the incongruent nonword preview *rall*. (Consistent with the regularity effect literature discussed in Chapter 3, one would expect the assembled phonological representation of *rall* to rhyme with *call*.) Ashby et al. found that fixation times on the target word were shorter with the congruent nonword preview, implicating some sort of assembled phonology in early phonological coding.

So far we have discussed phonological effects in reading solely at the phonemic level (e.g., manipulating the degree of phonemic overlap between preview and target). However, there are other levels of phonology: at a higher level, the syllable, and at a sub-phonemic level, distinctive features. One set of experiments examined the role of syllables by manipulating the initial syllable of the preview of a target word so that it matched or did not match the initial syllable of the target word (Ashby & Rayner, 2004). The target words had either a two- or three-segment initial syllable (e.g., *magic* or *magnet*) and the preview contained either the same first syllable of the target (e.g., *maxxx* as a preview for *magic, magxx* as a preview for *magnet*) or one letter more or fewer than the target's initial syllable (e.g., *magxx* as a preview for *magic, maxxxx* as a preview for *magnet*). The finding was the fixation time on the target word was shorter when the previews and target had matching initial syllables. This syllable facilitation effect was later replicated using the single-word version of the parafoveal boundary paradigm where the dependent variable was lexical decision time (Ashby & Martin, 2008) and in a masked-priming ERP experiment (Ashby, 2010). In the latter experiment the amplitude of an ERP component that appeared as early as 100 ms after the onset of the target word was smaller when the prime had a syllable structure that matched the syllable structure of the target than when there was a mismatch in syllable structure between prime and target. This indicates that a very early stage in processing the word was affected by syllable structure.

Ashby and Clifton (2005) examined whether the phonological code being extracted was merely a string of phonemes or syllables by manipulating the stress pattern of the word. They compared gaze durations on four-syllable target words that had either one or two stressed syllables (e.g., *intensity* vs. *radiation*). The rationale for this comparison is that there is evidence from the response programming literature (Sternberg, Monsell, Knoll, & Wright, 1978) that it takes longer to plan to say a word with two stressed syllables than with one. Ashby and Clifton found that gaze durations were longer on words with two stressed syllables, although there was no effect on first fixation duration. The gaze duration finding suggests that a phonological code that includes stress is computed during silent reading, and when a word includes an additional stressed syllable, the eye is more likely to refixate on it. The effect of number of stressed syllables did not simply reflect the duration of a pronounced word. Words with two syllables take longer to pronounce than one-syllable words, but Ashby and Clifton found that they were not fixated any longer.

Another study (Ashby, Sanders, & Kingston, 2009) indicated that a phonological feature below the level of the phoneme, voicing, also plays a role in the early stages of word encoding. As indicated in Chapter 2, the distinctive feature of voicing distinguishes several pairs of consonants: z, d, b, and, g, for example, are voiced but otherwise identical in sound to s, t, p, and k, respectively. The logic was similar to that of Ashby's (2010) ERP masked-priming study mentioned briefly above; however, in this study the comparison was between two primes that each had a phoneme different from the target word, but differed on whether they shared a distinctive feature with the target. For example, the target word *FAD* could be preceded either by *faz* or *fak*, but as *z* shares the voicing feature with *D*, one would expect it to be a better prime. As in Ashby (2010), a very early component of the ERP record (here, as early as 80 ms after target onset) was reduced in amplitude, indicating that the match in distinctive feature was "noticed" by the word-processing system this early even though subjects were not aware of the identity of the prime.

Meaning extraction

The above experiments indicate that phonological information is extracted early in the word identification process: early enough for it to affect the decision to move on to the next word (a decision that is plausibly made not much over 150 ms after a word is fixated). What we would like to document as well is that meaning extraction also occurs quite early and that phonological coding is involved in deciding on the meaning of a word. You may wonder why we are raising this issue here, as we have already documented in Chapter 4 that fixation time on a word is affected by variables such as the frequency of the word and whether it is predictable from the prior text. The reason we are doing so is that such effects don't necessarily indicate that the meaning of the word is extracted. That is, they may just imply that either the orthographic or phonological form of the word (or both) has been recognized. In other words, the reader may feel that it is safe to move the eyes forward when a judgment something like "I've seen that word before" has been made but before the meaning has been accessed.

Evidence that meaning is accessed during a fixation comes from a paradigm that examines the effects of prior context on the processing of homophones such as *port* that have two distinct and unrelated meanings (i.e., a type of wine or a harbor) (Duffy, Morris, & Rayner, 1988, see also Rayner & Duffy, 1986; Rayner & Frazier, 1989). (We will focus, for the moment, on cases where the two words are homophonic as well as being homographic.) First, consider the case of biased ambiguous words (e.g., *port*) where one meaning is much more frequent than the other. The gaze durations on these target words were compared to those on unambiguous control words (e.g., *wine*) matched on frequency that were in the same target location. In sentence 5.1 the disambiguation of the target word occurred after the target word appeared, whereas in sentence 5.2 the disambiguation occurred prior to the target word.

Of course the port (wine) was a great success when she finally served it to her guests.　(5.1)

When she finally served it to her guests, the port (wine) was a great success.　(5.2)

If fixation times on *port* only reflected the time to access the orthographic and phonological forms of the word, then the ambiguous word should be processed as quickly as the unambiguous control word and prior context should have no effect. On the other hand, if fixation time on *port* also reflects the time to access the meaning of the word, then one might expect that fixation time on *port* would be longer when the prior context was only consistent with the lower-frequency (wine) meaning of *port* than when the prior context was neutral. That is, if fixation time on a word reflects the accessibility of the meaning of a word as well as its orthographic and phonological form, then forcing the reader to have to extract a lower-frequency meaning should make fixation times on the word longer.

This is indeed what happens; gaze durations are longer on biased ambiguous words like *port* than on the unambiguous control words when prior context forces the reader to the less-frequent meaning (e.g., 5.2). Indeed a significant effect is also seen on first fixation durations (see Sereno, O'Donnell, & Rayner, 2006). This effect has been labeled the "subordinate bias effect" and been replicated a number of times (see Binder & Rayner, 1998; Rayner, Pacht, & Duffy, 1994; Rayner, Cook, Juhasz, & Frazier, 2006). In contrast to when the context instantiated the subordinate meaning, when there was a neutral prior context, gaze durations on the ambiguous and unambiguous words were about the same. This makes sense because the frequency of the wrong meaning (the *harbor* meaning, in this example) is about the same as that of the unambiguous word. However, if people encoded the more frequent meaning of the ambiguous word when there was no prior biasing context, one would expect that readers would run into trouble (e. g., and make regressions) when they reached the subsequent biasing context and were forced to retrieve the lower frequency meaning. This is in fact what the data showed. (In Duffy et al.'s materials, the lower frequency meaning was always consistent with the sentences.)

Duffy et al. (1988) also examined balanced ambiguous words such as *straw*—they also have two meanings, but the meanings are approximately equal in frequency (see sentences 5.3 and 5.4). For these words, it seems reasonable that one would observe a different pattern than for the biased words. First, consider when there is no prior biasing context (5.3). Given that each meaning of the ambiguous word is less frequent than the unambiguous control, and also because there might be competition between the two meanings, one would expect initial processing of the ambiguous word to be slower than the control word. This is what happened: gaze durations were significantly longer on the ambiguous word than on the control.

He put the remaining straw (ashes) away in the box after spreading some all over his garden.　(5.3)

After spreading some all over his garden, he put the remaining straw (ashes)
away in the box. (5.4)

In contrast, when the prior context biased the reader to one of the meanings (5.4), one would
expect the competition between the two meanings to decrease, and thus that there would be little
difference in gaze duration between the ambiguous word and the control word. In fact there was
no difference in gaze duration between the two for sentences like 5.4. As with the biased ambiguous words, there was a cost associated with the ambiguous word later in the sentence when the
ambiguity was resolved. However, the cost was significantly less for the balanced ambiguous words.
This difference makes sense if one assumes that the reader encoded the correct meaning about half
the time when the prior context was neutral for the balanced ambiguous words but only a small
percentage of the time for the biased ambiguous words.

Let's recap what these experiments tell us about the extraction of word meaning and how prior
context affects it. First, they clearly indicate that the meaning of a word is extracted early enough
to affect the gaze duration on the word. Second, they indicate a fairly interactive relationship
between bottom-up processes of meaning extraction and prior context. This is most clearly shown
with the balanced ambiguous words. That is, if there were a first step of meaning extraction in
which the word encoding system delivered the two meanings for later processing, it is hard to see
how there could be any early effects of prior context. Instead, it appears that the prior context
actually modulates the initial process of selecting the correct meaning. It apparently boosted the
strength of the meaning intended by the prior context enough so that there was little competition
between the two meanings. In contrast, for the biased ambiguous words, the prior context appeared
to decrease the strength of the incorrect meaning so that initial access of the meaning took longer
than when the prior context was neutral. This argument is a short-hand form of the reordered
access model (Duffy et al., 1988).

The above studies indicate that meaning is encoded early. But where does phonological coding
come into the process when people are reading text? This has been investigated in a similar paradigm using a different kind of ambiguous word: heterophonic homographs. These are letter strings
which have two different meanings but also have two different pronunciations (such as *bows*). Folk
and Morris (1995) embedded these words in neutral sentence frames (i.e., where both meanings
are consistent with the prior context) and compared them to control words matched on frequency
and length, e.g., *Mary knew that her bows/joke needed practicing before the last performance.* They found
quite huge differences in fixation times between these homographs and the control words. These
ambiguity effects were much larger (about 40 ms for first fixation duration and 80 ms for gaze
duration) than those for homophones like *bank*. These effects indicate that the extra time taken to
resolve the meaning ambiguity of the word is being hindered by early activation of the two
different phonological representations for the word.

The same issue was addressed from a slightly different angle by Folk (1999) using heterographic
homophones (e.g., *soul/sole*). Fixation times on these homophones were compared to those of
control words matched on frequency and length. She found, analogously to Duffy et al. (1988), that
gaze durations on the homophone were significantly longer than on an unambiguous control word
when the initial sentence context supported the less-frequent version of the homophone. That is,
it appears that the initial sentence context boosts the phonological representation of the less-
frequent homophone so that it interferes with extraction of the meaning of the printed word—
even though the less-frequent meaning is spelled differently than the word that is actually in the
sentence!

To summarize, there are two important conclusions that can be drawn from these data. The first
is that the gaze duration (and even the first fixation duration) on a word reflects more than just a

recognition process (i.e., "I've encoded the form and sound of the word") but also reflects whether the meaning has been encoded and whether this meaning agrees with prior context. Second, prior context doesn't merely wait until an initial encoding of the word occurs to guide the reader to the appropriate meaning; instead, it appears to be guiding the actual initial selection of the meaning of the word. For heterographic homophones, even though the printed word is unambiguous, the other homophone (and its meaning) is activated and appears to interfere with retrieving the contextually appropriate meaning. For heterophonic homographs, it appears that both phonological representations are activated on at least some percentage of the trials and the reader needs to decide between these phonological representations; this is a decision that doesn't need to be made with homophonic homographs such as *bank*. It is really quite amazing that all this processing can be occurring in the short amount of time needed to decide whether to fixate the next word. However, a major part of why this can occur is that processing of most words starts before they are actually fixated.

Automaticity of word encoding revisited: Does automaticity imply that more than one word is encoded at a time in reading?

In Chapter 3 we investigated the issue of automaticity of word encoding by looking at three issues. The first was whether people could process the meaning of a word without being aware of it and the answer was "yes." The second was whether people would process the meaning of a word even when they were not trying to—or probably, trying not to—process it. The answer to the second question was also "yes." In contrast, the answer to the question of whether a word could be processed without using central processing resources was probably "no." Indeed, the results from the visual search experiments discussed in Chapter 3 suggested that words had to be processed one at a time. Thus, if one had to extrapolate from this research to answer the question of whether more than one word at a time is processed in reading, the pattern of data seems potentially contradictory. That is, the first two findings seem to suggest that word processing is automatic and that all words that are within the perceptual span can be processed for meaning, whereas the latter experiments suggest that one needs to attend to one word at a time. However, this contradiction may be more apparent than real. That is, the data are consistent with the hypothesis that (spatial) attention to a word is a necessary condition for encoding the meaning of a word but that people may not always have perfect control over where their attention is allocated or to what aspect of the stimulus in a given location should be processed.

At this point, however, we expect you are thinking that the data presented in Chapter 4 contradict this assertion. First, there is a large body of data indicating that when word n is fixated, there is considerable processing of word n+1 (the word to the right). Surely this must mean that more than one word is being processed at a time! It clearly does mean that more than one word is being processed on a fixation; however, it does not necessarily mean that more than one word is processed at a time. Consider the following alternative. When readers fixate a word, the first order of business is to encode that word. However, when encoding of the word is completed, they shift their spatial attention to the next word and begin processing it before the saccade to the next word is executed. There is abundant evidence from the cognitive psychology literature (Posner, 1980) indicating that spatial attention can be shifted independently of where the person is fixating. Although the typical paradigms demonstrating such effects might be considered unnatural, in that they require the participant to fixate one location and attend to another location, they do demonstrate that where the eyes are fixated and where attention is directed can be different. As a result, because a covert attention shift can be executed more quickly than a saccadic eye movement, it makes sense in normal viewing (not only in reading) that spatial attention shifts usually precede the movement of the eyes. Another reason why spatial attention and where the eye is fixated in normal vision may be decoupled is that the saccade may not land where the viewer intended (due to programming error); thus, it would make sense for the viewer to direct covert attention to the region where the saccade was intended to land rather than to where it actually landed.

Second, Chapter 4 indicated that words are not infrequently skipped. This also would seem to argue for simultaneous processing of more than one word. Although a certain percentage of skips are likely due to errors in saccadic programming (Drieghe, Rayner, & Pollatsek, 2008), words are also skipped more often for "deeper reasons": either because they are frequent in the language or predictable from prior context. If so, this argues that words are skipped at least some of the time because they were processed quickly while fixating the prior word. Again, however, we will argue that this doesn't necessarily mean that the two words are processed simultaneously. That is, when words are skipped, the fixated word and the next word can perhaps both be processed sequentially on the same fixation if the next word is processed quickly enough. (We will discuss how this can occur in more detail in Chapter 6.)

Is there evidence for parallel processing of words?

The assumption we will adopt, that readers lexically process words sequentially, one at a time, is the basis of our model of reading, the E-Z Reader model, which will be discussed in detail in Chapter 6. However, this assumption is not universally agreed to and there are other models of eye movements in reading that posit parallel processing of words: Glenmore (Reilly & Radach, 2006) and SWIFT (Engbert, Nuthmann, Richter, & Kliegl, 2005). These models both posit massive parallel processing and a different view of how eye movements are controlled. First, these models posit that all words within the perceptual span are processed in parallel. Second, they each posit a very complex mechanism for how eye movements are controlled in which the levels of excitation for the various words that are being processed in parallel compete with each other and there is a complex decision rule involving this competition that triggers an eye movement. In other words, in contrast to the E-Z Reader model, the signal to move the eyes in these parallel models is nothing like recognition of word n, and thus the gaze duration on word n is a function of the frequency of word n is almost incidental.

We will return to a discussion of these models in the next chapter. Here, though, we concentrate on the empirical evidence about whether more than a single word is processed at any moment in time. First, as indicated in Chapter 4, there is indeed a close relationship between variables that plausibly influence the time to process the fixated word (e.g., its frequency in the written language) and the fixation time on that word (notably the gaze duration). Although, as we mentioned earlier, there are some effects of variables such as frequency that are delayed until the next word is fixated, they are generally quite small. In addition, the disappearing text experiments introduced in Chapter 4 argue even more strongly for serial processing of words in reading text. They not only demonstrate a tight coupling between fixation time on a word and the time to process the word, but they indicate that processing of the word to the right of fixation (word n+1) does not begin until late in the fixation on word n.

In these experiments (Blythe, Liversedge, Joseph, White, & Rayner, 2009; Liversedge, Rayner, White, Vergilino-Perez, Findlay, & Kentridge, 2004; Rayner, Liversedge, White, & Vergilino-Perez, 2003), participants read sentences, and the key manipulation is that a word or two either disappears or is replaced by a pattern mask at 50–60 ms after the beginning of the first fixation on a word. (The data are essentially the same when the region of text simply disappears or is replaced by a pattern mask.) The two conditions of greatest interest are (a) when the fixated word (word n) disappears and (b) when word n+1 disappears (see Table 5.1). Perhaps the most amazing finding

TABLE 5.1 Gaze duration (GD) on high- and low-frequency critical words when word n disappears after 60 ms and when word n+1 disappears after 60 ms

Measure	Condition	Word n disappears after 60 ms	Word n+1 disappears after 60 ms
GD on high-frequency word (ms)	Normal	295	245
	Disappearing	288	301
	Difference	−7	56
GD on low-frequency word (ms)	Normal	325	276
	Disappearing	329	355
	Difference	4	79
Normal text condition: Word frequency effect		*30*	*31*
Disappearing text condition: Word frequency effect		*41*	*54*

Adapted from: Rayner, K., Liversedge, S.P., & White, S.J. (2006). Eye movements when reading disappearing text: The importance of the word to the right of fixation. *Vision Research, 46,* 310–323.

from these experiments is that when the fixated word disappears after being fixated for only 50 or 60 ms, there is virtually no effect on fixation time on the word. Not only was the average fixation time unaffected by the disappearing text, the effect of word frequency was unchanged in the disappearing text condition. This argues strongly that the fixation time on the word is largely influenced by the time to process the fixated word as this quite salient low-level change in the display appears to have no effect on fixation time.

Perhaps of greater importance in distinguishing between serial and parallel processing is the finding that when word n+1 disappeared after 50–60 ms, there was a significant cost (i.e., longer fixation times on word n+1). This pattern of results seems hard for a parallel model to explain. That is, if all the words whose letters are legible during a fixation are processed in parallel, then there isn't any reason to expect word n+1 to suffer any more from the masking than word n. In contrast, the data are easily explainable if one assumes serial processing of words. That is, if one assumes (a) that words are attended to one at a time and (b) only attended words are transferred into a short-term memory storage, then there will be virtually no cost when word n is masked because this is virtually always attended to at the beginning of a fixation. In contrast, if attention shifts to word n+1 only after word n has been processed, then it makes sense that this shift will generally be too late to utilize the information when word n+1 has disappeared 60 ms after word n is fixated and thus this preview information will be lost.

One aspect of word processing that is often left quite vague in claims that more than one word is being processed at a time is how much processing is occurring in parallel. Certainly, any model of reading has to posit that some low-level visual information about the words subsequent to the fixated word is being processed, otherwise the reader would have no idea where to fixate next. And, as documented in Chapter 4, readers do get preview benefit from word n+1. Thus we think the key issue here is the level of processing from the subsequent word or words that is assumed to be occurring in parallel with processing of the fixated word. We think that the preponderance of the data indicates that the processing of word n+1 that is going on is usually at early levels (e.g., identifying letters and sounds). Such a pattern of data is consistent with a serial view of word processing: the initial agenda on a fixation is to process the fixated word, and if there is time at the end of a fixation, begin processing the next word. Among other things, this view is consistent with the data discussed in Chapter 4 that indicates that there is no facilitation if the reader sees, as a preview, a word semantically related to the target word.

A claim that more than one word at a time is being processed in reading is based on the assumption that there are "parafoveal-on foveal" effects (Kennedy, 1999). That is, it is claimed that lexical properties of words not yet fixated affect fixation time on a word. We will discuss the implications of this claim somewhat more fully in the next chapter, but if it is true that if the semantic properties of words not yet fixated has reliable effects on fixation time on a word, it would be problematic to maintain a view that words are processed one at a time. However, these effects are generally not very reliable, and sometimes they go one way and other times the other way (see e.g., Hyönä & Bertram, 2004). Moreover, the parafoveal-on-foveal effects that are more reliable (see Rayner, 2009) are those when the next word looks strange in some way (e.g., an unusual sequence of letters in the next word increases fixation duration on the current word). Thus it is unclear that these effects reflect accessing the meaning of the next word. Moreover, such effects generally are most reliable when the fixation point on word n is close to word n+1. In such cases, it is not clear whether the reader intended to fixate word n+1 but fell short and landed on word n. (See Drieghe, 2011, for an excellent review of this topic.)

We will discuss this serial–parallel issue again in the next chapter when we present our model of reading, the E-Z Reader model, which assumes that only one word is lexically processed at a time. As indicated above, this model can also explain why readers skip high-frequency words (which may seem like a parafoveal-on-foveal effect that a serial model cannot explain). However, this requires us to set up a lot of machinery that is beyond the scope of the current discussion. The main point we wish to make is that we see no compelling evidence against a serial (word-by-word) view of reading, and that, if there is no such evidence, it is parsimonious to assume serial processing (Reichle, Liversedge, Pollatsek, & Rayner, 2009). We also would like to comment that the effects of prior context that we discussed above (on the processing of homophones) and many that will appear in subsequent chapters are hard for a parallel processing model to explain. That is, if only partial processing of words occurs—so that one isn't sure, when word n is fixated, that all prior words have been processed—then it is far from clear (logically) how the meaning of the prior text could influence the processing of word n to such a great extent (Slattery, Pollatsek, & Rayner, 2007). In some cases, one might claim that the prior context might have been established well before word n; however, in other cases, this is a difficult claim to make.

Neighborhood effects and transposed letter effects in reading text

Neighborhood effects

In Chapter 3 we raised the question of whether word neighbors affect processing time on a word. As indicated there, the two variables studied most have been the number of neighbors a word has (neighborhood size), and whether a word has a higher-frequency neighbor. The data that we discussed there, which used lexical decision latency, indicated that the two variables produced opposite effects. That is, in those experiments, having a lot of neighbors speeded lexical decision time whereas having a higher-frequency neighbor slowed lexical decision time. These results are consistent with an interactive activation model (e.g., McClelland & Rumelhart, 1981) and most other models of word encoding discussed in Chapter 3. First, the presence of a lot of neighbors may facilitate the identification of the component letters of a word because the neighbors would lend support for the identification of many of the letters. However, if we assume that when a printed word is seen, not only the word itself is activated but similar words are also activated, then a higher-frequency neighbor could be inhibitory because its detector competes with the word detector of the actual word presented. We will adhere to the classic definition of "neighbor" presented in Chapter 3: a word that is identical to another word except that one letter in the same location is changed (e.g., *cord, ward*, and *work* are all neighbors of *word*).

One problem with an interpretation of these results is that they may be special to the lexical decision task and do not reflect how the presence of word neighbors affects encoding of words in reading. This problem was addressed in a series of experiments by Perea and Pollatsek (1998) and Pollatsek, Perea, and Binder (1999). Perea and Pollatsek investigated the role of having a higher-frequency neighbor, and target words were compared that either had one (or more) higher-frequency neighbors to those that had no higher-frequency neighbors. In a lexical decision experiment, they replicated the finding stated above: slower lexical decision times for words having higher-frequency neighbors. When they employed the same pairs of words as alternative target words in a sentence frame, they also observed an inhibitory effect of having a higher-frequency neighbor. However, the effect in reading was relatively late. That is, there was no effect of having a higher-frequency neighbor on the gaze duration on the target word. Instead, the inhibitory effect occurred a bit later, largely in the form of more regressions back to the target word after fixating the next word or two. This result suggested that the inhibitory effect of having a higher-frequency neighbor was not in delaying identification of the target word, but instead that the target word was sometimes mis-encoded as the higher-frequency neighbor. Then, when subsequent context indicated the wrong word had been encoded, the word had to be refixated in order to repair the damage.

Pollatsek et al. (1999), in a similar study, investigated the role of neighborhood size. As in Perea and Pollatsek, when these pairs of words were employed in a lexical decision task, they replicated the usual finding in the literature—lexical decision times were shorter when a word had more neighbors. However, when the same pairs of words were employed as target words in a sentence, quite a different pattern of results was observed. That is, the effect of a word having more neighbors was similar to that observed in Perea and Pollatsek: there was no effect of the number of neighbors on the gaze duration on the target word, but an inhibitory later effect largely in the form of more regressions back to the target word after fixating the next word or two. Sears, Campbell, and Lupker (2006) reported a failure to replicate the Perea and Pollatsek finding of inhibition from higher-frequency neighbors in a reading experiment. However, there were several aspects of the Sears et al. design that were not optimal, such as having target words in locations where there was a lot of variability in eye movements (e.g., right after a return sweep from a prior line of text), and the Perea and Pollatsek result was replicated by Slattery (2009). In addition, Slattery manipulated whether the higher-frequency neighbor was consistent with prior context. He found that when the higher-frequency neighbor was consistent with prior context, it produced a delayed interference effect (just as Perea and Pollatsek had observed) but that the interference effect went away when the higher-frequency neighbor was anomalous given the prior context. This suggests that prior context can prevent the incorrect word neighbor from being falsely identified.

These results suggest that neighbors mainly serve to confuse readers in actual reading and that the hypothesis that word neighbors facilitate early stages of word processing by helping to identify component letters was wrong. However, a preview experiment (Williams, Perea, Pollatsek, & Rayner, 2006) does show a facilitative effect of word neighbors in reading. The key comparison was between a parafoveal preview that was a word neighbor with a preview that was a nonword neighbor of the target word (e.g., for the target word *sleet*, the preview was either *sweet* or *speet*). In Experiment 1 fixation times on the target word were actually less on the target word when there was a higher-frequency word neighbor preview than when there was a nonword neighbor. However, in Experiment 2, when the preview and target word were reversed so that the preview was a lower-frequency neighbor of the target, there was no greater benefit for the word neighbor preview over the nonword neighbor preview. This result suggests that neighbors (especially higher-frequency neighbors) do facilitate early stages of word encoding in parafoveal processing.

Let's take stock of these results. First, we think there is a relatively straightforward explanation for why there is a different pattern of results in the lexical decision data than in the reading experiments: lexical decision time may not be a reliable index in these experiments of how long it takes to recognize a word. In particular, a model proposed by Grainger and Jacobs (1996) posits that a major cause of the facilitative effect of neighborhood size results from the sum of the excitation from all the lexical entries activated rather than the level of activation of the word actually presented. Thus, if a word has more neighbors, there is more total activation from word detectors, and thus it is easier to respond "word" in the lexical decision task; however, this may be irrelevant to the ease with which the actual word is identified.

Second, the Perea and Pollatsek and Pollatsek et al. reading data suggest that there is no clear pattern of having neighbors on the time to access a word. Although this result appears to go against models like the interactive activation model or the activation-verification model, one could argue that there are facilitating effects early in processing (as the Williams et al. experiment indicates) which are negated by later inhibitory effects caused by competition between the lexical entries of the word actually presented and those of its neighbors.

Letter position coding

In Chapter 3 we discussed how letter position was encoded in words, and expressed skepticism that it could be encoded perfectly, especially for longer words. The transposed letter experiments on single words in isolation supported our skepticism. That is, they indicated that the correct letters that appeared in the wrong location in a word were still, to some extent, processed as if they were in the correct locations. There were two primary lines of evidence for this; both involved stimuli with transposed letters (TL). The first was akin to some of the neighborhood effects discussed in the prior section. That is, for a word like *clam*, another word which has the same letters but in a different order (e.g., *calm*) could act as a neighbor. (Although we discussed some TL effects in Chapter 3 with transposed non-adjacent letters, the bulk of the research with isolated words and all the studies below only use transposed adjacent letters.)

As indicated in Chapter 3, the typical finding in both naming and lexical decision experiments is that a word with a high-frequency transposed-letter neighbor (like *clam/calm)* was responded to more slowly than a word with no such TL neighbors (like *clap*) (Andrews, 1996; Chambers, 1979; O'Connor & Forster, 1981; Perea, Rosa, & Gómez, 2005). Acha and Perea (2008) and Johnson (2009) examined the effect in reading (in Spanish and English, respectively) and also found that there was more difficulty reading a word with a TL neighbor than a control word when these words were embedded in a sentence. (As with all such experiments, the words were equated on frequency, length, and other relevant measures, and inserted into the same sentence frame; there was a separate rating study that assessed whether the words fit equally naturally in the sentence frame.) As with the above findings on neighborhood effects, however, the difficulty appeared late—mainly in regressions back to the target word after the reader had moved further in the text. Thus, as with the neighborhood effects in reading, the major effect of having a TL neighbor in reading appears to be that the reader occasionally misidentifies the word as its TL neighbor.

The second paradigm that was used to study TL effects for isolated words is masked priming (Forster & Davis, 1984). In that paradigm lexical decision times on a target word were assessed, and the key comparison was between transposed letter (TL) primes and substitute letter (SL) primes. (For example, *wrok* could be the TL prime for *work* and *wsak* could be the SL prime.) The finding that various response time measures (chiefly lexical decision time) are less for TL primes than for

SL primes is quite reliable (e.g., Andrews, 1996; Christianson, Johnson, & Rayner, 2005; Perea & Carreiras, 2006; Perea & Lupker, 2004; Schoonbaert & Grainger, 2004).

A paradigm in reading that similarly examines early stages of word processing is the boundary technique. There the parafoveal preview is analogous to a prime. The results seem similar in the parafoveal preview task in reading, although they are somewhat less robust. Johnson, Perea, and Rayner (2007) found reliable transposed letter effects and these were replicated in a recent study by Masserang, Pollatsek, and Rayner (2009).

To summarize, we are far from understanding how letter position is coded in visual word recognition. Certainly, the idea that each letter position is a separate channel and the letter information comes to that channel without error is wrong. This is seen most clearly in the masked priming and parafoveal preview data, which are consistent with each other: switching two letters has a much less disruptive effect than simply putting different letters into the two channels. This is likely because these tasks are examining the early stages of word processing and the participant is largely unaware of the manipulation. Thus the effects in both the single-word and reading paradigms are likely to be due to differences in word-encoding time rather than to differences in the time to make a response. The results from both paradigms indicate that there is quite a bit of uncertainty in the coding of letter position in the early stages of word processing as letters in the wrong place facilitate processing. Indeed, in the Masserang et al. (2009) study, where only internal letters were transposed, there was no difference between when the preview was the TL distortion of the target word and when the preview was identical to the target, suggesting that in very early stages of word processing, letter position (except for perhaps the first and last letters) may be encoded quite poorly.

The ultimate effect of having TL neighbors on word identification is somewhat less clear. Both the isolated word experiments and the reading data indicate that such neighbors interfere with word encoding. The isolated word experiments appeared to show that this effect was largely due to a competition process between a word and TL neighbor(s) that slowed encoding of the word. However, the reading experiments to date suggest that the interference is largely in the form of a word being occasionally misidentified as a TL neighbor.

The role of morphemes in encoding printed words

We briefly discussed the role of morphemes in Chapter 3. Our discussion was brief because the standard behavioral measures used there, lexical decision time and naming latency, seem inappropriate for studying longer words. For naming latency, the measure one has is the time to begin saying a word, and for longer words (especially those with identifiable subparts) this is likely not a good indicator of how long it takes to identify the whole word. For lexical decision time, there is a large problem in deciding what nonwords to use in the experiment. If the nonwords do not look much like real words, a "word" decision can be made well before identifying the whole word. On the other hand, if one uses very wordlike nonwords, the task is likely to become difficult or even irrelevant to retrieving the meaning of what is seen. For example, if you saw *overkill, unwrappable*, or *overbuttered* in a lexical decision task, would you respond "word" or "nonword"? (As the latter two have zero frequency in most of the standard word corpuses, the correct response should presumably be "nonword" even though they are clearly meaningful words.)

First, we should briefly discuss the three different ways in which a word can have more than one morpheme. (Although we will confine this discussion to English, virtually all of what we say applies to all Indo-European languages and much of it applies to all languages.) First there are prefixed words such as *replay*, which consist of a root morpheme and a prefix morpheme. Second, there are suffixed words, which fall into two categories. First there are *inflectional* suffixes that are (a) added to nouns that indicate whether they are singular or plural and (in many languages) also indicate whether the noun is the subject, object, or indirect object of a clause and (b) added to verbs to also indicate both whether the subject is singular or plural and the tense of the verb. (English has quite an impoverished set of inflectional suffixes compared to most European languages.) There are also derivational suffixes that usually convert the root morpheme from one part of speech to another (e.g., *compare* vs. *comparison, subject* vs. *subjective*). The third type of morphemically complex word is compound words such as *baseball* or *nightmare*, in which each morpheme is a word. Also, note that in this example, *base* by itself is a noun, so that the compound is not an adjective–noun combination. However, in English, the second morpheme is the head morpheme (e.g., a baseball is a type of ball). Obviously words can be morphemically complex in more than one way (e.g., *refinanced, baseballs, unlockable*) and thus have more than two component morphemes. As discussed in prior chapters, another type of morpheme, an infix, occurs in Semitic languages like Arabic and Hebrew but not in Indo-European languages. The root morpheme is a set of consonants (e.g., the consonants equivalent to *xbr* in English), expressing a meaning like "assembling," and the infix (an inflection or derivation) is a set of vowels that are interspersed among them (e.g., the added characters in *xibber*). We will discuss infixes later.

One important aspect of morphemically complex words probably occurred to you when reading the last paragraph: they vary in the transparency of their meanings. This is perhaps most obvious with compounds, where the meaning of *blackberry* is quite computable from the meaning of the parts whereas the meaning of *nightmare* has nothing to do with horses. In contrast, suffixes are usually completely transparent in meaning. Prefixes vary in transparency. Some are quite transparent, such as *mis, re, pre*, whereas others, such as *in*, can have several meanings and the meaning of the whole would be quite difficult to figure out from the root and the prefix (e.g., *information*). However, a point worth emphasizing is that, with the exception of inflections and some derivations, the meaning of morphemically complex words (even those that are classified as transparent) is rarely unambiguously computable from its parts. Even in the *blackberry* example, the meaning of *blackberry* is more than it is a berry that is black (i.e., there could be other black berries that are not blackberries). However, compound words are usually defined as transparent if the meaning of each morpheme is related to the meaning of the compound. Thus, *cowboy* is classified as transparent, even though it could mean a child who likes cows rather than a human being who deals with cows in a particular way. The same phenomenon also occurs with transparent prefixed words such as *misstep*. That is, it could mean that a step was taken when it shouldn't have been or that a step was taken in the wrong direction.

Two more related points should be made explicit about complex words. One is that some root morphemes do not exist as separate words (they are called bound morphemes). That is, we have *revolve, devolve*, involve, but no *volve*. Often this is a historical accident as *gruntled* (the root of *disgruntled*) used to be a word. The second is that some words look like they are composed of separate morphemes, but aren't, such as pseudosuffixed words (e.g., *corner*) and pseudocompound words (e.g., *carpet*).

Evidence for involvement of morphemes in encoding words in reading

At first blush it might appear that it is obvious that morphemes must be involved in the encoding of words. However, this is not logically the case. That is, if a person has seen a morphologically complex word and knows its meaning, there is no necessity to do a morphemic analysis as part of its encoding. Even if the morphological decomposition is completely transparent (e.g., for *sees*), there is no necessity to do morphological decomposition at the time of encoding. That is, one could have a lexical entry for *sees* in which one looks up the information that this is the third person singular form of *see*. Thus it is possible that morphemic decomposition only occurs after encoding. This is essentially the supra-lexical model of Giraudo and Grainger (2001). Given that there are a non-trivial number of opaque compound and prefixed words and pseudosuffixed and pseudocompound words, perhaps it doesn't make sense to try to morphemically decompose a word on encoding. On the other hand, how do you understand words such as *undoable* which you likely haven't seen before? One possibility is that existing words are looked up directly, and if the printed word isn't in your mental lexicon then you fall back on morphemic decomposition. Although this is a tempting hypothesis, we think the bulk of the data show that it is wrong, and that morphemic decomposition is part of the normal word-encoding process.

One paradigm that has provided evidence for the involvement of morphemes in the encoding of morphemically complex words is the comparison of two morphemically complex target words that are matched on the frequency of the whole word but which vary in the frequency of one of the morphemes. The most common experimental design is to place these words in the same sentence frame—of course, being careful that the two words fit equally well with the prior sentence context. A series of experiments with compound words was carried out in Finnish (for similar experiments in Dutch, see also Kuperman, Schreuder, Bertram, & Baayen, 2009). As with German, Finnish compounds are always written without spaces between the constituent morphemes, so that long compounds with two constituents are quite common. (Actually, the Finnish constituents were not all single morphemes; they frequently had inflectional endings, marking grammatical case.) The initial experiments, which employed compounds with 10 or more letters, found large effects on gaze duration on the word (about 100 ms) when the frequency of either the initial constituent or the final constituent was varied (Hyönä & Pollatsek, 1998; Pollatsek & Hyönä, 2005; Pollatsek, Hyönä, & Bertram, 2000). These data indicate that the constituents of these compound words are involved in the encoding of the words, especially as the frequency of the first constituent even influenced the duration of the first fixation on the word.

Encoding these words is not merely encoding the parts, however, as even for these long compound words the frequency of the whole word also had a large effect on the gaze duration (again about 100 ms) when the frequency of the constituents was equated (Pollatsek et al., 2000). This led Pollatsek et al. to propose a dual-route model, analogous to the one used to explain the phonological coding effect, in which there is both a whole-word route to encoding the word as well as a compositional route in which the constituents are separately encoded and then integrated. Although this hypothesis seems reasonable given the above data, we will see that it is quite unlikely that these routes operate independently of one another.

One relevant factor in encoding compound words appears to be length. Bertram and Hyönä (2003) varied the length of Finnish compounds and found, contrary to their results for longer compounds (average length about 12.5 letters), that first constituent frequency had virtually no effect on the gaze duration for their shorter compounds (average length about 7.5 letters) although the whole-word frequency did affect the gaze duration. This suggests that shorter compounds can be fairly easily processed as a unitary whole and the direct access of the word predominates, whereas for the longer words this is more difficult and a compositional process becomes involved in the encoding process. The modulation of the constituent frequency effect by length also may indicate why the analogous data in English are less clear cut (as English compounds are almost never as long as the long Finnish compounds in the above studies). In English, although the effects of the individual constituents are found (e.g., Andrews, Miller, & Rayner, 2004; Juhasz, 2007; Juhasz, Starr, Inhoff, & Placke, 2003), they are not nearly as big as in the Finnish studies, and the pattern of data varies from study to study.

Another possible explanation (besides word length) for the difference between the Finnish and English data is that compounding is much more productive in Finnish. Readers in Finnish are likely to encounter novel compounds daily and they are always written without a space between the constituents. (Although novel compounds are not rare in English, they would almost always be written with a space between the constituents.) Thus Finnish readers are likely to encounter unspaced compounds not knowing for sure whether they are novel, whereas English readers are virtually guaranteed that unspaced compounds are in their mental lexicon.

The pattern of data for English prefixed words is quite similar to that for Finnish compounds and also suggests a dual-route type of model. Niswander-Klement and Pollatsek (2006) varied both the frequency of the word for prefixed words and the frequency of the root morpheme (see Table 5.2). The prefixes (e.g., *mis, re*) were semantically transparent; furthermore, when two target words were compared, they had the same prefix so that the differences due to the difficulty of processing the prefix were controlled. As with the Finnish compounds, they found significant effects on gaze duration of both the frequency of the prefixed word and the frequency of the word that was the root. Moreover, consistent with the Finnish compound experiments, they found that the constituent frequency effect was larger for longer prefixed words. However, they also found that the word frequency effect was smaller for longer prefixed words (which was not the case for the Finnish compounds). There were also root frequency effects on gaze duration for suffixed words in English, although the effects were smaller (Niswander, Pollatsek, & Rayner, 2000).

A second type of paradigm used in the isolated word literature that has been used to document that morphemes are relevant in encoding of words is to see whether a morpheme primes a target that contains it. Masked priming (discussed in Chapter 3) is often used to study this. The basic finding is that showing a morpheme as a prime or preview facilitates processing of a target word (usually assessed by lexical decision time) more than a non-morphemic part of the word. This has been demonstrated in Indo-European languages (Dutch and German: Drews & Zwitzerlood, 1995; English: Forster & Azuma, 2000; Rastle, Davis, Marslen-Wilson, & Tyler, 2000; French: Grainger, Cole & Segui, 1991), although there have been failures to get significant effects as well (Masson & Isaak, 1999). What we would like to discuss here that is of additional interest is that this paradigm has been used to study morphological processing in Hebrew, which has a different type of morphology.

As indicated previously, in Hebrew (and in other Semitic languages), the morphemes are infixes. There is a root morpheme, which as in English expresses the basic meaning of the word, and a verbal or nominal pattern that does more or less the same work as suffixes do in English (e.g., giving the tense of verbs or whether the noun is nominative or accusative). For example, the root /xbr/ could combine with a nominal pattern to produce the spoken form /maxberet/ meaning

TABLE 5.2 Examples of materials from Niswander-Klement and Pollatsek (2006)

Longer prefixed words: Word frequency held constant

It was Robin's responsibility to [rearrange/reprocess] the employees' work schedules.

Shorter prefixed words: Word frequency held constant

Hugh asked Jake to [unfold/unroll] the dirty sleeping bag out on the porch.

Longer prefixed words: Root morpheme frequency held constant

The scientist set out to [disprove/discount] his rival's theories one by one.

Shorter prefixed words: Root morpheme frequency held constant

Jack and Fran tried to [relive/recall] the evening of their first kiss.

For all the examples, the lower-frequency instance is first.
When word frequency is held constant, the frequency manipulated is that of the root morpheme.
When root morpheme frequency is held constant, the frequency manipulated is that of the word.

"notebook" or with a verbal pattern to produce /xibber/ meaning "he combined." Another important feature of Hebrew and other Semitic languages is that consonants are always represented in the orthography but vowels are not. The root morpheme usually consists of three consonants (as in the above example); the verbal pattern mainly contains vowels, but can also have a consonant. Perhaps not surprisingly, the root morpheme presented alone (which is rarely a word) was a very effective prime for a word containing the root morpheme; the verbal pattern was a less effective prime, but there was no priming of a word from the nominal pattern (Deutsch, Frost, & Forster, 1998, Frost, Forster, & Deutsch, 1997).

The results from parafoveal preview experiments (Deutsch, Frost, Peleg, Pollatsek, & Rayner 2003; Deutsch, Frost, Pollatsek, & Rayner, 2005) produced similar results. Here the preview was not the isolated morpheme but another word that shared the morpheme with the target word. Control words were used that matched the preview word in the number of letters that were the same as the target word (although in both cases the positions of the letters in the preview and target were not necessarily the same). As in the masked priming experiments, a preview of both the root morpheme and the verbal pattern produced significant preview benefit, whereas a preview of the nominal pattern did not. These results argue that the benefit from morphemes does not depend on the morpheme being a consecutive series of letters but depends on something more fundamental in the structure of the word.

A second phenomenon with parafoveal preview argues in a different way for the relevance of morphemic decomposition in encoding words (Hyönä, Bertram, & Pollatsek, 2004). When the second half of a Finnish compound was replaced with "garbage" (i.e., incorrect letters) in a boundary change experiment, gaze duration on the first half was unchanged from a condition with normal preview. However, gaze durations on the second half were longer in the "garbage" preview condition. This is the pattern of data described earlier when the boundary is between separate words, and indicates that the second half of the compound is processed as a separate unit (for similar results in English, see also Drieghe, Pollatsek, Juhasz, & Rayner, 2010; Juhasz, Pollatsek, Hyönä, Dreighe, & Rayner, 2009).

The experiments in this section clearly indicate that morphemic parts of words are often processed as independent units and that the processing of these units feeds into the processing of the word as a whole. However, it is not clear at what level the processing of the constituent parts is feeding into encoding the word as a whole. One possibility is that the morphemes are merely familiar sequences of letters that are processed as units and then "glued" together at a relatively superficial level. A more interesting possibility is that this recombination of the component morphemes is, in some sense, a combination of meanings. One way this has been tested is by varying the semantic transparency of compound words. That is, if the recombination were going on at the level of meaning, when one encountered a compound word like *nightmare*, one would expect some sort of interference relative to a transparent word like *basketball*, because the composition of the meanings of the components of *nightmare* would not get you to the meaning of the word (as it has nothing to do with horses).

In the experiments examining semantic transparency, either a transparent compound word or an opaque compound word is inserted into a sentence frame; the sentence frame in the two cases is identical at least prior to the target compound word. (The two compounds are matched on word frequency and the frequency of the constituents.) The initial experiment in Finnish (Pollatsek & Hyönä, 2005) found no effect of transparency on gaze duration on the compound word or any other measure; however, there was an effect of the frequency of the first constituent on gaze duration on the compound word for both transparent and opaque compounds, indicating that the word encoding was (somehow) going through identification of the initial constituent. In English there is some suggestion of a transparency effect. Although Frisson, Niswander-Klement, and Pollatsek (2008) found no effect of semantic transparency for English compounds, Juhasz (2007) observed a significant, but relatively small, effect of semantic transparency on fixation time for English compounds.

Thus, perhaps surprisingly, the evidence for the morphemic composition process being at a deeper semantic level is not particularly strong. However, as pointed out above, transparency is not a simple construct as there is some sense in which there are few, if any, compounds in which the meaning can be completely constructed from the parts. For example, as indicated previously, *cowboy* is generally considered a transparent compound because both parts are related to the meaning of the compound, but it is unlikely that someone could figure out the meaning of *cowboy* from knowing the meaning of *cow* and *boy*. Thus perhaps there is little or no transparency effect for compounds because the meaning of the compound really has to be retrieved from the lexicon even for transparent compounds.

Another way in which the "depth" of the morphemic compositional process has been examined employed ambiguous trimorphemic words such as *unlockable*. For such words, the meaning of the word can depend on the order in which the parts are attached. For example, if one first attaches *un-* to *lock* and then attaches *-able* to get *(unlock)-able*, the word means "something that can be unlocked"; however if one does the attachment in the opposite order to obtain *un-(lockable)*, it means "something that can't be locked." This ambiguity raises the question of how the reader decides between these two possible attachment structures. Libben (2003) showed that participants who were asked to put a slash at the most natural division of the word generally put it between the prefix and the word (e.g., *re/lockable*). However, Pollatsek, Drieghe, Stockall, and de Almeida (2010) had people read such words (without the slashes) in an eye-tracking experiment, and found that reading was slowed when the prior context forced the un(lockable) meaning (something that cannot be locked), compared to when it forced the unlock(able) meaning (something that can be unlocked).

Assuming that this finding indicates that the preferred interpretation is the unX(able) meaning, it is analogous to Duffy et al.'s (1988) finding that when prior context strongly supported the lower-frequency meaning of an ambiguous word, it lengthened the fixation time on the word. There is a difference though: Duffy et al.'s effect appeared on gaze duration, while Pollatsek et al.'s effect was on a slightly later measure, go-past time (see Figure 4.1), indicating that readers in the latter experiment went back and re-read the context. Still, the (unX)able interpretation appears to be the preferred one—but why? The most likely explanation is the frequency of the components. That is, for virtually all the stimuli used in Pollatsek et al., the frequency of the *unX* component (e.g., *unlock*) was much higher than the frequency of the *Xable* component (e.g., *lockable*). Furthermore, the stimuli that showed the smallest preference effects were those that had the lowest frequencies for the *unX* component.

The effects of context on word identification

Some general issues

In Chapter 3 we argued that higher-order processes have a relatively minor effect on word identification. First, word identification in isolation is quite fluent and automatic for skilled readers so that it does not need much help in the first place. Second, variables such as word length and word frequency predict much of the variation in readers' eye fixations. Such a result would be inconsistent with a view in which most of the processing of words was coming from top-down sources, such as how well the word fit into the text. Such results (and others) led some (e.g., J. A. Fodor, 1983) to a more radical position (called modularity) in which it was argued that there is *no* influence of higher-order processes on word recognition. Since this position was forcefully advocated, and if true would help to simplify an analysis of the process of reading, we will discuss the evidence pertaining to whether top-down processes have any effect on word identification. The modularity debate has waned somewhat in recent years, but it is still instructive to consider some of the arguments that were made. Thus, we need to first clarify several points.

The first is that, as we will discuss later, there are uncontroversial effects of context on the time it takes to process a word. For example, a word that is highly predictable in text will be fixated for a shorter time than one that is not predictable. Partisans of the view that higher-order processes have no influence on word identification time do not dispute these data. What they claim is that the difference in time is not due to the ease of identifying the word, but to later processes, such as the time it takes to integrate the word into the ongoing discourse structures that are being built by the reader.

A second issue is whether there is a structural reason why higher-order processes do not affect word identification. For example, Fodor and others (e.g., Forster, 1979; Seidenberg, 1985) argued that lexical access is handled by a module of the information-processing system that cannot interact in any serious way with other systems or modules. In Fodor's theorizing (which is probably the most extreme position), the only communication between the lexical identification module and the rest of the language-processing system is that the lexical module sends the word that has been identified on for further processing, and if the rest of the system gets stuck (e.g., if a word is misread or mistyped) the higher-order processes could tell the lexical module to "try again" (although they could not tell the lexical module which word to look for).

At first blush, it might be hard to see how one can hold to that position. For example, in doing a crossword puzzle, if several letters of a word are filled in you can often fluently identify the correct word using the definition provided in the puzzle, whereas you would draw a blank if either the letters or the definition were missing. The definition and partial visual information appear to interact to produce lexical access. However, proponents of a modular view would likely argue that the context effect in such cases is not top-down. Instead, any effect on lexical access would be explained by invoking the mechanism of "spreading activation" wherein the lexical entries of related words in the definition would be activated and send automatic activation through links between them and the word being accessed, and this activation would help in access. Such a mechanism would be "intralexical" (totally within a lexical module) and hence not top-down.

An alternative to the view that top-down processes can in principle play no part in lexical access is that they play little part in fluent silent reading because the benefits are outweighed by the costs. That is, if lexical access can go on so well without any help (as with words in isolation) there may be little benefit in speeding it up, and there may be significant costs involved trying to use context in lexical access (Stanovich, 1980). This argument seems particularly telling, especially if the use of context is viewed as one of conscious prediction, as in the guessing game models of reading (Goodman, 1967, 1970; Hochberg, 1970; Levin & Kaplan, 1970). In these models, conscious prediction is seen as a major factor in identifying words in text, so that the visual information does not have to be fully processed. There seem to be two primary costs involved with such conscious prediction. The first is that such prediction is likely to be wrong; readers are usually not very good at predicting the next word, even with unlimited amounts of time (Gough, Alford, & Holley-Wilcox, 1981; McConkie & Rayner, 1976b). Second, one would expect that such prediction would take processing resources away from the higher-order processes needed to put the words together to form syntactic and semantic structures.

Does context affect the speed of lexical access?

This has been a major research question in cognitive psychology for well over 20 years, and the answer is still controversial. As we shall see, there is evidence for the beneficial effects of context on word identification; however, it is still unclear whether all of these effects can be ascribed to "intralexical" processes such as priming or whether an interaction between higher-order processes and lexical access needs to be invoked. A major problem in discussing the evidence is that the answer to whether context affects lexical access may depend on the situation. For example, context might have a large effect on lexical access in a situation like the crossword puzzle example where access is slow, but may not play any significant role in a fluent process such as normal silent reading where access is accomplished in a fraction of a second.

The first experiments attempting to demonstrate context effects in a reading-like situation (Morton, 1964; Tulving & Gold, 1963; Tulving, Mandler, & Baumal, 1964) were not too different from our crossword puzzle example. Participants read a sentence fragment such as:

The skiers were buried alive by the sudden (5.5)

The participants were then shown the target word *avalanche* very briefly in a tachistoscope. They were able to identify the target word at significantly briefer exposures when the context predicted it than when it was preceded by no context. These experiments were assumed to indicate that context affects the identification of words. However, many researchers question whether such situations have any bearing on normal reading, since the response in experiments with degraded stimuli is likely to be slow. Thus the response the participant selects may be the result of a conscious problem-solving process rather than perceptual identification.

Accordingly the procedure was modified so that the target word that appears after the sentence frame is not briefly shown and the participant makes a speeded response to it (Stanovich & West, 1983). Most of these experiments required the participants either to *name* (Becker, 1985; Stanovich & West, 1979) or make a *lexical decision* on the target word (Fischler & Bloom, 1979; Schuberth & Eimas, 1977). While this type of procedure alters the natural reading process, the timing relations are not too different from normal reading if the delay between the frame and the target word is relatively brief (some are as short as about 250 ms). In most of these experiments it has been shown that a highly predictive context in fact facilitates either naming or lexical decision latency relative to a neutral condition such as a frame like:

The next word in the sentence will be ... (5.6)

Context thus appears to facilitate the processing of words in a situation in which participants are making speeded responses to the words. There has subsequently been little controversy over that statement. Most of the controversy is over the two issues we discussed earlier: (1) Is lexical access the process that is facilitated or is it some later stage? (2) Is the effect of context really coming from a higher-order process such as prediction of the word in the sentence or is it due to an intra-lexical process such as spreading activation? We will defer discussion of the latter issue until later and concentrate for the moment on whether the speed of lexical access can be affected (in some way) by sentential context.

Although both lexical decision and naming tasks approximate fluent reading, there are some key differences. In both tasks there is an extraneous task that is interposed that is other than the understanding of discourse. In addition, a delay is usually introduced between the frame that contains the context and the target word. As a result, we think that the best way to study such effects in fluent reading is through the use of eye movements while people are reading for comprehension. Therefore we will focus on how eye movements have been employed to study context effects.

Effects of context in reading

The earliest experiment to investigate context effects in normal reading (Zola, 1984; originally reported in McConkie & Zola, 1981) employed a similar manipulation to the studies described above: the predictability of a target word was manipulated, and the average fixation time on the word and the probability of fixating on the target word were both measured. For example, a passage about the movie industry contained either the sentence

> Movie theatres must have buttered popcorn to serve their patrons. (5.7)

or the same sentence with *buttered* replaced by *adequate*. Zola found a surprisingly modest effect: fixation times were only about 15 ms shorter when the target word *popcorn* was highly predictable and participants were no more likely to skip the target word when it was predictable than when it was not. In the studies in this section, predictability is usually assessed in a norming study which precedes the actual experiment in which participants merely try to guess the target word given the prior context; highly predictable usually means that the target word was guessed by at least 60% of the participants.

In Zola's experiment the predictable context was always established by the adjective immediately preceding the target noun (*buttered* in the example above). Ehrlich and Rayner (1981) argued that this is not typical of context in reading, and that the predictability of many words is established by a more extended context segment. In their passages the target words were also either highly predictable or not predictable, but the context was established earlier (see Table 5.3). They found that readers skipped the target word more often when it was highly predictable than when it was not, and furthermore, when the target was fixated, the average fixation duration was shortened about 30–50 ms by predictability (or over twice as much as in Zola's experiment).

These studies, and others discussed below, thus establish that context does affect the amount of time spent on a word, although the effects are relatively modest. These results make the guessing game models of reading quite unlikely: that is, if guessing were an important part of word identification, one would expect bigger effects than these in the situations where the deck has been

---

TABLE 5.3 Passages from Ehrlich and Rayner (1981)

High constraint (Experiment 1)
He saw the black fin slice through the water and the image of shark's teeth came quickly to his mind. He turned quickly toward the shore and swam for his life. The coast guard had warned that someone had seen a *shark* off the north shore of the island. As usual, not everyone listened to the warning.

Low constraint (Experiment 1)
The young couple were delighted by the special attention they were getting. The zoo keeper explained that the life span of a *shark* is much longer than those of the other animals they had talked about. The scientists decided that this man would make a great ally.

High constraint (Experiment 2)
It is often said that dead men tell no tales. But Fred was very nervous as he put his shovel into the ground where he knew the makeshift grave was. He soon uncovered the skeletal remains and cleared the dirt away. He reached down and picked up one of the *bones* and quickly threw it aside realizing that it was not what he was searching for.

Constraint refers to the predictability of the target (italicized) word in the context (not italicized in the experiments). In the bottom example, the low constraint condition was created by replacing bones with boxes.

stacked to make guessing prevail. (As argued earlier, most content words are not nearly as predictable as the target words in these experiments.) However, these context effects are not necessarily due to speeded lexical access of the predictable word. It is possible that the predictable context speeds processing of the target word by allowing it to be fit into the sentence context more easily.

One way to test whether lexical access is affected by context is to look for interactions between context and purely visual aspects of a target word. An experiment by Balota, Pollatsek and Rayner (1985) manipulated visual information in the parafovea, using the boundary change procedure.

Since the wedding was today, the baker rushed the wedding cake (pies) to
the reception. (5.8)

One of two target words was present when the target location was fixated: _cake_, which is highly predicted by the prior context, or _pies_, which is not predicted by the prior context but is an acceptable word in that context. However, before a reader's eye movement crossed a boundary location, the string of letters presented initially in the target location (the _parafoveal preview_) could be different from the target word. The string could be identical to the target word (_cake_ as a preview for _cake_ or _pies_ for _pies_), visually similar to the target word (_cahc_ as a preview for _cake_ or _picz_ for _pies_), identical to the alternative word (_pies_ as a preview for _cake_ or vice versa), similar to the alternative word (_picz_ for _cake_ or _cahc_ for _pies_), or visually dissimilar and semantically unrelated (_bomb_ for either _cake_ or _pies_).

The highly predictable word and its visually similar misspelling (e.g., _cahc_) were skipped more often than the unpredictable word and its misspelling (_picz_) (as was previously found by Ehrlich & Rayner, 1981). Further, gaze duration on the target word reflected an interaction between predictability and visual aspects of the preview (see Table 5.4). Balota et al. argued that the best way to understand this interaction was to contrast the left two columns of Table 5.4 (where the preview and the target were the same or visually similar) with the right three columns (where the preview differed from the target; e.g., when the target was the high-predictable _cakes_, the preview could be _pies, picz_, or _bomb_). When the target was a high-predictable word, gaze duration on it was 43 ms shorter for an identical or visually similar preview than for a visually different preview. The difference was only 21 ms when the target was a low-predictable word. This result indicates that more letters were processed in the parafoveal stimulus when it (or a visually similar stimulus) was predictable.

A number of other studies (Ashby, Rayner, & Clifton, 2005; Drieghe, Brysbaert, Desmet, & De Baecke, 2004; Drieghe, Rayner, & Pollatsek, 2005; Kliegl, Nuthmann, & Engbert, 2006; Rayner, Ashby, Pollatsek, & Reichle, 2004; Rayner, Li, Juhasz, & Yan, 2005; Rayner, Slattery, Drieghe, & Liversedge, 2011; Rayner & Well, 1996; Schustack, Ehrlich, & Rayner, 1987; White, Rayner, & Liversedge, 2005a) have examined effects of predictability, showing that predictable contexts yield both shorter fixation times on a target word and more skipping of that target word. Three findings

TABLE 5.4 High and low predictability

	IDENT	VS	SR	VD	AN
High-predictable	232	284	280	280	292
Low-predictable	264	263	287	277	290

Mean gaze duration on the target word in the Balota et al. (1985) experiment, for high-and low-predictable target words (e.g., _cake_ and _pies_). Columns indicate preview condition: IDENT = identical, VS = visually similar (_cahc/cake, picz/pies_), SR = semantically realted (_pies/cake, cake/pies_), VD = visually different (_picz/cake, cahc/pies_), AN = anomalous (_bomb/cake, bomb/pies_).

from these studies are notable. First, Drieghe et al. (2005) reported a partial replication of Balota et al. (1985), examining only predictable target words. They found higher skipping rates for an identical preview than for any of several different previews (including those used by Balota et al.), but in contrast to Balota et al., the skipping rates for these different previews did not differ. They suggested that the differences between the two studies might be due to the fact that the quality of the display monitor used to present the stimuli had improved over the 20 years between the studies, and perhaps readers were able to extract parafoveal information more efficiently in the more recent study. Second, Rayner et al. (2004) found that while word frequency and word predictability interacted with respect to word skipping, they had additive effects on fixation time on a target word. Third, Rayner, Slattery et al. (2011) demonstrated that word predictability does not interact with word length for either skipping or fixation time on a target word. It is well known that the largest effect on word skipping is word length (Brysbaert & Vitu, 1998; Rayner & McConkie, 1976), so it is quite surprising that predictability would have similar effects on short (4–5 letters) and long words (9–13 letters).

Before leaving our discussion of context effects, it is worth noting that in addition to using cloze task values, researchers have used other ways to examine how context influences processing during reading. For example, McDonald and Shillcock (2003a, 2003b) argued for transitional probability, the statistical likelihood that a word will precede or follow another word. They argued that transitional probability operates independently from regular predictability effects, at least when predictability is low. In an experiment and a corpus analysis of eye movement data they presented evidence that readers spent less time looking at word n+1 when a count of frequencies in a corpus indicated that it was more likely to follow word n (note that their high transitional probability words had a transitional probability of only 1%, as opposed to 0.04% for their low transitional probability words). However, in a subsequent study, Frisson, Rayner, and Pickering (2005) replicated this result, but also demonstrated that it was more likely due to differences in predictability (as measured by a cloze procedure) than transitional probability. Finally, another approach to the study of context effects uses the syntax and semantics of prior context to estimate a quantity called "surprisal" (the negative log of the probability of the word given the analyzed context; Levy, 2008). Levy argued that words that are less likely in their particular context take longer to read.

To summarize, several studies have demonstrated that words are fixated for shorter periods of time and skipped more often when they are predictable from the sentential context. They also demonstrate that a predictable context modulates the extraction of visual information in the parafovea and thus indicate that context can affect lexical access during reading. They also suggest that the major locus of context effects in reading is speeding the extraction of visual information from the parafovea. This makes sense, since parafoveal visual information is not as good as foveal visual information, and thus more in need of context to help out.

What is the context mechanism?

There is no definitive answer to this question. While we have been referring to the context manipulation as predictability, the mechanism need not be prediction of the target word using higher-order processes. It could also be, at least in part, easier integration of predictable than unpredictable words into the representation of a text (see Chapters 8 and 9). Another explanation that has been offered for predictability effects is (intralexical) priming as discussed in Chapter 3. For example in sentence 5.8, perhaps the more efficient processing of *cake* is a result of semantic priming from the word *wedding* rather than of the high predictability of *cake* in that context. In fact Stanovich and West (1983) explained their predictability effects as the sum of priming effects from the words preceding the target word.

While such an explanation is plausible, there is no conclusive evidence that priming works in that fashion. First, priming by a related word rapidly dissipates in a lexical decision task even when only one or two words or pseudowords intervene between target and prime and the participant is required to make a lexical decision to each stimulus (Gough et al., 1981). If close contiguity of prime and target are required for priming, then it is unlikely that priming can account for most of the context effects in reading. However, the reading situation may be different than the laboratory lexical decision task, in that the reader may have the priming word active in short-term memory as a result of building the meaning of the sentence, and this active short-term memory representation may do the priming (Foss, 1982; Morris, 1994). Second, it is not at all clear that priming effects observed in the laboratory are necessarily due to an automatic associative mechanism. If a participant sees *doctor* as a priming stimulus, he or she may guess that the target will be *nurse* (i.e., priming may be due to prediction rather than vice versa; Neely, 1977).

Finally, the experiments on reading using eye movement measures suggest that the major effect of context on lexical access may be in the extraction of parafoveal information. First of all, the most dramatic effects of context observed are on word skipping. Moreover, since the Balota et al. experiment demonstrated that context was interacting with the extraction of *parafoveal* visual information, much of the savings in fixation time on a word is likely due to increased efficiency of extraction of visual information from the parafovea. In fact, at the level of word recognition, foveal information may be so good that applying context may be of little benefit (consistent with Stanovich's, 1980, view that context is mainly used when the visual information is degraded in some way).

Some conclusions, speculations, and a look ahead

What have we learned?

This chapter has focused on (a) what has been learned about the identification of words in experiments where people are reading text and (b) to what extent the conclusions that were drawn about word identification from experiments with isolated words needed to be modified. Let's start with an answer to (b). For many of the basic phenomena the answer is that the reading studies basically replicated the phenomena in the studies discussed in Chapter 3. A simple example is that the word frequency and word length effects demonstrated in Chapter 3 also appear in reading, as indicated in this chapter and Chapter 4. However, the sizes of the word frequency effects are larger (Schilling, Rayner, & Chumbley, 1998) in some of the single-word tasks (particularly lexical decision) than on gaze duration. This suggests that part of the word frequency effect in the lexical decision task is on the time to make a "word" decision rather than on the actual encoding time (Ratcliff, Gomez, & McKoon, 2004). Similarly, both single-word paradigms and reading studies indicate that access to phonology is an important component of word identification, affecting even the earliest stages of the process.

There is, however, an important way in which reading studies have advanced our knowledge. That is, the central questions that one wants to know about encoding of words are whether the meaning of a word is identified, how long meaning access takes, and what influences the time to access the meaning. It is hard to make a strong case that a naming or lexical decision response is necessarily triggered by accessing the meaning. In contrast, the experiments with ambiguous words show that fixation time on a word is definitely indexing whether the word's meaning was accessed. Given that this is the case, fixation time measures (particularly gaze duration on a word) seem like an excellent tool for studying the encoding of the meaning of a word in an ecologically valid paradigm for studying reading. Nonetheless, we need to make two important disclaimers. The first is that we are not claiming that gaze duration time equals the time to access the meaning of a word. Second, it is not necessarily true that if a variable affects the gaze duration on a word, it is affecting the time to access the meaning of the word (see Chapters 8 and 9).

The work discussed in the current chapter on neighborhood and transposed letter effects is also reasonably congruent with the work from the isolated word literature in that it indicates that (a) a word having neighbors influences word-encoding time and (b) that having correct letters in the wrong locations does facilitate word identification. However, unlike the results in the isolated word literature, it appears that the primary way in which neighbors influence reading is that they increase the probability that the word will be misidentified.

Our discussion of multimorphemic words supported several points. One is the conclusion that compound words are not processed in parallel, and that in some cases serial processing is not merely word by word but morpheme by morpheme. The second is that the data indicating that gaze duration on a word is influenced by both the whole-word frequency and the component morpheme frequencies indicate that the processing of polymorphemic words involves accessing both the whole word from the lexicon and accessing the components. However, the rest of the data (notably the fact that transparency effects are hard to document) indicate that how the component morphemes play a role in accessing the meaning of these complex words is far from clear.

A look ahead

At a few points in the chapter we mentioned phenomena (most notably word skipping) that are part of the reading process and are plausibly related to word identification. When we did so, we said that we would discuss them in Chapter 6, in which we outline a model of eye movement control in reading that explains such phenomena which is consistent with the hypothesis that we have adopted in this chapter—that words are generally processed one at a time in reading and that there is quite a tight linkage between when a word is identified and when the signal to move to the next word is given. We will move on to discuss this model which, among other things, will clarify how such phenomena can be explained. However, we need to emphasize (and will continue to do so in Chapter 6) that this model mainly accounts for how word identification is tied to how the eyes move in reading. It is clear that the model is not the whole story of eye movements in reading, as there is much in the comprehension of text that goes beyond understanding the meanings of individual words. These processes, understanding the syntax of a sentence and constructing the global meaning of a sentence or passage, also influence eye movement behavior and these phenomena will be discussed in detail in Chapters 8 and 9. Many of these phenomena are well beyond the scope of the model that we will present in Chapter 6.

6

A MODEL OF EYE MOVEMENTS IN READING

Chapters 3–5 have discussed word identification in isolation, many of the basics of eye movements in reading, and what we have learned about word identification when people read text. The present chapter will discuss a relatively simple model of eye movements in reading that we have developed, which can explain why there is such a tight linkage between word identification and where the eyes are fixating.

A central idea of the model that we will discuss in some detail—the E-Z Reader model (Rayner, Li, & Pollatsek, 2007; Reichle, Pollatsek, Fisher, & Rayner, 1998; Reichle, Rayner, & Pollatsek, 2003; Pollatsek, Reichle, & Rayner, 2006)—is that word identification is the basic force that is driving the eyes through the text when one reads for meaning. Of course, this does not mean that encoding the meaning of words is all there is to comprehending text. However, a key hypothesis of the model is that word identification is the basic engine that drives the eyes through the text and that the other processes generally lag behind the word-encoding process. (Chapters 8 and 9, however, will present some phenomena indicating that they sometimes are not lagging very much behind word encoding.) In earlier versions of the E-Z Reader model, these higher-order text comprehension processes were postulated to be continually operating but not affecting the forward progress of the eyes, however a later version (Reichle, Warren, & McConnell, 2009) has attempted to deal to some extent with how they can intervene and cause immediate regressions and lengthen fixation durations. As these phenomena are discussed in Chapters 8 and 9, we will largely restrict ourselves here to discussing the earlier versions that only model how word encoding drives eye movements in reading.

Why does such a model make sense? Consider the polar opposite: when a reader comes to each word, he or she has to ponder the deepest intentions of the author before going on to the next word. Such processing would take considerable time. We showed in Chapter 3 that tasks such as naming, lexical decision, and categorization take 500–700 ms to execute. Since the simple motor responses in these tasks take 200–300 ms, it appears to take several hundred ms to determine a word's identity and meaning. However, a skilled reader reads 250–350 words per minute (which is about 200 ms per word). Since the programming and execution of eye movements takes at least 150 ms, this leaves only 50 ms to identify the word. This doesn't seem long enough for the reader to determine an author's intentions. Thus we think it makes some sense for the system to do "good enough processing" to direct eye movements forward and rely on other clean-up operations when something goes wrong.

Before going on to outline the model we should emphasize one point that has already been made at the beginning of Chapter 3: the concept of word identification is quite fuzzy. Does it mean making contact with an entry in a mental dictionary, accessing the sound of the word, accessing its meaning, a sense of familiarity, or some complex combination of these? We do not pretend to have a definitive answer to the question of how much identification is good enough for the reader to move on in the text. Instead, E-Z Reader simply assumes that there are two levels of word identification that are relevant in the process of guiding the eyes: one produces a signal to make a saccade and the other, later, level produces a signal to shift covert attention to the next word. A second point that should also be emphasized is that, as we have noted earlier, the definition of "word" is by no means unambiguous, especially in languages such as Chinese where words are not demarcated by obvious markers such as spaces. However, the question is deeper than that. For example, for the purpose of word identification, is *basketball* one word or two? Moreover, we presented data in Chapter 5 (Drieghe, Pollatsek, Juhasz, & Rayner, 2010) indicating that there is a sense in which constituents of unspaced compound words may, to some extent, be processed as if they were two different words. However, for most of the rest of the chapter we will treat a word as "the sequence of letters between the spaces."

We now come to perhaps the key assumption of the model: that readers lexically process words in English (or any European language) one word at a time (i.e., serially) in the order they appear in the text. That is, according to the model, at any one time the letters of only one word are in a "spotlight" of an internal spatial attention mechanism and, for the purposes of recognizing a word, the other letters on the page are irrelevant. This is different from assuming that only one word is processed on a fixation; indeed the moving-window experiments discussed in Chapter 4 indicate that more than one word is typically processed on a fixation. Instead, what the model posits is that attention can shift during a fixation so that a reader may start the fixation by focusing attention on the fixated word, but when this word is identified this covert attention mechanism shifts to focus on the next word before the eyes actually move to that word. Indeed, the sequence described above—begin a fixation by attending to the fixated word but then shift attention at some time later in the fixation to the next word (i.e., the one to the right) and start to process that word—is what the E-Z Reader model predicts is the most common sequence of events on a fixation.

Why posit that words are encoded sequentially one word at a time? First, as indicated in Chapter 3, there is evidence indicating that when participants have to process words for meaning, the words are examined one at a time (Karlin & Bower, 1976; Reichle, Vanyukov, Laurent, & Warren, 2008). This is consistent with the general finding from visual search that objects are typically processed serially if the judgment is based on something more complex than detecting a single physical feature such as color (Treisman, 1988; Treisman & Gelade, 1980). Second, writing or print is an attempt to transcribe spoken language, which is the basic skill that we are more-or-less biologically programmed for and on which reading builds. Spoken language is something that unfolds in time, and although syllables or even words seldom have well-defined physical boundaries, one is still essentially processing one word at a time. Moreover, we have already encountered considerable evidence that even skilled readers are accessing the sounds of words, even if they are often not aware of it. Third, even if the serial assumption isn't exactly true (e.g., people might process *does not* as a single unit), the assumption makes understanding the reading process a conceivable undertaking. In contrast, if one assumes that several words at a time are partially activated, it would be hard to understand how one could build up a coherent representation of the text—especially if a word was encoded prior to a word to its left (e.g., see Rayner, Pollatsek, Liversedge, & Reichle, 2009; Reichle, Liversedge, Pollatsek, & Rayner, 2009). However, we should emphasize that our assumption is that words are lexically processed one at a time but that the letters within a word are all processed in parallel (at least for short- and medium-length words), which is consistent with the literature we discussed in Chapter 3.

A brief history and outline of the model

Why have a formal computational model?

Before starting to explain the E-Z Reader model, we should perhaps explain the purpose of such models, and in particular why we are spending a chapter describing this one. As we have argued above and in Chapters 4 and 5, there is a huge amount of evidence indicating that the time to encode a word influences the time spent fixating on the word. These data strongly suggest that the signal to move on to the next word is often something from the word encoding system indicating that the fixated word has been encoded and it's time to move to the next word. This seems to be quite consistent with the serial word-by-word processing assumption.

However, there are severe time pressures that make such a process difficult to explain. First, as we have seen, estimates of word-encoding time for most content words are about 200 ms. Then it takes time to program an eye movement. That is, the latency to move the eyes to a simple target (such as the onset of a light) takes about 150–175 ms (e.g., Becker & Jürgens, 1979; Rayner, Slowiaczek, Clifton, & Bertera, 1983). Even if some of this latter time is not programming the saccade but encoding the stimulus, a conservative estimate is that it takes nearly 100 ms between encoding the signal to move and actually moving the eyes. The sum of these two times thus appears to be greater than a typical fixation time in reading, which is typically just over 200 ms.

Of course, that's not the whole story, as a considerable amount of data from Chapters 4 and 5 indicated that processing of many words begins in the parafovea before they are fixated. Therefore it is possible that a serial model may be able to explain the eye movement data discussed in Chapters 4 and 5. However, saying that such a model is possible is a very weak argument. Thus the way to make a convincing argument that a serial model can explain the eye movement data is to actually implement such a model as a computer program or mathematical equation and see if it works. Indeed, when some of the present authors started developing E-Z Reader we were far from confident that we could get a model like the one described above to work if we made realistic assumptions about word-encoding time and the time to program a saccade. The fact that we have succeeded indicates that such a model is plausible. Furthermore, we will argue below that it gives the simplest account of the data and is a useful heuristic for thinking about eye movement data in reading.

Background

There are certain complexities of the model that will take a little time to explain, so perhaps the best way to start is to describe a somewhat simpler theory of eye movement control posited by Morrison (1984) that was in part the inspiration for the E-Z Reader model. Morrison never created a formal version of the model thus never tested it (although a version of it was tested by Pollatsek et al., 2006). However, the basic idea of the model is the core of the E-Z Reader model— with one key difference that we will soon come to. Morrison posited the following sequence of events on a fixation. First, the reader focuses attention on the word that is fixated. Second, when that word is identified, two events occur simultaneously: (1) a signal is sent out to the attentional system to shift attention to the next word, and (2) a signal is sent to the eye movement system to program an eye movement to the next word. If the attentional shift occurs quickly enough, processing of the next word will begin before the saccade is made and thus before it is fixated.

Thus such a model can account for the effects discussed in Chapters 4 and 5 indicating that you get a benefit from seeing a word before you actually fixate it.

Before going on, perhaps we should make some terminology clear. First, we will use the term *attention* to refer to an internal process that is focusing on one word at a time—but not necessarily where the eyes are pointed. Second, it will be convenient if we refer to the word that is currently fixated as word n, the word to the right as word n+1, the word after that as word n+2, etc.

So far we have a model that can explain several important aspects of reading. First, as we have documented, variables such as the frequency of a word in the language influence the time spent fixating the word. Morrison's model explains that naturally because identification of a word is the signal to make an eye movement to the next word. Second, as we indicated above, it also explains how one gets benefit from a preview of the word to the right. The model also explains why the word to the left of the fixated word doesn't affect eye movements, as moving-window experiments have documented. The model, as stated so far, however, has an obvious shortcoming: it doesn't explain how words can be skipped.

Morrison thought about this problem and incorporated an ingenious mechanism to explain word skipping. It was inspired by landmark experiments in saccadic control by Becker and Jürgens (1979). These experiments did not involve reading, but instead had participants make saccadic eye movements to points of light that jumped discretely. The key conditions in these experiment were "double-step" conditions in which the point of light moved from the original fixation location (location 1) to location 2 and then to location 3 (where all locations were on an imaginary horizontal line, with location 3 further from location 1 than location 2 was). The participants were initially fixating location 1 and then were asked to fixate location 2 and then location 3. Obviously, if the light appears in location 2 about 1 second after it appears in location 1 and then appears 1 second later in location 3, then the participant will first fixate location 2 and then fixate location 3. However, what happens if the light appears in location 3 soon after it appears in location 2? Will they still fixate location 2? Becker and Jürgens's data indicated that it depends on the timing: for long temporal gaps between locations 2 and 3, participants fixated location 2 and then location 3, whereas for short gaps, they only fixated location 3. (For some intermediate gaps they sometimes fixated an intermediate location, but neither Morrison nor our subsequent modeling attempted to incorporate this phenomenon as it would make the model much more complex and harder to use as an analytical tool.)

Morrison adapted the explanation that Becker and Jürgens developed for these data to reading. Becker and Jürgens claimed that when an eye movement is initially programmed it is in a labile state and can be interrupted or altered. Thus, if the light in location 3 appears early enough after the light in location 2 occurs, then the saccade that has been programmed to location 2 is cancelled and replaced by the program to make a saccade to location 3. On the other hand, if at some point the saccade program to location 2 has progressed far enough so that it is no longer labile or cancellable, then the execution of this saccade will go ahead, followed quickly by a saccade to location 3.

What does this all have to do with reading and skipping words? Words are typically skipped if they are easy to process: short, high frequency in the language, and/or predictable. Thus, consider what happens if word n+1 can be processed very quickly (e.g., if it is the word *the*). In that case the reader is fixating word n, and at some point shifts attention to word n+1 and programs a saccade to word n+1. But then word n+1 is quickly processed, and attention shifts to word n+2 and an eye movement is programmed to word n+2. If this second saccade program is initiated soon enough after the first, the first program will be cancelled and word n+1 will be skipped. Again, this would only happen when word n+1 can be processed very quickly. An intermediate state would be where word n+1 is fairly easy to process so that it is fully identified while still fixating word n (but not soon enough to cancel the saccade to word n+1), and then there would be a quite brief fixation on word n+1 followed by a saccade to word n+2.

We will return to this mechanism for skipping below, but for the moment please accept it as a plausible mechanism for how words can be skipped even though readers are only processing one word at a time. We have gone into Morrison's model in some detail to try to make clear that a serial processing model of word recognition with few assumptions has a serious chance of explaining how cognitive processing controls eye movements in reading. Specifically, it can, in principle, explain two of the important facts about reading: (1) some limited information ahead of the fixated word is processed—a word or at most two words; (2) words are skipped, and not randomly—short frequent words and predictable words are a lot more likely to be skipped than words that are more difficult to encode. However, as we will indicate below, there are problems with Morrison's model that indicate that its encoding assumptions are too simple. It also lacks any mechanism to explain why words are ever fixated more than once. Nonetheless, the E-Z Reader model can be viewed as an extension and an implementation of Morrison's model that can be used to fit and explain reading data quantitatively.

Outline of the model

Before getting into the details of the E-Z Reader model, we should state again what it is attempting to model. Specifically, it is not intended as a "deep" model of the cognitive processing that goes on during reading. The only important assumption in the model that bears on cognitive processing is that only one word is processed at a time. The model does not attempt to explain how words are identified or explain any other cognitive operation in reading. It merely assumes that these processes are somehow accomplished, but it does make some assumptions about how certain variables influence the speed of word identification. Thus it is primarily a model of how the cognitive processes that underlie word recognition talk to the eye movement system and control the pattern of eye movements.

We are not claiming that this model is accurate in every detail. However, we think it is a good approximation to reality and is a very good heuristic device for thinking about the patterns of eye movements in reading. Among other things, it provides a good framework for identifying those other patterns of eye movements in reading that cannot be explained by successful or unsuccessful identification of words, and it also provides a scaffold for thinking about how such phenomena do indeed influence the movement of the eyes during reading. An obvious phenomenon that is beyond the scope of the earlier versions of E-Z Reader is interword regressions (i.e., regressive eye movements back to a prior word). As a result, the bulk of the data that we have attempted to fit with E-Z Reader are the eye movement records from sentences in which there were no interword regressions. However, as noted earlier, a recent version of the E-Z Reader model has attempted to model some interword regressions (Reichle, Warren, & McConnell, 2009). We will briefly discuss this in a later section of this chapter.

Conceptually, the E-Z Reader model is basically the same as Morrison's model. There is only one key difference: E-Z Reader assumes that there are separate "triggers" for the shift of covert attention to the next word and for a saccade to be made to the next word. Other than that, it is just filling in needed detail and adding a mechanism to explain how words are refixated. As we argued above, this filling in of detail and quantitative modeling is important because it is a demonstration that such a serial processing model can explain how eye movements are controlled in reading. Among other things, this modeling shows that the fact that variables such as word length and word frequency have clear influences on measures such as gaze duration is not an accident; instead it indicates that these measures are very closely tied to (though not identical to) word-encoding time.

As indicated above, the key assumption of the E-Z Reader model that differs from Morrison's model is that there are separate triggers for shifting attention to the next word to the right and for programming a saccadic eye movement to that word (see Figure 6.1). We will first discuss why such an assumption seems plausible and then discuss the data that we think make it necessary. More specifically, the E–Z Reader model assumes that there are three stages of word processing. The first stage (V) is the extraction of the raw visual information from the retina when a new fixation begins. This can be conceived of as a roughly automatic stage that occurs in parallel across the retina. Among other things, such raw information about word n+1 is used in programming where to make the next fixation. However, the following two lexical processing stages, L_1 and L_2, require focused, attentional, processing. They are not conceptually distinct cognitive stages in the sense that

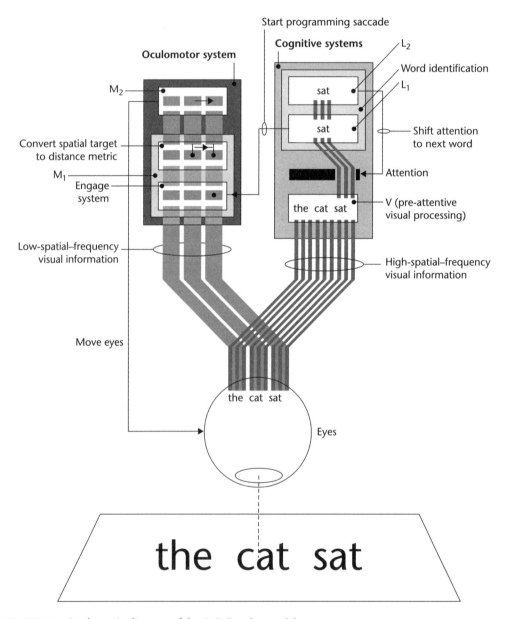

FIGURE 6.1   A schematic diagram of the E–Z Reader model

different types of processing are done in them, however. Instead, they are best conceived of as two different degrees of completion of the process of identification of a word. (We will return later to discuss why we think that there is no clear conceptual distinction between the processing that leads to the completion of L_1 and L_2.) By the end of the final stage, L_2, identification of the word is complete; thus attention can shift to begin processing the next word without any confusion. In contrast, the end of the first lexical stage of processing, L_1 is not a "magic moment" at which a word is identified. Instead it is a time when the cognitive system makes a decision that processing of the word is close enough to completion so that it is "safe" to program an eye movement to the next word.

We need to add a brief technical point here. For convenience in doing the modeling, we treat L_1 and L_2 as consecutive serial stages each having a duration influenced by various parameters of the words being read, such as their frequency in the language and the number of letters in them; however, we do not think of them as qualitatively different processes. Thus, in particular, not only is the duration of L_1 (i.e., the time when the reader knows that it is safe to program an eye movement) influenced by these variables, but the duration of L_2 (the time between when the eye movement is programmed and when the word is actually identified) is also influenced by these variables.

Why might such a two-stage mechanism evolve? Why not simply have a single signal do both jobs (as in Morrison's model)? We think that the reason that the system has an L_1 stage to trigger the eye movement rather than having the L_2 stage do both jobs is that the L_1 stage is a "cheat" that has evolved in the course of developing the highly practiced skill of reading, to speed up the process (Reichle & Laurent, 2006). This is plausible because there is a considerable latency between triggering a saccade to the next word and actually making the saccade (at least 100 ms). Thus, if one can reliably detect when processing of a fixated word is close to completion something like 100 ms before word identification is complete, processing of the fixated word will complete before the saccade occurs. More generally, unless arriving at the "safe to program a saccade" decision at the completion of L_1 is both slow and unreliable, this process will almost always allow time—both for completion of processing the fixated word and starting the processing of the next word— before actually making the eye movement to the next word. However, with such a cheat, readers will be fixating a word (where the visual information can be processed most rapidly) soon after attention has moved to that word. It is possible that beginning readers have not yet developed this strategy and thus do not have such a two-stage process. However, this hypothesis has not been tested.

The above argument indicates why separate mechanisms for shifting attention and programming saccades might be beneficial. In addition, when the model was developed, there were data indicating that separate mechanisms were necessary to explain the reading data. In particular, there was a finding by Henderson and Ferreira (1990) that has been replicated many times (Drieghe, Rayner, & Pollatsek, 2005; Kennison & Clifton, 1995; White, Rayner, & Liversedge, 2005b) indicating that when word n is more difficult to process (e.g., is a low-frequency word), the fixation times on not only word n but also on word n+1 are lengthened. (However, the frequency effect on word n+1 is considerably smaller than the effect on word n.) Such a spillover phenomenon (i.e., aspects of word n influencing fixation times on word n+1) is incompatible with Morrison's model. That is, if there were a single trigger for both the saccadic program to word n+1 and the shift of attention to word n+1, then attention would shift to word n+1 a fixed amount of time, T_a, after this "triggering moment." In turn, the actual eye movement to word n+1 would also occur a fixed amount of time, T_b, after the triggering moment. Thus the amount of time that the reader would have to preview word n+1 while fixating word n would simply be equal to T_b minus T_a and thus be independent of any characteristics of word n. This is not the case; the difficulty of processing word n+1 is affected by the difficulty of processing word n.

The E–Z Reader model explains the delayed effect of word n difficulty on fixation time on word n+1 by positing that the difference in time between the eye movement signal and the covert attention movement signal is determined by the duration of the L_2 stage, and that the L_2 stage (which is the difference in time between the eye movement signal and the shift of attention) is longer for more difficult words. Thus, when L_2 is long, the signal to shift attention to word n+1 and begin processing it is delayed relative to when the signal to move the eyes was sent out, and there is less time to process word n+1 before fixating it. This means that more time is needed to process that word when it is fixated. Explaining such spillover effects, however, is not the only reason why we now think that one needs to posit separate L_1 and L_2 stages in order to explain the reading data. When the E–Z Reader model was compared to a one-stage model like Morrison's (Pollatsek et al. 2006), it was found that, in order for a one-stage model to work, one needed to posit that information was extracted much too efficiently from the parafovea and, as a result, the preview benefit it predicted was far greater than that observed and reported in Chapters 4 and 5.

The assumption of separate L_1 and L_2 stages was tested in an experiment by Reingold and Rayner (2006) that followed from an ingenious prediction by Reingold (2003). He predicted that if a stimulus manipulation only affected the early stages of word identification, it should only affect the duration of the L_1 stage. If so, then this manipulation should only have an effect on processing time on the word manipulated and not affect any other aspects of eye movement behavior when reading a sentence. Although there may be no manipulation that completely meets this ideal, one of the manipulations that Reingold and Rayner employed was close. A given target word in a sentence was either presented in the normal font and normal contrast from the background or it was presented faintly (i.e., the contrast between the word and the background was significantly reduced). They found that the time spent fixating the faintly presented words was quite a bit greater than the normally presented target words (i.e., the gaze duration on the normal target word was about 260 ms whereas it was about 380 ms for the faintly presented target word). However, there was virtually no increase of fixation time on the next word for the faintly presented word, nor was there any other significant effect on any other subsequent eye movement measure. Thus, consistent with the two-stage encoding assumption of the E–Z Reader model, if only early processing stages of word encoding are affected by a stimulus variable, these effects will only be seen on fixation time measures on that word. More generally, of course, this result favors a model that processes words in series, as one would expect most parallel processing models to predict that the effect of the difficulty produced by making a word faint would be smeared out over the fixation times on several words.

This two-stage assumption of word processing, and how this processing is connected to the eye movement and internal attentional systems, is the only substantive difference between the E–Z Reader model and Morrison's model. What follows is mainly filling in details. The first important detail is that we have not indicated how the E–Z Reader model predicts that words are skipped. Although some skipping is the result of saccades that do not land where the reader targeted them (see below), the key mechanism for explaining skipping in the E–Z Reader model is that one saccade can cancel another (as outlined above when discussing Morrison's work). Formally, this is dealt with in the model by positing that there are two stages in a saccadic program (represented by M_1 and M_2 in Figure 6.1). Before the M_1 stage is completed, the saccade to word n+1 is still in its labile stage and can be cancelled by the initiation of a later saccadic program. However, after the M_1 stage is completed, the saccadic program can no longer be cancelled and will be executed when the M_2 stage is completed. The completed saccade is indicated in Figure 6.1 by the solid arrow from M_2 to the eye. If the M_2 stage of the program to fixate word n+1 is completed, this is a saccade to word n+1. However, if the signal to make a saccade to word n+2 occurs when the saccade program to word n+1 is still in the M_1 stage, the saccade will be to word n+2.

The second important detail is that we have not yet described a mechanism to explain why a word is ever refixated. The details of the mechanisms we have considered have changed slightly over iterations of the E–Z Reader model, but the basic idea of the mechanism is analogous to the mechanism described above to deal with word skipping. The saccadic program to refixate (like all saccadic programs) also is assumed to have an M_1 and an M_2 stage. The earlier versions of the model simply posited that, when one landed on a word, a refixation (directed to the center of the word) was automatically programmed. This would account for refixations (we discuss refinements below). However, the model doesn't predict that words are always refixated. When a word is relatively easy to process (e.g., when it is short and relatively high in frequency), the eye movement program to fixate word n+1 will come shortly enough after this automatic refixation program to be able to cancel it. However, if the word is harder to process, it is more likely that the refixation program proceeds to the M_2 stage before the L_1 stage of word identification is completed, and the refixation saccade is executed. Thus this mechanism can naturally explain why words that are easier to process are refixated less often.

This is the essence of the E–Z Reader model. There are a few further details that are worth spelling out because they are also relevant to some theoretical controversies and make an important practical point. They relate to where a saccade is targeted and where it actually lands. E–Z Reader assumes that the signal to make a saccade to word n+1 (the arrow between L_1 and the "engage system" box in Figure 6.1) is a signal to make a saccade to the middle letter of word n+1. (This assumption might be wrong for really long words, where the targeted location might be to somewhere to the left of the middle of the word.) This makes sense because, if you fixate on the middle of a word, you minimize the average distance the letters of the word are from the fixation point. As indicated in earlier chapters, the further letter information is from the fovea, the slower and less accurate the extraction of information is. E–Z Reader, as a result, posits that the further a letter is from fixation, the slower the processing of that letter is. This assumption is sufficient to explain both qualitatively and quantitatively why longer words take longer to process. As a result, the E–Z Reader model does not need to make an explicit assumption that longer words take more time to process; this relationship just follows from this loss of processing efficiency because the letters in longer words will be, on average, further from fixation than the letters of shorter words.

Eye movement execution, however, like any other motor act, is not perfect; thus the actual location of the next fixation is not necessarily where the eye movement is targeted. Instead, extensive analyses of eye movements by McConkie, Kerr, Reddix, and Zola (1988) indicate that there are two types of errors that are made in eye movement programming. The first, and obvious, kind of error is random error. That is, when one programs a fixation to a target, one doesn't hit it exactly. Instead, where the saccade actually lands is a roughly normal distribution of locations around a central value. The second type of saccadic error in reading is systematic error. In reading, the average length of a forward saccadic eye movement is approximately seven to eight letters. McConkie et al.'s data showed that eye movements in reading tended to regress to this value. That is, readers tend to overshoot intended short saccades and tend to undershoot intended long saccades. Therefore, in making a sequence of saccadic eye movements, there is a tendency for the length of the saccades to approximate the length of the average saccade. (This pattern is also true of many other motor movements when one is making a series of movements.) This tendency to overshoot short saccades is one reason why short words are skipped: sometimes, the reader may intend to fixate a short word but overshoot it and skip it. However, if this occurs, the reader's internal attention will be focused on the short word even though it was skipped. This is a special case of an important point about eye movements in reading: It is not always the case that the word that is fixated is the word attended to—even at the beginning of a fixation.

Another modification in later versions of the E–Z Reader model relates to the fact that the eyes are not usually exactly where the reader intended them to be. Earlier models assumed that there was an automatic refixation program to the center of the word that was initiated at the beginning of a fixation. This seemed too simplistic, and later versions posited that the refixations aimed at the center of the word are programmed probabilistically, with the probability of initiating a refixation program being greater the further the initial fixation is from the center of the word (which is the optimal viewing location; see Chapter 4). This assumption is consistent with the intuition that the more difficulty readers have extracting the information they want, the more quickly they sense a need to refixate. Moreover, it is consistent with the data that if an initial fixation is further from the center of a word (a) the probability of refixating the word is greater and (b) that the duration of the first fixation is shorter (Rayner, Sereno, & Raney, 1996; Vitu, McConkie, Kerr, & O'Regan, 2001).

We have now covered the essence of the E-Z Reader model. It has undergone several changes over the years since it was first proposed (for a comprehensive review, see Reichle, 2011). However, the basic assumptions have remained the same—most importantly the assumption that readers are only processing one word at a time. This book is not the appropriate place to detail the quantitative assumptions of the model. (For more details, see Reichle et al., 1998, and Pollatsek et al., 2006.) However, it may be worthwhile to spend some time indicating how one would test such a model. Before we do so, however, we review the key assumptions of the model:

1. An internal attention mechanism focuses on one word at a time, going through the words in the text in the order that they would be spoken (e.g., from left to right in English).
2. The signal to move the internal attention mechanism to the next word is completion of the identification of the attended word.
3. The signal to program a saccade to the next word is a less complete stage of identification of the attended word.
4. These processes continue so that it is reasonably likely that two words can be completely processed on a single fixation and a saccade program is initiated to word n+2. Moreover it is possible, though less likely, that attention could also shift to word n+2.
5. A later program for a saccade can cancel an earlier program if the later program occurs soon enough after the earlier program. Thus a word can be skipped if the program to fixate word n+2 occurs soon enough after the program to fixate word n+1.
6. Refixations are more-or-less automatically programmed when one lands on a word. However, if the program to fixate word n+1 occurs soon enough, the refixation saccade will be cancelled and the word will not be refixated.
7. The target for a saccade is the middle of a word. However, there are both systematic and random deviations of where the eye actually lands from this target point. Thus the actual pattern of fixation points is distributed across a word (although more probably somewhere near the center, or a little to left of center; Rayner, 1979). Also, because of these deviations, it is possible that the word landed on may be different from the one targeted.
8. Higher-order language processes intervene only when they sense that the meaning of the discourse is not being processed, and they generally either keep the reader at a location until the problem is solved or direct the reader back to the prior text to help resolve the difficulty. These assumptions have not been discussed yet. Although a full explanation of higher-order language processes is well beyond the scope of the model, there is some recent work (Reichle, Warren, & McConnell, 2009) that attempts to explain some regressions due to failures of understanding that we will briefly discuss at the end of the chapter.

The process of modeling reading behavior

So far, we have claimed that the E-Z Reader indeed predicts reading behavior quite well, but we have not been clear about what we mean by that. There are different ways to assess reading behavior, but the one we have generally chosen is the following. We have taken the reading data from experiments in which participants read a sentence for meaning. The set of data we have often attempted to model is by Schilling, Rayner, and Chumbley (1998) in which there are specific target words of varying frequency. In this original study the sentence contexts in which the target words appeared were not controlled. However, in a later study (Rayner, Ashby, Pollatsek, & Reichle, 2004) the contexts were controlled, and the data and the ability of the model to fit the data were quite similar. In the Rayner et al. study either a high-frequency word or a low-frequency word (of the same length) appeared in the same location in the sentence. The sentences were constructed so that the target words fit into the sentences equally well as verified by rating data. This manipulation allows us to assess the effect of a frequency of a word with everything else controlled. (However, a given participant saw only one version of the sentence.) Part of our test of the model was to examine how well the model could predict various measures on the target words such as gaze duration and first fixation duration. We also modeled the data from all the words of these sentences except for the first and last words. (The first words are excluded because the reader is taking time finding the word, and the last words are excluded because the trial ends with a manual response, indicating that the sentence has been comprehended, rather than by an eye movement trigger.) Obviously, relevant aspects of the non-target words were not as well controlled as the target words (such as how well they fit in the sentence), but we wanted to determine whether the E-Z Reader model was also giving a good global fit of all the data.

Our modeling then attempts to recapture the properties of the data in two ways. As in any model of this type, there are various free parameters such as the duration of the L_1 and L_2 stages, the time it takes to program a saccade, the duration during the saccade program when it can be cancelled by another saccade program, a parameter determining how rapidly acuity falls off as you go away from the fixation point. Some of these parameters are simply time values, but in other cases, such as the duration of the L_1 and L_2 stages, we assume a functional relation between an objective measure, such as word frequency, and the duration of the stages. (In this case we assume that the duration of the L_1 and L_2 stages are each linear functions of the logarithm of the frequency of the word.) In this case the free parameters are the slope and intercept of this linear function, but in general, parameters can be values in a function relating performance to an objective value such as the distance of a letter from the fixation point.

We then take the data and attempt to adjust the parameters of the model to come up with a best fit of the data. This fitting exercise attempts to minimize the sum of squared deviations between the observed value for a measure (such as gaze duration on a word) and what the model predicts. Moreover, the measure we are using for assessing goodness of fit is summing these squared deviations over all the words of the corpus and over a whole set of measures, such as first fixation duration, gaze duration, and the probability of fixating a word. The model is complex enough that there is no algebraic method for computing these best-fitting parameters. (This is typical for models like these.) Instead the way one determines the best-fitting parameter values is to do many simulations where one varies parameter values within a reasonable range (e.g., one would restrict the model's saccade latency parameter to the range 100–150 ms). One then takes the simulation with the best fit (i.e., the smallest summed squared deviations between predicted and observed values) as "the best simulation," and takes the parameter values from this simulation as the most likely parameter values.

Determining whether the model does a good job, however, is not merely looking at this goodness-of-fit value and seeing whether it is appropriately small. One wants to see whether the model accurately captures certain regularities. One we have focused on is whether the model accurately predicts the frequency effect (e.g., whether it correctly predicts the difference in gaze duration between high-frequency words and low-frequency words). For the Schilling et al. corpus, we attempted to answer that question in two ways. First, we divided all the words of the corpus (not only the target words) into five frequency classes and examined the mean observed and predicted values on a measure (such as gaze duration) for words of each of the frequency classes. Then we used these parameter values to predict the frequency effect for the target words, which were controlled on a number of variables (e.g., length in terms of number of letters). The E-Z Reader model indeed does a good job in capturing both the absolute values of fixation times and fixation probabilities and the size of the frequency effects, both on the actual word and spillover effects (see Table 6.1). In addition, the model (using the same parameters) also successfully predicts the variability in the fixation durations over participants and trials (see Figure 6.2). However, you may be wondering whether this is an empty exercise. That is, as we have explicitly built into the model that word-processing times are a function of word frequency and predictability, isn't it obvious that the model will predict this?

The answer is, in some sense, "yes and no." That is, because these assumptions were built into the model, it is essentially a given that it will be able to predict some sort of frequency effects. However, it is by no means a given that such a model could successfully predict the sizes of the frequency effects simultaneously with predicting the correct absolute values for the fixation times and fixation probabilities. More importantly, as indicated earlier, when we started on our modeling exercise we were by no means certain that any model that made these strong serial assumptions could predict reading data. That is, if one takes realistic values for word-encoding time and realistic values for eye movement programming time, it is by no means certain that there is room to predict that the processing of a word (and the duration of this processing as affected by word frequency) can act quickly enough to predict effects on fixation times that are on the order of 200–250 ms. However, we think the parameter values we selected are quite reasonable (see Table 6.2).

TABLE 6.1 Observed (Schilling et al., 1998) and predicted (E-Z Reader 9) mean fixation durations (ms) and fixation probability measures for five frequency classes of words

		Word frequency (# occurrences per million)				
		1–10	*11–100*	*101–1000*	*1001–10,000*	*10,001+*
Gaze durations	Observed	293	272	256	234	214
	E-Z Reader 9	295	275	241	220	216
First fixation durations	Observed	248	234	228	223	208
	E-Z Reader 9	251	239	225	217	214
Single fixation durations	Observed	265	249	243	235	216
	E-Z Reader 9	259	244	226	217	215
Probability of making one fixation	Observed	.68	.70	.68	.44	.32
	E-Z Reader 9	.75	.74	.75	.52	.42
Probability of making two fixations	Observed	.20	.16	.10	.02	.01
	E-Z Reader 9	.15	.13	.06	.01	.00
Probability of skipping	Observed	.10	.13	.22	.55	.67
	E-Z Reader 9	.09	.12	.19	.47	.58

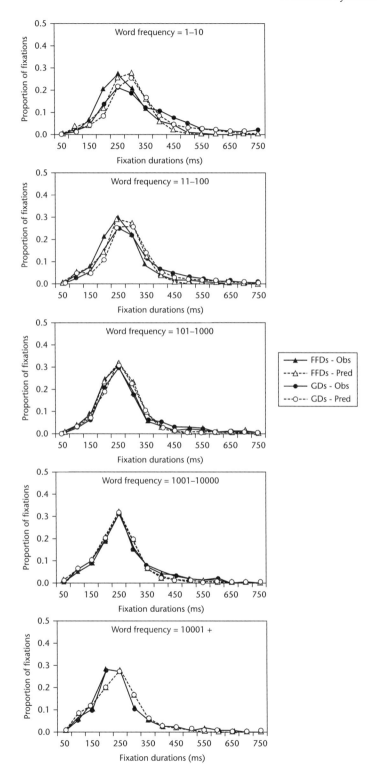

FIGURE 6.2 Observed (Schilling et al., 1998) and predicted (E-Z Reader 9) first fixation duration (FFD) and gaze duration (GD) distributions for five frequency classes of words

TABLE 6.2 E-Z Reader parameter interpretations and default values

Type of processing	Parameter	Interpretation	Default value[a]
Word identification	α_1	mean maximum L_1 time (ms)	98
	α_2	effect of $\log_e$ frequency on L_1 time (ms)	2
	α_3	effect of predictability on L_1 time (ms)	27
	Δ	proportional differences between L_1 and L_2 durations	0.25
	A	mean attention-shift time (ms)	50
Higher-level language processing	I	mean integration time (ms)	25
	P_F	probability of integration failure	0.1
	P_N	probability of regression being directed to prior word	0.5
Saccadic programming & execution	M_1	mean labile programming time (ms)	125
	ξ	proportion of M_1 allocated to "preparatory" sub-stage	0.5
	$M_{1,R}$	additional time rerquired for labile regressive programs (ms)	30
	M_2	mean non-labile programming time (ms)	25
	Ψ	optimal saccade length (character spaces)	7
	Ω_1	effect of launch-site fixation duration of systematic error	7.3
	Ω_2	effect of launch-site fixation duration of systematic error	3
	η_1	mean maximum random error (character spaces)	0.5
	η_2	effect of saccade length on random error (character spaces)	0.15
	λ	increase in refixation probability (character spaces)	0.05
	S	saccade duration (ms)	25
Visual processing	V	eye-to-brain transmission time (ms)	50
	ε	effect of visual acuity	1.15
General	σ_γ	standard deviation of gamma distributions	0.22

[a] There is no simple meaning to the "default" values of parameters. These values are all values that were used in obtaining the best-fitting values. Some of these values, such as α_1, α_2 and α_3, were allowed to vary during the simulation and are best-fitting values for this simulation. However, others such as V, S, and Ψ were chosen to be plausible values or estimated from prior literature.

A basic issue: What is the unit of processing that is driving the eyes?

Up until now we have assumed that a word is a sequence of letters between spaces and that the unit of processing that is being digested and allowing processing to continue is determined solely by spaces. In Chapter 5, however, we discussed experiments (e.g., Drieghe et al., 2010) that indicate that long compound words appear to be processed in segments. One indication of this is that participants are generally unaware of display changes. This was true even within the compound word, when the display change occurred on the saccade that took the reader from the first to the second constituent of the word. The second indication of it is that gaze duration on the first constituent of the word was unaffected by a "bad" preview of the second constituent. (However, gaze durations on the second constituent were substantially longer when the preview was bad.) Moreover, the gaze duration on the first constituent was affected by the frequency of this constituent as a word in isolation.

This pattern of results may almost seem like magic. That is, how can it be that there is no effect of the second constituent when the reader is fixating the first constituent given that he or she doesn't magically know that the word is a compound word when it is first fixated? There is a plausible explanation for the data; however, this is just a verbal explanation and hasn't been tested using the E–Z Reader model (but for a similar demonstration involving Finnish compound words, see Pollatsek, Reichle, & Rayner, 2003). The first step is to concede that the reader doesn't magically know the word is a compound word when it is first fixated, but that at some fairly early point in processing (perhaps helped out by processing of the word in the parafovea) the reader determines that the first part of the compound word is a word and narrows the window of attention to that region. This results in the following: (a) the trigger of a saccade to the next region is changed to the L_1 stage of processing the first constituent, (b) the target of that saccade is changed to the middle of the second constituent, and (c) the trigger for a shift of attention to the second constituent is the completion of the L_2 stage of the first constituent. In the Drieghe et al. (2010) experiment the preview effects on the gaze duration of the second constituent were quite a bit larger than for the usual preview effect (i.e., when the preview of word n+1 is manipulated). This is plausibly due to the initial period during the first fixation on the word (i.e., before the reader has segmented the word into the two constituents) when the letter information from all letters in the word was being extracted.

Experiments like this indicate that, in some cases, a unit smaller than the word may be the unit of processing and all that is attended to at one time. It also does not seem implausible that short frequent word combinations such as *to the* could be processed as units. Some support for such a word-grouping mechanism was provided by Radach (1996), who found a single normal distribution of initial landing sites on two adjacent words. However, Drieghe, Pollatsek, Staub, and Rayner (2008) replicated this finding when the first word was a three-letter article, but they did not replicate it when it was a content word. Drieghe et al.'s data show, at the least, that word grouping does not occur solely on the basis of word length, and they show further that the landing site distributions can be modeled by simply assuming that function words are skipped more often than content words. In addition, whether contractions such as *didn't* are processed as one word or as two is still an open question. Again, we emphasize that the E–Z Reader model was designed to be an approximation to reality and not an explanation of all phenomena in reading. At present it assumes that a word (the unit that is processed in parallel) is the sequence of letters between the spaces. The above data suggest that this is an oversimplification and it may have to be refined to handle polymorphemic words, highly frequent word combinations, and other delimiters such as hyphens and apostrophes.

More recent refinements of the model

One issue that we did not attempt to address in earlier versions of the model is the nature of the processing that leads to completion of the L_1 and L_2 stages. Instead we simply posited that their duration was a function of word frequency. However, that leaves open the question of what level of "identification" this represents. As indicated in Chapter 3, lexical decision and naming tasks are influenced by word frequency, even though one does not know for sure that the meaning of the word has been accessed when the program to make the response in these tasks has been initiated. Indeed, when we started our modeling enterprise we thought that an attractive possibility for the distinction between the L_1 and L_2 stages was that the former stage represented completion of a superficial level of identification (either the moment that you have made contact with the lexicon or that you have accessed the phonological representation) and that the latter stage represented the moment when one has accessed the meaning of the word.

In modeling the data of Duffy et al. (1988) on processing lexically ambiguous words such as *bank*, however, it became clear that this characterization had to be wrong. In particular, these data indicated that even the first fixation durations on the target word were influenced by whether the prior text disambiguated the meaning of the ambiguous word. Such a finding would be incompatible with the assumption that the L_1 stage was only sensitive to the orthographic or phonological identification of the word. These data, however, were successfully modeled by assuming that both the L_1 and L_2 stages were affected by getting to the word's meaning (Reichle, Rayner, & Pollatsek, 2007). In particular, Reichle et al. assumed that there was conflict between the two meanings that affected how long this semantic identification stage took. That is, when one of the meanings was much more frequent and the prior context was neutral with respect to which meaning was correct, the dominant meaning was recognized virtually as quickly as a word with a single meaning. In contrast, when the two meanings of the word were about equally frequent, there was conflict and thus meaning identification was slowed relative to an unambiguous word. However, when prior context favored the less frequent meaning, it increased the conflict and thus slowed the time to identify the meaning of the word. In contrast, when prior context favored one of the two meanings of an ambiguous word with equally frequent meanings, it reduced the conflict and shortened the fixation time on the word. Whether this is the ultimate explanation of these data is, of course, an open question. However, we are discussing it for two reasons. First, it indicates that it was not hard to adapt the E-Z Reader to explain phenomena that go beyond simple word frequency effects. Second, we hope it underlines the point that the eyes are extremely sensitive to the meaning of the text; not only is fixation time on a word influenced by the meaning of a word, but how this meaning interacts with the prior text.

As indicated earlier, a second refinement to the E-Z Reader model that has been made is to start to account for interword regressions due to failures of comprehension that go beyond the level of understanding the meanings of individual words (Reichle, Warren, & McConnell, 2009). As we have not yet discussed the experiments that this refinement deals with, we will just sketch the basic idea. The general phenomenon that we believe causes these interword regressions is when the reader encounters a word and comprehends the meaning of the word but that, in spite of that, the sentence including that word either does not make sense or does not seem grammatical.

A clear example of a word not making sense is *Jane used a pump to inflate the large carrot* (from Rayner, Warren, Juhasz, & Liversedge, 2004). Here the problem is not that the person is having trouble with knowing what *carrot* means; instead it is that it doesn't make sense given the prior context. Such anomalies cause extended gaze durations on the target word (e.g., *carrot*) and they also cause immediate regressions back to the prior text (Rayner et al., 2004). They also commonly result in the eyes moving forward to the next word in the text followed by a regression to prior text. It is quite remarkable that the response to such an anomaly is as rapid as it is. The way that Reichle, Warren, & McConnell, (2009) attempted to model such situations is to add another stage in the E-Z Reader model (the "integration" box at the top of Figure 6.3) that is after the L_2 stage; it decides whether the text up to this point "computes." There are two possible ways in which processing in this stage can produce a regression. One is that a decision is made that there is something wrong and a regression should be programmed. The second is that if the length of this third "integration" stage exceeds a threshold, a signal is made to the eye movement system to make a regression.

In short, Reichle et al. posited two checking mechanisms that monitor comprehension of the text beyond the level of the meaning of the word that is attended to. The first is a relatively rapid computation that there is something wrong (e.g., carrots can't be blown up with pumps) and thus

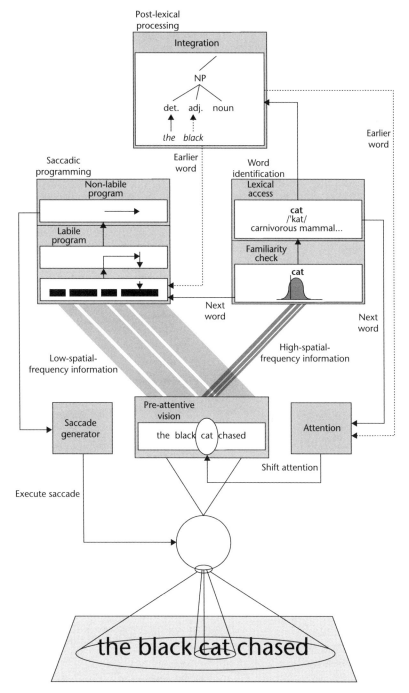

FIGURE 6.3   A schematic diagram of E-Z Reader 10

there is a need for immediate repair. The second is a more delayed mechanism where the reader is trying to fit the word into the prior context and realizes that the fitting operation still isn't complete after a reasonable amount of time (e.g., after the next word in the sentence has been identified), so that it is best to go back and determine what the problem is. As the next few chapters discuss, there may be a need for more than the second mechanism, as there are data indicating that the more serious the anomaly or problem, the more rapid the regression is. If the only mechanism causing regressions was one in which one decided to regress if too much time had elapsed and the text still didn't make sense, the seriousness of the problem might not affect the latency of the regression. Whether this particular mechanism is a good one for explaining regressions is another open question as it has not been seriously compared to other possibilities. However, it seems to be promising.

We need to make two points here about interword regressions. The first is that it is not strictly true to say that the basic E-Z Reader model does not predict any interword regressions. That is, because there are errors of targeting saccades, there are times when the reader intends to fixate word n but instead fixates word n+1. Especially if word n is difficult to process, a saccade program will occur to refixate it—because the initial saccade was on the wrong word, the refixation will be a regression from word n+1 to word n. However, because it seems clear that such a mechanism only accounts for a small percentage of interword regressions, we ignored sentences with interword regressions in our early modeling as being beyond the scope of the model.

The second point is that ultimately explaining and modeling the pattern of eye movements in sentences or passages that contain interword regressions is going to be quite complex. Reichle, Warren, & McConnell (2009) only attempted to model the regression and not the complete pattern of data after the regression. It seems clear that modeling the latter will be complex. First of all, a reader may realize that what has been read so far does not make sense, but may have little idea about where the source of the difficulty is. Did they just misidentify a key word? Did they get the wrong sense or meaning of a key word? Or is the problem more basic so that the whole passage needs to be reread? Even if readers have an idea of the source of difficulty (e.g., they misread a key word) they may have only an approximate idea of how far back that word was, and thus there will be considerable variability in where the regressive fixation goes. However, even if that problem is solved, one needs a good theory of "repair" to know what the subsequent series of eye movements would be. We are not claiming that explaining interword regressions is impossible—only that it is difficult and likely beyond our present understanding of how the meaning of text is computed.

Conclusions: E-Z Reader and other models

This chapter has introduced the E-Z Reader model in some detail, largely to provide you with a conceptual framework for thinking about how the pattern of eye movements is connected to cognitive processing. As we have tried to make clear in the chapter, we are not claiming that the model is the ultimate explanation of how the reading process works. However, we do feel that it is a plausible explanation for the forward movement of the eyes through the text, and that there are no data from the reading literature that seriously challenge it as an adequate model of that process, at least in alphabetic languages. Indeed, even though most of the tests of the E-Z Reader model have been in (American) English, it has been shown to give a good fit to French reading data as well (Miellet, Sparrow, & Sereno, 2007). Moreover, as indicated in the last section, we think that it can be built upon in the next 10 years to offer a more complete explanation for reading, especially when there are comprehension failures at a more global level such as those discussed in Chapters 8 and 9. An adequate model of reading in languages that have no spaces between words, such as Chinese, may be more difficult because it is less clear how saccades should be targeted. However, an extension of the E-Z Reader model (Rayner, Li, & Pollatsek, 2007) indicated that the basic ideas of the model may be applicable to Chinese.

As we noted in Chapter 5, there are alternative quantitative models of eye movements in reading that are well developed. They include Glenmore and SWIFT. These models differ from the E-Z Reader model largely because they posit that more than one word is processed at a time.

As a result, these models are far more complex than the E-Z Reader model. As we indicated in Chapter 5, we don't see any compelling evidence for such parallel processing. The SWIFT model (Engbert et al., 2005) posits that up to four words are processed at a time, and the Glenmore model posits that 30 letters plus spaces (or about four to five words) are processed at a time. We think that such extensive parallel processing is unlikely (Reichle, Liversedge et al., 2009). Moreover, one of the four words that they posit to be processed in parallel is word n-1; however, the moving-window experiments discussed in Chapter 4 indicate that generally little useful information is extracted from the left of the fixated word.[1] In addition, if several words are processed in parallel, the decisions of when and where to move the eyes become considerably more complex than in E-Z Reader. In the SWIFT model the decision to move is largely based on an autonomous "clock" mechanism that is modulated by the relative activation of the words that are being processed in parallel. The equations that handle this timing are quite complex and the pattern that they predict often depends on the particular parameter values that are used. In Glenmore the decision to move is based on increased excitation from a region in the parafovea. These two mechanisms are quite complex and how predictions follow from the model is often hard to understand. This contrasts with E-Z Reader (as we hope this chapter has illustrated), where the qualitative pattern of data that the model predicts is quite transparent. Of course, even in the E-Z Reader model, the details of how big an effect is depend on the parameter values selected to fit the data.

As indicated in Chapter 5, the evidence for such parallel processing that is usually put forward is "parafoveal-on-foveal effects" in which aspects of word n+1 influence fixation times on word n. We should quickly point out, however, that E-Z Reader does predict some effects that could be construed as parafoveal-on-foveal. The first is word skipping. The E-Z Reader model predicts that skipping occurs when word n+1 is processed rapidly enough so that a signal to fixate word n+2 cancels the saccade program to word n+1. Such a mechanism predicts that (everything else being equal), fixations on word n will be longer when word n+1 is skipped because a later eye movement program has cancelled an earlier eye movement program. This prediction has generally been borne out. The second way that the E-Z Reader model can predict an apparent parafoveal-on-foveal effect is in terms of mislocated fixations, to be discussed below.

The specific claim about parafoveal-on-foveal effects that would be evidence against the E-Z Reader model is that there are systematic effects of variables like the frequency of word n+1 on measures such as the gaze duration on word n. Indeed, if such effects were ubiquitous it would be evidence against the E-Z Reader model because the decision to move forward from word n in the E-Z Reader model is based on completion of the L_1 stage on word n. That is, there is no way within the E-Z Reader model that variables that affect the lexical processing of word n+1 can influence the duration of the L_1 stage on word n, because lexical processing of word n+1 does not begin until the completion of the L_2 stage on word n (which is even later in time than completion of the L_1 stage).

As we indicated in Chapter 5, however, it is by no means clear that such parafoveal-on-foveal effects are reliable (see Drieghe, 2011). Indeed, there are a number of studies that have found no influence of the frequency of the word to the right of fixation on the currently fixated word (see Rayner, 2009), although there are a few studies based on corpus analyses (in which all of the words in a text are analyzed rather than only words whose lexical properties are carefully controlled) that do show such an effect (see for example, Kliegl, Nuthmann, & Engbert, 2006). Moreover, we have indicated above that mislocated fixations might explain how there could be small apparent effects of this nature. That is, one might occasionally observe such effects when the reader intended to fixate word n+1, but undershot it and fixated word n instead. In that case, because attention is focused on word n+1, lexical properties of word n+1 would determine when a forward saccade is made. When a saccade is mistargeted like this, it is likely that the fixation on word n will be near the end of the word (as such targeting errors usually are not too large). This suggests that the most reliable parafoveal-on-foveal effects will occur when fixations are near the end of word n. We think the jury is still out on parafoveal-on-foveal effects, and that mislocated fixations may be able to account for the evidence that exists. However, if valid parafoveal-on-foveal effects are documented in the future, it would mean that the serial word-by-word processing assumption is not valid—at least in some circumstances. Until then, we see no reason to abandon this assumption.

It might be a worthwhile postscript to our discussion of parafoveal-on-foveal effects to compare and contrast three phenomena: (a) the frequency of word n+1 affecting fixation time on word n; (b) preview benefit; and (c) word skipping. That is, you might be wondering how E-Z Reader can easily predict (b) and (c) but not (a). First consider preview benefit. According to E-Z Reader, this occurs whenever attention shifts to word n+1 before the last fixation on word n has ended. This should occur most, if not all, the time, since the time spent fixating on word n between the signal to move to word n+1 and the beginning of the saccade is the time to program a saccade, which is usually about 100 ms in most of our simulations. The only way in which attention would not shift before that is if the duration of the L_2 stage was longer than that. Given that the typical L_2 stage duration in our model is 60–70 ms, this should rarely happen. (Given that both of these times are posited to vary randomly from fixation to fixation, it might occasionally happen, especially for a low-frequency word.)

Now consider word skipping. Intuitively this seems to implicate parallel processing even more than parafoveal-on-foveal effects do. However, it does not. Given the sequential processing assumption of E-Z Reader, it is possible that when word n is fixated, word n+1 can be processed up to the L_1 stage quickly enough to cancel the saccade program to word n+1 and replace it with a saccade program to word n+2. This does not happen all the time, as only very frequent, short, or predictable words are skipped more than 10% of the time. What distinguishes both of these phenomena from an effect of lexical properties of word n+1 on fixation durations on word n is that there is no "reach back." That is, both preview benefit and word skipping reflect how properties of the previous word or the word that is fixated affect the length of the fixation (or whether a fixation occurs at all), whereas the parafoveal-on-foveal effect would show that the lexical properties of an upcoming word affect fixation durations on the fixated word.

Another problem with parallel models is that, if words are processed in parallel, they can be processed out of order. However in most languages, especially a language like English that does not have much in the way of case marking (which indicates the syntactic role of a noun phrase), word order is important for understanding the meaning of a sentence (Rayner et al., 2009; Reichle, Warren, & McConnell, 2009). In addition it is hard to see how, if the order of encoding of words is not fixed, one can account for phenomena such as predictability effects. That is, predictability, as generally assessed, assumes that one has processed all the words prior to word n in order and is now predicting or somehow using this context to facilitate processing of word n. In E-Z Reader the covert attention mechanism ensures that the words in the text are processed in the correct sequence, and furthermore, except for mistargeting of saccades, it claims that all the words prior to word n have been processed prior to fixating word n+1. The E-Z Reader model does not explain how readers actually make predictions; it simply posits that there is such a computation with the hope that a deeper understanding of reading will lead to a mechanism. However, if the words prior to word n have all been processed and processed in sequence, it at least seems plausible that such a predictability computation can be done. In contrast, in parallel models one is not sure whether all of the words prior to word n have been processed. Furthermore, in these models one needs an additional mechanism for encoding the order of words in the text. As a result, if all the words prior to word n have not been fully processed (and possibly some of the sequencing information lost), it is much harder to see how the reader can predict upcoming material (Slattery, Pollatsek, & Rayner, 2007). We think that the burden of proof is on the architects of parallel models to show how such predictions can be made. We think the same problem will surface again in the phenomena discussed in the next two chapters, where many of the phenomena tacitly assume that all words prior to a target word have been processed and processed in order.

In summary, we have presented the E-Z Reader model in this much detail because we think it is a good heuristic framework for thinking about how the movement of the eyes relates to the cognitive processes underlying reading, notably to the encoding of the meanings of individual words. The next three chapters present many phenomena that go beyond this level of under-standing of the text and thus are largely beyond the current framework of the model. Nonetheless, we think that an understanding of the E-Z Reader model will serve as a good background for understanding these higher-level phenomena.

Note

1 This assumes that the text is being read left to right. As we indicated in Chapter 4, the pattern is the oppo-site in Hebrew (where the text runs right to left). There, little information is extracted to the right of the fixated word.

PART III

Understanding Text

You have probably had the experience of reading something and recognizing the words, but having little idea of the meaning of what you have read. This phenomenon indicates that understanding text is more than simply understanding the words it contains. Other processes are needed to form a more global meaning from the words in the stream of text, their order, and their grammatical markings.

The next three chapters are an introduction to understanding the "higher-order" processes that are an essential part of reading. The word *introduction* in the previous sentence should be kept in mind, since the topic is vast. If our brief discussion seems interesting, there are many excellent books on psycholinguistics you could study. Two handbooks of psycholinguistics are good starting places: Traxler and Gernsbacher, 2006, and Gaskell, 2007 (see Rayner & Clifton, 2002, for a modestly expanded treatment of some aspects of the present chapters). From these sources (and others, e.g., Cutler & Clifton, 1999) you will learn about the similarities and differences between written and spoken language. The goals of this book limit us to discussing written language.

Chapter 7 discusses the role of inner speech in silent reading. As we shall see, an important function of inner speech is in helping to integrate words into larger units. The inner voice we sometimes hear during reading both reflects and guides this structuring of the words we read. We review evidence for the existence and functional role of inner speech, and we argue that it can help comprehension of text.

Chapter 8 contains two main sections. The first begins with a very brief discussion of linguistics, and then examines how people "parse" sentences, i.e., determine the grammatical relationships among the words in the sentence. We discuss the two global theoretical positions that have guided much research on sentence parsing over the past few decades. The second section concerns "interpretation"—how we determine the meaning of sentences. Interpretation, as we will show, depends on the grammatical relationships that have been identified, but goes far beyond them.

Chapter 9 moves on to consider how units larger than sentences are comprehended. We consider ways of representing the knowledge a reader gets from reading an expository or narrative text. We discuss how readers tie the sentences of a text together into coherent wholes, covering such topics as anaphora, the use of connectives, and information structure. We address the question of what inferences readers make, under what conditions, then present an overview of "mental models," and conclude with a discussion of readability.

7

INNER SPEECH

When we read silently, we often experience the feeling of hearing our voice saying the words our eyes are falling on. Some readers actually move their lips at times during silent reading and there is a considerable amount of muscle activity in the speech tract that can be measured if not experienced as we read silently. What is the function of these activities? In Chapter 3 we argued that access to the lexicon can proceed via either a visual route or a phonological route. Yet most of the time we can clearly hear our voice saying the words in the text and for most readers there is evidence of much speech-like activity in silent reading. In this chapter we will discuss these speech-related activities in terms of the possible reasons for their occurrence.

Huey (1908) argued that the inner hearing or inner pronouncing (or both) that occur during reading represent a crucial constituent part of comprehending text. Ever since Huey's time the role of inner speech has been controversial and there has been a considerable amount of confusion about exactly what is being investigated in studies dealing with inner speech (McCusker, Bias, & Hillinger, 1981). A point that we wish to stress at the outset is that the auditory images we hear of our voice and the movements that occur in the speech tract may not necessarily be directly related to each other.

In this chapter we will refer to activity in the speech tract (either muscle movement or articulatory processes) as "subvocalization," while we will use the term "phonological coding" to refer to the mental representations of speech that can give rise to the experience of hearing sounds, but may not always lead to conscious experience. A variety of different labels have been used for what we shall call phonological coding: speech recoding (Kleiman, 1975; Martin, 1978), phonetic recoding (Taylor & Taylor, 1983), phonological recoding (Coltheart, Davelaar, Jonasson, & Besner, 1977), phonemic recoding (Baron, 1973; Baron & Strawson, 1976; Meyer et al., 1974), and deep phonemic recoding (Chomsky, 1970). The different labels that have been proposed carry with them certain implicit assumptions about the nature of the internal representation. "Speech recoding" suggests an internal representation similar to that subserving covert articulation; "phonetic recoding" suggests a process of converting written words into articulatory features; and "phonemic recoding" suggests a representation based on abstract theoretical units.

We will adopt the term "phonological coding" since it is relatively neutral. The issues about phonological coding that these other terms raise are interesting but, as we shall see, have not been resolved, since there is not any totally satisfactory way of identifying the exact form of inner speech during reading. Psychologists interested in the role of inner speech have also not been very successful in determining the extent to which phonological coding and subvocalization are related. As a result we will treat inner speech as a general phenomenon and adopt the convention of referring to both phonological coding and subvocalization as speech coding or inner speech. However, we will discuss attempts to differentiate between phonological coding and subvocalization.

One argument that is often advanced with respect to inner speech is that it is an "epiphenomenon" (i.e., a phenomenon that occurs but is of no real functional significance). According to this argument, inner speech is a by-product of the way we are taught to read—we learn to read orally before we learn to read silently, and inner speech during reading is merely a carryover from our initial form of reading. That is, inner speech represents a habit that persists but is of no value in silent reading and may even slow it down. While this argument is not implausible, it seems unusual that a process which is so pervasive would continue despite having little to do with understanding written text.

A direct way to demonstrate that inner speech is more than an epiphenomenon is to show that it does play a role in comprehending written text. There are three principal techniques that have been used to study inner speech in normal readers of English: (1) measuring whether muscles in the speech tract are moving during reading, (2) determining whether a task that makes it impossible to use the speech tract for inner speech interferes with reading, and (3) determining whether sound properties of the text (such as homophony or phonemic similarity) affect reading. We will also consider different reader populations, such as deaf readers and readers of ideographic languages such as Chinese. While the chapter concludes with an overall summary of the role of inner speech in reading, initially we would like to briefly raise some possibilities to frame the subsequent discussion.

Inner speech and comprehension

Some proponents of inner speech have argued that reading is little more than speech made visible. Children learning the reading process are known to sound out words and hence listen to themselves as they try to figure out new and unknown words. This is a prudent strategy in light of what the child brings to the process of learning to read (Rayner, Foorman, Perfetti, Pesetsky, & Seidenberg, 2001, 2002). That is, by the time a child begins to read, he or she is a fairly fluent user of the spoken language. Thus it is plausible that children should make the process of reading as similar to speech comprehension as possible in order to achieve a certain amount of cognitive economy (Gibson, 1965). It is similarly plausible that transforming printed words into auditory surrogates does not disappear for older readers, but simply becomes abbreviated and internalized. Indeed, as we shall see when we discuss electromyographic research (i.e., measurement of muscle activity), readers do subvocalize even when there is no overt speech behavior.

However, "speech made visible" cannot be exactly the same as overt speech since we can read silently much more quickly than we can read aloud. If reading necessitated obtaining the identical acoustic representations as in real speech, then we should read more slowly than we do. Oral reading rates are generally in the range of 150–200 words per minute and are a good approximation of speech rates (Rayner & Clifton, 2009), while silent reading rates for skilled readers are around 300 words per minute. But as we said before, inner speech of skilled adult readers is certainly compressed. If inner speech is not exactly overt speech, what is it? While it is possible that inner speech is used only for occasional difficult words, if you attend to the "voice in your head" while you read it seems to be more than that—you have the impression that the voice is saying most if not all words. It is possible, however, that your reading is slowing down to let the inner voice do this and that fewer words are said by your inner voice when you are not attending to it. Another possibility is that inner speech is some sort of shorthand form in which certain sounds are left out or shortened (e.g., vowels) or certain words are left out, such as function words. We will return to speculations about the form of inner speech at the end of the chapter.

At this point a thought experiment might be quite instructive in thinking about inner speech. Read the next several sentences to yourself silently, but make sure to hear them being said in your head. At the same time, say "blah–blah–blah" out loud over and over again as quickly as you can. The result, which may have surprised you, is that you can easily hear the voice in your head while your mouth is fully engaged with something else. Thus, as we argued earlier, subvocalization and phonological coding are not necessarily the same thing, since they can go on simultaneously. However, they might be closely tied in actual reading, with subvocalization being the main source of phonological coding. The relationship of subvocalization and phonological coding is a major issue in this chapter. The main thing to keep in mind at this point is that there can be a voice in your head that says at least most of the words you read, and furthermore it does not require any involvement of the speech musculature to produce it.

Another piece of evidence for the reality of inner speech was provided by Kosslyn and Matt (1977; see also Alexander & Nygaard, 2008; Kurby, Magliano, & Rapp, 2009). Kosslyn and Matt showed that the speed of silent reading of a passage was strongly influenced by the speaking rate of the person said to have written it. Prior to reading a passage, participants in the experiment heard the voice of the supposed author of the passage. If the supposed author was a fast speaker, participants read the passage quickly; if the author spoke slowly, they read it slowly. This evidence is also consistent with introspective accounts of inner speech. When you read a letter from someone you know very well, such as your mother, you often can hear her accent, or stress, or intonation pattern (Brown, 1970). Also, when you read text such as this book you do not hear your voice in a monotone (unless you always talk in a monotone). Rather, you are aware of providing stress and intonation patterns to the words.

Now that we have some feeling for the phenomenon of inner speech, let us briefly consider what role it might play in reading. One possibility is that inner speech helps the reader to access the meaning of words. The second is that it aids higher-order comprehension processes in reading. That is, after the meanings of words are accessed, there is some sort of "speech" representation of the words formed that aids in the processing of phrases, clauses, sentences, or other larger units.

The most popular view of why inner speech aids comprehension of text is that it aids higher-order comprehension by bolstering short-term memory. As we argued in Chapter 1, short-term memory is importantly (though not exclusively) acoustic in nature. Thus, while the meanings of individual words may be accessed without needing an acoustic representation, creating an acoustic or speech-like code may be beneficial for creating a short-term representation in which words are held while other tasks are done, such as working out the syntactic structure of the sentence or holding an easily accessible representation of nouns to search for the referent of a pronoun. Short-term memory may aid in such tasks because it is more easily accessible than long-term memory and also because temporal order is naturally stored in a speech-like representation.

A second view is that inner speech aids lexical access or post-lexical comprehension or both. As we shall see, a much clearer case can be made for the role of inner speech in post-lexical processes. This has led some researchers to conclude that there is no pre-lexical component to inner speech. Other evidence we will discuss, however, indicates that this conclusion is too strong. A third view is that the prosody of inner speech—its rhythm and melody, what words are emphasized, where pauses occur—can help determine the meaning of a sentence that is read. There is rather little compelling evidence that bears on this third issue, but it is a topic we will consider at the end of this chapter.

We now turn to the data. First we will present several lines of research that are aimed at determining whether inner speech plays any important role in normal reading. We will concentrate on methods that attempt to measure or to manipulate subvocalization and see how subvocalization is related to reading speed or comprehension. We will then briefly consider the nature of reading in people and in writing systems that apparently have only limited access to the phonology of spoken language. Finally, we will discuss the existing evidence about what roles inner speech might play in comprehending text.

Electromyographic recording

Electromyographic (EMG) records were, for a period of time, widely used to study the role of subvocalization in reading. By inserting needle electrodes inside the muscles or by placing surface electrodes on the speech organs (lips, tongue, chin, larynx, throat) it is possible to record the action potentials of the muscles during silent reading. EMGs taken during silent reading are then compared to EMGs in a condition in which participants are asked to sit quietly without thinking about anything. Generally, EMGs are also recorded from some other part of the body, such as the forearm, where muscle activity should have no relevance for reading. In fact, normal skilled readers show little forearm activity during reading, while EMG activity in the speech tract increases markedly during reading in comparison to the baseline condition (where the participant sits quietly). In contrast, deaf readers show a considerable amount of forearm activity during reading (we shall see the reason for that later in this chapter). In a review of EMG research, McGuigan (1970) found that almost all studies reviewed found an increase in speech tract activity during language tasks (be they reading or listening or thinking).

In addition, EMGs are clearly affected by the conditions of reading. For example, Edfeldt (1960) found that EMG activity was much greater for difficult text than for easy text. He also found that EMGs increased during the reading of intelligible foreign text, especially if the participant was unaccustomed to reading foreign text. Sokolov (1972) found that participants who were translating Russian into English had considerably more speech activity when reading difficult translations than when reading easy translations. Reading skill is also related to EMG activity. Beginning readers show more EMG activity than skilled readers. McGuigan (1967; McGuigan & Bailey, 1969) showed that the amount of EMG activity decreases as reading skill increases. Poor readers also show more EMG activity than do good readers (Edfeldt, 1960).

The above data indicate that subvocalization is a normal part of natural silent reading. To our knowledge there is little controversy about that assertion. What is less clear is whether subvocalization serves a useful purpose. Experimenters have attempted to assess the functional significance of subvocalization by determining what happens to reading when subvocalization is eliminated. One procedure for eliminating subvocalization involves giving participants feedback when their EMG activity exceeds a given level. This was done by buzzing a noxious noise into the participants' ears. In one experiment (Hardyck, Petrovinovich, & Ellsworth, 1966) it was found that a single session of such feedback was sufficient to eliminate subvocalization (or at least evidence of it in the EMG record). There was no evidence of subvocalization when participants were later retested. Aarons (1971) also reported that readers are responsive to feedback training and that reduction in subvocalization lasted beyond the training sessions. On the other hand, McGuigan (1971) contended that the effect of feedback training is short-lived and that subvocalizations occur again very soon after the training session. He tested participants via feedback training and found that, when retested, the level of EMG activity was the same as during the pre-training session. Thus he argued that the effects of feedback training are short-lived and transitory. We thus see that there is uncertainty about whether such training really can eliminate subvocalization for an extended period. However, for the moment, let us assume that the procedure can be effective.

Perhaps the most frequently cited study of EMG activity is that reported by Hardyck and Petrinovich (1970). The participants in the study were college students in a remedial English class.

They were asked to read selections of easy and difficult text under three different conditions: normal, feedback, and control. In the normal condition participants read the text while EMG activity in the speech tract was recorded. In the feedback condition everything was the same as the normal condition except that any increase in the amplitude of EMG activity above a predetermined relaxation level resulted in a noxious tone being sounded. Participants were told to keep the tone off as much as possible. In the control condition everything was the same as in the feedback condition except that the tone was triggered by an increase in the amplitude of the forearm flexor muscle over a predetermined relaxation level. Hardyck and Petrinovich found that when activity in the speech tract was decreased via feedback techniques, comprehension of the difficult passage suffered. In contrast, there was little comprehension loss for the easy reading selection (see Figure 7.1).

This study can be taken as evidence that comprehension (particularly of difficult text) requires subvocalization. When subvocalization was eliminated, comprehension suffered. However, the result does not necessarily indicate that subvocalization was essential for comprehension. Taylor and Taylor (1983) suggested that comprehension may have suffered simply because participants had to pay attention to the task of learning to eliminate muscle activity in the speech tract. A related difficulty with EMG suppression techniques is that, as text difficulty increases, overall muscle tone may increase and thus participants may have to work harder to keep their EMG activity down. Another general criticism of EMG studies is that while it is clear that activity in the speech tract increases, it is not always clear that such increases are due specifically to linguistic processing. However, Locke (1971) found that EMG activity in the lips was significantly greater in passages containing a larger number of bilabial consonants than in passages containing relatively few bilabial consonants. (The bilabial consonants, *b, v,* and *m*, require lip movement for oral pronunciation.) Garrity (1977) provided a review of EMG research which contains further evidence that EMG activity is at least partially speech specific.

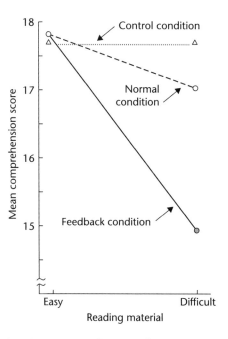

FIGURE 7.1   Reading comprehension score as a function of experimental condition in the Hardyck and Petrinovich (1970) study

Summary

EMG studies have provided some useful data concerning subvocalization in reading. It is clearly the case that less-skilled readers exhibit more EMG activity than skilled readers and that the rate of subvocalization increases as text difficulty increases. It is less clear what happens to reading comprehension when subvocalization is eliminated. It appears, at least, that when subvocalization is eliminated and the text is not easy to read, comprehension suffers.

It is interesting to note that studies utilizing EMG recordings have declined rather dramatically over the past 30 years. Some of the criticisms and uncertainties concerning various findings that we discussed above may be related to the fact that researchers are conducting fewer studies of this type. In some ways, EMG recording can be seen as a carryover from the behaviorist tradition in experimental psychology in which higher mental processes such as thinking or comprehension are thought of as internalized speech or behavior. Accordingly, the EMG research has focused on whether covert speech is occurring during reading, and models of the reading process based on this research have been very sparse in postulating cognitive processes that may be occurring during reading. A particularly thorny issue that will be discussed more fully in the next section is the relation of subvocalization to inner speech. We are not sure whether the lack of insight into cognitive processes lies with the EMG technique or with the orientation of EMG researchers. However, most cognitive psychologists interested in inner speech have turned to other techniques, to which we also now turn.

Concurrent articulatory activity

The feedback technique used in association with EMG studies represents one attempt to eliminate subvocalizations during reading. A second and more widely used technique is having the vocal tract engaged in other activity. The idea or rationale behind the suppression experiments is simple: if a reader's speech tract is somehow concurrently engaged during reading, he or she will not be able to subvocalize the text material. Other techniques have been used as well which attempted to keep the mouth immobile. First, experiments were undertaken around the end of the nineteenth century (see Huey, 1908) in which participants placed a balloon in their mouth (with a tube for breathing) and the balloon was inflated so that they could not move their speech musculature. Analogously, participants have been asked to bite into something and to clench their jaws so that articulation does not occur (Sokolov, 1972). These methods to restrict articulation via physical means were not particularly successful, are obviously unpleasant to the participant, and thus are generally not used very much these days. Thus we will focus on the "concurrent articulation" task as the technique to eliminate subvocalization.

The first type of experiment of this type was reported by Pintner (1913). Participants in his experiment were asked to count or pronounce the syllables *la-la-la* while reading text. Obviously if readers are forced to pronounce a well-rehearsed set of words (like a nursery rhyme) or to continuously repeat a meaningless set of sounds (like *la* or *blah*) or to count aloud, they cannot engage the articulatory apparatus for the text at the same time. Thus, according to the logic of the concurrent articulation paradigm, articulatory programs could not be set into motion for the words that are being read while engaged in the task of pronouncing words or phonemes unrelated to the text. The use of simple, well-learned, material to engage the articulatory apparatus is an attempt to minimize the extent to which the articulatory suppression task demands the participant's attention and hence competes for processing resources needed in the reading process. Thus, in the ideal suppression experiment, the suppression task would only interfere with the speech apparatus and with no other mechanism that subserves reading. How closely this ideal has been achieved is a major issue in this research.

The focus of many of the experiments using the concurrent articulation paradigm is whether recoding to speech during reading occurs before or after the meaning of a word is accessed from the lexicon (Besner, Davies, & Daniels, 1981; Chmiel, 1984; Martin, 1978). In this section we will begin by reviewing in some detail a classic concurrent articulation study (Kleiman, 1975) which led to the conclusion that post-lexical processing is primarily what is being affected by concurrent articulation. We will then discuss other studies using concurrent articulation, as well as discussing some general issues concerning its use.

Suppression while reading words and phrases

Kleiman's concurrent activity was "shadowing". In the shadowing task participants listen to digits and they repeat them aloud ("shadow them") in order to suppress subvocalization. The primary task (i.e., the one participants are supposed to attend to) involves making judgments about visually presented words or sentences as quickly as possible. The judgments are indicated by manual responses and timed. The basic measure of involvement of subvocal speech is thus how much slower responses are in the primary task when participants had to concurrently shadow the digits than when there is no concurrent shadowing task. Kleiman reasoned that the amount of interference due to shadowing ought to depend on the type of judgment being made. If the decision was about graphemic characteristics of words (how much words look alike), then little interference would be expected. On the other hand, if the decision was about phonemic characteristics of words (the extent to which words rhyme), then it should be quite difficult to make that decision while speaking at the same time.

In fact, Kleiman found that shadowing slowed down judgments of the visual similarity of two words only by about 120 ms, whereas it slowed down judgments about whether they rhymed by approximately 370 ms. You may be wondering why shadowing had any effect on the graphemic judgment. The answer probably has to do with the fact that any simultaneous task is likely to have some deleterious effect on performance unrelated to its putative primary purpose (in this case, vocal suppression). We will return to this point later in this section.

The most important question was what happened when the decision was based on the meaning of a word. If access to the lexicon depends on inner speech, then the meaning decision should be disrupted as much as the phonemic decision by concurrent articulation. If, on the other hand, access to meaning occurs independently of speech processing, then the judgments in the meaning task should resemble the graphemic judgment. In this latter case the conclusion would be that speech coding in reading occurs after lexical access. In fact, Kleiman found that the amount of interference in the graphemic task and the meaning task were about the same (see Table 7.1). This indicates that, in order to perform judgments of synonymy, it is not necessary to engage in the degree of inner speech that is necessary for the rhyme task. On the basis of these results, Kleiman argued that the meanings of individual words can be obtained without reference to inner speech.

To further test if speech recoding is used in the graphemic decision, participants in another experiment were asked to make the same types of visually similar judgments with and without shadowing. There were two types of stimuli requiring YES responses: phonemically similar (*BLAME–FLAME*) and phonemically dissimilar (*HEARD–BEARD*) word pairs. If participants use speech recoding when they are not shadowing, it should facilitate the decision about phonemically similar pairs relative to dissimilar pairs. The results of the experiment indicated that shadowing hindered both types of stimuli by the same amount, and thus support the argument that the interference observed in the visual comparison task is unrelated to speech recoding.

The pattern of results in another experiment using sentences was quite similar to that obtained when judgments about word pairs were required. In this experiment participants were given a

TABLE 7.1   Major results of Kleiman's first experiment

Task	Example of "Yes"	Example of "No"	Without shadowing	Change with shadowing
			ms	
Phonemic	TICKLE PICKLE	LEMON DEMON	1,137 (8.3)	+372 (+7.7)
Graphemic	HEARD BEARD	GRACE PRICE	970 (4.5)	+125 (+0.4)
Semantic	MOURN GRIEVE	DEPART COUPLE	1,118 (4.2)	+120 (+3.8)

Values in parentheses are error rates.

target word and then asked to read a sentence presented visually either while shadowing or not. The judgments were the same as in the word pair experiments. Thus, for example, participants might be given the target word *BURY* and asked if a graphemically similar word was in the target sentence (*YESTERDAY THE GRAND JURY ADJOURNED*). The participant then had to indicate a YES (as in this example) or NO judgment with a manual response as in the previous experiments. This experiment also included a condition in which participants had to make judgments of sentence acceptability (Is this a semantically acceptable sentence?). Thus the participant would respond YES to *NOISY PARTIES DISTURB SLEEPING NEIGHBORS* and NO to the anomalous sentence *PIZZAS HAVE BEEN EATING JERRY*. This condition was included in the experiment to test the notion that speech coding is used for short-term retention when a string of words has to be remembered. The acceptability judgment is likely to require working memory since the participant has to remember the subject noun of the sentence until the verb and object have been read if an accurate judgment is to be made. As can be seen in Table 7.2, Kleiman found that the sentence acceptability judgment was greatly interfered with by shadowing. In fact, there was even more interference than in the rhyme judgment.

Suppression while reading passages

The results of the sentence-reading experiments were taken by Kleiman as evidence that inner speech comes into use for the purposes of working memory and not for lexical access. Kleiman's results have been cited widely, and there are several other studies that support and extend this general conclusion. Since his studies were done with individual words, phrases, and individual sentences, it would be interesting to know whether blocking subvocalization would also result in interference when people are reading connected discourse. A major problem in studying reading comprehension for extended passages, however, is that it is very difficult to test for interference in comprehension—even without any interfering task, readers forget a lot of the detail of what they read. A compromise strategy that has been adopted is to have people read passages of about 5 to 10 sentences long and to test for memory of these materials immediately after each passage is read. The test after such a short interval of time should be sensitive to any interference with comprehension produced by the concurrent task. While the processing of these short passages is not exactly like reading real text, it's a reasonable approximation.

The typical procedure in these experiments is to have the sentences appear one at a time on a screen at a rate preset by the experimenter. The participant either reads silently or performs a concurrent vocal activity while reading (e.g., counting or repeating a nonsense phrase over and

TABLE 7.2   Major results of Kleiman's third experiment

Task	Examples of stimuli	Without shadowing	Change with shadowing
			ms
Phonemic	CREAM HE AWAKENED FROM THE DREAM (True) SOUL THE REFEREE CALLED A FOUL (False)	1,401(6.8)	312(+2.1)
Graphemic	BURY YESTERDAY THE GRAND JURY ADJOURNED (True) GATHER RUNNING FURTHER WAS TED'S MOTHER (False)	1,557(6.3)	140(+2.0)
Category	GAMES EVERYONE AT HOME PLAYED MONOPOLY (True) SPORTS HIS FAVORITE HOBBY IS CARPENTRY (False)	1,596(9.9)	78(−2.6)
Acceptability	NOISY PARTIES DISTURB SLEEPING NEIGHBORS (True) PIZZAS HAVE BEEN EATING JERRY (False)	1,431(7.3)	394(2.6)

Values in parentheses are error rates.

over). Thus, since reading speed is controlled, the experimenter measures whether comprehension of the passage suffers in any way from the concurrent vocal activity. As a control, Levy (1975, 1977) had participants listen to passages while counting aloud or being silent. One might think that counting aloud would interfere more with listening than with reading. However, Levy argued that if the speech coding involved in listening does not involve an articulatory component, whereas the speech coding involved in reading does (Baddeley, 1979), one might observe articulatory interference only in the reading task. Levy tested her participants' comprehension by giving them a recognition test containing either a sentence from the test paragraph or a sentence with a slight change in wording. The changes were either lexical (in which case a synonym was substituted for one of the words in the sentence) or semantic (in which case the subject and object nouns were switched). Levy found that vocalization affected comprehension for both types of test sentences in which there was a change if the participant was reading. However, no such decrement occurred during listening. Similarly, Baddeley, Eldridge, and Lewis (1981) found that articulatory suppression led to a clear decrement in the participants' ability to detect anomalous words or errors in word order.

   The picture gets more complicated when we consider other studies. In a later experiment Levy (1978) tested only for changes in meaning, found that concurrent vocal activity did not affect comprehension, and suggested that suppression may only hamper verbatim memory (which is contrary to her earlier results). However, in a subsequent study, Slowiaczek and Clifton (1980) demonstrated that while concurrent vocal activity did not affect memory for discrete propositions of the form "subject verb object" (which were the ones tested in Levy, 1978), it did affect comprehension of propositions when integration of information across sentences was required. A second complication is that Levy's original finding that there was no decrement due to suppression in the listening control has not usually been replicated. Thus the typical pattern in these studies (e.g., Slowiaczek & Clifton, 1980) is that there is a decrement in performance due to suppression in the listening condition, but it is less than the decrement in the reading condition.

It thus appears that suppression may only affect certain kinds of comprehension tasks: those that involve verbatim memory and those that require memory of the text in order for the reader to fully integrate the meaning of several sentences. Moreover, the effects of suppression appear to be greater for reading than listening, suggesting that the suppression is affecting the process whereby the printed text is converted to auditory form. Combined with the suppression studies using individual words (e.g., Kleiman, 1975), these results suggest that inner speech has little to do with accessing the meaning of individual words but is important in later memory processes that aid the comprehension of connected discourse.

Problems with the suppression technique

The usual interpretation of the suppression data presented above is not an unreasonable one. However, it would be misleading to leave the impression that the argument for it was close to airtight. There are two major methodological criticisms of the suppression technique.

Interference is not necessarily due to suppression

One problem with the technique is that a decrement, when observed, cannot necessarily be ascribed to the ability of the suppression task to use up the vocal apparatus and thus deny it to the reading process. First of all, when two tasks are performed simultaneously, some effort might be expended just for general bookkeeping needed to keep the two tasks distinct. Second, the suppression task itself may interfere not only with the vocal apparatus but with more general mental activity (Margolin, Griebel, & Wolford, 1982). In fact, as we have seen earlier with the Kleiman experiment, there was a 100-ms decrement in both the visual and semantic comparison tasks, which was analyzed as being due to either or both of these causes. It is possible to extend this argument to raise the possibility that "none" of the interference effects in reading are really due to suppression of subvocal speech and that all are due to interfering with more general mental activity.

How would such an argument go? Consider the Kleiman result that the rhyme judgment task is slowed by 300 ms. This extra interference may not necessarily be due to subvocalic suppression; it may be that the rhyming task takes more general mental activity than either the graphemic or the meaning judgment (synonymy) task. According to such an argument, tasks range in "difficulty" with more difficult tasks taking more general processing resources and hence interfering more with concurrent tasks.

The assumption that the rhyming task involves more general processing resources than the meaning task is somewhat ad hoc (although the absolute times for the rhyming task were longer than for the semantic judgment task). Is there any way to determine whether such a general interference explanation is to be preferred over the explanation that the interference effect is due to competition for the vocal tract? One experiment (Waters, Komoda, & Arbuckle, 1985) attempted to assess the general processing resources that various tasks take by assessing their interfering effects on another task that plausibly has nothing to do with phonology or speech (dot detection) and then subtracting out those effects from the interfering effects on reading (using a technique called analysis of covariance). The results, unfortunately, were mixed. Subtracting out the interfering effects on the dot detection task reduced the interfering effect of the shadowing task enough that it was not statistically significant. However, the effect was still fairly large (reading was slowed about 15% and comprehension suffered a bit).

An additional problem with the Waters et al. experiment is that they chose the shadowing task as concurring activity, while the other experiments that had participants read passages of text (e.g., Levy. 1977; Slowiaczek & Clifton. 1980) used a different task (either going through the numbers 1 through 10 or repeating a word or two over and over again). The shadowing task, unfortunately, is probably far from ideal to study subvocalic suppression. In Kleiman (1975) and in Waters et al. (1985) the fastest rate of shadowing single digits is one digit per two-thirds of a second. Since normal speech is at least 50% faster and probably usually about twice as fast, shadowing probably does not drive the vocal apparatus as continually as one might wish. The probable reason that such relatively slow rates are used is that the task is relatively demanding of general mental resources (as the interference in the visual and semantic comparison tasks of Kleiman's experiments indicates) and forcing the participant to go faster would probably cause a general breakdown in the shadowing task. A repetition task such as going *blah-blah-blah* over and over again, which was typically used in the passage comprehension studies (e.g., Levy, 1975), seems a much better approximation to the ideal of tying up the vocal apparatus with a minimum of use of general mental resources.

It appears that the decrements in reading observed with the suppression technique may not be due to suppression of subvocalization but to use of general mental resources. Similarly, a greater decrement in reading while shadowing than while performing some other concurrent task (such as finger tapping, used by Levy, 1981) may result from shadowing or talking using more general mental resources rather than more speech resources. At present, only one study (Waters et al., 1985) has seriously tried to assess the general mental resource demands of various concurrent tasks. The results were inconclusive, but suggested that shadowing has an effect beyond a general interference effect. No one has done a similar assessment of the repetition task. On the face of it, however, the repetition task seems to tie up vocal resources quite effectively without imposing substantial cognitive demands, and is thus a better candidate for a vocal suppression task.

The suppression task may not adequately suppress inner speech

The suppression task has been also attacked from the other side. That is, it has been argued that the absence of an interference effect does not necessarily mean that inner speech is not involved in the process of interest, such as in Kleiman's task where participants judge the synonymy of two words. How can it not interfere with inner speech, since the concurrent task is clearly tying up the vocal apparatus to a large extent? Remember, our intuitive demonstration earlier showed that phonological coding is possible while the vocal apparatus is completely tied up. Furthermore, most people's introspections are that it is not particularly difficult to hear the voice in the head while the mouth is saying something else. In other words, while a study like Kleiman's clearly demonstrates that subvocalization is not necessary for comprehension of the meaning of the two words, it may say little about whether inner speech (i.e., the voice in your head) is involved.

Let's expand the argument a bit. Assume that the data are: task X, such as comparing the meaning of two words, is unaffected by concurrent vocalization (this is an idealization of the real data). We can safely conclude that this means that subvocalization is not involved in task X, because even if the concurrent vocalization task doesn't completely suppress subvocalization (the participant might sneak it in a bit here and there), it would significantly disrupt subvocalization since the mouth can do only one thing at a time. When we consider the effect of concurrent vocal activity on phonological coding (the voice in the head), we are on much less solid ground because we know that the two activities can go on at the same time (at least on a global level). While we have the intuition that the sounds coming out of the mouth must have some interfering action on the voice in the head, we do not know for sure.

One possibility is that producing overt speech creates a second voice that interferes with listening to the inner voice. Studies in selective attention, however, indicate that if participants are trying to attend to an auditory message coming from one spatial location, a second auditory message (which the participant is told to ignore) coming from a second location produces little interference in comprehending the first message (Broadbent, 1958). Since the overt vocalizations appear to be coming from a different location than the inner voice, one may expect this "second voice" interference not to be important. What seems more plausible is that subvocalization may be needed to reinforce, extend, or perhaps adjust the inner speech being produced so that blocking subvocalization will lead to a more impoverished form of inner speech. However, if the participant can sneak in a little subvocalization, that may be good enough to produce adequate inner speech.

This leads to a second methodological criticism of the concurrent vocalization experiments. No study, to our knowledge, has made a serious attempt to measure a decrement (if any) in the concurrent vocal activity caused by the reading task (possibly caused by surreptitious subvocalization). This is especially a problem because there is evidence (e.g., Posner & Boies, 1971) that, in a dual-task situation, the task that is perceived as secondary is the one in which the major decrement is observed. That is, whenever the demands of the two tasks collide, the secondary one is usually the one to give. Since in this case the concurrent vocal activity is almost certainly perceived as secondary, one would expect subtle interference effects to show up in the concurrent vocal task rather than the reading task.

Summary

To summarize, interference due to concurrent vocalization may not be a sensitive measure of inner speech because (a) one thing can be phonologically coded while another is vocalized, and (b) subtle interference effects may be missed because the interference may be mainly in the vocalization task which is not carefully measured. We apologize for what might appear to be a lengthy methodological digression, but the concurrent task paradigm is complex enough that its problems needed some discussion. Our discussion indicates that few conclusions drawn from the concurrent task data are really solid. However, although the "general interference" explanation for positive effects cannot be ruled out, we feel that the data are reasonably convincing in demonstrating that both phonological coding and subvocalization are involved in short-term memory processes used in comprehending discourse. On the other hand, although the negative results indicate that subvocalization is probably irrelevant to accessing the meanings of words, they take nothing away from the evidence we presented in Chapters 3, 4, and 5 that shows that phonological coding is involved in word identification.

A similar argument was made by Besner et al. (1981; Besner & Davelaar, 1982) who distinguished between (1) phonological recoding from print for the purpose of lexical access and (2) buffer storage and/or maintenance of phonologically coded information derived from print. They claimed that only the latter is affected by subvocalization. They attempted to devise a task in which only the first (phonological coding) is tapped and determine whether there was an effect of concurrent articulation. Judgment of rhyming, one task used by Besner and his colleagues, does not meet this criterion. It requires both phonological coding and buffer storage since the first word would have to be coded in some auditory form, but then held in memory and compared with the second word. Thus it is possible that most of the interference observed with the rhyming task is not due to the encoding of the auditory forms but to the storage and comparison processes.

Besner et al. attempted to reduce the importance of buffer storage by having participants judge the homophony of two words, assuming that the memory comparison ("identical or not?") required by this judgment is simpler than that required by a rhyme judgment. They found a markedly reduced (but still significant) interference effect, suggesting that much of the interference in the rhyming task was due to processes beyond initial encoding.

Besner et al. attempted to remove all effects of buffer storage by using a task in which participants were asked to judge whether nonwords sounded like real words (i.e., were pseudohomophones). It is possible that this does not require any extensive storage or comparison of sounds, as the task only requires that a single sound be accessed and used to access a non-sound code (the lexical entry). Their results were mixed. They found interference in one task in which participants were suppressing as quickly as possible, while they found no interference in a task where participants were still going reasonably quickly (about three digits/second) but not quite as quickly as they could go.

Besner et al. concluded that the pseudohomophone task demonstrated that phonological encoding could go on without any interference effect. It could also be argued, however, that this was not sufficiently powerful to find the effect because the participant wasn't suppressing hard enough. In addition, they (like everyone else) did not look for effects on the secondary task. While the Besner et al. experiments have their problems, they do suggest that vocal interference tasks may produce much of their effects on the storage and manipulation of inner speech rather than the initial creation of it from text.

Phonological similarity effects

The third paradigm used to study inner speech during reading really consists of three separate techniques that share some common characteristics. We will refer to the general manipulation as "phonological similarity" since what is common across the three techniques is that the words that are used are homophones or words that are similar in sound. In the homophonic phrase technique participants are asked to judge the acceptability of phrases that have homophones (words that are spelled differently and mean different things, but sound the same such as *meet–meat*) replacing a critical word in the phrase. In the tongue twister and phonemic similarity techniques participants make acceptability judgments of sentences containing a number of words that sound very similar. As we shall see, the assumptions underlying the paradigms are similar and the results across the different paradigms are also rather consistent. The relation of phonological coding to subvocalization has been explored for each of these three paradigms by having participants engage in concurrent articulatory suppression.

Homophonic phrases

How easy do you find it to read the following two sentences? In each, pronunciation is preserved but the visual characteristics of the words are drastically altered.

> The bouy and the none tolled hymn they had scene and herd a pear of bear feat
> in the haul. (7.1)

> Iff yew kann sowned owt thiss sentunns, ewe wil komprihenned itt. (7.2)

In the first sentence (taken from LaBerge, 1972) most of the words are replaced by homophones so that the sentence sounds right but doesn't look right. In the second sentence (taken from

Baddeley et al., 1981) all of the words are misspelled (and most are nonwords) but you can still sound the words out and understand the sentence.

If reading relied totally on the use of a speech code, text that is altered but is still pronounced correctly (as in these examples), should be no harder to read than unaltered text. Following this reasoning, Bower (1970) used Greek letters to symbolize English words for Greek–English bilingual participants. Because the participants in his experiments found it very difficult to read such text, he concluded that speech recoding was not used in reading. However, one can only conclude from this result that speech recoding is not the *only* route to meaning. Another diagnostic use of homophones was provided by Baron (1973). He asked participants to judge the meaningfulness of phrases which contained either orthographically and phonetically incorrect words (such as *new I can't* or *I am kill*) or visually incorrect but phonetically correct words (such as *don't dew it* or *tie the not*). In the first case, the orthographically and phonetically incorrect words *new* and *kill* replace *no* and *ill*, and in the second case, the homophones *dew* and *not* replace *do* and *knot*. Participants were also given meaningful phrases (e.g., *I am ill*) on half the trials. Baron's reasoning was that, if speech recoding occurs, the correct sound of the homophonic errors should interfere with deciding that the sentence is not meaningful, and the homophonic errors would thus have longer reaction times for rejecting the sentence than the orthographic errors. If no recoding took place, the decision would be based on only visual features of the phrase and there would be no difference between the two conditions. Indeed, Baron found the latter pattern of results and argued that speech recoding is not necessary during reading.

It could be argued, however, that the reaction time data in Baron's experiment are not nearly as important as the error data. In fact, Baron also found that participants make more errors with the homophonic phrases (*tie the not*) than the nonhomophonic phrases (*I am kill*). Thus the error data provide support for the idea that speech recoding in reading does occur. Baron's finding of no differences in response times for rejecting phrases with homophone and nonhomophone words but more errors in the former case than in the latter case has been replicated by Doctor and Coltheart (1980) and by Banks, Oka, and Shugarman (1981). Furthermore, Treiman, Freyd, and Baron (1983), Treiman, Baron, and Luk (1981), Treiman and Hirsh-Pasek (1983), and Baron, Treiman, Freyd, and Kellman (1980) all reported more errors and longer response times in rejecting phrases containing homophones than in rejecting the control nonhomophone phrases. Thus it now seems clear that the phrase evaluation task involves speech recoding.

Although the phrase evaluation type of experiment was initially designed to investigate the role of speech coding in lexical access, we do not know whether the interference effects obtained are pre- or post-lexical. That is, the sound of the homophone may only interfere when the phrase as a whole (sitting in short-term memory) is evaluated for meaning. One interpretation of the pattern of results offered is that participants were often able to access the lexicon for the individual words (hence there would be no reaction time difference), yet the fact that post-lexical speech coding occurs would lead them to make errors when they had finished reading the entire phrase.

Tongue twisters

Another technique that has been used to examine speech coding in reading involves having participants read sentences that contain tongue twisters. Tongue twisters are sentences that contain a number of words with the same initial consonants. For example, the well-known tongue-twister that children (and adults) often try to say as fast as they can:

Peter Piper picked a peck of pickled peppers. (7.3)

It is obvious that oral reading of tongue twisters such as this would be slowed down by the same mechanisms that make them hard to say even if no reading is involved. That is, the parts of the speech musculature involved in articulatory programming are repeatedly involved in programming a phonetic sequence immediately after that same sentence has been produced. What is of interest is whether the difference between tongue-twister sentences and control sentences also occurs when participants read silently.

Haber and Haber (1982) gave participants tongue twister sentences like 7.4 and control sentences like 7.5:

Barbara burned the brown bread badly.   (7.4)

Samuel caught the high ball neatly.   (7.5)

They found that the tongue twisters took more time than the controls, and the difference between the two types of sentences was the same in both a silent reading condition and an oral reading condition. (Naturally, silent reading was faster than oral reading.) Ayres (1984) embedded tongue twisters in paragraphs and obtained the same results as Haber and Haber: paragraphs with tongue twisters took longer to read silently (and orally) than paragraphs with non-tongue twisters. The rationale in these experiments is that if articulatory programming is required in silent reading and cannot be suppressed, then the extra time to read a tongue twister silently as compared to its control should be the same as the difference between the times needed to read tongue twisters and control sentences orally.

A comprehensive study involving tongue twisters was reported by McCutchen and Perfetti (1982). Participants in their experiment silently read sentences and made semantic acceptability judgments of the sentences. Some of the sentences were tongue twisters which repeated initial consonants (such as sentences 7.3 and 7.4 above) and others were matched phonetically neutral sentences (where the word-initial consonants were not repeated). The authors found that semantic acceptability judgments were longer for the tongue twisters than the neutral sentences, and that concurrent vocalization with a tongue-twister phrase slowed performance. That is, when participants had to vocalize *Pack a pair of purple pampers* or *I owe you an I.O.U.* while making semantic acceptability judgments, response time was slowed down for both the tongue twisters and the neutral sentences that were being read. However, McCutchen and Perfetti found that the specific content of the concurrent vocalization had little effect on semantic acceptability judgment times. It mattered little whether or not the concurrently vocalized phrase contained consonants that were similar to the repeated consonant (e.g., the bilabial, /p/, in the tongue twister phrase, suggesting that the interference created by a tongue twister does not take place at the level of subvocal motor programs.

Recent research has explored the tongue twister effect in greater detail. Oppenheim and Dell (2008) examined specific errors made or reported in repeating lists of words like *lean reed reef leach* silently or aloud. They found that errors that resulted in real words (e.g., saying *leaf* rather than *reef*) occurred more frequently than errors that resulted in nonwords, both when reading aloud and when reading silently. However, decreasing the phonological similarity of the segments that could be confused with one another (e.g., replacing a liquid consonant with a stop consonant, so that *lean . . . leach* are replaced by *bean . . . beach* in the list) decreased errors in repeating aloud, but not silently. They concluded that inner speech lacks phonological detail, but still maintains information about phonemic identity. Acheson and MacDonald (2009), in a study aimed at understanding the nature of verbal working memory, examined errors made when strings of nonwords (like *shif seev sif sheeve*) were read aloud or remembered. The results they found for tongue twisters (like the list just given) indicated that working memory relies on the kinds of subvocal speech processes that seem to be implicated in silent reading.

Other research has asked whether the disruptive effect of tongue twisters appears at the level of reading individual words, or only more globally. Kennison and her colleagues (Kennison, 2004; Kennison, Sieck, & Briesch, 2003) used a phrase-by-phrase self-paced reading technique to measure reading speed for sentences with and without repeated initial phonemes, as in 7.6:

> Tina and Todd took the two toddlers the toys, despite the fact the weather was bad.
> Lisa and Chad sent the four orphans the toys, despite the fact the weather was bad.   (7.6)

They found slowed reading only after the end of the clause containing the repeated phonemes (after the comma in the example), suggesting that the tongue twister effect may involve only late processes of integration and memory rehearsal, and may not actually show the effect of inner speech on reading individual words and comprehending sentences. However, Warren and Morris (2009) recorded eye movements during silent reading of tongue twisters, and found that tongue twisters slowed both early and late measures of reading. It appears that tongue twisters do affect late stages of processing involved in attempting to remember a sentence, but also that, if sufficiently sensitive measures are used, tongue twisters can be shown to affect early stages of recognizing words and understanding sentences.

Tongue twisters thus do seem to slow reading both at a local and a global level, and interfere with comprehension of sentences and memory for sentences and word lists. The interference appears to be due to the overlap of the phonemic representations automatically activated during reading. However, the lack of specific interference between concurrent vocalization and the reading task (in McCutchen & Perfetti, 1982) and the lack of phonological similarity effects (in Oppenheim & Dell, 2008) suggests that these phonemic representations are not subvocal motor programs and lack phonetic detail.

Phonemic similarity effect

Closely related to the tongue twister effect is the phonemic similarity effect. Baddeley and Hitch (1974) first used the phonemic similarity effect, which has a powerful effect on memory span, in a reading study. They asked participants to make semantic acceptability judgments for sentences made up almost entirely of phonemically similar words. For example, consider sentences 7.7:

> Crude rude Jude chewed stewed food.
> Crude rude chewed Jude stewed food.   (7.7)

The first sentence is semantically coherent, while the second is not. Participants took longer to accept and reject sentences of this type than to process semantically equivalent sentences which contained words that were not phonemically similar. In a subsequent experiment Baddeley and Lewis (1981) asked participants to make the same types of semantic acceptability judgments while continually counting aloud. They found that articulatory suppression produced an increase in errors but did not influence the size of the phonemic similarity effect (which calls into question whether inner speech really is involved in the effect).

In a related study, Treiman et al. (1983) presented participants with a sentence fragment and then had them perform a forced-choice sentence completion task. For example, the fragment *He made a nasty hasty* was presented with a choice of two completions: *remark* or *profusely*. Participants had to choose the word that made a complete and meaningful sentence. Some of the fragments contained pairs of words with similar spellings, but different pronunciations (as in the *nasty–hasty* pair for the example). Other pairs consisted of similar spelling and similar pronunciation (as in *never–sever*). Treiman et al. found that the phonological relation between the members of a pair influenced performance: response times were longer when the pairs had similar spelling/different pronunciations than when the pairs were similar on both spelling and pronunciation. They also found in a sentence acceptability task that unacceptable sentences containing an exception word (e.g., *plaid*) whose regular pronunciation would be homophonic to a regular word (*played*) as in sentence 7.8 were harder to reject than those sentences containing the regular word as in sentence 7.9:

> The children plaid outdoors. (7.8)

> He wore a played shirt. (7.9)

The phonemic similarity effect studies are consistent with the idea that inner speech plays an important role in reading. In most of the studies the data are consistent with the hypothesis that inner speech is solely a post-lexical process involving holding words in working memory. However, Treiman et al.'s study suggests that inner speech is activated by non-lexical spelling-to-sound rules, since *plaid* would activate *played* only by such routes. This result reinforces the conclusion of Van Orden (1987) that phonemic codes are important in lexical access (see Chapter 3).

Summary

The research described in this section leads to the conclusion that inner speech is important in reading. The common thread running through the studies described here is that the sounds of words influence the speed and/or accuracy of silent reading. If a word that sounds the same as (or similar to) a target word in a phrase or sentence replaces the target word, participants have a harder time rejecting the phrase or sentence than when the target word is replaced by a word which does not sound the same. Additionally, sentences containing a number of words beginning with the same phoneme or a number of words that rhyme with each other are more difficult to read orally, but more interestingly, silently as well. Researchers investigating these issues and employing these paradigms have generally attributed the effects to post-lexical processing in working memory, although some research (Treiman et al., 1983; Warren & Morris, 2009) reinforces the conclusions of Chapters 3, 4, and 5 that indicate that there are early effects on lexical encoding.

Deaf readers

We have been pursuing the issue of how much normal silent reading relies on speech recoding for comprehension to occur. The common thread in all of the experiments that we have discussed is that researchers have tried to manipulate variables that might be related to inner speech (as, for example, by utilizing suppression studies to hinder articulatory recoding) or to find variables that might correlate with speech recoding (as in the EMG studies). A different way to pursue the issue is to investigate readers who presumably cannot fully engage in phonological speech recoding in processing text. Here, of course, we are referring to profoundly deaf individuals. There are various degrees of hearing loss. Some deaf people have mild to moderate hearing losses and can still perceive certain environmental sounds and some sounds of spoken language. The deaf readers we are most interested in are those that have little or no awareness of different speech sounds. Unless they see lips moving, they would not know someone in the room was speaking. The participants of most interest are also those that were either born profoundly deaf (10% of the time to deaf parents; Goldin-Meadow & Mayberry, 2001) or became profoundly deaf within the first year or so of life. Thus they would have had, at best, only limited exposure to a spoken language.

Can profoundly deaf people learn to read? If the answer were an emphatic "no" we would have some pretty good evidence that reading is only possible when speech coding is available. While most deaf children do, to some extent, learn to read, for the most part they do not read very well (Allen, 1986; Conrad, 1972). Conrad (1972; 1977) and Treiman and Hirsch-Pasek (1983) reviewed the characteristics of profoundly deaf readers and concluded that deaf readers do not cope well with the task of reading. They concluded that the average reading level observed for adult deaf readers was about fourth grade level and only about 25% of profoundly deaf people would be classified as functionally literate (where literacy is defined as fourth grade reading ability). About 50% of deaf people with hearing loss greater than 85 decibels have virtually no reading comprehension (Conrad, 1977).

The median reading-level of deaf high-school graduates has hovered around the third to fourth grade level for the past 40 years, despite much research focusing on this population and various approaches to reading instruction (Allen, 1986). Nevertheless, about 5% of deaf high-school graduates do reach expert reading skills matched to that of their hearing peers. Several factors seem to come into play when trying to identify the causes of overall poor reading skills in deaf people, including degree of hearing loss (Conrad, 1977), age of first language acquisition (Mayberry, 2007), and general language knowledge for oral and signed languages (Goldin-Meadow & Mayberry, 2001). One of the prevailing hypotheses to explain reading difficulties in the deaf population is related to their lack of access to the sounds of the language they learn to read (for a review see Perfetti & Sandak, 2000). A great deal of research has focused on whether or not deaf readers do use phonological codes when they read in tasks involving word recognition or short-term memory. However, some of these studies suggest a definite use of phonological codes during reading (Dyer et al., 2003; Hanson & Fowler, 1987; Hanson et al., 1991; Leybaert & Alegria, 1993; Transler & Reitsma, 2005; Transler, Gombert, & Leybaert, 2001; Treiman & Hirsh-Pasek, 1983) and others do not (Beech & Harris, 1997; Burden & Campbell, 1994; Harris & Moreno, 2004; Chamberlain, 2002; Mayberry et al., 2005). Additionally, very few studies have controlled for reading level. Despite this contradictory evidence and lack of tight control of reading level, it has been suggested that only the older (children), better deaf readers use phonological codes while reading (Hanson & Fowler, 1987; Perfetti & Sandak, 2000). Recent results suggest however that skilled and less-skilled deaf readers do not differ in their use of phonological codes in a masked primed lexical decision task and during a short-term memory recall task (Bélanger, Mayberry, & Baum, 2012).

That deaf people read poorly is not really surprising considering all the factors mentioned above. First, profoundly deaf people do not learn English through the normal channels and, lacking fully specified knowledge of the sound structure of English, they do not have an opportunity to benefit from an alphabetical writing system as hearing children do when they learn to read. Second, the main language used by a number of deaf people is not a spoken language but a signed language (American Sign Language or ASL, or some other sign language; e.g., England and Canada have different sign languages, although their spoken English is essentially the same as American English). ASL differs from English in that it is a visual-spatial language which is articulated mainly on the hands (and not the mouth), uses different morphological processes to combine simple morphemes, and also makes use of space as a syntactic process. Thus deaf people may have additional difficulties in reading besides their deafness, as they have to learn to read a language that is, in a sense, not their native language.

What is perhaps more surprising is the fact that some profoundly deaf people manage to read fairly well. Conrad (1977) estimated that by the end of their formal school training 4.5% of hearing-impaired students in England and Wales could read at a level commensurate with their age. Such good readers are less common among the profoundly deaf population than among those with some residual hearing (Conrad, 1977). Thus those who can benefit from some exposure to spoken language tend to be better readers. However, among the profoundly deaf population who have virtually no exposure to spoken English, those who have deaf parents tend to read better than those who have hearing parents, presumably because they learned ASL earlier, and at about the same time that hearing children learn a spoken language (Hoffmeister, 2000; Treiman & Hirsh-Pasek, 1983).

Investigations of profoundly deaf readers indicate that phonological coding may not occur as they read (Locke, 1978; Quinn, 1981; Treiman & Hirsch-Pasek, 1983). Given that their oral language is limited at best, this finding is not very surprising. Do they do any type of recoding of written language? Treiman and Hirsh-Pasek (1983) examined 14 congenitally and profoundly deaf adults who were native signers of ASL; 14 hearing participants with comparable reading levels were also tested. These participants took part in experiments that tested for the possibility of (1) recoding into articulation, (2) recoding into fingerspelling, (3) recoding into ASL, or (4) no recoding at all. The experiments used the phrase evaluation task with homophonic words and tongue twisters. Treiman and Hirsh-Pasek found that their deaf participants did not have the difficulty with homophonic words or tongue twisters that hearing participants do, suggesting limited recoding into articulation. In addition, there was no evidence that their deaf participants recoded printed words into fingerspelling. However, the deaf participants had considerable difficulty with sentences containing similar signs (i.e., "hand twisters"), indicating that they did decode using signs.

Thus second-generation profoundly deaf readers seem to consult their preferred language when reading English. Although their native language (ASL) bears no direct relation to the print, access to the language (possibly in a reduced "inner" form) seems to assist reading performance. As Treiman and Hirsh-Pasek pointed out, the comprehension and memory advantages provided by one's primary language certainly affect the choice of a recoding system.

In summary, that profoundly deaf people can read at all is sometimes taken as evidence that speech recoding in normal readers is optional (Conrad, 1972). However, as we have seen, very few deaf people read well and the best available evidence indicates that, when reading English text, deaf readers recode the printed information into their native language (ASL) for comprehension purposes. Since they have not experienced speech sounds, recoding into a phonological code is precluded in deaf readers. Instead the information is recoded into a manual form so as to aid with comprehension. The poor reading of deaf people is thus probably due in part to inner speech being a more efficient system of recording than inner and overt manual gestures.

The effects of the writing system

Treiman and Hirsh-Pasek's conclusion brings us to the issue of the effects of orthography on inner speech. As we saw in Chapter 2, some non-alphabetic systems rely much less heavily on representing sound with written symbols and rarely rely on grapheme–phoneme correspondence rules for pronunciation of words in the language. Observations such as this have frequently led to the suggestion that readers of languages that are primarily logographic (such as Chinese) go from print to meaning directly without any involvement of inner speech. There are two assumptions here that are at odds with the evidence presented earlier. First, it is assumed that the lexicon is always activated directly from the visual representation. However, we have seen in Chapter 2 that the system is not purely logographic and that the representation of some characters is (in principle) based on sound. Second, it is assumed that there is no benefit from post-lexical coding of information into sound codes to aid short-term or working memory.

It is clearly the case that speech recoding occurs among Chinese readers, since they make confusion errors in short-term memory for similar-sounding words and letters (Tzeng & Hung, 1980; Tzeng, Hung, & Wang, 1977; Yik, 1978) and, as we showed in Chapters 3–5, they use phonological coding in recognizing words in reading. However, some evidence suggests that speech recoding occurs to a lesser extent among readers of Chinese than among readers of English (Treiman et al., 1981). Thus, on the basis of the available data, it appears that once logographic characters are learned, they are phonetically recoded in working memory just as English words are (Erickson, Mattingly, & Turvey, 1977).

Readers of logographic systems such as Chinese can probably access the meaning of many printed characters directly from the visual representation. However, associations between the printed word and the appropriate pronunciation are activated during reading and appear to be important in comprehending text.

How inner speech affects reading

To this point, we have concentrated largely on describing and evaluating demonstrations that seem to show that inner speech does occur and does play a role in various decision and reading tasks. These demonstrations involve measuring and inhibiting implicit speech activity, suppressing inner speech, and presenting written materials that would be confusable if they were spoken We have also discussed the possible presence of inner speech in people with impaired hearing and in people whose writing system encodes speech in only a limited way. The weight of the evidence leads us to conclude that inner speech is not an epiphenomenon, but that it actually plays a role in reading comprehension. We have, however, given very little attention to the mechanisms that underlie inner speech. We turn to this topic in the remainder of the chapter.

The role of inner speech in encoding words

In Chapters 3, 4, and 5 we reviewed several lines of evidence that phonological representations play a role in recognizing words that are read. In particular, we showed that providing a parafoveal preview of a word that was phonologically similar, but not identical, to the word that is read facilitates reading the word (e.g., Pollatsek et al., 1992). Some of this research has probed rather deeply into just what kind of phonological information is extracted, showing that the syllable structure and the phonological (not necessarily orthographic) vowels of the parafoveal word are encoded. These results do show the importance of phonological encoding in normal reading. However, they do not necessarily implicate the little voice in the head that is inner speech. That is, people are generally not aware of the phonological nature of the parafoveal preview, but are often aware of inner speech.

One line of research that comes closer to showing the role that inner speech (as opposed to phonological encoding) plays in reading examines how phonological and phonetic properties of individual words affect the speed with which they are read. We have reviewed (Chapters 3, 4, and 5) how various lexical characteristics (e.g., frequency of occurrence) affect reading speed. Do these lexical characteristics include elements of the speech code? If execution of subvocal speech is actually necessary for reading, one would predict that words that take longer to pronounce would be read more slowly.

There is evidence that this is the case for individual word reading, at least when lexical decisions must be made. Abramson and Goldinger (1997) compared the time taken to make lexical decisions about words with phonetically long vs. phonetically short consonants and vowels. For instance, they compared mean lexical decision time for *game* (where the vowel is long because it precedes a voiced consonant) with the time for *tape* (with a phonetically short vowel, preceding a voiceless consonant). Lexical decision times were longer for words with phonetically longer segments. Abramson and Goldinger took this as evidence not only that inner speech is involved in reading, but that inner speech preserves the phonetic details of speech, not just phonemic identity (for which we have provided various sorts of evidence in Chapters 3–5). You may note that this seems to be inconsistent with the implicit recitation data of Oppenheim and Dell (2008), discussed earlier in this chapter. These latter authors concluded that inner speech, as involved in implicitly reciting tongue twisters, maintained phonemic identity but not phonetic detail. However, they were studying different phonetic properties, in different materials, using a different task, so any firm conclusions would be premature.

Even if the sheer length of time taken to utter a word affects its lexical decision time, it may not affect the time to read it in a sentence. Two-syllable words take longer to pronounce than one-syllable words. However, they take no longer to read silently (when length in characters is matched) than one-syllable words (Ashby & Clifton, 2005). On the other hand, Ashby and Clifton showed that words that have two *stressed* syllables take longer to pronounce, and to read silently, than words with one stressed syllable (e.g., *RA-di-A-tion* vs. *ge-O-met-ry*). The effect on reading speed was limited to gaze duration; it did not appear on first fixations, and thus implicated a process of refixating words more frequently, or longer, when they had more stressed syllables. The authors suggested that silent reading is affected by how long it takes to *prepare* the implicit speech representation of a word, not how long it takes to execute it. They appealed to work by Sternberg, Monsell, Knoll, and Wright (1978) who provided evidence that speech-programming time is a function of the number of stressed syllables being prepared.

A second phonological lexical property that appears to influence reading words in sentences is the stress pattern of a word, e.g., whether it is a first-syllable stressed word like the noun sense of *PRESent*, or a second-syllable stressed word, like the verb sense of *preSENT*. Breen and Clifton (2011) measured eye movements while people read limericks. Limericks have a very regular pattern of stresses that lead readers to anticipate that a word is stressed on a particular syllable. In 7.10 (the first two lines of a five-line limerick), the pattern of the first line leads the reader to anticipate strong stress on the last syllable on the second line (preSENT):

> There once was a clever young gent
> Who had a nice talk to present.   (7.10)

However, in 7.11 the first line leads the reader to anticipate weak stress on the last syllable of the second line (PRESent):

> There once was a penniless peasant
> Who went to his master to present.   (7.11)

These patterns of anticipated stresses are appropriate in 7.10, when the target word is a verb (note that verbs in noun–verb pairs like *PREsent/preSENT* generally have second syllable stress) but inappropriate in 7.11. Reading was disrupted on the last word of the second line in 7.11, as if the reader had to recode the anticipated noun form PREsent as the form preSENT to make it appropriate for the required verb sense of the word. Breen and Clifton claimed that this suggested that readers create an implicit metrical structure (stress pattern) while reading silently, and that eye movements are affected by the need to create a grammatically legitimate metrical structure.

The incomplete nature of inner speech

Ashby and Clifton (2005) suggested, in effect, that the phonological representation of inner speech during normal reading may be incomplete in that it may simply involve the preparation of a silent articulation but not the actual execution of a subvocalization. This suggestion is broadly consistent with an explicit proposal describing the characteristics of the phonological code activated during silent reading that has been made by Perfetti and McCutcheon (1982; McCutchen & Perfetti, 1982). Their argument is that, regardless of whether access to the lexicon is provided directly by the visual pattern of the printed word or indirectly through a rule-analogy system, a consequence of lexical access is an automatic activation of phonological information. However, they also suggested that a complete phonological representation for every word in the text does not occur because such detailed phonological activation would require too much time to be a part of efficient reading. Specifically, they suggest that phonetic specification is incomplete and biased toward the beginnings of the words (recall that Oppenheim & Dell, 2008, reached a similar conclusion). In addition, since function words (such as determiners, prepositions, conjunctions, etc.) are often reduced in spoken language, they may not require as elaborate phonetic representations as content words.

Perfetti and McCutchen argued that an abstract phonological representation containing information about the word-initial phoneme and general phonetic shape would be very useful during the integration process of comprehension. Together with abbreviated semantic information activated during the initial access of the lexicon, word-initial phonetic information could provide a concise index by which to re-access specific words if that were necessary during comprehension. Perfetti and McCutchen assumed that the codes used in the activation of the phonological representations are weighted to consonant features (in particular the distinctive articulatory features of consonants), rather than vowel sounds. This assumption was made for two reasons. First, consonants carry more linguistic information than vowels; consonants more specifically identify words so they would be more helpful in securing specific lexical reference. Second, consonants generally have a shorter acoustic duration than vowels and so would be more compatible with the speed at which silent reading occurs.

Perfetti and McCutchen's proposals are interesting. However, there are some potential problems. First, when you listen to the voice in your head, it does not appear to be in shorthand—all the sounds appear to be there, as do function words. Further, it is possible that when you become conscious of inner speech the process changes and the inner speech is less in shorthand but also slows down. The second problem is whether the shorthand form of the inner speech allows it to be sufficiently comprehensible. Function words are clearly critical to arriving at the proper interpretation of a sentence (Potter, Kroll, & Harris, 1980), and there is no direct evidence that they are less explicitly represented in memory than content words. It is possible that a phonological code should be activated for them as well. Of course, inner speech need not be the "only" memory representation that supports sentence comprehension.

Does inner speech lag behind the eyes?

Part of Perfetti and McCutchen's motivation for arguing that not all words have phonological codes activated during silent reading was to account for the discrepancy in reading rate between oral and silent reading. One thing, though, that we know about oral reading (see Chapter 4) is that the voice lags behind the eyes by about two words (about two fixations or about half a second) (Buswell, 1922; Inhoff, Solomon, Radach, & Seymour, 2011; Laubrock & Kliegl, 2011). While it is often emphasized that the eyes are ahead of the voice, it is important to realize that the eyes do not get very far ahead in oral reading; if they do, they remain in place so as not to get any further ahead. When we consider that part of the difference between the fixated word and the word that is spoken can be attributed to the fact that the motor programs involved in speech production are relatively slow, then the lag between voice and eyes may not be as great as it seems.

What about silent reading? Does inner speech lag behind the eyes? Introspection suggests that if there is a lag, it is quite small, because we seem to hear our voice pronouncing the word our eyes are looking at. But this may all be rather deceptive since all of these processes are occurring very quickly, and if we try to introspect on how well our eyes and inner voice are aligned, we probably are altering the process of silent reading.

An indirect but promising way to examine the time course of inner speech during silent reading is to measure eye movements while reading homophones. There is substantial evidence from eye movement studies using homographs that phonological codes are used in arriving at the meaning of a printed word (Folk & Morris, 1995; Inhoff & Topolski, 1994; Jared, Levy, & Rayner, 1999; Pollatsek, Lesch, Morris, & Rayner, 1992; Rayner, Pollatsek, & Binder, 1998; Rayner, Sereno, Lesch, & Pollatsek, 1995).

Here we will focus on the results reported by Rayner et al. (1998). They used homophone pairs that were either orthographically similar (*break–brake, meet–meat*) or orthographically dissimilar (*right–write, chute–shoot*), as well as pseudohomophones (*brane, skair*). They also varied the extent to which the prior context was highly constraining and made a given homophone highly predictable (i.e., a passage that clearly predicted *brake*); the predicted member of the pair (*brake*) could be present in the passage, or the alternative member (*break*) could be.

Rayner et al. found that, in the high-constraint, orthographically similar conditions of their experiment, there was no difference in early measures of reading (first fixation duration and single fixation duration) between the correct and incorrect homophones (e.g., *break* vs. *brake*). However, the spelling controls (words like *bread* or *meal*, which look like *break* and *meet*, but do not sound like them) received longer initial fixations. Such a pattern indicates that phonological analysis has progressed to the stage in which the target word "sounds wrong" by the time the decision is made to move the eyes, but orthographic analysis has not progressed to the stage where the target word "looks wrong." Moreover, in these conditions readers apparently failed to detect the incorrect homophone an appreciable fraction of the time. However, the anomaly of the incorrect homophone was discovered about half the time, occasionally indexed by a second fixation on the word and the lengthening of the gaze duration, but most often indexed by a regression back to it. This pattern of results suggests that, in the high-constraint situation, the access of semantics from phonology was faster than the access of semantics from orthography, and phonological coding (and perhaps inner speech) often progressed more quickly than extraction of all the information from the orthographic representation.

In contrast, in the low-constraint conditions and the orthographically dissimilar high-constraint conditions Rayner et al. found longer first fixations for incorrect than correct homophones, and even longer first fixations for the spelling controls. This pattern indicates that readers (at least on some fraction of the trials) detected both that the target word "sounds wrong" and that it looks wrong. It is possible that the high predictability of target words in the high-constraint passages speeded preparation of their inner speech representation, and it is also possible that the greater orthographic discrepancy of the "mis-spelled" target word (e.g., *write* for *right*) would be picked up quickly enough to interfere with speech encoding. It is unclear whether, in these conditions, phonology or orthography has faster access to semantics. All that can be said is that both have some access prior to the decision to move the eyes.

A final way that the time course of inner speech in reading has been examined was introduced by Inhoff, Connine, Eiter, Radach, and Heller (2004; see also Inhoff, Connine, & Radach, 2002). Their participants read sentences with predefined target words. When the eyes reached the target word, a spoken word was presented. The spoken word could be identical to the target word (*plate* was the target word and the word *PLATE* was heard), phonologically similar (*PLACE*), or dissimilar (*HORSE*). Inhoff and colleagues found that the identical word yielded shorter fixation times on the target word than the phonologically similar and dissimilar irrelevant spoken word, which did not differ. However, this pattern changed after the participants left the target word as they spent more time looking at the post-target word in the phonologically similar condition than in the identical and dissimilar conditions. According to Inhoff et al. a phonologically similar irrelevant word, compared to a phonologically dissimilar one, impeded the success with which a target word could be processed in working memory. However, in more recent work, Eiter and Inhoff (2010) argued that phonological codes influence both lexical access and a later occurring phonological code associated with keeping information active in working memory.

On the nature of the phonological code

We noted that Perfetti and McCutchen stressed acoustic durations and articulatory features as being important for the phonological code that is set up. Here the motivation appears to be for the phonological code in silent reading to be dependent on the speech code in general. While there is definitely a relationship between speech activity and the phonological code in silent reading, it is not clear that the latter should be totally identical to the former. For example, we pointed out that concurrent articulation interferes with subvocalization but not necessarily with phonological coding. If you are continually vocalizing *ba-ba-ba* and reading silently, you obviously cannot use the speech articulators to instantiate the phonological code. This may mean that the phonological code is somewhat independent of articulatory features and acoustic durations of overt speech. It is clear that considerably more work is necessary to completely specify the characteristics of the phonological code in silent reading and its relationship to overt speech.

In the absence of unambiguous data and theory on the issue, our suggestion is that word identification and lexical access result in automatic activation of a phonological code in silent reading that is somewhat independent from articulation processes (see also McCutchen & Perfetti, 1982; Perfetti, Bell, & Delaney, 1988). The phonological code is set up very quickly, and perhaps incompletely, for each word in the text. We want to suggest that the phonological code, abbreviated though it may be, that is established for words in silent reading results in your hearing a voice saying the words your eyes are falling on. This code is identical to the kind of code that occurs when you hear yourself think. This is not to say that all thinking is based on speech processes; purely visual thinking clearly occurs. But we want to argue that the kinds of phonological coding that occur during thinking and reading are one and the same. In this sense, we are totally comfortable with the metaphor of silent reading being "externally guided thinking" (Neisser, 1967).

How is the phonological code used for comprehension?

One way in which phonological codes could facilitate reading other than involvement in lexical access has been mentioned earlier in this chapter. A phonological representation could facilitate holding words and word order information in working memory. Because new words are processed very quickly, we would soon overload our short-term capacity if words were not chunked together in meaningful ways in working memory. Words in working memory are recoded into a phonological code and held there until meaningful units can be passed on to long-term memory. Since it is often the case that sentences have long distances between related words, having the words in a phonological code in working memory could help us to reinterpret an earlier part of a sentence in light of words that occur later in the sentence. You can always move your eyes back to the earlier part of the sentence and when the sentence is syntactically difficult readers often do (Frazier & Rayner, 1982; Kennedy & Murray, 1984). However, it might be more economical to use the information in working memory if it is there. Because working memory can represent temporal order information, it would readily have the information necessary for reinterpretation. Thus one way in which phonological codes in working memory could aid comprehension is by providing access to the order in which words were read, allowing us to restructure and reinterpret the words in light of new information in working memory.

It is possible, too, that inner speech can guide reading comprehension in ways beyond simply providing an effective memory store. Written language is impoverished in at least one way, when compared to spoken language. Spoken language has a distinctive, and informative, rhythm and melody (referred to as *prosody*). It is possible that readers, when they create an inner speech representation, add prosodic information, and that this prosodic information can affect how a sentence is interpreted.

Slowiaczek and Clifton (1980) made this suggestion to account for their finding that blocking subvocalization during silent reading impaired comprehension that required integration of information across clauses and sentences (even though it did not seem to impair memory for individual words and simple propositions). They proposed that prosody is needed for full comprehension of connected discourse. However, they did not have any direct evidence that prosody played a role in comprehension.

There is substantial evidence that sentence-level prosody does affect comprehension of spoken language (see, e.g., Frazier, Carlson, & Clifton, 2006; Carlson, 2009). The evidence that sentence-level prosody affects silent reading is intriguing, but only suggestive. Very little of this evidence provides the kind of on-line evidence that we favor. Bader (1998) is one of the rare exceptions. He used a self-paced reading procedure to show that reading a German sentence that required syntactic reanalysis (see Chapter 8) was slowed when the syntactic reanalysis also required prosodic reanalysis but not when it did not. Bader's participants read subordinate clauses (following a main clause), like those in 7.12:

... dass man (sogar) ihr Geld beschlagnahmt hat. (7.12a)

(... that someone (even) her money confiscated had.)

... dass man (sogar) ihr Geld anvertraut hat. (7.12b)

(... that someone (even) her money entrusted had.)

In 7.12a the pronoun *ihr* is the possessive pronoun "her," and the clause means "that someone had confiscated (even) her money." In 7.12b *ihr* is the indirect object "to her," and the clause means "that someone had entrusted money (even) to her." Bader claimed that the former interpretation of *ihr* is preferred to the latter (it is syntactically simpler; see Chapter 8). Adding the word *sogar* (a "focus particle") places focus on what follows it; it contrasts the following material with something else that is relevant in the context. Normally, Bader claimed, focus will be placed on the following noun *Geld*, not on the immediately following pronoun *ihr*, and further, Bader claimed, this focus will result in a marked pitch accent (sentence stress) in inner speech. This is appropriate for 7.12a, but not for 7.12b. When the verbal constituent *anvertraut hat* is read in the latter case, focus must be placed on the dative pronoun *ihr*; *sogar* is contrasting "her" with someone else. If readers do create implicit prosody in their inner speech, they will have to shift from the default accent on *Geld* to an accent on *ihr* in 7.12b, just in case *sogar* is present, and this should slow reading. Bader found just such an effect. (For research on focus particles that does not involve implicit prosody see Filik, Paterson, & Liversedge, 2005; Liversedge, Paterson, & Clayes, 2002.)

Most of the existing evidence that the prosody of implicit speech affects how sentences are comprehended comes from off-line judgment tasks and theorists' intuitions. Fodor (2002) reviewed much of this evidence, and proposed the implicit prosody hypothesis of 7.13:

> In silent reading, a default prosodic contour is projected onto the stimulus, and
> it may affect syntactic ambiguity resolution. (7.13)

This hypothesis claims that the inner speech that a reader creates while silently reading represents a grammatically and pragmatically acceptable prosody for what is read, and that this implicit prosody can affect how a sentence is understood. One illustrative line of evidence concerns how ambiguously attached relative clauses are interpreted (e.g., *The daughter of the colonel who was on the porch* could refer to a daughter on a porch, or a colonel on a porch). It turns out that readers are more likely to interpret the relative clause as modifying the first noun rather than the second one when the relative clause is long (as in 7.14) than when it is short (7.15) (Walther, Frazier, Clifton, Hemforth, Konieczny, & Seelig, 1999):

> The doctor met the son of the colonel who tragically died of a stroke. (7.14)

> The doctor met the son of the colonel who died. (7.15)

Fodor (2002) suggested that this is because a reader is more likely to place a prosodic boundary (a pause and distinctive tonal contour) in front of a long relative clause than in front of a short one. She provided evidence from listening experiments that placing a prosodic boundary in front of a relative clause increases the frequency with which it is taken to modify the earlier noun, and showed that this effect holds in various languages other than English. She claimed that cross-language differences in whether the relative clause tends to modify the first vs. the second of the preceding noun phrases can be attributed to cross-language differences in the prosody with which relative clauses are typically pronounced. However, it is not clear that these differences in how sentences are interpreted appear on-line. Do the preferences manifest themselves right when the eyes are fixating the relevant words, or are they put in place only later, after the sentence is read and thought about? Further, existing evidence does not even securely demonstrate that the preferences *are* due to implicit prosody as opposed to other effects that differences in length of clauses could have. Answers to questions about just what role the inner voice plays in guiding sentence interpretation clearly require additional research.

Summary

In this chapter we have considered the role of inner speech in reading. Evidence from a number of different types of experiments converge on the notion that inner speech serves a useful function in reading comprehension. Although the meanings of individual words can be determined without recoding written language into speech, phonological representations clearly affect how words are identified. Further, phonological codes appear to be activated for most words we read, and this phonological information is held in working memory and used to comprehend text. Although inner speech consists of articulatory movements (subvocalization) and phonological codes (hearing your voice), evidence suggests that interfering with subvocalization does not necessarily block the establishment of phonological codes, although it may interfere with some aspects of phonological representations (e.g., prosodic structure.) Finally, we considered the nature and role of phonological representations in some detail and suggested that, in addition to the role they play in recognizing individual words, they may be used to hold information about temporal order in working memory and to provide prosodic cues that are useful in comprehending the text.

8
WORDS AND SENTENCES

In the previous chapters of this book we have examined how the eyes move through text and how a reader recognizes the words that are seen. We have argued that reading is largely a word-by-word affair, and have discussed how the identification of words is affected by context. But we know that reading, and language comprehension generally, is more than identifying words. The words have to be put together into meaningful sentences, which then must be interpreted with respect to the context in which they occur and strung together into coherent discourses if the reading process is to be successful. While words are presumably stored as units in the lexicon (overlooking such things as novel compound words), there are too many sentences for there to be a "lexicon" of sentences. They must be built on the fly. Sentences have the property of compositionality; a reader or listener constructs, or "composes," the meaning of a sentence out of the meanings of the words it contains, plus their grammatical relationships. The current chapter explores how this is done.

Composing sentence meanings

Earlier in this book we gave a somewhat unsatisfactory account of what a word is—a series of letters between spaces. We could define a sentence in the same way—a string of words delimited by such devices as capitalization and a period. However, since Chomsky (1957), the major agenda of modern linguistics has been to construct a theory to explain what makes a string of words a grammatical sentence. Such a theory would take the form of a grammar; a collection of rules or principles that specify which strings of words are legal sentences in the language. To be grammatical, a sentence must follow the rules of syntax and morphology (where, roughly speaking, syntactic rules specify the possible structures sentences can take and morphological rules specify the possible forms of words, e.g., what forms inflections take). A simple sentence (one containing no embedded sentences) can correspond, roughly, to an idea unit, or more precisely a proposition, which can be defined as a symbolic object that can be true or false. You can read *The man bit the dog* and decide whether it is true or not, given the context in which it occurs (in which a dog actually bit a man). But a sentence is not just a collection of words. That sentence would be false, while the same words, arranged as *The dog bit the man*, expresses a true proposition. How the words are arranged (and in many languages, what morphological form they take) matters—usually (see the very end of this chapter for some discussion of how readers may engage in "good-enough" processing).

Linguists have long recognized that sentences have parts that are larger than words. These parts are called phrases. There are noun phrases, like *the dog*; even a single word like *Fido* or something as complex as *the dog that my brother told me was chasing him* can be a noun phrase as well. There are verb phrases, like *bit the man* (or *barked* or *acted like it had been hit with a rock*). Phrases, as these examples should make clear, can contain other phrases. A clause is a special kind of a phrase, one that contains all the elements of a sentence. One sentence can contain multiple clauses, e.g., *I thought that you said that the dog bit the man*; in effect, there can be sentences inside sentences ("embedded sentences"). A reader must decide how to group words into phrases, and what role each word plays in its phrase. This task is called "parsing." It uses the reader's implicit knowledge of syntax and morphology, together with other information, as will be discussed later.

A sentence does not have to be meaningful to be grammatical. One can parse a sentence and still not know what it means. Consider Chomsky's (1957) famous *Colorless green ideas sleep furiously* or Lewis Carroll's wonderful sentence in *Jabberwocky: 'Twas brillig and the slithy toves did gyre and gimbol in the wabe.* Most often, though, readers do understand what a sentence means. In the case of a simple, declarative sentence this amounts to determining the proposition that the sentence expresses, and perhaps evaluating its truth. In a complex sentence it can amount to deciding what state of affairs the combined propositions the sentence describes and, perhaps, whether this state of affairs corresponds to the real world.

The task of determining the meaning of a sentence is not simple. The order in which the words and phrases of a sentence appear (which, in English, largely specifies its syntax) does not, by itself, determine what the meaning of the sentence is. Consider the contrast between *The girl is eager to please* and *The girl is easy to please*. *The girl* plays the role of "agent" of *please* (the person doing the pleasing) in the former sentence, and the affected object or "undergoer" (arguably the "experiencer") of *please* in the latter. This difference is signaled by the words *eager* and *easy*. For another example, the role of the subject noun phrase *The girl* is very different in *The girl kissed the boy* and in *The girl liked the boy*. In the first example *the girl* is the agent; in the second *the girl* plays a different role, again an "experiencer." And in the ambiguous sentence *The girl frightened the boy*, *the girl* could be taken either to be an agent (who deliberately does something to frighten the boy) or the theme, in this case the non-agentive source of the boy's (an experiencer) fright. In some linguistic theories, these differences in meaning also appear as differences in syntactic relations, but for our purposes we will emphasize the difference in the meaning roles that the phrases play.

The reader may even go beyond identifying the grammatical structure of a sentence and the meaning that it explicitly expresses, and determine what additional propositions it implies. If you read *The man paid for the car*, you will very likely infer that he owns it; if you read *The man drove the car off the precipice into the thousand-foot deep canyon*, you may infer that the poor man is now dead. A reader may also decide that a sentence is being used to express something other than the proposition it appears to express. If you read a dialogue in which one person says *You could close that window, I think*, you probably won't take it as an observation about the addressee's abilities, but rather as a not terribly polite way of conveying a request (see Austin, 1962, for the seminal statement of the idea that people can apparently be saying one thing but are actually indirectly conveying a quite different message). Readers are also affected by how a sentence is related to its context (e.g., the reader can identify what information in the sentence is presented as old information and what is new, and try to understand the sentence accordingly). Such relations fall under the heading of "pragmatics." We will discuss the process of interpretation after we discuss parsing (but we will save some aspects of it, such as making inferences and processing pragmatic relations, for the following chapter).

Parsing

We use the term "parsing" to denote the process of identifying the parts (or phrases) of a sentence and the relations between them. Linguists have long recognized that sentences could be divided into their constituent phrases and represented as branching tree structures (as illustrated in Figure 8.1, using old-fashioned but easily understood labels), which capture many important syntactic relations among the words in a sentence. A tree structure describes a sentence (but as we will make clear later, does not directly specify how a sentence is parsed). The description is easily understood by starting at the top node S, which represents the whole sentence. The sentence is divided into parts, represented by "nodes" that are "daughters" of the parent node S. These nodes have labels like NP (noun phrase) and VP (verb phrase), and represent the constituents or phrases of the sentence. An important feature of the structure indicated by the tree is that some units are "further down" than others, so that, for example, the subject NP is just under the sentence node, while the object NP is "below" the VP and is thus in a more subordinate position to S. The structure goes down through potentially any number of daughter nodes until one reaches individual words or morphemes at the bottom. The tree structure provides part of the description of the grammatical relations among the words and phrases of a sentence.

Chomsky (1957, 1965, and many later works) revolutionized how linguists analyze these tree structures. He proposed that the task of linguistics was to formulate explicit rules that enumerate and describe ("generate") all and only the grammatical sentences of a language. He proposed that these rules amounted to a theory of the language, and that a language user had to have implicit knowledge of the rules. His claims about what rules are possible amounts to a theory of human languages, in general. In Chomsky (1957) he offered phrase structure rules, together with transformation rules, as his initial proposal for what the grammatical rules are.

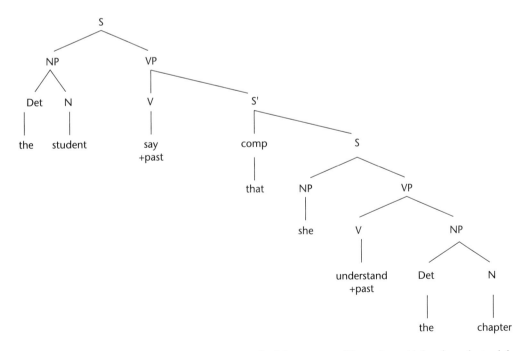

FIGURE 8.1 The syntactic structure (tree structure) of the sentence *The student said that she understood the chapter*

A phrase structure rule is a rule that rewrites one symbol (such as S) as one or more symbols (such as NP + VP). Such rules are written with the starting symbol on the left of a rewrite arrow, and the expanded symbols on the right of the arrow. A simple set of phrase structure rules, sufficient to generate the tree structure in Figure 8.1, appears in Figure 8.2.

Consider how these rules generate Figure 8.1. The first rule takes the presumed start symbol, S, as a given, and rewrites it as the sequence NP + VP. The second rule expands the node NP into its "daughter nodes," Det (determiner) and N (noun). These symbols are then rewritten as the words *the* and *student*. The third rule expands VP into V + S'. The fourth rule takes this S' (which is itself the parent or "mother" node for an embedded sentence) and rewrites it as a complementizer (a function word that introduces a sentence) plus a new S. Note that S is the original start symbol, so the whole process can start over again at this point, a process called recursion. This process is what lets sentences contain other sentences; it permits the rules to generate an infinitude of sentences, so you can have an S above an S above an S . . . without end. You can easily trace out the remaining steps yourself. These phrase-structure rules can generate an infinite number of sentences, but fall far short of generating all the sentences of English (e.g., in their current form, they have no way of generating sentences embedded within noun phrases, and thus cannot generate a phrase like *the sentence that you just read*, which is a noun phrase with a sentence—a relative clause—inside).

Chomsky (1957) used transformation rules to twist the trees generated by phrase structure rules into various non-simple sentences (e.g., to change a statement into a question, and even to put two sentences together). However, the transformation rules he used were soon recognized as being too powerful (they could generate languages that are entirely different from any human language, which is clearly undesirable if the theory of grammar is supposed to be a theory of natural human languages). Further, they were largely unnecessary, given that phrase structure rules can be recursive. An important remnant of transformation rules still exists in some grammars, in the form of movement rules. These rules move a symbol from one legal position in a phrase structure tree to another, permitting elements of a tree that are far removed from one another to depend on each other (e.g., *which book* in *Which book did the man read* depends on *read*; it is the underlying direct object and semantic theme—roughly "affected entity"—of *read*. It can be analyzed as having been generated as the direct object of *read* by the phrase structure rules and then moved to the front of the sentence, leaving an invisible "trace" behind, following *read*; often represented with a subscripted symbol *t* as in *Which book$_i$ did the man read t_i*).

Tree structures provide a very natural way of specifying some possible relations between words and phrases. These relations include parenthood and daughterhood (i.e., which phrases include,

$$S \longrightarrow NP + VP$$
$$NP \longrightarrow Det + N$$
$$VP \longrightarrow V + S'$$
$$S' \longrightarrow comp + S$$
$$VP \longrightarrow V + NP$$
$$Det \longrightarrow the$$
$$N \longrightarrow student, she, chapter$$
$$V \longrightarrow said, understood$$

FIGURE 8.2 An illustrative set of phrase structure rules sufficient to generate the tree structure in Figure 8.1 (overlooking inflectional morphology)

or are included in, which other phrases) and sisterhood (which parts are adjacent to each other, sharing the same superordinate node). But linguists have not limited themselves to such relations. Other relations recognized by some models of grammar include grammatical relations like subject-of and thematic relations like agent and theme or undergoer, as well as various sorts of dependency relations.

A couple of caveats are in order here. First, linguists do not claim that the rules of syntax are necessarily what is held up in school to be "good grammar". Linguists are not prescriptive grammarians. Instead they claim that speakers and writers (and listeners and readers) have implicit knowledge of rules that allow them to utter or interpret sentences in their own language, fully recognizing that different languages and even different dialects have different grammars. The second is that even the best speakers and writers among us are occasionally ungrammatical. However, this is viewed as a deficit in performance (i.e., a slip in execution) rather than a statement about the basic linguistic competence, since the speaker or writer would recognize their mistake if the utterance were "played back."

Early psycholinguists, upon reading Chomsky, conjectured that readers might somehow use the rules he postulated to build phrase structures for the sentences they read, thereby guiding their interpretation of the sentences. They did not claim that readers have any conscious awareness of phrase structure trees; they simply claimed that readers group words together into phrases and determine how the phrases are related to one another, and that the phrases and their relations are adequately represented by phrase structure trees. But until the late 1970s psycholinguists had few really good ideas about how readers used their implicit grammatical knowledge to parse sentences (for early but less than satisfactory attempts see Fodor, Bever, & Garrett, 1974; Miller, 1962). We will discuss various more satisfactory attempts below (for a more detailed introduction, see Pickering & van Gompel, 2006; van Gompel & Pickering, 2007).

But first, a few more cautionary notes. First, grammars have changed a lot since Chomsky (1957). Chomsky himself has made several radical changes in his theory (e.g., Chomsky, 1965, 1981, 1995). Phrase structure rules no longer play a role (although they still do, sometimes in different formal guises, in other contemporary grammars). Instead they have been replaced by very abstract and general principles restricting the possible shapes of phrase structure trees. Much of the detailed and specific information that the original phrase structure rules contained is now represented in detailed lexical entries. These entries amount to theories of how individual words can be used in sentences. Still, many psycholinguists find phrase structure rules useful in building theories of how people parse sentences. Frazier (1989), for instance, suggested that phrase structure rules may have psychological reality as the pre-compiled consequences of the abstract principles of some contemporary grammars, essentially templates for local configurations of phrases, and may be the grammatical knowledge that people actually use in parsing.

Further, note that a phrase structure tree represents both constituency (which words go together into which phrases, which phrases contain which other phrases) and order (which words occur before which other words). In some languages, like English, the order of words in a sentence provides important information about which words go together in phrases. The NP that precedes the verb is typically its subject; the NP that immediately follows the verb is normally its direct object. In other languages, though, word order does not provide clear information about syntactic structure. In German, for example, any NP can be moved to the initial position of a sentence, depending on pragmatic considerations such as focus (Hemforth & Konieczny, 2000). Its grammatical role is conveyed by the case marking specified by the ending of the word's determiner (which, to the dismay of students learning German as a second language, can be ambiguous; for instance, with a masculine noun like *Patient*, the determiner *der* indicates that it is nominative while *den* signals the accusative, but for a feminine noun like *Ärztin, die* works for both nominative and accusative). Japanese is even more extreme. The verb has to occur as the very last word in a clause (in contrast to English, where it is basically the first word in the VP), and the NPs that it is related to can occur in essentially any order, earlier in the sentence (as a result of a process called scrambling, which is dependent on the information structure of a discourse—e.g., the topic of the sentence can appear at the very start of the sentence, regardless of its grammatical role). It is obvious that users of different languages have to rely on very different sources of information to determine which words are related, and how, in phrases (see Bornkessel & Schlesewsky, 2006, for one parsing theory that is designed to apply to languages with very different grammars).

Finally, note that a reader must be sensitive to detailed aspects of syntax and morphology to understand sentences properly. Frazier (1983) presented some persuasive arguments that readers and listeners *must* use their knowledge of grammar to make distinctions between sentences that seem very similar but mean very different things. She noted that English readers form different interpretations of the baseball sentences in 8.1:

> The umpire helped the child to third base.
> The umpire helped the child on third base. (8.1)

The first of these sentences means that the umpire did something to help the child reach third base; the second means that the umpire did something to assist the child who was on third base. The difference between *to* and *on* makes a big difference.

Readers can also form three very different interpretations of the sentence in 8.2:

> He showed her baby pictures. (8.2)

In the first interpretation, the first example in 8.3, the baby of an unspecified woman is being shown some pictures; in the second example, some woman is being shown baby pictures; and in the third example, an unspecified person is being shown baby pictures that belong to someone (maybe her).

> He showed her baby the pictures.
> He showed her the baby pictures.
> He showed [someone] her baby pictures. (8.3)

The different interpretations of 8.1 and 8.2 reflect very minor differences in their lexical make-up or invisible differences in the syntax of the sentences. These differences, however, have major implications for grammatical structure. Why does syntax have to play such a core role in comprehension? Why can't we simply take what we read or hear to make sense in the situation? Perhaps Garrett (1976) put his finger on it, when he said that grammar exists to let us say surprising things, like *The man bit the dog*.

Methods

Before diving into theory and data about parsing, let us briefly consider the experimental methods used to study the topic. As will become apparent, we believe that measuring where and how long the eyes look during reading is the most illuminating method. Many of the questions about sentence parsing turn on how difficult it is to parse a sentence, which is reflected in how long it takes to read the sentence. In earlier chapters we have shown that eye fixations closely reflect word recognition processes. We will argue that the same is true of parsing: the duration of eye fixations and where the eyes move, can reflect the processes of parsing and interpretation. Because of this, a lot can be learned about parsing by measuring eye movements.

A researcher who is studying parsing and interpretation might rely on somewhat different eye movement measures than those that play a central role in studying word recognition. First-pass reading time (the summed fixation time on a region of a sentence from first entering it until first leaving it, which is the multi-word analog of gaze duration) is often more informative than first fixation duration or gaze duration on the first word of a region, since it may take more than one word to signal what a sentence is conveying. Go-past time—also called regression path duration—(the summed fixation duration from first entering a region to first exiting the region to the right and thus going further into the sentence) is very useful because it captures two consequences of processing difficulty: long fixations and regressions back to earlier text. The frequency of regressions out of a region, or regressions into another region, can be very informative. Second-pass reading time and total reading time on a region (see Chapter 4), can also provide information about how long it takes a reader to clear up processing difficulty. Many researchers have referred to first fixation duration and first pass time as "early" measures, and second pass time and total time as "late" measures, but there is no hard and fast relation between early and late processes and the different eye movement measures. All we can say for sure is that the time at which some parsing effect appears in the eye movement record puts an upper bound on when the process that underlies the effect took place.

Although eye movement measurement is the method of choice for studying parsing, other methods have also contributed a great deal to our understanding. In self-paced reading experiments readers press a button to make each successive word or phrase in a text appear (generally making previously read words disappear). They press at their own rate, controlling their reading rate, and the times at which the key is pressed are recorded by a computer. This method has uncovered a great many effects that have stood the test of time (Mitchell, 2004), but it has limitations. First, self-paced reading is slower than normal reading. An unfamiliar response has to be used to bring up new words, giving the reader extra time that could potentially be used to engage processes that normally do not take place, and the unfamiliarity of the task (as compared to normal reading) may also distort results in unknown ways. It does not provide parafoveal preview of upcoming words (see Chapter 4). Further, since it prevents regressive eye movements to earlier parts of the text, and because effects that should theoretically appear on one word in word-by-word self-paced reading often actually appear on the next word, it is not an ideal method. Nonetheless, it is easy to use and has proved useful in many domains.

Another method used to study parsing is cross-modal priming. In cross-modal priming, a participant reads a sentence, using word-by-word self-paced reading or experimenter-controlled word-by-word presentation, and at some point an auditory probe word is presented for some kind of task, e.g., lexical decision (see Swinney, 1982, for examples). If this probe word is related to what is in the reader's mind when it is presented (e.g., if it is semantically related to the current interpretation of the sentence), the decision about it may be facilitated. This permits the task to probe what mental representations the reader builds at any moment in a sentence.

Speed–accuracy trade-off measurement is yet another method. This paradigm visually presents a probe word at varying, short intervals after a target word, and the reader is forced to make an immediate decision about it (e.g., Does it fit into the sentence?). The sentence is presented word by word and the target word is generally the last word of a sentence. A response reflects the participant's best guess about how well the word fits. For a well-practiced participant, the accuracy of the decision starts out at chance at short delays between target and probe word, but grows over the course of the next few hundred ms. The rate and asymptote of this growth can inform us about the representation of the sentence and how it affects the decision (see Martin & McElree, 2008, for one example).

Finally, a good deal of recent research uses brain-imaging methods to study sentence comprehension. Electroencephalogram (EEG) recording measures the traces of brain electrical activity at the scalp, and the magnetoencephalogram (MEG) measures the magnetic field produced by brain activity. Functional magnetic resonance imaging (fMRI) measures the increased blood flow that goes to active parts of the brain. One very informative way of analyzing the EEG record is to look for event-related potentials (ERPs), which are typical waves of brain electrical activity time-locked to specific stimulus events, like the onset of a critical word in a sentence. Typical findings from ERPs are that a negative-going wave appears when an unexpected or semantically anomalous word is read (peaking at about 400 ms after the word onset, and termed the N400) and a positive-going wave appears in response to a grammatical misanalysis or an ungrammaticality (peaking at about 600 ms; the P600). These measures can be used to determine what words a reader finds to be anomalous and when a reader makes a parsing error that has to be corrected (for extended discussion of ERP methods see Kutas & Federmeier, 2007; Kutas, Van Petten, & Kluender, 2006).

There are other measures of value. Sometimes it is informative just to ask a reader how easy or natural a sentence seems to be, or what an ambiguous sentence means. Such questionnaire studies can be used to test theories of what sorts of structures are easy vs. hard to parse (e.g., Arregui, Clifton, Frazier, & Moulton, 2006) and what factors guide parsing decisions (Frazier & Clifton, 2005). And a great deal of current work measures where the eyes look when a listener is hearing a sentence that describes a scene being looked at (Tanenhaus & Trueswell, 2006). It turns out that listeners generally look at what is being talked about (Cooper, 1974), so the method can be used to learn what listeners think a sentence means at any moment of time. Because this technique studies listening, not reading, we will not discuss it further; however, we believe that the same parsing and interpretation processes take place in listening and in reading (a fact that is certainly related to the topics of phonological recoding and implicit speech, discussed earlier in Chapter 7), and we believe that much knowledge gained about listening will apply equally well to reading.

Serial modular models of parsing

The modern study of parsing began with the development in the 1970s of what came to be called serial, modular models (Forster, 1979; Frazier, 1979; Kimball, 1973). Frazier's version has been called the garden-path model, since it examines when a reader is "led down the garden path" (i.e., led astray) in processing a sentence and how the reader recovers. We will consider this model in detail, since it has had the most influence on psycholinguistic research on parsing, and since it was introduced to the psycholinguistic community in the same paper that stimulated the use of eye movement measurement to study parsing (Frazier & Rayner, 1982; for updated statements of garden-path theory see Frazier, 1987, 1990; Frazier & Clifton, 1996; for another parsing model that has some important serial and modular properties see Crocker, 1995).[1]

A core motivation behind garden-path theory is the realization that comprehension is nearly immediate. Parsing does not wait until the end of a clause, but is done almost word by word ("incrementally"). Most early psycholinguists did not think this was so, positing such things as clausal models which claimed that much of the process of comprehension and even parsing took place at clause boundaries (see J. A. Fodor et al., 1974, for extended discussion). But beginning with some early findings (Just & Carpenter, 1980; Marslen-Wilson, 1973), and continuing to the current time, it became clear that understanding the role a word plays in a sentence takes place very soon after reading the word. This is seen most clearly in studies that show how quickly a semantic anomaly is detected, since recognizing that a word doesn't make sense requires that the reader recognize the word, identify its syntactic role in the sentence, and recognize that the semantics of the word are inappropriate for this role. A clear recent example is found in Rayner, Warren, Juhasz, and Liversedge (2004), discussed in Chapter 6. They showed that eye movements were quickly disrupted upon reading *carrots* in sentences like 8.4:

> John used a pump to inflate the large carrots for dinner last night.   (8.4)

This disruption means that, before the reading of *carrots* was completed, the reader identified *the large carrots* as the direct object and semantic theme of *inflate* and (perhaps helped by how *use a pump* might lead them to anticipate *inflate*) determined that *carrots* are just not the kind of things you can inflate. (We will provide more details about this experiment later.)

Garden-path theory, as described by Frazier and Rayner (1982), claimed that readers (and listeners) use their implicit knowledge of phrase structure rules to build a syntactic tree (i.e., identify the phrases of a sentence and their relations to one another). The fundamental rule in garden-path theory governing how a phrase structure tree is built is "take the first available analysis" (Frazier, 1990; Frazier & Fodor, 1978). The assumption is that, in order to understand a sentence, you must first identify its syntactic relations. One cannot tell whether the relation between *inflate* and *carrots* is plausible or not without knowing whether or not *carrots* is the direct object of *inflate*.

According to garden path theory, a reader builds a syntactic tree quickly, word by word, first identifying the word's part of speech, and then implicitly scans all the phrase structure rules that could attach this word into the phrase structure tree built up to this point. If no phrase structure rule directly attaches the word into a phrase structure tree, the reader would implicitly scan the rules that would permit a multi-step attachment. For instance, no rule directly attaches a sentence initial *The* to the start symbol S, so that upon reading a sentence-initial *the*, the reader has to scan additional rules. These might be the rules that identify *the* as a Det(erminer) and project it into a larger phrase such as a NP (e.g., NP → Det + N) and then project the NP into S (e.g., S → NP + VP). Presumably, all rules are scanned in parallel. The first set of rules to attach the word into the tree wins.

Garden-path theory claims that only a single structure is built immediately, the first available structure. If later information arrives that indicates the structure is wrong, or if the interpretation of the structure is anomalous, it is rejected and another is built (reanalysis; see below). Because only one structure is built at a time, garden-path theory is a serial theory. It is also a modular theory (see J. A. Fodor, 1983, for an extended discussion of modularity) in the sense that the initial structure is built independently of any information that is not in the syntactic module (i.e., independent of meaning, plausibility, discourse, and the like). But keep this in mind: meaning, plausibility, discourse, etc. can have an effect on reading very quickly. It is not that they are processed slowly. Rather, their processing is logically dependent on the prior construction of a syntactic relation.

Garden-path theory posited two "strategies" for parsing, the Minimal Attachment and the Late Closure strategies. It is perhaps misleading to call them strategies, because they are not the result of any deliberate, strategic choice. Rather, they are simply consequences of the fundamental principle stated above: take the first available analysis. Minimal Attachment says "build the simplest possible structure." The simplest structure will generally be the one with the smallest number of phrase structure rule applications. Because each rule application presumably takes time, and because (as mentioned above) the fastest set of rule applications linking the word into the structure wins, the selected analysis will generally be the one with the smallest number of rules and the simplest structure. The second strategy is Late Closure, which says "attach a new word into the phrase or clause currently being analyzed if the attachment is grammatical." That is, garden-path theory says that if all else is equal, the fastest way to analyze a new word is to relate it to the phrase or clause being analyzed, just because this is the one most available in memory. Late Closure, like Minimal Attachment, is thus just a consequence of "take the first available analysis."

Frazier and Rayner (1982) provided evidence from eye movement measures for both strategies. Consider the sentences in 8.5:

> The girl knew the answer by heart. (Direct object)
> The girl knew the answer was wrong. (Sentence complement) (8.5)

In the former, *the answer* is the direct object of *know*; in the latter, it is the subject of an embedded sentence, the complement of *know*. Their tree structures appear in Figure 8.3.

Note that the structure of the sentence-complement sentence contains an extra node, the circled S′ node following the verb, compared to the first sentence. The first sentence is structurally simpler because *the answer* can be attached directly as the object of *knew* while the second sentence requires more rules (expanding VP into V + S′ and then expanding S′ into NP + VP). When faced with the need to attach *the answer* into the tree structure, Minimal Attachment says: take the simpler analysis (because it is made more quickly). But when the sentence continues *was wrong*, the reader knows he or she was "led down the garden path" (i.e., tricked) and must give up the initial analysis, slowing processing. (Note further that a great deal of parsing research has used temporarily ambiguous sentences like these, not because ambiguity is interesting in itself—even though it is—but because ambiguity lets the researcher study how parsing decisions are made.)

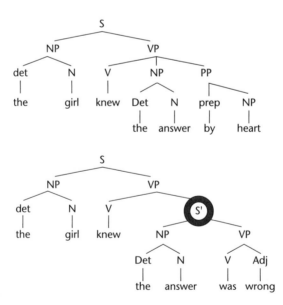

FIGURE 8.3 Tree structures for the sentences *The girl knew the answer by heart* (minimal attachment) and *The girl knew the answer was wrong* (non-minimal attachment). The circled node in the lower tree structure is not needed in the upper tree structure, making the latter simpler and temporarily preferred

Frazier and Rayner (1982) showed that Minimal Attachment predicted parsing difficulties, as measured by eye movements. They found that readers had difficulty with the sentence containing the sentence complement. Eye fixations were longer, and regressions increased in frequency, when the verb that indicated that there was a complement sentence was read, suggesting that the reader had to reanalyze the sentence (i.e., reject the initial analysis and construct a new one). You can see this in Figure 8.4, which shows the durations of the three fixations before the critical disambiguating phrase *was wrong* was fixated in a non-Minimal Attachment sentence, the duration of the first fixation on this phrase (D), and the durations of the next two fixations. Eye movements slow down very quickly when the disambiguating phrase is read and reanalysis must begin.

Frazier and Rayner also provided evidence for the operation of Late Closure. Consider the sentences in 8.6:

Since Jay always jogs a mile it seems like a short distance to him. (Late closure)
Since Jay always jogs a mile seems like a short distance to him. (Early closure)   (8.6)

Frazier and Rayner analyzed these sentences as equally complex syntactically (both have a subordinate clause followed by a main clause) and equally grammatical. However, the Late Closure principle claims that, rather than closing the first clause early and treating *a mile* as the subject of the second clause, a reader will attach *a mile* into the first clause as the object of jogs, delaying the closure of this clause. Of course, the reader might realize that a second clause is necessary, because the first clause was a subordinate clause that started with *Since*, but still it is faster and easier to attach *a mile* into the clause that is currently the focus of attention. Frazier and Rayner found severe disruption (long fixations and more frequent regressions) as soon as the disambiguating *seems* was read in the early closure sentence, compared to its reading in the late closure sentence ("...it seems ..."). This again indicated that the initial analysis followed the Late Closure principle, and it had to be given up and reanalyzed, taking time.

These results stimulated a great deal of experimental work, but also drew various criticisms. One criticism is that the early closure sentences like 8.6a usually have a comma after *jogs*, but the comma is actually not obligatory. Nonetheless it is true that the presence of the comma will reduce

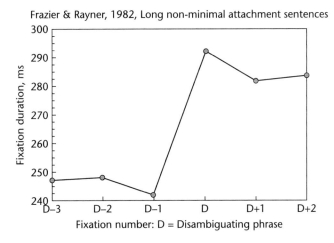

FIGURE 8.4   Reading time data from the Frazier and Rayner 1982 eye-tracking experiment, showing that reading is slowed at the disambiguating phrase for a non-minimal attachment sentence

or eliminate the difficulty of the early closure sentence. The comma provides relevant grammatical information. But the absence of the comma is not all that is going on. For example, the late closure sentence needs a comma after *a mile* just as much as the early closure sentence needs one after *jogs*. The absence of the comma in the late closure case does not seem to be disruptive. There is something special about the difficulty of the early closure case, and it is probably that the sentence violates the Late Closure principle. A second, similar, criticism is that inserting overt complementizers like *that* in non-Minimal Attachment sentences (*The girl knew that the answer was wrong*) eliminates their difficulty (Ferreira & Clifton, 1986; Mitchell & Holmes, 1985; Rayner & Frazier, 1987). However, sentences without overt complementizers are both grammatical and common in natural discourse, and the effect of the complementizer simply shows that it provides relevant grammatical information.

A third common criticism is that the parsing principles of Minimal Attachment and Late Closure would surely be overruled by meaning or plausibility or context. We will see later that there are cases where this may well be true. But a good deal of evidence shows that they are not easily overruled. Rayner, Carlson, and Frazier (1983) studied different kinds of sentences, including ones like *The boy hit the girl with the wart*. Under their syntactic assumptions, it is simpler (and hence preferred by Minimal Attachment) to analyze *with the wart* as a modifier of the verb than as a modifier of the noun, and hence the instrument analysis of *with the wart* will be preferred. But shouldn't the implausibility of this analysis block it? Rayner et al. showed that it did not. Readers' eye movements were disrupted on *with the wart*, just as if they had first interpreted it as an instrument (as predicted by Minimal Attachment) and then had to reanalyze this interpretation because of its implausibility.

An even stronger demonstration of the modularity of syntactic processing was provided by Ferreira and Clifton (1986). They studied the "reduced relative clause" construction, as exemplified by Bever's (1970) notorious sentence, *The horse raced past the barn fell*. (If you can't understand that sentence, try *The car that was driven down the road crashed*, then change that to *The car driven down the road crashed*, and then to *The car raced down the road crashed* and look for parallels to the "*horse raced*" sentence.) Ferreira and Clifton used eye-tracking to study sentences like 8.7:

> The defendant examined by the jury was misleading.
> The evidence examined by the jury was misleading. (8.7)

Minimal Attachment predicts that the first NP will be taken as subject of the main verb *examine* in both cases. This analysis is simpler than the reduced relative clause structure, in which *examine* is the verb of a relative clause that modifies the first NP (and in which the first NP is the object and theme of the verb). However, while it is plausible for a defendant to be the subject and agent of examining, it is implausible for evidence to be. So wouldn't the implausibility of the *evidence examined* analysis block the reader from making the simple subject-verb analysis? Ferreira and Clifton's (1986) evidence says that it does not (but see later in the chapter for some qualifications). Eye movements were disrupted at the disambiguating *by the jury* in both cases. This can be seen in Figure 8.5, which presents the mean first-pass reading time in three regions of the sentence. (Note that reading time is expressed in ms per character, which is a rough correction for differences in region length that is not often used any more.) Reading clearly slows down in the critical, disambiguating region of the sentence in both of the temporarily ambiguous (experimental) conditions, but not in the unambiguous (control) conditions with *that was*. Note also that reading time for *examined* was slow when it was read in the context *The evidence. . . .* this presumably was because *The evidence examined* is implausible on its subject-verb analysis. But this implausibility didn't eliminate the garden path; reading was still disrupted on *by the jury*.

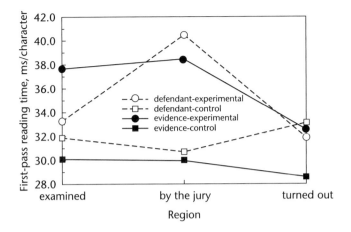

FIGURE 8.5   First-pass reading time data, expressed in ms/character, from Ferreira and Clifton, 1986

A great deal of research has stimulated modifications of the initial garden-path model. For instance, in its earliest versions, the only information about an individual word that was used was the word's part of speech. Transitive verbs (ones that can take a direct object noun phrase) like *kick* and *shout* were treated just like intransitive verbs like *sneeze* and *arrive* (ones that cannot take a direct object). The initial suggestion was that if any of these verbs were followed by a noun phrase, Minimal Attachment would take that noun phrase as a direct object. This now seems to be incorrect (for the most definitive evidence showing that readers are not garden-pathed by a noun phrase following an intransitive verb see Staub, 2007a; see also Pickering & Frisson, 2001). Advocates of garden-path theory now generally acknowledge that at least some more detailed lexical information, such as transitivity, is used in parsing. Further, it has become apparent that, while parsing and comprehension are very fast, they are not always immediate. For instance, Frazier and Rayner (1987) studied sentences like 8.8:

I know that the desert trains young people to be especially tough.
I know that the desert trains are especially tough on young people.   (8.8)

Note that *desert trains* is temporarily ambiguous between a noun + verb structure and a compound noun structure. Frazier and Rayner determined (using off-line methods) which structure was preferred. If the reader initially assigned the preferred structure (which might be the noun-verb structure for a given sentence) then reading should be slowed when the words *are especially tough* are read, since they disambiguate the sentence toward the other structure. Reading time on *are especially tough* was not slowed. And in fact, when the temporary ambiguity was eliminated by replacing the *the* with *this* or *these* (resulting in, e.g., . . . *this desert trains*, where *trains* has to be a verb, vs. . . . *these desert trains*, where *trains* has to be a noun), reading of *the desert trains* phrase actually slowed down. Frazier and Rayner suggested that, when faced with this particular ambiguity, readers actually delayed making any analysis. They could be sure that the material that immediately followed this ambiguity—a lexical category ambiguity (e.g., is *trains* a noun or a verb?)—would disambiguate it, and therefore they could safely delay analysis for a brief time, avoiding the possibility of being garden-pathed.

The principles of garden-path theory have been extended to numerous other constructions, including "filler-gap" constructions that have long distance dependencies (see Phillips & Wagers, 2007, for a recent discussion). For example, if a reader encounters a sentence like 8.9a, self-paced reading is slowed at the word *us*, compared to a sentence like 8.9b (Stowe, 1986):

My brother wanted to know who Ruth will bring us home to at Christmas.   (8.9a)

My brother wanted to know if Ruth will bring us home to Mom at Christmas.   (8.9b)

Why? It seems that the reader attempts to relate the sentence-initial *who* to the earliest place in the sentence where it can receive an interpretation (a thematic role) (note, this is another sign of immediate interpretation). Working through the sentence word by word, this is the word *bring*. But the following word *us* indicates that this is not possible; *us* occupies the needed position. Compared to a control sentence without *who*, reading is slowed at the word *us*, indicating that this word triggered a reanalysis of the initial assignment. The effect is called the "filled gap" effect (Stowe, 1986), and the principle governing it is the "active filler strategy" (Clifton & Frazier, 1989; Frazier & Flores d'Arcais, 1989) (with a generalization that includes other languages, called the minimal chain principle; De Vincenzi, 1991).

How does garden-path theory account for the apparent fact that readers and listeners do generally use all available information (meaning, discourse context, situation, plausibility, knowledge of the speaker, etc.) in arriving at the most likely meaning of a sentence, if this informa-tion is not used initially in parsing? Serial, modular models attribute this to reanalysis, a stage following the quick, initial, modular parse. Rayner, Carlson & Frazier (1983) discussed reanalysis, positing a thematic processor that searched for information that could refine the initial analysis. Other researchers have proposed various interesting ideas about how reanalysis takes place (for a collection of papers examining the topic see Fodor and Ferreira, 1998; for evidence that readers give up initial analyses only reluctantly see Schneider & Phillips, 2001; Sturt, Pickering, Scheepers, & Crocker, 2001).

One recent proposal (Levy, Bicknell, Slattery, & Rayner, 2009) suggests that reanalysis might be affected by a reader's realization that he or she might have misread a word earlier in the sentence. Levy et al. followed up a result reported by Tabor, Gallantuci, and Richardson (2004), who measured the reading of sentences like 8.10 using a self-paced reading task:

The coach smiled at the player tossed the Frisbee.   (8.10a)

The coach smiled at the player thrown the Frisbee.   (8.10b)

Tabor et al. found that reading was disrupted after *tossed* in 8.10a, compared to reading after *thrown* in 8.10b. Apparently, readers had some tendency to take *tossed* as a main verb with *the player* as its subject, which of course is ungrammatical, since *the player* is the direct object of the main clause of the sentence. This local coherence effect was blocked in 8.10b, because *thrown* cannot be a main verb; it is unambiguously a past participle. Levy et al. (2009) used eye-tracking measures to show that the local coherence effect was reduced, or even eliminated, when a critical word earlier in the sentence (*at* in 8.10) was replaced by a word like *toward* that has fewer similar words— neighbors—with which it could be confused. Apparently, when readers have some uncertainty about what an earlier word in a sentence is, later material that seems to be inconsistent with their initial analysis of the sentence is likely to make them consider reanalyzing earlier material, slowing reading. That is, readers check to be sure that the *at* they thought they read wasn't really a similar word, maybe *as*.

Interactive, constraint-based models of parsing

Not all researchers accept serial, modular theories like the garden-path theory as an accurate description of parsing. In fact, according to an authoritative review article (Pickering & Van Gompel, 2006) an alternative kind of theory that denies both modularity and a stage analysis of parsing is currently more popular. This kind of theory is generally called an interactive, constraint-based theory. It has precursors in early theories that claimed that (a) readers and listeners build or "project" grammatical structure from detailed information about individual lexical items (Ford, Bresnan, & Kaplan, 1982), (b) that readers and listeners use multiple sources of information simultaneously (Marslen-Wilson & Tyler, 1987), (c) that parsing is like a detective searching through all available cues (the detective model; Fodor et al., 1974), and (d) that these cues compete with one another to determine the meaning of a sentence (MacWhinney & Bates's, 1990, "competition model"). Theories positing such interactive, competitive integration of multiple sources of information received a huge impetus from the development of connectionist models in the 1980s (McClelland & Rumelhart, 1986) that were briefly discussed in Chapter 3.

Most contemporary interactive constraint-based theories have some properties in common (for reviews of such theories see MacDonald & Seidenberg, 2006; see also MacDonald, Pearlmutter, & Seidenberg, 1994; Trueswell & Tanenhaus, 1994). They are motivated by the acknowledged fact that language comprehension is generally successful in arriving at the most appropriate inter-pretation for a sentence, given the context in which it is used. These theories are generally lexi-calist, frequentist, and interactive. The theories are lexicalist in that a reader's implicit knowledge of linguistic structure is assumed to be stored with individual words, not as abstract phrase structure rules, and they generally assume parsing does not involve using rules to build structures. Instead, presumed networks of nodes, each of which might represent a concept or a word or part of a concept or word, are activated. Interactive constraint-based theories often assume that the frequency of experience with a given grammatical construction, and the frequency with which particular words occur in the construction, play an important role in parsing. This is an important and contentious claim, since one of Chomsky's (1957) core insights was that language structure was more than a simple sequence of statistical probabilities. The theories are interactive, in that they permit all kinds of knowledge—not just knowledge of grammar—to influence each other in making the very first parsing decisions. Parsing, according to them, can be guided by meaning and context and knowledge of the speaker and statistical information and so on.

The development of interactive, constraint-based parsing models has led to an explosion of research, much of it devoted to showing that various sorts of information do in fact influence parsing decisions. This research has been valuable in that it has provided empirical evidence about a wide range of phenomena involved in language comprehension, and it has put limitations on some extreme claims of modular, serial models. However, despite their heuristic value, such models should not be adopted uncritically. One problem is that it is difficult if not impossible to falsify the general claim that parsing is interactive and constraint-based. This claim by itself says little more than various things might matter in comprehending a sentence; it does not by itself make any clear predictions about which things actually matter, or how and when they have their influence. This is not a claim that can be shown to be wrong.

To their credit, interactive constraint-based theorists have implemented their theories compu-tationally. Figure 8.6 is a schematic presentation of the most influential implementation (McRae,

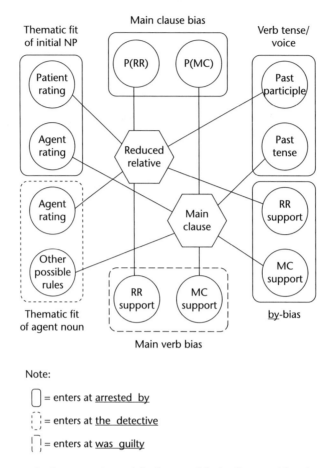

FIGURE 8.6 A connectionist constraint-satisfaction model, the "competition-integration" model, of McRae et al., 1998. Circles identify sources of information that activate the two analyses that a reader is claimed to choose between, the main clause and the reduced relative clause analyses

Spivey-Knowlton, & Tanenhaus, 1998). The two hexagons in the middle are nodes representing the two possible interpretations of the portion of a sentence that is ambiguously a main clause or a reduced relative clause (as was illustrated in 8.7, above). The theory does not explain where these two interpretations come from; it simply assumes that they exist, and are activated by various sources of information that favor one or the other. These sources of information include the higher frequency of main clause than reduced relative sentences, the relative thematic fit of the words as, e.g., subject or object, etc. All these sources of information compete with one another in a word-by-word fashion, raising or lowering the activation level of the two nodes in the middle, until some criterion of relative activation level is met—at which time, the parser commits to the more active interpretation, and moves on to the next word. An implemented model like this has the great virtue of making explicit predictions about interpretation difficulty (if the time to reach the activation criterion is longer, reading will be slower). We will argue later that not all of these predictions have been upheld.

Interactive constraint-based models de-emphasize the use of syntactic rules to create structures and instead emphasize the statistical aspects of language (how frequently particular structures are used) and lexically-specific knowledge (how particular words can be used). There is substantial evidence that more-frequent constructions are understood more easily than less-frequent ones. Consider the reduced relative clause construction discussed above (the *Horse raced* sentences). In such a sentence the temporarily ambiguous verb is in the passive voice, requiring the past participle form. For instance, in *The message recorded by the secretary could not be understood*, the word *recorded* is a past participle. Trueswell (1996) found that the difficulty normally observed in reading these sentences was reduced when the initial verb was one that occurs frequently in corpus counts as a past participle, compared to verbs (e.g., *searched*) that are used more often as simple past tense verbs.

Other constructions have been studied in which reading time might be affected by the frequency with which particular words occur in them. The direct object/sentence complement construction is one such, with a rather checkered history. This is a construction in which the word after the verb is temporarily ambiguous between its direct object (the simple Minimal Attachment analysis) and the subject of a complement sentence (e.g., *The waiter confirmed the reservation was made yesterday*). Ferreira and Henderson (1990) reported that the speed of reading sentences like these was not affected by how often the verb was used with a sentence complement vs. used with a direct object (e.g., *confirmed* is a verb that is often used with a direct object; *insisted* is more often used with a sentence complement). They argued that the Minimal Attachment strategy, not frequency of use, guided parsing decisions. Trueswell, Tanenhaus, and Kello (1993), in contrast, reported that reading speed did reflect frequency of use, and argued the opposite.

Kennison (2001) pointed out that neither of these experiments properly controlled plausibility. For example, in Trueswell et al., when a sentence contained a verb that was seldom used with a direct object, the following noun was implausible as a direct object. Kennison argued that this disrupted reading not because of parsing reasons but because the meaning of the phrase was implausible (e.g., in *The waiter insisted the reservation was made early* one cannot plausibly insist a reservation). When Kennison controlled plausibility, reading speed reflected the preferences predicted by Minimal Attachment, not those that reflect the frequency with which a verb is used with a direct object vs. a sentence complement. There are numerous other cases in which frequency of use in a particular construction affects reading time (e.g., Clifton, Frazier, & Connine, 1984; Garnsey, Pearlmutter, Myers, & Lotocky, 1997; Mitchell & Holmes, 1985; Snedeker & Trueswell, 2004), but also numerous cases where it does not (e.g., McKoon & Ratcliff, 2003; Pickering, Traxler, & Crocker, 2000; Staub, Clifton, & Frazier, 2006). Some recent approaches place great emphasis on the relative frequency of different words or word categories in very specific contexts, computing measures (e.g., surprisal) of how likely each possible word or word category is and in some cases claiming that these likelihood measures affect a reader's expectancies which in turn affect ease of reading (e.g., Hale, 2006; Jurafsky, 1996; Levy, 2008). Evidence from eye tracking of sentence corpora (Demberg & Keller, 2008) does suggest that these measures of frequency can play a role in predicting reading speed. Frequency clearly can matter; but there is a great deal left to learn about how and why it matters.

Meaning and plausibility clearly affect comprehension. The question is, how. Recall the Ferreira and Clifton (1986) result discussed earlier, in which the reading of sentences like *The evidence examined by the jury was unconvincing* was disrupted at the by-phrase, in spite of the fact that it is implausible for evidence to be the agent of examining (*evidence* is inanimate, for one thing, and a good theme but poor agent of *examine* as well). Trueswell, Tanenhaus, and Garnsey (1994) observed that a few of the Ferreira and Clifton sentences were in fact not implausible on their main verb reading (e.g., *The car towed by the truck* . . . was supposed to be implausible, but cars can tow things). They prepared a better set of sentences, carefully normed for plausibility, and re-did the Ferreira and Clifton study, using eye-tracking measures (as Ferreira and Clifton had done). Like Ferreira and Clifton, they found that when the sentence-initial noun was plausible as the agent of the first verb

(*The defendant examined* . . .), first-pass reading time on the disambiguating by-phrase (. . . *by the jury*) was disrupted compared to an unambiguous control condition (*The defendant that was examined* . . .). However, the first-pass time disruption effect disappeared when the initial noun was a plausible theme but not a plausible agent (. . . *evidence examined*). They claimed that this showed that semantics guided parsing, blocking the garden path.

Unfortunately for this straightforward story, Clifton, Traxler, Mohamed, Williams, Morris, and Rayner (2003) re-did the experiment, using the improved Trueswell et al. sentences, but performed additional analyses of the data (analyses that were not in common use in 1994). In particular, they examined both first-pass time and go-past time (regression path duration), and found, similar to Trueswell et al., that while first-pass disruption on the by-phrase was reduced when the initial noun was an implausible agent (actually, this reduction was non-significant, just as it was in Trueswell et al.), go-past time was not reduced at all. The eyes may have done slightly different things when the garden path was detected in the plausible and implausible agent cases—they lingered on the disambiguating material in the former case, and regressed back to re-read earlier material in the latter case—but reading was disrupted in both cases. Further, reading was slowed in the plausible agent, implausible theme (*defendant*) case regardless of whether or not there was any temporary ambiguity. That is, the meaning of the . . . *defendant (that was) examined* . . . sentences was difficult to grasp regardless of the presence or absence of *that was*. Clifton et al. took these results to be consistent with the claim that semantics was used to interpret unambiguous sentences and to reanalyze from a garden path, but not to block an initial implausible analysis (see Figure 8.7)

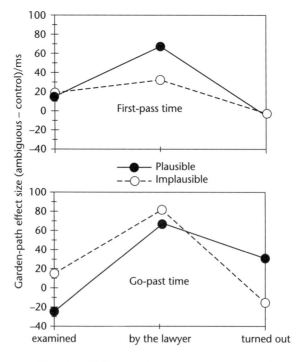

FIGURE 8.7   Garden-path effect sizes (differences in first-pass and go-past time in ms between ambiguous and unambiguous conditions) as a function of plausibility. Positive numbers indicate the presence of a garden path

The discourse context in which a sentence is read also affects comprehension, but again the question is: how and when? Crain and Steedman (1985) stimulated a long line of research when they proposed that apparent syntactic garden paths were actually semantic in nature. Consider the reduced relative clause garden path (the *horse raced . . .* sentences), discussed earlier. Crain and Steedman claimed that, when there is a single possible referent of the noun (just one horse), a restrictive relative clause is semantically inappropriate. They also claimed that a relative clause or some other modification is necessary when there are two or more potential referents. To paraphrase one of their examples, imagine you are reading a passage about two married couples and a therapist, where one couple is fighting with the therapist and the other couple is nice to him, and then read the sentence fragment in 8.11a. Crain and Steedman claimed that you will immediately take *that he was having trouble with* as a relative clause modifying wife in 8.11a, because there must be two wives involved, and the relative clause identifies which one is being referred to. In this case you will read the continuation in 8.11b very easily. However, if the continuation is 8.11c, which requires analysis as complement sentence and not a relative clause, you will have difficulty.

The psychologist told the wife that he was having trouble with. . . . (8.11a)

. . . to stop talking. (8.11b)

. . . her husband. (8.11c)

Crain and Steedman (1985) actually proposed a serial model, but one in which syntax initially proposes possible analyses and semantics comes along soon after to select the right one (see Townsend & Bever, 2001, for a roughly opposite claim, that semantics guides the initial analysis, which is then checked for syntactic legality). However, interactive constraint-based theorists took the Crain and Steedman result to support their claim that many different sources of information, including (in this case) whether the relative clause supports successful reference, affect parsing decisions. A good deal of research has shown that reference can matter, but the most commonly accepted conclusion is that while failure to refer does clearly affect comprehension (e.g., you can't write *the dog* when there are two or more dogs under discussion and nothing to indicate which one you are talking about; cf. Clifton & Ferreira, 1989), the presumed requirement to take a temporarily ambiguous phrase as a modifier can be overridden by syntactic requirements. The clearest example of this comes from Britt (1994), who showed that referential factors seemed to override weak syntactic parsing preferences but not strong ones. A verb like *put* requires a goal (i.e., where something is put). Even if the discourse context introduces two books, one of them about a battle, disruption is seen in a sentence like 8.12:

He put the book on the battle onto the chair. (8.12)

The phrase *on the battle* is initially taken to be the complement of *put*, satisfying that verb's requirement for a goal, and creates some reading difficulty when *onto the chair* is read. However, if the verb is one like *dropped*, which does not require a goal complement, the context seems to eliminate the syntactic misanalysis, and *onto the chair* is read quickly.

Context, thus, does have effects. Interactive constraint-based theory can simply say that its effects are weaker than syntactic requirements, so that strong syntactic requirements can override context effects. A modular, serial theory can simply say that the requirement that definite noun phrases have a unique, specific referent operates very quickly to correct an initial syntactic misanalysis. Which is the more satisfactory account? We think the complete story hasn't yet been told. But we do want to bring up two empirical sources of difficulty for interactive constraint-based theories. The first follows an argument advanced by Frazier (1995) who argued that both interactive and modular theories could account for fast effects of frequency or meaning or context overriding semantic preferences: interactive theories say these factors guide analysis, modular theories say they operate quickly in reanalysis. Frazier proposed that the real way to tell the theories apart is to look at their effects on the analyses that modular, serial theories claim to be preferred. She argued that, according to such theories, the analysis that honors Minimal Attachment or Late Closure is built regardless of frequency or meaning or context. That is, as long as the resulting interpretation is not semantically or pragmatically anomalous, the time to read the syntactically preferred analysis should not be affected by such factors. In contrast, she argued that interactive theories would have to predict that comprehension of the analysis that is preferred (according to modular theories) would be slowed down by factors of frequency or meaning or context if these same factors can be shown to speed up reading of the unpreferred analysis.

Binder, Duffy, and Rayner (2001), using eye movement data, showed that the disruption observed in reading a reduced relative clause sentence like 8.13a was reduced when it was presented in a discourse context that introduced a family with two troubled children, compared to a context in which there was only one child (all relative to control conditions in which the temporary ambiguity was eliminated by including *who was*). This is predicted by an interactive theory, but can also be explained in a modular theory by invoking fast reanalysis. However, Binder et al. found that if the critical sentence was a main verb sentence, such as 8.13b, the discourse context (one vs. two children) did not affect the difference in reading time between the syntactically ambiguous sentence and an unambiguous control condition. This result supports a modular theory but contradicts the predictions of an interactive theory. An interactive theory should claim that a factor (like discourse context) that facilitated one analysis (e.g., the reduced relative clause analysis) would interfere with inconsistent analyses (e.g., the main clause analysis) to more-or-less the same degree. Binder et al. implemented a computational version of such an interactive theory and showed that it did make the claimed predictions.

The teenager lectured by her stern parents left for school. (Relative clause)   (8.13a)

The daughter lectured her stern parents and left for school. (Main verb)   (8.13b)

Another source of difficulty for interactive, constraint-based models is that, for the most part, they involve multiple possible analyses competing with one another (directly or indirectly; cf. MacDonald & Seidenberg, 2006). Many of their predictions turn on the claim that more competition leads to longer decision time and slower or even disrupted reading. For instance, they uniformly account for garden-path effects by claiming that the available evidence at one point in the sentence provides strong support for one analysis, but later evidence provides conclusive support for a different analysis, and these two analyses compete, taking time. Given this analysis, competition between two analyses (or two sets of cues) at a point of ambiguity should disrupt reading (and is explicitly predicted to do so in some implemented interactive models; e.g., Elman, Hare, & McRae, 2004).

Unfortunately there is essentially no evidence that syntactic ambiguity per se slows reading (in contrast to lexical ambiguity, as discussed in Chapter 5) (see Clifton & Staub, 2008, for an extended discussion). In fact, the clearest available evidence indicates that syntactic ambiguity per se can actually speed reading. Traxler, Pickering, and Clifton (1998) and van Gompel, Pickering,

Pearson, and Liversedge (2005) carried out an extensive series of experiments with a relative clause or prepositional phrase attachment ambiguity and showed that reading was faster when attachment was ambiguous (as in 8.14a) than when attachment was unambiguous (as in 8.14b or 8.14c):

The son of the driver with the mustache . . .   (8.14a)

The driver of the car with the mustache . . .   (8.14b)

The car of the driver with the mustache . . .   (8.14c)

They argued for a race model, in which the parser tries to make both attachments in parallel (recall the "first available analysis" principle in the garden-path model). If both are acceptable as in the ambiguous case, the faster one wins; if the winner is anomalous, as could happen in the non-ambiguous case, reading is slowed down. Semantic implausibility does not seem to block an analysis in this case.

Our discussion has hardly exhausted the topic of parsing. We have had to overlook some very important approaches and phenomena and topics. For instance—this is not the only one—we have largely avoided discussing how memory considerations have an impact on parsing even though it is clear that they do. Since the earliest days of psycholinguistics, researchers have noted that some sentences place unbearably heavy loads on memory (e.g., multiply self-embedded sentences, which are grammatical but nearly incomprehensible; *The lawyer that the criminal that the judge disparaged attacked ran away*). Some researchers have proposed that an individual reader's memory span or reading span (measured as the ability to remember words from sentences being read) predicts aspects of parsing (Pearlmutter & MacDonald, 1995) while others have claimed that the memory used in sentence comprehension is, to an extent, distinct from normal working memory (Waters & Caplan, 1999). Theorists have built parsing theories based on the idea that processing load is increased when words that are dependent on each other are far apart in a sentence (Gibson, 1998). Others have proposed that interference in memory retrieval is responsible for some important processing effects (Gordon, Hendrick, & Johnson, 2001; Lewis & Vasishth, 2005).

Interpretation

We have already begun discussing some important parts of interpretation, namely the extent to which sentences are plausible as statements about the real world and the extent to which they are appropriate given the referential context of a discourse. There is more to meaning, however, than reference and plausibility. We will discuss a few contemporary approaches to studying how readers extract meaning from the sentences they have read and parsed (see Frazier, 1999, for a thorough and linguistically sophisticated treatment of earlier research on semantic interpretation).

Thematic roles and the argument–adjunct distinction

Semantics is actually a vast topic. We begin by discussing a concept we have already mentioned, thematic roles. Verbs (and other parts of speech) are thought to specify some semantic roles that the words they co-occur with (their arguments, such as their subject and their direct object) can take. In some accounts (Jackendoff, 1972) these are general but fairly detailed roles, such as agent (the intentional cause of an event; *The man* in *The man put the vase on the shelf*), patient or theme (the affected object; *the vase*), goal (*on the shelf*), source, experiencer, instrument, and so on. In other accounts thematic roles are very general, with only extremes (agent or doer vs. theme or undergoer; Bornkessel & Schlewesky, 2006; Dowty, 1991) being specified, and other roles representing blends of these. In still other accounts (Ferretti, McRae, & Hatherell, 2001; McRae, Ferretti, & Amyote, 1997), thematic roles are reflections of more detailed semantic knowledge of the situations in which verbs and other words are typically used. For instance, language users know not only that the verb *arrest* takes an agent and a theme; they also know that the agent of *arrest* is most likely to be an individual like a policeman, and the theme someone like a criminal, so that the comprehension of a sentence can be facilitated when these detailed relations are expressed.

In all these accounts there is a fairly close relation between syntactic relations and thematic roles. A subject is, by default, an agent (but it need not be an agent; e.g., it is an experiencer in *Jack liked Jill* and a theme in *Jack was pushed by Jill*). A direct object is, by default, a theme. An object of a preposition can very naturally either be a source or a goal. But, as mentioned earlier, thematic roles are not completely determined by syntactic relations. Lexical knowledge can also play a role (recall the earlier example of *The girl was easy to please* vs. *The girl was eager to please*). A theory that emphasizes the importance of thematic relations must describe how various sources of information are integrated to determine what thematic relations a sentence expresses.

Thematic roles have been studied in many ways (for early stimulating work see Carlson & Tanenhaus, 1988; for a promising recent approach see Ferretti et al., 2001). Here we will discuss a phenomenon we introduced earlier in this chapter, which we think has implications for how thematic roles are processed. Rayner et al. (2004) showed that, when one reads the sentence in 8.15a, gaze duration on the highly implausible (arguably, impossible) word *carrots* was lengthened, compared to the plausible use of *carrots* in 8.15b:

> John used a pump to inflate the large carrots for dinner last night. (8.15a)

> John used a knife to chop the large carrots for dinner last night. (8.15b)

> John used an axe to chop the large carrots for dinner last night. (8.15c)

As discussed earlier, this means that readers very quickly decided that *carrots* is the direct object and semantic theme of *inflate* and that such an interpretation makes no sense at all. Interestingly, there was also disruption in the possible but still implausible 8.15c; however, disruption was delayed, appearing only in the go-past time measure on the words immediately following the target word (and, with marginal significance, on the go-past measure on the target word itself).

Warren and McConnell (2007) showed that the really fast effects (first fixation and single fixation duration in their data) appeared only for sentences that expressed an impossible relation between the verb and its object.

> The man used a photo to blackmail the thin spaghetti yesterday evening. (8.16a)

> The man used a blow-drier to dry the thin spaghetti yesterday evening. (8.16b)

In 8.16a the grammatical object *spaghetti*, given what we know of the meanings of the words, cannot serve as the theme (affected object) of the verb *blackmail*. In contrast, merely implausible relations, as in 8.16b, resulted in regressive eye movements and long go-past times but not in an immediate disruption. Spaghetti can be blow-dried, but it usually isn't. It appears that violations of possible thematic relations may be detected more quickly than violations of more general world knowledge, suggesting that computing thematic relations may be an early step in interpretation.

What is the role of world knowledge? That's a very difficult question to answer, given that nobody is close to having a complete theory of world knowledge. But consider a result reported by Warren, McConnell, and Rayner (2008), who put sentences like the impossible event sentences used by Rayner et al. (2004) into fantasy contexts (e.g., Harry Potter doing magic), thereby changing what was possible in the world being talked about (see also Ferguson & Sanford, 2008). They showed that the fantasy context did not affect first-pass duration on the highly implausible phrase. However, the fantasy context did eliminate the disruption observed for go-past time. Warren et al. argued that the fantasy context did not affect the initial interpretation (we would say, did not affect the initial assignment of thematic roles), but did facilitate eventual integration.

Another line of evidence that supports the quick assignment of thematic roles comes from studies of the distinction between arguments and adjuncts. This distinction is basically a syntactic one. An argument of a word is a phrase that is a syntactic sister of that word, i.e., is immediately dominated by the same node. An adjunct is (typically) a modifier, and is syntactically attached at a higher level in a phrase structure tree. The interpretation of an argument is lexically specified by the word it is sister to; the interpretation of an adjunct is not closely dependent on the particular word it modifies, but is specified by fairly general principles. To take a simple example, in *John put the vase on the shelf in the morning, on the shelf* is an argument of *put. Put* requires a prepositional phrase argument, which specifies the goal of the act of putting. In contrast, the phrase *in the morning* is an adjunct that can modify essentially any word denoting an event. (For a detailed discussion of the linguistics of the adjunct/argument distinction, aimed at psycholinguists, see Schütze & Gibson, 1999; for discussions of related distinctions, based more on psychological principles, see Boland, 2004, Koenig, Mauner, & Bienvenue, 2003; for a proposal that adjuncts and other "non-primary" phrases do not receive the immediate kind of syntactic analysis that "primary" phrases do, see Frazier & Clifton, 1996.)

The main point is that arguments specify thematic roles whereas adjuncts do not. Our claims so far suggest that argument relations should be identified particularly quickly, and this seems to be the case. Clifton, Speer, and Abney (1991) used eye-tracking and self-paced reading measures to study the comprehension of sentences like those in 8.17. In both 8.17a and 8.17b, *in a wallet* is an argument of *interest*, even though *interest* is a verb in the former and a noun in the latter. They contrasted the reading of the prepositional phrases in these sentences with its reading in sentences where the prepositional phrase is an adjunct of a verb or a noun (8.17c and 8.17d):

The salesman tried to interest the man in a wallet. (Verb argument)   (8.17a)

The man expressed his interest in a wallet. (Noun argument)   (8.17b)

The man expressed his interest in a hurry. (Verb adjunct)   (8.17c)

The saleswoman tried to interest the man in his fifties. (Noun adjunct)   (8.17d)

Clifton et al. were testing a theory of Abney's (1989) which claimed that parsing decisions are made by preferring argument attachments to adjunct attachments, not by honoring the Minimal

Attachment principle discussed earlier. Minimal Attachment claims that syntactically attaching a prepositional phrase to a verb is simpler, and preferred, to attaching it to a noun; Abney's theory claimed that argument attachment would be faster than adjunct attachment, regardless of the part of speech of the host. Clifton et al. (1991) did find a small but significant early advantage for verb over noun attachment (which was not replicated by Schütze & Gibson, 1999, using word-by-word self-paced reading, or by Boland & Blodgett, 2006, measuring eye movements). More important for present purposes, however, Clifton et al. (1991) found a large and highly significant advantage for arguments of both nouns and verbs in later eye-tracking measures, in the sense that phrases that were temporarily ambiguous between arguments and adjuncts (e.g., . . . *man in a* . . . in 8.17a) were read faster when they were resolved as arguments than as adjuncts. In later research Speer and Clifton (1998) found a similar, large argument advantage when rated plausibility was controlled, and Boland and Blodgett (2006), using carefully normed materials, also found an argument advantage in first-pass time that was comparable to that reported by Clifton et al. (see Liversedge, Pickering, Branigan, & van Gompel, 1998, for a similar conclusion regarding the passive vs. locative uses of *by*-phrases). Apparently, when given a choice, readers take a phrase to be an argument rather than an adjunct.

Lexical complexity and lexical guidance

McKoon and Ratcliff (2003, cf. Gennari & Poeppel, 2003; McKoon & Macfarland, 2002) investigated one aspect of a verb's meaning (based on a linguistic analysis presented by Levin & Rappoport Hovav, 1996). The meaning of a simple change-of-state verb, like *bloom* or *arrive*, is claimed to be simpler than the meaning of a verb that denotes a causal agent causing a change of state (like *break* or *fade*). McKoon and Ratcliff provided evidence from self-paced reading and other techniques that verbs with the simpler meanings (event templates) were processed more quickly than verbs with the more complex event templates, even though they were carefully matched on numerous other variables. Further research may well uncover other effects of lexical semantic complexity on comprehension.

What linguistic devices beyond arguments vs. adjuncts and thematic roles affect sentence interpretation? Function words (little words like *and* and *or* and *some* and *not* and *may*, belonging to closed classes which are seldom expanded as language changes) certainly do. They often specify syntactic relations that have semantic consequences. The function word *not* was the subject of a great deal of research in the early days of psycholinguistics (e.g., Chase & Clark, 1972). Typical research used a sentence verification technique, in which a reader had to decide whether a sentence like *The plus is not above the star* is true of a picture. It found that responses were slowed down by the presence of the negation (but perhaps not when it is used to deny something that a reader or listener already had reason to believe; Wason, 1965).

More recently, Ferretti, McRae and their colleagues (Ferretti et al., 2001; Ferretti, Kutas, & McRae, 2007) have studied how auxiliary verbs that specify aspect affect sentence comprehension. Consider the difference between imperfective and perfective aspect, as illustrated in *The team is winning* (or *The team was winning*) vs. *The team has (had) won*. The former, imperfect, aspect denotes an ongoing action (which might be happening at some time other than the time the sentence is read or heard); the latter, perfect, aspect denotes an action that is completed. Ferretti et al. (2007) predicted that sentences in the imperfect aspect would highlight the location at which the action took place more than sentences with perfective aspect would, because the former denote an ongoing event with a time and a location, while the latter denote a completed event, with resultant state rather than time and location as a salient property. They found evidence supporting this conclusion in cross-modal priming, sentence completion, and ERP experiments. In the ERP experiment, for example, Ferretti et al. found a smaller N400 (indicating satisfaction of a semantic expectancy) to a word that denoted an expected location than to one that denoted an unexpected location (e.g., in *The weightlifter was exercising at the . . .* a smaller N400 was observed to the expected *gym* than at the plausible but unexpected *beach*). This difference held true only for sentences with imperfect aspect. With perfect aspect (*. . . had exercised . . .*), the difference disappeared. Ferretti et al. took this to mean that imperfect aspect highlights certain properties of the ongoing event, such as its location.

Semantic ambiguity

So far we have been describing how lexical information—including information about function words—can provide clear guidance to how a sentence should be interpreted. But what about semantic ambiguity? Just as there is lexical ambiguity (whose effects are fairly well understood; see the discussion in Chapters 4 and 5) and syntactic ambiguity (which has provided a tool to learn how syntactic decisions are made), there are ambiguities of semantic structure. How are they resolved? Are there preferred, default, resolutions?

Consider the ambiguity in *The wrestlers weighed 20 stone.* You may not know how much a stone is (it is 14 pounds, and is commonly used as a measure of body weight in the UK). If you didn't know that, you might wonder whether all the wrestlers together weighed 20 stone, or whether each one did. This is a semantic ambiguity. The former interpretation is called a collective reading; the latter, a distributive reading. Does a reader pick one interpretation, for some principled reason (or perhaps just pick randomly)? Does the reader consider both, attempting quickly to fix on one? Or does the reader just leave things vague until a decision is needed? It turns out (Frazier, Pacht, & Rayner, 1999) that, in cases of ambiguity like this, the reader tends first to take a collective ("all together") interpretation. When later information arrives that specifies a distributive interpretation (like the information about what a stone is, or to take an example from Frazier et al., first-pass reading time on *saved $1000 each* in *Lynne and Patrick saved $1000 each for their honeymoon* is slowed compared to when *each* is replaced by *together* (reading times were statistically adjusted for the difference in length between *each* and *together*). That is, participants read the word that supports the collective interpretation faster than one that requires the distributive interpretation. Why? It's not just that distributive meanings are hard to understand. No difference is apparent in an unambiguous baseline condition in which *each* or *together* appears before the verb (e.g., *Lynne and Patrick each saved $1000 for their honeymoon*). Instead, Frazier et al. suggested that, just as a reader must construct a single, explicit syntactic analysis so that its implications for the rest of the sentence are clear (as claimed in their garden-path model), the reader must construct a single semantic analysis. When there is a temporary ambiguity, the collective analysis is chosen because it is simpler and more quickly constructed than the distributive analysis (which, in the linguistic analysis assumed by Frazier et al., contains an additional semantic operator that specifies what is distributed over what). If later information forces this decision to be revised, reading is slowed down.

Semantic coercion

Reversing the resolution of a semantic ambiguity can slow reading. So can elaborating the semantic interpretation of a phrase in a sentence, a process that has been studied a good deal under the heading of coercion. Consider a sentence like *The man began the book.* The phrase *the book* refers to a concrete object; the verb *began* has to denote an event (like reading or writing a book). Linguists have argued that the semantic representation of *the book* must be elaborated, or coerced, into a representation of an event for the sentence to be understood; psycholinguists have demonstrated that this complement coercion process slows reading (the complement of the verb *begin* has to be coerced from being an entity to being an event). For instance, McElree, Traxler, Pickering, Seely, and Jackendoff, 2001, and Traxler, Pickering, and McElree, 2002, showed that self-paced reading and eye movements were slowed on or after a phrase like *the book* when complement coercion was required (as in *The man began the book*) but not when it was not (e.g., *The man read the book* or *The man began reading the book* and Frisson and McElree, 2008 found a similar effect in first-pass reading time using eye tracking).

A different kind of coercion, called aspectual coercion, was studied by Piñango, Zurif, and Jackendoff (1999). Participants were engaged in word-by-word reading and made a lexical decision to an unrelated auditory probe word. Lexical decision times to a probe following the word *until* were slowed in 8.18a compared to 8.18b:

The insect hopped effortlessly until it reached the far end of the garden . . .   (8.18a)

The insect glided effortlessly until it reached the far end of the garden . . .   (8.18b)

They argued that a verb like *hop* specifies a temporally bounded event, which is inconsistent with the fact that *until* is a durative adverb which must modify a temporally extended event, like gliding. A reader or listener must coerce *hop* into a temporally extended meaning, presumably an iterated series of events, and this coercion, like complement coercion, slows interpretation. (Note that Pickering et al., 2006, failed to find evidence for a cost of aspectual coercion in self-paced reading and eye tracking. See Pylkkänen and McElree, 2006, for extended discussion of coercion.)

Immediacy revisited

We have, to this point, emphasized the immediacy with which semantic interpretations are made. However, just as was the case in parsing (Frazier & Rayner, 1987), not all work is necessarily done without delay. The effects of complement coercion, just discussed, often show up a bit later in the eye movement record than effects of syntactic disambiguation, for example, and aspectual coercion may be delayed even further (Pickering, McElree, Frisson, Chen, & Traxler, 2006). Similarly, effects of semantic implausibility (as opposed to semantic impossibility; Warren & McConnell, 2007) and the effects of semantic disambiguation of postnominal modifier attachment (Traxler et al., 1998) appear with a slight delay in the eye-tracking record. We referred earlier to the clausal model of parsing, according to which parsing and interpretation are not completed until a clause boundary is reached. We argued that this is too extreme, and that most parsing decisions are made essentially without delay. But the clausal model may contain a bit of truth. The literature contains reports of decreasing availability of syntactic structure and increasing availability of semantic interpretation (as assessed by a memory test) after a clause boundary is crossed (Jarvella & Herman, 1972). Further, there is evidence (Townsend, 1978; Townsend & Bever, 1982) that verbatim memory for words that occur in a sentence-initial main clause (e.g., for the word *now* in 8.19a) is lost more quickly than when these words occur in a sentence-initial subordinate clause (8.19b):

Good jobs are now quite scarce in most large states, though there is . . .   (8.19a)

Though good jobs are now quite scarce in most large states, there is . . .   (8.19b)

Retention of verbatim information was greater when the subordinating conjunction was one like *though*, which denies a causal relation, than when it was one like *if*, which asserts such a relation. Townsend and Bever proposed that this is because a non-causal subordinate clause is interpreted only to a limited extent before the main clause is read.

The clearest evidence that some semantic interpretation is delayed to a clause boundary is the observation of "clausal wrap-up" effects (Just & Carpenter, 1980; Rayner, Kambe, & Duffy, 2000), in which reading is slowed at a clause boundary. However, the interpretation of even this evidence is in question; Hirotani, Frazier, and Rayner (2006) suggested that the effect of the punctuation that marks a clause boundary may not be due to semantic interpretation processes, but instead to implicit prosodic effects (see Chapter 7). In speaking, one typically pauses (introduces a prosodic boundary) at a comma or a period. Perhaps a reader pauses in a similar way. All that can be said for certain is that the topic of the time course of semantic interpretation is ripe for further study.

Good-enough processing

To this point we have discussed sentence parsing and interpretation as if it were an error-free process (or at least, when errors are made, they are made for good reasons and are efficiently corrected). We have viewed reading as a highly practiced, efficient, and useful skill, which it surely is. But some researchers have recently suggested that the errors we admittedly do make when we read do not simply reflect an overloaded system or an inattentive reader. They suggest instead that language comprehension is, deep down, just a means to a variety of ends—basically, getting enough out of what you read or hear to do whatever task is required (make conversation, find out where you need to go, learn how to put the kids' Christmas present together). Language comprehension is "good enough" (Ferreira, Bailey, & Ferraro, 2002). Ferreira and Patson (2007) provide a lucid overview of the claim; Frazier (2008) presents a careful critique. We will briefly review the issues involved.

One observation makes it clear that language comprehension is not always perfect. Readers quite frequently overlook the error in the question *How many animals of each kind did Moses take on the ark?* and answer "two" (Erickson & Mattson, 1981). A similar result appears when people are asked *After an air crash on the border of France and Spain, where should the survivors be buried?* (Barton & Sanford, 1993). Of course, people are not totally numb to what they are hearing or reading. If a non-biblical name is substituted for *Moses*, people detect the error, and say that Noah was the one with the ark; if *bicycle crash* is substituted for *air crash*, people recognize that you really shouldn't bury survivors. And if the critical word appears in a linguistically focused position (*It was Moses who put two of each kind of animal on the ark—True or false*) people are less likely to miss the error (Sturt, Sanford, Stewart, & Dawydiak, 2004). But it does seem clear that, sometimes, "close" is good enough.

Sometimes people really do seem numb. Ferreira (2003) had college students listen to sentences like *The dog was bitten by the man* and found a surprisingly high frequency of misidentification of the agent. Listeners reported that they thought they heard about a dog biting a man. As Frazier (2008) noted, such miscomprehension may simply reflect "experimental slop"; participants may not be bothering to listen carefully (a phenomenon every college lecturer—and student—is familiar with). But there are more subtle indications that comprehension falls far short of perfection. Christianson, Hollingworth, Halliwell, and Ferreira (2001) presented evidence that erroneous interpretations that are made while reading a garden-path sentence "linger" even after the error is corrected. For instance, after reading 8.20

While Mary bathed the baby played in the crib. (8.20)

readers are quite likely to report that Mary bathed the baby. This is the result of a Late Closure garden path. The phrase *the baby* is taken as direct object and theme of *bathe*, a misanalysis that should be corrected when *played* is read and *the baby* must be taken as its subject. There is evidence that this reanalysis is done; reading is in fact slowed at the disambiguating *played*. But something about the initial analysis lingers, even though the sentence does seem to be properly understood by the end (readers clearly know that the baby played in the crib, after 8.20). The something that lingers is likely to be a semantic interpretation, and perhaps not the original syntactic analysis (Sturt, 2007) (but see Staub, 2007b, for evidence that the initial syntactic misanalysis can still affect later syntactic processing). Still, it does appear that readers fall short of logical perfection.

Does this mean that language comprehension should not be viewed as the skilled use of implicit linguistic and non-linguistic knowledge, but instead as a heuristic, task-dependent, process? We agree with Frazier (2008) that the case is not yet made. Consider some of the most compelling pieces of evidence, e.g., the observation that interpretations based on temporary syntactic misanalyses (garden paths) seem to hang around (the *While Mary bathed the baby . . .* sentence). Note that the very existence of this misanalysis assumes that the reader is applying knowledge of possible syntactic structures in a principled way, described by Late Closure. And note that the erroneous interpretation is blocked by putting a comma after *bathed*, again indicating that the reader can use fairly sophisticated linguistic knowledge to guide interpretation.

Perhaps the best response to the arguments for good-enough processing would be to try to better understand how different goals for reading can affect the parsing and interpretation process. Many theorists have noted that readers can adopt many different goals—remembering the details of what they read, getting a vague sense of its gist, acknowledging its existence, etc.—and have suggested that these different goals may influence the reading process. A reader with very modest goals can give the appearance of good-enough processing. A few researchers have studied these influences. For instance, Swets, DeSmet, Clifton, and Ferreira (2008) showed that if experimental participants are asked detailed questions about the interpretation of the post-nominal modifier in the ambiguous-attachment sentences that were discussed earlier (the *The son of the driver with the mustache . . .* sentences; 8.14), the fast reading of ambiguous sentences, that is observed when simple and generic questions are asked, disappears.

It is also possible that readers and listeners might show a little charity toward an imperfect speaker or writer, and overlook aspects of what they read or hear that might be the result of production errors. Readers can make errors themselves, too. Consider, for instance, how readers comprehend sentences with ellipses, like 8.21:

The old schoolmaster praised the student and the advisor did too.   (8.21a)

The student was praised by the old schoolmaster and the advisor did too.   (8.21b)

The advisor praised the student and the old schoolmaster was too.   (8.21c)

Arregui et al. (2006) adopted linguistic analyses that claim that the elided material after *did* must match its antecedent structurally. It does, in 8.21a, which can be understood as *. . . and the advisor did [praise the student] too*. But the ellipsis does not match the antecedent in sentences like 8.21b or 8.21c. These sentences are, strictly speaking, ungrammatical. Arregui et al. used acceptability judgment tasks to show that sentences similar to these, where the antecedent does not have the right form for the ellipsis, are somewhat unacceptable and difficult to understand.

Arregui et al. additionally found higher rated acceptability for 8.21b, where a passive voice antecedent is followed by an active ellipsis, than for 8.21c, where an active antecedent is followed by a passive ellipsis. They suggested that this asymmetry could arise from memory errors, either on the part of the reader or the writer. Mehler (1963) demonstrated that people are more likely to recall passive sentences as actives than vice versa. A (careless) writer could start a sentence out with a passive (like 8.21b), misremember it as an active, and use an elliptical construction that requires an active antecedent. A reader could recognize this possibility and correct for it, or the reader could simply misrecall the initial passive as an active. Either of these would give the reader a reason to accept the active elliptical phrase. The converse process—misremembering an active as a passive— is less likely, and thus there is less reason to accept 8.21c.

The conclusion we draw from the research reviewed in this section is that readers do not mechanically apply their knowledge of a language to arrive at the proper understanding of a sentence. Sometimes their reading goals may lead them to fail to understand, or even to misunderstand, a sentence. Sometimes even when they do understand a sentence, traces of a temporary misunderstanding will remain. And sometimes they will understand a less than perfect sentence in a way that "cuts the speaker or writer (or themselves) some slack," as if they realize that speakers and writers and readers sometimes make errors that must be taken into account (see Frazier & Clifton, 2011, for further evidence about this last point).

Summary

We began this chapter claiming that readers have to put word meanings together to build sentence meanings, and we claimed that their knowledge of their language (grammar) constrains how they put the word meanings together. After a very brief discussion of how linguists analyze syntax, we turned to the topic of sentence parsing—how people identify the grammatical relations among words and phrases of a sentence. We claimed that a necessary step in understanding a sentence is identifying these relations. We considered two types of theories of sentence parsing, serial garden-path theories and interactive constraint satisfaction theories, presenting various kinds of evidence supporting and challenging each kind of theory. In the end we concluded that, while many kinds of evidence affect the eventual understanding of a sentence, information that is encoded into the grammar (e.g., what phrases and relations between them are possible) has a certain logical priority in comprehension. You cannot understand what happened to the poor dog in *John kicked the dog* without realizing that *the dog* is the direct object of *kicked*.

We then turned to the topic of sentence interpretation. A reader who has parsed a sentence is far from done. The reader must understand what the sentence means—a daunting task, actually. We discussed how the structural analysis provided by parsing feeds directly into the interpretation process, by e.g., constraining the possible thematic relations among phrases. We then examined several topics in interpretation. We discussed various views of how specific knowledge about lexical entries affects comprehension. We described how semantic ambiguities could have preferred resolutions (similar in some ways to the syntactic ambiguities discussed earlier in the chapter). We introduced the notion of semantic coercion, according to which some verbs require a reader to alter the semantic nature of their arguments, and we returned to the important question of how immediate semantic interpretation is, suggesting that some aspects take place essentially immediately, while others may be delayed. We concluded with a discussion of good-enough processing, considering the possibility that readers don't always make use of all the linguistic information that the text provides them, but instead sometimes process that information just well enough for the job at hand. Although this is probably true at times, readers are remarkably fast and effective at coordinating a vast range of linguistic and non-linguistic information in the task of understanding what sentences mean.

Note

1 For completeness, we note that earlier researchers used eye movements to study sentence comprehension (e.g., Mehler, Bever, & Carey, 1967), but Frazier and Rayner (1982) had the clearest lasting impact on the field.

9
COMPREHENSION OF DISCOURSE

Once a reader has parsed and interpreted a sentence, his or her work is probably not done. The reader must understand the text that includes the sentence; the meaning of a coherent text is more than the sum of the individual sentence meanings. The reader must knit the sentences together so that the propositions they contain can be combined as the writer intended. The reader must make inferences to fill in material that is only implicit in the text itself, and in doing this the reader often has to appeal to knowledge about the world, including the rest of the discourse. Ideally, the reader will understand the text in the sense of knowing what kind of real-world situation it is describing, or knowing how to do what the text is instructing the reader to do, or believing (or disbelieving) the claims it contains, and so on. Sometimes, the reader's prior knowledge distorts the text's message (Bartlett, 1932); nonetheless, what stays with the reader is generally the "gist" of the text.

Language contains devices that facilitate (but do not guarantee) accurate understanding of the text's message. Some of these devices become apparent when a text fails to use them. Consider the following malodorous passage:

> She set it down. Sue had gone to Kroger's to buy a bird. The day before, a mother
> had asked her to buy the turkey. The table's leg's collapsed. It had to be big enough
> to feed all of them. But it was too big for a table. She cleaned them from the floor.   (9.1)

There are so many things wrong with this passage! The first occurrence of *she* has no apparent referent; the second sentence talks, without warning, about an event that took place earlier than the preceding sentence; the third sentence talks oddly about *a*, not *her*, mother, and is the mother talking specifically about the turkey that Sue bought at Krogers? That's odd. And what made the table's leg collapse? And on and on.

We'll soon be discussing how people interpret pronouns and other anaphors, how they make inferences that go beyond the text, how they understand the sequence of events in an episode, and in general, how they glue a text together. But first, consider the following passage from Bransford and Johnson (1972):

> The procedure is actually quite simple. First you arrange things into different
> groups. Of course, one pile may be sufficient depending on how much there

is to do. If you have to go somewhere else due to lack of facilities, that is the next step, other wise you are pretty well set. It is important not to overdo things. That is, it is better to do too few things rather than too many. In the short run this may not seem important but complications can easily arise. A mistake can be expensive as well. At first the whole procedure will seem complicated. Soon, however, it will become just another facet of life. It is difficult to forsee any end to the necessity for this task in the immediate future, but then one can never tell. After the procedure is completed one arranges the materials in groups again. Then they can be put into their appropriate places. Eventually they will be used once more and the whole cycle will have to be repeated. However, this is part of life.   (9.2)

While you can understand the meaning of each sentence (in some sense) and even put the sentences together, the passage as a whole has no clear meaning. But if you were first told that it is describing doing your laundry, it becomes meaningful. This indicates that comprehending a text usually requires the reader to use real-world knowledge that includes plans, intentions, and causation. We will shortly discuss how readers integrate the text that they read with their knowledge of the real world and use both together to create a situation model or mental model that the reader takes as the meaning of the text. But first we will rather briefly discuss some analyses of what kind of representation readers have of a text that they read successfully.

Discourse representations

Kintsch's representations of discourse

Much of the experimental research on text comprehension was stimulated by a theory that Kintsch and his colleagues developed over a long period of time (Kintsch, 1974, 1988, 1994, 1998; Kintsch & van Dijk, 1978; van Dijk & Kintsch, 1983). One of the primary contributions of this theory was to distinguish between different mental representations of a text. These representations are called the surface representation, the propositional representation, and the situation model (Kintsch, 1994). The previous chapter focused on the first two representations, discussing how a reader goes from the printed text to a parsed representation of the form of a sentence (the surface representation) and then to a meaningful interpretation of the sentence (the propositional representation). Text and discourse processing researchers concentrate on how a reader puts the propositional representations of sentences in a text together to arrive at a representation of the situation that the text is describing (the situation model). In some versions of this theory, a distinction is made between "microstructure" and "macrostructure." Microstructure is a level of representation that puts the propositions together into a connected structure; macrostructure is the gist of the text, an edited version of the microstructure tied into schemas from long-term memory.

The typical way of representing a proposition, in approaches like Kintsch's, is as a predicate followed by its arguments. We will illustrate how this is done by sketching part of an analysis of the paragraph shown in Table 9.1. A predicate can be represented by the meaning of a verb (where meaningful concepts rather than words are indicated by UPPERCASE) and the arguments can be represented by the meanings of the nouns or prepositional phrases or adverbs that participate in the event denoted by the verb. For example (TEACH, SPEAKER, STUDENT) represents the proposition that some speaker is teaching some student(s). Other propositions represent adjective–noun combinations such as (VIOLENT, ENCOUNTER) and quantifier–noun combinations such as (ALL, STUDENT). Others represent ideas in phrases such as (OF REALITY, VOICE), others conjoin concepts such as (AND, STUDENT, SPEAKER), and others express location and time

TABLE 9.1 A paragraph and the propositions extracted from it

A series of violent, bloody encounters between police and Black Panther Party members punctuated the early summer days of 1969. Soon after, a group of Black students I teach at California State College, Los Angeles, who were members of the Panther Party, began to complain of continuous harassment by law enforcement officers. Among their many grievances, they complained about receiving so many traffic citations that some were in danger of losing their driving privileges. During one lengthy discussion, we realized that all of them drove automobiles with Panther Party signs glued to their bumpers. This is a report of a study that I undertook to assess the seriousness of their charges and to determine whether we were hearing the voice of paranoia or reality.

Proposition number	Proposition
1	(SERIES, ENCOUNTER)
2	(VIOLENT, ENCOUNTER)
3	(BLOODY, ENCOUNTER)
4	(BETWEEN, ENCOUNTER, POLICE, BLACK PANTHER)
5	(TIME: IN, ENCOUNTER, SUMMER)
6	(EARLY, SUMMER)
7	(TIME: IN, SUMMER, 1969)
8	(SOON, 9)
9	(AFTER, 4, 16)
10	(GROUP, STUDENT)
11	(BLACK, STUDENT)
12	(TEACH, SPEAKER, STUDENT)
13	(LOCATION: AT, 12, CAL STATE COLLEGE)
14	(LOCATION: AT, CAL STATE COLLEGE, LOS ANGELES)
15	(IS A, STUDENT, BLACK PANTHER)
16	(BEGIN, 17)
17	(COMPLAIN, STUDENT, 19)
18	(CONTINUOUS, 19)
19	(HARASS, POLICE, STUDENT)
20	(AMONG, COMPLAINT)
21	(MANY, COMPLAINT)
22	(COMPLAIN, STUDENT, 23)
23	(RECEIVE, STUDENT, TICKET)
24	(MANY, TICKET)
25	(CAUSE, 23, 27)
26	(SOME, STUDENT)
27	(IN DANGER OF, 26, 28)
28	(LOSE, 26, LICENSE)
29	(DURING, DISCUSSION, 32)
30	(LENGTHY, DISCUSSION)
31	(AND, STUDENT, SPEAKER)
32	(REALIZE, 31, 34)
33	(ALL, STUDENT)
34	(DRIVE, 33, AUTO)
35	(HAVE, AUTO, SIGN)
36	(BLACK PANTHER, SIGN)
37	(GLUED, SIGN, BUMPER)
38	(REPORT, SPEAKER, STUDY)

(Continued overleaf)

TABLE 9.1   *(Continued)*

Proposition number	Proposition
39	(DO, SPEAKER, STUDY)
40	(PURPOSE, STUDY, 41)
41	(ASSESS, STUDY, 42, 43)
42	(TRUE, 17)
43	(HEAR, 31, 44)
44	(OR, 45, 46)
45	(OF REALITY, VOICE)
46	(OF PARANOIA, VOICE)

Lines indicate sentence boundaries. Propositions are numbered for ease of reference and a number in a propositional argument refers to the proposition with that number. (The same numbers appear in Figure 9.1.) Adapted from Kintsch and Van Dijk (1978).

(TIME: IN, ENCOUNTER, SUMMER) or (LOCATION: AT, CAL STATE LOS ANGELES). In all cases the notation not only conveys that the concepts go together but contains some of the meaning. In (TEACH, SPEAKER, STUDENT), for example, TEACH is understood to be the verb, the second argument, SPEAKER, the agent, etc. See Table 9.1 for more examples of propositions.

As you can see in Table 9.1, a single sentence is usually broken down into several propositions. However, propositions can be built recursively so that a proposition can have other propositions as arguments. For example, in the proposition (COMPLAIN, STUDENT, 19), *19* stands for the proposition (HARASS, POLICE, STUDENT). Thus, by this recursive definition, a proposition can stand for a fairly complex thought. As you can also see in Table 9.1, many propositions are of this recursive type.

The microstructure of the text in Table 9.1 is a structure built out of the list of propositions in that table, and can be represented as a graph as in Figure 9.1. The graph is intended to capture the coherent relations among the propositions. Its structure is, in Kintsch's work, largely determined by how the propositions share concepts. Propositions with the same concept are said to overlap, and if the proposition that is being processed at one point in time shares a concept from a different proposition that is still in short-term memory, those two propositions can be linked together in the microstructure graph, from Kintsch and van Dijk (1978).

We will not review in detail the process by which Kintsch and van Dijk claim that such a coherence graph is created nor how a macrostructure is built up by attaching "important" aspects of the microstructure to a pre-existing "schema" (e.g., one's knowledge of what is likely to happen in a fairytale or a narrative about a visit to a restaurant). Suffice it to say that early research provided support for some of the predictions of the model, using measures of memory, of reading time, and of reaction time to probes, among other experimental methods. One prediction from their model is that propositions that overlap with many other propositions will appear high in the microstructure graph, and thus they are remembered better than lower-level propositions (e.g., Kintsch, Kozminsky, Streby, McKoon & Keenan, 1975; Meyer, 1975). A second prediction is that the reading time for a passage with more propositions is greater than for a passage with fewer propositions even when the number of words in the two passages is equal (Kintsch & Keenan, 1973).

A particularly interesting test of the Kintsch and van Dijk model was conducted by McKoon and Ratcliff (1980). Since this study is interesting methodologically as well, we will describe it in some detail. They used a variation of the priming technique (described below) to get at the structure of discourse memory. In one experiment, participants saw "paragraphs" like the following:

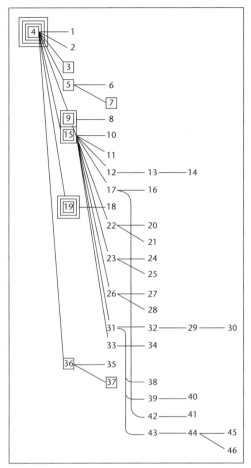

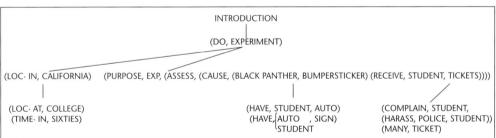

FIGURE 9.1   (Top) The complete "coherence graph" representing the microstructure of the "Bumperstickers" paragraph of Table 9.1. The numbers represent propositions and the number of squares around a proposition indicate the number of cycles it was held in STM for processing. (Bottom) The macrostructure for the Bumperstickers passage. The basic schema is a "scientific report" schema and the important propositions from the microstructure are incorporated into it. Reproduced from Kintsch and Van Dijk (1978) with permission from the American Psychological Association and the authors

(1) The businessman gestured to a waiter.
(2) The waiter brought coffee.
(3) The coffee stained the napkins.
(4) The napkins protected the tablecloth.

(5) The businessman flourished documents.
(6) The documents explained a contract.
(7) The contract satisfied the client. (9.3)

A propositional analysis of this paragraph is presented in Figure 9.2. The main feature of Figure 9.2 to notice is that Proposition 2 is closer to Proposition 5 in the microstructure than Proposition 4 is to Proposition 7 even though they are equally far apart in the surface representation of the text. Thus, the concepts WAITER and DOCUMENTS are closer in the microstructure than are the concepts NAPKINS and CLIENT (even though the two pairs of words are equally far in the surface text and the individual words in sentence 2 are not related to those in sentence 5). McKoon and Ratcliff tested for closeness using a recognition memory procedure. After reading the paragraph, participants saw a series of probe words, which they were to judge as having been present in the paragraph or not. (Their responses were timed.) Of primary interest was the effect of one probe word (the prime) on the response time to the following probe word (the target). The logic is that if responding to one probe word speeds up responding to a second probe word, then the words are closely linked in some memory structure, just as the phenomenon of *cat* priming *dog* in a lexical decision task argues that CAT and DOG are closely linked in some sort of memory structure. McKoon and Ratcliff found that *waiter* primed *documents* more than *napkins* primed *client* indicating that WAITER and DOCUMENTS were more closely linked in memory than NAPKINS and CLIENT (as predicted by the Kintsch and van Dijk model).

A problem with the above experiment is that the text was not very natural. Accordingly, McKoon and Ratcliff used more natural paragraphs such as the following:

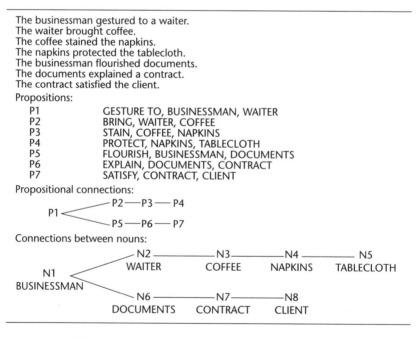

FIGURE 9.2 A paragraph from McKoon and Ratcliff (1980) together with the propositional analysis and propositional structure. Reproduced with permission from Academic Press and the authors

Early French settlements in North America were strung so thinly along the major waterways that land ownership was a problem. The Frenchmen were fur traders, and, by necessity, the fur traders were nomads. Towns were few, forts and trading posts were many. Little wonder that the successful fur trader learned to live, act, and think like an Indian. Circulation among the Indians was vital to the economic survival of the traders.   (9.4)

The probe task in the second experiment was also more meaningful, in that participants were given sentences such as *The fur traders were nomads* and asked to respond whether the idea was stated in the paragraph. (The probes essentially tested for memory of propositions.) Again, McKoon and Ratcliff looked at the effect of one probe on the next, and contrasted the priming effects of propositions that were near in the surface but far in the propositional structure with those that were near in the propositional structure but far in the surface. They found, for example, that *Circulation among the Indians was vital* which was near *The fur traders were nomads* in the propositional structure but far in the surface primed it more than *Land ownership was not a problem* which was near *The fur traders were nomads* in the surface but far in the propositional structure.

While all of these demonstrations are of interest in establishing the model, none provides definitive evidence in favor of it. The model does not have a fully adequate algorithm for creating a microstructure. Creation of a microstructure depends to a great extent on an experimenter's intuition. It is not enough to use algorithms that place propositions high in a microstructure simply because they share a noun phrase. Such algorithms may go wrong if the same noun phrase refers to different entities; propositions that share a noun phrase may involve different referents, and should not play a central role in the microstructure. Thus a successful demonstration that memory is better for propositions high in a microstructure may largely be due to the experimenter's intuitions about the importance of various propositions rather than to any intrinsic feature of the model. Similarly, the fact that reading time increases with the number of propositions could be due to the greater syntactic complexity and denseness needed to express more propositions with the same number of words. In summary, Kintsch and van Dijk's theorizing opened up the field of text processing to objective experimental study. Their representations of text captured some important aspects of a text (e.g., how propositions are linked together and how some are more central than others). Experimental work has provided support for many of the claims of the theory (e.g., the claim that some propositions are more central than others, that some propositions are closely linked to other, and that some sentences are easier to integrate into the structure of a text than others). Many of the core processing claims of the model are still widely accepted: readers are generally thought to encode the basic ideas (the propositions) in a text and to connect them together into more global, integrative structures using a limited-capacity processing system that forces integration to be selective. More recent work (some of which is discussed in the following pages) explores the details of how memory processes are involved in comprehending discourse and how the reader uses a rich knowledge base to guide comprehension (Gerrig & McKoon, 1998; Myers & O'Brien, 1998; Sanford & Garrod, 1998, 2005).

Schemas, scripts, and story grammars

It is interesting to compare the theories of sentence structure, discussed in the previous chapter, with the theories of discourse structure discussed in this chapter. The sentences of a language are described, in great detail, by the grammar of that language. Some sequences of words are grammatical; some are simply not sentences at all. Linguists have provided detailed rules that generate the sentences of a language—contentious rules, to be sure, but detailed and precise nonetheless. Psycholinguists have developed and tested explicit theories of how these rules are used and how they are integrated with nonlinguistic knowledge—contentious theories, again, but detailed and explicit.

Early discourse researchers attempted to analyze discourses in the way that linguists have analyzed sentences. They attempted, for instance, to devise grammars that would specify the permissible and impermissible structures of stories (e.g., Rumelhart, 1975; Thorndyke, 1977). Some rules specified the possible sequence of subsections of a story: SETTING, THEME, PLOT, RESOLUTION. Other rules specified how the plot subsection was to be divided into subsections, with such plot devices as goals and resolutions. Experimental research showed that disrupting the preferred order of a story (e.g., putting the theme last instead of first) disrupted memory for the story, and showed that if a superordinate proposition in a story were forgotten, its subordinates would tend to be forgotten (Thorndyke, 1977). However, most researchers now agree that while stories do have structure and violating the structure makes them less easy to comprehend, this structure is not like the grammar of a language. There is no clear line between a story and a non-story, as there is between a sentence and a non-sentence. Further, there is no evidence that readers of a story give priority to any story grammar rules in the same way that they seem to give priority to the rules of a sentence grammar; while they cannot legitimately understand *man bites dog* to mean that a dog bit a man, they can puzzle out stories presented in fascinatingly twisted ways.

A related approach to thinking about the structure of discourses and how people can use that structure to understand a text falls under the heading of schema theory (see the earlier discussion of Bransford & Johnson's 1972 "washing clothes" demonstration for an example). The fundamental claim of schema theories is that we have pre-stored, possibly elaborate, knowledge structures for different situations that guide how all the information in the text is understood and stored in memory. For example, in the laundry passage at the beginning of the chapter, the assumption of schema theorists is that you understand the passage (given the title *Laundry*) because the title allows you to retrieve a schema from your real-world knowledge for doing laundry. Once this schema is retrieved, you then tie the information in the passage into this schema.

A schema not only gives us the possibility of tying the propositions of a text down to a concrete type of situation; a schema can also let us fill in information that the writer of a text does not bother to include. Consider one specific example of a type of schema, namely the "script." A script is one's representation of a more-or-less stereotyped, socially sanctioned, series of actions appropriate to a given setting. Consider the restaurant schema or restaurant script (Bower, Black, & Turner, 1979; Schank & Abelson, 1977). When you recognize that a discourse is about visiting a restaurant, a restaurant script, essentially a structured sequence of events in a meal at a restaurant, is retrieved from memory, and certain "default values" for what happens are retrieved. The default values are presumably the actions that occur in your normal restaurant experience. The information from the script is then incorporated into your understanding of the story so that if the first sentence is about entering the restaurant and the second sentence is about ordering food, the script would fill in the missing steps, such as waiting to be seated, sitting down, getting menus, etc. Information that is redundant with the script (e.g., that the restaurant had menus) might not be explicitly added to the representation, but information that is inconsistent with the script (e.g., that the restaurant did not have menus) might be highlighted as being informative.

One of the reasons that schema theories attracted interest was that they appeared at a time when psycholinguistics had pretty much ignored the role of real-world knowledge in understanding discourse. A major thrust of these theories was to demonstrate that comprehension of a text does not follow automatically from knowing the literal meaning of its sentences, but instead has to rely on real-world knowledge such as what it is actually like to do laundry, why men go to jewelers, etc. But nobody has an adequate explicit theory of real-world knowledge, and it is not likely that one will appear in the foreseeable future. No "grammar of knowledge" is available. In retrospect, while schema theories probably captured something important and real about how we understand discourses, the predictions they made basically boil down to claiming that we are best at understanding what makes sense to us, and that what makes sense depends on what we know. (For an excellent discussion and critique of schema theories, see Alba & Hasher, 1983.)

Putting sentences together

Let us turn to a less ambitious project than explaining what knowledge is. Psycholinguists can say quite a lot about what linguistic devices make a text coherent and how readers use these devices. These devices let the reader know when something already familiar in the text is being referred to, and when something new is being introduced. They let the reader know the sequence of events and the causal relations among them. They support economy and efficiency—don't waste time saying what doesn't need saying—and, used properly, they can help the reader build a mental model of the situation being written about.

Pronominal anaphora

A third-person pronoun used in a text usually refers to an entity that has already been introduced in the text (which is termed anaphoric reference). Such pronouns contribute to the coherence of a text; they help tie the sentences in a text together. A reader's task upon encountering a pronoun is to determine what it refers to (see Garnham, 1999, for a thorough discussion).

When a pronoun has an antecedent in the text, the position and role of the antecedent can affect how a reader determines the referent of a pronoun. Early work showed that pronouns are read more easily when their antecedent is closer than when it is more distant in the text. Clark and Sengul (1979) found that as the distance between the pronoun and its antecedent increased, the reading time of the sentence containing the pronoun increased. Ehrlich and Rayner (1983) also varied the distance between pronoun and antecedent, and attempted to measure the time course of the effect by examining the pattern of eye movements on the sentence that contained the pronoun. There were three levels of distance: near, when the antecedent noun was the word immediately before the pronoun; intermediate, where about a line of text intervened; and far, where at least three lines of text intervened. A central purpose of the experiment was to test the immediacy hypothesis of Just and Carpenter (1980, see Chapter 4), which states that all linguistic operations, such as finding the antecedent of a pronoun, are completed before the eyes move on to the next word. A major problem in this research is identifying the fixation on which the pronoun is encoded, since it is usually fixated much less than half the time. Since the perceptual span extends to the right of the fixated word but not to the left of it (see Chapter 4), Ehrlich and Rayner assumed that if the pronoun was not fixated, then it was encoded on the fixation to the left of the pronoun. That is, the "encoding" fixation for a pronoun was either on the pronoun itself, or if it was not fixated on, the prior word.

There were two major findings. First, the fixation time on the encoding fixation was significantly longer (about 20 ms) than the previous one (in all distance conditions), suggesting that the reader was immediately starting to search for the antecedent in all conditions. However, in the immediate and near conditions, the two fixations following the encoding fixation returned to normal length, whereas these next two fixations in the far condition got even longer. The former finding is only suggestive, because the words being fixated are different. However, the latter finding strongly suggests that the process of searching for the antecedent may begin immediately, but in the case of the far condition, the search often continues for another fixation or two. This rules against a strong version of the immediacy hypothesis; at least some of the process of retrieving the antecedent of a pronoun is not immediate (see Carroll & Slowiaczek, 1987, for evidence that strengthens the case against the immediacy hypothesis).

However, the distance effect may not really be an effect of distance in the surface structure (i.e., how many words apart the pronoun is from the antecedent). Linguistic analyses of discourse structure (e.g., Grosz, Joshi, & Weinstein, 1983, 1995) have suggested that structural factors, not simple distance, determine the appropriateness of using a pronoun to co-refer with an antecedent noun phrase. Clifton and Ferreira (1987) tested the possibility that distance would not matter as long as the antecedent noun was still the "topic of the discourse" and thus still in some sort of active memory (see also, Garrod & Sanford, 1983). They tested this hypothesis using a phrase reading task, in which the reader saw a passage a phrase at a time and pushed a button to get the next phrase to appear. Reading time for a phrase was measured by the time between two button pushes. An example of one of their passages is as follows:

> Weddings can be / very emotional experiences for everyone involved. / The cigar smoking caterer / was obviously / on the verge / of tears, / and the others / were pretty upset too. / In fact, / the organist, / who was an old maid, / looked across the room / and sighed. / <u>She was / still looking for / a husband.</u> (9.5a)

(The slashes indicate the boundaries between phrases.) Of primary interest was the reading time for the underlined target sentence containing the pronoun *she*. In this example, *the organist* is the topic of the previous sentence and thus, according to this explanation, quite available as the antecedent for the pronoun *she* in the last sentence. On the other hand, if the middle two sentences are replaced by

> The cigar smoking caterer / was obviously / on the verge of tears, / having just noticed that / the organist, / who was an old maid, / was holding hands / with someone else. (9.5b)

the organist is not the topic of the sentence prior to the target sentence, and thus would not be available in active memory. Clifton and Ferreira found, in fact, that reading time for the sentence containing the pronoun was longer when the pronoun's antecedent was no longer the topic than when it was. As with the reading experiments measuring eye movements, a large portion of the effect was delayed, appearing after the phrase containing the pronoun. Clifton and Ferreira also varied how far back in the passage that the antecedent *organist* was, and found that distance, per se, had no effect on reading time for the target sentence as long as topic status remained the same.

Research by Gordon and his colleagues (Gordon, Grosz, & Gilliom, 1993; Gordon & Hendrick, 1997, 1998) has used a more precise and detailed analysis of the structural factors that affect finding the antecedent of a pronoun. They based their work on an analysis of "centering" by Grosz, Joshi, and Weinstein (1983, 1995) that combines linguistic and artificial intelligence approaches to language. This analysis draws on the idea that in a coherent discourse, sentences tend to keep talking about entities and events that were mentioned in earlier sentences. Centering theory (Grosz et al., 1983, 1995) defines a set of forward-looking centers, which are the entities and events in a sentence most likely to be referenced in future sentences, and a backward-looking center, which is the entity or event that is referenced in the current sentence that points back to a high-ranked forward-looking center of the previous sentence. The backward-looking center must be realized as a pronoun, if any element in its sentence is.

Gordon and his colleagues examined several implications of a psycholinguistic elaboration of this analysis, in which they proposed that a backward-looking center should generally be realized as a pronoun. One notable finding was the repeated name penalty. They measured the time to read passages like 9.6:

> Bruno was the bully of the neighborhood. He chased Tommy all the way home from school one day. He watched him hide behind a big tree and start to cry.   (9.6a)

> Bruno was the bully of the neighborhood. Bruno chased Tommy all the way home from school one day. Bruno watched Tommy hide behind a big tree and start to cry.   (9.6b)

The later sentences in 9.6b were read more slowly than those in 9.6a. Gordon et al. proposed that this was because the pronoun in the second sentence of 9.6a is an appropriate backwards-looking center, suitable to be realized as a pronoun. Realizing it as a full noun phrase, as in 9.6b, indicates that it is not the backwards-looking center, disrupting discourse integration. (Note that the third sentence in 9.6a is read quickly as well, indicating that if the backwards looking center of that sentence—its subject—is realized as a pronoun, other phrases can be as well. Thus, readers show no disruption upon reading the next pronoun, *him*, in this sentence.)

Although a pronoun is efficiently understood when its antecedent is a high-ranking forward-looking center of a previous sentence, other factors determine how and how easily it is understood. Morphological marking (for gender and number in English) clearly plays an important role. Sentences like 9.7a are read faster than 9.7b, presumably because gender-marking makes the former unambiguous while the reader has to resolve the ambiguity of reference in the latter even though it is probably clear that *he* refers to Ron (Ehrlich, 1980):

> Sally rewarded Ron because he was on time.   (9.7a)

> Sam rewarded Ron because he was on time.   (9.7b)

Vonk (1984) examined gender ambiguity in combination with another factor that has been shown to affect pronoun comprehension, implicit causality (Caramazza, Grober, Garvey, & Yates, 1977). She measured eye movements while participants read sentences that began like those in 9.8 and immediately afterwards named the antecedent of the pronoun:

> Mary won the money from John, because she . . .   (9.8a)

> Mary won the money from Jane, because she . . .   (9.8b)

> John punished Mary, because she . . .   (9.8c)

> Jane punished Mary, because she . . .   (9.8d)

These sentences contain verbs that implicitly specify the causal agent responsible for an action. Mary is the responsible agent in all these sentences (just as Ron is in 9.7), and therefore the preferred antecedent for the pronoun in the *because* clause. Vonk found that participants named the correct antecedent virtually all the time, even in sentences like 9.8b and 9.8d, when the gender of the pronoun did not disambiguate the assignment.

A very interesting finding emerged from the pattern of fixation times. Vonk distinguished between first-pass times (time spent fixating a region before any regressions from it) and second-pass times (time spent after a regression is made into the region; see Chapter 4). The first-pass times on the pronoun indicated that fixations were longer when the gender information made assignment unambiguous (i.e., when the gender of the two names was different) than when it didn't. In contrast, first-pass fixation times on the verb phrase following the pronoun as well as second-pass fixation times on the entire sentence were longer when only the implicit causality of the verb disambiguated the assignment. It appears that readers quickly assign the antecedent of a pronoun that is disambiguated by gender, but delay making the assignment when it is determined by implicit causality.

In the sentences that Vonk used, the pronoun could always co-refer to an appropriate antecedent. Koornneef and van Berkum (2006) measured reading time (using both self-paced reading and eye tracking) while people read sentences where the pronoun was either consistent or inconsistent with the implicit causality bias, such as the Dutch versions of those in 9.9:

> Linda praised David because he had been able to complete the difficult assignment with very little help. (9.9a)

> David praised Linda because he had been able to complete the difficult assignment with her help only. (9.9b)

The verb *praised* implicitly indicates that its direct object, the recipient of the praising, is the likely causal agent for a following *because* clause, and thus the preferred antecedent of the pronoun subject of that clause. Sentences like 9.9a, in which the gender of the pronoun was consistent with this assignment, were read faster than inconsistent sentences like 9.9b.

Many other factors have been found to affect the comprehension of pronouns. For instance, readers find it relatively difficult to "go inside" a conjoined noun phrase to find an antecedent for a singular pronoun (e.g., to refer to Mary as *she* following a phrase like *John and Mary went into town*; Albrecht & Clifton, 1998), although this difficulty does seem to depend on some subtle properties of the act that the conjoined pair of individuals are engaged in (Koh, Sanford, Clifton, & Dawydiak, 2008). Also, participants are faster to read a sentence containing a pronoun when its antecedent was introduced as a proper name as opposed to a descriptive noun phrase (Sanford, Moar, & Garrod, 1988). But we must turn to a discussion of other factors that affect the coherence of a text.

Nominal anaphora

Noun phrases as well as pronouns can refer to previously introduced referents. An indefinite noun phrase typically introduces a new referent into discourse, while a definite noun phrase frequently refers to a previously mentioned entity, especially when the referent is not salient enough for a pronoun to refer to it (cf. Almor, 1999). In contrast to pronouns, a definite noun phrase can refer to an entity that a reader could be expected to have inferred, as *the seat* in 9.10, or that the reader will recognize as unique, as *the biggest supermarket* in 9.11. (In passing, we have to say that the semantics of definiteness are actually quite complicated—try telling a speaker of languages that do not have definite vs. definite articles, e.g., Chinese, Japanese, or Korean, exactly when it is appropriate to use the definite article *the* and when it is not. See Heim & Kratzer, 1998, for discussion of the grammar of definiteness.)

Joe jumped into a nearby cab. The seat was disgustingly dirty. (9.10)

Mary looked for shallots in her local grocery store. Eventually she found them in the biggest supermarket in town. (9.11)

Despite these complexities, readers are exquisitely sensitive to whether a definite noun phrase has an appropriate antecedent in a discourse. Yekovich and Walker (1978) investigated two-sentence passages like 9.12a and 9.12b:

The accused youth sobbed quietly and asked for (the/an) attorney.
The attorney examined the statement of the arresting officer. (9.12a)

The contented mother rocked slowly and hummed (the/a) tune. The tune soothed the temper of the fussy newborn. (9.12b)

The second sentence of 9.12a was read more slowly when the first sentence had contained *an attorney* than when it had contained *the attorney*. Presumably, this is because simply asking for *an attorney* doesn't introduce some specific attorney into the discourse (although referring to *the attorney* in the first sentence does induce the reader to accommodate the existence of one, who can later be referred to with a definite noun phrase). However, no comparable difference was observed in 9.12b. This is most likely because *humming a tune*, unlike *asking for an attorney*, does introduce some specific tune into the discourse, providing *the tune* with a referent.

Quite often a superordinate noun phrase is appropriately used to refer to an entity previously introduced by a more specific noun phrase. Consider materials studied by Garrod and Sanford (1977), illustrated in 9.13:

A robin would sometimes wander into the house. The bird was attracted by the larder. (9.13a)

A goose would sometimes wander into the house. The bird was attracted by the larder. (9.13b)

They measured the reading time for each sentence. They found that readers took longer to read the second sentence in examples like 9.13b than 9.13a. If the concept in the first sentence is a less-typical member of the superordinate category, it is apparently accessed as a referent of the superordinate term *the bird* less quickly. But typicality only matters when the term in question actually provides the antecedent for the superordinate term. The second sentence in 9.14 was read no more quickly when the typical vehicle (a bus) was mentioned in the first sentence than when the less-typical vehicle was. The effect seen in 9.13 is not a simple matter of a more typical term priming its category more than a less-typical term.

A (bus,tank) came roaring round the corner.
It nearly hit a horse-drawn <u>vehicle</u>. (9.14)

Relations between propositions

Anaphora is not the only linguistic device that holds a text together. A readable text flows well from one proposition to the next. When the relation (causal, temporal, or otherwise) between two propositions is not obvious, a text can provide linguistic "connectives," like *because* and *so* and *but* and *however* that guide the reader in putting the sentences together (Halliday & Hasan, 1976).

Readers are sensitive to these relations and how they are signaled. Reading is slowed when the temporal order of propositions in a text does not match the chronological order of the events they denote (Mandler, 1986). Reading is also slower when there is a large time shift in the narrative than when events follow directly upon one another (Zwaan, 1996). For instance, 9.15a is read more slowly than 9.15b:

> Jamie turned on his PC and started typing. An hour later, the telephone rang. (9.15a)

> Jamie turned on his PC and started typing. A moment later, the telephone rang. (9.15

Thematic coherence matters too. Imagine you are reading a narrative about someone who is in a kitchen preparing dinner. In the middle of this narrative there is a sentence like either 9.16a or 9.16b:

> I cut up a slice of cooked ham. (9.16a)

> I took my moped from the garage. (9.16b)

Not too surprisingly the thematically incongruent sentence, 9.16b, is read more slowly than the congruent one, 9.16a (Bestgen & Vonk, 2000). Very interestingly, however, if the target sentence was preceded by a temporal adverb that indicates a change in time and possible setting (e.g., *Around 11 o'clock*), the reading time cost of the thematically incongruent sentence becomes smaller and non-significant.

Linguistic connectives are designed to guide a reader in identifying the relations among sentences, and readers do use them. Haberlandt (1982), for instance, had people read passages with causal or adversative connectives, such as 9.17:

> The passengers were terrified. They thought the plane would crash. (However),
> the pilot made a safe landing. (9.17)

Reading was faster when the connective (the adversative *however* in this example) was present than when it was not. Apparently, the connective speeded the task of determining how the last two sentences are related.

Information structure and the "given–new contract"

The syntax and morphology of a language provide ways to unambiguously encode the thematic roles that phrases play in sentences: "Who did what to whom." Languages also provide a variety of devices for linking sentences together in discourses. We have discussed anaphora as one such device, and the provision of connectives as another. Languages also have devices to encode the "information structure" of sentences. These devices signal distinctions that go by names like topic vs. comment, ground vs. focus, theme vs. rheme, given vs. new, old vs. new, etc. (see Vallduví & Engdahl, 1996, for a thorough discussion of these contrasts and how they are realized in different languages). These linguistic devices can all be seen as ways that a writer can aid a reader in relating the propositions in one sentence to the representation the reader has constructed for the preceding text (Clark & Haviland, 1977). They signal what information in a sentence should be considered new and informative, and what information the writer presupposes that the reader already has in the mental representation of the discourse.

These devices take different forms in different languages. In spoken English the most important devices are prosodic: New and focused information has to receive a "pitch accent" (generally a rise in pitch, sometimes accompanied by an increase in duration and/or amplitude; Selkirk, 2003). Other languages have specific syntactic structures for signaling what is given or topic and what is new or focus (Vallduvi & Engdahl, 1996). Even English has syntactic ways of encoding information structure. By default, a topic appears as the subject of a sentence, and a focused phrase appears as the final element of its clause. Focus can also be signaled by specific devices such as clefting; in a sentence like *It was the whiskey that made Tom sick*, the phrase *the whiskey* is focused, and it is presupposed that the reader knows that Tom was sick (in contrast to *What the whiskey did was make Tom sick*).

Psychologists have most often studied information structure from the standpoint of given vs. new information. Given information is information that the reader can be presupposed to already have in his or her mental model of the discourse. New information is information that is supposed to be added to the mental model, linked to the given information. Clark and Haviland (1977) proposed that there is an implicit "contract" between writer and reader (or speaker and hearer) to phrase sentences in a way that makes it clear what links to the prior discourse and what adds new information. Perhaps the clearest case of how this contract is realized can be seen in question–answer pairs. The pair in 9.18a respects the given–new contract. Tom is the topic or theme or given information in the answer, and *Tom* appears as the subject. *Whisky* is the focus or rheme or new information, and it appears as the predicate. But the pair in 9.18b violates the given–new contract. The information that is given in the text appears in the clefted position, where new information should appear, and the new information appears in the position that should contain given or presupposed information:

Q: What did Tom drink? A: Tom drank WHISKY. (9.18a)

Q: What did Tom drink? A: It was TOM who drank whisky. (9.18b)

The effects of such violations of information structure have most often been studied in spoken English (largely because, as mentioned earlier, the primary device English has for signaling focus is prosody). Violations of information structure (as in 9.18b) have been shown to impair auditory comprehension (Bock & Mazella, 1983; Birch & Clifton, 1995). Hornby (1974) showed that listeners seemed to pay less attention to material that was expressed as if it were given than if it were expressed as new information. For instance, if they had to decide whether or not a sentence they heard accurately described a briefly presented picture of a girl petting a cat, they were more likely to overlook the mismatch between the sentence and the picture if they had heard 9.19a than if they had heard 9.19b:

It is the girl that is petting the dog. (9.19a)

It is the boy that is petting the cat. (9.19b)

The difference is that in the former sentence, the critical information (about petting the dog) was presented as old, given information. In the latter sentence the critical information (about the boy doing the petting) was presented as new, focused information. A practical implication is that if you want to put something over on your reader without arousing the reader's critical faculty, express it as given information.

Reading experiments also show that focused information receives more attention. Birch, Albrecht, and Myers (2000) showed that recognition probes that were delayed 10 seconds after the end of a text were responded to more quickly when the word they probed had appeared in a focused position (e.g., an it-cleft, such as *mayor* in *It was the mayor who refused to answer a reporter's question* than if *mayor* had appeared in an unmarked subject position). In a reading time experiment Birch and Rayner (1997) demonstrated that readers fixated focused information longer than given information. In one experiment they measured eye movements while subjects read passages like 9.20, which began with one version of a focus-inducing question (Q-A or Q-B) and continued with an answer:

> Q-A. Where were the soldiers?
> Q-B. What were the soldiers playing?
> A. The soldiers in the underground bunker were playing cards to relieve
>   their boredom.   (9.20)

Following Q-A, the focused information was the phrase *in the underground bunker* (wide focus). Following Q-B, it was the single word *cards* (narrow focus). Gaze duration for the narrowly-focused word *cards* was not affected by the focus manipulation, although the word was re-read for a longer time when focused by Q-B. First pass time for the phrase that was the target of wide focus in Q-A (*in the underground bunker*) was increased by the focus. These data suggest that focused material receives more processing, consistent with an ERP result to be discussed soon. However, Birch and Rayner (2010) found faster reading time for material that they described as more "prominent" in the discourse, including material that would be considered to be focused, so the actual relation between focus, prominence, attention, and reading speed remains somewhat uncertain.

The information structure of a sentence ideally reflects how the sentence relates to the discourse structure, but it can also affect how a sentence is interpreted. Consider the Late Closure parsing preference discussed in the previous chapter. Sentences like 9.21a are read faster than sentences like 9.21b, because the former permits the final adverb phrase to be attached to the current clause (*she proposed . . .*) while the latter's tense forces it to modify the earlier clause (*Fiona will implement . . .*):

> Fiona will implement the plan she proposed to the committee last week.   (9.21a)

> Fiona will implement the plan she proposed to the committee next week.   (9.21b)

However, when Altmann, van Nice, Garnham, and Henstra (1998) had people read these sentences in a context like 9.22, the advantage of the late closure version (*last week*) disappears and is replaced with an apparent early closure (*next week*) advantage in several eye-tracking measures. What is going on here is that the discourse contains an indirect question (*The other committee members wonder when . . .*) about the time that the plan will be implemented, making the answer to this question (*She'll implement the plan . . . next week*) the focus of the final sentence. This focus seems to be sufficient to resolve the ambiguity of how the final adverb phrase will be attached. (Note, though, that to obtain this result, Altmann et al. had to insert a phrase *to the committee* between the adverb phrase and its most recent attachment site, which eliminated the normal late closure parsing preference.)

Last week, Fiona presented a new funding plan to her church committee. The other committee members wonder when Fiona will implement the plan she proposed. She'll implement the plan she proposed to the committee last week/next week, they hope. (9.22)

In an event-related potential (ERP) experiment Cowles, Kluender, Kutas, and Polinsky (2007) showed distinctive scalp electrical potential responses to information that appeared in a focused position. Their subjects read short passages like 9.23:

A queen, and advisor, and a banker were arguing over taxes. Who did the queen silence with a word, the advisor or a banker? It was the banker that the queen silenced. (9.23)

Cowles et al. showed that a word that appears in a focused position (e.g., the it-cleft, or even the final position of a sentence) elicited a brain electrical response (a P3b) that signals increased processing of the word. This is presumably related to Hornby's (1974) demonstration that listeners are more sensitive to focused than to presupposed information and to Birch et al.'s (2000) demonstration that probe responses can be faster to focused than non-focused information.

Not only do readers seem to pay more attention to new and focused information, they also seem to be disrupted, at least briefly, either if information that has not been presented in the preceding text appears as given information or if information that is given in the preceding text appears in a focused position. Haviland and Clark (1974) demonstrated the former by measuring the time to read the second sentence in short passages like 9.24:

Horace got some beer out of the trunk. The beer was warm. (9.24a)

Horace got some picnic supplies out of the trunk. The beer was warm. (9.24b)

Horace was especially fond of beer. The beer was warm. (9.24c)

In all cases, the phrase *the beer* appears as a definite noun phrase in the subject position of the second sentence, a signal to the reader that the phrase refers to given information. This is the case in 9.24a. However, no beer had been introduced in 9.24b. The reader has to make an inference that beer must have been included in the picnic supplies and add beer to the discourse representation. This takes extra time, slowing the reading of the second sentence of 9.24b compared to 9.24a. Similarly slowed reading was observed in 9.24c, where the word *beer* had appeared previously, but in a way that does not actually introduce a referent for *the beer*.

Cowles et al.'s (2007) study provides evidence that reading given information in a focused position can be disruptive. In the passage in 9.23, the answer *It was the banker that the queen silenced* has an appropriate information structure. The answer to the question, *the banker*, which should be focused, appears in the focused position in the it-cleft. However, in other passages, the information structure was inappropriate. Given information was presented in the focused position, e.g., *It was the queen that silenced the banker*. When such inappropriate information appeared in focused position, it elicited an N400 brain electrical response. The N400 is typically seen when an unexpected or semantically inappropriate word is read, suggesting that the readers took focusing a given term to be inappropriate.

Reinstatement from memory

We have seen how texts can provide a variety of aids to help a reader put information together, and how readers respond to such aids. But sometimes a text presents a reader with other challenges. For instance, a reader may be required to relate new information to some information that was presented so far back in the text that it is no longer easily available. You may have had the experience of reading a newspaper article and seeing a person's name mentioned, but not remembering who in the world that person was. You have to search the preceding text to recover that information. But there are circumstances in which material you read "automatically" calls to mind material to which it is related, even though that material occurred much earlier and is no longer in an active memory.

Some researchers propose that this reinstatement of earlier material occurs because of a passive "resonance" process (McKoon, Gerrig, & Greene, 1996; Myers & O'Brien, 1998). Such a process can account for data provided by Albrecht and O'Brien (1993), whose participants read long passages in which (for instance) the main character, Mary, was introduced as a strict vegetarian. After several filler sentences, which did not talk about Mary or her vegetarianism, the reader encountered a sentence that described Mary as ordering a cheeseburger and fries. This sentence was perfectly coherent with the preceding few sentences, but nonetheless was read more slowly than it was in a neutral passage that had given no information about Mary's eating habits. Albrecht and O'Brien proposed that the proposition about ordering a cheeseburger reactivated the information about Mary being a vegetarian through memory a resonance process, allowing the reader to detect the inconsistency in the text. Later research (O'Brien, Rizella, Albrecht, & Halleran, 1998) indicated that this resonance process is not particularly intelligent. A similar slowing of reading was observed even though the text that intervened between the mention of Mary's vegetarianism and the ordering of the hamburger explicitly said that Mary was no longer a vegetarian. (See O'Brien, Cook, & Guéraud, 2010, for further evidence confirming that information a reader knows is outdated still affects text comprehension.)

Other researchers grant readers more intelligence, and emphasize how the reader's search for meaning can hold a text together (Graesser, Singer, & Trabasso, 1994). Goals and causal actions play particularly important roles in this process. Suh and Trabasso (1993), for example, have shown that, in a text describing how a child wanted a new bicycle, memory for the bicycle goal was more salient if the goal was not yet satisfied than if it had been satisfied. Very likely both intelligent, meaning-guided, and rather dumb, resonance processes are involved in how memory helps glue texts together (Myers & O'Brien, 1998). Albrecht and Myers (1995) measured the time to read sentences in a story in which the protagonist was described as being successful or not in making an airline reservation late at night (thus satisfying or not satisfying a goal), followed by a target sentence that was inconsistent with the earlier goal not having been satisfied (stating that the protagonist was tired and decided to go to bed). When six or seven sentences that did not involve the goal followed the text about the goal, the target sentence was read equally fast regardless of whether or not the goal had been satisfied. Apparently, readers did not notice the inconsistency between not having made the airline reservations and going to bed. However, if some event was arbitrarily associated with making the airline reservation (e.g., sitting on a leather couch to look up the airline's phone number), calling this event to mind (by referring to the leather couch immediately before the target sentence) was enough to slow readers down on the target sentence if the goal of making an airline reservation had not been satisfied. Apparently, the arbitrary connection between the leather couch and the goal of making the reservation was enough to resonate with the goal statement, reminding the reader that the reservation had or had not been made. In sum, it appears that both passive resonance processes and active processes of meaningful interpretation play roles in text comprehension.

Inferences

A reader often has to do more than tie the sentences of a text together. The reader has to go beyond the information provided and add content that is only implicit in the text (see Singer, 2007, for an overview of inference processing in discourses). Much of the material earlier in this chapter has actually touched on inference processes. Deciding what the antecedent of a pronoun is can require inferences (e.g., in the fragment *Joe praised Tom because he . . .*, the referent of *he* is probably *Tom*, the person who did something that deserved praise; but this is an inference). Adding an entity to a discourse model to support a definite reference (e.g., *The beer was warm*) similarly requires going beyond the information presented, if the beer had not been mentioned before. Deciding that the protagonist of a story had not satisfied her goal of making an airline reservation because something had distracted her when she started to do it likewise requires an inference.

Making an inference takes time, and slows a reader down. An experiment reported by Haviland and Clark (1974) demonstrated that the second sentence of 9.25a:

> Last Christmas Emily went to a lot of parties.
> This Christmas she got very drunk again. (9.25a)

takes longer to read than the same sentence in the context 9.25b

> Last Christmas Emily became absolutely smashed.
> This Christmas she got very drunk again. (9.25b)

The latter text provides an explicit antecedent for *got very drunk again*, but the antecedent has to be inferred in the former text. The inference must not have always been made while reading the first sentence, because if it had been made, the second sentence should have been read equally fast in both contexts.

This example brings up the question of what inferences are made, and when. It is clear that a reader cannot make all possible inferences, or even the likely ones. There are just too many. A general conclusion from a lot of research is that readers are cautious. They often appear to wait until they must make an inference before they make it. But the detailed answer to what inferences are made, and when, appears to differ for different types of inferences. We will discuss two types of inferences: bridging inferences and elaborative inferences. A warning: Different experimental techniques seem to yield somewhat different results. The usual techniques that have been used to study the inferencing process include measuring the time to read a sentence whose interpretation requires that an inference is made (including measuring eye movements), the time to make a lexical decision or a naming response to a word that is presumably activated by an inference, the time to recall a sentence in response to a cue word that was presumably inferred, the time to verify the truth of a sentence that could have been inferred. When the results of different techniques all suggest that an inference has been made, one can have confidence in that conclusion. But quite often, techniques point in different directions, making conclusions uncertain.

Bridging inferences

A bridging inference is made when something has to be added to the discourse model to tie a new proposition into the previous model. Without such an inference the text would lack coherence. Anaphoric inference is an example of a bridging inference; a reader has to figure out who *he* refers to in *John praised Bill because he caught the pass* in order to make sense of that sentence. For another example, our discussion of Haviland and Clark (1974) presented the classic example of a bridging inference. You will recall that Haviland and Clark had participants read passages like 9.24 (repeated below) and found that the second sentence was read more slowly in 9.24b, where the reader had to infer that the picnic supplies contained beer, than in 9.24a:

> Horace got some beer out of the trunk. The beer was warm. (9.24a)

> Horace got some picnic supplies out of the trunk. The beer was warm. (9.24b)

The reader has to "bridge" the gap between *picnic supplies* and *the beer* to know what *beer* probably refers to. This requires the reader to use his or her background knowledge that beer is plausibly included in the picnic supplies. But note that the gap is not bridged until it must be; the reader generally does not infer that beer (and sausages and chips and ice and napkins . . .) is included in the picnic supplies until the inference is needed.

Another example of testing whether bridging inferences are made, perhaps after a delay, comes from Keenan and Kintsch (1974). They had people read passages like *Police are hunting a man in hiding. The wife of Bob Birch disclosed illegal business processes in an interview on Sunday.* One way of making sense of this passage is to infer that Bob Birch is the man in hiding. Readers apparently did this, at least by the time a verification test ("Was Bob Birch the man in hiding?") was given 15 minutes after reading the text. They were as fast verifying a statement like this as when it had been explicitly presented in the text.

Bridging inferences can involve goal-related and causal relations as well as identifying entities in the discourse. Myers, Shinjo, and Duffy (1987) had people read the sentence in 9.26b after reading one of the sentences in 9.26a:

> High relatedness: Tony's friend suddenly pushed him into a pond.
> Medium relatedness: Tony met his friend near a pond in the park.
> Low relatedness: Tony sat under a tree reading a good book. (9.26a)

> Test sentence: He walked home, soaking wet, to change his clothes. (9.26b)

The test sentence was read more slowly as the preceding sentence was less related to it. Presumably, the extra time was spent in trying to inferentially bridge the relation between the two sentences. Interestingly, when knowledge for how Tony got wet was later probed, recall was better in the medium relatedness passage than in either of the others. Apparently, the extra work done to bridge the two sentences enhanced memory, but only when it is successful (which was apparently not the case in the low relatedness passage).

A final example of a causal bridging inference comes from Singer and Halldorson (1996), who had participants read passages like 9.27:

> Terry was unhappy with his dental health.
> He phoned the dentist. (9.27a)

> Terry was unhappy with his dental bill.
> He phoned the dentist. (9.27b)

Three seconds after reading the second sentence, the participant was presented with a sentence like *Do dentists require appointments?* and asked to say whether it was true or false in general.

The decision was made more quickly following the passage in 9.27a than following the similar one in 9.27b. Apparently readers found a way to make a causal bridge between the two sentences. When the first concerned dental health, the inference that is made is that Terry called the dentist to make an appointment. However, when the first sentence concerned dental bills, the inference is that Terry called the dentist to complain. Making the bridge in the former case activated pre-existing knowledge that dentists require appointments, which in turn speeded verification.

Elaborative inferences

Sometimes inferences are made even before they are needed to make a text coherent. As an example, Garrod and Sanford (1982) had people read one of the sentences in 9.28a followed by 9.28b:

Explicit: Keith took his car to London.
Implicit: Keith drove to London. (9.28a)

Test: The car kept overheating. (9.28b)

The test sentence was read equally fast in both cases. This contrasts with the Clark and Haviland case (*The beer was warm*) discussed earlier. Apparently, the discourse representation constructed in the implicit version of 9.28a included a car (while the picnic supplies did not necessarily include beer). Still, since no car was explicitly mentioned in the text, its existence required an inference— and since its existence was not needed to make the sentence *Keith drove to London* coherent, it could not be considered a bridging inference. It is generally called an elaborative inference.

Such elaborative inferences are not always made. As indicated before, there may just be too many of them. But it is of interest to examine the conditions under which they are made. Consider an example discussed earlier, from Garrod and Sanford (1977), and shown in 9.13 (reproduced again below):

A robin/goose would sometimes wander into the house. The <u>bird</u> was attracted by
the larder. (9.13)

The reading time for the second sentence was longer when the preceding sentence contained the atypical *goose* than when it contained the typical *robin*, suggesting that the typical term was more likely to trigger an inference to the superordinate concept of bird. In addition, reversing the order of the specific and general terms, as in 9.29, increased reading time for the second sentence.

A bird would sometimes wander into the house. The <u>robin/goose</u> was attracted by
the larder. (9.29)

It appears that reading *robin* or *goose* in 9.29 requires that the reader add some specific information to the representation of the text, slowing reading compared to 9.13. Reading a word denoting a specific concept may not generally activate a specific example of the category, even a highly typical one (although reading was faster for *robin* than for *goose* in 9.29, suggesting that the inference that it is the bird previously referred to was easier for the more typical instance).

However, if the context is constraining enough, readers may make an elaborative inference from a general category to a specific example (Garrod, O'Brien, Morris, & Rayner, 1990). Participants read *The robin pecked the ground* about equally fast after 9.30a, where robin is only implicit, as after 9.30b, where it is explicitly mentioned:

> Julie was convinced that spring was near when she saw a cute red-breasted bird in her yard. (9.30a)

> Julie was convinced that spring was near when she saw a cute red-breasted robin in her yard. (9.30b)

Early work on elaborative inferences did suggest that such inferences were quite frequently drawn. Much of this work relied on assessments of memory for text. For instance, Johnson, Bransford, and Soloman (1973) gave participants passages like *The man dropped the delicate glass pitcher on the floor.* Later, they were about as likely to recognize an implication of this sentence, *The man broke the delicate glass pitcher on the floor,* as the actual sentence. However, later work (e.g., McKoon & Ratcliff, 1986) suggested that such memory effects did not demand the conclusion that the elaborative inference had been made when the passage had been presented. Instead, this later work suggested that the memory test could, instead, provide an effective retrieval cue when it expressed a predictable outcome. A similar conclusion was suggested by Corbett and Dosher (1978) in the domain of instrumental inferences (inferences made from a verb to a typical instrument) (see also Alba & Hasher, 1983).

Singer (1979) provided evidence from reading time measures that similarly indicated that instrumental inferences are not necessarily made at the time of reading. His participants read pairs of sentences such as 9.31a and 9.31b:

> The boy cleared the snow with a shovel. The shovel was heavy. (9.31a)

> The boy cleared the snow from the stairs. The shovel was heavy. (9.31b)

The reading time for the second sentence was longer in 9.31b than in 9.31a, indicating that integrating *shovel* with the prior sentence was more difficult when it was not explicitly mentioned. Singer reasoned that if readers had inferred *shovel* while reading the first sentence of 9.31b, then there should have been no difference.

However, it may be that instrumental inferences, like category-example inferences, are made only when they are highly constrained. Consider the passage in 9.32, from O'Brien, Shank, Myers, and Rayner (1988):

> All the mugger wanted was to steal the woman's money. But when she screamed, he stabbed her with his weapon in an attempt to quiet her. He looked to see if anyone had seen him. He threw the knife into the bushes, took her money, and ran away. (9.32)

The inference from *he stabbed her with his weapon* to the conclusion that the weapon was a knife is not a logical inference like knowing that a robin is a bird: the weapon could be an icepick, spear, or any other sharp instrument. However, O'Brien et al. measured eye movements while reading the last sentence of 9.32 and found fixation durations on *knife* were no longer than when the sentence followed a version of the passage in which *knife* had been explicitly mentioned previously (i.e., *weapon* was replaced with *knife*). In contrast, when the verb *stabbed* in the second sentence was replaced by a verb that did not strongly suggest a particular instrument (e.g., *assaulted*), gaze duration on *knife* was increased. It appears that readers do not always draw elaborative inferences when the context is unclear, and that the search for an antecedent of a definite noun phrase like *the knife* is begun immediately. Still, when a verb has a highly typical instrument, like the *stab–knife* pair, the instrumental inference may be made.

A different type of elaborative inference involves the causal relations in the situation a text describes. We have already discussed (in connection with 9.26 and 9.27) how causal inferences are made to bridge between two superficially unrelated sentences in a text. But we can also ask whether likely causal relations are inferred before they are required for discourse coherence. Consider passages like 9.33, as studied by Duffy (1986):

> John was eating in the dining car of a train. The waiter brought him a bowl of
> soup. Suddenly the train screeched to a halt. The soup spilled in John's lap.   (9.33)

After finishing this passage, careful readers undoubtedly make a causal link between the sudden halting of the train and the soup spilling. However, do they infer that the soup will spill in John's lap before they get to the last sentence? This type of inference is not logically required. The soup might not spill if the bowl isn't very full and it would only spill in John's lap if he were sitting on the forward side of the table. Yet the event of the soup spilling seems probable, and furthermore the narrative seems to be pointing in that direction.

Duffy (1986) distinguished between three possibilities of how such a causal link might be drawn. The first is backward inference or bridging: the reader waits until getting to the soup spilling sentence before searching back in the text for the cause or explanation of the event. The second is specific expectation, namely that the reader generates a specific expectation or prediction from the first three sentences that the soup is going to spill that is confirmed by the fourth sentence. The third is focusing, in which certain aspects of the text are so salient that they advertise themselves as things that are likely to be followed up on. When something comes up which has no transparent precedent, these salient items in memory are assumed to be the appropriate places to find the rationale for what follows. One might view this salience model as the reader using mental highlighter on some sentences in memory.

In one experiment Duffy presented participants with passages like the one above. For example, they read the first three sentences of 9.33 and then were shown the fourth sentence and asked to judge whether it was a good continuation of the passage. The control passage had a different third sentence, *The train began to slow down entering a station*, which makes the causal link less likely but still possible. Unsurprisingly, readers took less time in judging that the fourth sentence was an appropriate continuation of the first (*screeching to a halt*) version of the passage than of the second (*slow down*) version, indicating that they were making a causal inference at some point.

What was of greater interest was that when the fourth sentence was not a good continuation, such as *That night the whole forest burned down*, readers were quicker to judge that it was not a good continuation when the third sentence was the *screech to a halt* sentence than when it was the *slow down* sentence. This appears to rule out the backward inference model. If readers made such causal inferences merely searching back from the last sentence, then the time to judge that the "fire" sentence was not a good continuation should have been the same since there was nothing about fires in either version of the passage.

The difference indicates that readers are doing something active to the text that is shaping how they will process the next sentence they encounter. But are they actually generating a specific prediction of what is coming up next? Duffy assessed this by using a probe memory test. Participants read passages like the "soup" one and then, after either the *screeched to a stop* or the *slow down* sentence, they got a single probe word (*soup*) and judged whether it had been in the passage or not. The idea is that if the *screeched to a stop* sentence generated a specific prediction of soup spilling, *soup* should have been more available and hence easier to judge than it had been in the passage. In fact, there was no difference between the two conditions, suggesting that such an inference was not made. More recent work has suggested that while highly specific inferences (such as Duffy's inference about soup-spilling) are made only in highly constraining contexts, more general inferences involving categories of words or features of such categories are made in less-constraining contexts (Harmon-Vukic, Guéraud, Lassonde, & O'Brien, 2009; Lassonde & O'Brien, 2009).

Duffy's data thus suggest that the process of causal inference in reading is complex. It is neither sitting back and waiting until you don't understand why something is true and then searching, nor is it making uncertain guesses about what is going to happen as you go along. Instead, it appears to be a process of highlighting information that you are likely to need later on so that the highlighted information is readily accessible for future linkage. What indicates to the reader that the *screeching train* sentence should be highlighted? In this case it seems to be important because the topic apparently has been changed from the meal to the train even though there has been no closure on the eating episode. Thus the reader seems to be warned that the *screeching train* will be important, somehow.

A final type of inference is one that can be made by combining two or more propositions in the discourse, or one or more discourse propositions together with background knowledge, and deducing an implication. If readers do make the inference, reading of a later proposition in the text that contradicts it should be disrupted. Researchers have quite often failed to detect such disruption, but sometimes disruption is observed—e.g., when the subject matter is quite familiar to the reader or if the inference is specifically relevant to the goal of reading (see, e.g., Noordman, Vonk, & Kempff, 1992).

Another situation in which such deductive inferences are made is when all relevant information is presented in the text, in close enough contiguity to all be active in memory at one time. Wiley and Myers (2002) measured whole-sentence reading time of texts like 9.34a followed by a consistent (9.34b) or an inconsistent (9.34c) sentence:

> Seals are usually found in cold regions. Like most animals in such regions, they usually have to produce a lot of energy just to keep warm. Metabolic rate increases with energy needs. (9.34a)

> Seals have high metabolic rates. (9.34b)

> Seals have low metabolic rates. (9.34c)

The target sentence was read more slowly when it was inconsistent with a presumed implication of the preceding text (9.34c) than when it was consistent (9.34b). While this experiment does not conclusively show when the inference was drawn, it does show that it was made at least by the time the critical sentence was read.

To summarize, readers generally appear to be cautious about making inferences when they read (Corbett & Dosher, 1978; Duffy, 1986; McKoon & Ratcliff, 1986; Singer, 1979; Singer & Ferreira, 1983). Even such obvious elaborative inferences as instrumental inferences do not appear to be made much of the time. Instead, readers only appear to make inferences when the inference is highly constrained, or when the inference is needed to make the current text tie in with what has come before. Why are readers so cautious? One possibility is that reading is demanding enough of processing resources even without elaborative inferences; there are words to be encoded, sentences to be parsed, anaphoric antecedents to be searched, etc. A second possibility is that the costs of being wrong outweigh the benefits of being right. Many inferences that seem obvious when you know the answer are not in fact so obvious: the weapon didn't have to be a knife, the next sentence didn't have to be about soup spilling, it could have been about an accident or about robbers closing in on the train, etc. It seems likely that most real text is constructed so that there are very few sentences that merely confirm inferences that the reader has already made. Rather, as the given–new contract suggests, each sentence adds a new idea that the reader must tie in with what has gone on before.

Given the minimal effort view in the above paragraph, why does the reader bother to process certain passages more extensively ("highlight" them)? The answer may be that it is a good compromise between doing nothing and having to generate specific hypotheses. It may take little effort, and the hypothesis that something is likely to be used later on will be right much more often than a specific hypothesis about how it will be used. Clearly, much research is needed on what causes something to be made salient and targeted for future use as well as how backward search processes are influenced by what is salient. Duffy's (1986) experiment indicates that causal inferences make use of such highlighting, and our earlier discussion of centering and focusing indicates that potentially related processes play a variety of roles in helping a reader understand text.

Situation models

Many theorists argue that constructing a mental representation of the situation or scenario that is described is the principal goal of reading an expository text. Such a mental representation is often referred to as a "mental model" (Johnson-Laird, 1983); very similar concepts are termed situation models or discourse models (we will generally use the term situation model, but speak of mental model when we wish to emphasize the mental processes taking place). According to this view, a reader normally puts the sentences in an expository or narrative text together and makes at least the inferences needed for coherence with one primary purpose in mind: Constructing a situation model of what the text is about.

A situation model can represent a variety of aspects of a situation or event or scenario. It can represent the agents and objects that play roles in the situation. It can represent spatial relations among these agents and objects and it can represent visual and other sensory attributes of the situation. It can represent a situation from different perspectives. It can represent the motivations and the goals of the protagonists, and it can represent the causal relations between events that occur in the scenario. It can represent how a situation changes over time. A situation model, it seems, can represent anything we can know about a situation (see Zwaan & Radvansky, 1998, for one taxonomy of the types of information that situation models can represent).

A situation model is built up from the propositions contained in a text but it is both more and less than these propositions and the relations among them. It need not contain the details of how a situation was described, but it should represent the situation accurately. A compelling demonstration of how a mental model of a discourse goes beyond the propositions in the discourse is given by Sanford and Garrod (1998). If you read the short discourse *Harry put the wallpaper on the table. Then he put his mug of coffee on the paper*, everything seems fine. You understand the sentences, perhaps you create propositions like [ON, WALLPAPER, TABLE] and [ON, MUG, PAPER], and you interpret *paper* as anaphorically referring to the wallpaper. But now read *Harry put the wallpaper on the wall. Then he put his mug of coffee on the paper.* That does not compute! The propositions are nearly the same, but, because of background knowledge you bring to bear in constructing a representation of the situation being talked about, you know that the situation is impossible.

One way to experimentally study the role that memory models play in discourse comprehension is to study memory for texts. Consider an experiment by Garnham (1987), who had his participants read passages containing sentences like 9.35 (abbreviated from the original):

> The party had been in progress for about four hours. . . . By the window was a man with a martini. He commented on the decor to a woman. . . . She asked him if he had complemented the host on his taste. The man standing by the window shouted to the host. The other guests looked toward the pair. . . . [and so on].　　　(9.35)

Later, after an intervening task, the participants were asked whether the text contained the sentence *The man with the martini shouted to the host* or the sentence *The man standing by the window shouted to the host*. If the participants had been warned that there would be a verbatim memory test, they were generally accurate. However, if they had not been so warned they were almost equally likely to choose either of these two sentences. However, they were very accurate in rejecting other candidate sentences such as *The host shouted to the man standing by the window*. They had apparently formed an accurate mental model of what happened at the party, but lost most of the information about how the text described the events.

The operation of mental models can be observed during or shortly after the reading of a paragraph. Glenberg, Meyer, and Lindem (1987) had participants read passages like that in 9.36:

> John was preparing for a marathon in August. After doing a few warm-up exercises, he (took off/ put on) his sweatshirt and went jogging. He jogged halfway around the lake without too much difficulty. Further along the route, however, his muscles began to ache.　　　(9.36)

On key trials participants would be probed after reading the paragraph on whether the word *sweatshirt* had been in it. Glenberg et al. found that participants took longer to respond "yes" in a version of the paragraph where John took off his sweatshirt than in a version where he put it on. They argued that such a result indicates that, when John is said to put on his sweatshirt, the reader constructs a mental model with John wearing the sweatshirt. Since the paragraph is about John, John and his sweatshirt will both be part of the mental model that the reader constructs, even though the sweatshirt is never mentioned again. But if John had taken the sweatshirt off, the reader no longer includes it in the updated mental model, making it less available to memory.

Bower and Morrow (1990) presented probes during the reading of a passage to show that situation models containing spatial relations were constructed even while a passage was being read. Their participants first memorized a map describing the linear pathways through a series of rooms, together with the objects that were in the rooms. They then read a text that described the movement of a character through the rooms. Their reading was interrupted by the presentation of a pair of object names, and they were to decide whether or not the two objects were in the same room. Decisions were slower when the objects were further away from the room where the character was when the text was interrupted, strongly suggesting that participants were mentally representing the movement of the character through the mental map of the rooms.

Situation models can also represent the perspective that protagonists have on the situation. O'Brien and Albrecht (1992) had participants read passages like 9.37 (some with, some without, several sentences intervening between the initial and the target sentence):

> As Kim stood inside/outside the health club, she felt a rush of excitement. (. . .)

> She was getting anxious to start and was glad when she saw the instructor come
> in the door of the club. . . .   (9.37)

Line-by-line reading time was measured. The critical line included the information about the instructor coming in the door of the club. This is consistent with the perspective of the protagonist, Kim, when the first sentence said she was inside the club; it is inconsistent when the first sentence put Kim outside the club. Participants read the consistent line faster than the inconsistent line—but only when they were told that they should imagine that they were doing whatever the main character was doing. Thus, participants could take the perspective of that character, but they did not automatically do so.

This finding brings up the fact that constructing a situation model can take time and processing capacity. We have actually seen examples of this earlier, in our discussion of Mandler's (1986) and Zwaan's (1996) findings that passages are comprehended more quickly when events are described in the order in which they occur and when events that are described together take place close in time to one another. Time seems to be represented in situation models, and representing time is easier when the text maps naturally on to time relations.

An interesting experiment that appears to show influences of both lexical relations and of mental models was reported by Garrod and Terras (2000) (note, these authors did not discuss their data in terms of mental models). They measured eye movements while participants read passages that contained short texts like 9.38, after introducing a referent for the initial pronoun (e.g., a teacher):

> She was busy writing a letter of complaint to a parent. However, she was
> disturbed by a loud scream from the back of the class and the pen dropped
> on the floor.   (9.38a)

> She was busy writing a letter of complaint to a parent. However, she was
> disturbed by a loud scream from the back of the class and the chalk dropped
> on the floor.   (9.38b)

> She was busy writing an exercise on the blackboard by the door. However, she
> was disturbed by a loud scream from the back of the class and the pen dropped
> on the floor.   (9.38c)

> She was busy writing an exercise on the blackboard by the door. However, she
> was disturbed by a loud scream from the back of the class and the chalk dropped
> on the floor.   (9.38b)

There were also versions of the first sentence that explicitly mentioned a pen or chalk.

Facilitating effects of the lexical relation between *writing* and the typical instrument *pen* were apparent in measures of early reading on *pen dropped* and *chalk dropped* in the second sentence: *pen dropped* was read equally quickly whether or not a pen had been explicitly mentioned in the preceding text, but *chalk dropped* was read faster when chalk had been previously mentioned. Garrod and Terras suggested that this effect reflects a process of "bonding" an anaphor with a lexically related antecedent. Of more relevance to the current discussion of mental models, however, is the following. When the instrument was not explicitly mentioned in the first sentence, go-past time on the verb *dropped* was substantially longer for *pen dropped* following the blackboard context than following the letter of complaint context, and second-pass time on *pen* was longer as well.

While the go-past difference did not appear following *chalk dropped*, second-pass times on *chalk* were longer when *chalk dropped* had appeared in the letter of complaint context than in the blackboard context. Garrod and Terras referred to a process of resolution underlying these later effects. It appears that readers who read about writing a letter or writing on a blackboard form some sort of mental model with a plausible instrument, and text that is congruent with the typically formed mental model is read more fluently.

Readability

One would hope that, if we fully understood the process of reading and understanding texts, we would know how to construct texts that are easily understood—texts that are highly readable. Perhaps we could list all the aspects of text that can plausibly affect reading difficulty, starting with lexical variables such as the frequency of the words in the language, the length of the words, moving through syntactic variables measuring complexity of sentences such as the length of sentences, number of phrases in a sentence, number of clauses in a sentence, and then moving to more discourse-level variables such as the number of propositions, the complexity of the causal structure, etc. Then we could take all of these measures and see how well the combination can predict how difficult readers find the text.

Presumably, if you can come up with objective measures for each of the above predictor variables, and some combination of those variables in fact do a pretty good job of predicting how difficult readers find the text, then it would appear there is some sense in which you can say that you understand discourse processing. In addition, if you can find out which variables are doing most of the prediction, you can understand which text variables are really important in understanding discourse. Moreover, one would have a method for predicting difficulty of text that should have implications for helping to design educational curricula and other practical applications.

There is in fact, a reasonably large and fairly old literature on the topic (for reviews see Chall, 1958; Kintsch & Vipond, 1979). Most of the impetus was practical; people were trying to use objective techniques for measuring the relative difficulty of different texts for educational purposes. More recently, as correlational methods have become more sophisticated, the emphasis has been more on trying to understand which variables are the most important. While this enterprise is of some value, we think that the conclusions that can be drawn are limited. In this correlational procedure a set of passages are taken from various texts (let's say there are 50 such passages), and various objective indices, such as average word length, average word frequency, average sentence length, average number of phrases per sentence, etc., are computed for each of the paragraphs. Then a group of participants are asked to read the passages and some measure of reading difficulty (usually the average reading speed in words per minute) is computed for each passage. Finally, the reading times for the 50 passages are correlated with each of the objective indices one has computed, and the pattern of correlations is analyzed by a technique known as multiple regression, in order to achieve enlightenment.

One problem with the technique may already be apparent: why use reading speed as a measure of how much difficulty the reader is having? Presumably a measure of the reader's comprehension of the passage is needed as well. This leads to a very thorny issue: How does one measure comprehension? As you are probably aware from taking reading comprehension tests of various kinds, most reading comprehension questions tap many things besides your comprehension of the text. Testing readers for recognition of detail, such as dates and names of minor characters, does not seem to be testing for what one would want to call comprehension. Further, some people can answer questions that ask about content on the basis of prior knowledge, without much contribution from the passage.

In other words, if one wants to measure comprehension, it cannot be done in a vacuum; one needs a theory of what comprehension is (Kintsch & Vipond, 1979). Perhaps the solution is to use several measures of comprehension, each tapping a different facet of comprehension. For example, one would measure how many essential points of the story or passage are remembered, how much of the causal structure is remembered, the number of propositions that are recalled, how much lexical detail is remembered, etc. The problem with doing that is that most of the reason for the enterprise is then lost, since the goal we started with was to determine which variables are important for some global measure of readability. As a result, many experiments (e.g., Kintsch & Vipond, 1979) have measured readability using both reading speed and comprehension in terms of a memory test, in which memory has typically been measured in terms of something like number of idea units or propositions recalled (inspired by theories such as Kintsch & van Dijk's).

Even if one had the perfect behavioral measure of reading difficulty, there are still major difficulties in drawing any firm conclusions from the method. The basic one is that the method is correlational. As you undoubtedly know, it is difficult to draw causal inferences from correlational data. We will illustrate the problem by reviewing some of the findings. Many different educational researchers have come up with readability formulas, 50 or more of them (Kintsch & Vipond, 1979). Most are general-purpose, but some are intended to apply only to specialized areas such as chemistry texts. A major aspect of all of these measures is that simple low-level variables (especially the average word length and the number of words per sentence) are important components of the formulas, since they are highly predictive of how difficult the text is. (Usually, the average length of a word is the most predictive.) What can one infer from that? Unfortunately, very little.

First, let us take the average length of a word. As we indicated in Chapter 3, the average length of a word is highly correlated (negatively) with its frequency in the language. Thus, one cannot be sure whether the relation is due to the fact that longer words have more visual information, or because longer words are less frequent and thus harder to locate in the lexicon (see Chapter 3). There is no way to understand from correlational data which aspect is truly operative, or whether both are. (In contrast, as discussed in Chapter 1, one can experimentally control one variable and vary the other to get some idea whether the variables operating separately each have some effect.) The problem is worse when considered in the context of prose passages, however, since texts with longer words will also tend to have longer and more complex sentences, be expressing more complex ideas, etc. While multiple correlation techniques allow you to understand something about whether a variable has any effect when the effect of another is taken into account, it does not really allow you to say very much.

One reason why the low-level variables tend to do much of the predicting is that they are probably more reliable indices of the underlying psychological variables that they are measuring than are the higher-order ones. Word length is a reliable measure of the amount of visual information needed to be extracted in the word and also, since it is highly correlated with word frequency, a reliable predictor of lexical access time. In contrast, a complexity measure derived from existing analyses of discourse structure is probably at best capturing only part of what one would want to mean as "discourse complexity."

Another way to view the problem with the correlational method is to think about readability measures as a guide to the writer. Let's say that we know that text with shorter words and shorter sentences tends to be more readable than text with longer words and longer sentences. Does that mean that if we have a text with long words and long sentences, we should go about rewriting it so as to make both word and sentence length shorter? Perhaps, to some extent. If we have statements like *eschew obfuscation* and run-on sentences, it might be a good idea to change them. However, the underlying ideas that one is attempting to express in difficult text are often inherently complex.

Thus longer sentences and more-complex sentence structures are probably needed to explain these ideas, and they will take longer to read than simpler sentences expressing simpler ideas. Using simpler sentences will probably either make the text incomprehensible (if one is still trying to express the same ideas) or simplify the text at the expense of removing many of the ideas one was originally trying to express.

To summarize, readability formulas are of some value in allowing an educator to predict how difficult a group of participants will find a given text. However, the correlational data from which they are obtained are not of much help in understanding discourse processing. It is possible the situation may change as our understanding of the reading process increases and gets incorporated into theoretically motivated indices of readability. McNamara et al. (2010) present one example of a step in this direction. They describe a computational technique for integrating various measures of text cohesion and coherence with lower-level variables and using the result to predict comprehension of text. Another recent development with some promise has been to predict moment-to moment processing rather than global text comprehension. For example, the gaze duration on a word might be the variable that one is trying to predict, and then one would use indices such as word length, sentence length, position in sentence, etc. to predict gaze time. Using smaller units allows one to be more diagnostic, but does require accepting the "immediacy hypothesis" (i.e., that the time spent on a word reflects all the processing done on that word and only that word). As we discussed in Chapters 4 and 8, strong versions of the immediacy hypothesis overstate the actual facts and may seriously misrepresent the processing of complex discourse variables.

Summary

In previous chapters we discussed how readers recognize words, access their meaning, and use their knowledge of the structure of their language to put these meanings together in the process of understanding sentences. It is possible to provide fairly clear and explicit descriptions of the knowledge that readers bring to these tasks and to develop fairly clear and explicit theories of how they use this knowledge.

The present chapter discussed how readers put sentence meanings together into coherent representations of texts. The knowledge they use to do this is far more extensive, more amorphous in fact, than their knowledge of the lexicon and the grammar of their language, and theories of how they use this knowledge are accordingly far less constrained than theories of word recognition and sentence comprehension. Nonetheless, discourse comprehension researchers have been able to make substantial progress in understanding the process of comprehending texts. They have learned a good deal about how readers use anaphoric references to link sentences together. They have uncovered interesting facts about how readers use connectives like *because* and *later* to relate propositions in the text to one another and how they use the information structure of sentences (e.g., their given–new structure) to this end. Researchers have studied how memory for earlier material is accessed to make sense of what is currently being read. They have studied how readers go beyond what is literally said and make inferences that are required to tie a discourse together, and how they can (and sometimes do) make such inferences to enrich the description that the text provides. And they have shown how readers go beyond building networks of propositions and construct mental models that capture what anyone would want to call the meaning of a text.

We have to end with a cautionary note, however. The processes involved in comprehending text and making mental models of what is read use, in principle, all of our knowledge. And we have suggested that a mental model of a text can represent whatever a person knows about a situation. It is a daunting task to even contemplate building explicit models of what we know and how we use it (perhaps not even a possible task; J. A. Fodor, 1983; for discussion of problems and possible solutions see Koppen, Noordman, & Vonk, 2008). We have to accept that our theories of mental models and inference process, etc., are incomplete at best, and often vague and inexplicit. But even so we can look back at the research that has been done on text comprehension and know that it has taught us much that we did not previously know, and we can look ahead to future research with the same expectation in mind.

PART IV

Beginning Reading, Reading Disorders, and Individual Differences

Up to this point we have focused on skilled readers and on the kind of processing activities that they engage in during reading. However, we do not become skilled readers by accident. The task of learning to read involves a great deal of effort. In the process of becoming a skilled reader the cognitive activities involved in reading may change considerably, particularly in the recognition and identification of words. What might be a relatively automatic and effortless process for adults can be a plodding, time-consuming, and effortful process for young children. A key question is whether the reading process in children is just a slower version of what goes on in adults, or is qualitatively different.

Chapter 10 provides a description of the stages children go through in the process of learning to read. We briefly discuss the effects of different writing systems on these stages, and extensively describe the various cues that children use in reading. Developmental differences in comprehension and in such phenomena as the perceptual span (see Chapter 4) are also described.

Chapter 11 describes the processes of learning to read, and how different teaching practices affect these processes. We discuss the alphabetic principle that we described in Chapter 2 and the important role it plays in learning to read in our culture. We detail the cognitive foundations of learning to read, emphasizing the importance of phonological awareness in the process of learning to read. Chapter 11 provides a critical discussion of the concept of "emergent literacy" and examines the contributions of oral language comprehension to acquiring reading. We conclude with an extensive discussion of the research literature evaluating the effectiveness of different methods of reading instruction.

Chapter 12 turns to the topic of reading disorders, examining both acquired and developmental disorders. Different patterns of acquired dyslexia (reading disorders caused by brain injury) are described, and their relation to observed phenomena of developmental dyslexia (difficulty in learning to read in the absence of identified neurological, emotional, motivational, or cognitive handicaps) is discussed. We critically evaluate existing theories of developmental dyslexia and discuss issues in diagnosing dyslexia, concluding with a discussion of comprehension deficits.

Chapter 13 covers a variety of differences in reading skills and reading goals. We begin with a critical discussion of the claimed benefits of speed reading, suggesting that successful speed reading is generally a matter of successfully skimming material that the reader is already familiar with. Chapter 13 then reviews reading under various conditions in which meaning is not processed to any deep level, including proofreading and "mindless reading," and considers the effects of some differences in the goals for which material is read. We conclude by describing some of the correlates of individual differences in reading ability, and some of the changes that occur in reading with advancing age.

In sum, the focus in this section is not on the skilled reader but on "non-standard" readers: children learning to read, people who do not read well, people who report reading very quickly, and people reading for different purposes. Despite this focus it should be apparent that research on skilled readers has played a critical role in allowing us to understand the nature of "non-standard" reading.

10
STAGES OF READING DEVELOPMENT

Nothing is as central to the field of child development as the notion of stages. With respect to motor, cognitive, language, perceptual, and moral development, highly influential theories have been proposed in which children are seen as developing towards maturity by passing through a series of stages. While it might be quite easy to accept the idea of a natural sequence of stages that children pass through when beginning to walk or talk, there is no really compelling reason to expect the same to be true of learning to read. After all, reading is a product of cultural evolution rather than a biologically determined skill like walking or talking; it depends on cultural transmission for its continued existence. Rather than invariant, biologically driven sequence of stages, proposed taxonomies of stages in reading development are best viewed as convenient ways to describe how reading changes as children gain skill.

What it means to be a skilled reader changes over the lifespan. These changes are described in Chall's (1996) five stages of reading development, which extend from birth through adulthood. Chall's stages can be grouped into three general phases: Learning to Read, Reading to Learn, and Independent Reading (see Table 10.1). Essentially, children completing the Learning to Read phase can translate print into spoken language, comprehend text that contains familiar ideas, and spell. Note that children are expected to acquire basic reading skills fairly quickly, before reaching the middle of elementary school. By fourth grade, skilled readers use their basic reading skills to acquire new vocabulary and to build subject-area knowledge (Reading to Learn). These higher-order reading skills develop more slowly than basic reading processes, and continue to grow in the middle school years. By high school, reading proficiency entails advanced comprehension skills, such as the ability to understand multiple viewpoints. In college and the workplace, reading proficiency includes the ability to synthesize large amounts of material, detect bias, and integrate conflicting viewpoints from separate texts. Two main ideas appear consistently in Chall's discussion of reading stages: (a) higher levels of reading proficiency build incrementally on more basic foundation skills, which are necessary (but not sufficient) for continued reading progress; and (b) the goals of reading instruction shift as expectations change during a child's education. Although Chall's stages are broad in scope, they are familiar to educators and useful for conceptualizing the full trajectory of reading development from birth through adulthood.

TABLE 10.1 Three stages of reading development

Stage	Grade range	Characteristics
Learning to Read	1–3	Initial reading and decoding Building fluency Listening comprehension better than reading comprehension
Reading to Learn	4–9	Subject area reading Vocabulary expands through reading Reading comprehension equal to or better than listening comprehension
Independent Reading	10–College	Wide reading in different subjects and genres Continued vocabulary expansion Can integrate multiple viewpoints Reading is more efficient than listening

Adapted from Chall, 1996.

Stages of early reading development

Some investigators have developed focused descriptions of the early stages in which basic reading skill is acquired (Ehri, 1998, 2002; Gough & Hillinger, 1980; Marsh, Friedman, Welch, & Desberg, 1981; Mason, 1980). These theories can be situated within Chall's Learning to Read phase, as they describe changes in reading processes that typically occur between kindergarten and third grade. Anyone who has observed a child beginning to read can notice the apparently sudden changes that occur in the early elementary grades. Up through kindergarten, children memorize labels on food and signs on the road by their colors and shapes, then progress to memorizing books they have read. Then they may begin to notice the print as they are read to, pointing at words or turning the pages. When they begin to learn that print encodes speech and know some simple letter–sound correspondences, they may try to read some words on their own. In contrast to reading the words they've memorized, reading words sound by sound is laborious. At this point many children find reading to be a difficult task, but still enjoy hearing stories read to them. The plodding, labor-intensive work of decoding words may last up to a year or two, and it seems endless to some parents. Then suddenly the child begins reading text smoothly and with the correct intonation. At this point we say the child has begun to read. The stages of reading development we will discuss describe the cognitive changes that underlie these shifts in reading behavior. Although we do not think of these stages as biologically determined developmental sequences, most children experience the phases in the standard sequence we describe. In this section the phases of reading development proposed by Marsh et al. (1981) and Ehri (1998, 2002) are discussed, and then we address commonalities among stage models of early reading development.

Let's consider each of the stages in early reading proposed by Marsh et al. (1981): (1) linguistic guessing, (2) discrimination net guessing, (3) sequential decoding, and (4) hierarchical decoding (see Table 10.2). A young child at the linguistic guessing stage approaches the task of word recognition via a strategy of simple rote association (Gough & Hillinger, 1980). This rote association is between a previously unanalyzed visual stimulus (the printed word) and an oral response. At this point, the child is unable to consistently read words presented out of context, and does not recognize words presented in an unusual font or in uppercase letters (Mason, 1980). Children guess at words presented in a sentence or a story based on what makes sense in the linguistic context. Thus their errors tend to be syntactically and semantically appropriate for the sentence, but may not

TABLE 10.2 Stages of reading development

Stage	Description
Linguistic guessing	Glance and guess
Discrimination net guessing	Sophisticated guessing
Sequential decoding	Learns simple grapheme–phoneme correspondences
Hierarchical decoding	Skilled reading

Adapted from Marsh et al., 1981.

share any letters with the word in print. For example, if the text is: *Bob took his dog for a swim*, the child might read *Bob took his dog for a walk*. This phase corresponds with Ehri's pre-alphabetic phase, in which children are unaware that letters specify particular words. Instead, pre-alphabetic children recognize words by using semantic cues or default visual cues to identify words, such as the color of a label (Byrne, 1992). During this phase children become aware of environmental print and can recognize common labels and logos. Children with strong memories and high text exposure may memorize storybooks and practice "reading" to parents and siblings.

Children in the stage of discrimination net guessing typically respond to an isolated printed word with a spoken word that shares at least some of its letters. The term *discrimination net*, borrowed from computer science, means that the child processes graphemic cues only to the extent that they are necessary to discriminate one printed word from another. Whereas in the linguistic guessing stage a child is heavily influenced by the semantic-syntactic context of a word, a child in Stage 2 uses additional cues such as word shape, word length, and letter identity. The transition from linguistic guessing to discrimination net guessing is marked by a change in the nature of reading errors. As a child begins to use letter information to read words, error responses may be inconsistent with the surrounding context. Instead of guessing a word based on context and semantic properties, errors now share letters with the printed word. Thus errors that seem to be nonsensical may actually reflect the child's new prioritization of alphabetic information that supports the continued growth of word recognition skills. For example, if the text is: *Bob liked to read*, the child might read *Bob liked to ride*. This phase corresponds to the beginning of Ehri's partial alphabetic phase, in which children begin identifying isolated words based on some of the letters (Ehri & Wilce, 1985). Ehri notes that children in this phase use letter sounds to make connections between print and pronunciation. At this point default visual cues are replaced (or complemented) by partial phonetic cues (from any letters the child notices) to assist in word identification (De Abreu & Cardoso-Martins, 1998; Scott & Ehri, 1990; Treiman & Rodriguez, 1999).

According to Marsh et al., two factors underlie the shift from Stages 1 and 2 to the more analytic Stage 3. The primary factor is the increase in the number of words to which children are exposed. As long as word exposure is limited, a rote learning or discrimination net strategy is satisfactory. However, as the set of words encountered in print increases, memory load increases and whole word memorization has diminishing returns, as does the use of discrimination net guessing since exposure to more and more words invariably means that more of them will be graphically similar to each other. The second factor identified by Marsh et al. as underlying the shift from Stage 2 to Stage 3 is the increase in cognitive processing capacity as the child matures. Thus children in Stage 3 are able to process the order of a series of letters and to coordinate this series with a series of sounds. The sounding-out process in sequential decoding is said to work in a left-to-right manner, using simple, predictable relations between individual letters and sounds.

Marsh's third stage, sequential decoding, is characterized by the use of letter–sound correspondence rules which allow the child to decode novel words. Through increased exposure to printed words, explicit instruction, or self-teaching (Jorm & Share, 1983; Share, 1995), children learn that many letters are pronounced the same way in different words, and that it is possible to work out what a new word is by sounding it out. The child begins to recognize that letters encode sounds and, thereby, learns the alphabetic principle. The alphabetic principle simply means that alphabetic writing systems function to encode speech, and this is achieved through patterns of more or less regular letter-to-sound correspondences.

Whereas the decoding skills in Stage 3 reading are fairly basic, such skills become more sophisticated as the child gains more experience with decoding words in text. In Stage 4, hierarchical decoding, letter–sound correspondences become context sensitive so that, for example, the grapheme *c* is pronounced /s/ before *i*, but /k/ before *o*, and vowels are lengthened by a final *e*. It is during this stage that the child begins to use analogy as an alternative strategy for decoding. For example, if he/she recognizes the printed word *hand*, then he/she might recognize the *and* sequence in *band*. As we saw in Chapter 3, adult skilled readers use analogies to pronounce nonwords (and presumably words that they do not know).

Marsh et al.'s Stages 3 and 4 are included in Ehri's full alphabetic phase. At this point, children can decode new words and recognize them later when they appear in print. However, decoding might be slow initially and not always accurate. Word recognition is grounded in letter–sound relations and is not impaired by changing visual cues such as case or font changes. Such letter–sound relations support word recognition and spelling by enhancing memory for the order of letters within words beyond what can be achieved by visual memorization alone (Cunningham, Perry, Stanovich, & Share, 2002; Ehri, 2002). Paradoxically it is in the full alphabetic phase, when children are beginning to fully apply the alphabetic principle, that they may appear to struggle the most. They may read fairly accurately, but be slow and tire quickly. However, decoding words becomes faster with practice and continued reading exposes them to words repeatedly, and their speed gradually improves. Thus frequent reading of easy texts eventually ushers in the last of Ehri's phases: the consolidated alphabetic phase. Children in this phase recognize words quickly, apparently "by sight." Sight words are words that children can recognize after several exposures, without decoding them or using context cues (Ehri, 2002). The size of a child's sight word vocabulary is the main factor that allows a child to read accurately at a conversational rate and with appropriate intonation (Torgesen & Hudson, 2006). Once in the consolidated alphabetic phase, children become sensitive to frequent letter sequences such as *-nt* or *-ing* (Kessler, 2009). Words are read and spelled using groups of letters that indicate morphemes and syllables. In this way a child will suppose that the first syllable in *know*ledge is spelled *know*, rather than *no*. According to Ehri, the connections that support word recognition shift from primarily phonetic to being morphographic in nature. Similar to Marsh's Stage 4, children now read and spell unfamiliar words by analogy (Ehri & Robbins, 1992).

As we mentioned at the beginning of this section, the four different stages of early reading development that Marsh et al. (1981) identified may not necessarily be characteristic of every child (Stuart & Coltheart, 1988). Yet they do provide a reasonable description of the sequence of phases that normal children experience when learning to read in English. However, the period of time it takes to complete each phase varies widely among children, with some phases lasting longer than others for a particular child.

It is important to note that the five commonly cited stage models we have described posit a similar trajectory of early reading development (Chall, 1996; Ehri, 1998, 2002; Gough & Hillinger, 1980; Marsh et al., 1981; Mason, 1980). Initially children approach reading via the use of rote association and context cues. They may recognize a few high-frequency sight words by default visual cues. They cannot read unfamiliar words out of context. However, if an unfamiliar word is presented in a sentence or short story, they will respond with a word that fits semantically in the sentence. At the next stage children are attending to the letters and their sounds, and errors at this point are generally consistent with the graphemic characteristics of the word. For example, a child might read *worm* for *world*. As children are exposed to more print their responses to unknown words become consistent with letter cues and context, and they begin to recognize words automatically.

A major breakthrough in reading occurs when a child realizes that many letters are pronounced the same way in different words and that it is possible to determine what a new word is by sounding it out. In other words, the child understands that the alphabetic principle operates through patterns of sound-to-letter correspondences. Because of this principle, many spoken words can be written with one letter (grapheme) representing each sound (phoneme), as in *fly, begin*, and *giant*. Conversely, many written words can be read, or decoded. Young readers employ grapheme-to-phoneme correspondence rules to assign a certain sound to each letter, and then blend the sounds together to pronounce the word (e.g., *fist*). The term decoding is appropriate because a child in this stage can only deal effectively with invariant relations in the form of a simple code between letters and sounds. Unfortunately, English is a morphologically complex writing system that also contains numerous many-to-one mappings of letters to sounds (e.g., *thud, rain, pick*) as well as sounds-to-letters (e.g., *e* in *bed, began, like*) (see Chapter 2). Being able to use these many-to-one mappings to read and spell words marks a later stage of early reading development, in which children now use multi-letter units such as morphemes and syllables in reading and spelling, and they independently read new words by analogy. This occurs somewhere between the ages of 8 and 10, when a child has more or less acquired automatic word recognition skills. Those who complete this phase are ready to use their basic reading skills to learn new information in content-area subjects; they will move on to Chall's next phase of Reading to Learn.

Early reading development in other alphabetic writing systems

The studies providing empirical support for the early stages of reading development described by Marsh et al. (1981) and Ehri (1998, 2002) were conducted with children learning to read English. As reading is a product of culture, rather than a biological development, it seems reasonable to expect that the type of writing system could affect early reading development. If we view early reading as a process of learning the alphabetic code, then we might expect the orthographic-phonological consistency of a writing system to influence how reading develops. This section discusses how the early stages of reading development may differ for children learning more orthographically consistent writing systems than English. Table 10.3 lists several European languages in terms of their orthographic consistency. Highly consistent written languages are considered to have a shallow orthography, which is to say that the mapping of letters to sounds is very transparent (with one letter representing a single sound in the ideal case). Inconsistent languages have multiple sounds mapping onto a single letter (e.g., *c* in English) as well as multiple letters mapping onto one sound (e.g., *ph*); languages with these inconsistent mapping are considered to have a deep or opaque orthography.

TABLE 10.3   Writing systems categorized by orthographic depth

Shallow orthography				*Deep orthography*
Finnish	Greek	Portuguese	French	English
	Italian	Dutch	Danish	
	Spanish	Swedish		
	German			

Adapted from Seymour et al., 2003.

Several studies indicate that children learning to read in orthographically consistent writing systems may experience the early stages of reading differently from children learning to read in an inconsistent orthography like English. For example, Wimmer and Goswami (1994) compared the reading competence of children learning to read in English and in German. Children aged 7, 8, and 9 were given three tasks: numeral reading, number word reading, and pseudoword reading. Pseudowords were constructed using letter sequences found in the number words, and so could be read by analogy to the number words. Whereas reading rate and accuracy in the first two tasks were similar for readers of the two orthographies, the German children performed much better on the pseudoword reading task. Wimmer and Goswami interpreted these data as indicating early differences in word recognition strategies for readers in the two orthographies. German children appeared to use grapheme-to-phoneme correspondences (GPCs) and analogies to read the pseudowords correctly, in contrast to the early readers of English who did not use GPCs effectively to read unknown "words." This study provided initial evidence that the orthographic consistency of the writing system being learned can affect the early stages of reading development.

In order to compare reading development across several writing systems, a large-scale reading study was conducted across several European languages (Seymour, Aro, & Erskine, 2003). Children read lists of words and pseudowords, and accuracy rates were recorded. First- and second-grade readers in the 11 writing systems with consistent letter-to-phoneme GPCs (e.g., Spanish, Italian, Finnish) had accuracy rates above 85% for pseudoword reading, whereas accuracy rates were much lower in inconsistent writing systems such as Danish (54%) and English (29%). The higher accuracy rates for beginning readers of consistent scripts, as compared to less-consistent scripts like French or English, suggests that children learning to read in consistent writing systems enter the full alphabetic phase earlier than their English-reading peers. Aro and Wimmer (2003) report a similar pattern in the accuracy of nonword reading across languages among children in grades 1–4 (see Table 10.4).

At least two studies have attempted to control for possible sociocultural confounds in cross-language studies. Bruck, Genesee, and Caravolas (1997) studied the word and nonword reading of English- and French-speaking children living in the same province in Canada. The reading accuracy of English-speaking children was 24% lower for word reading and 27% lower for nonword reading (respectively) than the accuracy of French-speaking children. Ellis and Hooper (2001) conducted a study in north Wales that compared beginning reading in English and Welsh (a highly consistent orthography). After 2 years of reading instruction, Welsh readers could read about twice as many words as English readers on a frequency-matched test. These studies, discussed in Ziegler and Goswami (2005), suggest that the differences found in cross-language studies of word and nonword reading are unlikely to be accounted for completely by sociocultural differences.

TABLE 10.4   Percentage of pseudowords read accurately by children in grades 1–4

	Grade 1		Grade 2		Grade 3		Grade 4	
	M	SD	M	SD	M	SD	M	SD
Finnish	84.9	13.6	89.6	10.1	88.4	8.1	93.7	8.3
Spanish	87.3	12.2	90.4	8.1	90.9	6.8	90.6	8.2
Dutch	85.2	8.0	88.9	9.1	91.2	8.1	95.1	5.8
German	88.0	12.4	87.3	9.5	86.0	15.2	87.2	19.5
French	86.7	5.9	96.7	3.5	98.4	2.4	98.5	2.7
English	50.3	32.8	71.0	32.5	73.5	28.8	88.2	15.2

Adapted from Aro & Wimmer, 2003.

Whereas the data from cross-language studies seem to suggest that orthographic consistency affects the rate of reading development, it is not clear whether consistency affects the actual stages of early reading that children experience. If that were the case, then one might expect children learning to read in consistent orthographies to enter the alphabetic phase soon after reading instruction begins, whereas children reading in inconsistent scripts would initially experience the logographic and partial alphabetic phases. Share (2008) reviewed several studies that failed to find evidence of logographic and/or pre-alphabetic reading in orthographically consistent scripts such as German (Landerl, 2000; Mannhaupt, Janssen, & Marx, 1997; Wimmer & Hummer, 1990), Italian (Job & Reda, 1996, as cited in Job, Peressotti, & Mulatti, 2006), and Greek (Porpodas, 2006). However, Share also mentions studies in orthographically consistent scripts that report some early readers using logographic strategies (Cardoso-Martins, 2001; Share & Gur, 1999). Conversely, one longitudinal study of beginning reading in French did not find evidence for a logographic phase at any of the testing points between kindergarten and first grade, even though French is a relatively inconsistent script (Sprenger-Charolles & Bonnet, 1996). The inconclusiveness of these findings may be due to the influence of other uncontrolled factors, such as the type of early reading instruction and student demographics.

Ziegler and Goswami (2005) capture the idea of linguistic constraints on reading development in their psycholinguistic grain-size theory. This theory attempts to explain the role of orthographic consistency in reading development and skilled reading behavior (see also Katz & Frost, 1992). It claims that learning to read in more orthographically consistent languages involves a reliance on sublexical grapheme–phoneme correspondences (GPCs) that are fine grained and operate at the level of the phoneme. Children learning to read in consistent orthographies (such as Finnish) learn GPC mappings at one grain size (i.e., the phoneme–letter level), and they master this skill fairly quickly. The result is high accuracy rates for reading any letter string by the end of first grade (Seymour et al., 2003). Therefore the typical trajectory of early reading development in most consistent orthographies is hyperlexia; many children can read nearly any word or nonword they encounter by the end of first grade (Share, 2008).

In contrast, early readers of inconsistent orthographies like English may also need to use phonological mappings of a larger grain size to learn many of the irregular spelling patterns. For example, subjunctive modal verbs (i.e., *would, could, should*) share a consistent rime pattern (*_ould*) that makes their spelling and pronunciation more predictable. The consistency of print to sound mappings in English increases considerably when readers of English consider larger rime units as well as letter–phoneme correspondences (Kessler & Treiman, 2001). Studies indicate that readers facilitate word recognition by using the rime unit to predict the sound of ambiguous vowel patterns, such as *ea* in *head* or *eat* (Ashby, Treiman, Kessler, & Rayner, 2006; Treiman, Kessler, & Bick, 2003). Thus, in order to read words accurately, English readers must attend to multiple phonological grain sizes such as the syllable, rime, and phoneme. The need to learn mappings at several different grain sizes may slow their initial reading progress. Ziegler and Goswami (2005) noted that if young English readers are in fact using multiple levels of phonological coding (phoneme, rime, syllable), then reading accuracy should improve if nonwords were presented in blocks of uniform grain sizes. Goswami, Ziegler, Dalton, and Schneider (2003) tested this idea in an earlier experiment by presenting nonwords in lists that were either blocked by grain size or mixed. They measured reading accuracy for pseudowords presented in mixed lists (e.g., readers had to attend to rime as well as phoneme-level phonology to read the words accurately), and compared that to reading accuracy on blocked lists in which readers only had to attend to the rime or the phoneme level. Blocking improved the nonword reading performance of English readers, but not German readers. Goswami et al. interpreted this finding to indicate that the German children consistently relied on the processing of small (grapheme to phoneme) units, whereas the English readers processed several different grain sizes of phonology. Similarly, Goswami, Ziegler, Dalton, and Schneider (2001) found that young English readers were much better at reading pseudohomophones than control nonwords (*faik* vs *daik*). In contrast, the early German readers were as accurate reading the nonword controls as the pseudohomophones. The presence of a pseudohomophone advantage in nonword reading in English suggests that the readers of the inconsistent script used lexical-level analogies to read nonwords, whereas the German readers did not.

Whereas orthographic transparency may influence the grain size of phonological processing in young readers, and thereby affect specific early reading behaviors, it is not clear that the transparency of a writing system determines the path of cognitive development in reading. To examine the influence of orthographic consistency on the development of reading skill, Vaessen et al. (2010) conducted a longitudinal descriptive study of children in grades 1 through 4 learning to read in Hungarian (more consistent), Dutch, and Portuguese (more inconsistent). This study found that orthographic consistency mainly modulated how quickly children became fluent readers. Orthographic transparency did not affect the cognitive processes involved in reading, and the overall trajectory of reading development appeared similar across writing systems.

Early reading development in Chinese

The general process of learning to read in Chinese is quite different from the process of learning to read an alphabetic script, mainly because of the lack of a productive letter–sound mapping system. Recall that in Chinese the character is the main orthographic unit. Characters do not explicitly encode their pronunciation, although one portion of the character (the phonetic radical) does provide some pronunciation cues. Therefore character pronunciation (which is also the character name) must be memorized. In China this memorization process begins in kindergarten, when Chinese children are taught to memorize a basic set of characters. They are supposed to recognize and name these characters, but they don't have to write them. Although a limited number of characters can be learned through character–picture association, there is no visible way of encoding a character's pronunciation. To bridge that gap most schools in China teach the Pinyin system in first grade to help children memorize character pronunciations. At the time children learn Pinyin, they also learn how to write characters. Teachers show the order of writing each stroke within a character and teach the rules for writing with examples, such as from left to right, and top to bottom. Children keep learning new characters and how to write them throughout elementary school. Before they enter high school, Chinese children are supposed to know about 3000 characters and how to write 2500 of these characters.

Pinyin is implemented in different ways in the four main Chinese-speaking societies (Mainland China, Hong Kong, Singapore, and Taiwan), and the following description is of the common practice in mainland China. According to Cheung and Ng (2003), children are introduced to Pinyin at the very beginning of the Chinese (Mainland) Primary 1 book. The Pinyin system uses the Roman alphabet letters to transcribe the exact pronunciation of a character, including its lexical tone. Pinyin comprises 21 onsets (consonants), 35 rimes, and 4 indicators of lexical tone (Institute of Linguistics, Chinese Academy of Social Sciences, 2004, as cited in Lin et al., 2010). Children are expected to learn this alphabetic coding system within the first couple of months of instruction, and it is used almost immediately to teach simple, familiar characters. Typically, a character is introduced paired with its Pinyin transcription. Children first learn the simplest characters, such as 一 *yi* (one), 二 *er* (two), 三 *san* (three), and so on. One way this is done is that each character is presented on a card, with its Pinyin form and a picture for its meaning (e.g., one pencil for the character 一, etc.). The goal is for children to name the character on each card and build a connection between the visual character form, its pronunciation, and the pictured object.

Because native speakers already have associations between spoken word forms and their meanings, Pinyin provides a convenient way to identify unfamiliar characters (Fredlein & Fredlein, 1994, as cited in Lin et al., 2010), presumably by reactivating that spoken association and facilitating its link to the visual character form. Few studies have examined the effectiveness of Pinyin for learning to read in Chinese. Theoretically there is no reason to rule out the learning of direct character–meaning associations without the aid of a phonetic transcription. However, the "universal phonological principle" of reading contends that phonology is activated in word recognition across writing systems, even those that do not operate with an alphabetic principle (Perfetti & Tan, 1998). Lin et al. (2010) conducted a large-scale study of Beijing children to examine the relationship between Pinyin skills around age 6 and word reading 1 year later. They found that the accuracy of Pinyin invented spellings uniquely predicted word reading the next year, even when controlling for initial letter knowledge, phonological awareness, and word-reading performance. This result suggests that learning the alphabetic principle, as indicated by Pinyin mastery, facilitates early reading development even in writing systems that do not function as alphabets. On a more general level, the Lin et al. data offer converging evidence for a universal phonological principle in reading.

In summary, recent studies suggest that the nature of a writing system will influence the early stages of learning to read, and may leave developmental footprints that are detectable in cross-language comparisons of skilled word recognition (Share, 2008). Further investigation in naturalistic and laboratory settings is needed to clarify the role of linguistic constraints, such as orthographic consistency, versus more basic cognitive constraints on the phases of early reading development.

Word identification cues

Numerous naturalistic studies offer supporting evidence for the early stages of reading development described by Marsh et al. (1981) and Ehri (1998, 2001). As children learn to read English, their word recognition skills develop from the use of arbitrary visual cues and context, through simple letter–sound phonetic analysis, to complex morphological and phonological units (Ashby & Rayner, 2012; Barr, 1974; Biemiller, 1970; Cohen, 1974; Ehri & Wilce, 1987a, 1987b; Mason, 1980; Weber, 1970). In this section we turn our attention to experiments that examine how children develop the ability to use word identification cues to recognize unfamiliar words and to access the meanings of familiar words. We focus on laboratory experiments in which children with different levels of reading ability (in terms of the number of years that they have received formal instruction in reading) are tested on controlled tasks of "word" reading. (Many experiments actually use pseudowords; however, from the child's perspective, pseudowords are simply words they haven't seen before.) We discuss the role of four types of specific cues used in word identification: graphemic, orthographic, grapheme–phoneme correspondence, and context cues, then discuss experiments investigating the relative importance of these cues. Following this section, we describe research into what units of processing are used in beginning reading, reading comprehension, and the perceptual span.

Visual and graphemic cues

We have seen that children often substitute the actual word in a text with a word bearing some visual or graphemic relationship to it. Their errors provide some clue about what cues are being used. However, with more controlled tasks, it may be possible to be more diagnostic about what aspect or aspects of the word they are utilizing. Before we discuss this research, we need to make a distinction between visual and graphemic information. By visual information, we mean gross aspects of words that are independent of identifying letters; the two most frequently cited are word length and word shape. By graphemic information, we mean information specific to the letters making up a word, such as distinctive features of letters and the specific letters themselves.

Visual cues

The length of a printed word is a simple visual cue that even the youngest readers could try to apply to identifying a word. While it is simple, we will see (in Chapter 11) that prereaders do not use length to discriminate between words (Gleitman & Rozin, 1977). Children are likely to be able to make this discrimination in very early stages of reading. However, since word length is not a very useful cue in identifying words—far too many words share the same length—there has not been much interest in studying how sensitivity to this cue develops and whether it plays any role in word identification.

There has been more interest in word shape (Groff, 1975), since some researchers believe that word shape information is important in children's word identification (Haber & Haber, 1981). Usually word shape is defined by the pattern of ascenders and descenders in a word (i.e., the position of lowercase letters that extend above or below the line of print). Thus *shape* would have the same word shape as *clogs*. Since the word shape hypothesis has been investigated in conjunction with graphemic cues, we will discuss them together below.

Graphemic cues

As we mentioned before, children often focus on the initial letter of words. Most teachers are aware of this and many experimental studies have documented it. For example, Marchbanks and Levin (1965) and Williams, Blumberg, and Williams (1970) found that the first letter is the primary cue used in word identification by beginning readers. The task used in these studies was a delayed matching to sample test in which children were shown a pseudoword such as *cug*. They were then shown a response card with four alternatives on it and asked to point to the one most like the stimulus. Each of the alternatives was similar to the stimulus in a particular way. One alternative (*cak*) had the same first letter, the second (*tuk*) had the same second letter, the third (*ilg*) had the same third letter, and the fourth (*arp*) had the same overall word shape. Thus the alternative selected should reveal the most salient cue used by the child in word identification. Marchbanks and Levin found that the first letter was the most important cue and the last letter was the second most important cue for both kindergarten children and first-grade children while shape was the least used cue. Williams et al. (1970) replicated these findings for first-grade children. The kindergarten children in their study, however, showed no consistent selections. Williams et al. also used adults as participants and found that these proficient readers used complex strategies, including visual and phonetic matching as well as shape as a basis for choice. Both studies concluded that specific letters, and not the overall shape of the words, form the initial basis of word recognition.

In light of the above research it is not surprising that when beginning readers misread a word, the error often involves producing a word that begins with the same letter as the one in print (often ignoring other factors such as length). Is this because the first letter is graphically distinct or because of phonetic factors? When Ehri and Wilce (1985) tested kindergartners' memory for spelling a set of previously presented words, they found that initial letters were more salient than final letters. However, the initial letters were found to be more salient in the phonetic spellings (*cat*), but not in the non-phonetic spellings (*could*) that were more distinctive visually. This was true even among participants who had learned the visual spellings to criterion. In addition, initial letter salience was evident only among readers who could use phonetic cues effectively to learn words. Ehri and Wilce thus concluded that the salience of the initial letter in word learning is a result of phonetic recoding and is not due to any type of visual distinctiveness of the initial letters of words.

Gibson (1971) suggested that children perceive words by detecting the distinctive features of the letter-forms that spell the words, and changes in feature analysis enable older children to extract higher-order features. Rayner (1976) and Rayner and Hagelberg (1975) used the delayed matching to sample task described above to examine the use of distinctive features. In the experiments children were initially shown a stimulus such as *cug* and then asked to point to the response alternative most like the stimulus. Three of the six response alternatives (*cwq, ouq,* and *owg*) preserved many of the stimulus letters' distinctive features (e.g., a rounded letter at the beginning or a letter that descends below the base line) in the correct spatial location while three others did not (*cqn, jun,* and *jqg*). Notice that two of the alternatives maintained each letter in its correct serial position (for example, the *c* in the first position is preserved in *cwq* and *cqn*). Rayner and Hagelberg found that children at the beginning of kindergarten (without formal reading instruction) did not have a consistent pattern of responses, whereas first-grade children relied very heavily on the first letter. In a subsequent experiment, Rayner (1976) tested children from kindergarten through sixth grade. Kindergarten children (tested toward the end of the school year rather than near the beginning as in the Rayner and Hagelberg study) chose alternatives with the same beginning letter (e.g., chose either *cwg* or *cqn*) 48% of the time, whereas first-graders chose on the basis of the first letter 60% of the time. The same children chose alternatives that preserved the feature information of the second and third letters only 55% of the time (chance being 50%). Two clear developmental trends emerged from the data. First, there was a tendency for children to choose the response alternative with the same first letter as the stimulus up until the second grade, followed by a leveling off between second and fourth grade, and finally a decreasing tendency to rely on the first letter thereafter. The second major trend was an increasing tendency to choose response alternatives that preserved the letter feature information (so that either *cwq, ouq,* or *owg* was more likely to be chosen as similar to *cug* than *cqn, jun,* or *jqg*).

Research by Ehri (1980; Ehri & Wilce, 1979) demonstrates that beginning readers use information about the first two letters. Participants were taught to read several pseudowords (such as *wheople* or *weeple*) and knowledge about the orthography of these words was tested by having them spell the words after training in reading. Although many errors in spelling occurred, the children tended to retain the cues necessary for discriminating the words (as in the discrimination net stage). Every misspelling by those taught to read the pseudoword *wheople* began with *wh*, while every misspelling of *weeple* began with *we*. In addition, Reitsma (1983a, 1983b) found that young readers start early to produce a memory for word-specific letter patterns. Moreover, this memory for particular words was accurate enough for them to notice an alteration of only a single grapheme (even though the sound pattern was unaltered).

To summarize, there is strong evidence that beginning readers use the initial letter as an important cue, and often the sole cue, to word identification. As children progress they use more of the graphemic information in the word. In some of the studies above, the information being used could either be interpreted as word shape information or letter feature information. However, it seems to us more parsimonious to think of the relevant variable as letter feature information. First of all, when word shape is pitted against letter information (Feitelson & Razel, 1984; Marchbanks & Levin, 1965), word shape was hardly ever used. Since the external configuration is not a good differentiator of words, and thus not a good cue for word identification, it seems likely that children would attempt to use it mainly at the very beginning stages. Instead, as children progress beyond using the first letter to guess at a word, they extract progressively more information about the features of middle and ending graphemes.

Orthographic cues

Several studies suggest that children become increasingly aware of orthographic cues as reading develops. By orthographic cues we mean a sensitivity to letter sequences that enables a child to identify common letter sequences and discriminate legal from illegal spellings. Some studies used a search task in which children searched for a target letter in strings of words, pseudowords, and letter strings (Juola, Schadler, Chabot, & McCaughey, 1978; McCaughey, Juola, Schadler, & Ward, 1980). Kindergarten children, first-, second-, and fourth-graders, as well as adult participants took part in the experiments. The search time for the kindergarten and first-grade children did not differ between pseudowords and unpronounceable letter strings, indicating that they were unable to use orthographic structure to facilitate their search. The second- and fourth-graders searched faster through pseudowords than letter strings. This may indicate that these older readers used orthographic information to support their search, but it is also possible that the pronounceability of the pseudoword strings assisted their search.

One task that gets closer to the question of whether readers use orthographic information to identify words is the delayed matching to sample task. Doehring (1976) employed a matching to sample task in which participants indicated which of three alternative items was identical to a sample item. Using three-letter items, he showed that participants were faster on pseudowords than orthographically irregular letter strings from the second through the eleventh grade (considering every grade between). However, it is difficult to conclude whether readers used orthography or pronounceability to perform the task. In addition, numerous studies have used brief exposures to determine the extent to which orthographic cues are viable for beginning readers trying to recognize words (for an excellent review see Barron, 1981a). The results generally suggest that sometime between the second- and fourth-grade children can use some of the gross characteristics of orthographic structure in recognizing words. However, as the usual test for orthographic structure usually confounds the orthography of the string with its pronounceability (e.g., *dorch* vs *ohrdc*), it is difficult to confidently interpret these data as demonstrating orthographic effects.

From these studies one could easily argue that what appears to be the utilization of orthographic structure and more attention to all of the letters in a word (rather than just focusing all attention on the first letter) is little more than a byproduct of the fact that the child is learning to effectively read words. That is, as reading skill increases and word form knowledge increases, children will be bound to produce results in experiments that suggest the importance of these cues in their word identification. Whereas children clearly learn to utilize graphemic and orthographic cues as reading skill develops, neither of these cues in and of themselves will enable the child to identify new words. In order to do that, the child must master either grapheme–phoneme correspondence (GPC) rules or be able to make analogies from known words.

Grapheme-to-phoneme correspondence cues

As children become more proficient in identifying words, they become more sensitive to the alphabetic principle that governs reading and writing. As we mentioned earlier, English is a complex writing system in which the grapheme-to-phoneme correspondences (GPCs) can be inconsistent for basic, short words (e.g., *should, sleigh, either*) that dominate children's literature. In terms of reading, a letter may have several pronunciations (e.g., <u>c</u> as in *cat* and *face*). In terms of spelling, a single pronunciation may be written with several different letters (e.g., /z/ as in *Oz* or *nose*). Vowels in English are particularly inconsistent, as many have several pronunciations (e.g., *bed, flower, see*) and some vowel phonemes can be spelled many different ways (e.g., *goat, slow, toe*).

Ziegler, Stone, and Jacobs (1997) reported that 31% of monosyllabic English words were inconsistent in terms of their letter to pronunciation mappings. The number of such multiple mappings supports the claim that English is extremely inconsistent, relative to other alphabetic writing systems (Share, 2008).

Whereas multisyllabic English words with Greek and Latin roots tend to have fairly regular sound–spelling patterns (e.g., *adamant*), many single-syllable words of Anglo-Saxon origin have complex sound–spelling patterns (e.g., *thought*). The co-existence of these different etymological layers makes learning to read in English particularly difficult. A study conducted by Ziegler et al. (1997) indicates that the majority of monosyllabic English words (e.g., *big, so, frog, man*) are consistent for reading. However, many higher-frequency Anglo-Saxon words have irregular spellings or complex phonics patterns (e.g., *what*). These high-frequency words appear disproportionately often in the basal readers used in first and second grade. Around third or fourth grade, children begin to encounter multisyllable words of Latin or Greek origin, which are fairly consistent when syllable and morphological information is used to identify them (Aronoff & Koch, 1996; Moats, 2010). As we will discuss in the next chapter, giving beginning readers practice with controlled texts that present regular words that do follow GPC rules allows them to practice decoding words on the fly during reading. Once printed words are decoded into their spoken forms the meanings of familiar words are automatically available. In contrast, there is no connection between the simple visual cues in a word and its meaning (in alphabetic orthographies). When children become skilled in applying the alphabetic principle in context, then their reading material can vary to include irregular as well as regular words. As children are exposed to more words, they learn to combine letter–phoneme correspondence rules, rime units, and morphological forms to identify a unique lexical item, or the exact word in print.

Despite the fact that GPCs are the best cues for identifying a word in print, it takes children some time to identify regular correspondences and to learn how to apply them in reading. This is because reading differs from all other types of identification tasks that are familiar to children at this age. Children can identify and differentiate objects, people, textures, and actions by distinctive physical features. However, written words cannot be identified in this way. Visual and graphemic cues can be used to guess at a new word, but the only way to identify it for certain is to attend to all of the word's letters and map them onto sounds that blend together to produce the spoken word. A child who can use GPCs can tell the difference between many words that appear visually similar but differ considerably in meaning (e.g., *rink, ring, rank*).

At least two classic studies have tested the role of grapheme–phoneme correspondences in reading new words. Bishop (1964) trained college students to read eight Arabic words. One group was trained by whole-word memorization and the other was taught the letter–sound correspondences for the 12 letters in those words. At testing, the groups were compared on their ability to read other Arabic words that comprised those same 12 letters. The letter–sound group was better at reading the new words overall, but some of the whole-word readers performed as well as the letter–sound group. Later questioning about the strategies used indicated that 8 out of the 20 participants in the whole-word group failed to spontaneously apply the letter–sound correspondences to read the new words, even though they were already skilled readers of an alphabetic writing system (i.e., English). This result suggests that adults who implicitly understand the alphabetic principle may not transfer that understanding to a new writing system without specific instructions to do so. Perhaps it is not too surprising that many children do not discover the alphabetic principle without direct instruction. Jeffrey and Samuels (1967) examined the relative benefits of learning letter–sound correspondences using a set of specially constructed letters with kindergarteners (see Figure 10.1). The children who had learned grapheme–phoneme correspondences could read many more words than those whose training required them to learn whole words. Both groups of children went on to learn the intended pronunciation of the new words, but the word group needed twice as many trials as the letter group before they knew all of the words. The results of this study suggest that systematic teaching of specific grapheme–phoneme correspondences may be the best way of equipping children to recognize new words when they are encountered (see further evidence for this claim in Adams, 1990; Rayner, Foorman, Perfetti, Pesetsky, & Seidenberg, 2001, 2002).

Do children use grapheme–phoneme correspondences to process words that they have already seen? Backman, Bruck, Hebert and Seidenberg (1984) tested 7- and 8-year-olds on their ability to pronounce regular and irregular words. Backman et al. found that the children were more accurate in reading high-frequency regular words than in reading high-frequency irregular words, and tended to regularize the irregular words, usually by pronouncing the silent letters. The regularization of the unfamiliar irregular words indicates that children tended to use GPC rules to name them. However, they were not relying on these correspondences to name the familiar irregular words they read correctly. In contrast, older children (9- and 17-year-olds) were equally accurate in reading aloud regular and irregular words. This result suggests that, as reading develops, children become increasingly aware of GPCs that operate above the letter–sound level, such as rimes. Rather than processing rime units per se, it is more likely that children become sensitive to the consonant contexts that generally predict vowel sounds in English. Treiman, Kessler, Zevin, Bick, and Davis (2006) conducted a study of nonword naming with first-, third-, and fifth-grade children and high school students. The pronunciation of nonwords with ambiguous vowels (e.g., *oo*) was recorded to count the instances in which readers gave the pronunciation predicted by the consonant context. For example, the vowel *oo* in the context of a final *k* is pronounced as in *cook* more frequently than as in *spook*. Vowel sounds can also be predicted by the initial consonant in a word. For example, an initial *w* strongly predicts the pronunciation of the following *a* as in *want* and *wander*, in contrast to the typical *a* sound in *ant* and *sander*. Treiman et al. found that children increasingly used both initial and final consonant contexts to read ambiguous vowels in nonwords, and fifth-grade children's use of consonant contexts approached that of high school students and adults. This result is consistent with a number of previous studies that found that fifth-grade children show essentially the same pattern of responses as adults in tasks in which GPC rules can be applied (Pick, Unze, Brownell, Drozdal, & Hopmann, 1978; Snowling, 1980; Waters, Seidenberg, & Bruck, 1984).

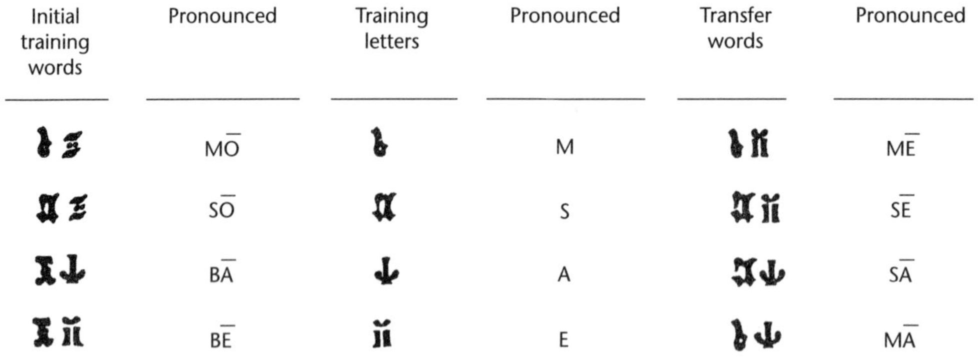

Initial training words	Pronounced	Training letters	Pronounced	Transfer words	Pronounced
░ ░	MŌ	░	M	░ ░	MĒ
░ ░	SŌ	░	S	░ ░	SĒ
░ ░	BĀ	░	A	░ ░	SĀ
░ ░	BĒ	░	E	░ ░	MĀ

FIGURE 10.1 Examples of stimuli used in the Jeffrey and Samuels (1967) study. (Reproduced with permission of Academic Press and the authors)

Evidence that even beginning readers are able to read unfamiliar words by analogy to other words comes from research by Goswami (1986). She showed young British children a clue word which they could not read (like *beak*), pronounced it, and then asked them to read other words. Some of these shared the same spelling patterns and had a sound in common with the original word (*bean, peak*), while others did not. She found that beginning readers were able to work out the analogical relationship for themselves. Some 5-year-old children on the verge of reading could even make analogies between the ends of words. Goswami's results show quite clearly that children are capable of using analogies at earlier stages in their reading development than many accounts of reading development would suggest (such as the model by Marsh et al., 1981, described earlier). However, clue word experiments do not examine analogical decoding during natural reading situations. During actual reading it is rare to have a clue word provided in the text that nearly matches an unfamiliar word that one is trying to decode (Treiman et al., 2006). Pick et al. (1978) also reported evidence that children can use analogies early in learning to read. Non-reading kindergarten children were taught to read 12 words, and then presented 18 transfer words which were composed of the same letters as the training words. The transfer words varied in terms of whether they shared an initial consonant–vowel combination, a final vowel–consonant combination, or no combination with the training words. Pick et al. found that beginning readers were much more likely to be able to read words that shared an initial consonant–vowel combination with the training words. Beginning readers' effective use of word-initial analogies in this experiment is consistent with our earlier point that these readers focus much of their attention on the beginning of words. As in Goswami (1986) however, the training set was limited and highly salient due to the proximity of its presentation relative to the transfer set.

Baron (1979) found that children use large unit analogies (like generalizing from *peak* to *beak* in Goswami's study). However, he also found evidence that smaller units (as in Pick et al.'s study) were used as well as large ones. One piece of evidence for this was that children made errors ignoring the presence or absence of final (silent) *e*. Baron suggested that method of reading instruction accounted for part of the variability in how much children rely on word-specific associations versus analogies. Whole-word methods were predicted to lead to the use of word-specific associations whereas phonics approaches would encourage the use of rules and analogies for reading nonwords. However, as Baron pointed out, it is also possible that quite apart from the method of instruction there are individual differences in the extent to which beginning readers rely on word-specific associations versus analogies in establishing words in the lexicon (Treiman, 1984; Treiman & Baron, 1983a). One thing that is clear from the research of Baron (1979) and Goswami (1986) is that the use of analogies is a strategy that can be taught to children as an approach to identifying new words. However, the ability of children to independently infer GPCs by analogy, to apply them when reading new words, and to remember them in subsequent reading has yet to be demonstrated. Perhaps the best conclusion that can be reached here is that children can use several mechanisms for reading words, including letter-to-phoneme GPCs and analogies using larger units such as consonant-vowel onsets and rimes.

Context cues

Earlier in this chapter we saw that the errors of beginning readers often fit with the context they are reading. A number of experimental studies have examined developmental changes in children's use of contextual information as they become more proficient readers. Ehrlich (1981) asked children in second, fourth, and sixth grade to read passages of text aloud in which certain target words were replaced by other words. The replacement words were either visually similar to the target (*house–horse*) or differed in overall word shape (*shark–sharp*) and were anomalous in the text.

Ehrlich found that beginning readers were much more likely to misread the replacement word as one predicted by the context than were the older children, and much less likely to pause before making an error. Ehrlich's study suggests that older readers have learned that context alone is rarely an effective cue for word identification. Perfetti, Goldman, and Hogaboam (1979) found that skilled 8- to 10-year-old readers made less use of sentence context in facilitating word naming than did children of the same age who were not as proficient in reading. These results indicate that beginning readers are more reliant on semantic cues and context to recognize words than are older readers, but the question is why. It is possible that around the age of 8, children's word identification processes become so efficient that they no longer need to rely on contextual information, but that context does support their identification of new words. Nation, Angell, and Castles (2007) examined the effect of context on novel word learning in 8- and 9-year-old children by presenting novel words in context and in isolation with one, two, or four exposures. They tested recall 1 day or 7 days later by asking children to identify the correct word in an array of visually and phonologically similar foils. Nation et al. found that the presentation condition did not affect word form learning, which suggests that context is little help in developing word recognition skill.

Reviewing the literature on the role of context in word recognition, Stanovich (1980) concluded that, within a given age range, less-skilled readers compensate for slower or poorer word identification skills by relying more on context to facilitate ongoing word identification than better readers do. Several studies have examined whether faster lexical access time can explain the relatively smaller context effects in skilled readers. For example, Stanovich, West, and Freeman (1981) asked children in second and fourth grade to read words preceded by either a congruous, incongruous, or neutral context. Each child was given practice recognizing one-half of the words in isolation before reading them in sentences. The effect of context on naming latency decreased with age and decreased for practiced words relative to unpracticed words. As expected, context effects increased with word difficulty (as measured by length and word frequency). In another study, Schwantes (1981) asked third-grade children and college students to make lexical decisions to words that were either visually degraded or undegraded. These decisions were made either with or without a congruous sentence context. In the undegraded condition the standard result was obtained: contextual facilitation of lexical decision times decreased with age. However, when word identification was slowed by degrading the target words, the context effect was as large for the skilled readers as for the third-graders. That is, degraded words made adults' use of context look like children's.

As the above studies suggest, the research on the use of contextual information is quite definitive and consistent with observational studies; as children gain more experience reading and word recognition processes become more automatic, their reliance on context decreases. The negative relationship between reading skill and the use of context cues undermines the validity of one of the most popular pedagogical tools for helping readers of all ages: the three cueing systems (Pearson, 1976; Routman, 1988). Essentially, the three cueing systems comprise semantic cues, syntax cues, and grapheme-to-phoneme correspondence cues. Although semantic and syntactic information clearly play a role in understanding the meaning of a text (see Chapters 8 and 9), there is reason to doubt that they are helpful in skilled word identification (Adams, 1998). The research findings we reviewed consistently show that better readers use such cues less than beginning and poor readers do in recognizing words.

Which cues are the most important?

We have seen that graphemic, orthographic, grapheme–phoneme correspondence cues, and context cues are used by children in learning to read. Consistent with the observational studies that we described earlier, children at the earliest stages of learning to read rely heavily on partial graphemic cues and context cues. As reading skill increases, children learn to attend to the entire word (including all of the letter features), its orthographic structure, and its grapheme–phoneme correspondences. Most of the studies that we have discussed up to this point examined the role of one particular type of cue. We now turn to some studies that have attempted to assess the relative importance of the different cues.

Ehri and Wilce (1985) tested the effectiveness of visual and phonetic cues with kindergarteners. They grouped children based on their ability to read words: "prereaders" (no words read), "novices" (a few words read), and "veterans" (several words read). The children were taught to read two kinds of words: simplified phonetic spellings whose letters corresponded to sounds (such as JRF for giraffe) and visual spellings whose letters bore no sound correspondence but were more distinct visually (see Table 10.5). Prereaders learned to read visual spellings more easily than phonetic spellings, while novices and veterans learned to read the phonetic spellings more easily. These results suggest that, as children advance in reading, they shift from using graphemic or visual cues to accessing words using phonetic cues as mediators.

A study by Beverly and Perfetti (1983) also examined the relative importance of different cues to second-grade, fourth-grade, and sixth-grade children. Participants judged the similarity of word pairs according to whatever criteria they chose to use. The visual, graphemic, and phonemic similarity of the pairs was systematically varied. For example, *new* and *sew* are identical in length and similar in word shape (visual cues) and share constituent letters (graphemic cues) but differ phonemically. *Sew* and *show*, on the other hand, are not similar in length or shape, but they have some graphemic similarity and high phonemic similarity. Given that the word pairs could vary in the similarity of visual, graphemic, and phonemic cues, what kinds of cues would be used to judge overall similarity? For second-graders, shared visual cues (word length), shared letters, and shared phonemes all contributed to perceived similarity, with shared letters receiving the most weight. In fact, shared letters, independent of shared phonemes, was the most important cue for all age groups, including adults. This finding is consistent with the findings reported by Rayner (1976) which we described in detail earlier. The weight given to shared phonemes depended on age and reading skill. While second-graders and less-skilled fourth-graders did not use phonemic similarity at all, adults and good fourth- and sixth-graders used shared phonemes as an important cue.

TABLE 10.5 Phonetic and visual spellings in the Ehri and Wilce (1985) study

Nouns	Phonetic spelling	Visual spellings
GIRAFFE SET		
knee	NE	FO
giraffe	JRF	WBC
balloon	BLUN	XGST
turtle	TRDL	YMP
mask	MSK	UHE
scissors	SZRS	ODJK
ELEPHANT SET		
arm	RM	FO
diaper	DIPR	XGST
elephant	LFT	WBC
comb	KOM	UHE
pencil	PNSL	ODJK
chicken	HKN	YMLP

Second-grade participants were quite unlikely to use vowel similarity as a cue. The results of this study suggest that beginning readers, unlike skilled readers, are typically more tuned to the way a word "looks" than the way it "sounds."

Finally, consider a study by Rayner (1988) that assessed which cues served as the basis for children's similarity judgments. Children participated in a delayed matching to sample task with three conditions: the response option that is "most like" the target word; the option that "sounds most like" the target word; or the option that "looks most like" the target word. In the first condition prereaders and beginning readers responded on the basis of word shape and the beginning letter. For them, the term *most like* clearly meant the option that looked most like the target. Even in the sounds-most-like condition, beginning readers continued to respond on the basis of visual and graphemic similarity. Intermediate readers (8 years old) in this most-like condition also chose the option that looked like the target. However, word shape was not a salient cue for them, whereas orthographic cues were; they tended to choose alternatives that conformed to English spelling rules. Few intermediate readers chose the phonemically similar word in the most-like condition, although they were able to in the sounds-like condition. In contrast, proficient 10-year-old readers tended to choose the response alternative which sounded most like the target in the most-like condition. This study suggests that the relevance of various cues changes with reading development. Beginning readers are not very flexible in their strategies, as they tended to rely on visual and graphemic cues to make similarity judgments in every condition. In contrast, children with at least 2 years of reading experience were very sensitive to orthographic structure. Their fairly high accuracy rates in the sounds-most-like condition indicate that they could use grapheme–phoneme correspondences when instructed to do so. Advanced readers' primary strategy for analyzing words clearly involved the use of grapheme–phoneme correspondences, although they could use orthographic cues as well.

Observing an increased reliance on orthographic and phonemic cues is an important aspect of early reading development, as these cues indicate that a child is attending to the full word form, not just a few of the letters. According to the lexical quality hypothesis (Perfetti & Hart, 2001, 2002), attention to the complete form enhances the quality of a person's mental representation of a word (the lexical representation). In turn, high-quality lexical representations support word recognition accuracy, reading fluency, and comprehension. Lexical quality has several dimensions. These include the obvious candidates of orthography, phonology, and meaning as well as a word's grammatical class and morphosyntactic inflections. Also, the binding of each of these constituents with the others is relevant. Examples of high- and low-quality representations in each dimension and the consequences for reading are described in Table 10.6 (Perfetti, 2007).

Share (1999) conducted a series of experiments to examine the role of visual input and phonological recoding in building high-quality orthographic representations of novel words. Second-grade Hebrew children read pseudowords that had been normed for spelling acceptability. In the first experiment they read fully pointed texts (i.e., texts with vowels included) that contained a pseudoword repeated several times, and then answered comprehension questions. After 3 days children were tested with several measures of orthographic learning: naming latency, spelling, and a forced choice recognition test that included (a) the original target spelling, (b) a homophonic spelling of the pseudoword, (c) a spelling with one letter substituted, (d) a spelling with two letters transposed. Share found shorter naming latencies and higher recognition accuracy for the pseudowords spelled as they appeared in the previously read texts. A second experiment tested whether the orthographic learning of novel words could be explained by visual exposure alone. Here a different group of children were exposed to the pseudowords under conditions designed to minimize phonological processing—they made lexical decisions to pseudowords and real words that appeared individually on the screen for 300 ms while simultaneously articulating

TABLE 10.6   Lexical quality and its consequences

Properties of a lexical representation	High quality	Low quality
Orthographic	Fully specified; letters are constants	Incompletely specified; some letter positions are variables
Phonological	Word-specific phonology; representation includes several layers of phonological information	Variable representations due to unstable grapheme–phoneme relations or incomplete phonology
Semantic	Full range of meanings specific enough to discriminate among semantic neighbors	Context-based, restricted range of meaning or very general sense of meaning
Morphosyntactic	Grammatical classes and inflections represented	Incomplete range of class and role information
Binding of these properties	Orthographic, phonological, semantic, and morphosyntactic properties tightly bound	Properties less tightly bound, activation of one does not consistently activate the others
Processing consequences for reading		
Stability	Higher: Words identified reliably and quickly from orthographic and phonological input	Lower: Word identification is slower and less reliable
Synchronicity	Properties are activated in tandem	Properties activated asynchronously

Adapted from Perfetti, 2007.

/*dubbadubbadubba*/ (see Chapter 7). Each pseudoword was presented six times during the experiment. Testing several days later indicated that primarily visual exposure to pseudowords had reduced recognition accuracy by 28% and spelling accuracy by 11% relative to the results of Experiment 1. In the third experiment Share presented the identical items for the same duration as in Experiment 2, but changed the task from lexical decision with concurrent articulation to naming in order to allow for phonological processing of the pseudowords. Recognition accuracy was significantly better here than in Experiment 2, although it was still 16% lower than in Experiment 1, and spelling accuracy was comparable to that found in Experiment 1. These results indicate that phonological processing plays an important role in children's formation of high-quality orthographic representations for novel words.

Cues for accessing the meaning of familiar words

So far in this chapter we have focused primarily on how children identify (or pronounce) new words. However, many of the words that children read are words that they already recognize in print. Here we turn to the issue of how children access the meanings of words that are already in their *print lexicon*. For the youngest beginning readers the print lexicon is almost totally the result of word-specific associations, in which the child associates some particular aspect of the word with its meaning and subsequently recognizes it on that basis. As reading skill increases, the print lexicon comes to contain information about orthographic patterns and the sound of the word, as well as its meaning (Ehri, 1983; Perfetti & Hart, 2001). Much of the research on children's access to word meanings has concerned whether there is a developmental shift in how word meanings are accessed.

This developmental shift hypothesis claims that novice readers rely mainly on phonological coding to access the meaning of words, whereas more skilled readers use both phonological and visual information (Barron, 1981a, 1986).

Several early studies called the developmental shift hypothesis into question by reporting findings indicating that not even novice readers use phonological coding to access word meanings (Barron & Baron, 1977; Condry, McMahon-Rideout, & Levy,1979; Rader, 1975). Jorm and Share (1983) pointed out that these studies used a restricted range of words (generally content words which were high in frequency and concreteness). Therefore they do not invalidate the developmental shift hypothesis as a whole. Rather, these early studies indicate that even beginning readers can and do use the visual route to access the meaning of common, high-frequency words. Jorm and Share also noted that using visual input to recognize high-frequency words does not necessarily imply that less-frequent and abstract words are processed in the same way; phonological coding may often be the first approach for processing such words before visual access becomes possible.

Backman et al.'s (1984) data from regular and irregular word naming support this idea. Backman et al. found that beginning readers rapidly learn to recognize high-frequency words from visual input alone, while at the same time they expand and consolidate their knowledge of spelling–sound correspondences. However, they also found that beginning readers have difficulty reading homographic spelling patterns (like *-ave, -own*) which have different pronunciations in different words (e.g., *have* vs *wave, town* vs *mown*), indicating that in such cases they did rely on phonological information in word decoding.

Picture–word interference

A number of studies have used a variation of the standard Stroop task that we described in Chapter 3 to investigate how beginning readers access word meanings. In the picture–word interference task (Rosinski, Golinkoff, & Kukish, 1975) participants are required to name a line drawing of a picture as rapidly as possible (see Figure 10.2). Printed inside the picture is a word or letter string which may or may not be related to the picture. Participants are faster naming the picture when the appropriate label is printed on the picture (the word apple inside a picture of an apple) than when the picture is presented alone (Ehri, 1976; Posnansky & Rayner, 1977).

FIGURE 10.2 Examples of stimuli in the picture–word interference task. The top row contains examples of incongruous words and pictures; the bottom row contains congruous examples

If the label printed inside the picture names another object, interference in naming the picture occurs.

Of present interest is the finding that when the picture and label printed on the picture are semantically incongruous (*house* printed on the picture of an apple), there is greater interference than when the label is semantically congruous (*fruit* printed on the picture of an apple). Rosinski (1977) used such a design to demonstrate that word labels in the semantic category of the picture produced more interference than word labels outside of the semantic category for second-, fourth-, and sixth-graders (and adults as well). This finding has been interpreted as indicating that the interference is semantically based and that word meaning access is not phonologically based even for beginning readers (Golinkoff & Rosinski, 1976; Rosinski et al., 1975). In subsequent research Guttentag and Haith (1978) tested end of first-grade, third-grade, and adult readers. They found that beginning readers showed more interference from semantically related than unrelated picture–word pairs, which suggests that beginning readers can access a lexical item described by a picture without necessarily processing the phonological information encoded in print. For third-graders and adults, however, pronounceable nonwords (*lart*) produced more interference than unpronounceable nonwords (*lbch*), which suggests that phonological activation from the label on the picture is automatic for older readers.

Posnansky and Rayner (1977) presented pictures with homophonic or non-homophonic nonword labels to beginning readers, older children, and adults. They found that beginning readers were faster naming the picture when the label had the same sound (e.g. *leef* or *lefe* on a picture of a leaf) than when it did not (*loef* or *lofe*). Participants were also faster when the label preserved most of the graphemic characteristics of the picture name (*leef*) than when it did not (*lefe*). In contrast to the previous study, the older children and adults showed essentially the same pattern as the beginning readers. Posnansky and Rayner's results suggest that visual information and the word-level phonological form are activated automatically irrespective of reading skill.

In summary, research on the development of word recognition provides little support for the hypothesis that there is a developmental shift away from reliance on phonological codes to the use of primarily orthographic codes. There is some evidence consistent with just the opposite hypothesis, namely that development proceeds from almost total reliance on graphemic information to the use of both phonological and visual codes. However, the most plausible hypothesis may be that beginning, as well as skilled, readers can use both graphemic and phonological information to access word meanings. Beginning readers may rely more on graphemic information when reading familiar words, before they have mastered analytic print-to-sound translation strategies. Once they have learned how to translate print into sound rapidly and accurately, they can use phonological coding to recognize unfamiliar words. As reading skill develops, they begin to activate phonological information automatically when they see a word.

Most of the results discussed in this section are consistent with the stages of early reading development described earlier, as well as with many of the observational studies upon which the stages are based. Together the results of these studies indicate that children move from almost total reliance on visual and graphemic cues to more phonological/orthographic strategies by the time they are beginning to read skillfully. Sensitivity to orthographic cues appears to evolve quite early (around the second grade of school). Second-grade readers appear to have some analytic strategies (such as the use of analogy and phonemic cues) available to them, but they are not as adept at using them as are 10-year-old readers. By fourth grade, children have developed and automatized the use of grapheme–phoneme correspondence rules so that they can read unfamiliar words and nonwords much like skilled readers do. They also can integrate orthographic, graphemic, and phonemic cues to build high-quality lexical representations that support efficient word recognition.

The studies discussed here question the viability of the developmental shift hypothesis (i.e., the idea that beginning readers use phonology to identify words whereas more-skilled readers rely on the direct orthographic route). In our view, the bulk of the present data suggest that word recognition skills develop from early logographic approaches for accessing the lexicon without phonology to the ability to use phonology as well as direct visual access. There are several sources of information consistent with this progression. First, as we saw in the section on word identification cues, children rely on visual or graphemic cues initially in reading, and move to phonological cues sometime in first grade. Second, children often enter reading instruction knowing the meanings of a small group of printed words, yet only have rudimentary knowledge of how to read words aloud except by associating whole words with their corresponding pronunciations, or by using a limited set of large unit analogies (Baron, 1979). Third, as we have also seen, learning to read words is often very difficult and time consuming and children who have trouble acquiring reading skill seem to be deficient in their use of print-to-sound translation procedures (Barron, 1981b; Bradley & Bryant, 1978; Perfetti & Hogaboam, 1975) and may be particularly reliant on visual cues when identifying words.

Lastly, experiments conducted using different paradigms converge on the automatic activation of phonology by skilled readers (see Chapter 5). Although some researchers and educators claim that skilled readers rely primarily on the direct route, behavioral and neurophysiological data do not seem to support that conclusion. Both eye movement and ERP studies found phonological priming effects early in word recognition, indicating that skilled readers typically engage phonological processes en route to word recognition during silent reading (Ashby, 2010; Ashby et al., 2009; Chace, Rayner, & Well, 2005; Lee, Binder, Kim, Pollatsek, & Rayner, 1999; Lee, Rayner, & Pollatsek, 1999; Pollatsek et al., 1992; Sereno & Rayner, 2000). Evidence from MEG experiments complements these findings by demonstrating concurrent activation in skilled word recognition; both the anterior orthographic-phonological pathway and the ventral orthographic-semantic pathway were active around 100 ms after a word was presented (Pammer et al., 2004; Wheat et al., 2010). However, some fMRI studies show reduced activation for skilled readers relative to dyslexic readers along the anterior phonological route (Pugh et al., 2001b). Initially, these data were interpreted as revealing skilled readers' shift from orthographic-phonological-semantic processing to orthographic-semantic processing. Yet reductions in activity could indicate more efficient phonological processing, as several perceptual and motor experiments have observed a reduction in the BOLD signal (blood flow to relevant cortical areas) when skills are practiced to the point of automaticity (Poldrack & Gabrieli, 2001; Ungerleider, Doyon, & Karni, 2002; Wang, Sereno, Jongman, & Hirsch, 2003). Sandak et al. (2004) found results consistent with increasingly efficient phonological activation in a training study that examined how reading circuits become tuned for word recognition; more efficient phonological processing in skilled readers manifests as reduced activation of anterior-dorsal phonological areas as letter strings became more familiar. Therefore the present neuroimaging data do not support the developmental shift hypothesis. In Chapter 11, however, we discuss data suggesting that an additional brain circuit becomes specialized for reading after age 10 in most children.

Units of processing and reading development

One major focus of reading research has been to determine what the unit of processing is for word recognition, and whether the unit size changes over time. Many previous studies were driven by speculation that the development of word recognition skill involves processing of progressively larger units (Gibson, 1971; LaBerge & Samuels, 1974). Typically, finding that word recognition becomes slower as word length increases is interpreted as indicative of letter-by-letter, small-unit processing. Several early studies examined developmental changes in units of processing, often producing inconsistent results (Barron, 1981a). Samuels, LaBerge, and Bremer (1978) found word length effects on the latency of semantic category decisions made by second-graders, but not those by adults. These results suggest either that children move from processing words letter-by-letter to processing words as wholes as reading skill increases, or that as reading skill increases children are able to process letters in parallel. In order to evaluate developmental changes in the processing units, Drewnowski (1978) used a letter detection task in which participants were to circle every instance of the letter *t* they found in prose passages, scrambled passages, and lists of words (see also Cunningham, Healy, Kanengiser, Chizzick, & Willitts, 1988; Mohan, 1978). Children in grades two through five and the adults made more errors in the prose passages when circling the *t*s in the word *the* as compared to *t*s in low-frequency words such as *thy*. The first-grade children, in contrast, performed similarly on both types of words. This pattern suggests that beginning readers are more likely to read letter-by-letter than skilled readers. As reading develops, readers begin to process some text in larger units. Barron (1981a) concluded that children develop the ability to attend to several units of processing (such as spelling patterns, syllables, some morphemes) as reading improves. More recent experiments with nonword reading indicate that children use consonant-vowel onsets and vowel-consonant codas to predict pronunciation as early as first grade, and this ability improves until about the fifth grade (Treiman et al., 2006). Alert readers will notice that these findings are consistent with the claim that readers of English learn to use several different grain sizes of phonological information to recognize words (Goswami, 2005).

It is likely that the sensitivity of the experimental paradigm influences what units of processing are identified. For example, experiments that examine length effects by measuring naming latency sometimes produce data that differs from those that measure eye movements. Two studies illustrate this point and shed light on the units of processing used by skilled adult readers. Weekes (1997) observed a length effect in naming latencies for low-frequency words but not high-frequency words, suggesting that adults process familiar words as wholes. In contrast, an eye movement study by Rayner, Sereno, and Raney (1996) found that fixation durations during silent reading increased steadily with word length for both high- and low-frequency words with 5 to 10 letters. Average word reading times increased 13 ms for each additional letter, irrespective of word frequency. This result indicates that skilled readers process each letter unit in skilled word recognition during silent reading. That is not to say that skilled readers only process letter units, or that they are necessarily processed in a distinctly serial fashion. Ashby et al. (2006) conducted an eye movement study which found that skilled readers also process larger units of print, such as onset-rime units, parafoveally during silent reading (see Chapter 5). Finding that skilled readers process letter units as well as larger patterns is consistent with the predictions of phonological grain size theory (Goswami, 2005).

Comprehension processes

We shall not have a great deal to say about the comprehension processes of children learning to read. We have suggested on a number of occasions in this chapter that, by fifth grade, children's word recognition processes are very much like those of adult skilled readers. We suspect that is also true of comprehension processes. This is not to say that fifth-grade children comprehend text as well as skilled readers. Certainly, if you give them difficult text to read (text that has many unfamiliar words and which is about an unfamiliar topic), they may not comprehend very much of it. Our point is that although children have less background knowledge to apply to the reading task than adults have, the way knowledge and strategies are brought to bear is similar for fifth-graders and adults (Bock & Brewer, 1985; Keenan & Brown, 1984).

Children younger than fifth grade do have problems comprehending text. Indeed, one can easily make the case that the younger the child, the more difficulties there may be in comprehension. But this general statement is quite independent of the modality of the discourse (i.e., reading or listening). Younger children also have more difficulty comprehending spoken stories and television shows than do older children. The reasons for this are fairly obvious: younger children do not have as much general knowledge about the world as do older children, and they have smaller vocabularies. Also, they are not as apt to infer motivational processes in characters in stories or infer why writers are presenting certain types of information as part of the plot development. By school age, most children have an adequate implicit knowledge of narrative forms (Stein & Glenn, 1979), but the richness of that knowledge continues to progress as they become more proficient in reading. Young children also often have difficulties in comprehending because they take everything quite literally; metaphors and idioms often go right over their heads. Therefore young children can have any of several language-based problems with comprehension that are not specifically related to reading and can be addressed through spoken language activities. Most children who are learning to read exhibit better listening comprehension than reading comprehension (Chall, 1996). As reading develops, the gap narrows and reading comprehension levels approach that of listening comprehension. Eventually, reading comprehension surpasses listening comprehension in skilled readers. With beginning readers, the better readers often have a smaller gap between their listening and reading comprehension than worse readers do. As beginning readers typically have better listening comprehension than reading comprehension when word reading is inaccurate (Curtis, 1980), a relative weakness in reading comprehension is not necessarily problematic early in reading development. Therefore, a reading comprehension deficit is best determined by comparing a child's understanding of text to that of his or her peers.

Of course, language comprehension problems do manifest in children's reading. When that happens, beginning readers can be quite oblivious to the fact that they do not understand the text. This brings us to another point about beginning readers: they are not very good at monitoring their own comprehension processes. A vast literature (Baker & Brown, 1984; Brown, 1980; Golinkoff, 1976; Markman, 1979, 1981; Myers & Paris, 1978; Ryan, 1982) on self-monitoring of comprehension has revealed that young children have deficits in this area; they are not aware of the extent to which they are understanding or misunderstanding a text. Some studies (Palinscar & Brown, 1984; Paris, Cross, & Lipson, 1984; Paris & Jacobs, 1984) have demonstrated that instruction in comprehension monitoring is quite beneficial, so it would seem that beginning readers can be capable of monitoring how well they are reading. Apparently, however, beginning readers typically do not do so unless specifically instructed. Why might this be?

When children are reading, comprehension may suffer from inefficient and cumbersome word identification processes. Baker and Brown (1984) argued that most beginning readers have little awareness that they must attempt to make sense of the text; rather they focus on reading as a decoding process and not as a meaning-gathering process. This may be because word identification is slow and effortful early in reading development. Beginning reading often sounds awkward, with the words being spoken in a staccato fashion and lacking the prosodic intonation that characterizes speech. Until word recognition processes become automatized, children must expend conscious effort attending to several aspects of reading (word identification and comprehension). In this respect, beginning to read is somewhat like trying to play basketball without knowing how to dribble well; it is difficult to focus on the ultimate objective of reading for meaning while simultaneously learning new decoding skills (Beck, 1998). For many children, instruction in comprehension monitoring improves their "game" by prioritizing comprehension monitoring at the cost of diminishing attention to fundamental skills. Alternatively, instruction that helps automatize word recognition processes can free up attention for comprehension while helping to strengthen lexical representations of printed words.

Omanson (1985) and Perfetti (1985) have argued that visual word recognition processes are heavily involved in reading comprehension. This explains why children's comprehension of text they hear generally exceeds their comprehension of text they read; a pattern that persists through the elementary grades (Curtis, 1980). As word recognition processes become more automatic, the resulting increase in efficiency allows readers to apply conscious effort to understanding the text. This idea is central to verbal efficiency theory (Perfetti, 1985). Verbal efficiency theory associates a reduction of the time and effort spent on word recognition with an increased capacity for text comprehension, and thereby provides a foundation for contemporary interest in reading fluency that is discussed in the next chapter.

Knowledge of word meanings also contributes to comprehension. If a text contains many long or unfamiliar words, even children with good word recognition skills will not understand it very well (Marks, Doctorow, & Wittrock, 1974; Wittrock, Marks, & Doctorow, 1975). If children are given vocabulary instruction, comprehension of texts that contain the instructed words improves significantly (Beck, Perfetti, & McKeown, 1982; Kameenui, Carnine, & Freschi, 1982; McKeown, Beck, Omanson, & Perfetti, 1983; Omanson, Beck, McKeown, & Perfetti, 1984). Thus it would seem that instruction that develops meaning vocabulary, automatizes word recognition, and helps monitor understanding can benefit children's comprehension processes.

Inner speech and reading comprehension

As we discussed in Chapter 7, inner speech processes support skilled reading comprehension. To what extent does inner speech aid beginning readers' text comprehension? This is not an easy area to evaluate because of the fact that many beginning readers practice reading orally as well as silently. Thus it is not surprising that EMG recordings during silent reading indicate more muscle activity in the speech tract of beginning readers than older children (Edfeldt, 1960; McGuigan, Keller, & Stanton, 1964). Perhaps much of this activity is merely a carryover from the more frequent oral reading that beginning readers engage in. It is probably the case that activity in the speech tract (i.e., subvocalization) is less important for comprehension processes than is phonological coding. Most of the research on speech processes associated with reading has focused on the role of pre-lexical phonology (or phonological processes that occur before a word is identified). In this section we are interested in phonological processes that operate post-lexically as identified words are integrated into sentences. Several studies indicate that post-lexical phonological recoding aids in comprehension.

Memory tasks are often used to identify phonological recoding strategies, and studies measure whether acoustically confusable material is more difficult to process than control material (i.e., a phonological similarity effect, see Chapter 7). A number of studies by Liberman and Shankweiler and their colleagues (Brady, Shankweiler, & Mann, 1983; Katz, Shankweiler, & Liberman, 1981; Liberman et al., 1977; Mann, Liberman, & Shankweiler, 1980; Mark, Shankweiler, Liberman, & Fowler, 1977; Shankweiler, Liberman, Mark, Fowler, & Fischer, 1979) and others (Byrne & Shea, 1979) demonstrated the importance of speech codes in the working memory processes thought to support comprehension. Liberman et al. found that good second-grade readers made more errors on rhyming sequences of letters than non-rhyming sequences, whereas poor readers made the same number of errors in both conditions. This suggests that good readers are more affected by the phonological properties of visually presented items and that they use speech codes in working memory more than do poor readers. Mark et al. (1977) conducted a follow-up study using a recognition memory paradigm that minimized rehearsal to test the locus of the phonological similarity effect. The result with the recognition task was similar to the previous recall study, which suggests that good readers have better access to phonological representations than do poor readers. Interestingly, when Hasselhorn and Grube (2003) tested the children in second through sixth grade, they found the magnitude of the phonological similarity effect to be independent of age and speech rate. These studies are consistent with the claim that inner speech is important for maintaining words in short-term memory, and that good beginning readers rely on inner speech more than poor beginning readers.

The above research demonstrates that inner speech is involved in the generation of short-term memory representations and, by extension, that inner speech supports reading comprehension. An alternative hypothesis is that the development of inner speech accompanies learning to read aloud with expression, or reading fluency (Beggs & Howarth, 1985). From this perspective, inner speech is a manifestation of the need to prestructure oral utterances (see also Slowiaczek & Clifton, 1980). Beggs and Howarth found that reading comprehension improved for beginning readers who read aloud text with the prosodic features marked (i.e., the stressed words written in boldface) as compared to unmarked text. Beggs and Howarth's inner speech hypothesis is also consistent with the results of Clay and Imlach (1971), who found that good 7-year-old readers read expressively, whereas less-skilled beginning readers did not.

A phrase-evaluation study reported by Doctor and Coltheart (1980) is one of the few developmental studies that obtained evidence relevant to the issue of post-lexical phonological recoding and reading comprehension. In Doctor and Coltheart's study, children 6 to 10 years old read phrases of the following types:

1. I have the time (meaningful sentences containing no homophones).
2. I have no time (meaningful sentences containing homophones).
3. I have know time (meaningless all-word sentences that sound correct).
4. I have blue time (meaningless all-word sentences that sound wrong).
5. I have noe time (meaningless sentences containing nonwords that sound correct).
6. I have bloo time (meaningless sentences containing nonwords that sound wrong).

When asked to judge whether the sentences were meaningful, beginning readers made more errors on phrases that sounded correct (*I have noe time* and *I have know time*) than with word phrases that sounded wrong (*I have blue time*). Additional experiments indicated that these errors were not based on visual similarity or poor knowledge of homophone spellings. However, the difference in error rates between the "sounds right" and "sounds wrong" conditions decreased with age. A follow-up study by Coltheart, Laxon, Keating, and Pool (1986) using Doctor and Coltheart's stimuli concluded that the previous phonological effects were due to post-lexical processing. Therefore it seems that beginning readers do rely on post-lexical phonological recoding to aid comprehension processes.

As we pointed out in Chapter 7, concurrent vocalization studies have been one source of information bolstering our knowledge of the role of phonological recoding in skilled reading. The concurrent vocalization technique has been used in only a few studies where children read meaningful text. Mayer, Crowley, and Kaminska (2007) studied the effect of concurrent vocalization on the reading comprehension of bilingual children in Wales: 7- and 11-year-old children read English and Welsh passages silently in each of three conditions; tapping their finger, repeating /lalalala/, or doing no additional task. After reading, which was self-paced, the children answered six questions about each of the six passages. Mayer et al. found that concurrent vocalization impaired the reading comprehension of the younger children more than the tapping did, for both the Welsh and the English passages. For the older children, however, concurrent vocalization only impaired reading comprehension for the Welsh passages. When reading English text, the comprehension of older children did not suffer in the concurrent vocalization condition as compared to the other two conditions. This result seems to indicate that when the older children read in English, they relied less on phonological coding than they did when reading Welsh. However, it is also possible that older readers continued to rely more on speech-tract activity for phonological coding when reading in Welsh, because it was first primary language, than when reading in English. This conclusion is consistent with research with proficient bilingual adults indicating that primary language (L1) characteristics influence word recognition data collected in the second language (L2) (Lemhöfer, Dijkstra, Schriefers, Baayen, Grainger, & Zwitserlood, 2008). Further research on the developmental relationship between speech-tract activity and comprehension with children whose primary language is English would be informative.

The small amount of research on inner speech during reading development suggests that as basic reading skills are acquired and initial reading experience accumulates, children become more proficient in using phonological coding as an aid for comprehension. Given that we have argued that adult skilled readers use inner speech to aid their comprehension, particularly of difficult text, it is likely that children do so as well. The role of inner speech in children's reading is an area that needs considerably more research before we will be able to completely understand the issue.

Summary

We have argued that many of the comprehension difficulties of beginning readers are not specific to reading: beginning readers have much less world knowledge and smaller meaning vocabularies than more skilled readers. Also, young children generally lack comprehension-monitoring strategies. Thus we would fully expect that younger children would not perform as well as older children on tests of comprehension (Keenan & Brown, 1984; Williams, Taylor, & DeCani, 1984). We have also suggested that major obstacles to comprehension in early readers are inefficient word recognition processes and limited vocabulary knowledge. Thus instruction aimed at improving children's comprehension monitoring strategies will aid understanding, but vocabulary instruction and the development of reading fluency will foster comprehension more effectively.

Eye movements and the perceptual span

As we noted in Chapter 4, beginning readers make more and longer fixations, shorter saccades, and more regressions than skilled readers. Beginning readers' average fixation duration is around 350 milliseconds, their average saccade length is between two and five characters, and about 25% of their eye movements are regressions. As children become better readers, their eye movement patterns show systematic changes: they make shorter fixations, longer (and fewer) saccades, and fewer regressions (Buswell, 1922; Rayner, 1978a; Taylor, 1965). Table 10.7 shows some summary statistics taken from Buswell and Taylor. Buswell (1922) observed that, by fifth grade, most of the indices of eye movements in reading have stabilized. The one aspect of eye movements that continues to change until the end of high school is the number of regressive eye movements.

Why do eye movement characteristics change as reading develops? Noting that the length of saccades increases with reading skill, many researchers have suggested that children beginning the reading process have smaller perceptual spans than their more-skilled counterparts. A generally accepted explanation for these phenomena is that beginning readers focus all of their attention on the fixated word and they are inefficient in the use of parafoveal and peripheral information, and hence have a smaller perceptual span than skilled readers (Fisher, 1979).

TABLE 10.7 Developmental characteristics of eye movements in reading

Article and characteristic	Grade level						
	1	2	3	4	5	6	Adult
S. E. Taylor (1965)							
Fixation duration (ms)	330	300	280	270	270	270	240
Fixations per 100 words	224	174	155	139	129	120	90
Frequency of regressions (%)	23	23	22	22	21	21	17
Buswell (1922)							
Fixation duration (ms)	432	364	316	268	252	236	252
Fixations per 100 words	182	126	113	92	87	87	75
Frequency of regressions (%)	26	21	20	19	20	21	8
Rayner (1986)							
Fixation duration (ms)	—	290	—	276	—	242	239
Fixations per 100 words	—	165	—	122	—	110	92
Frequency of regressions (%)	—	27	—	25	—	24	9
McConkie et al. (1991)							
Fixation duration (ms)	304	268	262	248	243	—	200
Fixations per 100 words	168	138	125	132	135	—	118
Frequency of regressions (%)	34	33	34	36	36	—	21
M							
Fixation duration (ms)	355	306	286	266	255	249	233
Fixations per 100 words	191	151	131	121	117	106	94
Frequency of regressions (%)	28	26	25	26	26	22	14

From Rayner (1998). Dashes indicate that data were not collected.

The technique most commonly used to assess the perceptual span in beginning readers involves simply dividing the number of words on a line by the number of fixations on the line. The problem with this approach is that it wrongly assumes there is no overlap of information from fixation to fixation. Another technique used to infer that children have smaller perceptual spans than skilled readers involves having participants read mutilated text, in which the spaces between words have been filled in with various types of letters or characters (Fisher & Montanary, 1977; Hochberg, 1970; Spragins, Lefton, & Fisher, 1976). The main problem with the mutilated text technique is that one cannot determine whether to attribute a slowdown in reading to difficulties related to processing information in eccentric vision or to difficulties associated with foveal word identification processes. Pollatsek and Rayner (1982) demonstrated that much of the difficulty in reading such text is a result of filling in the space to the right of the fixated word, and that much of the mutilation effect is likely due to disruption of identification of the fixated word rather than anything about the perceptual span.

Although the techniques described above are consistent in indicating that beginning readers have a smaller perceptual span than skilled readers, there are problems associated with each of them. Rayner (1986) used the moving-window technique described in Chapter 4 to investigate the size of the perceptual span of children at the beginning of the second, fourth, and sixth grade. Rayner found that the younger readers did have a slightly smaller perceptual span than skilled readers; the span of younger readers extends about 11 character spaces to the right of fixation in comparison to about 15 character spaces for skilled readers (see Chapter 4). Rayner also found that younger readers, like skilled readers, use word length information for determining where to look next, and that their perceptual span is asymmetric to the right of fixation (again like skilled readers). Apparently, 1 year of reading allows beginning readers to direct much of their attention to the right of fixation.

Whereas the perceptual span of younger readers was only slightly smaller than that of skilled readers in Rayner's study, reading in a moving window that restricted span to only five characters (two to the left and two to the right of fixation) slowed the reading rate of younger readers to just 62% of their normal reading rate. In comparison, fourth- and sixth-graders read with this size window at 40% and 44% of their normal rate, respectively, and adults read at 34%. As a reduced window slowed down the youngest readers the least (relative to their normal rate), it appears that their smaller perceptual span is due to the fact that they devote more attention to foveal word processing during a fixation than do skilled readers. Indeed, when fourth-grade children were given difficult text to read, the size of their perceptual span decreased to that of younger readers.

Häikiö, Bertram, Hyönä, and Niemi (2009) used a modified moving-window paradigm to examine the span for letter identity information in children 8, 10, and 12 years old as well as in adults reading Finnish. As Finnish is a more transparent orthography than English, it is possible that Finnish readers would have longer spans than readers of English. Rather than using Xs outside the window of visible text, Häikiö et al. used letter strings that preserved feature information about ascenders and descenders. This manipulation allowed testing of the letter identity span, which is smaller than the perceptual span (i.e., the area from which readers can extract useful information about letter features and word length). Their study replicates the Rayner (1986) findings discussed above, in that the better readers had larger letter identity spans than the poorer readers. In addition, the Häikiö et al. data suggest that, by age 12, children's letter identity span extends as far as the adult span, and that the letter identity span is comparable for skilled readers of Finnish (nine characters) and English (seven to eight characters). Therefore it seems that the orthographic consistency of a writing system does not impact parafoveal letter identification processes.

In summary, we can conclude that the perceptual span of beginning readers is slightly smaller than that of skilled readers (Häikiö et al., 2009; Rayner, 1986). However, neither the smaller perceptual span nor eye movements per se can fully account for younger readers' slower reading rate. Experiments with disappearing text indicate that children pick up basic visual information from the text nearly as quickly as do adults (Blythe et al., 2009). Mainly, it appears that children have significantly more trouble than adults in decoding single words. Younger children do read more slowly than older, more skilled children, but slow eye movements do not cause slow reading. They simply reflect the fact that central cognitive processes are slower in younger than older children and that many of the component processes in reading have not yet become automatized (LaBerge & Samuels, 1974). Consistent with that idea, Joseph et al. (2009) found that both children and adults had longer first fixations on words with more, as compared to fewer, letters. In children, however, the length effect appeared in other eye movement measures as well, such as refixations. Longer fixation durations, more fixations (resulting in shorter saccades), and more regressions all reflect the fact that encoding processes and word recognition processes require effortful processing for younger readers. Hence eye movements reflect the difficulties that younger readers have processing written language, but they are not the cause of their slower reading.

Summary

In this chapter we have described the stages of reading development across the lifespan, and discussed the early stages of reading development in some detail. We argued that these early stages of reading should not be thought of as a biological sequence that all children go through. Rather, we suggested that they should be viewed as a general developmental heuristic for describing a sequence of changes that occur in how children attempt to read words as their cognitive skills and reading experience increase. We then discussed data pertaining to several aspects of reading skill to support our claim that the basic processes fundamental to skilled reading have become pretty automatic and the basic strategies involved in comprehension of text are apparent by fifth grade in typically developing readers. Thus differences that exist between fifth-grade children and more advanced readers are primarily quantitative and not qualitative.

11

LEARNING TO READ

Learning to read is a complex and difficult task. Yet, for skilled readers, silent reading feels no more effortful than any other act of perception (e.g., listening). As we have seen in previous chapters, many component processes operate nearly automatically in skilled reading. These processes include recognizing familiar words, decoding new words, reading with intonation, comprehending the text, and learning the meaning of new words. The eventual automaticity of these processes in skilled readers underlies the common intuition that reading is an easy task. However, a few moments spent observing a beginning reader will reveal the tremendous effort that is initially expended when learning to read. Beginning readers often read aloud in a plodding, staccato fashion, pointing as they pronounce each individual word. Later, as children get faster at recognizing words, their reading becomes smoother and reflects the intonation patterns of speech, but many still misread and stumble over unfamiliar words for a few years. Thus we see the paradox of reading—that a skill that is so easy for adults can be quite difficult for children to learn.

In this chapter we examine a number of characteristics of learning to read, focusing on the component processes and cognitive skills that children must acquire to become skilled readers. While we touch on cross-cultural issues, this chapter is focused on the process of learning to read English. We begin by discussing the demands of an alphabetic system, then move to the foundations of reading development. Finally, we will discuss the various types of methods used to teach children to read.

The alphabetic principle

The nature of the writing system shapes the task of learning to read, yet the fundamental goals of reading are similar across systems. As we pointed out in Chapter 2, writing systems differ in terms of how they encode units of language. Alphabetic writing systems (e.g., English, Italian, Korean) use a limited number of graphemes (i.e., written symbols) to encode the basic phonemes of that language. In contrast, logographic writing systems (e.g., Chinese, Japanese Kanji) use a larger number of graphemes to record the semantic and phonetic properties of words. Between these two extremes lie *abjads*, which are alphabets that encode consonant phonemes but omit most vowel sounds (e.g., Hebrew, Arabic), and *syllabaries* that use graphemes to represent syllables (e.g., Japanese Kana). Alphabetic scripts have two advantages over logographic scripts. First, learning to read an alphabetic script requires knowing far fewer associations than learning to read a logographic script, in which each character encodes a word meaning. An alphabetic system gains this economy through predictable correspondences between letters and speech sounds; it takes advantage of the fact that speech is already associated with meaning in spoken language. Second, because alphabets encode basic phonemes, skilled readers of alphabetic scripts can pronounce unfamiliar words independently. In contrast, Chinese readers must memorize the pronunciation and form of thousands of characters in order to read text.

The different alphabets of the world are based on the same principle, despite differences in the appearance of the letters in Arabic, Cyrillic, and German script; written symbols are associated with phonemes, or speech sounds. The consistency of letter–sound associations is the major advantage of a productive alphabet, as it allows readers to pronounce words they have never seen before. This allows readers to assemble a phonological form that can be stored and retrieved from the lexicon, becoming part of the reader's language system. The consistency of grapheme–phoneme associations is referred to as the script's transparency. Italian, Spanish, Korean, and German are among the more transparent alphabetic scripts. However, many other alphabets represent the relation between letters and phonemes in more complex ways (e.g., the silent *e* in English). The English alphabet, for example, is considered to be morphophonemic in nature because it uses letters to indicate morphological as well as phonological information. Although letters roughly represent phonemes, exactly how the phonemes are spelled depends on the word's morphology (Perfetti, 2003). For example, the first syllables in *nature* and *natural* contain different phonemes, but they are spelled the same to indicate the morphological connection between these words. This morphophonemic characteristic of written English poses specific challenges to developing readers, and reading instruction should address these different layers of linguistic information. Therefore the sequence of reading instruction is more complex for non-transparent writing systems such as English, and the process of learning to read takes longer (Katz & Frost, 1992; Seymour et al., 2003; Share, 2008).

Despite the morphological complexity of English, the basic principle that letters represent phonemes, or single speech sounds, is the same across all alphabetic systems and this principle is the key to a "productive writing system" (Perfetti, 1985). A productive writing system is one that produces an indefinitely large number of words and morphemes from a small set of reusable symbols (or letters). For example, the four letters *p, s, t,* and *o* can encode *stop, pots, tops, top, pot, so, post, to,* and *sop*. Whereas the productive value of alphabetic scripts is economical for skilled readers, less-transparent alphabets can result in confusion for beginning readers. There are two reasons for confusion and difficulty in learning an alphabetic writing system in general, and English in particular: (a) the abstract nature of phoneme (especially consonants) and (b) the fact that English does not assign a unique symbol to each vowel sound. Let's consider each of these obstacles for children learning to read.

The first obstacle is that young children often have an imperfect idea of what phonemes are. This is because phonemes are abstractions rather than actual acoustic segments of the speech stream (Liberman, Cooper, Shankweiler, & Studdert-Kennedy, 1967). The phoneme /d/, for example, is an abstraction since both its perception and production are highly dependent on vowels that precede and follow it. First, the /d/ in *dime* is quite different acoustically from the /d/ in *dome* or the /d/ in *lid*. Second, you can't say /d/ by itself. When a teacher tries to explain that the word *dime* begins with the phoneme /d/ there will be a problem because she or he will produce /d/ plus a bit of the following vowel, as some vocalization is necessary. If the vowel sound /ay/ (pronounced *eye*) is added after the /d/, it will be correct for *dime* but not for *dome*. If the teacher tries to omit the subsequent vowel, then /d/ will probably be produced as *duh*, and the resulting sound will not be a component of either *dime* or *dome*.

The abstract nature of phoneme segments helps to account for beginning readers' difficulty with phonological awareness. Phonological awareness is the umbrella term for being able to identify the sound structure of language at the syllable, rime, or phoneme level. Phonemic awareness refers to the conscious awareness of single speech sounds that allows the segmentation, storage, and manipulation of the phonemes in words they hear (e.g., the ability to answer the question, What is /spot/ without the /s/?). A good deal of research has shown that phonemic awareness predicts success in learning to read. Learning to apply the alphabetic principle involves associating the abstract phoneme /d/ (or any other consonant) with a specific grapheme, in this case the letter *d*. Associating two elements may be especially difficult for the child if he/she only understands one of them, knowing the letter *d* but not being certain about the abstract phoneme.

It can be difficult for skilled readers to appreciate children's lack of understanding about how print relates to spoken language. Rozin, Bressman, and Taft (1974) conducted a study that illustrates the extent to which knowledge of the alphabetic principle develops over the course of learning to read. Children saw two cards, one containing (for example) the word *mow* and the other *motorcycle*. Both words were pronounced carefully by the experimenter before children were asked to point to the card containing the appropriate word. If children understand that *motorcycle* has a longer pronunciation (with more phonemic segments) than *mow*, they should be able to easily choose the correct card. Rozin et al. found that prereaders performed at chance on this task, indicating that they did not understand that words with more speech sounds had more letters. In contrast, most second-graders could perform the task accurately. By this time they had learned to read and developed an understanding of the relationship between spoken sounds and printed letters.

The second obstacle for children learning to read, the fact that alphabets do not spell each of the vowels with a unique symbol, is greater in some alphabetic scripts than others. For example, in written Finnish most vowel sounds are spelled with distinct letters, making it one of the most transparent orthographies. As we mentioned earlier, the English writing system is not very transparent. Part of the reason for its complexity is that American English has over a dozen vowel sounds but only five standard vowel letters. That means that *a, e, i, o*, and *u* have to do double and triple duty, even with some help from *y* and *w*. For example, *cat, cake, car*, and *call* each use the letter *a* for a different vowel phoneme. Few of these differences are arbitrary, however. Rather, the regularity of pronunciation appears to be governed by larger phonological units: the pronunciation of the *a* in *cake* is determined by the presence of the final *e*, and the pronunciation of the *a* in *car* is determined by the presence of the following *r*. These examples illustrate the results of corpus studies in English, which indicate that vowel phonemes become more predictable when the vowel letter is considered in the context of surrounding consonants (Kessler & Treiman, 2001; Treiman, Mullennix, Bijeljac-Babic, & Richmond-Welty, 1995). Consonants that follow a vowel have a particular influence over its pronunciation; as the previous examples indicate, the letter *a* may have several possible pronunciations, but the possibilities narrow if the reader also considers the letter following the vowel (i.e., the coda). Notice the consistency in the /a/ sound in the words *hall, wall*, and *small*. Here, words sharing the same rime unit (i.e., the vowel + the following consonants) are spelled consistently, and this contributes to orthographic-phonological transparency. Eye movement experiments indicate that skilled readers are sensitive to vowel context, as they use coda information when activating phonological vowel information parafoveally, during the initial phases of lexical access (Ashby, Treiman, Kessler, & Rayner, 2006). The consistent pronunciation of rime units also holds for many words that we think of as being spelled irregularly (e.g., *could, should, would*). It is therefore not accurate, as some have argued, to say that English spelling is chaotic. Rather, all alphabets value economy (e.g., 26 letters) and achieve that through complexity (i.e., the mapping of multiple sounds to one letter). However, languages with fewer vowel sounds, like Spanish and Italian, do require fewer of these multiple mappings than does English. Not surprisingly, children learning to read writing systems with simpler mappings achieve proficiency before those learning to read in systems such as English (Aro & Wimmer, 2003; Seymour et al., 2003).

Discerning patterns of orthographic-phonological regularity at the phoneme, rime, and syllable level is one of the primary challenges of learning to read in English (Ziegler & Goswami, 2005). Whereas children who have memorized words may appear to be "reading", building knowledge of the alphabetic principle is key to developing a facility with orthographic-phonological coding to support truly independent reading—or the ability to read words never seen before. Surprisingly, then, many first-grade readers who struggle to master orthographic-phonological coding, and read laboriously while they are doing so, may be more on track for becoming independent readers than readers who memorize whole words and disregard the alphabetic principle. Early readers who understand the alphabetic principle learn to attend to all the letters in a word as they enter the full alphabetic phase, in order to differentiate the lexical representations of similar-looking words, such as *winter* and *wonder* (Ehri, 1980, Perfetti, 1992; Venezky & Massaro, 1979). Beck (2006) observed that some readers, who seem to be reading well initially due to their memorization of whole words, may begin to flounder as reading begins to entail the recognition of longer words that look and sound very similar (e.g., *wonder* and *wander*).

In summary, understanding the alphabetic principle and automatizing the common orthography-to-phonology mappings make learning to read in English a challenging task. As we've argued, there are two major problems: (1) phonemes are perceptual abstractions and (2) most alphabets sacrifice phoneme explicitness for symbol economy or morphological transparency, thereby complicating the orthography. Numerous studies make it clear that discovering the alphabetic principle is the key to successfully learning to read (Backman, 1983; Bradley & Bryant, 1978; Bruce, 1964; Calfee, Chapman, & Venezky, 1972; Calfee, Lindamood, & Lindamood, 1973; Fox & Routh, 1975, 1976, 1984; Helfgott, 1976; Juel, Griffith, & Gough, 1986; Liberman, 1973; Lundberg, Olofsson, & Wall, 1980; Torneus, 1984; Wagner & Torgesen, 1987; Zifcak, 1981). The morphophonemic nature of the English writing system results in less orthographic transparency, which makes learning to read in English more difficult than learning to read in many other languages. Ehri (1979, p. 63) has stated, "If the light were not so gradual in dawning, the relationship between speech and print might count as one of the most remarkable discoveries of childhood."

Emergent literacy

Children in every country develop spoken language spontaneously as a natural part of being immersed in a language community. The concept of emergent literacy is rooted in the idea that children will also learn to read spontaneously as a result of being part of a community that values and practices literacy. Although a literacy community can motivate children to learn to read, most children do not become readers automatically. Unlike speech, an ability that is hard-wired in the human brain, reading is a learned skill (Gough & Hillinger, 1980). The term *emergent literacy* (Clay, 1991) is used to describe the knowledge and attitudes that children develop prior to formal literacy instruction (Storch & Whitehurst, 2002; Whitehurst & Lonigan, 1998). In the preschool years children begin to understand the significance of their writing system and how it operates. The central idea of emergent literacy is that literacy, although possibly not hard-wired in the brain, emerges as part of natural developmental processes, taking various forms before it becomes conventional reading. In this sense it is somewhat of a catch-all term that refers to any literacy-related competence before age 6, from how to hold a book to naming letters. Children's performance on literacy-like tasks is taken as an indicator of their progress on a continuum of competencies that precede conventional reading and writing development.

The period of emergent literacy extends from birth through age 6, and it involves the growth of spoken language skills and a dawning awareness of print in the surrounding environment. Informal observations have led to the recognition of standard benchmarks that preschool children should reach under normal circumstances. Before the age of 4 children discover the function of print by noticing print in the environment. At this point they recognize words by using the visual cues on labels, rather than the print itself. This has been demonstrated by studies in which children failed to reject labels in which the initial letter had been altered (e.g., *Pepsi* to *Xepsi*), even though they noticed the letter change (Masonheimer, Drum, & Ehri, 1984; McGee, Lomax, & Head, 1988). Around 4 years of age children begin to understand the figural aspects of print (e.g., word shape). Gradually they begin to develop an awareness of letters as word constituents and the importance of letter orientation. By 5 years of age, children should know where to find the beginning and end of a storybook. They also begin to identify letters, especially the letters in their name.

Few quantitative studies have investigated the developmental course of emergent literacy using a standard set of tasks. Levy, Gong, Hessels, Evans, and Jared (2006) conducted a cross-sectional, descriptive study of 474 children between the ages of 4 and 6. They administered a variety of experimental tasks and standardized tests to children in order to better understand the trajectory of emergent literacy. The study focused on how print knowledge and phonological awareness develop as well as the relationship between this knowledge and word reading skills. Print knowledge was examined through a discrimination task in which children looked at pairs of items (see Table 11.1) and identified which one "Mommy would like to read" (p. 72). Children worked at their own pace through cards that tested their ability to detect print violations in words and sentences, including linearity, spacing, letter–number combinations, and upside-down and backward print. Phonological awareness, letter recognition, and single-word reading were assessed with standardized tests.

Levy et al. (2006) found that knowledge of print developed quickly in 4-year-olds. By the age of 4 children knew that the conventions of writing differ from those of drawings. Their detection of print violations indicated an understanding of many abstract print conventions, such as letter spacing and linearity. That knowledge was related to their ability to read letters, but not to their phonological awareness. Few children at this age could read any single words, suggesting that knowledge of print conventions develops prior to word reading. By 5 years of age virtually all of the children could detect word-shape violations like linearity and spacing. Five-year-olds could detect letter orientation violations, and they started to focus on letter sequences. The violation-detection task indicated growth in their knowledge of letter constituents (e.g., consonant and vowel variation) and spelling (e.g., acceptable letter strings) that predicted variance in word reading beyond that accounted for by phonological awareness alone. For 6-year-old children, spelling knowledge became a stronger predictor of word reading than it was for the 5-year-olds,

TABLE 11.1   Example items from a discrimination task

Violation type	Correct choice	Incorrect choice
Linearity	Grass is green.	G a i g e n. r s s r e
Spacing	Farmers pick apples.	Fa rm ers p i c k app les.
Multiplicity	Flowers smell good.	F s g.
Variety	Owls dislike rats.	Oooo dddd rrrr.

From Levy et al., 2006.

contributing 19% of the unique variance after accounting for phonological awareness and age. These data suggest that children's knowledge of how words are coded in writing becomes increasingly specific over time and that the specificity of this knowledge is related to word reading skills in first grade.

The Levy et al. (2006) data suggest a difference between the awareness of print and knowing how to use it to read. Although 4-year-olds knew that the letters in a word occur in a single line of text with no spaces between them, these figural aspects of print did not mediate their reading achievement. Rather it was their attention to the internal constituents of words (i.e., vowels and consonants) that predicted reading in 4-, 5-, and 6-year-olds. Therefore basic print awareness (e.g., word shape, linearity of text, knowledge of functions of print) may precede reading chronologically, without necessarily contributing much to early reading per se. Despite the limited ability of many emergent literacy skills to predict early reading, they clearly mark the developmental trajectory that leads to it.

Whereas the bulk of the classic emergent literacy research mainly focused on pre-alphabetic skills, in more recent literature the term "emergent literacy" encompasses a broad set of skills that includes the awareness of sound sequences and letter–sound correspondences (or code-based skills). Admittedly, the inclusion of these skills under a catch-all term of emergent literacy captures the continuum of development from understanding speech to reading print. However, this broadening of the term may also carry some costs. First, the broad use of the term "emergent" literacy implies that phonological awareness, letter identification, and orthographic knowledge emerge naturally in children. We question whether current research actually supports the claim that these skills usually develop spontaneously without instruction. Whereas a general awareness of print in the environment (e.g., recognizing labels) may emerge naturally, the claim that alphabetic skills emerge naturally from experience with spoken language is not consistently supported by the data (e.g., Levy et al., 2006; Lonigan, Burgess, & Anthony, 2000; Sénéchal, LeFevre, Thomas, & Daly, 1998). Certainly, some children develop alphabetic skills from everyday experiences and without explicit instruction. However, many children do not. For example, a review of the Early Childhood Longitudinal Study indicates that nearly 30% of children living *above* poverty level did not recognize all the alphabet letters by the start of kindergarten (Douglas & Montiel, 2008). Therefore the broad use of the term emergent literacy tends to minimize the importance of explicit instruction in building the alphabetic skills that support beginning to read.

Treating emergent literacy as a unitary process can have the effect of masking the relatively distinct phases in reading development, which we discussed in Chapter 10. The behaviors characteristic of each phase have been observed in several studies. In many cases these behaviors indicate the typical development of the neural networks underlying reading. Conversely, the absence of certain behaviors at a particular phase in reading development can be diagnostic of reading problems. Therefore viewing the process of learning to read as a unitary process of emergent literacy may not be in the best interest of those seeking to understand reading development or identify reading difficulties.

Lastly, classrooms organized around the emergent literacy concept tend to emphasize communication opportunities (e.g., storybook reading by the teacher, picture drawing, and journal writing). Often these classrooms do not provide many children with sufficient systematic instruction about the letter–sound correspondences that constitute the alphabetic principle. Emergent literacy classrooms are very good at getting children to experience literacy-like activities and see how exciting literacy can be. Even though this result has positive consequences, such classrooms may incur an unanticipated cost: some children may attend to the functions of print at the expense of learning the process of how to read words. Children who love books do not necessarily have the understanding of the alphabetic principle that is needed to read new words independently and become fluent readers. The following sections discuss the empirical evidence for how two central themes of emergent literacy education, storybook reading and spoken language, relate to word-reading skills in elementary school.

Listening to storybooks

Advocates of the emergent literacy perspective often focus on the importance of a child's home environment in setting a foundation for later reading development. Since the 1980s, educators have emphasized the importance of having children's books in the home and reading aloud to children in order to develop oral language and print awareness. For this reason, emergent literacy classrooms emphasize teachers reading storybooks to children as a central activity. Whereas storybook reading is a popular and valuable activity for parents and teachers, recent studies suggest the connection between storybook reading and early alphabetic skills (e.g., letter identification, letter sounds, and basic word reading) may not be as substantial or direct as is frequently thought.

The initial field studies of storybook exposure reported inconclusive findings about whether parent storybook reading predicted later emergent literacy skills in children (e.g., Bus, van Ijzendoorn, & Pellegrini, 1995; Scarborough & Dobrich, 1994). In retrospect, the predictive relationships found were apparently due to the practice of including storybook-reading time as the sole index of the influence of the home environment. Such studies found a modest association between the time parents spent reading to their children and the development of early literacy skills. More recent field studies included several variables to index aspects of home environment in order to distinguish the predictive value of storybook reading from other variables such as parent expectations, size of spoken vocabulary, time spent on reading and writing activities, and degree of task-focused behavior (Evans, Shaw, & Bell, 2000; Levy et al., 2006; Sénéchal et al., 1998; Stephenson, Parrila, Georgiou & Kirby, 2008). In studies that include these other variables, storybook reading fails to account for much unique variance in early literacy development (although it does support the development of spoken vocabulary). Instead, the time children spend on reading and writing activities is consistently predictive of early reading development. In other words, it is the child's engagement in reading and writing activities that is key, not the time spent listening to storybooks. Therefore it seems that the later phases of emergent literacy (e.g., print recognition, letter discrimination, and letter sounds) do not necessarily develop spontaneously through frequent storybook listening; these skills are learned as children actively engage in reading and writing activities at home and at school.

Empirical studies of where children look when listening to storybooks suggest why storybook reading does not directly support the development of early literacy skills. Evans and Saint-Aubin (2005) conducted the initial experiments that monitored the eye movements of 4-year-olds as they listened to their mother read a storybook. To determine whether the nature of the text and illustrations had any effect on children's attention to print, the authors used several different types of text placement, such as text-left or text-below the pictures and text boxes (as in comic strips). Evans and Saint-Aubin found that children rarely looked at the text, even when portions of it were in all capital letters. Further, the time spent on the text was not affected by the layout of the book or the attractiveness of the illustrations. When children spent additional time on a page, that time was spent inspecting the pictures, not the text. In another eye movement study Justice, Skibbe, Canning, and Lankford (2005) found that children spent more time looking at the text when parents read print-salient books than picture-salient books, but the percentage of fixations on print was still quite small (13%).

Several studies indicate that adult readers rarely engage with children to draw their attention to print (Ezell & Justice, 2000; Phillips & McNaughton, 1990; Yaden, Smolkin & Conlon, 1989). To investigate this, Justice, Pullen, and Pence (2008) conducted an eye movement study to examine whether differences in the style of storybook reading affected the time preschool children spent looking at the print. Four-year-olds were read four storybooks by trained readers, each in one of four conditions in a counterbalanced, within-participants design. In one condition the reader made general comments about the text (e.g., "This is my favorite part.") In another condition comments referred specifically to the pictures or the print in the storybook (e.g., "The cat looks really mad!"). In the last condition the reader made general comments and tracked the text with her finger and pointed to phrases in the text. General comments about the print somewhat increased the time children spent looking at it. However, it was the last tracking and pointing condition that was most effective in increasing the time children attended to print. This is an important finding for parents and teachers who hope to increase print awareness through storybook reading. Whether parents and teachers actually use these attention-directing behaviors once they learn them is a topic for future research.

Developing spoken language

In the years prior to learning to read, children accrue at least 3 or 4 years of language experience. Children generally begin to talk between 12 and 18 months of age, with girls usually being more precocious than boys. By the time they are 5 years old they have an extensive vocabulary. While syntactic and semantic development of language processes is not yet complete, children are fairly proficient language users. Although they are certainly not as skilled in the use of language as adults, they can communicate quite effectively.

How important is oral language competence in the process of learning to read? Several studies suggest that children with limited spoken vocabularies experience difficulty learning to read (Nation & Snowling, 1998, 2004; Ouellette, 2006). In preschool, semantic and syntactic skills have been found to predict early phonological awareness (Chaney, 1992). Children's knowledge of syntax and concepts frequently correlates with early reading development as well (Bishop & Adams, 1990; Gillon & Dodd, 1994; Vellutino, Scanlon, & Spearing, 1995). Catts, Fey, Zhang, and Tomblin (1999) found that kindergarten oral language skills predicted later visual word recognition skills. One reason for these correlations may be that a larger vocabulary demands the development of more specific phonemic representations in order to differentiate similar words in memory, such as *fine* and *mine* (Jusczyk, Pisoni, & Mullennix, 1992; Metsala & Walley, 1998; Walley, 1993). Thus children with larger vocabularies develop detailed phonological representations earlier, and these representations support their performance on phonological awareness tasks (Garlock, Walley, & Metsala, 2001). Spoken vocabulary provides a foundation for accurate lexical representations of words in print. The number of high-quality lexical representations, in turn, enables efficient word recognition processes that allow readers to allocate most attention to understanding the text (Perfetti, 1998; Samuels & Flor, 1997). Conversely, children with poor vocabularies may have difficulty with reading comprehension (Beck, Perfetti, & McKeown, 1982).

Studies that have systematically investigated whether the development of oral language skills in preschool contributes to early reading achievement in the primary grades do not find compelling evidence for a direct connection. Storch and Whitehurst (2002) followed a sample of low-income children from preschool to fourth grade and used structural equation modeling to map the connection between early language ability and learning to read. Oral language skills included vocabulary, one-word picture naming, and the ability to recall a story they had heard. Reading measures tested first-graders' ability to match words with pictures and older students' ability to read words aloud accurately. Their analyses indicated that oral language development and code-based skills (e.g., recognizing letters, discriminating print from pictures, identifying sounds, and segmenting sentences) are highly correlated during preschool, with oral language predicting 48% of the variance in code-based skills prior to kindergarten. However, this relationship decreased in subsequent grades. In kindergarten oral language accounted for only 10% of the variance in code-related skills, and there was no significant relationship by the first and second grades. Therefore the Storch and Whitehurst data indicate that oral language mainly affects early reading development through its influence on the acquisition of code-related skills during preschool and kindergarten. This finding is consistent with Carroll, Snowling, Stevenson, and Hulme (2003), who found vocabulary size to be associated with syllable awareness in preschool, which predicted phoneme awareness at age 5. It is also consistent with other studies that found little correlation between oral language skills and reading in first and second grade (Curtis, 1980; Lonigan et al., 2000; Schatschneider, Fletcher, Francis, Carlson, and Foorman, 2004). In contrast to oral language skills, the Storch and Whitehurst study found a fairly tight correlation between code-based skills and early reading. Code-related abilities in kindergarten accounted for 58% of the variance in Grade 1 reading and 30% of the variance in Grade 2 reading. Together, Lonigan et al. (2000), Schatschneider et al. (2004), and Storch and Whitehurst (2002) indicate a direct relationship between code-related skills in kindergarten and success in learning to read. Thus there appears to be few empirical data to indicate that an emphasis on spoken language skill in the primary grades, in and of itself, results in measurable gains in early reading. However, Storch and Whitehurst found that the contribution of oral language to reading achievement picks up again in grades three and four, although the main predictors of comprehension skill were prior reading achievement and current reading accuracy. Their data are consistent with earlier studies that identify stronger correlations between oral language and reading in the later school years (Sticht & James, 1984).

Are there aspects of oral language that support automatic word recognition? Nation and Cocksey (2009) divided the construct of oral language vocabulary into two categories, knowledge of a word's meaning and familiarity of its phonological form, and examined the influence of each factor on regular and irregular word reading. Of particular interest was whether semantic knowledge would predict accuracy in isolated word reading, especially for irregular words. Phonological familiarity was indexed by accuracy in an auditory lexical decision task and semantic knowledge was assessed by a definitions task. Seven-year-olds were tested in three sessions, each of which used the same set of regular and irregular words. The first session involved auditory lexical decision, the second measured reading accuracy, and in the third children defined the words. Item-level analyses indicated that both semantic knowledge and phonological familiarity predicted word reading accuracy for regular and irregular words. This is not too surprising, given that children tend to know the spoken form of a word if they know its meaning. However, subsequent hierarchical regression analyses indicated that semantic knowledge did not account for any additional variance in irregular word reading accuracy, beyond that which was taken up by phonological familiarity alone. This suggests that the critical factor in irregular word reading for younger readers is familiarity of the phonological form.

These data and those of a similar study with regular words by McKague, Pratt, and Johnston (2001) are consistent with educators' claim that children initially use familiar phonological forms to bootstrap visual word recognition, making partial decoding attempts and matching them with words they have heard (Jorm & Share, 1983; Share, 1995). The Nation and Cocksey study also holds interesting implications for the interpretation of previous studies that reported a relationship between vocabulary knowledge and word-reading accuracy (e.g., Nation & Snowling, 1998, 2004; Ouellette, 2006; Ricketts, Nation, & Bishop, 2007). Given that McKague et al. and Nation and Cocksey failed to find evidence for a unique contribution of semantic knowledge in visual word recognition accuracy, it is possible that the vocabulary assessments in previous studies were actually tapping the more critical variable of phonological familiarity (in addition to semantic knowledge).

Further research is needed to determine whether preschool vocabulary growth contributes to early reading mainly by establishing a large store of familiar spoken word forms onto which children can map print that they attempt to decode. In addition, it may be that the relationship between semantics and word identification develops along with reading skill, and therefore is more likely to appear in studies involving older children.

In summary, oral language development has an impact on learning to read in different ways at different stages of reading development. As children's spoken vocabularies expand, they acquire more words that are similar to each other, and thus may become increasingly sensitive to phonological information in the speech stream. Spoken language and early code-based skills are highly correlated during preschool; however, spoken language development does not seem to predict reading success in the primary grades in studies that also include phonological awareness as a separate factor. Rather, it is the code-based skills acquired in kindergarten that lay the foundation for subsequent reading development.

Becoming conscious of words as units

It is sometimes assumed that spoken words are perceptual units and that young children beginning the reading process (who speak quite fluently) are aware of the separate words they are combining and recombining in their speech. However, as Ehri (1979) pointed out, more careful consideration of children's experiences with words and relationships between words and meanings raises some doubts about the plausibility of this assumption. Young children typically experience most words in the context of other words, and their attention is centered on the meanings conveyed by these spoken combinations, not on their linguistic structure. Moreover, there are no auditory signals that segment speech into word units. Thus, in normal spoken language, words as individual components are neither salient nor clearly marked (see Figure 11.1).

There is substantial evidence to indicate that children are not conscious of separate words before they begin learning to read. For example, when non-reading children are asked either to tap or to

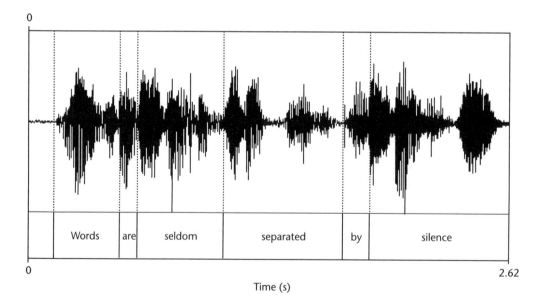

FIGURE 11.1   The wave-form (sound amplitude as a function of time) of the sentence *Words are seldom separated by silence* illustrates that the presence of pauses does not reliably indicate word boundaries

point as each word is spoken, they do not perform very well (Huttenlocher, 1964; Holden & MacGinitie, 1972; Ehri, 1975, 1976). In the Holden and MacGinitie study, kindergarteners repeated sentences they heard, assigning one poker chip to each word unit they perceived. Most children failed to segment the sentences into the correct number of words. Words with greater lexical meaning were sometimes isolated accurately, but function words were frequently combined with adjacent units and included in one chip. Whether function words were isolated or combined with other words seemed to be primarily dependent on the rhythmic pattern imposed on the sentence by the child. Similarly, studies in which children marked the word boundaries in normal written sentences also reveal a lack of word consciousness in beginning readers (Holden & MacGinitie, 1972; Meltzer & Herse, 1969; Mickish, 1974). On the basis of these data, it is questionable whether very early beginning readers can be regarded as possessing a definitive notion of word units, even when they are looking at words separated by spaces in print. Given that beginning readers have spent hours looking at pages of storybooks as they were read to by parents, one might expect them to develop some awareness of word units. However, their lack of attention to the print and the absence of obvious word segmentation cues in parents' speech help to account for the slowly dawning realization that words are the fundamental units of spoken and written language.

Pick et al. (1978) examined the development of children's awareness of word units. In this study 3- to 8-year-old children were shown letter strings varying in length, and asked to judge if each string was a word or not. Prereaders had a tendency to say the string was a word irrespective of whether or not it was, particularly if the string was more than one letter. Table 11.2 shows the different responses to different types of letter strings by the different groups of participants. Between nursery school and kindergarten, the ability to discriminate nonwords from words clearly improved as evidenced by decreasing error rates. As reported in Levy et al. (2006), it appears that by kindergarten most children understand the characteristics of printed words even though they do not yet know how to read. They know that letters have a correct orientation. They also learn something

TABLE 11.2   Percentage of children responding that a stimulus was a word

	Single-letter words	Single-letter nonwords	Long words	Long nonwords	Five-letter words	Unfamiliar words	Familiar initials
3–4 years	48	54	85	87	81	80	77
5 years	14	6	88	75	86	81	75
Kindergarteners	26	29	59	53	66	66	59
Grade 1	62	16	50	34	63	35	41
Grades 2, 3	58	23	58	8	82	22	29

	Meaningful nonwords	Pronounceable clusters: Nonwords	Consonant clusters	Vowel clusters	Misoriented letters (could be words)	Misoriented letters (could not be words)
3–4 years	85	83	80	80	73	72
5 years	87	80	83	71	61	56
Kindergarteners	59	62	59	51	38	35
Grade 1	51	30	23	17	35	30
Grades 2, 3	29	18	5	4	20	2

From Pick et al. 1978.

about the combinations of letters of which words are composed (that, for example, words are not composed of all consonants or all vowels).

Summary

The emergent literacy literature has contributed rich observational data that deepen our understanding of the skills which precede actually beginning to read. However, the studies discussed above suggest that at least three aspects of the emergent literacy perspective are problematic. First, the initial phases of print awareness, such as knowledge of print linearity and spacing, do not predict the development of early word reading. Second, time spent listening to storybooks does not increase print awareness (e.g., the ability to count the words in a written sentence), and children rarely look at print during this activity. Third, studies consistently find that code-based skills like letter knowledge and phoneme awareness are better predictors of reading in first and second grade than are oral language skills. Together, these points suggest that children need more than a rich language environment in order to be successful in learning to read. In other words, it is not clear what is "emergent" about emergent literacy. At the present time there is little evidence that the fundamental emergent skills, such as awareness of print in the environment or the structure of a storybook, predict early reading achievement. Conversely, the skills that children learn from parents and teachers about letters and sounds do predict early reading (e.g., print recognition, letter discrimination, and letter sounds). Emergent literacy, then, may describe the process by which children become aware of literacy, but not the process by which they learn to read. As we see in the next section of this chapter, learning to read involves knowing letter–sound relationships and understanding the alphabetic principle.

Beginning to read

Children who develop emergent literacy skills and fundamental print skills before entering first grade have several advantages in learning to read. First, they know that print occurs in different forms (e.g., lists, poems, and stories), and they implicitly understand how the writing system operates. Second, they are familiar with the letter forms and sequences that support early writing and spelling. Third, they have started to think about how words sound, and to realize that some words sound more alike than others (*cat*/*mat* vs. *kitty*/*rug*). These foundation skills help to develop recognition of a word as an orthographic unit that has a spoken form and meaning.

It is tempting to assume that intelligence plays a critical role in learning to read. In cases of extremely low IQ, this might be the case. However, three types of evidence indicate that the relationship between intelligence and reading in the primary grades is generally quite weak. First, studies of early readers fail to indicate a strong relationship between IQ and early reading, as many children who are early readers do not have high IQs (Briggs & Elkind, 1973; Durkin, 1966). Second, evidence from several studies of reading in first and second grade indicates that IQ is only weakly related to early reading achievement (for reviews see Stanovich, Cunningham, & Cramer, 1984; Tunmer, Herriman, & Nesdale, 1988). Third, children who have difficulty initially learning to read often have above-average IQs (e.g., Rawson, 1995). There is some reason to suspect that the relation of IQ and reading ability changes with age, as empirical studies do indicate a moderate relationship between IQ and reading achievement after first grade (e.g., Scarborough, 1991).

Beginning to read is marked by the transition from print awareness to print processing. To process print and read new words independently, readers develop an understanding of the letter–sound connections that exemplify the alphabetic principle. Gaining this fundamental understanding hinges on the development of two knowledge sets: letter knowledge and phonological awareness

(Chall, 1996; Juel et al., 1986; Share, Jorm, MacLean, & Matthews, 1984). Letter–sound connections form most efficiently when children can recognize letters in the alphabet and attend to the sounds of spoken language. We refer to these skills as the cognitive foundations of learning to read.

Cognitive foundations of learning to read

Phonological awareness

Phonological awareness is one type of linguistic awareness; or the knowledge of the sound structure of spoken words that is at least partly accessible to awareness (Liberman, Liberman, Mattingly, & Shankweiler, 1980; Mattingly, 1972; Rozin & Gleitman, 1977). Spoken language has several levels of structure: phonological, morphological, and syntactic. Beginning to read depends on being able to map written symbols onto a spoken word form, and this requires sensitivity to the phonological structure of spoken language. The mapping of orthography to speech is involved in learning to read in any language (Hu & Catts, 1998), so it is not surprising that cross-cultural studies find that phonological awareness predicts early reading in logographic languages such as Chinese as well as in alphabetic systems such as English (McBride-Chang & Kail, 2002).

As we pointed out in an earlier section of this chapter, the discovery and application of the alphabetic principle are not always easy for beginning readers. The ease with which many children learn the alphabetic principle rests on a foundation of phonemic awareness, which is phonological awareness at the level of individual speech sounds. Phonological awareness is the general term for understanding several aspects of the sound structure of language: syllable, rime, and phoneme. Research indicates that phonological awareness supports early reading by facilitating the use of letter–sound correspondences to decode new words (Baron, 1979; Byrne & Field-Barnsley, 1991; Goswami, 1993; Tangel & Blachman, 1992; Walton, 1995). The level of phonological awareness needed to support early reading depends on the nature of the writing system. Because alphabetic writing systems operate at the letter–sound level, it is phonemic awareness that best predicts early reading in English (Adams, 1990). In contrast, it is syllable sensitivity that predicts early reading in written languages like Chinese that represent the syllable orthographically (McBride-Chang & Kail, 2002). Whereas children develop some degree of phonological awareness without instruction, many children do not develop the fine-grained phonemic awareness skills necessary for learning to read without explicit instruction (Adams, Treiman, & Pressley, 1998).

Simple spoken language tasks are used to measure phonological awareness (see Goswami, 2000). Despite different aspects of phonological structure, phonological sensitivity appears to be a unidimensional construct that develops in a roughly sequential manner (Anthony, Lonigan, Burgess, Driscoll, Phillips, & Cantor, 2002; Bradley & Bryant, 1978; Goswami & Bryant, 1990). Developmentally, children become aware of larger sound units earlier than smaller ones, so phonological awareness assessment begins at the syllable level, continues at the rime level, and completes at the level of individual phonemes (Schatschneider, Francis, Fletcher, Foorman, & Mehta, 1999). This is also the course of phonological awareness instruction (Fox & Routh, 1975; Liberman, Shankweiler, Fisher, & Carter, 1974; Stanovich, 1992). The example tasks that follow are used for diagnostic and training purposes. At the syllable level, tasks include syllable counting, syllable deletion, and syllable blending. Instruction at this level would include clapping out the syllables as a word is spoken, removing one syllable from a spoken word (picnic − pic = nic), and putting two spoken syllables together to form a word (doc + tor = doctor). At the level of rime, children can discriminate whether two words rhyme or not, and generate words that rhyme. Recognizing syllable and rime is fairly easy for most children by the time kindergarten begins. However, it is mastery of the next level (phonemic awareness) that appears to be most important for learning the alphabetic principle (Lonigan, Burgess, Anthony, & Barker, 1998; Muter, Hulme, Snowling, & Taylor, 1997; Nation & Hulme, 1998). The easiest phonemic task is matching, in which children say whether /meat/ and /mop/ start with the same sound. Although this task may seem easy, its initial difficulty for children indicates that awareness of the detailed form of spoken words does not develop spontaneously. With practice, most children learn to pick the "odd man out" among three words, first in terms of initial sound (e.g., /meat/ /pan/ /mop/; the answer is /pan/) and later based on the final sound. This type of task involves segmenting the last phoneme. Full segmentation tasks require the division of a spoken word into its component phonemes. In blending tasks a child combines a /n/ sound and an /o/ sound to produce /no/. The most advanced phonemic awareness tasks involve phoneme manipulation. Examples include saying /snap/ without the /n/ or moving the /s/ at the end of /tops/ to the initial position to form /stop/. Because sounds in speech are ephemeral, children have to detect phonemes quickly and hold the segments in memory. Colored blocks or other items can be effective tools for concretely representing phoneme segments as children hear them, in order to support working memory (Castiglioni-Spalten & Ehri, 2003; Elkonin, 1973; Lindamood & Lindamood, 1998; McGuiness, McGuiness, & Donohue, 1995; Wise, Ring, & Olson, 1999).

Observers of early readers have noted that they initially have problems with phonological awareness below the level of the syllable (Calfee et al., 1972; Savin, 1972). It is also known that children with well-developed reading skills are better at phonological awareness tasks than beginning readers (Golinkoff, 1978). There has been some debate, however, about the appropriate interpretation of this latter finding. Does phonological awareness assist in reading development, or does learning to read improve children's awareness of words as sequences of sounds?

In the remainder of this section we focus on this chicken–egg issue of whether phonological development aids reading or vice versa. It is notable that phonological awareness studies yield consistent results despite the fact that different tasks have been used. A review of this literature indicates that level of phonological awareness before learning to read is the most reliable predictor of early reading achievement yet to be identified. Initial studies of the relationship between phonemic awareness and reading conducted by Liberman and her colleagues found that children who are good at segmenting are also good at reading (e.g., Liberman et al., 1977). Bradley and Bryant (1983) conducted a longitudinal study to test the role of phonological awareness in early reading. Here 4- and 5-year-old children were orally presented three or four words each. The child's task was to identify the "odd man out." For example, if presented with /cot/, /not/, /got/, and /hat/, the child should choose /hat/ as the odd one. If presented with /win/, /sit/, /fin/, and /pin/, the correct choice is /sit/, which differs in its final phoneme. Bradley and Bryant found that performance on this task before learning to read was a good predictor of how well the child would read 3 or 4 years later. Stanovich et al. (1984) administered 10 different phonological awareness tasks to a group of kindergarten children whose reading ability was assessed 1 year later. The tasks used were similar to those described earlier in this chapter. Whereas performance on rhyming tasks did not correlate with subsequent reading progress, the performance on the combined phonemic awareness tasks was a very strong predictor of subsequent reading progress. Impressively, phonemic awareness was a better predictor of early reading achievement than more global measures of cognitive skills such as IQ. Thus tests of phonemic awareness seem to be measuring an important factor in reading development.

Liberman and Shankweiler (1979) proposed that phonological awareness is a necessary prerequisite for learning to read. Experimental evidence has accumulated in support of the claim that phonemic processing problems are a core cause of poor reading (Fletcher et al., 1994; Foorman, Francis, Fletcher, & Lynn, 1996; Stanovich & Siegel, 1994; Wagner, Torgesen, & Rashotte, 1994). Fortunately several training studies have demonstrated that phonemic awareness skills can be successfully taught to prereaders (Bentin & Leshem, 1993; Content, Kolinsky, Morais, & Bertelson, 1986; Hurford, Shauf, Bunce, Blaich, & Moore, 1994; Lean & Arbuckle, 1984; Lewkowicz, 1980; Treiman & Baron, 1983b; Williams, 1980; Wise et al., 1999). One such study is Bradley and Bryant (1983). Children with poor phonological awareness skills who performed poorly on the odd man out task were trained in 40 sessions over a 2-year period to select which of a set of pictures of common objects had the same beginning, middle, or final sounds. (The training involved no experience with printed words or letters.) At the end of the study these children were reading better than a group given no training, who were matched for age, verbal IQ, and initial phonological awareness. The treatment-control group was trained to classify pictures into categories (such as "farm animal"). In contrast, training for this group had no effect on their reading. A final group was taught to identify matching sounds in words and then taught which letters represented the sounds. These children fared the best of all the groups in reading at the end of the study. Recent studies continue to demonstrate that instruction can improve phonological awareness and, in turn, improve early word-reading skills (Ball & Blachman, 1988; Ehri, Nunes, Stahl, & Willows, 2001; Perfetti, Beck, Bell, & Hughes, 1988;Vellutino & Scanlon, 1991).

Overall, an extensive body of research provides consistent evidence for a causal role for phonemic awareness in learning to read. Longitudinal research indicates that phonemic awareness impacts early reading achievement by affecting the ease with which children learn letter–sound correspondences (e.g., Hulme, Snowling, Caravolas, & Carroll, 2005). Thus, phonemic awareness may have direct and indirect influences on reading (see the Figure 11.2).

In addition to research demonstrating that phonemic awareness impacts reading development, two lines of evidence suggest that reading experience plays a role in phonemic awareness. We discussed the first earlier in this chapter: longitudinal studies of early readers indicate that phonemic awareness develops as children learn to read an alphabetic orthography (e.g., Perfetti et al., 1987; Rozin et al., 1974). The second line of evidence for a reciprocal relationship between learning to read and phonological awareness comes from studies of illiterate adults. In an influential study Morais, Cary, Alegria, and Bertelson (1979) compared the segmenting ability of literate adults in Portugal with other adults who had never learned to read. Those who could not read were not nearly as good at phonemic segmentation tasks as those who could read. Furthermore, as illiterate adults learned to read, their ability to segment words into phonemes improved as well. This finding has been taken as evidence that learning to read (and write) makes one more aware of the sound and/or formal properties of language. A number of researchers have thus concluded that segmenting ability is strongly influenced by learning to read, and that reading leads to segmenting

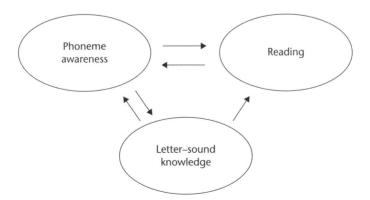

FIGURE 11.2   An illustration of the direct and indirect effects of phonological awarenesss on early reading (adapted from Hulme et al., 2005)

ability (e.g., Bertelson, Morais, Alegria, & Content, 1985a; Ehri, 1983, Ehri & Wilce, 1987b; Perfetti et al., 1987).

The data we discussed here indicates a reciprocal relationship between reading and phonemic awareness. Bradley and Bryant's study is important because it provides clear evidence that building phonemic awareness in non-reading tasks will also help them learn to read (see Ehri et al., 2001, for a meta-analysis). As children who do well on phonemic awareness tests in kindergarten pick up reading fairly easily by the end of first grade, the concept of phonemic awareness is central to understanding the development of early reading skill in alphabetic writing systems.

Letter knowledge

Letter knowledge has been recognized as a predictor of early reading achievement for more than 60 years (Bond & Dykstra, 1967; Chall, 1967, 1983; Durrell, 1958; Juel, Griffith, & Gough, 1986; Scanlon & Vellutino, 1996; Schatschneider et al., 2004; Stevenson, Parker, Wilkinson, Hegion, & Fish, 1976). Accuracy in letter naming is important, and the speed of letter naming is also a predictor of success on literacy tasks in kindergarten and beyond (Badian, 1998; Blachman, 1984; Speer & Lamb, 1976; Stanovich, Cunningham, & Cramer, 1984; Tunmer et al., 1988). Before a child actually learns to read, letter-naming speed and accuracy indicate how well they have learned to identify letters. Children with better letter knowledge are less likely to misidentify letters, and therefore less likely to misread words. Also, because the names of some letters relate closely to their sounds (*b* /b/), children can use the letter names to bootstrap learning of a letter's sound (Bowman & Treiman, 2002). Thus learning letter names may constitute a first step toward understanding the alphabetic principle.

Although it is essential for a child to be able to recognize the 26 letters of the alphabet, there is little evidence that teaching children letter names will substantially improve reading. This may be because letter naming is not directly involved in the reading process. It appears that letter-naming skill in prereaders might indicate a child's overall familiarity with print, including the letter forms (Adams, 1990; Chall, 1983). In children who are already reading, letter-naming speed may index a more general ability to name items quickly and effortlessly (Denckla & Rudel, 1976a, 1976b; Kail & Hall, 1994).

Letter-naming speed is measured by rapid automatized naming (RAN) tasks, in which children name rows of letters as quickly as possible (Denkla & Rudel, 1976a). Performance on the RAN is highly correlated with early reading achievement in both cross-sectional and longitudinal studies (Compton, 2003a; de Jong & van der Leij, 1999; Schatschneider et al., 2004; Wagner, Torgesen, Rashotte, Hecht, Barker, Burgess, et al., 1997; Wolf & Bowers, 1999). Since naming speed for abstract symbols (i.e., letters and numbers) predicts reading achievement better than do color- and object-naming speed (e.g., Lervåg & Hulme, 2009; Wagner et al., 1997), this indicates that rapid letter naming reflects more than processing speed. Several studies indicate that rapid letter naming indexes the efficiency of mapping written symbols onto phonological forms, among other processes involved in word recognition (Vellutino, Fletcher, Snowling, & Scanlon, 2004; Wagner & Torgesen, 1987; Wimmer, Mayringer, & Landerl, 2000). It may be that the rate of serial naming speed taps central processes that underlie reading fluency, given its power to predict reading achievement even beyond the elementary grades (Felton, Wood, Brown, Campbell, & Harter, 1987; Vellutino & Scanlon, 1987; Wolf & Obregón, 1992).

Exactly what is involved in learning to recognize letters? Letter recognition involves discriminating the distinguishing features of letters. In learning to recognize letters it is common for typically developing readers to initially confuse letters that look alike, so that *b* and *d* are often confused, as are *p* and *q*. Presumably this is because these pairs of letters differ only in the placement of a single visual feature. In learning to recognize letters, children must be able to determine the features that differentiate one letter from another.

Nodine and his colleagues compared prereaders and beginning readers with older children, using eye movement patterns to reveal what features are attended to (Nodine & Evans, 1969; Nodine & Lang, 1971; Nodine & Simmons, 1974; Nodine & Steurele, 1973). (Very large letters were used in order for the experimenters to be able to determine which feature was fixated.) Children in these experiments were asked to make same–different judgments about pairs of letters, letter-like symbols, or letter strings as their eye movements were recorded. When children were shown nonword pairs, for example, containing middle letters of either high visual confusability (e.g., *ZPRN*) or low visual confusability (e.g., *EROI*), several differences between third-grade readers and prereading kindergarten children were found. First, older children looked more frequently at those parts of the strings relevant for making an accurate decision. Second, older children were more proficient at processing distinctive feature information. Also, the younger children shifted their fixation back and forth between the stimuli more than the older children and did not look as frequently at that part of a letter which distinguished it from a similar letter (e.g., *G* and *C*). While the same–different task is not actual reading, Nodine's research suggests that, for the child who is beginning to read, letter recognition involves being able to identify the critical features that distinguish visually similar letters. When this skill is acquired, same–different judgments of visually similar strings (*PAT* and *RAT*) are made quite easily. Before this skill is acquired, the discrimination is quite difficult.

It is common for children to have trouble discriminating letters that are mirror images of each other (e.g., *b* and *d*) in addition to letters with many similar visual features (e.g., *m* and *n*). The source of this problem is not yet known; however, many researchers have suggested that it is one specific instantiation of a general problem children have with attending to spatial orientation. This problem is often not apparent until children are learning the abstract letter symbols, because most objects in the world do not change identity when rotated in space. A truck is a truck, irrespective of whether it is viewed from the right side or the left side. Upon beginning school the child has to learn the directional constraints of print (Clay, 1979). From an adult perspective, a child must learn that the printed page is made up of lines, words, and letters, each of which must be processed in a set direction. As children begin reading they often have problems keeping their place on the page. Beginning reading books are often printed in large letters and with only a few words on each page (the remainder of the page being occupied with pictures) to help children discriminate the letters as well as to reduce the problems of keeping their place.

For children who enter school with poor directional skills, the process of learning to read can build those directional skills implicitly. For example, Elkind and Weiss (1967) found that children who were beginning readers reported a series of pictured objects arranged along the sides of a triangle from left to right rather than in sequence around the triangle. Elkind and Weiss suggested that the act of learning to read dominated the perceptual exploration of most two-dimensional materials during the acquisition of directional behavior. Also, many adults tend to scan complex pictures in the direction in which they read text, which is likely a carryover from their silent reading experiences (Rayner, 1998, 2009). How eye movements change during reading development is discussed in the next section.

Despite the recognition that children learn the directionality of print during the process of learning to read, longitudinal studies often fail to find a significant relationship between directional skills and beginning reading. For example, McBride-Chang and Kail (2002) assessed the visual-perceptual skills of kindergarteners in China and the U.S. by measuring their performance on a same–different task that required the discrimination of the directionality of orthographic strings. Directional skills did not predict first-grade reading for either the Chinese or the U.S. children, whereas phonological awareness did. Thus it is the linguistic aspects of learning to read, rather than visual-spatial skills that determine early reading success. It appears that directional skills develop as a result of learning to read, and need not be a major focus of instruction.

What about eye movements?

Children's eye movements change as they learn to read. Prior to learning to read, children rarely have to focus their attention so precisely upon a specified region of a stimulus array as they do when reading text. There is some indication that prereading children have difficulty controlling their eye movements because they have a hard time holding fixation on a target (Kowler & Martins, 1982), and saccadic latency in simple oculomotor tasks is longer in younger children than in older children (Cohen & Ross, 1977; Groll & Ross, 1982). We pointed out when discussing Nodine's research in the previous section that the scanning strategies of the older children were more planned and deliberate than those of prereaders (see also Vurpoillot, 1968). These experiments suggest that, as children's cognitive processes develop to deal with progressively more complex stimuli, their eye movement patterns change as their scanning strategies become more systematic and efficient. Eye movements thus provide valuable evidence concerning the cognitive processes employed during reading. Indeed eye movement patterns during reading show a steady progression, so that as reading skill increases, the number of fixations decreases, the saccade length increases, fixation duration decreases, and the number of regressions decreases (Rayner, 1986; Rayner, Foorman, Perfetti, Pesetsky, & Seidenberg, 2001, 2002). These changes in eye movement behavior correspond to other cognitive changes that are taking place as children become more proficient in the task of reading.

Through the process of learning to read, children become more adept at controlling their eye movements, focusing on specific words, and moving in a left-to-right direction. All too often, well-meaning educators recommend oculomotor training for children who struggle with learning to read, in order to improve their eye movement patterns. Given that better eye movement control is a result of learning to read, oculomotor training is often an unnecessary intervention for children with early reading problems. For most children who struggle with learning to read, the main challenges are focusing attention on the relevant part of the word or text and processing information more effectively during eye fixations. Interested readers will find an in-depth discussion of the role of eye movements in reading disorders such as dyslexia in Chapter 12.

When should reading instruction begin?

Everyone would agree that learning to read involves developing many skills. What is more controversial is whether learning these skills depends on the child reaching a certain stage of cognitive development. This idea is central to the issue of "reading readiness," or the idea that reading instruction should begin when a child reaches certain cognitive or behavioral benchmarks. Consequently, there is often little concern about reading difficulties prior to age 7, due to the belief that general cognitive maturation will resolve early reading problems. This belief does not appear to be supported by empirical longitudinal studies indicating that word recognition skills as early as first grade can predict how much reading students will do in high school as measured by the Author Recognition Test (e.g., Cunningham & Stanovich, 1997). As the following discussion shows, the roots of the "reading readiness" concept reach far back into education history, and perhaps that is why this belief is still prevalent among teachers today. Some developmental psychologists and teachers contend that children must attain a "concrete operations" stage of cognitive development before they can learn to read successfully, and this usually occurs around the age of 7.

The notion of concrete operations is best exemplified by the famous conservation experiments that test children's understanding of the concept of invariance (Piaget, 1952). Piaget claimed that his experiments demonstrated that the concept of "invariance" (the idea that quantities remain the same even when their form changes) develops as children get older. His observations suggested, for example, that younger children believe that lengthening a row of coins by spreading them out farther actually increases their number, whereas older children understand that quantities do not change unless something is added or taken away.

Piaget's work has had a widespread influence on teachers and psychologists, many of whom use it as a basis for claiming that the concrete operations stage is necessary for children to learn to read. This approach implies that reading instruction will not be fruitful until the child has reached the concrete operations stage of development. Therefore advocates of reading readiness often attribute early reading problems to a lack of maturity, and can be reluctant to recommend early intervention for reading difficulties (see Chapter 12).

The age of 7 is also consistent with the classic observation of Dolch and Bloomster (1937), who assessed the IQ of 115 first- and second-graders, provided them with phonics instruction, and measured their ability to match printed words with spoken words. They found that very few of the children with a mental age lower than 7 years could perform the matching task, and concluded that children under 7 could not use phonics. This finding is often cited as evidence that children under the age of 7 will not benefit from phonics instruction (Dolch, 1948). However, a later review of the Dolch and Bloomster study noted that their sample of children was taught phonics incidentally in the course of reading for meaning (Brown, 1958; Chall, 1967). In other words, these children were taught phonics haphazardly in the course of reading, rather than receiving systematic phonics lessons. Therefore the Dolch and Bloomster finding merely indicated the ineffectiveness of non-systematic phonics instruction for children in first and second grade; however, this limitation of the Dolch finding is rarely mentioned. As we discuss in the following section, several empirical studies have established the effectiveness of systematic phonics instruction with younger children (Adams, 1990; Ehri et al., 2001). Therefore it appears that age-appropriate pedagogy can facilitate reading development at an early age, irrespective of cognitive "readiness."

If reading readiness were a valid biological construct, then one might expect reading instruction to begin at a similar age in different cultures. Yet the age at which children receive their first formal reading instruction varies considerably from country to country. In England, for example, reading instruction generally begins around 5 years of age, and in Denmark and Sweden it generally begins around 7 years of age. In France and Japan formal instruction begins at the age of 6. Looking across cultures, it seems that the age reading instruction begins is not too important in terms of predicting how well children will read in third grade (for example), as compared to the transparency of the orthography, for example (see Chapters 2 and 10 for a discussion of various writing systems). Cultural variations in the onset of formal reading instruction fly in the face of a biologically programmed version of reading readiness. These variations suggest that cultural expectations are an important determiner of when children begin to read. If we take the idea of reading readiness seriously, then we should expect more reading problems in cultures that begin reading instruction early than in those that begin later. Yet the rate of reading problems in England is similar to that in the United States (6–15%), even though reading instruction typically begins 1 year earlier in England. Also, one might expect to see effects of age when instruction begins on the cognitive underpinnings of reading development, such as phonological awareness, but that does not seem to be the case. For example, Vaessen et al. (2010) did not find effects of age that were independent of years of instruction in their study of reading development in Hungarian, Dutch, and Portuguese.

Therefore there are several problems with the idea that a lack of cognitive maturity is the root of early reading difficulties. What emerges most clearly from the research is that phonological awareness and letter naming are the strongest predictors of how easily a child will learn to read. Whereas most teachers agree that knowledge of letter names should precede reading instruction, children with partial phonemic awareness skills often benefit from systematic phonics instruction (National Reading Panel, 2000). Further, such instruction benefits kindergarten children as much as first-graders (Ehri et al., 2001). Once children know their letters and have started to attend to individual speech sounds, then they are ready to learn about the letter–sound relationships that constitute the alphabetic principle. Learning how printed symbols encode the sound patterns of English, applying that knowledge to read words that are visually unfamiliar, and beginning to recognize familiar words quickly are fundamental tasks in learning to read. We now discuss different instructional methods for teaching reading, and then describe research that compares the effectiveness of these methods.

Methods of teaching reading

The method used to teach reading in the U.S. varies depending on the preferences of the individual teacher, the published reading program purchased by the school district, and the culture of the school. Before we discuss specific pedagogical differences, it may be helpful to provide a general example of how initial reading instruction usually proceeds, irrespective of the particular pedagogical approach. When children enter school in first grade, the teacher spends a great deal of time reading to them. Stories are often read to the children in order to encourage further language development and to cultivate a desire on the part of the child to want to discover what is within a book. This is further encouraged by using books with attractive illustrations. Children also receive instruction to help them gain complete knowledge of letter names and continue to develop phonemic awareness. Written words are introduced gradually, perhaps starting with the name of the child written on his/her exercise book. Initially, many teachers have children dictate stories that the teacher writes down. The child may draw something and then is asked to tell a story about the object he or she has drawn. After a text is dictated, the teacher might read it to the student, emphasizing key words, and then ask the child to "read" the passage. In this way, written labels are provided for all sorts of objects in the child's environment. Then 10 to 20 words are introduced over several weeks, and the child memorizes these. This is typically referred to as the child's initial "sight" vocabulary. At some time during this initial stage, the first reading primer or reading workbook is introduced by the teacher. From this point forward, instructional practices diverge depending on the approach used in a particular classroom.

Reading philosophies and district-mandated curricula vary widely, but these approaches to reading instruction can be roughly categorized as either having a meaning-emphasis or a code-emphasis. These approaches can be roughly categorized as either meaning-emphasis or code-emphasis approaches to reading instruction. Code-emphasis approaches to early reading instruction emphasize the importance of learning the letter–sound correspondences that make up written English and developing proficient decoding skills that will bootstrap future reading achievement. Meaning-emphasis approaches minimize the importance of early decoding practice, and focus primarily on exposing first-grade children to a variety of reading and writing tasks such as daily journals and keeping lists. In this section we describe the main aspects of these approaches and their strengths and weaknesses. We conclude the section with a discussion of recent laboratory and classroom studies that investigate the relative merits of different instructional methods for teaching children to read.

Reading instruction with an emphasis on cracking the alphabetic code

To become a proficient reader a child must learn some very specific skills. These skills mainly involve understanding the relationship between printed symbols, phonological forms, and semantic referents. In other words, children learn to map the unfamiliar letter strings they find in print onto words in their spoken vocabulary. This mapping of letters onto sounds marks the beginning of reading development, and mastery of that alphabetic principle is a critical bridge to getting meaning from print. Before the alphabetic principle is mastered, children's reading errors indicate the pre-alphabetic phase, in which they may read /hat/ for *heat* or /back/ for *black*. The process of decoding draws children's attention to letter sequences in the middle of words, and helps usher in the full alphabetic phase of reading, which is necessary for building high-quality lexical representations that enable children to progress to the consolidated phase of efficient word recognition (Ehri, 1999, 2002). It is accurate and efficient word recognition that enables readers to quickly get meaning from print (Ehri, 1980; Perfetti, 1992; Torgesen, Rashotte, & Alexander, 2001). In that respect, one can view the building of automatic decoding skills as a necessary foundation for reading comprehension. Revisiting the analogy mentioned in Chapter 10 might help clarify this point. The importance of automatic decoding in early reading parallels the role of the fundamental skill of dribbling in basketball (Beck, 1998). Dribbling is not sufficient to score points, but it is necessary to play the game. Developing a solid dribble does not make one a star player, but having a weak dribble will prevent one from becoming a star player.

Code-emphasis approaches recognize that a mastery of letter–sound correspondences supports accurate and fast word recognition, which is a fundamental skill for reading fluently and with comprehension. Young readers begin with stronger skills in spoken language comprehension than in reading comprehension, and the initial roadblock to understanding print is the struggle to translate words on the page into their spoken forms (Curtis, 1980). Once they can decode the written word into its spoken form, most children understand what they are reading. The sooner children know the basic letter–sound pairs, the more they can practice sounding out words in text. Practice at decoding builds efficiency, and reading a word accurately several times enables children to develop consolidated representations that support quick word recognition, which increases reading fluency (Torgesen & Hudson, 2006). Thus mastery of decoding skills provides a foundation for automatic word recognition that frees children to focus on the meaning of the text they are reading. Just as stronger basketball players generally play more than weaker players, stronger readers read more often and, thereby, get exposed to more orthographic patterns and new vocabulary than do weaker readers (Stanovich, 1986). Thus early mastery of letter–sound correspondences provides a powerful tool that children use to further their own reading development (Jorm & Share 1983; Share, 1995). In contrast, children who cannot decode unfamiliar words either skip over them or guess them. Skipping and guessing strategies leave word identification to chance and do not encourage attention to word-specific orthographic and phonological information. This can result in reading inaccuracies, which hinder the building of high-quality lexical representations that support efficient word recognition processes (e.g., Perfetti, 2007). Because word recognition is less efficient, it is more effortful and leaves children with fewer cognitive resources to devote to comprehension (Perfetti, 1985).

There are several types of code-emphasis approaches, which generally share the following characteristics: they directly teach letter–sound correspondences in a sequence from simple to complex in order to build mastery of the alphabetic principle and children practice decoding by reading words, sentences, and stories that contain phonics patterns that have been learned. In other words, systematic phonics instruction explicitly teaches the alphabetic principle that is fundamental to learning to read. Code-emphasis pedagogy is generally defined by three assumptions: (a) reading is not a natural, developmental process, therefore children must be taught to read (Gough & Hillinger, 1980; Rayner et al., 2001, 2002); (b) initial reading instruction should include teaching phonics patterns systematically and (c) practice with controlled texts is important for building fluent decoding skills.

Code-emphasis programs stress the mapping of sounds to letters in our writing system by including phonics instruction as a daily part of the reading lesson. Systematic phonics instruction teaches letter–sound correspondences directly, and has been shown to reduce the number of children who struggle with beginning to read (Bos, Mather, Dickinson, Podhajski, & Chard, 2001; Ehri et al. 2001; Foorman, Francis, Fletcher, Schatschneider, & Mehta, 1998). The effectiveness of phonics in preventing reading failure could be attributed to many factors. Phonics draws attention to the alphabetic principle, as it emphasizes the relationship between printed letters and speech sounds. It is not surprising that several studies have found that phonics instruction improves phonemic awareness (Alegria, Pignot, & Morais, 1982; Baron & Treiman, 1980).

In code-emphasis programs, reading instruction time is spent learning to decode text and listening to children's literature. The phonics lesson is the time when children learn the letter–sound correspondences that are the foundation of the alphabetic principle and how to use these to help them identify unfamiliar printed words. In its purest form, phonics begins with a limited set of letters which can be combined into many different kinds of words. The individual letters are taught by the sounds they make, and then children practice blending the sounds of novel letter combinations. For example, children who learn two vowels and three consonants can read and spell *top, pot, pat, tap, sat, stop, pots, spat*, etc. Gradually more letters are added and then the children learn more complex patterns, such as consonant digraphs (e.g., *th, sh*) and vowel teams (e.g., *oi, ai*). With continued phonics instruction children learn more letter–sound patterns that help them read and spell many more words. Teaching phonics directly and providing plenty of practice draws children's attention to the productivity of our alphabetic writing system. Through the repetition of some words, children also develop a sight vocabulary as they build lexical–orthographic connections that will eventually support accurate spelling (Stanovich & West, 1989).

Code-emphasis programs teach children to recognize printed words primarily by converting letters to speech sounds, and then blending those together. This process is commonly referred to as "sounding-out" a word. When children misread or stumble on a word, the teacher will typically cue them to produce the initial sounds in the word (e.g., /s/n/ for snail), then look at the vowel or rime pattern (ail) to see if it is similar to any other words they know. The goal is to teach children a strategy for independently reading unknown words (Jorm & Share, 1983). In the process of decoding, children attend to all of the letters in a word, which enables them to form precise representations of new words they encounter (Ehri, 1992; 1998; Perfetti, 1992).

In the process of learning several letter/sound combinations each day, children in code-emphasis classrooms practice reading and writing words with those patterns (e.g., *plain, sail, pail, train*) both in lists and in controlled text. Controlled text is text that is written to maximize the use of words with regular phonics patterns in order to provide practice in decoding words. High-frequency, irregular words (*beautiful*) do appear in controlled texts, but the majority of the words are decodable. Using controlled text is one way to provide practice decoding words with straightforward orthography-to-phonology mappings, and thereby emphasize common spelling patterns that clearly illustrate the alphabetic principle. Although children may initially work harder to decode a text word-by-word than to read a text composed of memorized words, the letter-by-letter processing involved is important for building the high-quality lexical representations needed to support quick and accurate reading (Ehri, 1980, 2002; Perfetti, 1992; Venezky & Massaro, 1979).

Chall's (1967) review of several reading studies indicated that the time children spent reading learned letter–sound patterns was key to their early progress in reading. Reading controlled text aloud allows children to practice decoding in an environment where they will be successful, rather than frustrated by the oddly spelled high-frequency words that are common in early readers. Beck (1981) found that 79% to 100% (depending on the specific program) of the words in code-based readers were decodable on the basis of taught correspondences. Because the text is simplified, most words can be read successfully by beginning readers. For example, if a child has learned that *e* encodes the sound in *egg* and *o* encodes the sound in *on*, he or she would practice reading controlled text, such as 11.1:

Ben wanted a pet. He got his net and went to the pond.   (11.1)

Using these controlled texts provides children with practice at sounding-out words on the fly while reading sentences. As the quality of lexical representations improves, words become more familiar and are read more quickly (Rayner et al., 2001, 2002). The result of this process is reading fluency, or the ability to read text quickly and with appropriate intonation. During the first year of reading instruction the decoding process can be laborious. Because decoding is effortful, children may fatigue quickly when reading (as they do when learning any new skill, such as playing the piano). Children benefit from repeatedly reading text that they have decoded (Meyer & Felton, 1999). Repeated readings of a sentence or paragraph allow readers to practice consistent input–output mappings of print to speech, which helps build automatic word recognition processes (National Reading Panel, 2000; Schneider & Shiffrin, 1977). However, some research suggests that the gains from repeated reading are comparable to gains achieved when reading similar amounts of non-repeated text (e.g., Kuhn & Stahl, 2003). As decoding becomes automatized through the increased volume of reading, children become more fluent readers, with more resources left to devote to comprehending and enjoying text (Curtis, 1980; Perfetti, 1985).

Code-emphasis classrooms also include time for listening to children's literature. Children are exposed to a language-rich environment and listen to storybooks read aloud by the teacher, in order to build attention, awareness of plot, and spoken vocabulary. Storybook time is where children experience the vivid language and memorable plot lines available in children's literature. By exposing early readers to both literature and controlled text, code-emphasis programs give children the opportunity to experience vocabulary-rich literature and to practice their reading in simplified texts to develop decoding skills that support accurate reading.

Reading instruction with an emphasis on meaning

For our purposes, this pedagogical category prioritizes teaching higher-order comprehension strategies to early readers (over decoding)—based on the belief that such strategies are the most important contributors to skilled reading (Routman, 1991). The central assumption that children learn to read best without systematic code instruction drives meaning-emphasis programs to stress the linkage between a child's oral language and literacy experiences. One common activity in first grade is to have early readers keep a journal in which they record their experiences with the help of a teacher. The teacher reads back the words that the child has dictated and helps him or her learn to recognize the written form of these spoken words. Written words are typically taught by a teacher showing the child a flash card with a word on it, pronouncing the word, and asking the child to say it as well. Generally the teacher starts with a small set of words, and this set is gradually expanded on. Children are taught to recognize words by a combination of whole-word memorization and using sentence context to predict word identity. The alphabetic principle is implied in word study activities, but phonics is not taught in a systematic way.

One historical trend in meaning-emphasis instruction is to emphasize the memorization of whole words. A possible advantage of the whole-word method is that it promotes smooth reading very early in reading development. When a child has developed a small sight vocabulary, this vocabulary can be deployed in various combinations to construct meaningful sentences that children can read quickly as they recognize the memorized words. The pronunciation of the word is initially provided by the teacher, and such sight words are posted on a word wall in the classroom, grouped by part-of-speech or semantic category for later reference. However, any early advantage of whole-word instruction can backfire when a child's sight vocabulary increases to the point where many words become confusable (usually by the end of first grade). A whole-word approach may work well within a restricted set of words that children can quickly recognize at the start of reading instruction. Problems may arise if children continue with a whole-word memorization strategy, as many children do not attend to the internal letter sequence when words are memorized as wholes (Beck, 2006; Gough & Hillinger, 1980). This can lead to the misreading of words that begin or end with similar letters (e.g., *stick* and *stock*). As a child's sight word vocabulary expands, it necessarily begins to include many words that differ from each other only in terms of one or two internal letters. As more reading further increases the number of similar word forms stored, some teachers observe an unexpected decline in reading accuracy as children become confused by more frequent misreadings that mar text coherence and impair comprehension. Therefore a child with strong visual memory processes may be able to "read" by accurately retrieving memorized words in the early grades, but may begin to falter when reading demands the accurate recognition of multisyllable words that have many more letters.

A main rationale behind using the whole-word approach is that children initially do not recognize that letters represent sound units, and so the entire pattern of letters is taught holistically as representing a particular word. The experiments of Cattell (1886) and Reicher (1969) have been cited as support for the whole-word approach. However, these experiments have only a tenuous connection to how reading instruction should proceed since they do not imply that words are processed as gestalt visual patterns (see Chapter 3).

A second historical trend in meaning-emphasis instruction is the use of a basal reading program, which presents high-frequency words in story contexts. Many high-frequency words have irregular spelling patterns. Thus children using high-frequency basal reading programs memorize regular words that follow common phonics rules, such as *bike*, along with irregular, opaque words such as *should* (Willows, Borwick, & Hayvren, 1981). As the goal of whole-word, basal programs is to introduce in print words that are already part of the child's spoken vocabulary, the stories read at the start of first grade contain many words that cannot be easily decoded (Beck, 1981; Willows et al., 1981). A first-grade, whole-word basal reader might contain:

> Pam likes to read at night. "I like the big bird in this book," she said. (11.2)

Notice that the high-frequency words used here have complex spelling patterns (such as *oo* and *ea*) that are associated with multiple sounds (e.g., *great* and *read*). Beck (1981) concluded that whatever gains that meaning-emphasis basal readers help children achieve by presenting familiar words, these are likely to be offset by the limited opportunity to practice the decoding skills that support independent word reading. Because whole-word basal programs make it difficult for beginning readers to recognize the alphabetic principle and to learn that unfamiliar words can be decoded on the basis of the relationship between the letters and their associated sounds, it is not surprising that children taught to read with high-frequency, basal programs performed worse than those who learned to read with any other approach (Bond & Dykstra, 1967, 1997). Basal reading programs, or core reading curricula, are still used in most classrooms today for reading practice. However, current programs range widely in terms of the degree to which they use high-frequency irregular words. Some modern basal readers even use mainly decodable text, although those would not be used in a meaning-emphasis classroom.

Whole language is a common meaning-based approach used to teach reading in the U.S. today. Whole language incorporates some whole-word memorization, but the approach emphasizes reading practice with children's literature and mini-books. Several texts describe the whole-language philosophy at length (e.g., Routman, 1991; Weaver, 1994), but the critical elements can be summarized as follows. First, the whole-language philosophy claims that learning to read, like learning to speak, is a natural ability that develops spontaneously through a child's interaction with text (Goodman, 1967; Routman, 1991; Smith, 2004). This view of the reading process is quite different from that held by most psychologists, who view learning to read as a process of skill acquisition that generally requires some assistance from teachers (Gough & Hillinger, 1980; Rayner et al., 2002). As we mentioned earlier, the claim that alphabetic skills emerge naturally from experience with spoken language is not consistently supported by the data (Levy et al., 2006; Lonigan, Burgess, & Anthony, 2000; Sénéchal, LeFevre, Thomas, & Daly, 1998). A belief in the "naturalness" of reading acquisition may provide a rationale for the resistance to the systematic, teacher-directed instruction that characterizes code-emphasis approaches to early reading. In whole-language classrooms, the teacher serves as facilitator and children initiate their own learning experiences. Reading, spelling, and writing are experienced in the context of meaningful literacy activities. Children's construction of meaning is central, as opposed to building accurate and efficient word recognition (Routman, 1991).

The development of the whole-language approach was informed by several reading theorists (e.g., Goodman, 1967; Smith, 1971, 1973; Smith & Goodman, 1971). Goodman (1970) viewed the reading process as a "psycholinguistic guessing game" in which the reader tries to predict words based on the surrounding context. This guessing game supposedly involves three types of cues: "syntactic", "semantic", and "graphophonic". As we discussed in Chapter 10, the teacher facilitates a child's ability to read unfamiliar words by modeling a strategy known as the "three-cueing system," which uses the above three cues to identify unfamiliar words during reading (see Adams, 1998; Routman, 1991). The idea that readers should use all of these cues to comprehend text is intuitively sensible. In practice, however, the cueing system is taught primarily as a method of identifying printed words. When children come upon a word they don't recognize, teachers prompt them to use the three-cueing system (Weaver, 1994). Despite decades of eye movement evidence indicating that skilled readers recognize words automatically in about a quarter of a second, whole-language teachers present word identification as a guessing process that involves the conscious application of these cueing systems.

The main problem with the three-cueing system approach to word reading is that it does not prioritize the most reliable cue to word identification—the letters themselves (Adams, 1998). Although the representation of words can be built through several mechanisms, phonological recoding of letter sounds is the most effective (Share & Stanovich, 1995). In practice, teachers of meaning-based approaches encourage readers to predict upcoming words from context, rather than decode unfamiliar words. One problem with this approach is that most content words in print are not very predictable, and those that are (such as function words) are probably already in the child's sight vocabulary. Guessing from context may work in the predictable stories read in the early grades, but that strategy becomes far less effective later in elementary school when children begin reading to learn new information in social studies, science, and math. Context is of little use in word identification when the topic is unfamiliar. Therefore it is not too surprising that better readers rely less on context than poor readers (Share & Stanovich, 1995). Even when early readers are successful at guessing words from context, the value of this approach is questionable because it encourages the habit of guessing first and then looking at the letters later. During this process the child's attention is initially distributed over the context surrounding the word, rather than on the alphabetic structure of the word they are trying to read. Also, the typical emphasis on semantic and syntactic cues to word identification can disadvantage low-income children, who often enter school with limited background knowledge and/or less experience with spoken English at home.

In addition to the three-cueing system, whole-language teachers may help students identify print words by teaching some letter–sound relationships in the context of reading, based on mistakes made by the reader (Weaver, 1994). Whereas some whole-language advocates take the extreme position that "the sounds associated with letters are largely irrelevant" (Smith, 2004, p. 7), others claim that children should discover the alphabetic principle naturally through their exposure to text (Weaver, 1994). The practice of teaching letter–sound relations in response to reading errors is known as "embedded phonics." For example, when a child pauses on the word *snow*, the teacher might point out that it rhymes with the word *grow*. The advantage of embedded phonics is that it is quick and helps the child to say the current word. However, the unsystematic nature of embedded phonics has several drawbacks. Although teaching phonics patterns as they occur in meaningful texts may seem like a good idea, this approach can pose several problems for young readers who have not yet mastered the alphabetic principle. First, the richness of the language that makes children's literature appealing depends on a wide variety of words with more- and less-consistent spelling patterns. Because the content of instruction is driven by reading errors, such phonics instruction lacks systematicity and sequence. That is to say, embedded phonics instruction does not begin with easy words (e.g., *cat, hat, bat*) and then progress to more complex patterns (e.g., *that, trap, hand, sail*) because instruction occurs on the fly in response to student errors. Second, embedded phonics can make it difficult to generalize phonics patterns to a group of words. For example, a child who is taught how the *ow* at the end of *snow* is pronounced might see *snow* several times during a reading session and will probably learn to recognize it by sight, but he may not see other words that share the same pattern during that session (*blow, glow, show*). As the ability to read similarly spelled words by analogy is fundamental to the alphabetic principle, one consequence of this lack of generalization is to make the alphabetic principle less obvious than it might otherwise be. Lastly, children may be exposed to many letter patterns each day in their reading, and not get enough practice with reading and writing a specific pattern to remember the letter–sound correspondence.

The last characteristic of whole-language, meaning-based classrooms we will discuss is the use of children's literature for reading practice. Children learn to preview a book first, looking at the pictures to get an idea of the story plot. Then they might follow along as the teacher reads the story aloud first. Finally, they practice reading the story aloud and silently. If they make errors when reading, or stumble on a word, they are encouraged to guess what the word is by looking at the picture or using the three-cueing system. Reading fluency improves through repeated exposures to the book, as a child memorizes the words in the text and begins to recognize them rapidly.

The use of children's literature alone for early reading practice can be problematic for some children, despite its intuitive appeal for adults. One issue is the difficulty of finding literature that fits with children's developing skills. Consider this sample of text from children's literature discussed in Beck (1998):

> Hattie was a big black hen. One morning she looked up and said, "Goodness gracious me!" (11.3)

Although this sentence is easy enough to understand when read by an adult, the range of spellings and length of some words will prevent many children from reading it independently. Also, the number of irregular words (e.g., *was, one, looked, said, gracious*) prevents children from applying code-based strategies to identify the words successfully. Instead they may guess the words based on what makes sense. Beck (1998) emphasizes the importance of considering the purpose of the text to be used for reading practice, as well as its overall quality. Children certainly benefit from listening to literature as it is read aloud, but the words it contains are often too complex to be read by early readers. Such texts develop spoken vocabulary and interest in books, but do not provide children with practice applying the alphabetic principle to recognize printed words. Instead children may rely on guessing strategies and whole-word memorization by using picture cues to guess at the printed words, but this does little to focus their attention on the internal structure of words. In this way, the overuse of complex texts can discourage children from transitioning from the partial-alphabetic to the alphabetic phase of reading, in which they attend to all of the letters in a word and develop high-quality lexical representations.

Children who enter school with good emergent literacy skills and those who learn to read easily seem to enjoy whole-language instruction, as do their peers who struggle to learn the alphabetic principle. The clear strength of whole language resides in its immersion of children in a language-rich classroom environment that emphasizes pleasurable literacy experiences. The use of entertaining stories and beautifully illustrated books does get children excited about reading. Controlled classroom studies that compare whole-language with decoding-based methods indicate that whole language results in more positive attitudes toward reading (Foorman et al., 1998; Stahl, McKenna, & Pagnucco, 1994). However, its effectiveness in helping children learn to read is less clear. Positive effects on attitude do not necessarily translate into reading improvement, as the ability to enjoy listening to children's literature is quite different from being able to read it. We discuss this point further in the last section of this chapter.

A more recent development in meaning-emphasis approaches to reading instruction is known as balanced literacy (e.g., Fountas & Pinnell, 2006, 2008). As its name implies, balanced literacy claims to combine skill instruction with the use of "authentic" texts (as opposed to basal readers). With this approach, teachers model literacy behaviors for children. They read aloud to the children and demonstrate writing about a book. During guided reading, which is the core activity, children work in small groups silently reading an authentic text chosen by the teacher, who guides their practice of a particular reading strategy. Finally the teacher observes as children read and write independently and share their work with the class.

This approach draws heavily from the writing workshop model, in which children write, confer with a teacher, and revise their writing projects. From our perspective, it is not clear why a model that is successful for teaching writing would help children develop early reading skills. The writing workshop model teaches children the processes that skilled writers use to produce text, but what is the connection with learning to read?

According to a web-based publication by Pinnell and Fountas (2000), a balanced literacy program provides students with a variety of contexts for reading. Each context includes specific instructional components such as reading aloud to the children, phonics and spelling instruction, book club, guided reading, independent reading, and conferring. At first glance, this may seem like a good balance between code-emphasis and meaning-based approaches to reading instruction. However, our review of several balanced literacy publications suggests that teaching the alphabetic principle and phonics plays a surprisingly small role in this approach. For example, Pinnell and Fountas (2000) include a framework that describes the components of balanced literacy: phonics and spelling instruction are mentioned, but together they account for one-sixth of the instructional components. Also, it is interesting to note that teaching the alphabetic principle is not mentioned here as an instructional goal, although teaching comprehension and language skills are stated goals. Likewise, a recent teacher guide focused on helping struggling readers in grade K–3 comprised 520 pages, but only 6 pages described methods of phonics instruction (Fountas & Pinnell, 2008). Although it is difficult to quantify the weight that any approach gives to phonics and decoding practice, there is little written evidence that balanced literacy places much emphasis on the development of fluent decoding.

Given the abundance of research that indicates the importance of fluent decoding in developing reading, using a balanced literacy approach to teach reading before Grade 3 raises several concerns. In previous chapters you have read about scores of studies indicating the automaticity of word recognition in skilled reading. When printed words are identified, young readers can usually build meaning from text easily. However, children in balanced literacy classrooms are taught to make meaning from text by deliberately applying higher-order strategies, rather than by relying on straightforward word identification. Children may learn to apply phonics skills in the context of the day's reading, but embedded phonics instruction is likely to have limited effectiveness for many children due to its lack of sequence, adequate practice, and opportunities for generalization. If children are not provided with systematic instruction to promote mastery of the alphabetic principle, and cannot identify printed words accurately, then understanding text does indeed become a difficult task.

In summary, the specific pedagogical practices of meaning-emphasis approaches can present a variety of problems for early readers. In our opinion, these practices are not necessarily problematic in and of themselves. Rather it is the timing of these practices that is at issue. Recall from Chapter 10 that all four of Ehri's phases of early reading development occur in the period of Learning to Read that extends from kindergarten to Grade 3. Passage through the pre-alphabetic, partial-alphabetic, and full alphabetic phases entails mastering the alphabetic principle and applying it to read words accurately and quickly. Therefore it seems that code-based instruction would best support reading growth in these early grades. In contrast it seems likely that higher-order strategies contribute to reading comprehension once children begin to use reading to learn new information around Grade 3. Thus teaching with a meaning-based approach once children have mastered decoding seems appropriate in middle elementary school. However, practices such as unsystematic phonics and the cueing systems simply are not very effective (relative to code-based approaches) for teaching alphabetic decoding skills to children who have not yet developed those skills (Ehri et al., 2001). In our opinion it is the application of meaning emphasis approaches across the board (i.e., even for beginning and struggling readers) that can exacerbate some children's struggle with learning to read. Intensive intervention studies indicate that if children are not fluent readers by the third grade it is unlikely that they will ever catch up to their peers (e.g., Torgesen, Alexander et al., 2001). Therefore it seems especially important for early reading instruction to develop the alphabetic decoding skills that are the foundation of fluent reading.

The debate about early reading instruction

The teaching of reading has a long history of contentious debate (Adams, 1990; Goodman, 1993; Grundin, 1994; Rayner et al., 2001; Stahl et al., 1994; Stahl & Kuhn, 1995; Weaver, 1994). Although the argument has taken on many different forms, the critical issue is whether or not decoding (phonics) should be taught systematically or incidentally to children who are beginning to read. Code advocates contend that the mapping of letters onto sounds marks the beginning of reading development, and mastery of that alphabetic principle is a critical bridge to getting meaning from print that enables children to identify unfamiliar written words independently. Meaning advocates claim that decoding instruction distracts children from the meaning-making process, and teaches a skill that good readers don't often use (Smith, 2004). Code advocates note that readers initially have stronger skills in spoken language comprehension than in reading comprehension, and the initial roadblock to understanding print is the struggle to translate words on the page into their spoken forms (Curtis, 1980). Meaning advocates counter that concern with letter–sound mappings is responsible for relatively poor reading comprehension in new readers (Weaver, 1994). And so the debate continues. Fortunately, empirical studies conducted over the past two decades provide data to help differentiate the valid from the invalid claims.

Models of skilled word recognition are invoked to support both sides of this debate. For example, some connectionist PDP models of word recognition (see Chapter 3) propose that word recognition in skilled reading results from the cooperative activation of the direct (orthographic-semantic) and indirect (orthographic-phonological-semantic) pathways. Therefore these "triangle" models are often invoked to support code-emphasis approaches to reading instruction that encourage children to practice letter–sound mappings and apply decoding skills. In contrast, dual-route theories (e.g., Coltheart, Rastle, Perry, Langdon, & Ziegler, 2001) propose a direct access account of skilled word recognition, in which readers rely primarily on the orthographic-semantic route to identify most words. Thus dual-route models may be used to justify reading methods that de-emphasize decoding instruction. For example, Smith (1973) forcefully argued that direct access to word meaning via orthography is necessarily more efficient because it does not require an extra phonological-recoding step, and this assumption is fundamental to meaning-emphasis approaches, which oppose the systematic teaching of phonics.

The greater efficiency of the direct (orthographic-semantic) route seems intuitively obvious, as this path involves two processors rather than three. However, that intuition does not fit well with data from computational models of reading. Computer models have demonstrated an ability to simulate human reading data fairly well based on the assumption of parallel processing (e.g., Harm & Seidenberg, 2004). If reading processes do operate in parallel, then route efficiency cannot be gauged based on the number of processors (two routes can operate in parallel in the same amount of time as a single route).

Still, a couple of important pedagogical questions remain. If skilled readers access word meaning directly from orthography, then why should teachers emphasize laborious decoding processes? If the experimental evidence indicated that the orthographic-semantic route was sufficient for skilled word recognition, then it might be appropriate to minimize code instruction or to teach phonics incidentally. Although there is evidence that skilled readers utilize the direct route from orthography to semantics (Cohen & Deahene, 2009), there is a growing body of evidence that they engage the orthographic-phonological pathway as well. As we discussed in Chapters 5 and 10, eye movement and ERP studies have found effects of phonological processing in skilled readers during silent reading and in word identification tasks. Initial MEG data demonstrate concurrent activation of two pathways—both an anterior orthographic-phonological pathway and the ventral orthographic-semantic pathway (Pammer et al., 2004; Wheat et al., 2010). In addition, computer simulations have demonstrated superior word recognition performance from input that results from the cooperation between pathways (for a review see Rueckl & Seidenberg, 2009). Based on the data currently available, skilled readers appear to use both the orthographic-phonological-semantic and the orthographic-semantic paths in word recognition.

Some may argue that even though skilled readers typically use the orthographic-phonological pathway in reading, there remains a question of whether it is developmentally appropriate to teach letter–sound relationships to young children in kindergarten and first grade. Pedagogical concerns about phonics instruction take several forms. Some educators expect that children will find phonics too difficult to learn, or believe that even when learned, phonics will not be helpful. The concern that young children do not benefit from code instruction dates back to research conducted many decades ago suggesting that children under the age of 7 will not benefit from phonics instruction (Dolch & Bloomster, 1937; Dolch, 1948). However, as we indicated earlier in this chapter, the children in this research were taught phonics incidentally rather than systematically, which suggests that Dolch and Bloomster's finding merely indicated the ineffectiveness of embedded phonics for first-grade children (Brown, 1958; Chall, 1996).

Neuroimaging studies that track the development of reading circuitry in the brain provide some evidence that early phonics instruction is neurodevelopmentally appropriate for beginning readers. These studies indicate that dorsal and anterior systems involved in orthographic-phonological processing are most active in beginning readers (Frost et al., 2009). For example, Shaywitz et al. (2002, 2007) conducted an fMRI study to measure brain activity as children read real words and pronounceable nonwords. They found that younger readers used a diffuse network of brain areas in both the right and left hemispheres. Activation became lateralized to the left hemisphere as reading skill developed, and the dorsal and anterior (orthographic-phonological-semantic) systems were more active than the ventral (orthographic-semantic) circuit for reading words in children under 10 years old.

The neuroimaging data make two important contributions to our discussion of reading development. Finding activation in younger children primarily in the anterior and dorsal circuits involved in orthographic-phonological processing indicates that, when children begin to read, their brains develop the circuitry to process the letter–sound mappings, and these mappings are the focus of phonics instruction. Second, Frost et al. (2009) suggest that children who can read accurately and fluently develop the neural circuitry to access whole-word forms through the ventral pathway. This developmental pattern of initial activation in orthographic-phonological circuits followed by activation along the ventral route (once the occipital-temporal (OT) area is tuned to word recognition) is compatible with a phonics approach to early reading instruction. Letter–sound associations are taught and practiced in order to develop fluent decoding skills that support the accurate and fast recognition of words. Therefore it appears that early phonics instruction is compatible with the development of reading circuits in the brain.

Although the neuroimaging evidence indicates that code-based instruction is appropriate for beginning readers, there remains a concern that systematic phonics will not benefit children's reading. In part this concern stems from the perceived irregularity of English spelling (Kessler & Treiman, 2003). The present literature indicates that, after learning to read, most children learn complex spelling patterns implicitly through exposure to print (for a review see Kessler, 2009). However, only children who have developed reading fluency to a level that supports wide reading achieve adequate print exposure. Code-based reading instruction contributes to these implicit learning processes in several ways. First, it establishes an awareness of the alphabetic principle that provides a reason to attend to the internal letters in words (Ehri, 1992). Second, children use letter–sound mappings as a self-teaching mechanism to bootstrap their recognition of unfamiliar words and to consolidate their lexical representations of familiar words (Ehri, 2002; Jorm & Share, 1983; Share, 1999). Third, the ERP, MEG, and eye movement data from skilled readers indicate that automatic phonological processes operate on advance word form information to facilitate lexical access (Ashby, 2010; Ashby & Rayner, 2004; Ashby et al., 2009; Wheat et al., 2010). In other words, once the orthography-to-phonology connections become automatized they are typically used for the parafoveal processing of words when silently reading text. As we have discussed in Chapter 4, parafoveal processing reduces word recognition time substantially. Thus code-based approaches help build the reading fluency needed for children to read widely enough that they can implicitly learn the morphological patterns that govern much of English spelling. Having highlighted some of the issues in the debate about early reading instruction and the effects of different approaches on the processes underlying reading development, we now turn to discuss empirical studies and meta-analyses that examined how meaning-based and code-based approaches to reading instruction affect reading achievement in the classroom.

Empirical studies of meaning-emphasis and code-emphasis approaches

Today, meaning-emphasis programs are widely used in whole-language/language-experience classrooms. However, there has also been a growing awareness of the importance of systematic and early phonics instruction that explicitly teaches the alphabetic principle (e.g., Moats, 2010; Rayner et al., 2001). Both meaning-emphasis and code-emphasis approaches are effective forms of instruction, in that the performance of students often reflects the goals of each approach. First-graders taught in a meaning-emphasis program tend to read fluently, but develop a habit of guessing at words and may struggle to read accurately. This is especially true when the text is unfamiliar. Children in code-emphasis programs read accurately, but their reading may initially be labored until they reach fluency during the second year of reading instruction. Because meaning-emphasis and code-emphasis approaches hold different goals, it is not possible to determine a priori which is the more valid educational philosophy. However, it is possible to empirically evaluate which approach is most effective with most children.

In addressing the question of which approach is more effective for teaching children to read in the primary grades, we mostly refer to classroom-based research. Whereas laboratory tasks may be carefully designed to elicit evidence of cognitive processes, such research cannot assess which type of reading instruction is best for most children. Our discussion begins with two longitudinal studies, and then broadens to include the meta-analysis of studies conducted in the 1990s by the National Institute of Child Health and Human Development (the National Reading Panel; NICHD, 2000).

Evans and Carr (1985) evaluated two programs in 20 first-grade classrooms. Half of these were traditional teacher-directed classrooms in which instruction used a reading program with phonics drills and applications. The other half of the classrooms were taught in less-traditional student-centered classrooms in which teacher instruction constituted only 35% of the day's activity. In the latter, reading was taught primarily by an individualized language-experience method in which students produced their own workbooks of stories and banks of words to be recognized. Evans and Carr (1985) characterized these two groups as decoding–oriented and language-oriented. Despite differences in emphasis, the two groups spent similar amounts of time on reading tasks. The two groups were also matched on relevant social-economic variables, IQ, and spoken language development. The clear result was that the decoding group scored higher on year-end reading achievement tests, including comprehension tests. Additionally, the language-experience group did not show any higher achievement in oral language measures based on a storytelling task. Similar results were found in the Pittsburgh Longitudinal Study (see Lesgold & Curtis, 1981; Lesgold & Resnick, 1981). Perfetti (1985) summarized these results, which indicate that instruction that emphasizes the alphabetic principle does not produce "word callers" who are insensitive to the meaning of print. These studies clearly indicate that phonics instruction is beneficial to comprehension as well as word recognition.

Meta-analyses of a group of reading studies can provide critical evidence about effects of instruction, as they consolidate the findings of many individual studies to determine the predominant data pattern. In a widely cited study, Chall (1967) reviewed reading research conducted through the mid-1960s and concluded that early systematic phonics instruction led to better achievement in reading than approaches that used unsystematic phonics or taught phonics later. This finding has been upheld in reviews of reading research that have been conducted since then (Adams, 1990; Anderson, Hiebert, Wilkinson, & Scott, 1985; Balmuth, 1982; Dykstra, 1968; Rayner et al., 2001). However, Chall's review also indicated that the teacher may be as important as the specific type of instruction used. In contrast, Williams (1979) concluded that the measurable advantages of code-based programs for reading achievement were small and confined to word recognition and spelling, primarily during the first 2 years of school. However, she also concluded that there was no measurable advantage of meaning-based approaches even in measures of comprehension.

The previous edition of this text noted that few meta-analyses had been conducted prior to 1990 to compare the effectiveness of meaning-based vs. code-based approaches. Since that time

Congress directed the formation of the National Reading Panel (NRP) to assess the effect of various approaches to reading instruction, and several large-scale studies have been conducted to further examine the effectiveness of phonics instruction (e.g., Foorman et al., 1998; Torgesen, Wagner, Rashotte, Rose, Lindamood, Conway, 1999). These studies used stronger experimental designs than were used in some previous studies, such as random assignment to treatment conditions and a comparable control group. After these more recent studies were conducted, Congress convened a National Reading Panel to review the vast body of reading research, to conduct a meta-analysis of all the school-based research conducted thus far, and to make recommendations for empirically supported effective practices for teaching children to read. The subpanel charged with studying the effectiveness of systematic phonics instruction produced a review article describing the methods and results of their meta-analysis in detail (Ehri et al., 2001).

For the meta-analysis the National Reading Panel searched the literature and identified 38 studies that provided 66 control–treatment comparisons of reading gains for children taught by systematic phonics instruction with the gains of children taught with any other method. Of those studies, 28 were conducted between 1990 and 2000. In some studies the comparison group received no phonics instruction, but in others the control children were taught with non-systematic, or embedded, phonics. Control groups included those learning to read with a whole-language approach, basal program, or whole-word method. The meta-analysis included several different moderator variables, including socio-economic status, grade level, type of phonics program, and instructional group size. The duration of instruction was not included as a variable, given that many studies were vague about the time devoted to phonics instruction. Reading gains were measured by reading real words, reading pseudowords, reading aloud, and comprehending text. Effect size served as the main statistic, indicating whether the reading achievement of the systematic phonics group differed from the control group and by how much. When multiple assessments were administered in a study, the NRP calculated effect sizes for each measure and then averaged these together to obtain a single effect-size for that study. This ensured that each study contributed equally to the meta-analysis.

The results of the NRP meta-analysis were fairly clear "... systematic phonics produced better reading than every program taught to control groups" (p. 430). Across the 66 treatment–control comparisons, systematic phonics was more effective at helping children learn to read than any of the control approaches, including whole language. Further, the study indicated who was helped and when the phonics instruction was most effective. Phonics helped children from middle- as well as low-income families, children at risk for reading failure because of poor phonological awareness or incomplete letter knowledge, and older elementary students with reading disabilities. Individual tutoring in phonics was not found to be more effective than instruction in larger groups. In many cases, effects of phonics instruction persisted after the end of the intervention, continuing to support growth in decoding, isolated word reading, and comprehension for many students. Thus there seems to be no way of getting around the conclusion that systematic phonics instruction is the most effective approach for helping children become better readers (Rayner et al., 2001).

The impact of phonics in kindergarten and first grade

Larger effects were observed when instruction began before or during first grade, rather than in later grades, indicating that systematic phonics instruction is most effective in the first 2 years of reading instruction. Effect sizes were comparable in kindergarten and first grade, ranging from moderate to large on most measures of reading proficiency (see Figure 11.3). Moderate to large effect sizes in early readers indicate that using a phonics approach for beginning reading instruction provides the support necessary to prevent reading problems in children who enter school with

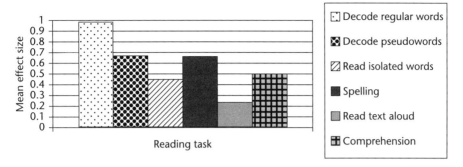

FIGURE 11.3 Effects of phonics instruction in K-1 (based on Ehri et al., 2001)

poor letter knowledge and phonological awareness skills. Phonics instruction benefitted both isolated word reading and text comprehension. In addition, phonics helped young children understand the alphabetic principle, as evidenced by progress in phonetic spelling and pseudoword decoding.

Finding larger effect sizes for systematic phonics when it is taught to children initially as they learn to read may surprise some readers. Ever since Dolch (1948) many educators have held the mistaken belief that young children do not benefit from phonics instruction. The present finding of greater benefits of systematic phonics in kindergarten and first grade reaffirms Chall's conclusion that the Dolch and Bloomster (1937) data only speak to the limited effectiveness of incidental, or embedded, phonics instruction for children under 7. Rather, the NRP report clearly suggests that children who receive systematic phonics instruction as they begin learning to read will benefit most. By extension, it seems that instruction which highlights the alphabetic code and teaches children how to decode words should be a priority in K-1 classrooms. Irrespective of how teachers feel about systematic phonics, the NRP data indicate that this approach is best for teaching children to read. While many children may discover some letter–sound correspondences without phonics instruction, teaching methods that make the alphabetic principle explicit provide a key to our writing system that produces better readers overall. Of course, the most effective reading instruction includes both systematic decoding instruction and activities that expose children to good, age-appropriate literature. The NRP report simply provides empirical support for the benefit of systematic phonics instruction as a component of early reading instruction.

The impact of phonics on older readers

Systematic phonics instruction helped children in grades two through six improve their reading, although the benefit over other types of instruction was smaller here than in beginning readers. This is not surprising, given that more than 75% of the students in these studies were reading-disabled and low-achieving readers (who are more difficult to remediate). As with the younger children, phonics instruction improved performance on several measures of reading proficiency. However, basic phonics did not improve the spelling of older children, perhaps because their writing vocabulary consisted of proportionally more irregular words and multisyllable words.

Many good teachers are eclectic in their approach, and realize that phonics is important to help children discover the alphabetic principle, but they also recognize that when learning is made meaningful and exciting, children learn much more. It might be tempting to conclude that since most teachers use some form of phonics instruction, the major difference between the code-emphasis and meaning-emphasis approaches to reading instruction is best thought of in terms of the relative amount of time given to the phonics component. However, data indicate that the main difference in the effectiveness of each approach resides in the *nature* of the phonics instruction. The NRP report clearly indicates that systematicity is the critical factor in maximizing the positive effect of phonics on early reading achievement.

Teaching systematic phonics requires that teachers possess an explicit knowledge of our writing system, so that they can teach children how it operates. This explicit knowledge includes an understanding of the alphabetic principle and phonemic awareness, a vocabulary for describing the different layers of language as well as the linguistic terms specific to each layer (e.g., digraph), and a command of a sequence of phonics principles that allows instruction to proceed from simple to complex decoding concepts. For teachers in kindergarten and the primary grades, this is the core linguistic knowledge for teaching reading effectively. Intervention studies have found correlations between teachers' command of the linguistic knowledge used in explicit decoding instruction and student performance in reading (McCutchen & Berninger, 1999; Moats & Foorman, 2003; Spear-Swerling & Brucker, 2003). You may not be surprised that teachers need a foundation of linguistic knowledge in order to be effective reading teachers—just as they need an understanding of number systems, one-to-one correspondence in counting, and a pedagogical order of operations in order to teach math. What is surprising is that only a handful of teacher education programs offer courses that teach this linguistic knowledge. One possible reason for this dearth of instruction is that certification programs are highly invested in whole-language pedagogy, which does not value the systematic teaching of phonics.

Several studies have examined the linguistic knowledge base that teachers bring to early reading instruction in their elementary school classrooms. According to Moats (1994), basic linguistic knowledge includes knowledge of language structure and its application to teaching phonics, such as phonology and morphology. A complex writing system like English requires teacher-guided explicit instruction to help children learn simple letter–sound mappings first (e.g., m says /m/) and more complex ones later (e.g., kn says /n/). Whereas this knowledge is not necessary for skilled readers, it is difficult to imagine how teachers can explain the regularities in our writing system to new readers without having command of it themselves. On surveys that test explicit knowledge of phonics, few teachers can identify a consonant digraph or explain when *ck* is used in spelling (Bos et al., 2001; Cunningham, Perry, Stanovich, & Stanovich, 2004; Fielding-Barnsley & Purdie, 2005; Moats, 1994; Moats & Foorman, 2003). Joshi, Binks, Hougen, Dahlgran, Ocker-Dean, and Smith (2009) surveyed the linguistic knowledge of teacher educators and found similar results. The majority of those surveyed performed poorly on morphemic and phonemic analysis tasks and defined phonological awareness inaccurately.

The importance of having a command of linguistic knowledge in order to teach systematic phonics and decoding has been recognized by several researchers as well as being noted in the National Reading Panel report (Rayner, Foorman et al., 2001; Darling-Hammond, 2006; McCardle & Chhabra, 2004; NICHD, 2000). The actual performance of teachers on measures of linguistic knowledge indicates that there are several obstacles to implementing systematic phonics instruction in elementary classrooms. In addition to potential conflicts with whole-language philosophy, many of today's teachers cannot demonstrate the necessary core knowledge of the linguistic structure of English.

Summary of methods of teaching reading

In this section we have reviewed the major instructional approaches used to teach children to read. We described the methods and materials used in meaning-emphasis and code-emphasis approaches, illuminating their points of similarity and differences. In particular, we discussed whole-language and systematic phonics methods. Finally we reviewed the meta-analysis of experimental, classroom-based reading studies conducted by the National Reading Panel. The NRP results indicate that teaching systematic phonics is the most effective approach to reading instruction. The reason for this is, of course, that phonics approaches make the alphabetic principle explicit. Unfortunately, surveys of teachers' knowledge of the English writing system indicate that many teachers lack the core linguistic knowledge that is used to teach systematic phonics.

Summary

In this chapter we have discussed several aspects of early reading development. We began with a discussion of the alphabetic principle and the challenges of learning to read in a morphophonemic writing system such as English. The concept of emergent literacy was discussed, focusing on the contribution of spoken language skills and storybook reading to early reading development. Overall, it appears that storybook reading does not contribute much to print-related emergent literacy skills. It does help to build vocabulary, but vocabulary does not predict reading achievement until after second grade. Therefore we drew a distinction between two phases of experience in learning about our writing system: (a) awareness of story structure and the functions of writing (emergent literacy), and (b) print processing (learning to read). The "beginning to read" section discussed the fundamental role that phonemic awareness and letter knowledge play in learning to read, which is supported by numerous studies. Understanding the alphabetic principle, or the association of written symbols with specific phonemes, represents the major hurdle for children learning to read. In contrast, there is a notable lack of empirical research support for a critical role of cognitive maturity in learning to read. Finally we described two general approaches to early reading instruction (meaning-emphasis and code-emphasis), before discussing the laboratory and classroom-based studies that clearly demonstrate that systematic phonics instruction is the most effective way to teach children how to read.

12
READING DISORDERS

In the preceding chapters we discussed the process of learning to read. As we pointed out there, despite some variation in teaching methods and cultural approaches to teaching reading, most children do learn to read quite well. However, this process is a struggle for many children, and a number of these do not learn to read very well and may even reach adulthood without being able to read proficiently. Part of the problem for some children with reading difficulties may be tied to general cognitive aptitude (or IQ). Low verbal IQ does tend to be associated with deficits in comprehension and vocabulary. But the biggest hurdle that most children with reading difficulties must overcome involves word decoding. Most of the children who have difficulty learning to decode words experience problems with reading speed and/or comprehension, despite scoring in the average range or better on intelligence tests. To complicate matters further, the correlation between IQ and reading difficulties tends to appear later in elementary school, which suggests that years of poor reading can suppress performance on aptitude tests (Hoskyn & Swanson, 2000; Siegel, 1992; Stanovich, 1986; but see B.A. Shaywitz et al., 1995). Thus the causal relationship between IQ scores and reading difficulties may be bidirectional, since reading becomes a main avenue for acquiring new vocabulary and general knowledge around third grade (Chall, 1967, 1983).

However, we're getting ahead of ourselves. This chapter discusses three main types of reading disorders: acquired dyslexia, followed by developmental dyslexia, and hyperlexia. The term dyslexia is used to describe individuals who have difficulty reading words accurately and fluently. In cases of acquired dyslexia the reading problems result from brain damage caused by a stroke or accident in an individual who read normally prior to the stroke. We discuss acquired dyslexia first because of the impact that case studies of acquired dyslexia have had on theories of skilled reading and the diagnosis of developmental dyslexia. Developmental dyslexia occurs in childhood, with the child usually experiencing extreme decoding problems when reading instruction begins. The reading disorder hyperlexia is also developmental in nature, but it is characterized by relatively strong single-word reading skills accompanied by lower reading comprehension.

From our point of view, developmental dyslexia is the most interesting type of reading difficulty because the biological factors underlying its etiology have proved to be extremely complex. Dyslexia is continuous in nature, which is to say that dyslexia occurs along a continuum from mild (perhaps only affecting spelling) to severe (posing extreme difficulties in both reading and writing tasks). In addition to its varying degrees of severity, dyslexia often co-occurs with other non-linguistic impairments, such as attention-deficit disorder or motor sequencing problems. Despite the complexity of dyslexia, great gains have been made since 1990 in understanding the epidemiology and treatment of this reading disorder. Therefore our primary focus in this chapter will be on developmental dyslexia and we will discuss other types of reading disorders in contrast to developmental dyslexia.

Cognitive psychologists are only one of many types of researchers interested in reading disorders. Educators, neurologists, pediatricians, epidemiologists, statisticians, behavioral geneticists, educational psychologists, neuropsychologists, and developmental psychologists are all keenly interested in reading difficulties. In discussing reading disabilities it is necessary to be somewhat interdisciplinary in focus, and we will borrow from related fields as necessary, but we will rely most heavily on the work of cognitive psychologists.

Acquired dyslexia

Many cognitive processes are lateralized, so they occur mainly in the left or mainly in the right hemisphere of the brain. Most aspects of language processing are lateralized to the left hemisphere of the brain (in most people). As a consequence, injuries to the left hemisphere of the brain that result from stroke or other head injuries often result in language problems. Disorders of speech comprehension or production occurring as a result of brain damage are known as aphasias. There are several recognized varieties of aphasia depending on the precise nature of the language problem (Coslett, 2000; Kertesz, Harlock, & Coates, 1979; Lenneberg, 1967). Aphasic patients often experience reading difficulties as part of their more general language impairment. However, speech systems sometimes remain intact and reading problems are the predominant (or only) symptom of brain injury (e.g., Broadbent, 1872; Kussmaul, 1877), and these acquired dyslexia syndromes are the focus of this section.

Case studies of acquired dyslexia have had a strong influence on models of normal reading (Beaton, 2004). The general approach that cognitive psychologists have taken is to ask how the component processes involved in normal reading might be organized such that they would be prone to the distinctive types of reading errors that emerge among people with acquired dyslexia. The three major acquired dyslexia syndromes that are most often considered in discussions of developmental dyslexia are surface dyslexia, phonological dyslexia, and deep dyslexia (Beaton, 2004; Coslett, 2000). People with surface dyslexia can decode unfamiliar regular words and nonwords, but struggle with irregular and exception word reading. Those with phonological dyslexia struggle with decoding nonwords but can read familiar words. People with deep dyslexia also struggle with decoding, but they make semantic substitution errors. In fact, few pure cases of these types of dyslexia have been reported, and the fact that most reports are individual case studies makes it difficult to estimate the relative rates of occurrence of each type. Nonetheless, these differences in error patterns have been interpreted as evidence for two independent routes to word recognition: (1) a sublexical route using grapheme–phoneme correspondence rules (which is preserved in surface dyslexia) and (2) a direct route from orthography to meaning (which is preserved in phonological dyslexia) (Coltheart, 2005; Coltheart & Rastle, 1994; Coltheart, Rastle, Perry, Ziegler, & Langdon, 2001; Marshall & Newcombe, 1973; Shallice & Warrington, 1980; see Chapters 3 and 5 for further discussion).

Surface dyslexia

Much of the interest in acquired dyslexia stems from a seminal paper by Marshall and Newcombe (1973) in which surface dyslexia was described, along with deep dyslexia. As we mentioned above, people with surface dyslexia typically exhibit better nonword and regular word reading than irregular word reading, which seems to indicate their reliance on a sublexical route of letter–sound correspondences. A person reading in this way should be more likely to arrive at the correct pronunciation when the word shown is a regular word than when it is an irregular word. For example, Shallice and Warrington (1980) found that their patient read 36 out of 39 regular words correctly, but only 25 out of 39 irregular words correctly. How to interpret such data is unclear. If the "sublexical route" were all that was available, presumably those with surface dyslexia should mispronounce all of the irregular words. The fact that some irregular words were read correctly indicates that lexical information was available for some words. Thus we see that the typical pattern of reading impairment after a stroke consists of relative strengths and weaknesses.

Surface dyslexia has been intensively studied (Patterson, Marshall, & Coltheart, 1985) and some interesting patterns have emerged. The characteristic error type made by surface dyslexic readers is the phonologically plausible reading of an irregular word. Sometimes these errors produce nonwords, such as reading *island* as is-land/; and sometimes the errors are words, such as reading *disease* as /decease/. In both cases the errors can be described as phonic approximations in which the pronunciation is based on treating the target word as if it were regular or orthographically transparent. The meaning people with surface dyslexia ascribe to a word follows from the pronunciation they give to it. For example, a patient who read *begin* as /beggin'/ said "that's collecting money" (Marshall & Newcombe, 1973). Surface dyslexic readers sometimes make visual errors as well (such as misreading *precise* as /precious/ and *foreign* as /forgiven/), but these also tend to be phonologically similar to the target word.

Phonological dyslexia

In contrast to surface dyslexia, people with phonological dyslexia struggle to read unfamiliar words and pseudowords, which must be sounded out, but they can read familiar irregular words (e.g., Beauvois & Derouesne, 1979; Funnell, 1983; Patterson, 1982; Shallice & Warrington, 1980). As Ellis (1984) pointed out, it is unlikely that phonological dyslexia would have been detected if researchers had not been on the lookout for it, since reading of known words was unimpaired in many cases.

The main symptom of phonological dyslexia is the inaccurate reading aloud of even simple nonwords such as *pib* or *cug* that must be decoded. This error pattern has generally been taken as resulting from substantial damage to sublexical reading processes that compute letter–sound correspondences, despite the fact that these people can read (and understand) familiar words. Relatively accurate reading of familiar words suggests primary use of the direct route to the lexicon, which seems preserved in phonological dyslexia.

Deep dyslexia

A great deal of attention has been paid to the deep dyslexia syndrome (Coltheart, Patterson, & Marshall, 1980). Similar to phonological dyslexia, people with deep dyslexia make most reading errors on new words and nonwords, indicating damage to the sublexical route. In contrast, their reading of familiar words is usually preserved. Unlike phonological dyslexia, those with deep dyslexia make characteristic semantic errors, known as semantic paralexias. For example, when shown the word *kitten* they may respond /cat/, *ape* is read as /monkey/, or *forest* is read as /trees/. Additionally, semantic properties such as imageability or concreteness may affect the accuracy of a deep dyslexic person's word reading. Other symptoms include visual errors (where the error response is visually similar to the word shown), morphological errors (adding a suffix or prefix), and a greater facility with content words than function words.

Marshall and Newcombe (1966) provided the first full description of the symptoms of deep dyslexia. Nearly 50 years later the cause of reading errors made by people with deep dyslexia has yet to be determined. Marshall and Newcombe suggested that those with deep dyslexia have lost the capacity for grapheme–phoneme conversion, arguing that the direct route to the lexicon may be inherently prone to substituting incorrect pronunciations that are similar in meaning to the target word. In terms of normal reading, their interpretation suggests that the simultaneous activation of sublexical and direct routes helps to prevent semantic errors. Shallice and Warrington (1980) developed the alternative idea that general language-based retrieval processes contribute to these errors, consistent with Friedman and Perlman's (1982) observation of paralexias when a deep dyslexic patient named objects as well as words, which indicated that general semantic processes were impaired. The main characteristic to keep in mind is that deep dyslexic patients can read many words they knew before their injury, their errors are often semantically related to the target word, and they have difficulty reading even short nonwords.

To summarize, people with surface dyslexia have relatively preserved sublexical processes for decoding regular words and nonwords, but they struggle to read irregular words. In contrast, those with phonological dyslexia and deep dyslexia can read regular and irregular words that they knew before their injury, but have impaired sublexical processes that interfere with reading nonwords and words they haven't seen before. Given the similarity in the reading patterns in phonological and deep dyslexia, some researchers conceptualize the two syndromes as ends of a single continuum, in which deep dyslexia is considered a severe form of phonological dyslexia (Cloutman, Newhart, Davis, Heidler-Gary, & Hillis, 2009; Crisp & Ralph, 2006; Glosser & Friedman, 1990).

Although studies of acquired dyslexia have been influential in developing theories of reading, we feel that a certain amount of caution is necessary when interpreting case study data. Our major concern about generalizing from work on acquired dyslexia to normal reading is that it involves a certain amount of faith that the processes involved in normal reading can be accurately inferred on the basis of major injuries to the brain. First, the very serious reading problems that people with acquired dyslexia have sets limits on how data can be collected. For example, patient research has focused on single-word reading out of necessity, since reading connected text is almost impossible for most of these patients. Some see this as a virtue of the research, while others see it as somewhat problematic; as we have pointed out before, reading involves more than just stringing together the meanings of individual words.

The second source of our concern with inferring normal reading processes from case study patient data stems from the likelihood that the processes that people with acquired dyslexia adopt to cope with the task of reading after a stroke may be quite different from those used to read silently before the stroke occurred. One example of this is seen in letter-by-letter reading (Patterson & Kay, 1982; Rayner & Johnson, 2005; Johnson & Rayner, 2007). Some patients with acquired dyslexia can identify most words only by consciously processing each letter, making reading extremely laborious. When normal readers read silently with a one-letter window, their gaze durations and number of fixations per word approximated that of G.J., a letter-by-letter reader (Rayner & Johnson, 2005). In other words, an experimental manipulation of how much text is available induced eye movement behaviors in normal readers that mimicked the effect of brain-injured reading. However, when Rayner and Johnson expanded the window to three letters, the reading rate of the normal readers increased dramatically as the number of fixations decreased. Thus, when the text presentation was normalized, skilled readers abandoned their letter-by-letter reading in a way that G.J. could not, suggesting that his brain injury forced him to resort to a letter-by-letter reading strategy (see also Rayner & Bertera, 1979).

A related concern is that case study research does not systematically account for the duration of the recovery period, or the time between when the stroke occurred and the data were collected.

This makes it difficult to distinguish behaviors caused by the stroke itself from behaviors resulting from the neural rewiring that occurs during stroke recovery (e.g., Cloutman et al., 2009b). Most of the published patient data consists of observations taken months or years after the stroke occurred (e.g., Dickerson & Johnson, 2004; Gerhand & Barry, 2000; Miozzo & Caramazza, 1998; Rastle, Tyler, & Marslen-Wilson, 2006). Therefore, it seems important to also consider data gathered from large-scale studies of acute stroke patients, who are observed shortly after the injury occurred.

In one such study Cloutman et al. (2009b) presented 112 patients with word and nonword stimuli within 48 hours of their stroke. Control tasks included naming pictures and matching pictures to words they heard. Based on their performance, patients fell into five possible categories: (a) nonword deficit—patients with at least twice as many nonword errors as word errors; (b) word deficit—patients with at least twice as many word errors as nonword errors; (c) general deficit—patients who made errors on both words and nonwords; (d) phonological/visual—patients who made only phonological/visual errors in reading; (e) no reading errors.

Several findings from this study are of interest, and we will focus on the first three categories of word identification errors shown in Table 12.1. This table indicates that patients are distributed quite unevenly across the different categories of typical errors. The largest proportion of patients (46%) had nonword-reading deficits similar to those of traditional phonological dyslexic patients. This group made nearly five times as many errors on average when reading nonwords as compared to words, which is consistent with damaged sublexical processing. Among patients who had reading errors, the next largest group (17%) was the general deficit group, who read only about half of the words and nonwords correctly on average. The general deficit group thus showed evidence of impaired word reading as well as nonword reading, which suggested some damage to both the lexical and sublexical routes. This group had the highest error rates, as one might expect given that both sublexical and lexical processes were impaired. Thus Cloutman et al. observed reading impairments that could be at least partially attributed to damaged sublexical processes in 63% of their acute stroke sample. In contrast to finding a large proportion of acute patients with damaged sublexical decoding processes, only 4% of their sample exhibited poorer word reading than nonword reading. These patients had only mildly impaired reading, making no errors at all in nonword reading and few errors in word reading (< 2%). The pattern of intact sublexical processes that resulted in accurate nonword reading differs from the error patterns in the nonword deficit group and the general deficit group, and so it might be tempting to consider these readers as the equivalent of surface dyslexic. However, Cloutman et al. note that few of these patients exhibited any phonologically plausible errors, which is a key characteristic of surface dyslexia (Patterson et al., 1985). The overall low error rates and few phonic-type errors indicates that the word-reading deficit group was not relying primarily on sublexical processes to recognize words during the acute phase of their stroke. Similarly, Cloutman et al. also did not observe a single semantic paralexia during the word-naming task, although semantic paralexias occurred frequently in the picture-naming task. Now we consider the implications of these data gathered from acute stroke patients.

TABLE 12.1 Percentage of acute patients with errors on the word naming task

Nonword deficit	Word deficit	General deficit	Phonological/visual only	No reading errors
46%	4%	17%	15%	18%

Adapted from Cloutman et al., 2009.

Although Cloutman et al. used a non-traditional framework to interpret the data collected from their acute patients, they identified distinct error patterns that were similar to those observed in traditional case studies. In addition, this large scale study sheds light on the prevalence of each type of acquired dyslexia. A majority of readers demonstrated impaired sublexical processing that hampered nonword reading. In addition, a very small group of patients had intact sublexical processes with only mildly damaged lexical processes. However, the low error rate for this word-deficit group suggests that these patients did not rely primarily on sublexical processes within the first 48 hours after their stroke. If they had, error rates on word reading would be expected to be much higher, as readers would make phonic-type errors when reading irregular words. So this study did not find evidence of a surface dyslexia syndrome. Cloutman et al. also failed to find any cases of deep dyslexia in this sample, nor did they observe a single instance of semantic paralexias in word reading. Failure to find error patterns that indicate either surface dyslexia or deep dyslexia in this large sample suggests, at minimum, that these syndromes are extremely rare among acute stroke patients. In addition, finding null effects in the first 48 hours post-stroke raises the possibility that either or both syndromes actually reflect the operation of compensatory processes that patients learn to rely on in the course of their recovery from stroke. In contrast, frequent observations of errors reading nonwords in the nonword-deficit and general-deficit groups indicates that the most common acute symptom of acquired dyslexia is damage to sublexical reading processes.

Summary of acquired dyslexia

Acquired dyslexia is generally studied via observations of individual patients with brain damage from stroke or other trauma. Neuropsychologists have done rather thorough investigations of an individual's ability to perform various language-related tasks. For people with acquired dyslexia, the focus has been on their ability to read words and nonwords. Over the years a number of these case studies have been documented and categorized primarily in terms of the types of reading errors found (although sometimes also on the basis of the locus of the brain damage).

Although we have described three of the several different types of acquired dyslexia, this does not mean that every patient that has been identified falls neatly into one or another of the recognized categories. Indeed patients often show mixed symptoms, and the cases described in the literature tend to be the relatively small proportion of pure cases. Even among the pure cases, there are individual differences between patients grouped together as deep dyslexic or surface dyslexic (e.g., Funnell, 1983; Patterson, 1982). The existence of multiple forms of acquired dyslexia with separate symptoms can be taken as support for the notion that normal reading, once it has developed, involves the activity of separate components which are occasionally dissociable despite a fair amount of concerted and orchestrated activity (Ellis, 1984). The high rate of phonological dyslexia relative to surface and deep dyslexia indicates that sublexical processes are more vulnerable to damage from brain injury than lexical processes. Cloutman et al. (2009b) propose that this is due to the location of sublexical processes in the brain. As damage to the sublexical route is more common, it is not surprising that these patients would come to rely on lexical processes to compensate for that loss. It is difficult to determine whether the syndromes of surface dyslexia and deep dyslexia are very rare results of brain injury or whether they actually reflect patients' compensatory reorganization of reading processes during later phases of stroke injury. Either way, stroke patient data continue to make fundamental contributions to understanding how reading happens in the brain (Dehaene, 2009). Our intention here is not to become engaged in a debate concerning the relative merits of studying brain-damaged individuals versus studying normal readers. Rather, the primary focus of this chapter is how research with acquired dyslexic patients can enlighten us with respect to the problem of developmental dyslexia.

Developmental reading disorders

The reading difficulties that many children experience stem from three main sources (Gabrieli, 2009). Most commonly, children struggle when learning to decode and spell unfamiliar words. Other children may grasp decoding fairly quickly, but have problems understanding text. Still other children may fall behind their peers because they lack the motivation to read. The children in the first group are described as suffering from developmental dyslexia, which is the primary focus of this section.

Some may argue that the notion of reading difficulties is a statistical phenomenon (see Figure 12.1). How well a child is progressing in reading is indicated by how well he or she does on standardized tests of reading skill that are routinely administered in elementary school. Let's say that the test is given to 1000 second-graders in the middle of the school year and the average reading level obtained is 7 years 6 months (90 months). The standard deviation of the test scores is 12 months. This represents how much variability there is in the different test scores that our second-graders obtain. Since random error is usually assumed to follow the normal (or bell-shaped) distribution, 68% of the children taking the test will score between 78 months and 102 months on the test (the mean minus or plus 1 standard deviation). In this example, those scoring 78 months or less on the test have reading difficulties, relative to the rest of the children in their grade. Therefore the extent of a child's reading problem is determined in part by the relationship of their reading ability to the ability of others comparable in age. Similarly, a person is called obese if his or her weight substantially exceeds the average weight of a person of the same height and sex. As with obesity, the dividing line between reading difficulties and normal reading development is arbitrary; one can raise or lower the percentage of people who are considered dyslexic simply by altering the criteria. Understanding this fact does not invalidate the concept of dyslexia any more than it invalidates the concept of obesity (Ellis, 1984). The important point to remember is that although estimates of the incidence of reading disorders and descriptions of the symptoms may vary, reading problems at any age persist and can lead to negative educational and psychological outcomes if they go unaddressed.

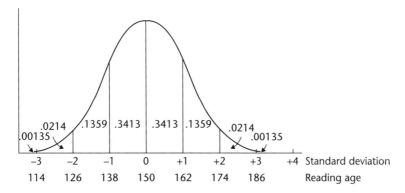

FIGURE 12.1 A hypothetical frequency distribution of reading scores. Values within different regions represent the percentage of students falling between the two scores (e.g., roughly 34% between 150 and 162)

Identifying reading disorders

There is agreement among most psychologists that the data gathered thus far on children's reading problems indicate that comprehension problems in elementary school stem from two sources:

(a) word-level deficits in reading and/or spelling or (b) problems with language comprehension (for examples of this position see Nation, 2005; Snowling & Hulme, 2005). Therefore understanding a particular child's instructional needs requires consideration of his or her relative strengths and weaknesses in the component areas of word recognition, spelling, comprehension, and vocabulary. Group-administered silent reading tests indicate a child's independent reading level relative to their age and grade, but they do not provide information about the development of underlying skills that contribute to that overall reading score. This is because an overall reading comprehension score can reflect the summed outcome of any number of different patterns of strengths and weaknesses in component skills. For example, if a fourth-grader's overall reading score on a test of silent reading comprehension falls in the bottom 25th percentile, this does not typically indicate a specific deficit in reading comprehension per se. Most children who score poorly on tests of reading comprehension do so because they struggle with isolated word recognition (Leach, Scarborough, & Rescorla, 2003; Perfetti, 1985; Shankweiler, Lundquist, Katz, Stuebing, Fletcher, Brady, et al., 1999). A minority of children do have global language comprehension deficits that yield problems in understanding both spoken and written language, and we will return to consider those language-based deficits later in the section that follows our discussion of dyslexia.

The converse also holds; children who experience word recognition difficulties often struggle to comprehend texts written at grade level (Gough & Tunmer, 1986; Hoover & Gough, 1990; Snowling, 2000a;Vellutino, Scanlon, & Tanzman, 1994;Vellutino, Scanlon, Sipay, Small, Pratt, Chen, et al., 1996). In the lower grades, children with poor word recognition skills may be able to comprehend predictable texts by compensating with guessing, using picture cues, memorizing, or applying background knowledge. By the middle of elementary school, however, comprehension may falter as texts become more abstract and deliver new information. To be able to use reading to learn new information, readers need to rely on strong word recognition skills. Words are the fundamental units of meaning, and identifying words accurately is fundamental for understanding a text. Despite the ample evidence that supports a close connection between efficient word recognition and text comprehension, our experience suggests that teachers tend to respond to low comprehension scores by intensifying their teaching of metacognitive strategies (such as posing questions to monitor comprehension), rather than by improving the weak component skills that interfere with getting meaning from text (such as inaccurate or slow word recognition). If word-level reading problems are not addressed, they persist and continue to interfere with reading fluency and comprehension (Perfetti & Hogaboam, 1975; Perfetti, 1985; Stanovich, 1986). Affected children continue to read in a labored fashion and devote a disproportionate amount of resources to decoding, which leaves fewer cognitive resources available for comprehending text (Curtis, 1980; Perfetti, 1988). Even though strong word recognition skills are not sufficient for comprehension, word recognition and decoding provide a necessary foundation for growth in reading comprehension.

Developmental dyslexia

If you were to ask your neighbors what a dyslexic reader is, they may well respond by describing someone who could not read because they saw words and letters backwards. In reality there is little evidence to support such a notion, but many myths and ill-conceived notions about developmental dyslexia exist. With respect to confusing the direction or orientation of words and letters, beginning readers who are dyslexic do not make such mistakes any more frequently on average than other beginning readers (Liberman, Shankweiler, Orlando, Harris, & Berti, 1971; Lyle, 1979; Lyle & Goyern, 1968). In this section we will describe the present definition of dyslexia and its characteristics, theories about the causes of dyslexia, issues in the diagnosis and identification of dyslexia, and theories of dyslexia subtypes. Table 12.2 describes some adult developmental dyslexic

TABLE 12.2   Descriptions of four developmental dyslexic readers

These cases are presented to give some indication of the range of the nature of reading problems and to illustrate how people can cope with reading problems.

Tom. Tom is a very proficient computer programmer, but his reading ability is very limited. Notes left for him were often not replied to because he could not read the words. Messages that were left had to be printed in large letters. Even though his father was a professor at a well-known university, Tom dropped out of school at the beginning of high school. His academic career was very undistinguished and what progress he made in school was done by listening carefully. Eventually, he found the whole routine of school life rather depressing and left. Yet, he was fully conversant with world and local events (via watching the news on television). Casual conversations with him would not lead anyone to suspect that he had a major disability. He had no problems with mathematical concepts or with the type of logic necessary for programming. Examination of his eye movements as he read indicated that he fixated on almost every other letter and generally could not report the sentence that had been presented.

Dave. Dave owns his own auto repair shop and is doing quite well in his chosen vocation. His reading was quite a bit better than Tom's, but yet he read no better than fifth-grade level. In spite of that, he graduated from high school with an average between B and C. He claimed to have developed very sophisticated listening strategies during school. He was further helped by sympathetic friends who shared their class notes with him and read the assigned readings to him. IQ tests showed him to be normal and any casual conversation with him would lead to the conclusion that he was a very well-informed and friendly individual. When he was presented text that was at his reading level, his eye movement patterns were very much like those of a typical adult reader. When presented text more in line with his chronological age, his eye movement patterns became fairly chaotic and looked very much like those of children presented with text that was above their reading level.

Steve. Steve is a university professor in a field that demands a lot of reading. As a youth he attended a special school for dyslexic children. His intelligence is very high, and he does well in his field because he has exceptional listening scores (scoring in the 99.9th percentile). When it comes to reading, he scores at about the 10th percentile. He relies on his wife who reads all professional related materials to him. Testing revealed two striking characteristics. First, he was able to identify words and letters further from fixation than were control participants. Second, when reading in the moving-window paradigm (see Chapter 4), his best performance was with a one-word window with Xs outside the window. As the window got larger, his reading performance (both in terms of speed and comprehension) grew poorer.

Jane. Jane's intelligence was quite high as measured by standardized tests, but her reading performance was around fifth-grade level when she read text in its normal orientation. Although she was diagnosed as dyslexic, she has a variety of problems that are not typical of dyslexia, and perhaps is better diagnosed as having a very rare disorder: developmental Gerstmann's syndrome. She has problems with spatial orientation tasks and has a difficult time remembering her left from her right. Another striking characteristic of Jane is that she produces mirror writing. She is left-handed and when writing twists her hand around; if you are sitting opposite her the script is written perfectly normally from your perspective, yet is a mirror reversal from her own perspective. If a text is rotated so that it is upside down, her reading skill improves markedly. She reported that in school she often turned the book upside down to read, but teachers continually told her that you cannot read with the book upside down. When reading text in its normal orientation, Jane shows a tendency right-to-left eye movements as she reads, sometimes at the end of the line and sometimes not. Interestingly, when the text was turned upside down, her eye movements looked quite normal (apart from the fact that they progressed from right-to-left across the line). We emphasize that Jane's reading behaviors are not typical of dyslexic people, and describe them only to illustrate that reading problems may take a wide variety of forms and have many different causes. Hearing about impaired readers with vivid symptoms like Jane's has led some people to propose that these symptoms are at the root of dyslexia. They are not.

See Pirozzola and Rayner, 1977, 1978 and Rayner, 1983, 1986; Rayner, Murphy, Henderson, and Pollatsek, 1989 for further discussion.

people that we have met over the years. All of them are intelligent people who have serious problems reading; their problems were identified when they were children and continued on into adulthood. The interesting aspect of these dyslexic readers is that they vary quite a bit in terms of what might be their underlying problem, although they all obviously had problems reading.

Defining dyslexia

The term "developmental dyslexia" implies that a child does not acquire reading very easily, and the word "developmental" implies that the problem is in the initial learning. Incidentally, *dyslexia* simply means "difficulty with reading." Sometimes the problem is not simply reading, but also includes spelling, writing, and other aspects of language. Since this book is about reading, however, we will focus on the issue of reading and not say much about spelling and writing.

The first case of developmental dyslexia was reported in a British medical journal (Morgan, 1896). Not surprisingly, this case involved a striking contrast between the overall intellectual abilities of P.F. (age 14) and his inability to learn to read. Since that time thousands of studies have examined many dimensions of dyslexia in order to advance our understanding of this reading disorder and improve our ability to identify dyslexic children. The current definition of dyslexia from the National Institutes of Health reflects the dominant understanding of dyslexia as a neurobiological disorder that results in a particular pattern of reading difficulties (Lyon, Shaywitz, & Shaywitz, 2003).

> Dyslexia is a specific learning disability that is neurobiological in origin. It is characterized by difficulties with accurate and/or fluent word recognition and poor spelling and decoding abilities. These difficulties typically result from a deficit in the phonological component of language that is often unexpected in relation to other cognitive abilities and the provision of effective classroom instruction. Secondary consequences may include problems in reading comprehension and reduced reading experience that can impede the growth of vocabulary and background knowledge.

At this point in time, the above definition is widely accepted in the U.S. Its central claim is that deficits in the phonological language system lie at the core of reading difficulties (Morton & Frith, 1995). Cumbersome though it is, this definition includes several important concepts about dyslexia that may not be obvious. There are three keys points here. First, the symptoms of dyslexia are behavioral, although the bases of these symptoms may be neurological or genetic. Due to the behavioral nature of dyslexia symptoms, early educational interventions can be effective in helping dyslexic children become better readers. Second, reading difficulties mainly result from phonological processing problems, as opposed to visual or auditory perceptual deficits (Fletcher, Lyon, Fuchs, & Barnes, 2007; Vellutino & Fletcher, 2005; White, Milne, Rosen, Hansen, Swettenham et al., 2006). Third, problems in reading comprehension and vocabulary are secondary results of a main impairment in single-word reading (Stanovich, 1986).

Dyslexia can be operationally identified as a substantial deficit in word recognition and/or spelling. Convergent evidence suggests that for most children with dyslexia this word recognition deficit stems from difficulty learning the letter–sound mappings that allow the accurate identification of unfamiliar words (Fletcher, Foorman, Francis, Shaywitz, & Shaywitz, 1994; Liberman & Shankweiler, 1979, 1991; Stanovich & Siegel, 1994; Torgesen, Alexander, Wagner, Rashotte, Voeller, et al., 2001; Vellutino, 1979; Vellutino, Scanlon, & Spearing, 1995; Torgesen, Wagner, & Rashotte, 1994). In turn, the difficulty in phonological coding seems to stem from phonological awareness problems, given the abundant evidence that training in phonological awareness and letter–sound correspondences improves word recognition skill (Blachman, 2000; Foorman et al.,

1998; Hatcher, Hulme, & Ellis, 1994; Torgesen, Wagner, Rashotte, Rose, Lindmood, Conway, et al., 1999;Vellutino & Scanlon, 1987). Thus it appears that most children who perform poorly on reading comprehension tests struggle with the alphabetics component of learning to read, which includes phonemic awareness and phonics skills. Fletcher et al. (2007) note that studies consistently identify single-word decoding as the major deficit exhibited by dyslexic readers (Olson, Forsberg, Wise, & Rack, 1994; Perfetti, 1985; Shaywitz & Shaywitz, 2004; Stanovich, 1986), and they sensibly recommend that the term *word-level reading disability* (WLRD) be used to describe dyslexic readers. As phonological awareness and orthographic awareness work together to build a growing sensitivity to orthographic patterns, deficits in phonological awareness often result in lower ortho-graphic knowledge as well (Bruck, 1990;Vellutino et al., 1994; Katzir, Kim, Wolf, Kennedy, Lovett et al., 2006). Therefore a word-level reading disability is often accompanied by spelling problems. In languages with more transparent orthographies, it is common to find that slow reading rate is the main marker of dyslexia (Wimmer & Mayringer, 2002).

Phonological deficit theory of dyslexia

The phonological deficit theory contends that dyslexic readers' difficulties with reading and spelling words stem directly from a deficit in the processing of the abstract speech sounds or phonemes that make up words (I .Y. Liberman, 1973; Murphy, Pollatsek, & Well, 1988; Stanovich, 1988). As we discussed in Chapter 11, problems with the storage, access, and conscious manipulation of spoken phonemes constitute a deficit in phonemic awareness, which is the type of phonological awareness that is necessary for learning to read in alphabetic writing systems. Spoken phonemes are coarticulated with their neighbors and thus a given phoneme has different acoustic properties in different environ-ments. They are, therefore, abstract entities that have to be learned, not acoustic objects that can be defined psychophysically. Dyslexic readers have indistinct cognitive representations of the phonemes and phoneme sequences that make up a spoken word form. Although they typically understand speech adequately, they have difficulty consciously processing and manipulating its segments.

According to the phonological–core deficit model, most poor readers share a phonological deficit that can manifest in any number of reading problems. To be sure, other models do exist that propose multiple, independent etiologies for reading problems (e.g. the double-deficit hypothesis; Wolf & Bowers, 1999). We discuss those in a later section of this chapter. However, we believe that the phonological–core deficit model (e.g., Stanovich, 1988) best accommodates converging evidence that most poor readers have difficulty segmenting, blending, and manipulating the phonemes that they hear in a spoken word. This difficulty is apparent in phonological awareness tasks that require a spoken response, but also in tasks that do not, such as matching two pictures that start with the same sound. A phonological deficit in speech processing makes the individual phonemes difficult to discern and hinders the learning of letter–sound correspondences. In addition, the model recognizes that this core problem can manifest itself in different behaviors with different degrees of severity. The phonological–core deficit model laid the groundwork for an extensive body of research indi-cating that dyslexia is not a categorically different condition from poor reading (Hoskyn & Swanson, 2000). Rather, numerous studies have found that the risk of reading failure occurs along a continuum, with dyslexia being the left-most tail in the normal distribution of reading skill (see Figure 12.1; Gayán & Olson, 2001; Scarborough, 1990; Snowling et al., 2003; Stanovich & Siegel, 1994).

How does phonological processing interfere with learning to read?

The specific way(s) in which phonological processing deficits impair reading development is still under debate, but most of the empirical data indicate that poor performance on phonological awareness tasks that require the isolation of individual phonemes reflects problems with underlying phonological representations that interfere with reading development (Beaton, 2004; Snowling, 2000b). Phonological deficits can distort the underlying phonological representations in several ways, making these representations weak, unstable, or indistinct (Blomert & Mitterer, 2004; Boada & Pennington, 2006; Breier, Fletcher, Denton, & Gray, 2004; Godfrey, Syrdal-Lasky, Millay, & Knox, 1981; Perfetti & Hart, 2001; Swan & Goswami, 1997). Because these representations support a variety of tasks (such as reading, writing, and naming), low-quality phonological representations contribute to performance deficits in several areas (Hulme & Snowling, 1992). Within the domain of reading, deficient phonological representations seem to impede grapheme–phoneme translation and efficient word recognition (Griffiths & Snowling, 2002; Perfetti, 1985; Rack, Snowling, & Olson, 1992; Rugel, 1974; Share, 1995; Swan & Goswami, 1997). Phonological deficits also impact performance on verbal short-term memory and naming tasks (Berninger et al., 2006; Brady, Shankweiler, & Mann, 1983; Bruck, 1992; Wolf & Bowers, 1999). Therefore the presence of weak, unstable, or indistinct representations is the central processing problem faced by dyslexic readers, according to phonological-core deficit theory (Elbro, 1996; Hulme & Snowling, 1994; Katz, 1986).

Before leaving this discussion, we note two points. First, the severity of the reading disorder and the age of the child can modulate the relative impact of the phonological deficit. Thus, mild dyslexic readers may experience impaired reading, whereas more extreme dyslexic readers with more pronounced phonological deficits may also be impaired on speech perception tasks (Bruno, Manis, Keating, Sperling, Nakamoto, et al., 2007; Harm & Seidenberg, 1999; McBride-Chang, 1996). Proficient readers with a family history of dyslexia may still struggle with spelling (e.g., Frith, 1980). Our second point is that phonological-core deficit theory does not claim that dyslexic readers have only a phonological deficit. Rather, it recognizes that some dyslexic readers present additional cognitive deficits, but questions the causal role of such additional deficits in word recognition-based reading disorders (Ramus, 2004a; Rochelle & Talcott, 2006; White et al., 2006). The strongest evidence presently available indicates that the word-level reading problems in dyslexia can be accounted for primarily by phonological deficits (Brady, 1997; Fowler, 1991; Ramus, 2003; Snowling, 2000a; Stanovich & Seigel, 1994; Wagner & Torgesen, 1987).

You should note, however, that the direct contribution of phonological deficits to word recognition disorders does not imply that phonological deficits always culminate in reading problems. In other words, a phonological deficit is a necessary but not sufficient contributor to dyslexia. Gallagher, Frith, and Snowling (2000) conducted a longitudinal study to compare the phonological development of children from families with a history of reading problems (the at-risk group) with children from families with no such risk (the control group). Performance on reading, spelling, and phonological awareness tasks was assessed at 3 years 9 months, 6 years, and 8 years of age. A literacy-impaired group was identified at age 8, then the earlier data were analyzed. At age 3 the unimpaired and impaired at-risk readers scored similarly low on the basic phonological memory task of nonword repetition. At age 6 the impaired at-risk readers scored lower on phonemic segmentation tasks (see Chapter 11) than their unimpaired counterparts, who also scored somewhat lower than the controls with no family history of dyslexia. In other words, the earliest phonological tasks did not predict which children would become impaired readers, but children with the poorest phonological awareness at 6 years old did develop reading problems by age 8. Furthermore, children from families at risk for dyslexia performed worse on most phonological tasks than control children, irrespective of whether they developed typical reading skills or impaired reading. Therefore these data indicate that although phonological awareness at age 6 usually is predictive of early reading achievement, some children from at-risk families seem to overcome their phonological deficits and become normal readers.

Are dyslexic readers really different from poor readers?

Vellutino and Fletcher (2005) discuss the mounting evidence that difficulties with phonological decoding are common to most children with reading problems. Despite the fact that a small minority of struggling readers receive a diagnosis of dyslexia, the difference between dyslexia and other word recognition problems that impair early reading progress is not obvious. For some non-dyslexic children, phonological difficulties may arise due to environmental factors such as inadequate reading instruction or second language issues, in which case they are likely to show rapid improvement in reading when provided with appropriate, code-emphasis instruction. In the case of a dyslexic child, the phonological deficit is rooted in the cognitive systems, and dyslexic children often experience weaknesses in word recognition and spelling that persist into adulthood (Hatcher, Snowling, & Griffths, 2002; Pennington, Van Orden, Smith, Green, & Haith, 1990; Shaywitz et al., 1999). In other words, reading problems may be more persistent, or may be more likely to be reported as persistent, among readers who are formally diagnosed as dyslexic. However, whether a child receives a diagnosis of dyslexia depends on many factors, including family income and education level.

At this time there is little research evidence to support the common perception that the reading problems of dyslexic children are categorically different from those of other children who struggle with learning to read. Vellutino et al. (1996) conducted a longitudinal study that examined differences between children with environmentally and cognitively based reading difficulties. Letter-naming and phonological awareness skills were substandard in nearly all of the kindergarten children who were later identified as poor readers in the middle of first grade. For 70% of those children one semester of tutoring in first grade was enough to bring them into the average range of reading achievement, and that was maintained through the fourth grade. However, those readers who were difficult to remediate (the remaining 30%) continued to perform poorly on phonological tests into the third grade. The Vellutino et al. study complements other intervention studies showing that most impaired readers can develop average-level reading skills if they are identified early and receive the appropriate instruction (Iverson & Tunmer, 1993; Scanlon, Boudah, Elksnin, Gersten, & Klingner, 2003; Torgesen, Alexander et al. 1999, 2001). Therefore it appears that most children with early reading problems benefit from supplemental decoding instruction, whether or not they are diagnosed with dyslexia.

Should children fail to receive appropriate instruction, however, they do not appear to grow out of their reading difficulties simply with the passage of time. The Connecticut Longitudinal Study followed a representative sample of 445 children from kindergarten through high school (Shaywitz et al., 1999). Children who met the criteria for persistently poor reading were compared to a group of non-disabled average readers and superior readers in terms of their reading achievement in Grade 9. This study found very little change in readers' achievement over time relative to the reading of their peers. In other words, the children who exhibited initial reading difficulties continued to read poorly into the high school years, and rarely caught up with their peers. This finding is consistent with other longitudinal studies that indicate the long-term persistence of reading problems (Bruck, 1992; Felton, Naylor, & Wood, 1990; Francis, Shaywitz, Stuebing, Shaywitz, & Fletcher, 1996; Snowling, Nation, Moxham, Gallagher, & Frith, 1997). Thus, when children fall behind in reading, it is rarely due to a temporary lag in their cognitive development, and they are unlikely to catch up to their peers without effective intervention.

What is the incidence of developmental dyslexia?

It is estimated that dyslexia occurs in 5% to 17% of all children, making it one of the most prevalent neurobehavioral disorders (Shaywitz, 1998). Even if only 5% of children could be categorized as severely dyslexic, we are talking about a large number of children. Epidemiological studies indicate that children with dyslexia range from being severely impaired in their reading to only mildly impaired. The continuous nature of dyslexia can make it seem like a fuzzy concept, as there is no absolute list of symptoms beyond a marked difficulty with decoding and encoding written language. In fact, many deny the existence of a group of readers who have a learning disability. Our own casual observation is that researchers who work primarily with young children may be inclined to think of reading difficulties as occurring along a continuum, whereas those who work with older disabled readers tend to believe that there is a definite group of children with reading disabilities. The reasons for this developmental difference are complex. For one, older children with persistent reading problems are by definition more difficult to remediate, and thus are likely to have more severe problems (Ehri et al., 2001). Also, persistent reading problems deter children from reading independently and this can hinder the development of other cognitive skills, such as vocabulary (Hoskyn & Swanson, 2000; Stanovich, 1986). The combined influence of these factors (and others) may make older children with reading disorders seem more distinct from typical readers than their younger counterparts.

Dyslexia is a heritable trait

DeFries, Singer, Foch, and Lewitter (1978) studied the families of over 100 children with reading difficulties and found preliminary evidence suggesting that dyslexia runs in families. It is not easy to determine whether dyslexia has a genetic component, because families share environments as well as genes. Twin studies have been conducted to disentangle these two factors, based on the rationale that monozygotic twins should have a higher incidence of dyslexia than dizygotic twins if genetics plays a role. A large twin study was conducted at the Colorado Learning Disabilities Research Center to examine dyslexic twin pairs and pairs of younger, normal readers in a reading-level matched design. This Colorado Twin study found evidence for a genetic component to word recognition deficits in both male and female twins (Olson, Wise, Conners, & Rack, 1989). Olson et al. (1989) measured phonological coding as the ability to read nonwords aloud accurately (*strale*) and orthographic coding as the ability to identify words among homophonic nonwords (*rain* vs. *rane*). Orthographic coding and phonological coding made independent contributions to word recognition skill, and phonological coding accounted for nearly the full heritable component of variance in word recognition. Later studies with a larger sample suggested that orthographic coding abilities are also inherited (Fisher, Stein, & Monaco, 1999; Gayán & Olson, 2001). As many as half of the children with a dyslexic parent will develop dyslexia themselves (Gilger, Hanebuth, Smith, & Pennington, 1996; Locke, Hodgson, Macaruso, Roberts, Lambrecht-Smith, et al., 1997; Scarborough, 1990).

Genetic studies consistently implicate chromosomes 2, 3, 6, 15, and 18 in transmitting dyslexia from one generation to the next (Fisher & DeFries, 2002). At this time, it is not known whether the multiple loci involved are responsible for a single phenotype or if they transmit different types of dyslexia (Shaywitz & Shaywitz, 2005). The role of multiple genes in passing dyslexia on from one generation to the next helps account for the number of children affected and variety of symptoms observed. Note, however, that these genes are unlikely to have any direct link with reading skill, as specific reading genes could not have evolved in the short time since the beginning of writing systems some 6000 years ago (Beaton, 2004). Still, the identification of possible genetic contributions to dyslexia holds the promise of providing more accurate early diagnosis and intervention.

Traditionally dyslexia was thought to occur much more commonly in males than in females, yet several studies now indicate that the ratio of male to female dyslexic readers is relatively representative of the gender distribution in the population as a whole (DeFries & Gilllis, 1991; Shaywitz, Shaywitz, Fletcher, & Escobar, 1990; Wood & Felton, 1994). The disparity in the traditionally reported 4:1 ratio of male to female dyslexics may have resulted from referral bias, as boys tend to show externalizing behaviors that lead to clinical and school referrals more often than do girls (Fletcher et al., 2007; Hallgren, 1950). The failure of genetic studies to find evidence for a sex-linked aspect of dyslexia is consistent with this referral-bias theory (Plomin & Kovas, 2005). However, an analysis of four epidemiological studies conducted by Rutter et al. (2004) found a gender ratio of male to female ranging from 1.4:1 to 2.7:1. Beaton's (2004) review of the sex ratio debate proposes that the gender ratio among dyslexic readers may vary depending on the diagnostic criteria used for selecting dyslexic participants. Samples of readers with severe deficits and higher than normal IQs seem to comprise a higher proportion of males than females, even in initially gender-balanced studies such as the Colorado Reading Project. Therefore the current data seem to indicate that dyslexia may be slightly more common in males, that it is under-diagnosed in females, and that the sex ratio may vary with the severity of the reading problem.

The neurobiological basis of dyslexia

Given that dyslexia is a cognitive learning disorder with high heritability rates, it must logically have a neurobiological origin. Evidence for differences in the brain anatomy of dyslexic and normal readers has been brought forth and debated for decades (Drake, 1968; Galaburda & Kemper, 1979; Leonard, Eckert, Lombardino et al., 2001; Luttenberg, 1965; Rumsey, Dorwart, Vermess, Denckla, Kuesi, & Rappaport, 1986; Schultz, Cho, Staib, & Kier, 1994). Several neurological differences may differentiate dyslexic from normal readers, including differences in hemisphere volume and the asymmetry of cortical structures like the planum temporale as well as differences in the size of the insula, anterior and superior cortex, and Broca's area. Promising as some anatomical studies seem, the evidence is inconsistent overall, due in part to the small *N* in many studies and differences in the selection criteria for dyslexic participants.

For example, classic theories of dyslexia emphasized the role of mixed hemispheric dominance in dyslexia (e.g., Orton, 1928). In other words, poor reading was thought to result from an underdevelopment of the left hemisphere, which allowed the right hemisphere to activate competing perceptual signals. More recently, research has investigated whether the incomplete lateralization of language functions is responsible for word recognition and spelling problems. Lateralization is the process by which a set of cognitive functions becomes situated primarily in one hemisphere or the other, with greater lateralization being indicated by asymmetries in the size of brain structures in the two hemispheres. In normal readers most of the activation involved in reading and language processes has been observed in the left hemisphere (see Beaton, 2004). The thinking is that mixed-dominance reflects an incomplete lateralization of language processes that could be observed in the relative symmetry of brain structures in the two hemispheres. The relation between the relative size of cortical structures in each hemisphere and the degree to which language processes were lateralized was fueled by a seminal study by Geschwind and Levitsky (1968). They found that an area of the temporal lobe called the planum temporale was longer on the left side of the brain than on the right side in 65% of normal adults. Given modern estimates that 90% of the population is left-lateralized for language (Knecht, Deppe, Drager, Bobe, Lohman, et al., 2000), the relationship between planum temporale asymmetry and the lateralization of language must be fairly loose (Beaton, 2004). Still, developments in brain-imaging technology in the 1980s supported a plethora of studies on brain asymmetry that often yielded inconsistent results. Interested readers should see Chapter 9 of Beaton (2004) for a comprehensive discussion of this literature.

The task of identifying consistent differences in the asymmetry of dyslexic and normal brains is made more challenging by the general variance observed in the size of brain structures (Phinney, Pennington, Olson, Filley, & Filipek, 2007). For example, gender and handedness contribute to the relative size of brain structures in each hemisphere (Preis, Jänke, Schmitz-Hillebrecht, & Steinmetz, 1999; Zetzsche et al., 2001). Apparently females exhibit greater leftward asymmetry than males and left-handed people tend to exhibit more symmetry or inverse asymmetry as compared to right-handed people. Therefore, gender and handedness factors can blur differences between dyslexic and normal individuals, especially when studies use a small number of participants. The problem is further compounded by the use of varying selection criteria for dyslexic participants across studies and by disagreements about the correct boundaries of structures like the planum temporale. For example, studies that include the surface of the supramarginal gyrus as part of the planum temporale do not find significant asymmetry in either dyslexic participants or controls (Green et al., 1999; Rumsey et al., 1997). Studies that examined other possible anatomical differences, such as whether the corpus callosum was larger in dyslexic than normal readers also report inconsistent findings (Duara, Kushch, Gross-Glenn, & Barker, 1991; Pennington et al., 1999; Robichon & Habib, 1998; von Plessen et al. 2002).

Whereas the findings for differences in the size and asymmetry of specific brain structures are not conclusive, research has identified at least two neurobiological differences between dyslexic and normal readers: differences in predictors of overall cerebral volume and differences in the neural activation patterns that indicate networks used for reading. Phinney et al. (2007) investigated differences in predictors of brain volume between dyslexic and normal readers by conducting MRI scans of 167 poor readers and 92 good readers in the Colorado Twin Study. The twins were administered an IQ test, reading achievement tests of word recognition and comprehension, phonological awareness tasks, an orthographic choice task, and a rapid naming task. Individual regression analyses tested for correlations between performance on these tests and total cortical volume, neocortical volume, and subcortical volume. Phinney et al. found that phonological aware-ness (PA) interacted with reading ability, such that PA was positively correlated with total cerebral volume for good readers but not for poor readers. Phinney et al. mention that the effect size of the interaction was very small. Nonetheless, the observation that PA is differentially predictive of total cerebral volume in good but not poor readers appears inconsistent with the presently accepted claim that poor readers are part of a continuum of reading ability in the general population. Phinney et al. reconcile this conclusion with the Shaywitz, Fletcher, Holahan, and Shaywitz (1992) claims of a continuous distribution by noting that their poor readers had a higher genetic risk of dyslexia, and therefore may have been more severely impaired than the readers in the Connecticut Longitudinal Study.

Several brain-imaging studies have identified different patterns of neural activation in dyslexic and normal brains during reading (Pugh et al., 2001a,b; for a review see Gabrieli, 2009). Normal readers utilize multiple brain areas to form a network for word recognition: an anterior circuit that activates the inferior frontal gyrus and a posterior circuit that activates both ventral (occipito-temporal regions and Wernicke's area) and dorsal (temporo-parietal) regions (Pugh et al., 2001). As compared to normal readers, dyslexic readers exhibit different patterns of activation in both the anterior and posterior circuits as well as differences in connectivity within the posterior circuit. In the posterior reading network several imaging experiments found reduced activation when dyslexic participants read unfamiliar words and pseudowords that required decoding (Brunswick, McCrory, Price, Frith, & Frith, 1999; Helenius, Tarkiainen, Cornelissen, Hansen, & Salmelin, 1999; Pugh et al., 2000a,b; Rumsey, Andreason, Zametkin, & Aquino, 1992; Shaywitz, 1998; Simos et al., 2000). Rumsey et al. (1997) found fewer correlations between activity in the left angular gyrus and activity in other reading areas for dyslexic as compared to normal readers, which suggests that dyslexic participants had fewer functional connections between the brain areas that form their posterior reading network. Activity differences also were observed in the anterior reading network, with dyslexic readers showing greater activation of the inferior frontal gyrus and the dorso-lateral prefrontal cortex than normal readers during word and pseudoword reading (Brunswick et al., 1999; Pugh et al., 2000a,b; Rumsey et al., 1997). Recent research suggests that differences in anterior circuit activation reflect dyslexic participants' less-efficient phonological processing, rather than an over-reliance on phonological processing (see Frost et al., 2009). It is interesting to note that at least two fMRI studies have reported that effective reading interventions with dyslexic readers altered their brain activation patterns such that these patterns more closely resembled those of normal readers (Shaywitz et al., 2004; Temple et al., 2003).

In summary, decades of research into possible neuro-anatomical differences between dyslexic and normal readers has yielded few consistent findings. It appears that there is a positive correlation between phonological awareness and overall cerebral volume in good readers, but not in poor readers. Also, there is accumulating evidence that dyslexic readers exhibit different patterns of activation in reading circuits than normal readers do, and that improved reading is accompanied by changing patterns of brain activation.

Alternative theories of dyslexia

Developmental dyslexia is one of the most prevalent learning disorders, and the quest to identify its cause has generated a large literature over the past few decades. The bulk of the evidence from laboratory and classroom studies supports the phonological-core deficit model (Beaton, 2004; Snowling, 2000a). However, there are a number of alternative theories that claim to identify other cognitive processes that are fundamental to the disorder. These theories can be grouped under the umbrella term of sensorimotor deficits (Ramus, 2003). Essentially these theories contend that problems with processing speed underlie the learning difficulties of people with dyslexia. These temporal processing problems seem to impair auditory processing, vision, and/or motor control when stimuli are presented quickly. Stein (2001) described these theories together under the umbrella of magnocellular theories of dyslexia. Sensorimotor theories are appealing because of their ability to account for apparent differences among dyslexic readers.

We prefer to use the term sensorimotor, rather than magnocellular, to avoid confusion with the initial construct of magnocellular theory, which attributed dyslexia primarily to deficits in the visual system. For example, Livingstone, Rosen, Drislane, and Galaburda (1991) reported finding smaller evoked potentials (ERPs) in dyslexic than typical readers in response to rapidly presented, low-contrast stimuli. Histological comparisons of the magno cells in five dyslexic and five control brains found abnormalities in the magnocellular, but not parvocellular, layers of the lateral geniculate nuclei. The Livingstone et al. data were taken to suggest that dyslexic readers' problems with processing quickly presented visual stimuli arise early in the visual system (i.e., before V1) due to abnormalities in the magnocellular system. Present-day sensorimotor theories extend the original magnocellular theory of Livingstone et al. (1991) to claim that processing problems in dyslexia are caused by basic deficits in the visual system, auditory system, and cerebellum (White et al., 2006). Therefore we use the term sensorimotor deficit because it encompasses the idea of a deficit in one or more perceptual/motor system (Ramus, 2003).

Sensorimotor theories of dyslexia claim that the word-level reading problems cannot be accounted for primarily by a core phonological deficit. Instead they propose that the root of dyslexia for some children resides in temporal processing problems that can manifest in the auditory, visual, and/or motor systems and arise when processing quickly presented stimuli, such as a rapid sequence of speech sounds or dots in motion (Tallal, 1980a; Lovegrove, Bowling,

Badcock, & Blackwood, 1980; Nicolson, Fawcett, & Dean, 2001). Rather than attempt to discuss the large experimental literature in rapid auditory processing, magnocellular visual processing, and motor/cerebellar problems, we refer interested readers to Beaton (2004) for a thorough review of the literature in each domain. This discussion will highlight data patterns and issues that appear consistently in the sensorimotor research. One such pattern is that sensorimotor deficits seem to be distinct from phonological deficits, as several studies that tested dyslexic participants failed to find a correlation between their performance in sensorimotor domains and their phonological processing (Chiappe, Stringer, Siegel, & Stanovich, 2001; Kronbichler, Hutzler, & Wimmer, 2002). Another consistent pattern is that about a third of dyslexic participants who were tested in a single domain had a deficit in that domain (Ramus, 2003). However, studies testing for processing deficits across domains found overlapping deficits, with some dyslexic participants exhibiting deficits in multiple sensorimotor domains and others exhibiting a single, core deficit in phonological representation (e.g., Amitay, Ben-Yedudah, Banai, & Ahissar, 2002; Witton et al., 1998).

Several issues in the literature appear to raise doubt about a causal role for sensorimotor deficits in reading disorders, according to Beaton (2004). First, it is not unusual to find that a sensorimotor deficit fails to predict reading achievement after controlling for IQ (e.g., Hulslander et al., 2004; Share, Jorm, Maclean, & Matthews, 2002; White et al., 2006). In other words, sensorimotor deficits may be relatively common among dyslexic readers, but these deficits are not tightly correlated with reading problems. Second, a number of studies with groups of dyslexic readers have failed to find auditory perception deficits in tasks that require speech processing at the sensorimotor level (Adlard & Hazan, 1998; Heath, Hogben, & Clark, 1999; Joanisse, Manis, Keating, & Seidenberg, 2000; Manis & Keating, 2005; Marshall, Snowling, & Bailey, 2001). Third, sensorimotor deficits also appear in children with specific language impairment (SLI) and those with autism (Hill, 2001; Milne, Swettenham, Hansen, Campbell, Jeffries, & Plaisted, 2002; Robertson, Joanisse, Desroches, & Ng, 2009). Therefore the literature presently indicates that some dyslexic readers have sensorimotor deficits, but not all of those with sensorimotor deficits are dyslexic.

Even when dyslexic readers with sensorimotor deficits are identified, it is not clear that these deficits result from problems processing quickly presented stimuli. Several studies have reported sensorimotor deficits in tasks that use longer stimulus presentation times and interstimulus intervals (Amitay et al., 2002; Chiappe et al., 2001; Olson & Datta, 2002; Rosen & Manganari, 2001; Sperling, Lu, Manis, & Seidenberg, 2005). Sperling et al. (2005) proposed an alternative theory that accounts for much of the sensorimotor data, claiming that people with dyslexia have a general deficit in perceptual filtering. Sperling et al. (2005, 2006) manipulated the background noise that was present when good and poor readers were making perceptual judgments about dot motion or grating detection. Good and poor readers had comparable detection thresholds in the low-noise and no-noise conditions, but poor readers performed significantly worse in the high-noise condition. Ziegler and his colleagues reported similar findings on tests of speech perception. In the high-noise condition, poor readers were worse at detecting place of articulation differences (*ba-da*) than were good readers, but no group differences were found in the no-noise condition (Ziegler, Pech-Georgel, George, & Lorenzi, 2009). These data indicate that what many regard as a sensorimotor deficit may actually be a noise-exclusion deficit that affects both reading and spoken language skills in children.

In summary, the research literature confirms the existence of phonological and/or sensorimotor deficits in some dyslexic readers. There is a general consensus in the field that phonological deficits form the core of dyslexic readers' difficulty with grapheme to phoneme translation, efficient word recognition, and spelling. In addition to a phonological deficit, some dyslexic children exhibit processing problems in one or more sensorimotor systems. These sensorimotor deficits may contribute to their learning problems, but these deficits do not appear to directly affect reading achievement. Evidence that sensorimotor deficits result from a difficulty with processing fast or transient stimuli is inconclusive at the present time. There is evidence that some people with dyslexia have perceptual problems under high noise conditions. However, we still do not know the percentage of dyslexic readers who exhibit these noise exclusion deficits nor how to remediate them.

The combination of a phonological deficit with one or more sensorimotor deficits does account for the phenotypic variety observed in the dyslexic population. Also, the identification of sensorimotor deficits may eventually lead to the development of instructional practices that are more tailored to individual patterns of difficulty. However, the identification of phonological deficits as the proximal cause of dyslexia has already informed a host of effective practices that can be implemented to help dyslexic readers strengthen their reading skills.

Subtypes of dyslexia

Those who have spent time teaching dyslexic readers have experienced the diversity of this population first-hand. Although most dyslexic children have an underlying phonological deficit, no one child has quite the same needs or abilities as another. This phenotypic diversity can be accounted for by the interaction of a phonological deficit with other cognitive factors, as well as the social and emotional problems that are unique to each child. Such is the nature of developmental disorders. Within this variety, however, one often perceives groups of children who seem similar to each other. It is possible that such perceived groupings stem from differential causes of dyslexia, and that identifying subtypes could be an initial step in thinking about separate causal mechanisms (Seymour & Evans, 1994). Formalizing subtypes can also lead to more effective treatments of some learning disorders, such as the differentiation between children who have attention deficits with and without hyperactivity. Therefore identifying valid subtypes of dyslexia could inform the development of better interventions (Morris et al., 1998). Thus the quest to identify dyslexia subtypes seems both intuitively sensible and potentially useful.

Unfortunately, most historical attempts to classify dyslexic readers into subtypes have been subject to several criticisms, including small sample size, a priori selection, and incomplete classification (Beaton, 2004). Early subtyping schemes proposed by Johnson and Myklebust (1967) and Boder (1973) tended to be based on clinical observations of relatively small numbers of dyslexic participants that made it difficult to generalize to the wider population of dyslexic readers. In these clinical samples, subtypes were typically identified by performing cluster analyses of individual's scores on a battery of tests in order to see how children with similar abilities grouped together. Because people with dyslexia were identified a priori with this approach, it was not possible to know whether these subtype characteristics also existed in normal readers. Another problem with this approach is that the particular tests employed in a study largely determined which characteristics could define subtypes in that study. For example, much of the subtyping research was conducted prior to widespread recognition of phonological deficits as central to dyslexia, therefore tests of phonological awareness were often not administered as part of these batteries. As a result, these subtyping schemes were organized on theoretical bases that proved to be only tangentially related to the current knowledge about reading processes (Stanovich, Siegel, & Gottardo, 1997). Snowling (2001) questioned the usefulness of subtype schemes because no particular taxonomy seems able to classify the full population of dyslexic readers. Despite these concerns, two subtyping schemes persist in the current research literature: subtypes of developmental dyslexia based on the reading patterns of acquired dyslexia and subtypes based on performance on rapid-naming tasks.

Acquired dyslexia subtypes

Castles and Coltheart (1993) attempted to extend the subtypes established in case studies of patients with acquired and phonological dyslexia to a population of developmental dyslexic readers. Children read lists of exception words and pseudowords, and subtypes were identified based on relative imbalances in reading performance on these lists, as compared to normal readers of the same age. Children in the surface dyslexia group demonstrated age-appropriate pseudoword reading, but impaired exception word reading relative to age-matched controls. Conversely, children in the phonological dyslexia group demonstrated age-appropriate exception word reading, but impaired pseudoword reading. Out of the 53 dyslexic children studied, Castles and Coltheart identified 16 with surface dyslexia and 29 with phonological dyslexia, finding that the majority of their dyslexic participants fell under one these two subtypes. For a time, the results of this study seemed to indicate that normal reading, reading problems acquired as a result of stroke, and developmental dyslexia could all be understood using a single heuristic consistent with the dual-route model. Subsequent research, however, cast doubt on this approach.

Several papers followed Castles and Coltheart (1993), presenting two main criticisms of their research methodology. The first point emphasized the importance of understanding dyslexia from a developmental perspective, and questioned the value of imposing characteristics of acquired reading difficulties on cases where reading development had gone awry (Snowling, Bryant, & Hulme, 1996). The second criticism concerned the use of age-matched controls to define impaired reading (Manis, Seidenberg, Doi, & McBride-Chang, 1996; Snowling et al., 1996). Consistent with earlier evidence from Bryant and Impey (1986), these papers argued that the balance between decoding and other word recognition processes changes as reading develops, and therefore strengths or weaknesses in reading skills should be determined relative to reading-level matched controls. Several studies have found that changing the type of control group from age-matched children to reading-level-matched children had interesting effects on the subtypes observed. For example, Manis et al. (1996) compared dyslexic children to both their age-matched peers and their reading-level peers (who averaged 8.5 years of age, 4 years younger than the dyslexic children). They found that fewer children were captured by each subtype when reading-level-matched peers provided the baseline than when age-matched peers were compared. The number of surface dyslexic children shrank most dramatically; only 1 of the 15 readers who met the criteria for surface dyslexia with age-matched controls also met the criteria when compared to reading-level-matched controls.

Stanovich, Siegel, and Gottardo (1997) conducted a study to examine the effect of using reading-level-matched controls on subtype identification First, they re-analyzed the Castles and Coltheart (1993) data using reading-level-matched controls from the original sample, and found that 14 of the 16 surface dyslexic children identified in the original study no longer qualified for this subtype. A second experiment tested the validity of the phonological and surface subtypes with a large sample of third-graders reading below the 25th percentile. The pseudoword and exception word reading of these children was compared to that of their age-matched peers as well as to their reading-level-matched peers. With age-matched controls, the proportion of identified phonological dyslexic children was lower (25%) than in previous studies, but proportion of surface dyslexic choildren (22%) was similar. Using reading-level matched controls did not change the incidence of the phonological subtype, but the number of surface dyslexics was reduced to one. As in Manis et al. and the re-analysis of the Castles and Coltheart data, comparing dyslexic readers to peers reading at a similar level virtually eliminated the surface dyslexia subtype.

Stanovich et al. (1997) concluded that, of the two subtypes, only phonological dyslexia reflected a true deficit in reading development. The surface dyslexia subtype, in contrast, seemed to arise from a delay in reading development, as it essentially disappeared from two sets of data when a reading-level-matched control group was used. Therefore it seems likely that the surface subtype reflects a byproduct of reading difficulties, which is reduced time spent reading. Due to their limited exposure to text, many dyslexic readers lack the word-specific knowledge which is particularly helpful for reading irregular words and that becomes available with wide reading (Snowling, 2001). This evidence suggests that the surface subtype is environmentally based, rather than constitutional in origin. This is consistent with the findings from a behavioral-genetic study of these subtypes conducted with the Colorado Twins data (Castles, Datta, Gayan, & Olson, 1999). Castles et al. found that genetics had a much stronger influence in phonological dyslexia than did shared environment (roughly 2:1), whereas the inverse was observed for surface dyslexia. The stronger influence of shared environment in surface dyslexia parallels, perhaps coincidentally, the conclusion from behavioral studies that the surface subtype captures a delay in exposure to text rather than a different type of dyslexia (Manis et al., 1996; Sprenger-Charolles, Cole, Lacert, & Serniclaes, 2000; Stanovich, Seigel, Gottardo, Chiappe, & Sidhu, 1997).

In summary, several tests of the acquired dyslexia subtype scheme yielded one stable dyslexia subtype, that of phonological dyslexia. In the Stanovich et al. data over 30% of the children studied experienced difficulty reading both words and nonwords, which could indicate a phonological deficit in conjunction with low text exposure. If we add these children to the group of phonological dyslexic readers (25%), who mainly struggled with reading pseudowords, then some deficit in phonological processing accounted for over half of the poor readers in this sample of 68 children. In contrast, one child struggled to read exception words only and the remainder of the children had difficulties in other areas. Therefore Stanovich et al.'s data cast doubt on the viability and usefulness of sub-typing developmental dyslexic children based on the reading patterns of adults with acquired dyslexia. One limitation of this approach is that only a single subtype appeared stable in the population of developing readers. Another is that when struggling readers were compared to age-matched controls, the acquired dyslexia subtypes excluded nearly half of the struggling readers.

Rapid-naming subtypes

Denckla and Rudel (1974, 1976b) conducted the initial research in rapid serial naming by studying how tests of serial naming speed correlated with reading achievement in dyslexic children. Tests of serial naming speed typically present 50 items (objects, colors, digits, or letters) arranged in a five-row grid. Children are timed while naming the items aloud, and the rate of naming speed is highly correlated with reading achievement. Since the Denkla and Rudel studies, rapid automatized naming (or RAN) has been tested in typically developing readers as well as dyslexic children. Color- and object-naming speed in preschool and kindergarten predicts reading achievement in first grade (deJong & van der Leij, 1999; Landerl & Wimmer, 2008; Lervåg & Hulme, 2009). After children learn their letters, naming times for the letter and digit matrices become more predictive of variance in reading than the objects and color RAN tasks (Compton, 2003b; Lervåg & Hulme, 2009; Torgesen, Wagner, Rashotte, Burgess, & Hecht, 1997). Serial naming speed continues to predict reading in the later grades (Meyer, Wood, Hart, & Felton, 1998), after the influence of phonemic awareness diminishes. In writing systems with more transparent orthographies than English, serial naming serves as a better long-term predictor of reading achievement than phonemic awareness (e.g., Furnes & Samuelsson, 2010). In such writing systems, slow reading speed is the main indicator of dyslexia whereas in English dyslexic readers have impaired accuracy as well (Share, 2008). Thus the correlations between rapid naming speed and reading development contribute to our understanding of reading in several ways, including raising awareness about the importance of reading fluency and revitalizing investigations into the role of orthographic awareness in reading development.

RAN research has also broadened our conception of the factors that contribute to dyslexia. Since Denkla and Rudel identified rapid naming deficits in dyslexic children, researchers have pursued the idea that dyslexic children can be divided into accuracy-disabled and rate-disabled readers (e.g., Lovett, 1984). Accuracy-disabled readers had difficulty recognizing words accurately, whereas rate-disabled readers could recognize words accurately, but read them more slowly than most children did. As with other subtyping schemes, this one was unable to account for a large proportion of poor readers. However, the idea of rate-disabled readers foreshadowed the double-deficit hypothesis, which proposes that dyslexic readers can be grouped by those with slow naming speed, those with poor phonemic awareness, and those with a combined deficit (Wolf & Bowers, 1999). Unlike other subtype schemes, the double-deficit hypothesis is able to account for the vast majority of poor readers by considering naming speed deficits as well as phonological deficits (Katzir, Kim, Wolf, Morris, & Lovett, 2008). Genetic studies conducted by Compton, Davis, DeFries, Gayan, and Olson (2001) support the existence of two distinct genetic contributors to dyslexia, as indicated by separate heritability patterns for phonemic awareness and RAN speed.

The double-deficit hypothesis contributes to our understanding of dyslexia in several important ways. First, differences in naming speed differentiate among groups of dyslexic readers in transparent as well as opaque writing systems (for a review see Wolf, Bowers, & Biddle, 2000). Second, it identifies a probable additional source of variance in reading achievement that, in most studies, differentiates dyslexic readers from reading-level matched controls (Ackerman & Dykman, 1993; Segal & Wolf, 1993). In other words, it passes the test that acquired dyslexia subtypes do not. Most importantly, the identification of double-deficits may help schools to identify children in kindergarten who are likely to struggle the most in learning to read—those with phonological deficits combined with slow serial naming. Subtypes based on a combination of rapid naming and phonemic awareness account for 90% of the poor readers in second and third grade (Katzir et al., 2008; cf. Murphy, Pollatsek, & Well, 1988).

A correlational study by Katzir et al. (2008) indicates that about 70% of poor readers are affected by a phonological deficit either alone or in conjunction with slow naming. This proportion aligns with previous research on phonologically based reading deficits conducted by researchers who favor a core phonological deficit model of dyslexia (e.g., Stanovich, Siegel, & Gottardo, 1997). Finding a similar incidence of phonological deficits (measured with two different constructs and from divergent theoretical perspectives) suggests that RAN and phonologically based studies are tapping similar populations of poor readers and, thereby, lends credibility to the double-deficit perspective.

In some respects, then, a given cohort of poor readers resembles a deck of cards that can be sorted in a number of different ways. The sort could involve two categories (e.g., phonological deficit or not) or three categories (e.g., phonological deficit only, serial naming deficit only, or a double deficit). The value of one sorting scheme over another is probably relative to the purpose of the sort. For example, if the goal of the sort is to maximize the number of readers categorized, then the double-deficit subtype scheme appears to be a stronger construct than the core phonological deficit approach. However, if the goal of the sort is to deliver effective reading interventions, then it is not clear what additional benefits are to be gained by the use of RAN subtypes over a core phonological deficit approach that ignores subtypes. Given the lack of a straightforward connection between RAN performance and reading intervention, it is unclear how impaired RAN performance informs a child's intervention program. Evidence of interventions that improve reading through gains in serial naming speed is not yet forthcoming, and initial studies have not demonstrated that training in rapid naming or gains in reading fluency translate into faster RAN performance (deJong & Vrielink, 2004; Lervåg & Hulme, 2009). Nor has research consistently identified the processes underlying naming speed that could affect word recognition and word analysis. For example, Carver (1997) claimed that slow processing speed may be a factor in poor RAN performance, but the findings have been inconsistent. Several studies have found processing speed to be slower in some children with dyslexia (Breznitz & Meyler, 2003; Kail, Hall, & Caskey, 1999; Nicolson & Fawcett, 1994; Stringer & Stanovich, 2000), but other studies did not find significant differences in processing speed between dyslexic readers and age-matched controls (e.g., Bonifacci & Snowling, 2008; Wimmer & Mayringer, 2001). However, it is possible that a better understanding of the cognitive components of RAN performance will some day yield implications for reading instruction.

Issues in the diagnosis of dyslexia

In this section we discuss two common practices that are problematic in diagnosing dyslexia and ensuring that children get effective reading instruction. The first practice is a traditional one of using an IQ–achievement discrepancy to identify which children are dyslexic and will receive special education services. The other practice is the initial referral of children who are identified as dyslexic to vision therapy, under the assumption that problems with eye movement control are the cause of their reading problems.

Discrepancy-based definitions of dyslexia

For most of the past 30 years dyslexia was diagnosed primarily based on the observation of a significant discrepancy between a child's reading level and his or her aptitude as assessed by an IQ test. With this traditional approach, dyslexia was typically diagnosed when the reading score was one or two standard deviations below the IQ. According to Fletcher et al. (2007), this practice can be harmful to children in several ways. First, the discrepancy formula over-identified very bright children who were reading at an average level early in elementary school, as their IQs were substantially above their level of reading achievement. Second, the formula under-identified children with average range IQs, because floor effects in early reading development can prevent a significant discrepancy from being detected. Also, using a discrepancy-based formula to diagnose reading problems can have unfortunate consequences for children who need supplementary reading instruction, as it can delay the identification of a reading problem serious enough to warrant special education services. Stuebing, Fletcher, LeDoux, Lyon, Shaywitz, and Shaywitz (2002) describe this all-too familiar scenario, which we paraphrase here.

> Jack's second-grade teacher notices his reading problems in the middle of the school year. His reading aloud is slow and labored, and he struggles to read new words accurately. After a parent–teacher conference in which Jack's parents express concern about his reading progress, the various specialists in the school convene a meeting to discuss Jack's instructional needs. At this conference the teacher shares a portfolio of Jack's spelling and writing samples and observes that he struggles in these areas as well as reading. She also notes that he performs better in math and other activities that do not involve writing and reading. The reading specialist notes that Jack's difficulties were recognized early in first grade, when he was referred for a supplemental reading program. Although his reading improved somewhat, progress was slower than expected. Given this history and his present struggles, the school decides to conduct an evaluation to determine whether Jack is dyslexic. To qualify for special education services, Jack's IQ must be one standard deviation (15 points) higher than his reading achievement. Unfortunately, the evaluation found only a 10-point discrepancy,

which is not adequate to qualify him as having a reading disability or to receive special education services. Instead, the school develops a plan for accommodations that includes having more time on tests and listening to books on tape during silent reading time. Jack continues to struggle in school, resulting in another evaluation in grade four. At this point, he has fallen far enough behind in reading to exceed the 15-point discrepancy criterion, and he begins receiving special education services.

In essence, the use of a discrepancy-based formula delayed the identification of Jack's reading disability by two critical school years. The reason for this is that children fall behind in reading gradually, starting from when instruction begins in first grade. It often takes some time for them to get far enough behind, relative to their IQ, to qualify for remedial reading instruction. In addition to the years of struggle that Jack experienced unnecessarily while waiting to qualify as dyslexic, his late diagnosis has further implications for his future school performance. By fourth grade, other children his age are using reading to learn new information whereas Jack is still in the process of learning to read. While he spends his school hours improving his reading (hopefully), he will be missing content-area classes that contribute to the expanding vocabularies and general knowledge of his classmates.

In addition to the harmful effects of discrepancy-based diagnoses, there is accumulating evidence that the fundamental assumption behind the formula may be incorrect. Meta-analyses of reading studies have found that the symptoms of poor word reading and spelling persist across the range of normal and above-normal IQs, and are uncorrelated with the discrepancy between individual IQ and reading achievement (e.g., Stuebing et al., 2002). Children who have a discrepancy between their IQ and their reading achievement may have a more obvious disability, but discrepancy criteria do not predict what instructional techniques will be effective (Hatcher & Hulme, 1999; Hoskyn & Swanson, 2000). In addition, a study by Vellutino et al. (1996) found that IQ did not distinguish the children who were easily remediated from those who were not. As Figure 12.2 illustrates, the

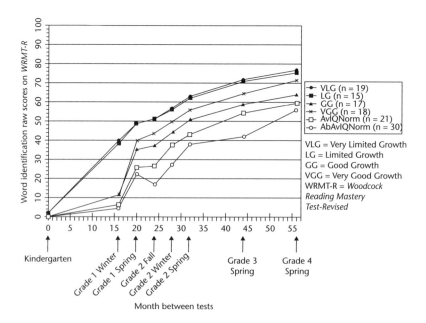

FIGURE 12.2 Growth curves for mean raw scores on the word identification subtest (WRMT-R) for normal and tutored poor readers with IQs in the average (open square) and above average (open circle) range. (Adapted from Vellutino & Fletcher, 2005)

growth curve for the average IQ group was comparable to that of the above-average group at several time points. This finding has been validated by later studies that confirmed that readers with higher IQs than their reading scores (i.e., discrepant readers) could not be differentiated from readers with comparable IQs and reading scores (i.e., non-discrepant readers) in terms of their response to intervention (Fletcher et al., 2002; Lyon et al., 2001; Stanovich, 2005). These individual studies are consistent with two meta-analyses that show negligible differences in the IQs of those who benefit readily from intervention vs. those who continue to struggle (Hoskyn & Swanson, 2000; Stuebing et al., 2002). Therefore, it is difficult to justify the use of IQ to distinguish between poor readers and dyslexic children based on the accumulated data, even though this practice continues to occur in many schools (Fletcher et al., 2007).

Do faulty eye movements cause reading problems?

This is technically possible, in that individuals with oculomotor disorders such as saccade intrusions (Ciuffreda, Kenyon, & Stark, 1983) or congenital jerk nystagmus have accompanying difficulties with reading. Obviously, if a person has difficulty controlling the eye movements that are necessary for reading to proceed smoothly, then learning to read would present enormous difficulties. However, the balance of the evidence indicates that most instances of dyslexia are not caused by faulty eye movements. The eye movements of dyslexic readers and normal readers *do* differ during reading. Dyslexic readers make many more fixations per line and have longer fixation durations, shorter saccades, and a higher frequency of regressions than normal readers (Rayner, 1978a, 1998, 2009). However, the real issue is whether these erratic eye movements are the cause of dyslexia or a consequence of the failure to learn to read. If you think about it, it should be obvious that if you tried to read Hebrew or Japanese (assuming that you cannot read either of these languages) your eye movement pattern would be pretty erratic (i.e., different from skilled readers of those languages).

In a classic summary of eye movement research, Tinker (1958) argued quite strongly that eye movements were not a cause of reading problems, but rather were a reflection of other underlying problems. The possibility of a causal role for eye movement control in dyslexia was dramatically brought back into the spotlight by Pavlidis (1981, 1985). He reasoned that if the cause of dyslexia is constitutional in nature (e.g., due to a sequential disability or oculomotor malfunction), such problems should manifest in non-reading tasks in which sequencing and eye movements are important. Thus, Pavlidis asked his dyslexic participants to fixate continuously on a fixation target that jumped from left to right or right to left across a screen. He reported that when the target moved from left to right, dyslexic participants showed significantly more right-to-left saccades than did normal readers. However, other studies did not find this result (Black, Collins, De Roach, & Zubrick, 1984; Brown, Haegerstrom-Portnoy, Adams, Yingling, Galin, Herron, & Marcus, 1983; Olson, Kliegl, & Davidson, 1983; Stanley, Smith, & Howell, 1983). Although Stanley et al. (1983) failed to find differences in eye movements in a non-reading task, the eye movements of dyslexic and normal readers differed markedly when asked to read text, and this suggests there is something about the act of reading that influenced the different eye movements of dyslexic readers. Hyönä and Olson (1995) measured the eye movements of dyslexic and normal readers when reading texts that contained words of different length and frequency. The eye movement patterns of both groups of readers changed as the texts contained longer and less familiar words. Therefore, it appears that most of the variation in eye movements stems from difficulty with word recognition.

What can we conclude about the relationship between eye movement control and developmental dyslexia? While some dyslexic readers show erratic eye movement patterns in non-reading tasks, it is clearly the case that most do not. However, even for those who exhibit unusual eye movement patterns in reading and non-reading tasks, the eye movements in and of themselves are not the cause of the reading problem (see Rayner, 1983, 1985; Stanovich, 1986). Of course, we accept that improvements in visual acuity can be expected to improve performance on visual tasks to some degree. To the extent that a child with reading problems also has problems associated with binocular disparity or the development of eye dominance (Stein & Fowler, 1982, 1984), opthalmological exercises may be helpful. However, at least one eye movement study now indicates that the binocular disparity problems dyslexic readers may have are unlikely to be rooted in eye movement control systems. Kirkby, Blythe, Drieghe, and Liversedge (submitted) tested whether dyslexic children have binocular disparity problems when compared to normal readers their age (see Figure 12.3). Kirkby et al. found that the eye movements of dyslexic and normally reading children were comparable on a dot-scanning task, and differed on the reading task. These

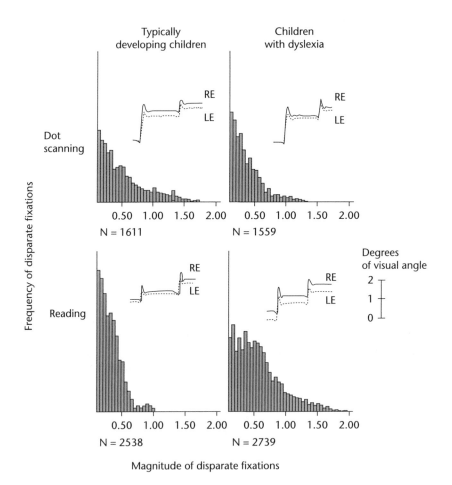

FIGURE 12.3 Histograms represent the frequency of disparate fixations of increasing magnitude. Eye movement traces from an individual participant's right eye (RE) and left eye (LE), are also presented. These traces are representative of the mean fixation disparity for each participant group. The top graphs present data from typical and dyslexic children collected during a dot-scanning task. The bottom graphs present data from typical and dyslexic children during a reading task. Solid lines represent the movements of the right eye and dotted lines represent eye movements of the left eye, and the difference between the two reflects disparity between the two eyes. (Adapted from Kirkby et al., submitted.)

data suggest that when binocular coordination issues are observed in dyslexic children, they are specific to the context of their reading difficulties.

The American Academy of Pediatrics (AAP) and the American Academy of Opthalmologists have issued repeated statements warning parents about the unproven benefits of vision therapy (AAP, 1999, 2009). The title of their statement makes the point: "Vision problems don't cause dyslexia." Although dyslexic children may suffer from vision problems, using vision therapy as a primary response will not remediate core reading difficulties. In practice, children may participate in vision therapy for several months "to see if it helps" their reading. The result is to delay their access to effective educational interventions in the critical early years of learning to read.

Parent attitudes

One problem with the term dyslexia is that many parents and teachers think of it as a pathology, and as a result believe that the child can never learn to read, write, and spell. There is no need for such a hopeless prognosis, if the child can be identified before third grade and provided with the appropriate educational services (Torgesen, 2004; Torgesen & Hudson, 2006). Even with remediation, parents may assume that a dyslexic child will struggle to accomplish the many reading and writing tasks included in a school curriculum. We've heard many parents say, "My child has dyslexia" just as if they were saying "My child has the measles." While dyslexia may be due to some type of abnormality in the way the brain processes information, it is not a virus. Rather, it is a chronic condition with its own set of specific challenges, not unlike diabetes. It would be more appropriate to say "My child is dyslexic," just as we would say "My child is diabetic." The use of parallel grammatical constructions here indicates the recognition of dyslexia as an ongoing neurological state that gives rise to certain symptoms, such as early reading difficulty. If effective educational interventions occur early enough, then normal reading skills may be acquired. In that case, the child becomes asymptomatic, similar to a diabetic who carefully controls insulin levels. However, both children suffer from conditions that pose persistent challenges.

Summary of developmental dyslexia

In the previous sections we have discussed a portion of the developmental dyslexia research, attempting to focus on the central issues that have occupied scientists for the past 30 years. The dominant concept of dyslexia is that it is a code-based word reading disorder that stems from a core deficit in phonological processing. Dyslexia occurs on a continuum of severity, ranging from mild problems with spelling to severe reading impairments that persist into adulthood. The severity of dyslexic symptoms is not correlated with IQ. Dyslexia is a heritable disorder that is passed from one generation to the next on several different chromosomes, and it occurs in girls almost as often as in boys. Researchers have found some neurobiological differences between dyslexic readers and typical readers, particularly in the patterns of activation during word reading. Dyslexic readers exhibit reduced activation in the posterior word reading network relative to typical readers. Psychological research has also been able to resolve some diagnostic issues that permit earlier identification of, and more effective treatment for, dyslexic readers. At this time, the evidence for alternative theories of dyslexia, such as the impact of sensorimotor deficits, is inconclusive. Lastly, our review of the two main subtyping schemes for dyslexia found problems with both, although either may bear fruit for improved intervention with certain dyslexics in the future. Now we turn to discuss another main type of developmental reading disorder.

Reading comprehension deficits

Approximately 10–25% of children with reading disorders can read single words accurately and fluently, but have problems understanding the meaning of text (Aaron, Joshi, & Williams, 1999; Leach et al., 2003). This difficulty was initially termed *hyperlexia*. Roughly speaking, hyperlexic children show the inverse pattern of strengths and weaknesses that characterize cases of dyslexia. Rather than weak coding skills and strong comprehension, hyperlexics tend to have weak comprehension accompanied by relatively strong decoding and word recognition skills. Another difference between hyperlexia and dyslexia is that dyslexic readers have problems reading text but understand spoken information relatively well, whereas the comprehension problems of hyperlexic readers occur during listening as well as reading (Nation, Clarke, Marshall, & Durand, 2004). A third difference is that the gap between word recognition and comprehension tends to increase over time in dyslexia and decrease over time in hyperlexia. Longitudinal studies indicate that relative strengths in word recognition tend to appear by age 6 in hyperlexia and often decline over time, whereas comprehension deficits tend to remain stable over the course of reading development (Grigorenko, Klin, & Volkmar, 2003; Sparks, 2001).

Snowling, Nation, and colleagues have helped to set methodological standards for psychological research with this population. Using independent measurements to assess word recognition and comprehension, Nation (2005) defined poor comprehenders as readers who perform at an age-appropriate level on a standardized test of nonword decoding but have low scores on a test of reading comprehension. Furthermore, their experiments match poor comprehenders with controls matched for nonword reading ability and non-verbal cognitive ability (Nation & Snowling, 1998). Given the proportion of poor comprehenders with low cognitive abilities, controlling for non-verbal ability is especially important (Nation, 2005).

There is debate about the definition of reading comprehension deficits, however. Although researchers generally agree that a comprehension deficit is characterized by weaker text comprehension than single-word reading skills, some researchers focus on the comprehension weaknesses relative to IQ and word reading, whereas others focus on the relative strength of word reading, or hyperlexia. Therefore there is some debate about whether children with superior word reading who lag in comprehension should be considered to have a super-ability or a deficit (Grigorenko, Klin, & Volkmar, 2003). The term hyperlexia is often used by researchers who prefer the super-ability concept, and these researchers are often interested in hyperlexia as it is exhibited by some autistic children. In contrast, many researchers who espouse a deficit model tend to refer to these children as poor comprehenders. Here, we will use both terms (hyperlexia and poor comprehenders) to refer to children who have age-appropriate word-reading skills accompanied by delayed text comprehension ability.

Initial research in this area observed that some low-IQ children developed stronger single-word reading skills than expected given their cognitive ability (e.g., Bender, 1955; Kanner, 1943; Parker, 1919). Evidence suggests that these hyperlexic readers recognize words in a similar fashion to normal readers (Cobrinik, 1974; Healy, Aram, Horowitz, & Kessler, 1982; Mehegan & Dreifuss, 1972). In a study that compared dyslexic and hyperlexic readers, Frith and Snowling (1983) found that, unlike dyslexic readers, hyperlexic readers were similar to normal readers in their proficient nonword decoding, their irregular word reading, and their demonstration of frequency and imageability effects. Therefore hyperlexic readers appear to use normal phonological and orthographic processes to recognize single words, so the unusual behavior they exhibit is in the area of comprehension.

In contrast to the ample research which has illuminated the core deficits of dyslexia, the sources of comprehension problems in hyperlexics are still under investigation. Nation (2005) provides a cogent discussion of the multiple processing deficits that may contribute to the comprehension problems that these children experience both when listening and reading. At a lexical level, hyperlexic children exhibit impaired semantic processing of words and pictures (Nation, Marshall, & Snowling, 2001; Nation & Snowling, 1998, 1999). Research on possible working memory problems generally indicates deficits in verbal working memory among poor comprehenders (Nation & Snowling, 1999; Seigneuric, Erlich, Oakhill, & Yuill, 2000; Yuill, Oakhill, & Parkin, 1989).

In addition to lexical processing and working memory, difficulty with discourse-level processes (such as drawing inferences and comprehension monitoring) is also evident in poor comprehenders. Research suggests that poor comprehenders have problems drawing inferences from text relative to younger normal readers matched for comprehension ability (Cain & Oakhill, 1999; Cain, Oakhill, Barnes, & Bryant, 2001). Later in elementary school, when children mainly expand their vocabularies by inferring the meaning of new words encountered while reading, problems drawing inferences can hamper vocabulary growth (Cain, Oakhill, & Elbro, 2003). Poor comprehenders are also less likely to monitor their understanding of text when reading anomalous passages (Oakhill & Yuill, 1996; Yuill & Oakhill, 1991). Whereas some researchers may regard limited discourse-level processes as causal contributors to poor comprehension, we tend to agree with Perfetti's (1994) suggestion that these are manifestations of the comprehension deficit itself. In other words, the failure of higher-order discourse processes is likely to be a result of underlying weaknesses in semantic and syntactic processes (Perfetti, Marron, & Foltz, 1996).

Today, research on hyperlexia often focuses separately on children diagnosed with autism and children with low verbal IQs. Case and group studies have documented a higher incidence of hyperlexia among children diagnosed with autism (Grigorenko, Klin, Pauls, Senft, Hooper, et al., 2002; Patti & Lupinetti, 1993; Siegel, 1984). Yet hyperlexia has also been diagnosed in children with Tourette's, Turner's syndrome, and mental retardation (Burd & Kerbeshian, 1988; Fontanelle & Alarcon, 1982; Temple & Carney, 1996). Therefore hyperlexia is generally considered an independent, language-based learning disorder that does not result directly from developmental social disabilities but may co-occur with them (Goldberg, 1987; Snowling & Frith, 1986; Whitehouse & Harris, 1984). However, preliminary research into possible subtypes of hyperlexia has identified a number of children with non-verbal learning disabilities who also have stronger word recognition than comprehension skills, and thus fit the hyperlexia profile of reading skills (Richman & Wood, 2002).

Irrespective of a common association between hyperlexia and autism, research that includes both autistic and non-autistic children rarely yields differences in the reading performance of these two groups. For example, Snowling and Frith (1986) did not find differences in their study of comprehension in autistic and non-autistic hyperlexic readers. Both groups could match pictures to sentences that they read or heard at a level predicted by their IQ. The more able children (autistic or not) used sentence context to pronounce homographs (e.g., *tear*), just as the reading-matched normal IQ controls did, and their ability to comprehend sentences and paragraphs was also comparable to normal children. In contrast, the autistic and non-autistic children with lower verbal ability performed much worse on comprehension tasks than normals. Thus Snowling and Frith found that "true" hyperlexia, or an unexpected ability to read single words that exceeds one's comprehension level, was marked by low verbal cognitive ability rather than by the presence or absence of autism.

Saldaña, Carreiras, and Frith (2009) conducted a small-scale study that examined the phono-logical, orthographic, rapid naming, and memory skills in typical children and children with autism, half of whom were hyperlexic. All three groups were matched for age and word-reading scores, and no significant differences in performance were found on any of these tasks between groups.

Some differences did appear within the autistic group. The hyperlexic children, as defined by at least a 10-point discrepancy between their word reading and verbal IQ, performed better on lexical decision and pseudohomophone identification tasks than the non-hyperlexic children. However, the two groups performed similarly on sublexical phonological tasks (e.g., nonword repetition), rapid naming, and digit span tasks. These data contrast with Newman et al. (2007), which reported that hyperlexic autistic children were superior to non-hyperlexic autistic children on phonological processing tasks. However, Newman et al. (2007) did not match their groups with respect to word reading level.

Can an early focus on letter–sound correspondences produce readers with a comprehension deficit?

Niensted (1968) informally reported a higher incidence of hyperlexia among children enrolled in a phonics-based program as compared to children taught reading with a basal reading series. Training in reading comprehension techniques resulted in comprehension gains for the hyperlexic children in that particular school. Some educators continue to assert that phonics instruction is likely to contribute to deficits in reading comprehension. We suspect that it is simply likely to enhance word-decoding skills relative to comprehension, which may develop normally, but we acknowledge that this is an empirical question worth investigating.

Do word recognition and comprehension develop in tandem in normal readers, and does the lag of one skill behind the other indicate future reading problems? With respect to the first point, there is little reason to expect that comprehension and word recognition would develop in lockstep, because the cognitive processes that support the two competencies probably differ (Landi & Perfetti, 2007; Oakhill, 1984; Oakhill, Cain, & Bryant, 2003). Therefore there may be phases in normal reading development in which one leads the other. For example, children initially learning to read often struggle more with word recognition than comprehension, as indicated by their quick realization of the meaning of the sentence after the printed words have been laboriously identified. Conversely, it is fairly unusual to find a child who can read a passage in English smoothly without understanding it—behavior that could be taken as indicative of a relative comprehension deficit. If that behavior was observed, should it raise the concern of parents? This question is best answered empirically, but it is interesting to consider that the pattern of nearly asymptotic word reading accompanied by age-appropriate comprehension is frequently observed in children learning to read in orthographically transparent writing systems, such as Spanish, Finnish, and Italian (Share, 2008). In these orthographically transparent writing systems, children can identify most printed words accurately and fluently by the end of first grade and they typically have word recognition skills that exceed their comprehension and meaning vocabulary. In other words, normal readers can read text aloud that they cannot understand. Similarly, systematic phonics teaching may yield relative strengths in decoding and word recognition relative to comprehension, but this should not be a cause for concern as long as comprehension levels are age-appropriate.

Summary

To close this chapter, let us briefly review the topics discussed: acquired dyslexia, developmental dyslexia, and comprehension deficits. Of these three areas, the topic of acquired dyslexia has been under investigation the longest, and one can trace the roots of this area back to the nineteenth century. The three subtypes of acquired dyslexia are characterized by different patterns of reading errors and the data are usually reported as case studies. Recent studies of large groups of acquired dyslexic individuals shortly after they experienced their brain injury are beginning to alter our understanding about the prevalence of each subtype as well as the effect of coping strategies on observations of patients' reading. In acute patients, phonological dyslexia accounts for more than half of the reading disorders, and the semantic paralexias that characterize deep dyslexia rarely occur.

Developmental dyslexia and reading comprehension deficits affect children's reading. Of the two topics, far more research has been conducted into the former than the latter. Dyslexia refers to a deficit in recognizing single words that usually stems from an underlying core deficit in phonological processing. Children as young as 3 years old can be identified as being at risk for dyslexia based on their success on phonological awareness tasks such as nonword repetition. Although most dyslexic children have a phonological deficit, the impairment is graded so that some mildly impaired children may have spelling problems with intact reading, whereas more severely impaired children may have persistent reading and writing problems. In addition to a core phonological deficit that is causally related to reading achievement, some dyslexic children may also have sensorimotor deficits. Although these deficits may affect their learning in general, we do not yet know how they may contribute to a word-level reading disorder. Some dyslexic children exhibit slow serial naming speed in addition to a phonological deficit, and these children tend to be the most difficult to remediate. Whereas naming speed and the degree of phonological impairment can predict how quickly a child's reading will be remediated, overall intelligence (IQ) is not a reliable predictor of either the risk of reading failure or response to intervention. Developmental reading disorders do not appear to be grounded in basic visual systems that control eye movements. Early identification and treatment are key to helping dyslexic readers, and interventions received in first and second grade are often most effective.

Comprehension deficits are defined as intact word reading and decoding accompanied by delayed text comprehension. As a research topic this area is the newest, so definitional and methodological issues are still being sorted out. In general, researchers compare comprehension-impaired children with control children matched for performance IQ and word-reading ability. Children with comprehension deficits are often referred to as hyperlexic readers in reference to their relatively stronger word-reading skills. However, few studies have found any consistent differences between typical readers' and hyperlexic children's word identification processes. Both groups show frequency and length effects in word recognition. What does seem to differentiate the hyperlexic readers is difficulty comprehending spoken and written language.

13

SPEED READING, PROOFREADING, AND INDIVIDUAL DIFFERENCES

Throughout most of this book we have discussed reading as the careful processing of written material. As we said in Chapter 1, we have approached reading in terms of someone carefully reading a textbook or a newspaper article or a novel (which you must read carefully in order to pay attention to the plot). However, it is clearly the case that we can read in different ways under certain conditions. For example, when you read a novel that is not particularly intellectually stimulating, but which has a certain amount of entertainment value (or "escapism") associated with it, you may be aware of reading much more quickly than you normally do. If you think carefully about it, your introspections may suggest that you are skipping over large sections of the text. You probably do this because many parts of such novels are either totally predictable or very redundant. We would want to classify your reading behavior in such a situation as a mixture of reading (where you are carefully processing the text) and *skimming*. By skimming we mean the type of reading activity in which you skim over the text without really deeply comprehending it. In this chapter we review alternatives to the type of careful reading that we have been discussing in the rest of this book. In particular, we begin the chapter by discussing speed reading, followed by a discussion of research on proofreading and mindless reading. Along the way we discuss the concept of skimming on a number of occasions. We conclude the chapter by discussing individual differences in reading.

Individual differences are important to consider because of the possibility that different readers are doing different things or using different processing strategies. If this were the case, then it would seem unlikely that any single model of reading would be able to capture the essence of these individual differences. From a great deal of research on memory processes, cognitive psychologists know that, while there are similar memory structures, different individuals use different strategies in trying to store information in these structures. Is it possible that people read in vastly different ways? As we shall see, the available evidence indicates that there are individual differences in reading rate and comprehension processes. However, it appears that speed of encoding written material, the reader's background knowledge of the subject, and perhaps the size of working memory can effectively account for much of these differences and that most readers are doing pretty much the same thing when they read. But we're getting ahead of ourselves. Let's first consider speed reading.

Speed reading

Perhaps nothing related to reading is as controversial as the topic of speed reading. As we saw when we discussed the process of learning to read, there is a great deal of emotion and evangelism associated with that topic. With the topic of learning to read there are primarily professional educators involved in the nature of the debates and there can be little doubt that such individuals do have the interests of children uppermost in their hearts (though some of them may be misguided). With the topic of speed reading, however, the fickle finger of profit making is involved and various types of advertisements are used to encourage the unsuspecting public to accept the claims of speed-reading proponents. It is quite likely that somewhere in the community where you go to school or live there is some type of profit-making organization advertising for you to visit them to learn how to speed read.

Let's examine the claims of speed-reading proponents and then consider these claims in light of the research evidence that is available. We begin by noting that there is not very much in the way of good research on the topic of speed reading per se. By this we mean that much of the research that has been done on speed reading is flawed, either because the researchers did not accurately measure comprehension or reading speed, or because they did not test appropriate control groups (to compare speed readers with normal readers, for example). The good research that is available tends to shed serious doubt on the claims of speed-reading proponents.

Speed-reading proponents claim that you should be able to increase your reading speed from 200–400 words per minute (*wpm* from here on), which is the normal range for college students, to 2000 wpm or even faster. There have been speed readers who purport to have reading rates in excess of 10,000 wpm! Central to the claim of speed-reading proponents is the idea that our brain is rather lazy and we only process effectively a small proportion of what it is capable of doing. In particular, speed-reading proponents argue that reading speed can be increased by taking in more information per eye fixation and by eliminating inner speech, which is seen as a drag on reading speed. By processing more per fixation the brain is presumably forced to operate closer to maximal capacity, and supposedly there will be no loss of comprehension. In order to process more per fixation, speed readers are often taught to move a finger rapidly across a line. The eyes are supposed to keep up with the finger so that the speed of visual processing is increased. Eventually the finger is used as a pointer as it zigzags down the page with the reader taking in large chunks of information. The important claim of speed-reading proponents is thus that reading speed can be dramatically increased without any penalty on (or loss of) comprehension.

According to speed-reading proponents, readers can take in a large number of words on each fixation. If you think back to Chapter 1 where we discussed the problems associated with acuity, you will recall that the evidence indicates the ability to resolve the details of letters presented parafoveally and peripherally with respect to the fixation point is severely limited. Thus we make eye movements every 250 milliseconds (on average) to bring a given region of text into foveal vision. If you recall the research we described in Chapter 4 dealing with the size of the perceptual span, you will remember that the results clearly document that the area from which a college student (reading at average reading speeds) obtains useful information is relatively small. In experiments using the moving-window technique (DenBuurman et al., 1981; McConkie & Rayner, 1975; Miellet et al., 2009; Rayner, 1984; Rayner & Bertera, 1979; Rayner, Well, & Pollatsek, 1980; Rayner et al., 1981, 2009a; Underwood & McConkie, 1985) it has been found that readers are generally not influenced by erroneous material lying more than 4 letter spaces to the left of fixation (or the beginning of the currently fixated word) or more than 15 letter spaces to the right of fixation (or more than three words to the right of fixation).

While the moving-window experiments are compelling evidence against the idea that readers can obtain information from an entire line of text in a single fixation, it could be argued that the experiments can't be generalized to speed readers. Perhaps speed readers do something very different from normal readers on each fixation. Indeed, some data that have been obtained on the eye movements of speed readers suggest that speed readers *are* doing something very different. Llewellyn-Thomas (1962) and McLaughlin (1969) each recorded the eye movements of a speed reader. The mean fixation duration was normal or slightly above normal for both readers, and they both moved their eyes down the middle of the left-hand page and then up the middle of the right-hand page, skipping a number of lines per saccade and only fixating once on each line that they fixated on. Notice that this peculiar pattern of eye fixations actually results in the reader processing half of the material in the opposite sequence that the author intended. That is, when the speed reader moves up the right-hand page, he or she is processing the textual information in a different order than the author intended to convey it. McLaughlin concluded that speed reading has only limited usefulness because of confused and sometimes fabricated recall. He suggested that it is possible, and implied peripheral vision and parallel processing as explanatory mechanisms. However, given what is known about peripheral vision and parallel processing, his arguments are not very compelling.

In contrast to Llewellyn-Thomas and McLaughlin, Taylor (1962) recorded the eye movements of graduates of a speed-reading course and reported very little indication of a vertical line of progression. Those participants who showed the greatest tendency to move down the center of the page had the poorest scores on a true–false test of the content of what they had read, scoring no better than chance. Taylor (1965) and Walton (1957) concluded that eye movement patterns of speed readers closely resemble the eye movement patterns produced during skimming of text. More recently, Calef, Pieper, and Coffey (1999) recorded the eye movements of a group of students prior to enrolling in a speed-reading class and after they completed the class. They also compared the speed readers to a control group who did not take the speed-reading course. In the pre-test (see below for further discussion) both groups of readers read at a rate of about 280 wpm. After the speed-reading course, the speed readers read at a rate of about 400 wpm, making fewer fixations (and regressions) per 100 words and shorter fixation durations (228 ms after compared with 241 ms before). Interestingly, their comprehension score on the pre-test was 81% correct, but on the post-test it was 74%. So, while those who took the speed-reading course did read at a faster rate, they certainly didn't reach the astronomical rates typically advertised for such courses. And their comprehension got slightly worse. This certainly coincides with the view expressed by Carver (1985) that reading rates above 400 wpm with good comprehension are quite unlikely.

The most complete study of the eye movement characteristics of speed readers was carried out by Just, Carpenter, and Masson (1982; see also Just & Carpenter, 1987). In their study the eye fixations of speed readers (reading at rates around 600–700 wpm) and normal readers (reading around 250 wpm) were compared. In addition, normal readers were asked to skim the text (producing "reading" rates around 600–700 wpm). When tested after reading, the speed readers did as well as the normal readers (when reading at their normal speed and not skimming) on general comprehension questions or questions about the gist of the passage. On the other hand, when tested about details of the text, speed readers could not answer questions if they had not fixated on the region where the answer was located. Normal readers, whose fixations were much denser than the speed readers, were able to answer the detail questions relatively well. When normal readers were asked to skim the text, both their eye movement patterns and comprehension measures were very similar to those of speed readers.

In general, the results of research investigating the characteristics of speed readers' eye move-ments is consistent with the idea that they are skimming the text and not really reading it in the sense of reading each word. Apparently, they are doing a lot of filling in on the basis of what they already know about the topic being read or what they can surmise from those portions of the text they have actually read.

Although we have never tested speed readers using the moving-window paradigm, it is our observation that fast readers (reading rates around 400–500 wpm) may not be better in the use of peripheral vision than are slower readers (reading rates around 200 wpm). For example, in the type of study in which a foveal mask moved in synchrony with the eyes (Rayner & Bertera, 1979), it was the fast readers that were most disturbed by this situation, not the slower readers. If fast readers are fast because they can use parafoveal and peripheral vision more effectively than slow readers, we would expect that they should do better than slow readers when foveal vision is masked because they should be able to read more effectively from nonfoveal vision. But in fact they were more disrupted than the slower readers. Also, Underwood and Zola (1986) found that fast and slow readers did not differ in the span of letter recognition during eye fixations.

On the other hand, when faster readers were compared to slower readers in a moving-window experiment, Rayner, Slattery, and Bélanger (2010; see also Häikiö, Bertram, Hyönä, & Niemi, 2009) found that fast readers have a larger region of effective vision than slower readers. It is certainly the case that fast readers have fewer fixations per line than slow readers (Rayner, 1978a, 1998, 2009) and they skip over short words more frequently than slow readers do. But what evidence we do have is not necessarily consistent with the notion that fast readers can use parafoveal and peripheral vision more effectively than slow readers. In the Rayner et al. study (2010) it is highly likely that the slower readers had more difficulty processing the fixated words and hence they were able to process words to the right of fixation less efficiently. The conclusion that fast readers don't necessarily use eccentric vision more effectively than slow readers is also consistent with the finding that attempts to train readers to use peripheral vision effectively have not been successful and the comprehension assessments have been equivocal (Brim, 1968; Sailor & Ball, 1975).

Let's turn now to the second major claim of speed-reading proponents. As we suggested earlier, advocates of speed reading claim that reading speed can be dramatically increased by eliminating inner speech. As we pointed out in Chapter 7, we all hear an inner voice pronouncing the words that our eyes are traversing as we read. As we indicated in that chapter, it is not at all clear what the relationship is between the voice that we hear and activity in the speech tract and/or auditory images. Speed-reading proponents are generally not very clear about what they have in mind when they suggest that we should eliminate inner speech, but the idea seems to be that we should be able to read via a purely visual mode and that an involvement of speech processes will slow us down. In essence, the argument seems to be that inner speech is a carryover (or habit) from the fact that we are taught to read orally before we read silently.

Just as the research evidence on eye movements and speed reading does not seem to be consistent with the speed-reading position, so the evidence on elimination of inner speech and reading comprehension does not seem consistent with the position. As reviewed in Chapter 7, the general finding is that if the text is anything but rather simple prose then an attempt to eliminate inner speech results in marked impairments in comprehension. In principle, while purely visual reading might be possible, the bulk of the evidence indicates that inner speech plays a critical role in comprehending most written discourse.

Why do so many people believe speed reading is effective? The reason is that speed reading is portrayed as increasing speed without decreasing comprehension. However, a major problem is assessing comprehension. Let's consider some anecdotal accounts about speed reading that may be relevant. First, consider some observations from a psychologist who enrolled in a speed-reading program and then described his experiences (Carver, 1971, 1972). Students in speed-reading programs are typically given a test (called a *pre-test*) prior to beginning their program that measures both their reading speed and their comprehension. At the end of their training program they are given another test measuring these same two components (called a *post-test*). One observation concerning these two types of tests is that the pre-test is often harder than the post-test. Sometimes trainees are tested repeatedly on the same material in the pre-test and the post-test so that it is inevitable that their performance will improve with training.

More serious is another problem related to the manner in which performance is assessed. A new student in a speed-reading course is typically asked for his or her speed of reading. This is generally measured in a straightforward way and turns out to be in the range of 200 to 400 wpm. After the course, what is usually measured is the Reading Efficiency Index (which we'll call the *RE Index*). The RE Index is based on the argument that rapid reading rates should be qualified by the percentage of the material that the reader is able to comprehend. Students in the program thus have their comprehension measured with a post-test and the reading rate is multiplied by a percent score on the comprehension test. Thus, if a reader had a reading rate of 5000 wpm and scored 60% on the comprehension test, his or her RE Index would be 3000 wpm (5000 × .60). Unfortunately we seldom know how well a person would score on the comprehension test if they had not read the passage. If a multiple-choice test with four questions is used, chance performance (assuming that the person knew none of the material being tested) would be 25% and thus a person who "read" at 5000 wpm and understood absolutely nothing would get a score of 1250 wpm. Since people cannot be assumed to know nothing of the tested material before they read the passage, even this 25% figure is an underestimate of "chance" performance. Should a score of .60 be multiplied by a very rapid reading rate (such as 5000 wpm) to yield a RE Index of 3000 wpm? It doesn't seem quite fair.

Using this line of reasoning, Carver reanalyzed a study (Liddle, 1965) that is widely cited by speed-reading proponents as support for speed reading. In Liddle's study graduates of a speed-reading program were compared to readers who had signed up for the program, but had not yet taken the course. This is in fact a good control group because people who elect to take speed-reading courses could conceivably be different in some important dimensions from other people. Both groups of participants were tested for both speed and comprehension on reading selections using both fictional and non-fictional material. The reading rates were between 300 and 1300 wpm faster for the graduates than the control group. However, there was actually a significant decline in comprehension for the graduates on the fictional test material (an outcome that is not emphasized in the commercial publicity). Indeed, much has been made of the fact that the comprehension scores were not reliably different from each other in the tests of the non-fictional material—the speed readers scored 68% correct and the control group scored 72% correct.

Carver administered the same comprehension test to a group of participants who had never read the passage. These people obtained a score of 57% correct. Common sense and guessing apparently allowed participants who had never read the material to score only a bit below those who had read the material. If we take this new control group's score (57%) as the zero point against which to evaluate the results of Liddle's study, a different conclusion emerges. The control participants who read the passages scored 15 percentage points above the chance level and the speed readers scored only 11 percentage points above it. From this perspective, the speed-reading course can be said to have caused a decline in comprehension of 4/15 (or 27%). While the difference is quite small, it does qualify the conclusion that there was no comprehension loss for the non-fictional material (and we already know that the comprehension loss caused by speed reading was statistically significant for the fictional material). More generally, Carver's observations raise serious questions about the methods by which reading efficiency is measured. The RE Index, in particular, in the context of speed reading, is a dubious measure that may only be limited by the rate at which people can turn pages of text (Crowder, 1982).

Our second anecdotal account is from Crowder (1982) and is based on a case history from the *Journal of Reading*. This observation deals with a performance contract between a speed-reading firm and a school district. The contract called for a dramatic increase in the reading skills for the entire seventh grade of the school district in return for a fee of $110,000. The terms of the contract specified that of the 2501 children in the seventh grade of the district, 75% or more would quintuple their reading speeds (or better) and at the same time these same children would gain at least 10% in comprehension scores. In order to accomplish this, the students were each to spend 24 hours in classroom instruction and 22 hours outside of class practicing what they learned in the reading class.

Reading performance for the entire seventh-grade class is shown in Table 13.1. The first column shows performance on a vocabulary test. As you can see there was an increase in this measure, but we would anticipate that children of this age would show an increase on this measure anyway. The second column shows a large increase in reading speed; in fact, there was a quadrupling in the post-test over the pre-test. The measure shown is an actual wpm measure and does not involve the Reading Efficiency Index that we mentioned earlier. The third column of the table shows that overall comprehension scores were low (about 33% correct), and that there was little difference between the pre-test and the post-test.

How do these performance measures square with the agreed-upon contract? Of all of the 2501 seventh-graders in the district, 259 students both quintupled their reading speed and also increased their comprehension scores by 10%. Thus only about 13% of the children involved met the objectives set out by the contract. At face value these data are certainly problematical for the speed-reading firm. But the problem is even worse than it appears. For one thing, the standardized test used to obtain these results has a leaflet that goes with it stating that the reading rate results are not useful unless comprehension rates are 75% or better. As can be seen in Table 13.1, the obtained scores were more like 33% and so the reading speed measures are not really interpretable. Furthermore, as we discussed above, we have no idea how well people would do on the comprehension test if they had never read the passages. Would such a control group be able to score 33% correct?

A problem even more serious than those we have already discussed is that the measurement procedure was changed from the pre-test to the post-test. (We mentioned this general problem earlier.) The reading rates were supposed to be measured on a 3-minute sample of reading and this was done on the pre-test. However, the speed-reading firm argued for a shorter reading period on the post-test because the full passages used in the test contained only 1000 words. Thus anyone reading faster than 333 wpm would finish before 3 minutes were up and therefore his or her true reading rate would be indeterminate. Of course, one way to solve this problem would be to have

TABLE 13.1   Results of speed-reading program

	Performance measure		
Test	*Vocabulary*	*Words per minute*	*Comprehension*[a]
Pre–	21.5	155	5.2
Post–	24.4	657	4.9

Adapted from Crowder (1982).
[a] Maximum possible = 15.0.

a clock in the reading room and have students write down the time that they finished reading. Such a procedure would probably involve lots of monitors to ensure that students actually finished when they said they did. So the speed-reading firm proposed instead to sample reading for 30 seconds on the post-test and then double the obtained figure to get an estimate of wpm. The school district agreed to this proposal, but it was probably a mistake to do so.

One thing that years and years of research on tests and measurement has told us is that a short test of anything is less likely to be reliable than a longer test. Later on, 440 of the seventh-graders who had participated in this program were asked to read, and estimated reading rates were obtained based upon either a 30-second sample of reading or a 3-minute sample. The short reading test gave a mean rate of 780 wpm while the long test gave a mean rate of 205 wpm (with all tests taken from the same materials). This result certainly makes the results shown in Table 13.1 unconvincing. There may have been other questionable activities and abuses involved in this particular example, but you probably have the point. The school district settled for an award of $99,000 rather than the contracted $110,000—the rate of return for the speed-reading firm would have been about $2500 for each $75 invested (Crowder, 1982).

You may want to argue that the examples we have provided represent isolated, dishonest, business marketing tactics and that such isolated cases of malicious business ethics should not discredit the true value of the product being sold. We would not want to argue that all speed-reading firms are dishonest in their approach. Our point is that as consumers we should be aware of what can and cannot be accomplished in speed-reading programs. Unfortunately the average person in the street does not have the specialized knowledge needed to evaluate the types of claims made by many speed-reading programs.

Our own impressions concerning speed-reading programs are that such programs can improve reading speed. However, it is not necessary to pay exorbitant fees to increase your reading speed. By simply practicing reading more quickly you can learn to increase your reading speed dramatically (Glock, 1949; Tinker, 1958). Reading speeds of 600–800 wpm may be obtainable with reasonably good comprehension provided that the reading material is very easy going—when the text gets difficult we often need to slow down to comprehend effectively, as we have already seen. While we have been very negative about speed-reading programs, they probably do provide training that has a very specific value. Skimming, after all, is a very important skill in our society. In careers that depend on the written word there is simply too much information to be assimilated thoroughly and we are often forced to constantly be selecting what we look at. Someone unable to skim material would find that they spent their entire day reading.

In the 1960s there was a lot of publicity (often from speed-reading firms) about high government officials (including President Kennedy) who were purported to be speed readers. It was argued that such officials could pick up a copy of the *Washington Post* or the *New York Times* and read the front section from front to back in a few minutes. However, before we become too gullible and believe that these officials were actually reading, consider the knowledge and information that such an official would bring to the task. The government official is probably being briefed each day before looking at the newspaper about important world events. Indeed, he or she may well be involved in establishing policy matters and would have first-hand knowledge about many of the events reported in the front section of the newspaper. In contrast, the average person would come to such a situation with very few facts at his or her disposal and would probably have to read it fairly carefully in order to completely understand any given article about it. On the other hand, suppose that you had watched the New Orleans Saints victory over the Indianapolis Colts in the 2010 Super Bowl. Having watched the game first-hand you can read the *Times* report of the game fairly quickly, and a week later when *Sports Illustrated* ran its story on the game you could quickly skim the article looking for some information that you did not previously have (such as an interview with a player or coach that occurred 3 days after the game was completed). While this particular example is related to sports, we all have pockets of specialized knowledge (the stock market, music, movies, experimental psychology, politics, etc.). There is written information in all areas that is prepared for the general reader. For those areas where you already have specialized knowledge, or those areas where you already know most of the facts (as in our Super Bowl example) you can skim over the material quite easily.

Conversations that we have had with graduates of speed-reading courses also lead us to believe that what is effectively being taught is a method for skimming. Most graduates of such courses point out that their reading speed increased as a result of taking the course and most of them acknowledge that they learned to skim effectively. However, with respect to the more extreme claims of speed-reading programs (namely, that the program really teaches people to *read*, not skim, at very fast rates), graduates are somewhat divided. Some insist that the program does not work or that they cannot read at fast rates. And a few say that they could read at astronomical rates but they stopped doing it. According to these people, speed reading was like "gobbling down mashed potatoes" and they had to stop because reading lost its appeal. Finally, there do appear to be a small percentage of the graduates of speed-reading courses who insist that they can do it, and they appear to be rather aggressive about asserting that they can.

This is probably a good place to bring up one final anecdote about speed reading. One of the authors of this book was once interviewed (along with a number of other psychologists who had done research on the process of reading) by the *Washington Post* for an article on speed reading. Many of the points that have been brought out in this section were brought out by the psychologists interviewed. At the end of the article (after all of the points about eye movements and acuity had been discussed) your author and a couple of other psychologists were asked, "Is speed reading really possible?" Your author's response was rather cautious and was something like the following: "I have not directly done research on speed readers, but based on all of the research that I and others have done on eye movements in reading and from what is known about the visual system and acuity, I can't imagine that reading rates of over 800 wpm are really possible." The article appeared in the *Post* and many other newspapers around the country. A number of letters were received from irate speed readers around the country including one who wrote: "Just because you can't imagine something, doesn't mean that it can't happen. Quit living in an ivory tower and learn the joys and ecstasy of speed reading."

Those letters are securely locked away in a file cabinet, yet we continue to maintain that the kinds of reading rates advertised by speed-reading programs are not possible. Speed readers appear to be intelligent individuals who already know a great deal about the topic they are reading and are able to successfully skim the material at rapid rates and accept the lowered comprehension that accompanies skimming (Carver, 1985).

Perhaps it is appropriate to end this discussion of speed reading with Woody Allen's classic line: "I took a speed reading course and read *War and Peace* in two minutes. It's about Russia."

Summary

Although the topic of speed reading receives a great deal of publicity and interest, the available evidence suggests that "speed readers" are skimming the material and not really reading. Successful speed readers appear to be intelligent individuals who already know a great deal about the topic they are reading. When so-called speed readers are given material to read they often do quite well on questions dealing with the gist of the passage, but they cannot answer questions dealing with details unless they fixated in the region where the information to answer the question was located. Also, as we have seen previously, comprehension of difficult material requires the capability of recoding the visual information into subvocal speech. Thus speed readers can skim easy material much more readily than they can skim difficult material.

Proofreading, visual search, and mindless reading

While there has been very little good research on speed reading, there has been a great deal of good research on the process of proofreading. Research on proofreading typically involves appropriate experimental controls and well-designed studies. Thus psychologists who are experienced in issues concerning experimental design would not have the same kind of uneasy feelings about the research that they have about speed-reading research. However, from our point of view, there is a problem with research on proofreading—many researchers who study proofreading presume that the results of their studies inform us about the process of normal reading. While it is possible that results of research on proofreading have important implications for reading, the two tasks are quite different.

When you read a passage of text, your primary goal is to comprehend the passage. When you proofread a passage you are generally looking for typographical errors, misspellings, and omitted words, and as a result comprehension is not the goal. Sometimes proofreading is very much like a visual search task (indeed, in many experimental instantiations of proofreading, participants are asked to search for the presence of certain target letters), and other times it is very much like skimming. While we do not doubt that at times comprehension processes get in the way of proofreading (so that you inadvertently start paying more attention to the meaning of what you are proofreading than the task at hand), we are suspicious about the extent to which results of experiments on proofreading can inform us about reading. To be fair, though, Greenberg, Inhoff, and Weger (2006) demonstrated that eye movements were quite similar when people read passages of text and when they did a letter cancellation task. But although eye movements may look similar in two tasks, that is no guarantee that participants are doing similar things (see Rayner & Fischer, 1996).

Let's make an analogy here. You have probably had the experience of reading some material and after some time realizing that you have been daydreaming and understood nothing of what you have "read." Your eyes kept moving over the text and you may have even been conscious of a few of the words in the text. But, in point of fact, you may have gone through a whole page in "daydream mode" and not comprehended much of the passage at all. Would we want to entertain the possibility that "reading" under such circumstances could inform us about the process of normal reading? Perhaps we might learn something about such "mindless" reading, but the odds are that the results of such research (if we could experimentally induce people to read in "daydream mode" in the first place) would not be very informative. Indeed, research (Reichle, Reineberg, & Schooler, 2010) aimed at detecting when people "zone out" (using self-reports or failure to respond to a probe) has demonstrated that "reading" under these circumstances is much different from normal reading; among other things, the word frequency effect (where readers look at low-frequency words longer than high-frequency words) disappears (which is evidence that the words are not being processed very deeply in daydream mode). This conclusion is also consistent with research showing that during a visual search task (in which participants have to search for a target word in text), the word frequency effect disappears (Rayner & Fischer, 1996; Rayner & Raney, 1996); in a search task through text, participants do not have to process the meaning of the text. With these caveats in mind, let's review some of the research on proofreading and the general conclusions that can be reached from the research.

Widespread interest in proofreading originated with some experiments reported by Corcoran (1966, 1967). We should point out that the task Corcoran and most later researchers favored, while similar to proofreading (i.e., detection of misspellings and other mistakes), was really a slightly different task: visual search. He asked participants to go through a passage and mark off all instances of the letter *e*. What he found was that participants missed silent *e*s nearly four times as often as pronounced *e*s. In a second experiment Corcoran used a real proofreading task: participants were asked to mark as quickly as possible places in text where letters were missing. He found that an absent silent *e* went unnoticed significantly more often than an absent pronounced *e*. Corcoran originally interpreted his findings as evidence of the importance of acoustic coding in a visual task like reading (see Conrad, 1972). However, subsequent research has suggested that while acoustic codes may play some part in the "proofreader's error," they are not the primary source of the problem (see Smith & Groat, 1979).

Try counting the number of occurrences of the letter *f* in Table 13.2. Count them once, and do not go back and count them again. When presented with short passages such as this, participants tend to overlook the *f* in the word *of*. Most people will say that there are three or four instances of the letter *f* in the passage. Actually, there are six—most people miss the *f* in *of*, in part because *f* is pronounced as *v* (but that isn't the whole problem because participants miss the *t, h*, and *e* in *the* as well). Indeed, if participants are asked to count the number of times that the word *of* occurs, they come up short there also.

There is now a rather substantial literature (see Drewnowski & Healy, 1977, 1980; Haber & Schindler, 1981; Healy, 1976, 1980; Healy & Drewnowski, 1983) showing that proofreaders tend to miss letters in short function words like *of, the*, and *and*. That the effect has something to do with reading is clear from the finding that errors on such words occur much more frequently when the function word is embedded in coherent text than when it occurs in scrambled text or in word lists (Schindler, 1978). Thus it appears that, with coherent text, it may be difficult for readers to turn off their reading habits which are so deeply ingrained. It might be tempting to think that participants miss the letters in function words because they skip over them (or do not fixate on them). However, some recent eye movement experiments (for a summary see Saint Aubin, Kenny, & Roy-Charland, 2010) demonstrate that while function words (like *the, and, for*) are more likely to be skipped than control content words (*tie, ton, toe, fun, fat, fog*) and there are more omissions for skipped than for fixated words, the missing-letter effect (more omissions for function than for content words) was found for both the subset of skipped and the subset of fixated words.

On the basis of this type of research there has been a great deal of theorizing about perceptual units in reading. But, again, our impression is that task differences make generalizations from proof-reading to normal reading somewhat dubious. If experiments force readers to fixate on every func-tion word (as in Schindler's word list arrangement), the proofreader's error decreases markedly. We know that, in reading, short function words are often not fixated (see Chapter 5), and the fact that participants miss target letters in such words is probably highly related to where they fixate (Saint Aubin et al., 2010). Proofreading errors of this type can thus be explained in terms of a model such as that of Paap et al. (1982) (see Chapter 3) without having to postulate special perceptual units for short, common function words. Presumably it takes less perceptual evidence to fire off the lexical entry of a predictable function word, and participants who skip the function word do receive less perceptual evidence. In Paap's model, letters can be identified either because their detectors are

TABLE 13.2 Count the number of Fs in this passage

FINISHED FILES ARE THE RESULT OF YEARS
OF SCIENTIFIC STUDY COMBINED WITH THE
EXPERIENCE OF YEARS.

---

activated, or because the word that contains them is activated. But if target letters are identified largely on the basis of the activation of letter detectors, one would predict poorer identification of letter targets in function words.

Most subsequent research in the area used the visual search task. The metaphor that reading is "visual search for meaning" that has occasionally been made goes too far: reading is more of a construction of meaning than a search for a pre-stored meaning (see Chapters 8 and 9). However, studies comparing visual search and reading have revealed some interesting findings. For example, Spragins, Lefton, and Fisher (1976) asked participants to search through text for a target word, and compared eye movement characteristics to when these same participants read text. Table 13.3 shows the differences in primary eye movement characteristics and search (or reading) rate in the two different conditions. Notice that search rate was considerably faster than reading rate. Participants achieved the faster rate in the search condition primarily by moving their eyes a greater distance with each saccade than in reading. In essence, participants' performance in the search task appears to be quite similar to that of participants who are skimming text. As in situations in which reading and skimming are compared (see Just et al., 1982), Spragins et al.'s data suggest that more information is being processed per fixation in their search task than in reading. However, it is not clear that more visual information is really processed per fixation in the search task (Rayner & Fisher, 1987). First, as we argued earlier, the perceptual span in reading is appreciably larger than the average size of a saccade; thus it is hazardous to infer the amount of visual information extracted from the size of a saccade. In addition, at least some of the difference in the speed of the tasks is due to discourse comprehension processes; it seems quite likely that if a surprise comprehension test were given, participants in the reading condition would do considerably better than those in the search condition.

Another point that should be stressed is that the speed of search varies widely from task to task. For example, the more visually similar the target is to the distractors (that is, non-target letters), the slower the search is and the shorter the saccades are (Rayner & Fisher, 1987). In addition to being influenced by changes in the materials, the rate at which participants are able to process information in visual search tasks depends a great deal on exactly what they are asked to do. When participants are asked to count all occurrences of given targets, their "reading" rate may be as slow as 50–80 wpm. When they are asked to search for a given target word, their rate may be as fast as 400–500 wpm.

As we pointed out in the prior section, the speed of "reading" also depends on the exact task. When people skim text their "reading" rates range between 500 and 1000 wpm, whereas in normal reading, reading rates for college age students typically range between 200 and 350 wpm. Some people might want to argue that results from these different tasks are generalizable to one another. However, our inclination would be to argue that each involves different strategies and processes on the part of the participant. Thus we might well have a model of proofreading for misspellings that differs from a model of proofreading (or searching) for a target word. And both types of models would be different from a model of reading in which the goal is to comprehend the text.

TABLE 13.3   A comparison of reading and search for a target word

	WPM	Words per fixation	Saccade length	Fixation duration
Reading	256	1.2	5.6	234
Search	435	2.2	10.1	244

From Spragins, Lefton, and Fisher 1976.

Flexibility in reading

We have been discussing tasks that are ostensibly related to reading, yet which still differ in critical ways from reading, and we have argued that strategies that you may adopt in such tasks result in critical processing differences from normal reading. To what extent are we able to vary our strategies within the task of reading itself? Do we read in different ways depending on our purpose? We suggested at the outset of this chapter that we can. In fact it has long been recognized that people have some flexibility in the way they read a passage. In addition it is generally accepted that the ability to be flexible in reading is a characteristic of better, more mature readers. Walker (1938) found that skilled readers are more adaptive to the nature of the material than less-skilled readers, in that the skilled readers' eye movement patterns were more disrupted by comprehension failure than were those of less-skilled readers.

A number of studies have been aimed at assessing the degree to which readers demonstrate flexibility in reading. One measure that has often been used to assess such flexibility is reading rate. The efficient reader is thought to be one who will modify his or her reading rate according to the difficulty of the material being read, the familiarity of the material, or the purpose of reading (whether seeking to gain only an overview of the passage or to understand and remember factual details from the passage). Studies that have investigated the effects of these variables, however, have found surprisingly small changes in reading rate. Although most of the studies have found some changes in reading rate resulting from the manipulations of passage difficulty or of instructions to the readers, this change has usually been quite small (Carillo & Sheldon, 1952; Rankin, 1970).

Aside from being admonished to vary their reading rate, readers are also advised to focus on the acquisition of different types of information from passages, depending on their purposes in reading them (Tinker, 1965). That readers are able to do this is nicely demonstrated in studies by Anderson and Pichert (1978) and Pichert and Anderson (1977). In these studies participants were asked to read stories from two different perspectives. Thus a story was read about two boys playing hooky from school who go to one of the boys' homes because his mother is never there on Thursday. The story describes quite a bit about the house that they are playing in. For example, since the house is quite old it has some defects, such as a leaky roof, a damp and dusty basement, and so on. On the other hand, because the family is quite wealthy they have a lot of valuable possessions, such as ten-speed bikes, a color TV set, a rare coin collection, and so on. Half of the participants in the experiment were asked to read the passage from the perspective of a homebuyer and half from the perspective of a burglar. Clearly, a leaky roof is important to a homebuyer, but unimportant to a burglar. The reverse is true of a color TV set or rare coin collection. Anderson and Pichert found that what readers could remember from the passage was influenced by the perspective that they had been asked to take.

In an experiment designed to investigate the flexibility of reading strategies, McConkie, Rayner, and Wilson (1973) asked groups of readers to read a series of passages. Each group only had to answer one type of question after each passage. For example, some participants were consistently given questions testing numerical facts presented in the passage, others were consistently given recognition questions, and some were given questions that tested higher-order understanding of the passage. After a number of passages, participants were given all three types of questions in a surprise test. McConkie et al. found that readers were able to adopt different strategies as evidenced by their reading rate and by the types of questions that they could answer. They found that when readers were given a certain type of question (e.g., high-level vs. low-level) consistently after each passage, they were able to increase reading speed and still answer that type of question quite well. However, on the surprise test the participants had a difficult time answering questions of the type different from those they had been experiencing. However, participants who were given question types that encouraged them to read more slowly and carefully were better able to answer questions that were different from those they had been receiving.

We can see, then, that skilled readers are able to be quite flexible in their approach to reading. What readers can remember from text appears to be a sensitive indicator of their purpose in reading. Thus, strategies involved in storing text information in memory clearly exist. Variations in reading rate across different strategies are not quite as obvious, however, which may imply that (within a broad range) when the reader is trying to comprehend some aspect of the text, reading rate will not vary too much. However, again, when the purpose is to read for very specific types of information or to skim the material, reading rate increases rather dramatically over the reading rate evident where more general comprehension processes are involved.

Individual differences

As we saw in Chapter 12, the question of what differentiates a good reader from a poor reader is an important one and one to which considerable attention has been paid. In this section, however, we will not devote much space to that question. An excellent book by Perfetti (1985) goes into great detail about differences between good and poor readers. Essentially, much of the literature suggests that differences in "intelligence" and in short-term memory can account for endpoint differences in the reading achievement of good and poor readers. All other things being equal (which they probably never are), someone with an IQ score of 120 will be a better reader as an adult than someone with an IQ score of 90. IQ scores and various measures of skilled reading ability are known to be highly correlated, and undoubtedly intelligence can account for much of the difference between people who might be classified as good and poor readers. Perfetti's (and others') analyses lead to the striking conclusion that when IQ differences are taken into account, differences in short-term memory processing can account for much of the difference between adult good and poor readers.

Our primary concern in this section will be to examine the extent to which there are differences among readers that we would generally consider to be good readers. In essence, throughout this book we have been discussing reading as if the processes and strategies involved were very much the same for all people. Is it possible that readers are doing somewhat different things and still coming out with the same end product, namely comprehension of the text?

Let's begin this discussion at the most basic level. We know that, during reading, eye movements are very important in the sense that they serve as the means by which readers are able to acquire new information from the text. We also know, as we pointed out in Chapter 4, that there are differences in the eye movement characteristics of good vs. poor readers. If you look at Table 13.4 it is obvious that some people read quickly because they make fewer fixations than readers who are not quite so fast, while others may read a bit more quickly by making shorter fixations. In fact, while reading rate can be increased by making either fewer fixations or shorter fixations (or both), most of the increase is generally due to making fewer fixations. In light of the individual differences that are evident in Table 13.4, and on the basis of data collected in his lab, Rothkopf (1978; Rothkopf & Billington, 1979) suggested that individual differences in eye movement patterns are extremely important. Rothkopf reported what appear to be marked differences in readers in both their eye movement patterns and their responses to changes in reading task demands, and has warned that eye movement patterns of different individuals may not be sufficiently alike to warrant a single theoretical model of reading processes. On the other hand, on the basis of a large-scale examination of individual differences in eye movement patterns as participants read easy

TABLE 13.4 Mean fixation duration, mean saccade length, proportion of fixations that were regressions, and words per minute (WPM) for 10 good college-age readers

Participant	Fixation duration[a]	Saccade length[b]	Regressions (%)[c]	WPM
KB	195	9.0	6	378
JC	227	7.6	12	251
AK	190	8.6	11	348
TP	196	9.5	15	382
TT	255	7.7	19	244
GT	206	7.9	4	335
GB	205	8.5	6	347
BB	247	6.7	1	257
LC	193	8.3	20	314
JJ	241	7.2	14	230
Mean	215.5	8.1	10.8	308

From Rayner,1978a. For these participants there was a correlation between mean fixation duration and mean saccade length of .81; that is, the faster readers had shorter mean fixation durations and longer mean saccade lengths. Thus the WPM score correlates about .89 with both mean fixation duration (− .89) and mean saccade length.
[a] In ms.
[b] In character spaces (4 character spaces = 1° of visual angle).
[c] Percentage of total fixations that were regressions.

and difficult text under six different experimental conditions, Fisher (1983) concluded that the extent of individual differences in reading styles is not sufficient to challenge the validity of a general model of reading behavior. Fisher found that most individual differences in terms of eye movement behavior are found at the level of main effects and do not interact with task demands. In other words, there are differences between readers, but these differences remain when the task is changed from reading to search, for example.

Our contention is that, although there are clearly individual differences in eye movement characteristics and patterns among good readers, in terms of eye movements most good readers are pretty much doing the same thing. For the most part this observation derives from the large number of studies we have done using the moving-window paradigm. In those studies the effect of a restricted window affects all readers in pretty much the same way. That is, as small windows are presented, readers decrease saccade length (and make more fixations) and increase fixation duration in comparison to when larger windows are presented. Thus, while there are indeed individual differences in eye movement characteristics, our sense is that they may not be particularly important in explaining reading performance. In large part this is because of the anatomy of the eye in which the distinction between foveal, parafoveal, and peripheral regions of text holds for all readers. We have already noted that Rayner, Slattery, and Bélanger (2010) found that slower readers have a smaller perceptual span than fast readers, but this probably has more to do with difficulties encoding fixated words than differences in peripheral acuity.

In an attempt to determine what differentiates a good fast reader from a good slower reader, Jackson and McClelland (1975) tested participants on a number of information-processing tasks. Table 13.5 and Figure 13.1 show some of the primary results from the experiment. Let's run through the different tasks that were used. First, however, note that the mean reading speed (wpm) for the average readers was 260 wpm and the mean reading speed for the fast readers was 586 wpm.

In the free report task that was used, five-word sentences such as *Dan fixed the flat tire* were presented for 200 milliseconds. All the sentences contained short words such as in the example.

TABLE 13.5   Individual participant results[a]

Participant	Speed	Comprehension	Effective reading speed	Free letters	Report words	Sentences	Threshold	Overall span	Unrelated letters	Forced choice
JC	206	70	144	43	37	0	64.5	79	53	57
MS	242	85	206	86	83	40	54.0	94	47	82
MW	257	80	206	65	63	15	49.0	81	52	65
PS	299	70	210	41	36	0	50.5	77	50	68
EM	268	80	215	62	61	20	44.0	88	57	76
JS	286	90	260	66	66	20	54.5	88	59	79
Mean	260	79	207	61	58	16	52.7	85	53	71
MT	451	80	361	82	74	25	46.5	88	71	79
CG	525	80	420	78	70	15	50.5	73	63	75
SH	615	70	430	90	88	50	50.2	81	66	79
GS	528	90	475	93	89	45	57.0	88	66	79
FM	542	90	487	87	83	40	42.0	85	61	81
BG	855	90	769	93	87	50	49.5	92	57	83
Mean	586	83	490	87	82	39	49.3	85	64	79

From Jackson and McClelland (1975).

[a] All numbers are percentage correct except Speed and Effective reading speed (words per minute) and Threshold (milliseconds).

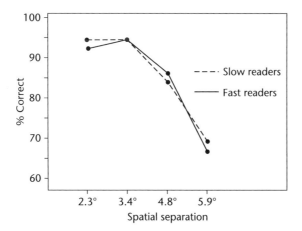

FIGURE 13.1   Percentage of letters correctly reported in letter separation task for each spatial separation. Means for fast readers and slow readers are plotted separately. From Jackson and McClelland (1975).

Participants were asked to fixate on a target point and then the sentence was presented around the fixation. After each exposure, participants wrote down as much of the sentence as they could. They were instructed to write down any letters they saw whenever they recognized letters without identifying the whole word. The number of letters reported and the number of words reported are in the columns labeled *Free letters* and *Report words* in Table 13.5, respectively. The column labeled *Sentences* presents the percentage of time that participants were able to report all five words from the sentence. In a single-letter threshold task, capital letters were presented starting at 20 milliseconds and participants were asked to report the letter. If the participant could not report the letter, the duration of the exposure was increased incrementally until the participant could report it. The row labeled *Threshold* presents the average of the final 20 trials participants were given in which they could identify the target letter.

In the unrelated letter task, eight randomly chosen letters (all consonants) were presented for 200 milliseconds. After each exposure, participants wrote down eight letters in any order, guessing if necessary. The results of this task are shown in the column labeled *Unrelated letters.* In the forced-choice test, participants were shown a sentence such as *Kevin fired a new worker* for 200 milliseconds and then asked to indicate if the word *fired* or *hired* was present in the sentence. In all of the tasks in which stimuli were presented for 200 milliseconds the exposure of the stimuli was preceded and followed by a mask consisting of overlapping Os and Xs. In the final letter separation task two letters were presented at different distances to the left and right of fixation for 200 milliseconds and participants had to write down the letters. The results of this task are shown in Figure 13.1.

Jackson and McClelland found that there were no differences between the fast and slow readers in what they termed the *sensory tasks*. That is, on the single-letter threshold task, thresholds for the two groups did not differ. Also, on the letter separation task there was likewise no difference between the two groups. On all other tasks, however, there was a difference in favor of the fast readers. Jackson and McClelland concluded that breadth of field from which the reader can utilize visual information was approximately the same for the fast-reader group and the slow-reader group. What apparently distinguishes the two groups is that faster readers are able to encode more of the contents of each fixation, whether or not higher-order linguistic structure is present. The results of the study also suggested that differences in reading speed are not due to the reader's ability to infer or fill in missing information (in contrast to our earlier claims that speed readers are successful to the extent that they can fill in information without reading it).

Jackson and McClelland's analysis that differences in reading speed were not due to basic sensory skills is consistent with what we have been arguing in this section. A large number of other studies (Baddeley, Logie, Nimmo-Smith, & Brereton, 1985; Carr, 1981; Daneman & Carpenter, 1980, 1983; Frederiksen, 1982; Jackson, 1980; Jackson & McClelland, 1979; Masson & Miller, 1983; Palmer, MacLeod, Hunt, & Davidson, 1985) have been undertaken to examine how relatively good readers may differ from each other in component skills related to reading. The primary approach taken by these different investigators has been to present participants with a large battery of tests (as in Jackson & McClelland) and then to determine how the different tasks (and differences on these tasks) correlate with some measure of reading performance.

Rather than reviewing all of the types of tasks that have been used and the general outcome of each study, we will present the important points to be gleaned from this research. The tasks that have been used in these studies include tests of sensory functions, verbal and quantitative reasoning skills, memory span, listening comprehension, visual letter matching, lexical decision, naming ability, picture–sentence verification, semantic categorization, and so on. Among the important results that have emerged from this research are the following. First, reading performance on these various information-processing tasks correlates rather well when words are used as stimuli, but not so well when letters are used (Palmer et al., 1985). Second, reading speed and comprehension have different correlations with the information-processing measures (Jackson & McClelland, 1979; Palmer et al., 1985). This finding basically suggests that factors that affect reading speed may differ somewhat from those factors that affect comprehension processes. Third, much of the variability in reading speed appears to be due to the speed with which participants can access memory codes for meaningful material as in word identification (Jackson, 1980; Jackson & McClelland, 1979). Fourth, much of the variability in comprehension processes appears to be due to working memory differences between fast and average slow readers (Baddeley et al., 1985; Daneman & Carpenter, 1980, 1983; Masson & Miller, 1983). For example, the research tends to suggest that readers with small working memories devote so many resources to the decoding aspects of reading that they have less capacity for retaining earlier verbatim wording in working memory. Finally, while reading speed is only moderately correlated with listening comprehension, reading comprehension ability is apparently indistinguishable from listening comprehension ability (Jackson & McClelland, 1979; Palmer et al., 1985).

In essence, the evidence from these studies dealing with individual differences suggests that good readers do not differ at the basic sensory or perceptual level in terms of what they perceive in a fixation. Rather, the speed with which material can be encoded and accessed in memory appears to play a part in determining reading speed, and the size of working memory appears to play a role in determining comprehension processes. As such, these data do not imply that fast and average/slow readers (all of whom we would want to categorize as relatively good readers) are doing vastly different things. Readers may use sophisticated strategies that help them remember things that they have read, and some may be more adept than others in using these strategies. When we examine individual differences in terms of on-line and immediate processing of text, it appears that most good readers are doing essentially the same thing; some may do it a bit slower (hence their reading speed will be slower) and some may not have as good working memory abilities (hence their comprehension will not be quite as good) as others. Yet the bottom line is that there are many more similarities than differences, and hence it is justifiable to try and specify a general model of the reading process.

More recently a handful of studies have examined eye movements in the context of individual differences. Schilling et al. (1998) found that participants tended to rank themselves consistently in both overall speed and in the size of the word frequency effect across naming and lexical decision tasks and eye fixation time measures. Several studies have examined working memory, via the use of the Daneman and Carpenter (1980) sentence span task. Thus, Clifton et al. (2003) found that low-span readers spent more time re-reading the ambiguous region of reduced relative clause sentences than high-span readers. Traxler, Williams, Blozis, and Morris (2005) initially reported that working memory span predicted syntactic and semantic effects on eye fixations during reading. Traxler (2007) found that low-span readers had more difficulties (expressed as longer go-past times and total fixation time) integrating relative clauses with preceding sentence fragments if these clauses had an ambiguous attachment. However, Kennison and Clifton (1995) examined whether differences in working memory capacity correlate with parafoveal preview and found no effect. One of the problems with determining effects of working memory span is that working memory capacity correlates with other reading variables (e.g., reading speed, vocabulary, and print exposure). One way to tease apart the influence of correlated variables is through a statistical analysis termed *hierarchical linear modeling* (HLM). Traxler et al. (in press) applied HLM techniques to re-analyze the Traxler et al. (2005) data. When reading speed was entered into the statistical model along with working memory span, span did not interact with the influence of syntactic and semantic variables on eye movements. Rather, reading speed provided the better model for these data. The eye movement measures indicated that slower readers had more difficulty reading sentences with animate subjects and object relative clauses than did faster readers. Future research will determine whether other results attributed to working memory span may also be better accounted for by simple reading speed.

Kuperman and Van Dyke (2011) have recently reported a large-scale study of how individual differences in reading-related tasks affect eye movement control during reading. They used a sample of 16–24-year-old not-college-bound participants, and used a large battery of tests that they then related to their participants' eye movements during reading. They found that individual scores in rapid serial naming (the RAN test; see Chapter 11) and standardized word recognition tests were the only measures from their battery that reliably predicted fixation durations and re-reading patterns. They also found that the effect sizes of these two variables were larger in magnitude than established effects due to word length and word frequency. Finally, they found that poorer readers tended to fixate at an earlier position in a word (see also Hawelka, Gagl, & Wimmer, 2010).

Other studies have used scores on the Nelson-Denny test, which provides a standardized measure of reading comprehension, to identify individual differences in reading skill. Ashby, Rayner, and Clifton (2005) used this test in an investigation of highly skilled and average college readers' word recognition processes. They compared the eye movements of the two groups that were recorded as they read high- and low-frequency words in predictable, unpredictable, and neutral contexts. In the neutral and predictable contexts both groups of readers fixated low-frequency words longer than the high-frequency words (the typical frequency effect). In unpredictable contexts frequency effects appeared for the highly skilled readers but the average readers did not fixate the low-frequency words any longer than the high-frequency words. The re-reading patterns of the average readers indicated that their eyes left low-frequency predictable words before recognition was complete and re-read the sentence contexts, which suggests that they relied on context to recognize less-familiar words. In contrast, finding comparable frequency effects across different predictability conditions for the highly skilled readers indicates that their automatic word recognition processes were resilient to changes in text predictability. Therefore Ashby et al. (2005) demonstrated that the best college readers maintain stable, automatic word recognition processes, although they may adjust their conscious reading strategies for different types of text.

Three other studies used the Nelson-Denny test to examine the phonological processing of high- and low-skilled college readers. Jared, Levy, and Rayner (1999) measured eye movements as good and poor readers read sentences that contained a correctly spelled target, a homophone of the target, or a misspelled control. They found that poor readers were less likely to notice homophone errors than the misspelled controls. In contrast, the good readers had comparable gaze durations in the homophone and misspelled conditions—both of which were longer than gaze times on the correct target. Unsworth and Pexman (2003) conducted a lexical decision study that demonstrated poor readers were more likely to accept pseudohomophones as words than non-homophone controls. Whereas these two studies (and several others) indicate that poor readers rely more on phonological processes to identify words than good readers do, the third experiment provides an important caveat to that conclusion. Chace, Rayner, and Well (2005) conducted an eye movement study to examine whether differences in reading skill affect parafoveal word recognition processes during silent reading. Sentences were presented that contained a target for which the parafoveal preview was either the identical word (*beach–beach*), a homophone (*beech–beach*), an orthographic control (*bench–beach*), or a consonant string (*jfzrp*). Chace et al. found that the gaze durations of the more-skilled readers were comparable in the homophone and identical preview conditions, and shorter there than in the control and consonant string conditions. In contrast, the less-skilled readers had roughly comparable mean gaze durations in all four conditions. Finally, the gaze durations of the two groups of readers did not differ in the orthographic and consonant string conditions. In sum, the Chace et al. data indicate that phonologically similar parafoveal previews reduced word recognition time for the better readers only, and that the worse readers did not benefit from any parafoveal information. Together, the findings from Jared et al. (1999), Unsworth and Pexman (2003), and Chace et al. (2005) suggest that more-skilled readers primarily process phonological information parafoveally whereas less-skilled readers are more susceptible to foveal phonological effects.

As a final discussion point concerning individual differences, let's consider older readers in comparison to young college-aged skilled readers. Older readers tend to read more slowly than younger readers; their fixation durations are longer and they make more regressions (Laubrock, Kliegl, & Engbert, 2006; Rayner, Reichle, Stroud, Williams, & Pollatsek, 2006). However, their reading comprehension is typically as good as, or better than, younger readers. Older readers have a smaller and more symmetric perceptual span (Rayner, Castelhano, & Yang, 2009a) than younger readers, and on some fixations they obtain less preview benefit than younger readers (Rayner, Castelhano, & Yang, 2010). While the older readers apparently do not take longer to encode words in the disappearing text paradigm than younger readers (Rayner, Yang, Castelhano, & Liversedge, 2010), it is interesting that they show less disruption to the sudden onset of a mask during reading than younger readers. The general conclusion reached by Rayner et al. is that older readers tend to read more slowly than younger readers (presumably due to some type of general cognitive slowing). In order to circumvent the slower reading, the older readers engage in guessing strategies concerning what the next word is more frequently than younger readers. This results in longer average saccades for older readers (Laubrock et al., 2006; Rayner, Reichle, et al., 2006) but, because they are sometimes wrong about their guess, it also results in them making more regressions than younger readers. The main point to be gleaned from this discussion is that while older readers are quite similar to younger readers in many ways, they engage in a more risky reading strategy to try to compensate for the fact that they read more slowly than they previously did.

Summary

In this chapter we discussed alternative types of "reading" such as speed reading, skimming, and proofreading. We also discussed individual differences in reading. With respect to speed reading, we concluded that adults who read at very fast rates are primarily skimming the text, picking up the general gist of what they are reading as well as a few details. However, they are not able to get all of the detail from the text that normal readers do, and they are more willing than normal readers to accept the lowered comprehension that accompanies skimming.

In proofreading the usual task is to look for spelling or grammatical mistakes and/or to ensure that each sentence makes sense. However, most of the research on proofreading has used a visual search variant of the task in which participants search for all instances of a given target letter or target word. We argued that the link between these types of tasks and reading is somewhat tentative. However, all the work on skimming and proofreading (as well as research in which readers are instructed to read for different purposes) does demonstrate that skilled readers are quite flexible in the range of reading or reading-like behaviors they can employ; they can modulate the "reading" speed as a function of their task or goal. Also, what they can comprehend from the passage will be influenced by the reading task or their goal; participants reading for a specific type of information may not be able to remember much of the information unrelated to the type of information they were trying to acquire.

In the final section of the chapter we reviewed research dealing with individual differences. There are clear individual differences in adult reading speed: some people read more slowly than others, and the slower readers make shorter saccades (or more fixations), have smaller perceptual spans, and/or have longer fixations. However, in terms of basic perceptual processes, the data suggest that all skilled readers are doing much the same thing. Readers undoubtedly use sophisticated strategies to help them remember what they have read, but the basic way in which information is initially encoded and processed is quite similar for all skilled readers. Thus we suspect that it is reasonable to attempt to specify a single general model of the process of reading that will be appropriate for virtually all skilled readers.

14

FINAL OVERVIEW

Our goal in this final chapter is simply to summarize some of the things that we know about reading and to highlight what has yet to be learned. Throughout this book we have concentrated on presenting you with what is known about reading. In many cases, however, the data were incomplete or equivocal, and so we summarized the best available evidence. When it was necessary to provide some theoretical interpretation we did so, and our interpretations have been guided by an implicit general theory of the reading process.

It would be nice if we had a comprehensive model of the reading process. However, despite the fact that there has been considerable accumulation of knowledge of the reading process, for the most part the advances have come from the development of specific aspects of the process, such as models of word recognition, eye movement control, sentence parsing, and discourse processing (see Rayner & Reichle, 2010; Reichle, 2012, for further discussion of the development of such models). In the earlier edition of the present book we presented a number of "models" of the reading process, including one of our own, but we clearly noted that all of the models were really inadequate. Unfortunately things haven't changed that much in the 20-plus years since the original version was published. Rather than describing in any detail models that we clearly view as inadequate for capturing the reading process, we will provide some general comments concerning possible classes of models of the reading process, briefly discussing the notions of top-down, bottom-up, and interactive models of reading. We will also briefly describe the model that we presented in the previous edition. These models of the reading process are typically so-called box-and-arrow type models, which are not nearly as fashionable as the types of computer and mathematical simulations that predominate cognitive psychology these days (like the model described in Chapter 6). We think, though, that they are still useful in laying out the basic claims about what kinds of processes a more formal model has to implement.

Top-down models

The primary characteristic of top-down models is that the "top" of the information-processing system, which in reading is the part that represents the meaning of a passage, controls the information flow at all levels. A model proposed by Goodman (1970) is generally considered to be a prototypical top-down model. As we indicated in Chapter 1, a major motivation for top-down models is the belief that the reader needs to overcome various bottlenecks in the bottom-up processing system, by using general world knowledge and contextual information from the passage being read to make hypotheses about what will come next during reading. The reader is generally seen as engaging in a cycle which involves generating an initial hypothesis of what will be read next, confirmation of the hypothesis by minimally sampling the visual information on the printed page, and then the generation of a new hypothesis about the next material to be encountered.

One difficulty with this class of models is that their proponents have never been very explicit about what kinds of hypotheses are being entertained. Despite all of the boxes and arrows typically associated with such models, they do not really specify much about the reading process. For example, they do not specify how the various non-visual sources of information are drawn upon and used to modulate the formation of the perceptual image of the text. Nor do they specify how the system deals with graphic cues that are encountered in successive fixations. At the word recognition level, such models list some of the sources of information that might be used to make a tentative choice about the identity of the word, but they do not specify how this information is used to facilitate the choice, and they do not indicate if some types of information are more important than other types. Similarly, processes beyond the level of word recognition are likewise very vague. Before it is possible to check that the identified word is compatible with prior context, it is necessary for the reader to parse and interpret the part of the sentence analyzed to date. However, top-down models make no provisions for procedures of this kind or how they might work, nor do the models really explain how the meaning that is currently analyzed is assimilated with prior meaning. This lack of precision is undoubtedly due, in part, to how little we know about how "higher-order" processes work (see Chapters 8 and 9), and is a feature shared by all of the types of models we discuss. However, this lack of precision is a particular problem for a model that relies so heavily on top-down mechanisms to explain the reading process.

Bottom-up models

As we pointed out in Chapter 1, bottom-up models generally argue that processing is very fast and that information flows through the processing system in a series of stages. A prototypical bottom-up model was proposed by Gough (1972). The basic idea is that visual information is initially sampled from the printed page and the information is transformed through a series of stages, with little (if any) influence from general world knowledge, contextual information, or higher-order processing strategies. The bottom-up models that have been proposed generally are not comprehensive models of the reading process and have often been criticized because of the lack of flexibility that is attributed to the reader. One virtue of bottom-up models is that they are much better at making clear and testable predictions than is generally the case with top-down models. Unfortunately they fail to provide accounts of many documented facts about how higher-order information affects the reading process.

Interactive models

When the original version of this book was written, interactive models had a great deal of currency in cognitive psychology. In interactive models, readers are usually assumed to be drawing on both top-down and bottom-up information before eventually settling on an interpretation of the text. A comprehensive model of the reading process that is primarily interactive in flavor was presented by Just and Carpenter (1980). Some of these models have been implemented as computer simulations which have mimicked human performance. The major criticism of interactive models has been that it is not clear what they predict about various types of processes during reading. The problem is that they can account for all sorts of data, but with different choices of parameters (e.g., how heavily different sorts of information are weighted in arriving at a decision about what some text means); they could equally well account for patterns of data that are not observed. That is, the extent to which they can provide a clear prediction of the outcome of an experiment is very uncertain. To a certain extent this criticism is unfair, because it may well be that many of the complex processes that occur during reading cannot be specified without much more psychological experimentation. The traditional tests of a model in experimental psychology have always been (1) how well the model can predict behavior (as well as explain it) and/or (2) how much research it generates. While interactive models have generated a great deal of research, they may fall short at predicting behavior, at least at their current level of development.

The Rayner and Pollatsek (1989) model

We have been quite critical in our evaluation of models of the reading process. Likewise, in the previous edition of this book we were also quite critical and we also clearly acknowledged that many of the criticisms directed at the other models could be directed at the model we presented (especially our vagueness about higher-order processes). Although we are not satisfied with the model, we will present it here (with some changes that reflect changes in our thinking) because it reflects our theoretical biases and how we interpret the majority of the evidence on the reading process. We are definitely not tied to this model as the truth about reading. Instead, we see it as a working model or convenient way of summarizing the evidence that we place the most credence in. Thus, we view the model as part of the process of understanding reading, and the criticisms we have just discussed in connection with interactive models are valid for our model; it summarizes our way of viewing reading rather than making explicit predictions. We will come back again at the end to a discussion of why the development of a model of the reading process per se has lagged behind the development of models of the component parts of the process.

As we indicated in Chapter 1, our model is primarily a bottom-up model, but top-down processes do interact with bottom-up processes. We suspect that making the relationship explicit between eye movements and other processing stages is a strength of our model. What we will present here is a sketch, and thus we could easily be criticized for the lack of detail in the model. In our defense, many of the details can be found in other chapters and thus the model is, in some sense, distributed through the book. However, like all models, ours will be somewhat vague about the role of higher-order processes. In essence we see the model as a way of identifying which aspects of reading we have a secure understanding of, as well as identifying those aspects of the reading process where our understanding is weak.

The various components that are shown in Figure 14.1 represent different aspects of the reading process. We follow the convention of using hexagons to indicate processes, square boxes to represent knowledge sources, boxes with rounded corners to represent events, and a diamond to reflect the outcome of a decision.

The processing sequence begins during an eye fixation with the initial encoding of the printed words. The initial encoding process can be thought of as two separate processes occurring in parallel, "foveal word processing" and "parafoveal pre-processing." The former process is concerned with processing the letters (in parallel) in the word that the eye is fixated on. Parafoveal processing involves extracting visual and phonological information to the right of fixation. The visual information includes both word/letter information and word length information that is used in determining where to look next. The phonological information includes syllable as well as phonemic information that is used to facilitate word recognition. The size of the perceptual span in skilled readers extends from the beginning of the currently fixated word to about 14–15 character spaces

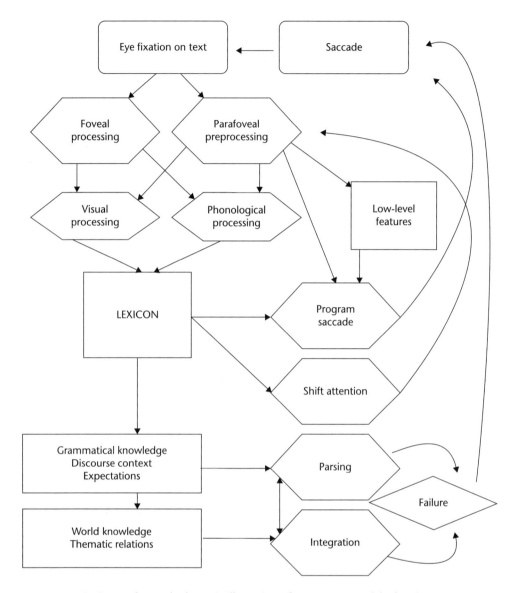

FIGURE 14.1 An incomplete and schematic illustration of our current model of reading.

to the right of fixation for skilled readers. Perceptual span is influenced by visual and phonological processing activities that we described in Chapters 4 and 5.

Turning our attention to the fixated word, visual and phonological processes provide access to the lexicon. We take no strong position on whether or not these are separate kinds of processes (e.g., learned associative processes vs. rule-governed processes), but we are committed to the importance of both. After the initial registration of visual information, lexical access may occur rapidly, especially if it is aided by parafoveal information from the prior fixation. The meaning of the word (in addition to syntactic information such as its part of speech) is obtained from the lexicon. Phonological forms that are constructed from letter information as well as forms that are retrieved from the lexicon activate phonological codes (and speech tract activity) that we characterized in Chapter 7 as inner speech. Inner speech is used as a system for temporarily holding information for comprehension processes because it holds a sequential and relatively literal record of the recently read information in working memory, apparently including some representation of the prosody of speech.

When lexical access of the fixated word (word n) has reached some degree of completion (referred to as the L1 stage in the E-Z Reader model described in Chapter 6), a saccade to word n+1 is programmed. Low-level visual features that were processed parafoveally guide the target of the saccade. When lexical access has reached a greater degree of completion (L2), attention is shifted to the next word, word n+1, but if L2 is not reached before the saccade is initiated, the saccade can be cancelled. Thus the duration of both L1 and L2 affects fixation times. If, however, L2 is short and attention is shifted quickly, word n+1 can be identified before the saccade is initiated. In this case the saccade can be re-programmed so that the word is skipped and the eye goes directly to word n+2 (see Chapter 6 for details). This canceling of the first saccade is not without cost, however, and the duration of the fixation will be increased (by about 30 milliseconds) preceding a skip. If the program for the saccade to word n+1 is far enough along that it cannot be cancelled, the reader will fixate on word n+1 and with a very short latency move to word n+2. This parallel programming mechanism for saccades can account for the very short fixations that sometimes occur in the eye movement record during reading.

While the parallel saccade programming mechanism can account for important aspects of the eye movement record, most of the time the sequence of events on a fixation is the following. First, there is processing of the attended word (which is usually the fixated word and hence in the fovea) together with low-level parafoveal processing to identify the target of the next saccade. Then there is tentative identification of the attended word, which leads to programming of the saccade to the next word, followed by complete identification of the attended word, which leads to an attention shift to the word in the parafovea. The saccade is then usually executed after the attention shift, and the cycle starts again (with the preview benefit that takes place after the attention shift useful in speeding up the initial foveal processing).

When lexical access is completed, not only does attention shift to the next word, but the lexical item that was accessed is also integrated into an ongoing representation of the sentence that is being built. The first stage of this process is termed *parsing*. The parsing device parses strings of words into their appropriate syntactic constituents and identifies the relationships among these constituents. The parser receives input from the lexicon about the syntactic class of each word (plus more detailed lexical information) as it is read, and on the basis of this information together with knowledge of the grammar and the discourse context, and perhaps other sources of information, constructs a syntactic representation. In general the parser constructs only one syntactic representation of a sentence and does so as quickly as possible after lexical access, resulting in choices such as those described in Chapter 8 as following the Minimal Attachment and Late Closure principles. This parsing is generally fast and arguably automatic, but it may be delayed or disrupted when certain kinds of ambiguity are encountered or when its initial decisions must be revised. When information later in the sentence, or information provided by world knowledge and other sources, conflicts with the initial analysis adopted by the syntactic parser, the reader may be garden-pathed and have to engage in costly reanalysis of the sentence (see Chapter 8). This results in the "failure" shown in Figure 14.1, with consequent refixations or regressions, resulting in slowed reading.

Identifying the syntactic structure of a sentence and assigning thematic roles still leaves the language comprehension system short of knowing the meaning of a sentence. The meaning includes the propositions the sentence expresses, what the sentence refers to, whether it is true or not, and perhaps what other propositions it entails. We have only limited knowledge of how this happens. Prior context appears to disambiguate the meanings of ambiguous words pretty quickly, and implausibility or impossibility is detected quickly, so one might assume that construction of meaning is reasonably on-line and does not usually wait for the end of a clause or sentence. However, effects of meaning on interpretation often seem to appear only in refixations or second-pass reading times, so that the construction of meaning appears to wait for at least some syntactic units to be constructed.

As you can see we are getting into deeper and deeper water, and things get worse when we consider how sentences are integrated into larger discourses (as discussed in Chapter 9). Our knowledge of the world plays a substantial role in this process of interpretation and integration (recall the discussion of schema theory in Chapter 9), and our knowledge of discourse structure provides some guidance in how to link sentences. For instance, it provides us some guidance in finding the proper antecedent of an anaphor, and the information structure of sentences—e.g., what is signaled as given and what is new—also guides integration. It is not clear just how far understanding goes; readers seem to compute some of the implications of what they read, but not all, and it is not clear how quickly these inferences are made. The end result of comprehension of expository or narrative text may be the construction of a mental model of the world, some sort of representation that uses various sources of information to represent the reader's understanding of the part of the world the text was describing.

To summarize, the situation is pretty murky after we leave the lexicon. Processing is probably quite interactive (although syntactic processing appears to be logically prior to most of the semantic interpretation) and reasonably on-line (although some semantic processing probably lags behind the eye by at least one fixation). Unfortunately it is premature to draw any more definite conclusions than that about how semantic processing works or what it constructs.

How are readers likely to differ? First, let us consider variation among the population that would be considered skilled readers. As we noted in Chapter 13, we think there is likely to be little difference among skilled readers in the way early processing is done, although there is evidence that there are differences in the speed of lexical access and the relative weight placed on the direct and indirect routes (Baron & Strawson, 1976). In contrast, skilled readers undoubtedly differ markedly in both the knowledge and the comprehension strategies they bring to bear on text. Of course, an individual reader will vary similarly from text to text depending on his or her reading goals and knowledge of the world that the text is describing. We have also seen in Chapter 13 that older readers adopt a somewhat different (and more risky) reading strategy than younger readers. It is less clear whether readers also differ markedly in their strategies of syntactically parsing text.

How does the reading process change for skilled readers when they skim as opposed to read carefully? There is little hard information on this. We assume that lexical access is pretty much the same in the two conditions, at least to the extent that skimmers actually look at words, but the details of higher-order processing must differ considerably. While it is often assumed that readers fill in a lot of the details when they skim, it may be that much of the detail is just lost. The exact nature of the filling in process in skimming is not clear. For example, do readers attempt to fill in everything on the basis of accessing key content words, or do they read small areas carefully and then skip over relatively large areas of text until they stop to "graze" in another important area? We suspect that the latter mechanism is more prevalent.

Is the basic mechanism of reading different for children? The evidence indicates that children can be reading just about like adults by the time they reach the fifth grade, and probably well before that. The perceptual span for children appears to be the same as that for adults by the fourth grade, as long as they are reading easy text. However, it appears (see Chapters 10 and 11) that the process of lexical access develops over time, involving the need for more careful visual analysis of the stimulus as well as phonemic awareness to fully involve the indirect route. The fact that developing this indirect route seems to be so closely involved with developing the skill of reading suggests to us that the indirect route is quite important even in skilled reading (contrary to some current beliefs). Of course, children will differ markedly from adults in terms of the knowledge they bring to bear or in terms of their comprehension strategies (e.g., they are often oblivious to the characters' motivations in stories).

Do people with reading difficulties differ qualitatively from normal readers? As described in Chapter 12, much of the interest in adult acquired dyslexic readers has, historically, been focused on subtyping readers who have damaged routes to the lexicon as either surface dyslexics or phonological dyslexics. Research in developmental dyslexia indicates that the subtype of dyslexia most commonly found in children is the phonological subtype (i.e., a deficit in decoding skills). Most of the children identified in research on developmental dyslexia have a core deficit in phonological processing. This deficit may be accompanied by other processing deficits in some children, but dyslexic children usually do not differ from normal readers in terms of eye movement control or IQ. However, reading contributes to the growth of many cognitive skills. Thus, children with reading difficulties may fall behind in skills like working memory, attention, and vocabulary. In addition to dyslexic children, there are children who can decode adequately but suffer comprehension deficits. These children have general language processing deficits that interfere with listening as well as reading, and they often have lower verbal IQs than normal readers.

Final thoughts

We end with a final note about models and theoretical development. In this book we have provided you with an overview of important sub-components of the reading process. While we acknowledge the importance of putting all of the information together to have an overall model of the reading process, as we conjectured in the earlier version of this book, so far the greatest advances in understanding reading have come via researchers working on each sub-component process (for extended discussions of models of the component processes in reading see Rayner & Reichle, 2010; Reichle, 2012). In other words, we suspect that great breakthroughs in understanding reading will not come from a group of researchers proposing an overall model of the reading process that explains everything about reading. Rather, as we understand each of the component processes in reading better, we will be able to put them together to understand the big picture. Certainly, the past 50 years of research on reading attests to the fact that cognitive psychology is a cumulative science, and that each small step we make in understanding the component processes of the comprehension of text takes us one step closer to solving the fascinating puzzle of how the mind works during reading.

REFERENCES

Aaron, P. G., Joshi, M., & Williams, K. A. (1999). Not all reading disabilities are alike. *Journal of Learning Disabilities*, *32*(2), 120–137.

Aarons, L. (1971). Subvocalization: Aural and EMG feedback in reading. *Perceptual and Motor Skills*, *33*, 271–306.

Abney, S. (1989). A computational model of human parsing. *Journal of Psycholinguistic Research*, *18*, 129–144.

Abramson, M., & Goldinger, S. D. (1997). What the reader's eye tells the mind's ear: Silent reading activates inner speech. *Perception & Psychophysics*, *59*(7), 1059–1068.

Acha, J., & Perea, M. (2008). The effect of neighborhood frequency in reading: Evidence with transposed-letter neighbors. *Cognition*, *108*, 290–300.

Acheson, D. J., & MacDonald, M. C. (2009). Twisting tongues and memories: Explorations of the relationship between language production and verbal working memory. *Journal of Memory and Language*, *60*, 329–350.

Ackerman, P. T., & Dykman, R. A. (1993). Phonological processes, confrontational naming, and immediate memory in dyslexia. *Journal of Learning Disabilities*, *26*(9), 597–609.

Adams, M. J. (1979). Models of word recognition. *Cognitive Psychology*, *11*, 133–176.

Adams, M. J. (1990). *Beginning to read: Thinking and learning about print*. Cambridge, MA: MIT Press.

Adams, M. J. (1998). The three-cueing system. In J. Osborn & F. Lehr (Eds.), *Literacy for all: Issues in teaching and learning* (pp. 73–99). New York: Guilford Press.

Adams, M. J., Treiman, R., & Pressley, M. (1998). Reading, writing, and literacy. In I. E. Sigel (Series Ed.) & K. A. Renninger (Vol. Ed.), *Handbook of child psychology volume 4: Child psychology in practice* (pp. 275–355). New York: Wiley.

Adlard, A., & Hazan, V. (1998). Speech perception in children with specific reading difficulties (dyslexia). *Quarterly Journal of Experimental Psychology A: Human Experimental Psychology*, *51A*(1), 153–177.

Alba, J. W., & Hasher, L. (1983). Is memory schematic? *Psychological Bulletin*, *93*, 203–231.

Albert, M. (1975). Cerebral dominance and reading habits. *Nature*, *256*, 403–404.

Albrecht, J. E. & Clifton, C. Jr. (1998). Accessing singular antecedents in conjoined phrases. *Memory & Cognition*, *26*(3), 599–610.

Albrecht, J. E., & Myers, J. L. (1995). Role of context in accessing distant information during reading. *Journal of Experimental Psychology: Learning, Memory, and Cognition*, *21*, 1459–1468.

Albrecht, J. E., & O'Brien, E. J. (1993). Updating a mental model: Maintaining both local and global coherence. *Journal of Experimental Psychology: Learning, Memory, and Cognition*, *19*, 1061–1070.

Alegria, J., Pignot, E., & Morais, J. (1982). Phonetic analysis of speech and memory codes in beginning readers. *Memory & Cognition*, *10*, 451–456.

Alexander, J., & Nygaard, L. C. (2008). Reading voices and hearing text: Talker-specific auditory imagery in reading. *Journal of Experimental Psychology: Human Perception and Performance*, *34*, 446–459.

Allen, T. (1986). A study of the achievement patterns of hearing-impaired students: 1974–1983. In A. N. Schildroth & M. A. Karchmer (Eds.), *Deaf children in America* (pp. 161–206). San Diego, CA: College-Hill.

Alleton, V. (1970). *L'ecriture Chinoise. Que sais-je?, 1374.* Paris: Presses Universitaires de France.

Allport, D. A. (1977). On knowing the meaning of words we are unable to report: The effects of visual masking. In S. Dornic (Ed.), *Attention and performance VI.* Hillsdale, NJ: Lawrence Erlbaum Associates Inc.

Almor, A. (1999). Noun-phrase anaphora and focus: The informational load hypothesis. *Psychological Review, 106,* 748–765.

Altarriba, J., Kambe, G., Pollatsek, A., & Rayner, K. (2001). Semantic codes are not used in integrating information across eye fixations in reading: Evidence from fluent Spanish–English bilinguals. *Perception & Psychophysics, 63,* 875–890.

Altmann, G. T. M., van Nice, K. Y., Garnham, A., & Henstra, J-A. (1998). Late closure in context. *Journal of Memory and Language, 38,* 459–484.

American Academy of Pediatrics, Committee on Children with Disabilities. (1999). The pediatrician's role in development and implementation of an individual education plan (IEP) and/or an individual family service plan (IFSP). *Pediatrics, 104,* 124–127.

American Academy of Pediatrics, Section on Ophthalmology, Council on Children with Disabilities, American Academy of Ophthalmology, American Association for Pediatric Ophthalmology and Strabismus and American Association of Certified Orthoptists. (2009). Learning disabilities, dyslexia, and vision. *Pediatrics, 124,* 837–844.

Amitay, S., Ben-Yehudah, G., Banai, K., & Ahissar, M. (2002). Disabled readers suffer from visual and auditory impairments but not from a specific magnocellular deficit. *Brain: A Journal of Neurology, 125*(10), 2272–2284.

Anderson, J. R. (1976). *Language, memory, and thought.* Hillsdale, NJ: Lawrence Erlbaum Associates Inc.

Anderson, J. R. (2010). *Cognitive psychology and its implications: Seventh edition.* New York: Worth Publishing.

Anderson, R. C., Hiebert, E. H., Wilkinson, I. A. G., & Scott, J. (1985). *Becoming a nation of readers.* Champaign, IL: National Academy of Education and Center for the Study of Reading.

Anderson, R. C., & Pichert, J. W. (1978). Recall of previously unrecallable information following a shift in perspective. *Journal of Verbal Learning and Verbal Behavior, 17,* 1–12.

Andrews, S. (1989). Frequency and neighborhood effects on lexical access: Activation or search? *Journal of Experimental Psychology: Learning, Memory, and Cognition, 15,* 802–814.

Andrews, S. (1992). Frequency and neighborhood effects on lexical access: Lexical similarity or orthographic redundancy? *Journal of Experimental Psychology: Learning, Memory, and Cognition, 18,* 234–254.

Andrews, S. (1996). Lexical retrieval and selection processes: Effects of transposed-letter confusability. *Journal of Memory and Language, 35,* 775–800.

Andrews, S. (1997). The effects of orthographic similarity on lexical retrieval: Resolving neighborhood conflicts. *Psychonomic Bulletin & Review, 4,* 439–461.

Andrews, S., Miller, B., & Rayner, K. (2004). Eye movements and morphological segmentation of compound words: There is a mouse in mousetrap. *European Journal of Cognitive Psychology, 16,* 285–311.

Andriessen, J. J., & de Voogd, A. H. (1973). Analysis of eye movement patterns in silent reading. *IPO Annual Progress Report, 8,* 29–35.

Angele, B., & Rayner, K. (2011). Parafoveal processing of word n+2 during reading: Do the preceding words matter? *Journal of Experimental Psychology: Human Perception and Performance, 37,* 1210–1220.

Angele, B., Slattery, T. J., Yang, J., Kliegl, R., & Rayner, K. (2008). Parafoveal processing in reading: Manipulating n+1 and n+2 previews simultaneously. *Visual Cognition, 16,* 697–707.

Antes, J. R. (1974). The time course of picture viewing. *Journal of Experimental Psychology, 103,* 62–70.

Anthony, J. L., Lonigan, C. J., Burgess, S. R., Driscoll, K., Phillips, B. M., & Cantor, B. G. (2002). Structure of preschool phonological sensitivity: Overlapping sensitivity to rhyme, words, syllables, and phonemes. *Journal of Experimental Child Psychology, 82,* 65–92.

Aro, M., & Wimmer, H. (2003). Learning to read: English in comparison to six more regular orthographies. *Applied Psycholinguistics, 24*(4), 621–635.

Aronoff, M., & Koch, E. (1996). Context-sensitive regularities in English vowel spelling. *Reading and Writing: An Interdisciplinary Journal, 8*(3), 251–265.

Arregui, A., Clifton, C. Jr., Frazier, L., & Moulton, K. (2006). Processing elided verb phrases with flawed antecedents: The recycling hypothesis. *Journal of Memory and Language, 55,* 232–246.

Ashby, J. (2010). Phonology is fundamental in skilled reading: Evidence from ERPs. *Psychonomic Bulletin & Review*, *17*, 95–100.

Ashby, J., & Clifton, C. Jr. (2005). The prosodic property of lexical stress affects eye movements during silent reading. *Cognition*, *96*, B89–B100.

Ashby, J., & Martin, A. E. (2008). Prosodic phonological representations early in visual word recognition. *Journal of Experimental Psychology: Human Perception and Performance*, *34*, 224–236.

Ashby, J., & Rayner, K. (2004). Representing syllable information in word recognition during silent reading: Evidence from eye movements. *Language and Cognitive Processes*, *19*, 391–426.

Ashby, J., & Rayner, K. (2012). Learning to read in an alphabetic writing system: Evidence from cognitive neuroscience. In M. Anderson (Ed.), *Cognitive Neuroscience: The good, the bad, and the ugly*. Oxford: Oxford University Press.

Ashby, J., Rayner, K., & Clifton, C. Jr. (2005). Eye movements of highly skilled and average readers: Differential effects of frequency and predictability. *Quarterly Journal of Experimental Psychology*, *58A*, 1065–1086.

Ashby J., Sanders L. D., & Kingston J. (2009). Skilled readers begin processing phonological features by 80 msec: Evidence from ERPs. *Biological Psychology*, *80*, 84–94.

Ashby, J., Treiman, R., Kessler, B., & Rayner, K. (2006). Vowel processing during silent reading: Evidence from eye movements. *Journal of Experimental Psychology: Learning, Memory, and Cognition*, *32*, 416–424.

Austin, J. L. (1962). *How to do things with words*. Cambridge, MA: Harvard University Press.

Ayres, T. J. (1984). Silent reading time for tongue-twister paragraphs. *American Journal of Psychology*, *97*, 605–609.

Baayen, R. H., Piepenbrock, R. & Gulikers, L. (1995). *The CELEX Lexical Database* [CD–ROM]. Philadelphia: University of Pennsylvania, Linguistic Data Consortium.

Backman, J. E. (1983). Psycholinguistic skills and reading acquisition: A look at early readers. *Reading Research Quarterly*, *18*, 466–479.

Backman, J., Bruck, M., Hebert, M., & Seidenberg, M. S. (1984). Acquisition and use of spelling–sound correspondences in reading. *Journal of Experimental Child Psychology*, *38*, 114–133.

Baddeley, A. D. (1979) Working memory and reading. In P. A. Kolers, M. E. Wrolstad, & H. Bouma (Eds.), *Processing of visible language*. New York: Plenum.

Baddeley, A. D., Eldridge, M., & Lewis, V. (1981). The role of subvocalization in reading. *Quarterly Journal of Experimental Psychology*, *33A*, 439–454.

Baddeley, A., & Hitch, G. (1974). Working memory. In G. Bower (Ed.), *The psychology of learning and motivation (Vol. 8)*. New York: Academic Press.

Baddeley, A., & Lewis, V. (1981). Inner active processes in reading: The inner voice, the inner ear, and the inner eye. In A. M. Lesgold & C. A. Perfetti (Eds.), *Interactive processes in reading*. Hillsdale, NJ: Lawrence Erlbaum Associates Inc.

Baddeley, A., Logie, R., Nimmo-Smith, I., & Brereton, N. (1985). Components of fluent reading. *Journal of Memory and Language*, *24*, 119–131.

Bader, M. (1998). Prosodic influences on reading syntactically ambiguous sentences. In J. Fodor & F. Ferreira (Eds.), *Reanalysis in sentence processing* (pp. 1–46). Dordrecht: Kluwer.

Badian, N. A. (1998). A validation of the role of preschool phonological and orthographic skills in the prediction of reading. *Journal of Learning Disabilities*, *31*(5), 472–481.

Baker, L., & Brown, A. L. (1984). Metacognitive skills and reading. In P. D. Pearson, R. Barr, M. L. Kamil, & P. Mosenthal (Eds.), *Handbook of reading research*. New York: Longman.

Ball, E. W., & Blachman, B. A. (1988). Phoneme segmentation training: Effect on reading readiness. *Annals of Dyslexia*, *38*, 208–225.

Balmuth, M. (1982). *The roots of phonics: A historical introduction*. New York: McGraw-Hill.

Balota, D. A. (1983). Automatic semantic activation and episodic memory encoding. *Journal of Verbal Learning and Verbal Behavior*, *22*, 88–104.

Balota, D. A., & Chumbley, J. I. (1984). Are lexical decisions a good measure of lexical access? The role of word frequency in neglected decision stage. *Journal of Experimental Psychology: Human Perception and Performance*, *10*, 340–357.

Balota, D. A., & Chumbley, J. I. (1985). The locus of word-frequency effects in the pronunciation task: Lexical access and/or production? *Journal of Memory and Language*, *24*, 89–106.

Balota, D. A., Pollatsek, A., & Rayner, K. (1985). The interaction of contextual constraints and parafoveal visual information in reading. *Cognitive Psychology, 17,* 364–390.

Balota, D. A., & Rayner, K. (1983). Parafoveal visual information and semantic contextual constraints. *Journal of Experimental Psychology: Human Perception and Performance, 9,* 726–738.

Balota, D. A., Yap, M. J., Cortese, M. J., Hutchison, K. A., Kessler, B., Loftis, B., et al. (2007). The English lexicon project. *Behavior Research Methods, 39,* 445–459.

Banks, W. P., Oka, E., & Shugarman, S. (1981). Recoding of printed words to internalize speech: Does recoding come before lexical access? In O. J. L. Tzeng & H. Singer (Eds.), *Perception of print.* Hillsdale, NJ: Lawrence Erlbaum Associates Inc.

Baron, J. (1973). Phonemic stage not necessary for reading. *Quarterly Journal of Experimental Psychology, 25,* 241–246.

Baron, J. (1979). Orthographic and word specific mechanisms in children's reading of words. *Child Development, 50,* 60–72.

Baron, J., & Strawson, C. (1976). Use of orthographic and word-specific knowledge in reading words aloud. *Journal of Experimental Psychology: Human Perception and Performance, 2,* 386–393.

Baron, J., & Thurston, I. (1973). An analysis of the word superiority effect. *Cognitive Psychology, 4,* 207–228.

Baron, J., & Treiman, R. (1980). Use of orthography in reading and learning to read. In J. F. Kavanagh & R. L. Venezky (Eds.), *Orthography, reading, and dyslexia.* Baltimore: University Park Press.

Baron, J., Treiman, R., Freyd, J., & Kellman, P. (1980). Spelling and reading by rules. In U. Frith (Ed.), *Cognitive processes in spelling.* London: Academic Press.

Barr, R. (1974). The effect of instruction on pupil's reading strategies. *Reading Research Quarterly, 10,* 555–582.

Barron, R. W. (1981a). The development of visual word recognition: A review. In G. E. MacKinnon & T. G. Waller (Eds.), *Reading research: Advances in theory and practice* (Vol. 3). New York: Academic Press.

Barron, R. W. (1981b). Reading skill and reading strategies. In A. M. Lesgold & C. A. Perfetti (Eds.), *Interactive processes in reading.* Hillsdale, NJ: Lawrence Erlbaum Associates Inc.

Barron, R. W. (1986). Word recognition in early reading: A review of the direct and indirect access hypothesis. *Cognition, 24,* 93–119.

Barron, R. W. & Baron, J. (1977). How children get meaning from printed words. *Child Development, 48,* 587–594.

Bartlett, F. (1932). *Remembering: A study in experimental and social psychology.* Cambridge, UK: Cambridge University Press.

Barton, S. B., & Sanford, A. J. (1993). A case study of anomaly detection: Shallow semantic processing and cohesion establishment. *Memory & Cognition, 21,* 477–487.

Bauer, D., & Stanovich, K. E. (1980). Lexical access and the spelling-to-sound regularity effect. *Memory & Cognition, 8,* 424–432.

Beaton, A. A. (2004). *Dyslexia, reading and the brain: A sourcebook of psychological and biological research.* Florence, KY: Taylor & Francis/Routledge.

Beauvois, M. F., & Derouesne, J. (1979). Phonological alexia: Three dissociations. *Journal of Neurology, Neurosurgery and Psychiatry, 42,* 1115–1124.

Beck, I. L. (1981). Reading problems and instructional practices. In G. E. MacKinnon & T. G. Waller (Eds.), *Reading research: Advances in theory and practice.* New York: Academic Press.

Beck, I. L. (1998). Understanding beginning reading: A journey through teaching and research. In J. Osborn & F. Lehr (Eds.), *Literacy for all: Issues in teaching and learning* (pp. 11–31). New York: Guilford Press.

Beck, I. L. (2006). *Making sense of phonics.* New York: Guilford Press.

Beck, I. L., Perfetti, C. A., & McKeown, M. G. (1982). Effects of long-term vocabulary instruction on lexical access and reading comprehension. *Journal of Educational Psychology, 74,* 506–521.

Becker, C. A. (1985). What do we really know about semantic context effects during reading? In D. Besner, T. G, Waller, & G. E. MacKinnon (Eds.), *Reading research: Advances in theory and practice (Vol. 5).* New York: Academic Press.

Becker, W., & Jürgens, R. (1979). An analysis of the saccadic system by means of double-step stimuli. *Vision Research, 19,* 967–983.

Becker, M. W., Pashler, H., & Lubin, J. (2007). Object-intrinsic oddities draw early saccades. *Journal of Experimental Psychology: Human Perception and Performance, 33,* 20–30.

Beech, J. R., & Harris, M. (1997). The prelingually deaf young reader: A case of reliance on direct lexical access? *Journal of Research in Reading, 20,* 105–121.

Beggs, W. D. A., & Howarth, P. N. (1985). Inner speech as a learned skill. *Journal of Experimental Child Psychology, 39*, 396–411.

Bélanger, N. N., Mayberry, R. I., & Baum, S. R. (2012 in press). Reading difficulties in adult deaf readers of French: Phonological codes, not guilty! *Scientific Studies of Reading*.

Bender, L. (1955). Twenty years of clinical research on schizophrenic children. In G. Caplan (Ed.), *Emotional problems of early childhood*. New York: Basic Books.

Bentin, S., Bargai, N., & Katz, L. (1984). Orthographic and phonemic coding for lexical access: Evidence from Hebrew. *Journal of Experimental Psychology: Learning, Memory, and Cognition, 10*, 353–368.

Bentin, S., & Leshem, H. (1993). On the interaction between phonological awareness and reading acquisition: It's a two-way street. *Annals of Dyslexia, 43*, 125–148.

Berninger, V. W., Abbott, R. D., Thomson, J., Wagner, R., Swanson, H. L., Wijsman, E. M., et al. (2006). Modeling phonological core deficits within a working memory architecture in children and adults with developmental dyslexia. *Scientific Studies of Reading, 10*(2), 165–198.

Bertelson, P., Morais, J., Alegria, J., & Content, A. (1985a). Phonetic analysis capacity and learning to read. *Nature, 313*, 73–74.

Bertelson, P., Mousty, P., & D'Alimonte, G. (1985b). A study of Braille reading: Patterns of hand activity in one-handed and two-handed reading. *Quarterly Journal of Experimental Psychology, 37A*, 235–256.

Bertram, R., & Hyönä, J. (2003). The length of a complex word modifies the role of morphological structure: Evidence from eye movements when reading short and long Finnish compounds. *Journal of Memory and Language, 48*, 615–634.

Besner, D., Coltheart, M., & Davelaar, E. (1984). Basic processes in reading: Computation of abstract letter identities. *Canadian Journal of Psychology, 38*, 126–134.

Besner, D., & Davelaar, E. (1982). Basic processes in reading: Two phonological codes. *Canadian Journal of Psychology, 36*, 701–711.

Besner, D., Davies, J., & Daniels, S. (1981). Reading for meaning: The effects of concurrent articulation. *Quarterly Journal of Experimental Psychology, 33A*, 415–437.

Besner, D., & Hildebrandt, N. (1987). Orthographic and phonological codes in the oral reading of Japanese Kana. *Journal of Experimental Psychology: Learning, Memory, and Cognition, 13*, 335–343.

Besner, D., Risko, E., & Sklair, N. (2005). Spatial attention as a necessary preliminary to early processes in reading. *Canadian Journal of Experimental Psychology, 59*, 99–108.

Bestgen, Y., & Vonk, W. (2000). Temporal adverbials as segmentation markers in discourse comprehension. *Journal of Memory and Language, 42*, 74–87.

Bever, T. G. (1970). The cognitive basis for linguistic structure. In J. R. Hayes (Eds.), *Cognitive development of language*. New York: Wiley.

Beverly, S. E., & Perfetti, C. A. (1983). *Skill differences in phonological representation and development of orthographic knowledge*. Paper presented at the Biennial Meeting of the Society of Research in Child Development, Detroit, MI.

Biemiller, A. (1970). The development of the use of graphic and contextual information as children learn to read. *Reading Research Quarterly, 6*, 75–96.

Binder, K., Duffy, S., & Rayner, K. (2001). The effects of thematic fit and discourse context on syntactic ambiguity resolution. *Journal of Memory and Language, 44*, 297–324.

Binder, K. S., Pollatsek, A., & Rayner, K. (1999). Extraction of information to the left of the fixated word in reading. *Journal of Experimental Psychology: Human Perception and Performance, 25*, 1162–1172.

Binder, K. S., & Rayner, K. (1998). Contextual strength does not modulate the subordinate bias effect: Evidence from eye fixations and self-paced reading. *Psychonomic Bulletin & Review, 5*, 271–276.

Birch, S., Albrecht, J. E., & Myers, J. L. (2000). Syntactic focusing strategies influence discourse processing. *Discourse Processes, 30*, 285–304.

Birch, S., & Clifton, C. Jr. (1995). Focus, accent, and argument structure. *Language and Speech, 33*, 365–391.

Birch, S., & Rayner, K. (1997). Linguistic focus affects eye movements during reading. *Memory & Cognition, 25*, 653–660.

Birch, S., & Rayner, K. (2010). Effects of syntactic prominence on eye movements during reading. *Memory & Cognition, 38*, 740–752.

Bishop, C. H. (1964). Transfer effects of word and letter training in reading. *Journal of Verbal Learning and Verbal Behavior, 36*, 840–847.

Bishop, D.V., & Adams, C. (1990). A prospective study of the relationship between specific language impairment, phonological disorders and reading retardation. *Journal of Child Psychology and Psychiatry, 31*, 1027–1050.

Blachman, B. A. (1984). Relationship of rapid naming ability and language analysis skills to kindergarten and first-grade reading achievement. *Journal of Educational Psychology, 76*, 610–622.

Blachman, B. A. (2000). Phonological awareness. In M. L. Kamil, P. B. Mosenthal, P. D. Pearson, & R. Barr (Eds.), *Handbook of reading research, Vol. III* (pp. 483–502). Mahwah, NJ: Lawrence Erlbaum Associates Inc.

Black, J. L., Collins, D. W. K., DeRoach, J. N., & Zubrick, S. (1984). A detailed study of sequential saccadic eye movements for normal and poor reading children. *Perceptual and Motor Skills, 59*, 423–434.

Blanchard, H. E. (1985). A comparison of some processing time measures based on eye movements. *Acta Psychologica, 58*, 1–15.

Blanchard, H. E., Pollatsek, A., & Rayner, K. (1989). The acquisition of parafoveal word information in reading. *Perception & Psychophysics, 46*, 85–94.

Blomert, L., & Mitterer, H. (2004). The fragile nature of the speech-perception deficit in dyslexia: Natural vs. synthetic speech. *Brain and Language, 89*(1), 21–26.

Blythe, H. I., Liversedge, S. P., Joseph, H. S. S. L., White, S. J., & Rayner, K. (2009). Visual information capture during fixations in reading for children and adults. *Vision Research, 49*(12), 1583–1591.

Boada, R., & Pennington, B. F. (2006). Deficient implicit phonological representations in children with dyslexia. *Journal of Experimental Child Psychology, 95*(3), 153–193.

Bock, J. K., & Brewer, W. F. (1985). Discourse structure and mental models. In T. C. Carr (Ed.), *The development of readings skills*. San Francisco: Jossey-Bass.

Bock, K., & Mazella, J. R. (1983). Intonational marking of given and new information: Some consequences for comprehension. *Memory & Cognition, 11*, 64–76.

Boder, E. (1973). Developmental dyslexia: A diagnostic based on three atypical reading–spelling patterns. *Developmental Medicine and Child Neurology, 15*, 663–687.

Boland, J. (2004). Linking eye movements to sentence comprehension in reading and listening. In M. Carreiras & C. C. Jr. (Eds.), *The on-line study of sentence comprehension* (pp. 51–76). New York: Psychology Press.

Boland, J., & Blodgett, A. (2006). Argument status and PP attachment. *Journal of Psycholinguistic Research, 35*, 385–403.

Bond, G. L., & Dykstra, R. (1967). The cooperative research program in first-grade reading instruction. *Reading Research Quarterly, 2*(4), 5–142.

Bond, G. L., & Dykstra, R. (1997). The cooperative research program in first-grade reading instruction. *Reading Research Quarterly, 32*(4), 345–427.

Bonifacci, P., & Snowling, M. J. (2008). Speed of processing and reading disability: A cross-linguistic investigation of dyslexia and borderline intellectual functioning. *Cognition, 107*(3), 999–1017.

Bornkessel, I., & Schlesewsky, M. (2006). The extended argument dependency model: A neurocognitive approach to sentence comprehension across languages. *Psychological Review, 113*, 787–821.

Bornkessel-Schlesewsky, I., & Friederici, A. D. (2007). Neuroimaging studies of sentence and discourse perception. In G. Gaskell (Ed.), *The Oxford handbook of psycholinguistics* (pp. 407–424). Oxford, UK: Oxford University Press.

Bos, C., Mather, N., Dickson, S., Podhajski, B., & Chard, D. (2001). Perceptions and knowledge of preservice and inservice educators about early reading instruction. *Annals of Dyslexia, 51*, 97–120.

Bouma, H., & de Voogd, A.H. (1974). On the control of eye saccades in reading. *Vision Research, 14*, 273–284.

Bower, G. H., Black, J. B., & Turner, T. J. (1979). Scripts in memory for text. *Cognitive Psychology, 11*, 177–220.

Bower, G. H., & Morrow, D. G. (1990). Mental models in narrative comprehension. *Science, 247*, 44–48.

Bower, T. G. R. (1970) Reading by eye. In H. Levin & J. P. Williams (Eds.), *Basic studies on reading*. New York: Basic Books.

Bowman, M., & Treiman, R. (2002). Relating print and speech: The effects of letter names and word position on reading and spelling performance. *Journal of Experimental Child Psychology, 82*, 305–340.

Bradley, D. (1979). Lexical representations of derivational relations. In M. Aranoff & M. Kean (Eds.), *Juncture*. Cambridge, MA: MIT Press.

Bradley, L., & Bryant, P. E. (1978). Difficulties in auditory organization as a possible cause of reading backwardness. *Nature, 271*, 746–747.

Bradley, L., & Bryant, P. E. (1983). Categorizing sounds and learning to read – A causal connection. *Nature, 301*, 419–421.

Bradshaw, J. L. (1974). Peripherally presented and unreported words may bias the meaning of a centrally fixated homograph. *Journal of Experimental Psychology, 103*, 1200–1202.

Brady, S., Shankweiler, D., & Mann, V. A. (1983). Speech perception and memory coding in relation to reading ability. *Journal of Experimental Child Psychology, 35*(2), 345–367.

Brady, S. A. (1997). Ability to encode phonological representations: An underlying difficulty of poor readers. In B. A. Blachman (Ed.), *Foundations of reading acquisition and dyslexia: Implications for early intervention* (pp. 21–47). Mahwah, NJ: Lawrence Erlbaum Associates Inc.

Bransford, J. D., & Johnson, M. K. (1972). Contextual prerequisites for understanding: Some investigations of comprehension and recall. *Journal of Verbal Learning and Verbal Behavior, 11*, 717–726.

Breen, M., & Clifton, C. Jr. (2011). Stress matters: Effects of anticipated lexical stress on silent reading. *Journal of Memory and Language, 64*, 153–170.

Breier, J. I., Fletcher, J. M., Denton, C., & Gray, L. C. (2004). Categorical perception of speech stimuli in children at risk for reading difficulty. *Journal of Experimental Child Psychology, 88*(2), 152–170.

Breznitz, Z., & Meyler, A. (2003). Speed of lower-level auditory and visual processing as a basic factor in dyslexia: Electrophysiological evidence. *Brain and Language, 85*(2), 166–184.

Briggs, C., & Elkind, D. (1973). Cognitive development in early readers. *Developmental Psychology, 9*, 279–280.

Brim, B. J. (1968). Impact of a reading improvement program. *Journal of Educational Research, 62*, 177–182.

Britt, M. A. (1994). The interaction of referential ambiguity and argument structure in the parsing of prepositional phrases. *Journal of Memory and Language, 33*, 251–283.

Broadbent, D. E. (1958). *Perception and communication.* London: Pergamon.

Broadbent, D. E. (1984). The Maltese cross: A new simplistic model for memory. *Behavioral and Brain Sciences, 7*, 55–94.

Broadbent, W. H. (1872). *On the cerebral mechanism of speech and thought. Proceedings of the Royal Medical and Chirurgical Society of London* (pp. 25–29). London: Anonymous.

Brooks, L. (1977). Visual pattern in fluent word identification. In A. S. Reber & D. L. Scarborough (Eds.), *Toward a psychology of reading.* Hillsdale, NJ: Lawrence Erlbaum Associates Inc.

Brown, A. L. (1980). Metacognitive development and reading. In R. J. Spiro, B. C. Bruce, & W. F. Brewer, (Eds.), *Theoretical issues in reading comprehension.* Hillsdale, NJ: Lawrence Erlbaum Associates Inc.

Brown, B., Haegerstrom-Portnoy, G., Adams, A. J., Yingling, C. D., Galin, D., Herron, J., et al. (1983). Predictive eye movements do not discriminate between dyslexic and normal children. *Neuropsychologia, 21*, 121–128.

Brown, R. (1970). Psychology and reading. In H. Levin & J. P. Williams (Eds.), *Basic studies on reading.* New York: Basic Books.

Brown, R. W. (1958). *Words and things.* New York: Free Press.

Bruce, D. J. (1964). The analysis of word sounds by young children. *British Journal of Educational Psychology, 34*, 158–170.

Bruck, M. (1990). Word-recognition skills of adults with childhood diagnoses of dyslexia. *Developmental Psychology, 26*(3), 439–454.

Bruck, M. (1992). Persistence of dyslexics' phonological awareness deficits. *Developmental Psychology, 28*(5), 874–886.

Bruck, M., Genesee, F., & Caravolas, M. (1997). A cross-linguistic study of early literacy acquisition. In B. A. Blachman (Ed.), *Foundations of reading acquisition and dyslexia: Implications for early intervention* (pp. 145–162). Mahwah, NJ: Lawrence Erlbaum Associates Inc.

Bruno, J. L., Manis, F. R., Keating, P., Sperling, A. J., Nakamoto, J., & Seidenberg, M. S. (2007). Auditory word identification in dyslexic and normally achieving readers. *Journal of Experimental Child Psychology, 97*(3), 183–204.

Brunswick, N., McCrory, E., Price, C. J., Frith, C. D., & Frith, U. (1999). Explicit and implicit processing of words and pseudowords by adult developmental dyslexics. *Brain: A Journal of Neurology, 122*(10), 1901–1917.

Bryant, P. E., & Impey, L. (1986). The similarities between normal readers and developmental and acquired dyslexics. *Cognition, 24*, 121–137.

Brysbaert, M., Drieghe, D., & Vitu, F. (2003). Word skipping: Implications for eye movement control in reading. In G. Underwood (Ed.), *Cognitive processes in eye guidance*. Oxford, UK: Oxford University Press.

Brysbaert, M., & New, B. (2009). Moving beyond Kucera and Francis: A critical evaluation of current word frequency norms and the introduction of a new and improved word frequency measure for American English. *Behavior Research Methods, 41*, 488–496.

Brysbaert, M., & Vitu, F. (1998). Word skipping: Implications for theories of eye movement control in reading. In Underwood, G. (Ed.), *Eye guidance in reading and scene perception* (pp. 125–147). Amsterdam: Elsevier.

Burd, L., & Kerbeshian, J. (1988). Familial pervasive development disorder, Tourette disorder, and hyperlexia. *Neuroscience and Biobehavioral Reviews, 12*, 233–234.

Burden, V., & Campbell, R. (1994). The development of word-coding skills in the born deaf: An experimental study of deaf school-leavers. *British Journal of Developmental Psychology, 12*, 331–349.

Bus, A. G., van Ijzendoorn, M. H., & Pellegrini, A. D. (1995). Joint book reading makes for success in learning to read: A meta-analysis on intergenerational transmission of literacy. *Review of Educational Research, 65*(1), 1–21.

Buswell, G. T. (1922). *Fundamental reading habits: A study of their development*. Chicago: Chicago University Press.

Byrne, B. (1992). Studies in the acquisition procedure for reading: Rationale, hypotheses, and data. In P. B. Gough, L. C. Ehri, & R. Treiman (Eds.), *Reading acquisition* (pp. 1–34). Hillsdale, NJ: Lawrence Erlbaum Associates Inc.

Byrne, B., & Fielding-Barnsley, R. (1991). Evaluation of a program to teach phonemic awareness to young children. *Journal of Educational Psychology, 83*, 451–455.

Byrne, B., & Shea, P. (1979). Semantic and phonetic memory codes in beginning readers. *Memory & Cognition, 7*, 333–338.

Cain, K., & Oakhill, J. V. (1999). Inference making ability and its relation to comprehension failure in young children. *Reading and Writing, 11*(5–6), 489–503.

Cain, K., Oakhill, J. V., Barnes, M. A., & Bryant, P. E. (2001). Comprehension skill, inference-making ability, and the relation to knowledge. *Memory & Cognition, 29*(6), 850–859.

Cain, K., Oakhill, J. V., & Elbro, C. (2003). The ability to learn new word meanings from context by school-age children with and without language comprehension difficulties. *Journal of Child Language, 30*, 681–694.

Calef, T., Pieper, M., & Coffey, B. (1999). Comparisons of eye movements before and after a speed-reading course. *Journal of the American Optometric Association, 70*, 171–181.

Calfee, R. C., Chapman, R., & Venezky, R. (1972). How a child needs to think to learn to read. In L. W. Gregg (Ed.), *Cognition in learning and memory*. New York: Wiley.

Calfee, R. C., Lindamood, P., & Lindamood, C. (1973). Acoustic–phonetic skills and reading: Kindergarten through twelfth grade. *Journal of Educational Psychology, 64*, 293–298.

Campbell, F. W., & Wurtz, R. H. (1978). Saccadic omission: Why we do not see a grey-out during a saccadic eye movement. *Vision Research, 18*, 1297–1303.

Caramazza, A., Grober, E. H., Garvey, C., & Yates, J. (1977). Comprehension of anaphoric pronouns. *Journal of Verbal Learning and Verbal Behavior, 16*, 601–609.

Cardoso-Martins, C. (2001). The reading abilities of beginning readers of Brazilian Portugese: Implications for a theory of reading acquisition. *Scientific Studies of Reading, 5*(4), 289–317.

Carillo, L. W., & Sheldon, W. D. (1952). The flexibility of the reading rate. *Journal of Educational Psychology, 43*, 299–305.

Carlson, G. N., & Tanenhaus, M. K. (1988). Thematic roles and language comprehension. In W. Wilkins (Ed.), *Syntax and semantics: Thematic relations* (pp. 263–300). New York: Academic Press.

Carlson, K. (2009). How prosody influences sentence comprehension. *Language and Linguistics Compass, 3*, July.

Carr, T. H. (1981). Building theories of reading ability: On the relation between individual differences in cognitive skills and reading comprehension. *Cognition, 9*, 73–114.

Carr, T. H. (1982). What's in a model: Reading theory and reading instruction. In M. H. Singer (Ed.), *Competent reader, disabled reader: Research and application*. Hillsdale, NJ: Lawrence Erlbaum Associates Inc.

Carr, T. H., Davidson, B. J., & Hawkins, H. L. (1978). Perceptual flexibility in word recognition: Strategies affect orthographic computation but not lexical access. *Journal of Experimental Psychology: Human Perception and Performance, 4*, 674–690.

Carr, T. H., McCauley, C., Sperber, R. D., & Parmelee, C. M. (1982). Words, pictures, and priming: On semantic activation, conscious identification, and the automaticity of information processing. *Journal of Experimental Psychology: Human Perception and Performance, 8*, 757–777.

Carr, T. H., & Pollatsek, A. (1985). Recognizing printed words: A look at current models. In D. Besner, T. G. Waller, & G. E. MacKinnon (Eds.), *Reading research: Advances in theory and practice* (Vol. 5). Orlando, FL: Academic Press.

Carreiras, M., Duñabeitia, J. A., & Molinaro, N. (2009). Consonants and vowels contribute differently to visual word recognition: ERPs of relative position priming. *Cerebral Cortex, 19*, 2659–2670.

Carreiras, M., Perea, M., & Grainger, J. (1997). Effects of orthographic neighborhood in visual word recognition: Cross-task comparisons. *Journal of Experimental Psychology: Learning, Memory, and Cognition, 23*, 857–871.

Carroll, J. M., Snowling, M. J., Stevenson, J., & Hulme, C. (2003). The development of phonological awareness in preschool children. *Developmental Psychology, 39*, 913–923.

Carroll, P., & Slowiaczek, M. L. (1987). Modes and modules: Multiple pathways to the language processor. In J. Garfield (Ed.), *Modularity in knowledge representation and natural language processing*. Cambridge, MA: MIT Press.

Carver, R. P. (1971). *Sense and nonsense in speed reading*. Silver Spring, MD: Revrac.

Carver, R. P. (1972). Speed readers don't read; they skim. *Psychology Today*, 22–30.

Carver, R. P. (1985). How good are some of the world's best readers? *Reading Research Quarterly, 4*, 389–419.

Carver, R. P. (1997). Reading for one second, one minute, or one year from the perspective of rauding theory. *Scientific Studies of Reading, 1*, 3–43.

Castiglioni-Spalten, M. L., & Ehri, L. C. (2003). Phonemic awareness instruction: Contribution of articulatory segmentation to novice beginners' reading and spelling. *Scientific Studies of Reading, 7*(1), 25–52.

Castles, A., & Coltheart, M. (1993). Varieties of developmental dyslexia. *Cognition, 47*(2), 149–180.

Castles, A., Datta, H., Gayan, J., & Olson, R. K. (1999). Varieties of developmental reading disorder: Genetic and environmental influences. *Journal of Experimental Child Psychology, 72*(2), 73–94.

Cattell, J. M. (1886). The time it takes to see and name objects. *Mind, 11*, 63–65.

Catts, H. W., Fey, M. E., Zhang, X., & Tomblin, J. B. (1999). Language basis of reading and reading disabilities: Evidence from a longitudinal investigation. *Scientific Studies of Reading, 3*(4), 331–361.

Chace, K. H., Rayner, K., & Well, A. D. (2005). Eye movements and phonological preview benefit: Effects of reading skill. *Canadian Journal of Experimental Psychology, 59*, 209–217.

Chall, J. S. (1958). *Readability: An appraisal of research and application*. Columbus, OH: Ohio State University.

Chall, J. S. (1967/1996). *Learning to read: The great debate* (3rd ed.). Fort Worth, TX: Harcourt Brace.

Chall, J. S. (1983/1996). *Stages of reading development*. Orlando, FL: Harcourt–Brace.

Chamberlain, C. (2002). *Reading skills of deaf adults who sign: Good and poor readers compared*. Unpublished Ph.D., McGill University, Montreal.

Chambers, S. M. (1979). Letter and order information in lexical access. *Journal of Verbal Learning and Behavior, 18*, 225–241.

Chaney, C. (1992). Language development, metalinguistic skills, and print awareness in 3-year-old children. *Applied Psycholinguistics, 13*(4), 485–514.

Chase, W. G., & Clark, H. H. (1972). Mental operations in the comparison of sentences and pictures. In L. W. Gregg (Ed.), *Cognition in learning and memory*. New York: Wiley.

Cheesman, J., & Merikle, P. M. (1984). Priming with and without awareness. *Perception & Psychophysics, 36*, 387–395.

Chen, H-C., & Tang, C-K., (1998). The effective visual field in Chinese. *Reading and Writing, 10*, 245–254.

Cheung, H., & Ng, L. K. H. (2003). Chinese reading development in some major Chinese societies: An introduction. In C. McBride-Chang & H-C. Chen (Eds.), *Reading development in Chinese children* (pp. 3–17). Westport, CT: Greenwood Press.

Chiappe, P., Stringer, R., Siegel, L. S., & Stanovich, K. E. (2002). Why the timing deficit hypothesis does not explain reading disability in adults. *Reading and Writing, 15*(1–2), 73–107.

Chmiel, N. (1984). Phonological recoding for reading: The effect of concurrent articulation in a Stroop task. *British Journal of Psychology, 75*, 213–220.

Chomsky, N. (1957). *Syntactic structures*. The Hague, Netherlands: Mouton.

Chomsky, N. (1959). A review of Verbal Behavior by B. F. Skinner. *Language, 35*, 26–58.

Chomsky, N. (1965). *Aspects of the theory of syntax*. Cambridge, MA: MIT Press.

Chomsky, N. (1970). Phonology and reading. In H. Levin & J. P. Williams (Eds.), *Basic studies on reading*. New York: Basic Books.

Chomsky, N. (1981). *Lectures on government and binding: The Pisa lectures*. Dordrecht: Foris.

Chomsky, N. (1995). *The minimalist program*. Cambridge, MA: MIT Press.

Chomsky, N., & Halle, M. (1968). *The sound pattern of English*. New York: Harper & Row.

Christianson, K., Hollingworth, A., Halliwell, J., & Ferreira, F. (2001). Thematic roles assigned along the garden path linger. *Cognitive Psychology: Learning, Memory, and Cognition, 42*, 368–407.

Christianson, K., Johnson, R. L., & Rayner, K. (2005). Letter transpositions within and across morphemes. *Journal of Experimental Psychology: Learning, Memory, and Cognition, 31*, 1327–1339.

Chumbley, J. I., & Balota, D. A. (1984). A word's meaning affects the decision in lexical decision. *Memory & Cognition, 12*, 590–606.

Ciuffreda, K. J., Kenyon, R. W., & Stark, L. (1983). Saccadic intrusions contributing to reading disability: A case report. *American Journal of Optometry and Physiological Optics, 60*, 242–249.

Clark, H. H., & Haviland, S. E. (1977). Comprehension and the given–new contract. In R. O. Freedle (Ed.), *Discourse production and comprehension*. Norwood, NJ: Ables.

Clark, H. H., & Sengul, C. J. (1979). In search of referents for nouns and pronouns. *Memory & Cognition, 7*, 35–41.

Clay, M. M. (1979) *Reading: The patterning of complex behavior*. Auckland, New Zealand: Heinemann Educational Books.

Clay, M. M. (1991). *Becoming literate: The construction of inner control*. Portsmouth, NH: Heinemann.

Clay, M. M., & Imlach, R.H. (1971). Juncture, pitch and stress as reading behavior variables. *Journal of Verbal Learning and Verbal Behavior, 10*, 133–139.

Clifton, C. Jr., & Ferreira, F. (1987). Discourse structure and anaphora: Some experimental results. In M. Coltheart (Ed.), *Attention and performance 12* (pp. 635–654), Hove, UK: Lawrence Erlbaum Associates Ltd.

Clifton, C. Jr., & Ferreira, F. (1989). Ambiguity in context. *Language and Cognitive Processes, 4*, 77–104.

Clifton, C. Jr., & Frazier, L. (1989). Comprehending sentences with long-distance dependencies. In G. Carlson & M. Tanenhaus (Eds.), *Linguistic structure in language processing* (pp. 273–318). Dordrecht: Kluwer Academic.

Clifton, C. Jr., Frazier, L., & Connine, C. (1984). Lexical expectations in sentence comprehension. *Journal of Verbal Learning and Verbal Behavior, 23*(6), 696–708.

Clifton, C. Jr., Speer, S., & Abney, S. (1991). Parsing arguments: Phrase structure and argument structure as determinants of initial parsing decisions. *Journal of Memory and Language, 30*, 251–271.

Clifton, C. Jr., & Staub, A. (2008). Parallelism and competition in syntactic ambiguity resolution. *Language and Linguistics Compass, 2*, 234–250.

Clifton, C. Jr., Traxler, M., Mohamed, M. T., Williams, R. S., Morris, R. K., & Rayner, K. (2003). The use of thematic role information in parsing: Syntactic processing autonomy revisited. *Journal of Memory and Language, 49*, 317–334.

Cloutman, L., Goettesman, R., Chaudhry, P., Davis, C., Kleinman, J. T., Pawlak, M., et al. (2009a). Where (in the brain) do semantic errors come from? *Cortex, 45*(5), 641–649.

Cloutman, L., Newhart, M., Davis, C., Heidler-Gary, J., & Hillis, A. E. (2009b). Acute recovery of oral word production following stroke: Patterns of performance as predictors of recovery. *Behavioural Neurology, 21*(3–4), 145–153.

Cobrinik, L. (1974). Unusual reading ability in severely disturbed children: Clinical observation and a retrospective inquiry. *Journal of Autism and Childhood Schizophrenia, 4*(2), 163–175.

Cohen, A. S. (1974). Oral reading errors of first grade children taught by a code emphasis approach. *Reading Research Quarterly, 10*, 616–650.

Cohen, L., & Dehaene, S. (2009). Ventral and dorsal contributions to word reading. In M. S. Gazzaniga (Ed.), *Cognitive neuroscience* (4th ed.). Cambridge, MA: MIT Press.

Cohen, L., Dehaene, S., Naccache L., Lehricy, S., Dehaene-Lambertz, G., Henaff, G. M. A., et al. (2000). The visual word form area: Spatial and temporal characterization of an initial stage of reading in normal subjects and posterior split-brain patients. *Brain, 123*, 291–307.

Cohen, M. E., & Ross, L. E. (1977). Saccade latency in children and adults: Effects of warning interval and target eccentricity. *Journal of Experimental Child Psychology, 23*, 539–549.

Coltheart, M. (1978). Lexical access in simple reading tasks. In G. Underwood (Ed.), *Strategies of information processing*. London: Academic Press.

Coltheart, M. (1980). Iconic memory and visual persistence. *Perception & Psychophysics, 27*, 183–228.

Coltheart, M. (1981). Disorders of reading and their implications for models of normal reading. *Visible Language, 15*, 245–286.

Coltheart, M. (2005). Analyzing developmental disorders of reading. *Advances in Speech Language Pathology*, 7(2), 49–57.

Coltheart, M., Davelaar, E., Jonasson, J. T., & Besner, D. (1977). Access to the internal lexicon. In S. Dornic (Ed.), *Attention and performance VI*. London: Academic Press.

Coltheart, M., & Freeman, R. (1974). Case alternation impairs word recognition. *Bulletin of the Psychonomic Society*, 3, 102–104.

Coltheart, M., Patterson, K., & Marshall, J. (1980). *Deep dyslexia*. London: Routledge & Kegan Paul.

Coltheart, M., & Rastle, K. (1994). Serial processing in reading aloud: Evidence for dual-route models of reading. *Journal of Experimental Psychology: Human Perception and Performance*, 20(6), 1197–1211.

Coltheart, M., Rastle, K., Perry, C., Langdon, R., & Ziegler, J. (2001). DRC: A dual route cascaded model of visual word recognition and reading aloud. *Psychological Review*, 108, 204–256.

Coltheart, V., Laxon, V. J., Keating, G. C., & Pool, M. M. (1986). Direct access and phonological encoding processes in children's reading: Effect of word characteristics. *British Journal of Eductional Psychology*, 56, 255–270.

Compton, D. L. (2003a). Modeling the relationship between growth in rapid naming speed and growth in decoding skill in first-grade children. *Journal of Educational Psychology*, 95(2), 225–239.

Compton, D. L. (2003b). The influence of item composition on RAN letter performance in first-grade children. *Journal of Special Education*, 37(2), 81–94.

Compton, D. L., Davis, C. J., DeFries, J. C., Gayan, J., & Olson, R. K. (2001). Genetic and environmental influences on reading and RAN: An overview of results from the Colorado Twin Study. In M. Wolf (Ed.), *Extraordinary brain series: Time, fluency, and developmental dyslexia* (pp. 277–303). Baltimore, MD: York Press.

Condry, S. M., McMahon-Rideout, M., & Levy, A. A. (1979). A developmental investigation of selective attention to graphic, phonetic, and semantic information in words. *Perception & Psychophysics*, 25, 88–94.

Conrad, R. (1972). Speech and reading. In J. F. Kavanagh & I. Mattingly (Eds.), *Language by ear and by eye*. Cambridge, MA: MIT Press.

Conrad, R. (1977). The reading ability of deaf school-leavers. *British Journal of Educational Psychology*, 47, 138–148.

Content, A., Kolinsky, R., Morais, J., & Bertelson, P. (1986). Phonetic segmentation in prereaders: Effect of corrective information. *Journal of Experimental Child Psychology*, 42, 49–72.

Cooper, R. M. (1974). The control of eye fixation by the meaning of spoken language: A new methodology for the real-time investigation of speech perception, memory, and language processing. *Cognitive Psychology*, 6, 84–107.

Corbett, A. T., & Dosher, B. A. (1978). Instrument inferences in sentence encoding. *Journal of Verbal Learning and Verbal Behavior*, 17, 479–491.

Corcoran, D. W. J. (1966). An acoustic factor in letter cancellation. *Nature*, 210, 658.

Corcoran, D. W. J. (1967). Acoustic factor in proofreading. *Nature*, 214, 851–852.

Coslett, H. B. (2000). Acquired dyslexia. In M. J. Farah, & T. E. Feinberg (Eds.), *Patient-based approaches to cognitive neuroscience* (pp. 235–246). Cambridge, MA: MIT Press.

Cowan, N. (1984). On short and long auditory stores. *Psychological Bulletin*, 96, 341–370.

Cowan, N. (2000). The magical number 4 in short-term memory: A reconsideration of mental storage capacity. *Behavioral and Brain Sciences*, 24, 87–185.

Cowles, H. W., Kluender, R., Kutas, M., & Polinsky, M. (2007). Violations of information structure: An electrophysiological study of answers to wh-questions. *Brain and Language*, 102, 228–242.

Craik, F. I. M., & Lockhart, R. S. (1972). Levels of processing: A framework for memory research. *Journal of Verbal Learning and Verbal Behavior*, 11, 671–684.

Crain, S., & Steedman, M. (1985). On not being led up the garden path: The use of context by the psychological parser. In D. Dowty, L. Karttunen, & A. Zwicky (Eds.), *Natural language processing: Psychological, computational, and theoretical perspectives*. Cambridge, UK: Cambridge University Press.

Crisp, J., & Ralph, M. A. L. (2006). Unlocking the nature of the phonological–deep dyslexia continuum: The keys to reading aloud are in phonology and semantics. *Journal of Cognitive Neuroscience*, 18(3), 348–362.

Crocker, M. (1995). *Computational psycholinguistics: An interdisciplinary approach to the study of language*. Dordrecht: Kluwer.

Crowder, R. G. (1982). *The psychology of reading: An introduction*. New York: Oxford University Press.

Crowder, R. G., & Wagner, R. K. (1992). *The psychology of reading*. Oxford, UK: Oxford University Press.

Cunningham, A. E., Perry, K. E., Stanovich, K. E., & Share, D. L. (2002). Orthographic learning during reading: Examining the role of self-teaching. *Journal of Experimental Child Psychology, 82*(3), 185–199.

Cunningham, A. E., Perry, K. E., Stanovich, K. E., & Stanovich, P. J. (2004). Disciplinary knowledge of K-3 teachers and their knowledge calibration in the domain of early literacy. *Annals of Dyslexia, 54*, 139–167.

Cunningham, A. E., & Stanovich, K.E. (1997). Early reading acquisition and its relation to reading experience and ability 10 years later. *Developmental Psychology, 33*(6), 934–945.

Cunningham, T. J., Healy, A. F., Kanengiser, N., Chizzick, L., & Willitts, R.L. (1988). Investigating the boundaries of reading units across ages and reading levels. *Journal of Experimental Child Psychology, 45*, 175–208.

Curtis, M. E. (1980). Development of components of reading skill. *Journal of Educational Psychology, 72*, 656–669.

Cutler, A., & Clifton, C., Jr. (1999). Blueprint of the listener. In P. Hagoort & C. Brown (Eds.), *The neurocognition of language* (pp. 123–166). Oxford: Oxford University Press.

Daneman, M., & Carpenter, P. A. (1980). Individual differences in working memory and reading, *Journal of Verbal Learning and Verbal Behavior, 19*, 450–466.

Daneman, M., & Carpenter, P. A. (1983). Individual differences in integrating information between and within sentences. *Journal of Experimental Psychology: Learning, Memory, and Cognition, 9*, 561–584.

Darling-Hammond, L. (2006). No child left behind and high school reform. *Harvard Educational Review, 76*(4), 642–667.

Davis, C. J. (2010). The spatial coding model of visual word identification. *Psychological Review, 117*, 713–758.

Davis, C. J., Perea, M., & Acha, J. (2009). Re(de)fining the orthographic neighbourhood: The role of addition and deletion neighbours in lexical decision and reading. *Journal of Experimental Psychology: Human Perception and Performance, 35*, 1550–1570.

de Abreu, M. D., & Cardoso-Martins, C. (1998). Alphabetic access route in beginning reading acquisition in Portuguese: The role of letter–name knowledge. *Reading and Writing, 10*(2), 85–104.

de Jong, P. F., & van der Leij, A. (1999). Specific contributions of phonological abilities to early reading acquisition: Results from a Dutch latent variable longitudinal study. *Journal of Educational Psychology, 91*, 450–476.

de Jong, P. F., & Vrielink, L. O. (2004). Rapid automatic naming: Easy to measure, hard to improve (quickly). *Annals of Dyslexia, 54*, 65–88.

DeFries, J. C., & Gillis, J. J. (1991). Etiology of reading deficits in learning disabilities: Quantitative genetic analysis. In J. E. Obrzut & G. W. Hynd (Eds.), *Neuropsychological foundations of learning disabilities: A handbook of issues, methods, and practice* (pp. 29–47). San Diego, CA: Academic Press.

DeFries, J. C., Singer, S. M., Foch, T. T., & Lewitter, F. I. (1978). Familial nature of reading disability. *British Journal of Psychiatry, 132*, 361–367.

Dehaene, S. (2009). *Reading in the brain.* Toronto, Canada: Viking Press.

Dehaene, S., & Cohen, L. (2007). Cultural recycling of cortical maps. *Neuron, 56*, 384–398.

Demberg, V., & Keller, F. (2008). Data from eye-tracking corpora as evidence for theories of syntactic processing complexity. *Cognition, 109*, 193–210.

DenBuurman, R., Boersma, T., & Gerrissen, J.F. (1981). Eye movements and the perceptual span in reading. *Reading Research Quarterly, 16*, 227–235.

Denckla, M. B., & Rudel, R. (1976a). Naming of pictured objects by dyslexics and other learning disabled children. *Brain and Language 3*, 1–15.

Denckla, M. B., & Rudel, R. (1976b). Rapid "automatized" naming (RAN): Dylexia differentiated from other learning disabilities. *Neuropsychologia, 14*, 471–9.

Denckla, M. B., & Rudel, R. G. (1974). Rapid "automatized" naming of pictured objects, colors, letters and numbers by normal children. *Cortex, 10*(2), 186–202.

Dennis, I., Besner, D., & Davelaar, E. (1985). Phonology is visual word recognition: Their is more two this than meats the I. In D. Besner, T. G. Waller, & G. E. MacKinnon (Eds.), *Reading research: Advances in theory and practice* (Vol.5). New York: Academic Press.

Deutsch, A., Frost, R., & Forster, K. I. (1998). Verbs and nouns are organized and accessed differently in the mental lexicon: Evidence from Hebrew. *Journal of Experimental Psychology: Learning Memory, and Cognition, 24*, 1238–1255.

Deutsch, A., Frost, R., Peleg, S., Pollatsek, A., & Rayner, K. (2003). Early morphological effects in reading: Evidence from parafoveal preview benefit in Hebrew. *Psychonomic Bulletin & Review, 10*, 415–422.

Deutsch, A., Frost, R., Pollatsek, A., & Rayner, K. (2000). Early morphological effects in word recognition in Hebrew: Evidence from parafoveal preview benefit. *Language and Cognitive Processes, 15*, 487–506.

Deutsch, A., Frost, R., Pollatsek, A., & Rayner, K. (2005). Morphological parafoveal preview benefit effects in reading: Evidence from Hebrew. *Language and Cognitive Processes, 20*, 341–371.

DeVincenzi, M. (1991). *Syntactic parsing strategies in Italian.* Dordrecht: Kluwer Academic.

Dickerson, J., & Johnson, H. (2004). Sub-types of deep dyslexia: A case study of central deep dyslexia. *Neurocase, 10*(1), 39–47.

Diringer, D. (1962). *Writing.* London: Thames & Hudson.

Doctor, E. A., & Coltheart, M. (1980). Children's use of phonological encoding when reading for meaning. *Memory & Cognition, 8*, 195–209.

Dodge, R. (1900). Visual perception during eye movement. *Psychological Review, 7*, 454–465.

Dodge, R. (1906). Recent studies in the correlation of eye movement and visual perception. *Psychological Bulletin, 13*, 85–92.

Doehring, D. G. (1976). Acquisition of rapid reading responses. *Monographs of the Society for Research in Child Development, 41*, No. 165.

Dolch, E. W. (1948). *Helping handicapped children in school.* Oxford, UK: Garrard Press.

Dolch, E. W., & Bloomster, M. (1937). Phonic readiness. *The Elementary School Journal, 38*, 201–205.

Douglas, K., & Montiel, E. (2008). *Learning to read in American elementary school classrooms: Poverty and the acquisition of reading skills.* Retrieved from www.reading.org/Libraries/SRII/ECLS-K_SES_Report.sflb.ashx

Downing, J., & Leong, C. K. (1982). *Psychology of reading.* New York: Macmillan.

Dowty, D. (1991). Thematic proto-roles and argument selection. *Language, 67*, 547–619.

Drake, W. E. (1968). Clinical and pathological findings in a child with a developmental learning disability. *Journal of Learning Disabilities, 1*(9), 486–502.

Drewnowski, A. (1978). Detection errors on the word the: Evidence for the acquisition of reading levels. *Memory & Cognition, 6*, 403–409.

Drewnowski, A., & Healy, A. F. (1977). Detection errors on the and and: Evidence for reading units larger than the word. *Memory & Cognition, 5*, 636–647.

Drewnowski, A., & Healy, A. F. (1980). Missing -ing in reading: Letter detection errors in word endings. *Journal of Verbal Learning and Verbal Behavior, 19*, 247–262.

Drews, E., & Zwitserlood, P. (1995). Morphological and orthographic similarity in visual word recognition. *Journal of Experimental Psychology: Human Perception and Performance, 21*, 1098–1116.

Drieghe, D. (2011). Parafoveal-on-foveal effects in eye movements during reading. In S. P. Liversedge, I. D. Gilchrist, & S. Everling (Eds.), *Oxford handbook on eye movements* (pp. 839–855). Oxford, UK: Oxford University Press.

Drieghe, D., Brysbaert, M., Desmet, T., & De Baecke, C. (2004). Word skipping in reading: On the interplay of linguistic and visual factors. *European Journal of Cognitive Psychology, 16*, 79–103.

Drieghe, D., Pollatsek, A., Juhasz, B. J., & Rayner, K. (2010). Parafoveal processing during reading is reduced across a morphological boundary. *Cognition, 116*, 136–142.

Drieghe, D., Pollatsek, A., Staub, A., & Rayner, K. (2008). The word grouping hypothesis and eye movements during reading. *Journal of Experimental Psychology: Learning, Memory, and Cognition, 34*, 1552–1560.

Drieghe, D., Rayner, K., & Pollatsek, A. (2005). Eye movements and word skipping during reading revisited. *Journal of Experimental Psychology: Human Perception and Performance, 31*, 954–969.

Drieghe, D., Rayner, K., & Pollatsek A. (2008). Mislocated fixations can account for parafoveal-on-foveal effects in eye movements during reading. *Quarterly Journal of Experimental Psychology, 61*, 1239–1249.

Duara, R., Kushch, A., Gross-Glenn, K., & Barker, W. W. (1991). Neuroanatomic differences between dyslexic and normal readers on magnetic resonance imaging scans. *Archives of Neurology, 48*(4), 410–416.

Duffy, S. A. (1986). Role of expectations in sentence integration. *Journal of Experimental Psychology: Learning, Memory, and Cognition, 12*, 208–219.

Duffy, S. A., Morris, R. K., & Rayner, K. (1988). Lexical ambiguity and fixation times in reading. *Journal of Memory and Language, 27*, 429–446.

Duffy, S. A., & Rayner, K. (1990). Eye movements and anaphor resolution: Effects of antecedent typicality and distance. *Language and Speech, 33*, 103–119.

Durkin, D. (1966). *Children who read early*. New York: Teachers College, Columbia University.

Durrell, D. D. (1958). First grade reading success study: A summary. *Journal of Education, 140*, 2–6.

Dyer, A., MacSwenney, M., Szczerbinski, M., Green, L., & Campbell, R. (2003). Predictors of reading delay in deaf adolescents: The relative contributions of rapid automatized naming speed and phonological awareness and decoding. *Journal of Deaf Studies and Deaf Education, 8*(3), 215.

Dyer, F. N. (1973). The Stroop phenomenon and its use in the study of perceptual, cognitive and response processes. *Memory & Cognition, 1*, 106–120.

Dykstra, R. (1968). The effectiveness of code- and meaning-emphasis beginning reading programs. *Reading Teacher, 22*(1), 17–23.

Edfeldt. A. W. (1960). *Silent speech and silent reading*. Chicago: University of Chicago Press.

Egeth, H., Jonides, J., & Wall, S. (1972). Parallel processing of multi-element displays. *Cognitive Psychology, 3*, 674–698.

Ehri, L. C. (1975). Word consciousness in readers and prereaders. *Journal of Educational Psychology, 67*, 204–212.

Ehri, L. C. (1976). Do words really interfere in naming pictures? *Child Development, 47*, 502–505.

Ehri, L. C. (1979). Linguistic insight: Threshold of reading acquisition. In T. W. Waller & G. E. MacKinnon (Eds.), *Reading research: Advances in theory and practice*. New York: Academic Press.

Ehri, L. C. (1980). The role of orthography in printed word learning. In J. G. Kavanaugh & R.L. Venezky (Eds.), *Orthography, reading, and dyslexia*. Baltimore: University Park Press.

Ehri, L. C. (1983). Influence of orthography of phonological and lexical awareness in beginning readers. In J. Downing & R. Valtin (Eds.), *Language awareness and learning to read*. New York: Springer-Verlag.

Ehri, L. C. (1992). Reconceptualizing the development of sight word reading and its relationship to recoding. In P. B. Gough, L. C. Ehri, & R. Treiman (Eds.), *Reading acquisition* (pp. 107–143). Hillsdale, NJ: Lawrence Erlbaum Associates Inc.

Ehri, L. C. (1998). Grapheme–phoneme knowledge is essential to learning to read words in English. In J. L. Metsala, & L. C. Ehri (Eds.), *Word recognition in beginning literacy* (pp. 3–40). Mahwah, NJ: Lawrence Erlbaum Associates Inc.

Ehri, L. C. (1999). Phases of development in learning to read words. In J. Oakhill & R. Beard (Eds.), *Reading development and the teaching of reading: A psychological perspective* (pp. 79–108). Oxford: Blackwell Science.

Ehri, L. C. (2002). Phases of acquisition in learning to read words and implications for teaching. In R. Stainthorp & P. Tomlinson (Eds.), *Learning and teaching reading*. London: British Journal of Educational Psychology Monograph Series II.

Ehri, L. C., Nunes, S. R., Stahl, S. A., & Willows, D. M. (2001). Systematic phonics instruction helps students learn to read: Evidence from the National Reading Panel's meta-analysis. *Review of Educational Research, 71*(3), 393–447.

Ehri, L. C., & Robbins, C. (1992). Beginners need some decoding skill to read words by analogy. *Reading Research Quarterly, 27*(1), 12–26.

Ehri, L. C., & Wilce, L. S. (1979). The mnemonic value of orthography among beginning readers. *Journal of Educational Psychology, 71*, 26–40.

Ehri, L. C., & Wilce, L. S. (1985). Movement into reading: Is the first stage of printed word learning visual or phonetic? *Reading Research Quarterly, 2*, 163–179.

Ehri, L. E., & Wilce, L. S. (1987a). Cipher versus cue reading: An experiment in decoding acquisition. *Journal of Educational Psychology, 79*, 3–13.

Ehri, L. E., & Wilce, L. S. (1987b). Does learning to spell help beginning readers learn to read words? *Reading Research Quarterly, 22*, 47–65.

Ehrlich, K. (1980). Comprehension of pronouns. *Quarterly Journal of Experimental Psychology, 32*, 247–255.

Ehrlich, K., & Rayner K. (1983) Pronoun assignment and semantic integration during reading: Eye movements and immediacy of processing. *Journal of Verbal Learning and Verbal Behavior, 22*, 75–87.

Ehrlich, S. F. (1981). Children's word recognition in prose context. *Visible Language, 15*, 219–244.

Ehrlich, S. F., & Rayner, K. (1981). Contextual effects on word perception and eye movements during reading. *Journal of Verbal Learning and Verbal Behavior, 20*, 641–655.

Eiter, B. M., & Inhoff, A. W. (2010). Visual word recognition in reading is followed by subvocal articulation. *Journal of Experimental Psychology: Learning, Memory and Cognition, 36*, 457–470.

Elbro, C. (1996). Early linguistic abilities and reading development. A review and a hypothesis. *Reading and Writing, 8*(6), 453–485.

Elkind, D., & Weiss, J. (1967). Studies in perceptual development. III: Perceptual exploration. *Child Development, 38,* 553–561.

Elkonin, D. B. (1973). U.S.S.R. In J. Downing (Ed.), *Comparative reading* (pp. 551–579). New York: Macmillan.

Ellis, A. W. (1984). *Reading, writing and dyslexia: A cognitive analysis.* Hove, UK: Lawrence Erlbaum Associates Ltd.

Ellis, N. C., & Hooper, A. M. (2001). Why learning to read is easier in Welsh than in English: Orthographic transparency effects evinced with frequency-matched tests. *Applied Psycholinguistics, 22*(4), 571–599.

Elman, J. L., Hare, M., & McRae, K. (2004). Cues, constraints, and competition in sentence processing. In M. Tomasello & D. Slobin (Eds.), *Beyond nature–nuture: Essays in honor of Elizabeth Bates.* Mahwah, NJ: Lawrence Erlbaum Associates Inc.

Engbert, R., Nuthmann, A., Richter, E., & Kliegl, R. (2005). SWIFT: A dynamical model of saccade generation during reading. *Psychological Review, 112,* 777–813.

Erdmann, B., & Dodge, R. (1898). *Psychologische Untersuchungen uber das Lesen.* Halle, Germany: M. Niemeyer.

Erickson, D., Mattingly, I. G., & Turvey, M. T. (1977). Phonetic activity in reading: An experiment with Kanji. *Language and Speech, 20,* 384–403.

Erickson, T. D., & Mattson, M. E. (1981). From words to meaning: A semantic illusion. *Journal of Verbal Learning and Verbal Behavior, 20,* 540–551.

Evans, M. A., & Carr, T. H. (1985). Cognitive abilities, conditions of learning, and the early development of reading skill. *Reading Research Quarterly, 20*(3), 327–350.

Evans, M. A., & Saint-Aubin, J. (2005). What children are looking at during shared storybook reading: Evidence from eye movement monitoring. *Psychological Science, 16,* 913–920.

Evans, M. A., Shaw, D., & Bell, M. (2000). Home literacy activities and their influence on early literacy skills. *Canadian Journal of Experimental Psychology, 54*(2), 65–75.

Evett, L. J., & Humphreys, G. W. (1981). The use of abstract graphemic information in lexical access. *Quarterly Journal of Experimental Psychology, 33A,* 325–350.

Eysenck, M. W., & Keane, M. T. (2010). *Cognitive psychology: A student's handbook* (6th ed.). Hove, UK: Psychology Press.

Ezell, H. K., & Justice, L. M. (2000). Increasing the print focus of adult–child shared book reading through observational learning. *American Journal of Speech–Language Pathology, 9,* 36–47.

Feinberg, R. (1949). A study of some aspects of peripheral visual acuity. *American Journal of Optometry and Archives of the American Annals of Optometry, 26,* 49–56, 105–119.

Feitelson, D., & Razel, M. (1984). Word superiority and word shape effects in beginning readers. *International Journal of Behavioral Development, 7,* 359–370.

Feldman, L. B. (2000). Are morphological effects distinguishable from the effects of shared meaning and shared form? *Journal of Experimental Psychology: Learning, Memory, and Cognition, 26,* 1431–1444.

Feldman, L. B., & Turvey, M. T. (1983). Word recognition in Serbo-Croatian is phonologically analytic. *Journal of Experimental Psychology: Human Perception and Performance, 9,* 288–298.

Felton, R. H., Naylor, C. E., & Wood, F. B. (1990). Neuropsychological profile of adult dyslexics. *Brain and Language, 39*(4), 485–497.

Felton, R. H., Wood, F. B., Brown, I. B., Campbell, S. K. & Harter, M. R. (1987). Separate verbal memory and naming deficits in attention deficit disorder and reading disability. *Brain & Language, 31,* 171–184.

Ferguson, H. J., & Sanford, A. (2008). Anomalies in real and counterfactual worlds: An eye-movement investigation. *Journal of Memory and Language, 58,* 609–626.

Ferreira, F. (2003). The misinterpretation of noncanonical sentences. *Cognitive Psychology, 47,* 164–203.

Ferreira, F., Bailey, K. G. D., & Ferraro, V. (2002). Good-enough representations in language comprehension. *Current Directions in Psychological Science, 11,* 11–14.

Ferreira, F., & Clifton C. Jr. (1986). The independence of syntactic processing. *Journal of Memory and Language, 25,* 75–87.

Ferreira, F., & Henderson, J. (1990). The use of verb information in syntactic parsing: Evidence from eye movements and word-by-word self-paced reading. *Journal of Experimental Psychology: Learning, Memory, and Cognition, 16,* 555–568.

Ferreira, F., & Patson, N. D. (2007). The 'good enough' approach to language comprehension. *Language and Linguistics Compass, 1,* 71–83.

Ferretti, T. R., Kutas, M., & McRae, K. (2007).Verb aspect and the activation of event knowledge. *Journal of Experimental Psychology: Learning, Memory, and Cognition, 33,* 182–196.

Ferretti, T. R., McRae, K., & Hatherell, A. (2001). Integrating verbs, situation schemas, and thematic role concepts. *Journal of Memory and Language, 44,* 516–548.

Fielding-Barnsley, R., & Purdie, N. (2005). Teachers' attitude to and knowledge of metalinguistics in the process of learning to read. *Asia-Pacific Journal of Teacher Education, 33*(1), 65–76.

Filik, R., Paterson, K. B., & Liversedge, S. P. (2005). Parsing with focus particles in context: Eye movements during the processing of relative clause ambiguities. *Journal of Memory and Language, 53,* 473–495.

Fine, E. M., & Rubin, G. S. (1999). Reading with a central field loss: number of letters masked is more important than the size of the mask in degrees. *Vision Research, 39,* 747–756.

Fischer, I., & Bloom, P. (1979). Automatic and attentional processes in the effects of sentence context on word recognition. *Journal of Verbal Learning and Verbal Behavior, 18,* 1–20.

Fisher, D. F. (1979). Dysfunctions in reading disability: There's more than meets the eye. In L. B. Resnick & P. A. Weaver (Eds.), *Theory and practice of early reading* (Vol. 1). Hillsdale, NJ: Lawrence Erlbaum Associates Inc.

Fisher, D. F., & Montanary, S. P. (1977). *Spatial and contextual factors in beginning reading: Evidence for PSG-CSG complements to developing automaticity?* (pp. 247–251). Hillsdale, NJ: Lawrence Erlbaum Associates Inc.

Fisher, D. G. (1983). An experimental study of eye movements during reading. Unpublished manuscript. Murray Hill, NJ: Bell Laboratories.

Fisher, S. E., & DeFries, J. C. (2002). Developmental dyslexia: Genetic dissection of a complex cognitive trait. *Nature Reviews Neuroscience, 3,* 767–80.

Fisher, S. E., Stein, J. F., & Monaco, A. P. (1999). A genome-wide search strategy for identifying quantitative trait loci involved in reading and spelling disability (developmental dyslexia). *European Child & Adolescent Psychiatry, 8*(3), III–47–III/51.

Fletcher, J. M., Foorman, B. R., Francis, D. J., Shaywitz, B. A., & Shaywitz, S. E. (1994). Treatment of dyslexia. In K. P. van den Bos, L. S. Siegel, D. J. Baker, & D. L. Share (Eds.), *Current directions in dyslexia research* (pp. 223–233). Lisse, Switzerland: Swets & Zeitlinger.

Fletcher, J. M., Lyon, G. R., Barnes, M., Stuebing, K. K., Francis, D. J., Olson, R., et al. (2002). Classification of learning disabilities: An evidenced-based evaluation. In R. Bradley, L. Danielson, & D. Hallahan (Eds.), *Identification of learning disabilities: Research to practice* (pp. 185–250). Mahwah, NJ: Lawrence Erlbaum Associates Inc.

Fletcher, J. M., Lyon, G. R., Fuchs, L. S., & Barnes, M. A. (2007). *Learning disabilities: From identification to intervention.* New York: Guilford Press.

Fletcher, J. M., Shaywitz, S. E., Shankweiler, D. P., Katz, L., Liberman, I. Y., Stuebing, K. K., et al. (1994). Cognitive profiles of reading disability: Comparisons of discrepancy and low achievement definitions. *Journal of Educational Psychology, 86,* 6–23.

Fodor, J. A. (1983). *Modularity of mind.* Cambridge, MA: MIT Press.

Fodor, J. A., Bever, T. G., & Garrett, M. (1974). *The psychology of language.* New York: McGraw-Hill.

Fodor, J. D. (2002). Prosodic disambiguation in silent reading. In M. Hirotani (Ed.), *Proceedings of the North East Linguistics Society* (Vol. 32, pp. 112–132). Amherst, MA: GSLA.

Fodor, J. D., & Ferreira, F. (Eds.). (1998). *Sentence reanalysis.* Dordrecht: Kluwer Academic.

Folk, J. R. (1999). Phonological codes are used to access the lexicon during silent reading. *Journal of Experimental Psychology: Learning, Memory, and Cognition, 25,* 892–906.

Folk, J. R., & Morris, R. K. (1995). Multiple lexical codes in reading: Evidence from eye movements, naming time, and oral reading. *Journal of Experimental Psychology: Learning, Memory, and Cognition, 21,* 1412–1429.

Fontenelle, S., & Alarcon, M. (1982). Hyperlexia: Precocious word recognition in developmentally delayed children. *Perceptual and Motor Skills, 55,* 247–252.

Foorman, B. R., Francis, D. J., Fletcher, J. M., & Lynn, A. (1996). Relation of phonological and orthographic processing to early reading: Comparing two approaches to regression-based, reading-level match designs. *Journal of Educational Psychology, 88*(4), 639–652.

Foorman, B. R., Francis, D. J., Fletcher, J. M., Schatschneider, C., & Mehta, P. (1998). The role of instruction in learning to read: Preventing reading failure in at-risk children. *Journal of Educational Psychology, 90,* 37–55.

Ford, M., Bresnan, J., & Kaplan, R. (1982). A competence-based theory of syntactic closure. In J. Bresnan (Ed.), *The mental representation of grammatical relations.* Cambridge, MA: MIT Press.

Forster, K. I. (1976). Accessing the mental lexicon. In R. J. Wales & E. C. T. Walker (Eds.), *New approach to language mechanisms*. Amsterdam: North-Holland.

Forster, K. I. (1979). Levels of processing and the structure of the language processor. In W. E. Cooper & E. Walker (Eds.), *Sentence processing: Psycholinguistic studies presented to Merrill Garrett*. Hillsdale, NJ: Lawrence Erlbaum Associates Inc.

Forster, K. I., & Azuma, T. (2000). Masked priming for prefixed words with bound stems: Does submit prime permit? *Language and Cognitive Processes, 15*, 539–562.

Forster, K. I., & Davis, C. (1984). Repetition priming and frequency attenuation in lexical access. *Journal of Experimental Psychology: Learning, Memory, and Cognition, 10*, 680–698.

Foss, D. J. (1982). A discourse on semantic priming. *Cognitive Psychology, 14*, 590–607.

Fountas, I. C., & Pinnell, G. S. (1996). *Guided reading: Good first teaching for all children*. Portsmouth, NH: Heinemann.

Fountas, I. C., & Pinnell, G. S. (2006). *Teaching for comprehending and fluency: Thinking, talking, and writing about reading, K-8*. Portsmouth, NH: Heinemann.

Fountas, I. C., & Pinnell, G. S. (2008). *When readers struggle: Teaching that works*. Portsmouth, NH: Heinemann.

Fowler, A. E. (1991). How early phonological development might set the stage for phoneme awareness. In S. A. Brady & D. P. Shankweiler (Eds.), *Phonological processes in literacy: A tribute to Isabelle Y. Liberman* (pp. 97–117). Hillsdale, NJ: Lawrence Erlbaum Associates Inc.

Fowler, C., Wolford, G., Slade, R., & Tassinary, L. (1981). Lexical access with and without awareness. *Journal of Experimental Psychology: General, 110*, 341–362.

Fox, B., & Routh, D. K. (1975). Analyzing spoken language into words, syllables, and phonemes: A developmental study. *Journal of Psycholinguistic Research, 4*, 331–342.

Fox, B., & Routh, D. K. (1976). Phonetic analysis and synthesis as word attack skills. *Journal of Educational Psychology, 68*, 70–74.

Fox, B., & Routh, D. K. (1984). Phonemic analysis and synthesis as word attack skills: Revisited. *Journal of Educational Psychology, 76*, 1059–1064.

Francis, D. J., Shaywitz, S. E., Stuebing, K. K., Shaywitz, B. A., & Fletcher, J. M. (1996). Developmental lag versus deficit models of reading disability: A longitudinal, individual growth curves analysis. *Journal of Educational Psychology, 88*(1), 3–17.

Francis, W. N., & Kučera, H. (1982). *Frequency analysis of English usage: Lexicon and grammar*. Boston: Houghton Mifflin.

Frazier, L. (1979). *On comprehending sentences: Syntactic parsing strategies*. Bloomington, IN: Indiana University Linguistics Club.

Frazier, L. (1983). Processing sentence structure. In K. Rayner (Ed.), *Eye movements in reading: Perceptual and language processes* (pp. 215–236). New York: Academic Press.

Frazier, L. (1987). Sentence processing: A tutorial review. In M. Coltheart, (Ed.), *Attention and performance XII*. Hillsdale, NJ: Lawrence Erlbaum Associates Inc.

Frazier, L. (1989). Against lexical generation of syntax. In W. Marslen-Wilson (Ed.), *Lexical representation and process* (pp. 505–528). Cambridge, MA: MIT Press.

Frazier, L. (1990). Exploring the architecture of the language system. In G. Altmann (Ed.), *Cognitive models of speech processing: Psycholinguistic and computational perspectives* (pp. 409–433). Cambridge, MA: MIT Press.

Frazier, L. (1995). Constraint satisfaction as a theory of sentence processing. *Journal of Psycholinguistic Research, 24*, 437–468.

Frazier, L. (1999). *On sentence interpretation*. Dordrecht: Kluwer Academic.

Frazier, L. (2008). Is good-enough parsing good enough? In L. Arcuri, P. Boscolo, & F. Peressotti (Eds.), *Cognition and language: A long story. Festschrift in honour of Ino Flores d'Arcais* (pp. 13–29). Department of Psychology, University of Padua.

Frazier, L., Carlson, K., & Clifton, C. Jr. (2006). Prosodic phrasing is central to language comprehension. *Trends in Cognitive Sciences, 10*, 244–249.

Frazier, L., & Clifton, C., Jr. (1996). *Construal*. Cambridge, MA: MIT Press.

Frazier, L., & Clifton, C. Jr. (2005). The syntax–discourse divide: Processing ellipsis. *Syntax, 8*, 154–207.

Frazier, L., & Clifton, C. Jr. (2011). Quantifiers undone: Reversing predictable speech errors in comprehension. *Language, 87*, 158–171.

Frazier, L., & Flores d'Arcais, G. B. (1989). Filler driven parsing: A study of gap filling in Dutch. *Journal of Memory and Language, 28*, 331–344.

Frazier, L. & Fodor, J. D. (1978). The sausage machine: A new two-stage parsing model. *Cognition, 6*, 291–326.

Frazier, L., Pacht, J. M., & Rayner, K. (1999). Taking on semantic commitments. II: Collective versus distributive readings. *Cognition, 70*, 87–104.

Frazier, L., & Rayner, K. (1982). Making and correcting errors during sentence comprehension: Eye movements in the analysis of structurally ambiguous sentences. *Cognitive Psychology, 14*, 178–210.

Frazier, L., & Rayner, K. (1987). Resolution of syntactic category ambiguities: Eye movements in parsing lexically ambiguous sentences. *Journal of Memory and Language, 26*, 505–526.

Frederiksen, J. R. (1982). A componential model of reading skills and their interrelations. In R. J. Sternberg (Ed.), *Advances in the psychology of human intelligence*. Hillsdale, NJ: Lawrence Erlbaum Associates Inc.

Friedman, R. B., & Perlman, M. B. (1982). On the underlying causes of semantic paralexias in a patient with deep dyslexia. *Neuropsychologia, 20*, 559–568.

Frisson, S., & McElree, B. (2008). Complement coercion is not modulated by competition: Evidence from eye movements. *Journal of Experimental Psychology: Learning, Memory and Cognition, 34*, 1–11.

Frisson, S., Niswander–Klement, E., & Pollatsek, A. (2008). The role of semantic transparency in the processing of English compound words. *British Journal of Psychology, 99*, 87–107.

Frisson, S., Rayner, K., & Pickering, M. J. (2005). Effects of contextual predictability and transitional probability on eye movements during reading. *Journal of Experimental Psychology: Learning, Memory, and Cognition, 31*, 862–877.

Frith, U. (1980). *Cognitive processes in spelling*. London: Academic Press.

Frith, U., & Snowling, M. (1983). Reading for meaning and reading for sound in autistic and dyslexic children. *British Journal of Developmental Psychology, 1*(4), 329–342.

Frost, R., Forster, K. I., & Deutsch, A. (1997). What can we learn from the morphology of Hebrew: A masked priming investigation of morphological representation? *Journal of Experimental Psychology: Learning Memory, and Cognition, 23*, 829–856.

Frost, S. J., Sandak, R., Mencl, W. E., Landi, N., Rueckl, J. G., Katz, L., et al. (2009). Mapping the word reading circuitry in skilled and disabled readers. In K. Pugh & P. McCardle (Eds.), *How children learn to read: Current issues and new directions in the integration of cognition, neurobiology and genetics of reading and dyslexia research and practice* (pp. 3–19). New York: Psychology Press.

Funnell, E. (1983). Phonological processes in reading: New evidence from acquired dyslexia. *British Journal of Psychology, 74*, 159–180.

Furnes, B., & Samuelsson, S. (2010). Predicting reading and spelling difficulties in transparent and opaque orthographies: A comparison between Scandinavian and US/Australian children. *Dyslexia: An International Journal of Research and Practice, 16*(2), 119–142.

Gabrieli, J. D. (2009). Dyslexia: A new synergy between education and cognitive neuroscience. *Science, 325*, 280–283.

Galaburda, A. M., & Kemper, T. L. (1979). Cytoarchitectonic abnormalities in developmental dyslexia: a case study. *Annals of Neurology, 6*(2), 94–100.

Gallagher, A., Frith, U., & Snowling, M. J. (2000). Precursors of literacy delay among children at genetic risk of dyslexia. *Journal of Child Psychology and Psychiatry, 41*(2), 202–213.

Garlock, V. M., Walley, A. C., & Metsala, J. L. (2001). Age of acquisition, word frequency, and neighborhood density in spoken word recognition by children and adults. *Journal of Memory and Language, 45*, 468–492.

Garnham, A. (1987). *Mental models as representations of discourse and text*. Chichester, UK: Wiley.

Garnham, A. (1999). Reference and anaphora. In S. Garrod & M. J. Pickering (Eds.), *Language processing* (pp. 335–362). Hove, UK: Psychology Press.

Garnsey, S. M., Pearlmutter, N. J., Myers, E., & Lotocky, M. A. (1997). The contributions of verb bias and plausibility to the comprehension of temporarily–ambiguous sentences. *Journal of Memory and Language, 37*, 58–93.

Garrett, M. F. (1976). Syntactic processes in sentence production. In R. J. Wales & E. Walker (Eds.), *New approaches to language mechanisms. A collection of psycholinguistic studies*. Amsterdam: North-Holland.

Garrity, L. I. (1977). Electromyography: A review of the current status of subvocal speech research. *Memory & Cognition, 5*, 615–622.

Garrod, S., O'Brien, E. J., Morris, R. K., & Rayner, K. (1990). Elaborative inferencing as an active or passive process. *Journal of Experimental Psychology: Learning, Memory, and Cognition, 16*, 250–257.

Garrod, S., & Sanford, A. J. (1977). Interpreting anaphoric relations: The integration of semantic information while reading. *Journal of Verbal Learning and Verbal Behavior, 16*, 77–90.

Garrod, S., & Sanford, A. J. (1982). The mental representation of discourse in a focused memory system: Implications for the interpretation of anaphoric noun-phrases. *Journal of Semantics, 1*, 21–41.

Garrod, S., & Sanford, A. J. (1983). Topic dependent effects in language processing. In G. B. F. d'Arcais & R. J. Jarvella (Eds.), *The process of language understanding*. Chichester, UK: Wiley.

Garrod, S., & Terras, M. (2000). The contribution of lexical and situation knowledge to resolving discourse roles: Bonding and resolution. *Journal of Memory and Language, 42*, 526–544.

Gaskell, M. G. (Ed.). (2007). *The Oxford handbook of psycholinguistics*. Oxford: Oxford University Press.

Gayán, J., & Olson, R. K. (2001). Genetic and environmental influences on orthographic and phonological skills in children with reading disabilities. *Developmental Neuropsychology, 20*(2), 483–507.

Gelb, I. J. (1963). *A study of writing, 2nd ed.* Chicago: University of Chicago Press.

Gennari, S. P., & Poeppel, D. (2003). Processing correlates of lexical syntactic complexity. *Cognition, 89*, B27–B41.

Gerhand, S., & Barry, C. (2000). When does a deep dyslexic make a semantic error? The roles of age-of-acquisition, concreteness, and frequency. *Brain and Language, 74*(1), 26–47.

Gerrig, R. J., & McKoon, G. (1998). The readiness is all: The functionality of memory-based text processing. *Discourse Processes, 26*, 67–86.

Geschwind, N., & Levitsky, W. (1968). Human brain: Left–right asymmetries in temporal speech region. *Science, 161*(3837), 186–187.

Gibson, E. (1998). Linguistic complexity: Locality of syntactic dependencies. *Cognition, 68*, 1–76.

Gibson, E. J. (1965). Learning to read. *Science, 148*, 1066–1072.

Gibson, E. J. (1971). Perceptual learning and the theory of word perception. *Cognitive Psychology, 2*, 351–368.

Gibson, E. J., & Levin, H. (1975). *The psychology of reading*. Cambridge, MA: MIT Press.

Gilger, J. W., Hanebuth, E., Smith, S. D., & Pennington, B. F. (1996). Differential risk for developmental reading disorders in the offspring of compensated versus noncompensated parents. *Reading and Writing, 8*(5), 407–417.

Gilger, J. W., Pennington, B. F., & DeFries, J. C. (1991). Risk for reading disability as a function of parental history in three family studies. In B. Pennington (Ed.), *Reading disabilities: Genetic and neurological influences*. Boston: Kluwer Academic.

Gillon, G., & Dodd, B. J. (1994). A prospective study of the relationship between phonological, semantic and syntactic skills and specific reading disability. *Reading and Writing, 6*(4), 321–345.

Giraudo, H., & Grainger, J. (2001). Priming complex words: Evidence for supralexical representation of morphology. *Psychonomic Bulletin & Review, 8*, 127–131.

Gleitman, L. R., & Rozin, P. (1977). The structure and acquisition of reading I: Relations between orthographies and the structure of language. In A. S. Reber & D. L. Scarborough (Eds.), *Toward a psychology of reading*. Hillsdale, NJ: Lawrence Erlbaum Associates Inc.

Glenberg, A. M., Meyer, M., & Lindem, K. (1987). Mental models contribute to foregrounding during text comprehension. *Journal of Memory and Language, 26*, 69–83.

Glock, M. D. (1949). The effect upon eye-movements and reading rate at the college level of three methods of training. *Journal of Educational Psychology, 40*, 93–106.

Glosser, G., & Friedman, R. B. (1990). The continuum of deep/phonological alexia. *Cortex, 26*(3), 343–359.

Glushko, R. J. (1979). The organization and activation of orthographic knowledge in reading aloud. *Journal of Experimental Psychology: Human Perception and Performance, 5*, 674–691.

Glushko, R. J. (1981). Principles for pronouncing print: The psychology of phonography. In A. M. Lesgold & C. A. Perfetti (Eds.), *Interactive processes in reading*. Hillsdale, NJ: Erlbaum.

Godfrey, J. J., Syrdal-Lasky, A. K., Millay, K. K., & Knox, C. M. (1981). Performance of dyslexic children on speech perception tests. *Journal of Experimental Child Psychology, 32*(3), 401–424.

Goldberg, T. E. (1987). On hermetic reading abilities. *Journal of Autism and Developmental Disorders, 17*(1), 29–44.

Goldin-Meadow, S., & Mayberry, R. I. (2001). How do profoundly deaf children learn to read? *Learning Disabilities Research and Practice, 16*(4), 222–229.

Golinkoff, R. M. (1976). A comparison of reading comprehension processes in good and poor comprehenders. *Reading Research Quarterly, 11,* 623–669.

Golinkoff, R. M. (1978). Critique: Phonemic awareness skills and reading achievement. In F. B. Murray & J. J. Pikulski (Eds.), *The acquisition of reading: Cognitive, linguistic and perceptual prerequisites.* Baltimore, MD: University Park Press.

Golinkoff, R. M., & Rosinski, R. R. (1976). Decoding, semantic processing, and reading comprehension skill. *Child Development, 47,* 252–258.

Gómez, P., Ratcliff, R., & Perea, M. (2008). The overlap model: A model of letter position coding. *Psychological Review, 115,* 577–601.

Goodman, K. S. (1967). Reading: A psycholinguistic guessing game. *Journal of the Reading Specialist, 6,* 126–135.

Goodman, K. S. (1970). Reading: A psycholinguistic guessing game. In H. Singer & R.B. Ruddell, R.B. (Eds.), *Theoretical models and processes of reading.* Newark, DE: International Reading Association.

Goodman, K. S. (1993). *Phonics phacts.* Portsmouth, NH: Heinemann.

Gordon, P. C., Grosz, B. J., & Gilliom, L. A. (1993). Pronouns, nouns, and the centering of attention in discourse. *Cognitive Science, 17,* 311–349.

Gordon, P. C., & Hendrick, R. (1997). Intuitive knowledge of linguistic co-reference. *Cognition, 62,* 325–370.

Gordon, P. C., & Hendrick, R. (1998). The representation and processing of co-reference in discourse. *Cognitive Science, 22,* 389–424.

Gordon, P. C., Hendrick, R., & Johnson, M. (2001). Memory interference during language processing. *Journal of Experimental Psychology: Learning, Memory, and Cognition, 27,* 1411–1423.

Goswami, U. (1986). Children's use of analogy in learning to read: A developmental study. *Journal of Experimental Child Psychology, 42,* 73–83.

Goswami, U. (1993). Toward an interactive analogy model of reading development: Decoding vowel graphemes in beginning reading. *Journal of Experimental Child Psychology, 56,* 443–475.

Goswami, U. (2000). Phonological and lexical processes. In M. L. Kamil, P. B. Mosenthal, P. D. Pearson, & R. Barr (Eds.), *Handbook of reading research* (Vol. 3, pp. 251–267). Mahwah, NJ: Lawrence Erlbaum Associates Inc.

Goswami, U. (2005). Synthetic phonics and learning to read: A cross-language perspective. *Educational Psychology in Practice, 21*(4), 273–282.

Goswami, U., & Bryant, P. (1990). *Phonological skills and learning to read. Essays in developmental psychology.* Hillsdale, NJ: Lawrence Erlbaum Associates Inc.

Goswami, U., Ziegler, J. C., Dalton, L., & Schneider, W. (2001). Pseudohomophone effects and phonological recoding procedures in reading development in English and German. *Journal of Memory and Language, 45,* 648–664.

Goswami, U., Ziegler, J. C., Dalton, L., & Schneider, W. (2003). Nonword reading across orthographies: How flexible is the choice of reading units? *Applied Psycholinguistics, 24*(2), 235–247.

Gough, P. B. (1972). One second of reading. In J. F. Kavanagh & I. G. Mattingly (Eds.), *Language by ear and by eye.* Cambridge, MA: MIT Press.

Gough, P. B., Alford, J. A., & Holley-Wilcox, P. (1981). Words and contexts. In O. L. Tzeng & H. Singer (Eds.), *Perception of print: Reading research in experimental psychology.* Hillsdale, NJ: Erlbaum.

Gough, P. B., & Hillinger, M. L. (1980). Learning to read: An unnatural act. *Bulletin of the Orton Society, 20,* 179–196.

Gough, P. B., & Tunmer, W. E. (1986). Decoding, reading, and reading disability. *RASE: Remedial & Special Education, 7*(1), 6–10.

Graesser, A. C., Singer, M., & Trabasso, T. (1994). Constructing inferences during narrative text comprehension. *Psychological Review, 101,* 371–395.

Grainger, J. (1990). Word frequency and neighborhood frequency effects in lexical decision and naming. *Journal of Memory and Language, 29,* 228–244.

Grainger, J., Cole, P., & Segui, J. (1991). Masked morphological priming in visual word recognition. *Journal of Memory and Language, 30,* 370–384.

Grainger, J., & Jacobs, A. M. (1996). Orthographic processing in visual word recognition: A multiple read-out model. *Psychological Review, 103,* 518–565.

Grainger, J., Rey, A., & Dufau, S. (2008). Letter perception: From pixels to pandemonium. *Trends in Cognitive Science, 12,* 381–387.

Grainger, J., & Segui, J. (1990). Neighborhood frequency effects in visual word recognition: A comparison of lexical decision and masked identification latencies. *Perception & Psychophysics, 47*, 191–198.

Grainger, J., & Whitney, C. (2004). Does the huamn mnid raed wrods as a whole? *Trends in Cognitive Sciences, 8*, 58–59.

Green, R. L., Hustler, J. J., Loftus, W. C., Tramo, M. J., Thomas, C. E., Silberfarb, A. W., et al. (1999). The caudal infrasylvian surface in dyslexia: Novel magnetic resonance imaging-based findings. *Neurology, 53*, 974–981.

Greenberg, S. N., Inhoff, A. W., & Weger, U. W. (2006). The impact of letter detection on eye movement patterns during reading: Reconsidering lexical analysis in connected text as a function of task. *Quarterly Journal of Experimental Psychology, 59*, 987–995.

Griffiths, Y. M., & Snowling, M. J. (2002). Predictors of exception word and nonword reading in dyslexic children: The severity hypothesis. *Journal of Educational Psychology, 94*(1), 34–43.

Grigorenko, E. L., Klin, A., Pauls, D. L., Senft, R., Hooper, C., & Volkmar, F. (2002). A descriptive study of hyperlexia in a clinically referred sample of children with developmental delays. *Journal of Autism and Developmental Disorders, 32*(1), 3–12.

Grigorenko, E. L., Klin, A., & Volkmar, F. (2003). Hyperlexia: Disability or superability? *Journal of Child Psychology and Psychiatry, 44*(8), 1079–1091.

Groff, P. (1975). Research in brief: Shapes as cues to word recognition. *Visible Language, 9*, 67–71.

Groll, S. L., & Ross, L. E. (1982). Saccadic eye movements of children and adults to double-step stimuli. *Developmental Psychology, 18*, 108–123.

Grosz, B., Joshi, A., & Weinstein, S. (1983). Providing a unified account of definite noun phrases in discourse. *Proceedings of the Association for Computational Linguistics* (pp. 44–50). Cambridge, MA: MIT Press.

Grosz, B. J., Joshi, A. K., & Weinstein, S. (1995). Centering: A framework for modeling the local coherence of discourse. *Computational Linguistics, 21*, 203–225.

Grundin, H. (1994). If it ain't whole, it ain't language—or back to the basics of freedom and dignity. In F. Lehr & J. Osborn (Eds.), *Reading, language, and literacy* (pp. 77–88). Mahwah, NJ: Lawrence Erlbaum Associates Inc.

Guttentag, R. E., & Haith, M. M. (1978). Automatic processing as a function of age and reading ability. *Child Development, 49*, 707–716.

Haber, R. N. (1983). The impending demise of the icon: A critique of the concept of iconic storage in visual information processing. *Behavioral and Brain Sciences, 6*, 1–54.

Haber, R. N., & Haber, L. R. (1981). The shape of a word can specify its meaning. *Reading Research Quarterly, 16*, 334–345

Haber, R. N., & Haber, L. R. (1982). Does silent reading involve articulation? Evidence from tongue-twisters. *American Journal of Psychology, 95*, 409–419.

Haber, R. N., & Schindler, R. M. (1981). Error in proofreading: Evidence of syntactic control of letter processing? *Journal of Experimental Psychology: Human Perception and Performance, 7*, 573–579.

Haberlandt, K. (1982). Reader expectations in text comprehension. In J. F. L. Ny & W. Kintsch (Eds.), *Language comprehension* (pp. 239–249). Amsterdam: North-Holland.

Häikiö, T., Bertram, R., Hyönä, J., & Niemi, P. (2009). Development of the letter identity span in reading: Evidence from the eye movement moving window paradigm. *Journal of Experimental Child Psychology, 102*, 167–181.

Halderman, L. K., Ashby, J., & Perfetti, C. A. (2012). Phonology: An early and integral role in identifying words. In J. S. Adelman (Ed.), *Visual word recognition*. Hove, UK: Psychology Press.

Hale, J. (2006). Uncertainty about the rest of the sentence. *Cognitive Science, 30*, 643–672.

Hallgren, B. (1950). Specific dyslexia ("congenital word-blindness"): A clinical and genetic study. *Acta Psychiatrica et Neurologica, Suppl. 65*, 1–287.

Halliday, M. A. K., & Hasan, R. O. (1976). *Cohesion in English*. London: Longman.

Hanson, V., Goodell, E. W., & Perfetti, C. (1991). Tongue-twister effects in the silent reading of hearing and deaf college students. *Journal of Memory and Language, 30*(3), 319.

Hanson, V. L., & Fowler, C. A. (1987). Phonological coding in word reading: Evidence from hearing and deaf readers. *Memory & Cognition, 15*, 199–207.

Hardyck, C. D., & Petrinovich, L. F. (1970). Subvocal speech and comprehension level as a function of the difficulty level of reading material. *Journal of Verbal Learning and Verbal Behavior, 9*, 647–652.

Hardyck, C. D., Petrinovich, L. F., & Ellsworth, D. W. (1966). Feedback of speech muscle activity during silent reading: Rapid extinction. *Science, 154,* 1467–1468.

Harm, M. W., & Seidenberg, M. S. (1999). Phonology, reading acquisition, and dyslexia: Insights from connectionist models. *Psychological Review, 106*(3), 491–528.

Harm, M. W., & Seidenberg, M. S. (2004). Computing the meanings of words in reading: Cooperative division of labor between visual and phonological processes. *Psychological Review, 111,* 662–720.

Harmon-Vukic, M., Guéraud, S., Lassonde, K. A., & O'Brien, E. J. (2009). The activation and instantiation of predictive inferences. *Discourse Processes, 46,* 467–490.

Harris, M., & Moreno, C. (2004). Deaf children's use of phonological coding: Evidence from reading, spelling, and working memory. *Journal of Deaf Studies and Deaf Education, 9,* 253–268.

Hasselhorn, M., & Grube, D. (2003). The phonological similarity effect on memory span in children: Does it depend on age, speech rate, and articulatory suppression? *International Journal of Behavioral Development, 27*(2), 145–152.

Hatcher, P. J., & Hulme, C. (1999). Phonemes, rhymes, and intelligence as predictors of children's responsiveness to remedial reading instruction: Evidence from a longitudinal study. *Journal of Experimental Child Psychology, 72*(2), 130–153.

Hatcher, P. J., Hulme, C., & Ellis, A. W. (1994). Ameliorating early reading failure by integrating the teaching of reading and phonological skills: The phonological linkage hypothesis. *Child Development, 65*(1), 41–57.

Hatcher, P. J., Snowling, M. J., & Griffiths, Y. M. (2002). Cognitive assessment of dyslexic students in higher education. *British Journal of Educational Psychology, 72*(1), 119–133.

Haviland, S. E., & Clark, H. H. (1974). What's new? Acquiring new information as a process in comprehension. *Journal of Verbal Learning and Verbal Behavior, 13,* 512–521.

Hawelka, S., Gagl, B., & Wimmer, H. (2010). A dual-route perspective on eye movements of dyslexic readers. *Cognition, 115,* 367–379.

Hawkins, H. L., Reicher, G. M., Rogers, M., & Peterson, L. (1976). Flexible coding in work recognition. *Journal of Experimental Psychology: Human Perception and Performance, 2,* 380–385.

Healy, A. F. (1976). Detection errors on the word the: Evidence for reading units larger than letters. *Journal of Experimental Psychology, 2,* 235–242.

Healy, A. F. (1980). Proofreading errors on the word the: New evidence on reading units. *Journal of Experimental Psychology: Human Perception and Performance, 6,* 45–57.

Healy, A. F., & Drewnowski, A. (1983). Investigation the boundaries of reading units: Letter detection in misspelled words. *Journal of Experimental Psychology: Human Perception and Performance, 9,* 413–426,

Healy, J. M., Aram, D. M., Horowitz, S. J., & Kessler, J. W. (1982). A study of hyperlexia. *Brain and Language, 17*(1), 1–23.

Heath, S. M., Hogben, J. H., & Clark, C. D. (1999). Auditory temporal processing in disabled readers with and without oral language delay. *Journal of Child Psychology and Psychiatry, 40*(4), 637–647.

Heim, I., & Kratzer, A. (1998). *Semantics in generative grammar.* Malden, MA: Blackwell Publishers.

Helenius, P., Tarkiainen, A., Cornelissen, P., Hansen, P. C., & Salmelin, R. (1999). Dissociation of normal feature analysis and deficient processing of letter-strings in dyslexic adults. *Cerebral Cortex, 9*(5), 476–483.

Helfgott, J. (1976). Phonemic segmentation and blending skills of kindergarten children: Implications for beginning reading acquisition, *Contemporary Educational Psychology, 1,* 157–169.

Hemforth, B., & Konieczny, L. (2000). *German sentence processing.* Dordrecht: Kluwer.

Henderson, J. M., Dixon, P., Petersen, A., Twilley, L. C., & Ferreira, F. (1995). Evidence for the use of phonological representations during transaccadic word recognition. *Journal of Experimental Psychology: Human Perception and Performance, 21,* 82–97.

Henderson, J. M., & Ferreira, F. (1990). Effects of foveal processing difficulty on the perceptual span in reading: Implications for attention and eye movement control. *Journal of Experimental Psychology: Learning, Memory, and Cognition, 16,* 417–429.

Henderson, J. M., Weeks, P. A., & Hollingworth, A. (1999). The effects of semantic consistency on eye movements during complex scene viewing. *Journal of Experimental Psychology: Human Perception and Performance, 25,* 210–228.

Henderson, L. (1982). *Orthography and word recognition in reading.* New York: Academic Press.

Henderson, L. (1984). *Orthographies and reading.* Hillsdale, NJ: Lawrence Erlbaum Associates Inc.

Hill, E. L. (2001). Non-specific nature of specific language impairment: A review of the literature with regard to concomitant motor impairments. *Journal of Language and Communication Disorders*, *36*, 149–171.

Hintzman, D. L., Carre, F. A., Eskridge, V. L., Owens, A. M., Shaff, S. S., & Sparks, M. E. (1972). "Stroop" effect: Input or output phenomenon? *Journal of Experimental Psychology*, *95*, 458–459.

Hirotani, M., Frazier, L., & Rayner, K. (2006). Punctuation and intonation effects on clause and sentence wrap-up: Evidence from eye movements. *Journal of Memory and Language*, *54*, 425–443.

Hochberg, J. (1970). Components of literacy: Speculations and exploratory research. In H. Levin & J. P. Williams (Eds.), *Basic studies on reading*. New York: Basic Books.

Hoffmeister, R. J. (2000). A piece of the puzzle: ASL and reading comprehension in deaf children. In C. Chamberlain, J. P. Morford, & R. I. Mayberry (Eds.), *Language acquisition by eye* (pp. 143–163). Mahwah, NJ: Lawrence Erlbaum Associates Inc.

Hohenstein, S., Laubrock, J., & Kliegl, R. (2010). Semantic preview benefit in eye movements during reading: A parafoveal fast-priming study. *Journal of Experimental Psychology: Learning, Memory, and Cognition*, *36*, 1150–1170.

Holden, M. H., & MacGinitie, W. H. (1972). Children's conceptions of word boundaries in speech and print. *Journal of Educational Psychology*, *63*, 551–557.

Holender, D. (1986). Semantic activation without conscious indentification in dichotic listening, parafoveal vision, and visual masking: A survey and appraisal. *Behavioral and Brain Sciences*, *9*, 1–66.

Holt, E. B. (1903). Eye-movement and central anaesthesia. *Psychological Monographs*, *4*, 3–48.

Hoover, W. A., & Gough, P. B. (1990). The simple view of reading. *Reading and Writing*, *2*, 127–160.

Hornby, P. A. (1974). Surface structure and presupposition. *Journal of Verbal Learning and Verbal Behavior*, *13*, 530–538.

Hoskyn, M., & Swanson, H. L. (2000). Cognitive processing of low achievers and children with reading disabilities: A selective meta-analytic review of the published literature. *School Psychology Review*, *29*(1), 102–119.

Hu, C. F., & Catts, H. W. (1998). The role of phonological processing in early reading ability: What we can learn from Chinese. *Scientific Studies of Reading*, *2*(1), 55–79.

Hubel, D. H., & Wiesel, T. N. (1962). Receptive fields, binocular interaction and functional architecture in the cat's visual cortex. *Journal of Physiology*, *160*, 106–154.

Huey, E. B. (1908). *The psychology and pedagogy of reading*. New York: Macmillan. [Republished: Cambridge, MA: MIT Press, 1968.]

Hulme, C., & Snowling, M. (1992). Deficits in output phonology: An explanation of reading failure? *Cognitive Neuropsychology*, *9*(1), 47–72.

Hulme, C., & Snowling, M. (1994). *Reading development and dyslexia*. London: Whurr Publishers.

Hulme, C., Snowling, M., Caravolas, M., & Carroll, J. (2005). Phonological skills are (probably) one cause of success in learning to read: A comment on Castles and Coltheart. *Scientific Studies of Reading*, *9*(4), 351–365.

Hulslander, J., Talcott, J., Witton, C., DeFries, J., Pennington, B., Wadsworth, S., et al. (2004). Sensory processing, reading, IQ, and attention. *Journal of Experimental Child Psychology*, *88*(3), 274–295.

Humphreys, G. W., & Evett, L. J. (1985). Are there independent lexical and nonlexical routes in word processing? An evaluation of the dual-route theory of reading. *Behavioral and Brain Sciences*, *8*, 689–740.

Hung, D. L., & Tzeng, O. J. L. (1981). Orthographic variations and visual information processing. *Psychological Bulletin*, *3*, 377–414.

Huntsman, L. A., & Lima, S. D. (1996). Orthographic neighborhood structure and lexical access. *Journal of Psycholinguistic Research*, *25*, 417–429.

Huttenlocher, J. (1964). Children's language: Word–phrase relationship. *Science*, *143*, 264–265.

Hurford, D. P., Schauf, J. D., Bunce, L., Blaich, T., & Moore, K. (1994). Early identification of children at risk for reading disabilities. *Journal of Learning Disabilities*, *27*, 371–382.

Hyönä, J., & Bertram, R. (2004). Do frequency characteristics of nonfixated words influence the processing of fixated words during reading? *European Journal of Cognitive Psychology*, *16*, 104–127.

Hyönä, J., Bertram, R., & Pollatsek, A. (2004). Are long compound words identified serially via their constituents? Evidence from an eye-movement contingent display change study. *Memory & Cognition*, *32*, 523–532.

Hyönä, J., & Häikiö, T. (2005). Is emotional content obtained from parafoveal words during reading? An eye movement analysis. *Scandinavian Journal of Psychology*, *46*, 475–483.

Hyönä, J., & Olson, R. K. (1995). Eye fixation patterns among dyslexic and normal readers: Effects of word length and word frequency. *Journal of Experimental Psychology: Learning, Memory, and Cognition, 21*(6), 1430–1440.

Hyönä, J. & Pollatsek, A. (1998). Reading Finnish compound words: Eye fixations are affected by component morphemes. *Journal of Experimental Psychology: Human Perception and Performance, 24*, 1612–1627.

Ikeda, M., & Saida, S. (1978). Span of recognition in reading. *Vision Research, 18*, 83–88.

Inhoff, A. W. (1982). Parafoveal word perception: A further case against semantic pre-processing. *Journal of Experimental Psychology: Human Perception and Performance, 8*, 137–145.

Inhoff, A. W. (1987). Lexical access during eye fixations in sentence reading: Effects of word structure. In M. Coltheart (Ed.), *Attention and performance 12*. Hove, UK: Erlbaum.

Inhoff, A. W. (1989a). Lexical access during eye fixations in reading: Are word access codes used to integrate lexical information across interword fixations? *Journal of Memory and Language, 28*, 444–461.

Inhoff, A. W. (1989b). Parafoveal processing of words and saccade computation during eye fixations in reading. *Journal of Experimental Psychology: Human Perception and Performance, 15*, 544–555.

Inhoff, A. W., Connine, C., Eiter, B., Radach, R., & Heller, D. (2004). Phonological representation of words in working memory during sentence reading. *Psychonomic Bulletin & Review, 11*, 320–325.

Inhoff, A. W., Connine, C., & Radach, R. (2002). A contingent speech technique in eye movement research on reading. *Behavior Research Methods, Instruments, & Computers, 3*, 471–480.

Inhoff, A. W., & Liu, W. (1998). The perceptual span and oculomotor activity during the reading of Chinese sentences. *Journal of Experimental Psychology: Human Perception and Performance, 24*, 20–34.

Inhoff, A. W., & Rayner, K. (1980). Parafoveal word perception: A case against semantic preprocessing. *Perception & Psychophysics, 27*, 457–464.

Inhoff, A. W., & Rayner, K. (1986). Parafoveal word processing during eye fixations in reading: Effects of word frequency. *Perception & Psychophysics, 40*, 431–439.

Inhoff, A. W., Solomon, M., Radach, R., & Seymour, B. A. (2011). Temporal dynamics of the eye–voice span and eye movement control during oral reading. *Journal of Cognitive Psychology, 23*, 543–558.

Inhoff, A. W., & Topolski, R. (1994). Use of phonological codes during eye fixations in reading and in on-line and delayed naming tasks. *Journal of Memory and Language, 33*, 689–713.

Ishida, T., & Ikeda, M. (1989). Temporal properties of information extraction in reading studied by a text-mask replacement technique. *Journal of the Optical Society A: Optics and Image Science, 6*, 1624–1632.

Iverson, J. A., & Tunmer, W. E. (1993). Phonological processing skills and the Reading Recovery Program. *Journal of Educational Psychology, 85*, 112–125.

Jackendoff, R. (1972). *Semantic interpretation in generative grammar*. Cambridge, MA: MIT Press.

Jackson, M. D. (1980). Further evidence for a relationship between memory access and reading ability. *Journal of Verbal Learning and Verbal Behavior, 19*, 683–694.

Jackson, M. D., & McClelland, J. L. (1975). Sensory and cognitive determinants of reading speed. *Journal of Verbal Learning and Verbal Behavior, 19*, 565–574.

Jackson, M. D., & McClelland, J. L. (1979). Processing determinants of reading speed. *Journal of Experimental Psychology: General, 108*, 151–181.

Jared, D., Levy, B. A., & Rayner, K. (1999). The role of phonology in the activation of word meanings during reading: Evidence from proofreading and eye movements. *Journal of Experimental Psychology: General, 128*, 219–264.

Jarvella, R. J., & Herman, S. J. (1972). Clause structure of sentences and speech processing. *Perception & Psychophysics, 11*, 381–384.

Jeffrey, W. E., & Samuels, S. J. (1967). The effect of method of reading training on initial reading and transfer. *Journal of Verbal Learning and Verbal Behavior, 6*, 354–358.

Joanisse, M. F., Manis, F. R., Keating, P., & Seidenberg, M. S. (2000). Language deficits in dyslexic children: Speech perception, phonology, and morphology. *Journal of Experimental Child Psychology, 77*(1), 30–60.

Job, R., Peressotti, F., & Mulatti, C. (2006). The acquisition of literacy in Italian. In R. M. Joshi & P. G. Aaron (Eds.), *Handbook of orthography and literacy* (pp. 321–338). Mahwah, NJ: Lawrence Erlbaum Associates Inc.

Johnson, D., & Myklebust, H. (1967). *Learning disabilities: Educational principles and practices*. New York: Grune & Stratton.

Johnson, M. K., Bransford, J. D., & Soloman, S. K. (1973). Memory for tacit implications of sentences. *Journal of Experimental Psychology, 98*, 203–215.

Johnson, N. E, & Pugh, K. R. (1994). A cohort model of visual word recognition. *Cognitive Psychology*, *26*, 240–346.

Johnson, R. L. (2009). The quite clam is calm: Transposed-letter neighborhood effects on eye movements during reading. *Journal of Experimental Psychology: Learning, Memory, and Cognition, 35*, 943–969.

Johnson, R. L., Perea, M., & Rayner, K. (2007). Transposed letter effects in reading: Evidence from eye movements and parafoveal preview benefit. *Journal of Experimental Psychology: Human Performance and Perception, 33*, 209–229.

Johnson, R. L., & Rayner, K. (2007). Top-down and bottom-up effects in pure alexia: Evidence from eye movements. *Neuropsychologia, 45*, 2246–2257.

Johnson-Laird, P. N. (1983). *Mental models*. Cambridge, MA: Harvard University Press.

Johnston, J. C. (1978). A test of the sophisticated guessing theory of word perception. *Cognitive Psychology, 10*, 123–153.

Johnston, J. C., & McClelland, J. L. (1974). Perception of letters in words: Seek and ye shall not find. *Science, 184*, 1192–1193.

Jorm, A. F., & Share, D. L. (1983). Phonological recoding and reading acquisition. *Applied Psycholinguistics, 4*, 103–147.

Joseph, H. S., Liversedge, S. P., Blythe, H. I., White, S. J., & Rayner, K. (2009). Word length and landing position effects during reading in children and adults. *Vision Research, 49*(16), 2078–2086.

Joshi, R. M., Binks, E., Hougen, M., Dahlgren, M. E., Ocker-Dean, E., & Smith, D. L. (2009). Why elementary teachers might be inadequately prepared to teach reading. *Journal of Learning Disabilities, 42*(5), 392–402.

Juel, C., Griffith, P. L., & Gough, P. B. (1986). Acquisition of literacy: A longitudinal study of children in first and second grade. *Journal of Educational Psychology, 78*, 243–255.

Juhasz, B. J. (2007). The influence of semantic transparency on eye movements during English compound word recognition. In R. van Gompel, M. Fischer, W. Murray, & R. Hill (Eds.), *Eye movements: A window on mind and brain* (pp. 373–389). New York: Elsevier.

Juhasz, B. J., Liversedge, S. P., White, S. J., & Rayner, K. (2006). Binocular coordination of the eyes during reading: Word frequency and case alternation affect fixation duration but not fixation disparity. *Quarterly Journal of Experimental Psychology, 59*, 1614–1625.

Juhasz, B. J., Pollatsek, A., Hyönä, J., & Rayner, K. (2009). Parafoveal processing within and between words. *Quarterly Journal of Experimental Psychology, 62*, 1356–1376.

Juhasz, B. J., & Rayner, K. (2003). Investigating the effects of a set of intercorrelated variables on eye-fixation durations in reading. *Journal of Experimental Psychology: Learning, Memory, and Cognition, 29*, 1312–1318.

Juhasz, B. J., & Rayner, K. (2006). The role of age-of-acquisition and word frequency in reading: Evidence from eye fixation durations. *Visual Cognition, 13*, 846–863.

Juhasz, B. J., Starr, M., Inhoff, A. W., & Placke, L. (2003). The effects of morphology on the processing of compound words: Evidence from naming, lexical decisions, and eye fixations. *British Journal of Psychology, 94*, 223–244.

Juhasz, B. J., White, S. J., Liversedge, S. P., & Rayner, K. (2008). Eye movements and the use of parafoveal word length information in reading. *Journal of Experimental Psychology: Human Perception and Peformance, 34*, 1560–1579.

Juola, J. F., Schadler, M., Chabot, R. J., & McCaughey, M. W. (1978). The development of visual information processing skills related to reading. *Journal of Experimental Child Psychology, 25*, 459–476.

Jurafsky, D. (1996). A probabilistic model of lexical and syntactic access and disambiguation. *Cognitive Science, 20*, 137–194.

Jusczyk, P. W., Pisoni, D. B., & Mullennix, J. (1992). Some consequences of stimulus variability on speech processing by 2-month-old infants. *Cognition, 43*(3), 253–291.

Just, M. A., & Carpenter, P. A. (1980). A theory of reading: From eye fixations to comprehension. *Psychological Review, 87*, 329–354.

Just, M. A., & Carpenter, P. A. (1987). *The psychology of reading and language comprehension*. Newton, MA: Allyn & Bacon.

Just, M. A., Carpenter, P. A., & Masson, M. E. J. (1982). *What eye fixations tell us about speed reading and skimming*. Eye-Lab Technical Report, Carnegie-Mellon University.

Justice, L. M., Pullen, P. C., & Pence, K. (2008). Influence of verbal and nonverbal references to print on preschoolers' visual attention to print during storybook reading. *Developmental Psychology, 44*, 855–866.

Justice, L. M., Skibbe, L., Canning, A., & Lankford, C. (2005). Preschoolers, print, and storybooks: An observational study using eye-gaze analysis. *Journal of Research in Reading, 28*, 229–243.

Kail, R., & Hall, L. K. (1994). Processing speed, naming speed, and reading. *Developmental Psychology, 30*, 949–954.

Kail, R., Hall, L., & Caskey, B. (1999). Processing speed, exposure to print, and naming speed. *Applied Psycholinguistics, 20*, 303–314.

Kambe, G. (2004). Parafoveal processing of prefixed words during eye fixations in reading: Evidence against morphological influences on parafoveal preprocessing. *Perception & Psychophysics, 66*, 279–292.

Kameenui, E. J., Carnine, D. W., & Freschi, R. (1982). Effects of text construction and instructional procedures for teaching word meanings on comprehension and recall. *Reading Research Quarterly, 17*, 367–388.

Kanner, L. (1943). Autistic disturbances of affective contact. *Nervous Child, 2*, 217–250.

Karlin, M. B., & Bower, G. H. (1976). Semantic category effects in visual word search. *Perception & Psychophysics, 19*, 417–424.

Katz, L., & Feldman, L. B. (1983). Relation between pronunciation and recognition of printed words in deep and shallow orthographies. *Journal of Experimental Psychology: Learning, Memory, and Cognition, 9*, 157–166.

Katz, L., & Frost, R. (1992). Reading in different orthographies: The orthographic depth hypothesis. In R. Frost & L. Katz (Eds.), *Orthography, phonology, morphology, and meaning* (pp. 67–84). Amsterdam: Elsevier North-Holland Press.

Katz, R. B. (1986). Phonological deficiencies in children with reading disability: Evidence from an object-naming task. *Cognition, 22*(3), 225–257.

Katz, R. B., Shankweiler, D., & Liberman, I. Y. (1981). Memory for item order and phonetic recoding in the beginning reader. *Journal of Experimental Child Psychology, 32*, 474–484.

Katzir, T., Kim, Y., Wolf, M., Kennedy, B., Lovett, M., & Morris, R. (2006). The relationship of spelling recognition, RAN, and phonological awareness to reading skills in older poor readers and younger reading-matched controls. *Reading and Writing, 19*(8), 845–872.

Katzir, T., Kim, Y., Wolf, M., Morris, R., & Lovett, M. W. (2008). The varieties of pathways to dysfluent reading: Comparing subtypes of children with dyslexia at letter, word, and connected text levels of reading. *Journal of Learning Disabilities, 41*(1), 47–66.

Keele, S. W. (1972). Attention demands of memory retrieval. *Journal of Experimental Psychology, 93*, 245–248.

Keenan, J. M., & Brown, P. (1984). Children's reading rate and retention as a function of the number of propositions in a text. *Child Development, 55*, 1556–1569.

Keenan, J. M., & Kintsch, W. (1974). The identification of explicitly and implicitly presented information. In W. Kintsch (Ed.), *The representation of meaning in memory* (pp. 153–165). Hillsdale, NJ: Lawrence Erlbaum Associates Inc.

Kennedy, A. (1999). Parafoveal-on-foveal effects in reading and word recognition. In W. Becker, H. Deubel, & T. Mergner (Eds.), *Current oculomotor research: Physiological and psychological aspects* (pp. 359–367). New York: Plenum.

Kennedy, A., & Murray, W. S. (1984). Inspection times for words in syntactically ambiguous sentences under three presentation conditions. *Journal of Experimental Psychology: Human Perception and Performance, 10*, 833–849.

Kennison, S. M. (2001). Limitations on the use of verb information during sentence comprehension. *Psychonomic Bulletin & Review, 8*, 132–137.

Kennison, S. M. (2004). The effect of phonemic repetition on syntactic ambiguity resolution: Implications for models of working memory. *Journal of Psycholinguistic Research, 33*, 493–516.

Kennison, S. M., & Clifton, C. Jr. (1995). Determinants of parafoveal preview benefit in high and low working memory capacity readers: Implications for eye movement control. *Journal of Experimental Psychology: Learning, Memory, and Cognition, 21*, 68–81.

Kennison, S. M., Sieck, J. P., & Briesch, K. A. (2003). Evidence for a late-occurring effect of phoneme repetition in silent reading. *Journal of Psycholinguistic Research, 32*, 297–312.

Kertesz, A., Harlock, W., & Coates, R. (1979). Computer tomographic localization, lesion size, and prognosis in aphasia and nonverbal impairment. *Brain and Language, 8*(1), 34–50.

Kessler, B. (2009). Statistical learning of conditional orthographic correspondences. *Writing Systems Research, 1*(1), 19–34.

Kessler, B., & Treiman, R. (2001). Relationship between sounds and letters in english monosyllables. *Journal of Memory and Language, 44*, 592–617.

Kessler, B., & Treiman, R. (2003). Is English spelling chaotic? Misconceptions concerning its irregularity. *Reading Psychology*, *24*(3–4), 267–289.

Kimball, J. (1973). Seven principles of surface structure parsing in natural language, *Cognition*, *2*, 15–47.

Kintsch, W. (1974). *The representation of meaning in memory*. Hillsdale, NJ: Lawrence Erlbaum Associates Inc.

Kintsch, W. (1988). The use of knowledge in discourse processing. *Psychological Review*, *95*, 163–182.

Kintsch, W. (1994). Text comprehension, memory, and learning. *American Psychologist*, *49*, 294–303.

Kintsch, W. (1998). *Comprehension: A paradigm for cognition*. Cambridge, UK: Cambridge University Press.

Kintsch, W., & Keenan, J. (1973). Reading rate and retention as a function of the number of propositions in the base structure of sentences. *Cognitive Psychology*, *5*, 257–274.

Kintsch, W., Kozminsky, E., Streby, W. J., McKoon, G., & Keenan, J. M. (1975). Comprehension and recall of test as a function of content variables. *Journal of Verbal Learning and Verbal Behavior*, *14*, 196–214.

Kintsch, W., & van Dijk, T. A. (1978). Toward a model of text comprehension and production. *Psychological Review*, *85*, 363–394.

Kintsch, W., & Vipond, D. (1979). Reading comprehension and readability in educational practice and psychological theory. In L-G. Nilsson (Ed.), *Perspectives on memory research*. Hillsdale, NJ: Lawrence Erlbaum Associates Inc.

Kirkby, J. A., Blythe, H. I., Drieghe, D., & Liversedge, S. P. *Reading text increases binocular disparity in children*. Submitted to PL oS One.

Kirkby, J. A., Webster, L. A., Blythe, H. I., & Liversedge, S. P. (2008). Binocular coordination during reading and non–reading tasks. *Psychological Bulletin*, *134*, 742–763.

Kleiman, G. M. (1975). Speech recoding in reading. *Journal of Verbal Learning and Verbal Behavior*, *14*, 323–339.

Kliegl, R. (2007). Toward a perceptual–span theory of distributed processing in reading: A reply to Rayner, Pollatsek, Drieghe, Slattery, and Reichle (2007). *Journal of Experimental Psychology: General*, *136*, 530–537.

Kliegl, R., Nuthmann, A., & Engbert, R. (2006). Tracking the mind during reading: The influence of past, present, and future words on fixation durations. *Journal of Experimental Psychology: General*, *135*, 12–35.

Kliegl, R., Olson, R. K., & Davidson, B. J. (1982). Regression analyses as a tool for studying reading processes: Comments on Just and Carpenter's eye fixation theory. *Memory & Cognition*, *10*, 287–296.

Kliegl, R., Risse, S., & Laubrock, J. (2007). Preview benefit and parafoveal-on-foveal effects from word n+2. *Journal of Experimental Psychology: Human Perception and Performance*, *33*, 1250–1255.

Knecht, S., Deppe, M., Drager, B., Bobe, L., Lohmann, H., Ringelstein, E., et al. (2000). Language lateralization in healthy right-handers. *Brain: A Journal of Neurology*, *123*(1), 74–81.

Koenig, J-P., Mauner, G., & Bienvenue, B. (2003). Arguments for adjuncts. *Cognition*, *89*, 67–103.

Koh, S., Sanford, A., Clifton, C. Jr., & Dawydiak, E. J. (2008). Good-enough representation in plural and singular pronominal reference: Modulating the conjunction cost. In J. Gundel & N. Hedberg (Eds.), *Reference: Interdisciplinary perspectives* (pp. 123–142). Oxford, UK: Oxford University Press.

Kolers, P. (1972). Experiments in reading. *Scientific American*, *227*, 84–91.

Koornneef, A. W., & van Berkum, J. J. A. (2006). On the use of verb-based implicit causality in sentence comprehension: Evidence from self-paced reading and eye tracking. *Journal of Memory and Language*, *54*, 445–465.

Koppen, M., Noordman, L. G. M., & Vonk, W. (2008). World knowledge in computational models of discourse comprehension. *Discourse Processes*, *45*, 429–463.

Kosslyn, S. M., & Matt, A. M. (1977). If you speak slowly, do people read your prose slowly? Person-particular speech recoding during reading. *Bulletin of the Psychonomic Society*, *9*, 250–252.

Kowler, E., & Martins, A. J. (1982). Eye movements of preschool children. *Science*, *215*, 997–999.

Kronbichler, M., Hutzler, F., & Wimmer, H. (2002). Dyslexia: Verbal impairments in the absence of magnocellular impairments. *Neuroreport*, *13*(5), 617–620.

Kuhn, M. R., & Stahl, S. A. (2003). Fluency: A review of developmental and remedial practices. *Journal of Educational Psychology*, *95*, 3–21.

Kuperman, V., Schreuder, R., Bertram, R., & Baayen, R. H. (2009). Reading polymorphemic Dutch compounds: Toward a multiple route model of lexical processing. *Journal of Experimental Psychology: Human Perception and Performance*, *35*(3), 876–895.

Kuperman, V., & Van Dyke, J. A. (2011). Effects of individual differences in verbal skills on eye-movement patterns during sentence reading. *Journal of Memory and Language*, *65*, 42–73.

Kurby, C. A., Magliano, J. P., & Rapp, D. N. (2009). Those voices in your head: Activation of auditory images during reading. *Cognition*, *112*, 457–461.

Kussmaul, A. (1877). Word deafness and word blindness. In H. von Ziemssen & J. A. T. McCreery (Eds.), *Cyclopedia of the practice of medicine* (pp. 770–778). New York: William Wood.

Kutas, M., & Federmeier, K. (2007). Event–related brain potential (ERP) studies of sentence processing. In M. G. Gaskell (Ed.), *The Oxford handbook of psycholinguistics* (pp. 385–406). Oxford, UK: Oxford University Press.

Kutas, M., & Hillyard, S. A. (1980). Reading senseless sentences: Brain potentials reflect semantic incongruity. *Science, 207*, 203–205.

Kutas, M., Van Petten, C., & Kluender, R. (2006). Psycholinguistics electrified II (1994–2005). In M. A. Gernsbacher & M. Traxler (Eds.), *Handbook of psycholinguistics* (2nd ed., pp. 655–720). New York: Elsevier.

LaBerge, D. (1972). Beyond auditory coding. In J. F. Kavanagh & I. G. Mattingly (Eds.), *Language by ear and by eye*. Cambridge, MA: MIT Press.

LaBerge D., & Samuels, S. J. (1974). Toward a theory of automatic information processing in reading. *Cognitive Psychology, 6*, 293–323.

Landerl, K. (2000). Influences of orthographic consistency and reading instruction on the development of nonword reading skills. *European Journal of Psychology of Education, 15*, 239–257.

Landerl, K., & Wimmer, H. (2008). Development of word reading fluency and spelling in a consistent orthography: An 8-year follow-up. *Journal of Educational Psychology, 100*(1), 150–161.

Landi, N., & Perfetti, C. A. (2007). An electrophysiological investigation of semantic and phonological processing in skilled and less skilled comprehenders. *Brain and Language, 102*, 30–45.

Lassonde, K. A., & O'Brien, E. J. (2009). Contextual specification in the activation of predictive inferences. *Discourse Processes, 46*, 426–438.

Laubrock, J., Hohenstein, S., & Kliegl, R. (2010). Semantic preview benefit in eye movements during reading: A parafoveal fast-priming study. *Journal of Experimental Psychology: Learning, Memory, and Cognition, 36*, 1150–1170.

Laubrock, J., & Kliegl, R. (2011). *The eye–voice span in oral reading.* Manuscript submitted for publication.

Laubrock, J., Kliegl, R., & Engbert, R. (2006). SWIFT explorations of age differences in eye movements during reading. *Neuroscience and Biobehavioral Reviews, 30*, 872–884.

Leach, J. M., Scarborough, H. S., & Rescorla, L. (2003). Late-emerging reading disabilities. *Journal of Educational Psychology, 95*(2), 211–224.

Lean, D. S., & Arbuckle, T. Y. (1984). Phonological coding in prereaders. *Journal of Educational Psychology, 76*, 1282–1290

Lee, H., Rayner, K., & Pollatsek, A. (1999). The time course of phonological, semantic, and orthographic coding in reading: Evidence from the fast priming technique. *Psychonomic Bulletin & Review, 5*, 624–634.

Lee, Y., Binder, K. S., Kim, J., Pollatsek, A., & Rayner, K. (1999). Activation of phonological codes during eye fixations in reading. *Journal of Experimental Psychology: Human Perception and Performance, 25*(4), 948–964.

Lemhöfer, K., Dijkstra, T., Schriefers, H., Baayen, R. H., Grainger, J., & Zwitserlood, P. (2008). Native language influences on word recognition in a second language: A megastudy. *Journal of Experimental Psychology: Learning, Memory, and Cognition, 34*(1), 12–31.

Lenneberg, E. H. (1967). *Biological foundations of language*. New York: Wiley.

Leonard, C. M., Eckert, M. A., Lombardino, L. J., Oakland, T., Kranzler, J., Mohr, C. M., et al. (2001). Anatomical risk factors for phonological dyslexia. *Cerebral Cortex, 11*(2), 148–157.

Lervåg, A., & Hulme, C. (2009). Rapid automatized naming (RAN) taps a mechanism that places constraints on the development of early reading fluency. *Psychological Science, 20*(8), 1040–1048.

Lesch, M. F., & Pollatsek, A. (1998). Evidence for the use of assembled phonology in accessing the meaning of printed words. *Journal of Experimental Psychology: Learning, Memory and Cognition, 24*, 573–592.

Lesgold, A. M., & Curtis, M. E. (1981). Learning to read words efficiently. In A. M. Lesgold & C. A. Perfetti (Eds.), *Interactive processes in reading*. Hillsdale, NJ: Lawrence Erlbaum Associates Inc.

Lesgold, A. M., & Resnick, L. B. (1982). How reading disabilities develop: Perspectives from a longitudinal study. In J. P. Das, R. Mulcahy, & A. E. Wall (Eds.), *Theory and research in learning disability*. New York: Plenum.

Levin, B., & Rappaport Hovav, M. (1996). Lexical semantics and syntactic structure. In S. Lappin (Ed.), *The handbook of contemporary semantic theory* (pp. 487–508). Oxford, UK: Blackwell.

Levin, H., & Kaplan, E. L. (1970). Grammatical structure and reading. In H. Levin & J. P. Williams (Eds.), *Basic studies on reading*. New York: Basic Books.

Levy, B. A. (1975). Vocalization and suppression effects in sentence memory. *Journal of Verbal Learning and Verbal Behavior, 14,* 304–316.

Levy, B. A. (1977). Reading: Speech and meaning processes. *Journal of Verbal Learning and Verbal Behavior, 16,* 623–638.

Levy, B. A. (1978). Speech analysis during sentence processing: Reading and listening. *Visible Language, 12,* 81–101.

Levy, B. A. (1981). Interactive processes during reading. In A. M. Lesgold & C. A. Perfetti (Eds.), *Interactive processes in reading.* Hillsdale, NJ: Lawrence Erlbaum Associates Inc.

Levy, B. A., Gong, Z., Hessels, S., Evans, M. A., & Jared, D. (2006). Understanding print: Early reading development and the contributions of home literacy experiences. *Journal of Experimental Child Psychology, 95,* 78.

Levy, R. (2008). Expectation-based syntactic comprehension. *Cognition, 106,* 1126–1177.

Levy, R., Bicknell, K., Slattery, T. J., & Rayner, K. (2009). Eye movement evidence that readers maintain and act on uncertainty about past linguistic input. *Proceedings of the National Academy of Sciences, 106,* 21086–21090.

Lewis, R. L., & Vasishth, S. (2005). An activation-based model of sentence processing as skilled memory retrieval. *Cognitive Science, 29,* 375–420.

Lewkowicz, N. K. (1980). Phonemic awareness training: What to teach and how to teach it. *Journal of Educational Psychology, 72,* 686–700.

Leybaert, J., & Alegria, J. (1993). Is word processing involuntary in deaf children? *British Journal of Developmental Psychology, 11,* 1–29.

Li, X., Liu, P., & Rayner, K. (2011). Eye movement guidance in Chinese reading: Is there a preferred viewing location? *Vision Research,* 51, 1146–1156.

Libben, G. (2003). Morphological parsing and morphological structure. In A. Egbert & D. Sandra (Eds.), *Reading complex words* (pp. 221–239). Amsterdam: Kluwer.

Liberman, A. M., Cooper, F. S., Shankweiler, D. P., & Studdert-Kennedy, M. (1967). Perception of the speech code. *Psychological Review, 74,* 431–461.

Liberman, I. Y. (1973). Segmentation of the spoken word and reading acquisition. *Bulletin of the Orton Society, 23,* 65–77.

Liberman, I. Y., Liberman, A., Mattingly, I., & Shankweiler, P. (1980). Orthography and the beginning reader. In J. Kavenagh & R. Venezky (Eds.), *Orthography reading and dyslexia.* Baltimore, MD: University Park Press.

Liberman, I. Y., & Shankweiler, D. (1979). Speech, the alphabet, and teaching to read. In L. Resnick & P. Weaver (Eds.), *Theory and practice of early reading* (Vol. 2). Hillsdale, NJ: Lawrence Erlbaum Associates Inc.

Liberman, I. Y., & Shankweiler, D. (1991). Phonology and beginning reading: A tutorial. In L. Rieben & C. A. Perfetti (Eds.), *Learning to read: Basic research and its implications* (pp. 3–17). Hillsdale, NJ: Lawrence Erlbaum Associates Inc.

Liberman, I. Y., Shankweiler, D., Fischer, F. W., & Carter, B. (1974). Explicit syllable and phoneme segmentation in the young child. *Journal of Experimental Child Psychology, 18,* 201–212.

Liberman, I. Y., Shankweiler, D., Liberman, A. M., Fowler, C., & Fischer, F. W. (1977). Phonetic segmentation and recoding in the beginning reader. In A. S. Reber & D. Scarborough (Eds.), *Towards a psychology of reading.* Hillsdale, NJ: Lawrence Erlbaum Associates Inc.

Liberman, I. Y., Shankweiler, D., Orlando, C., Harris, K. S., & Berti, F. B. (1971). Letter confusion and reversals of sequence in the beginning reader: Implications for Orton's theory of developmental dyslexia. *Cortex, 7,* 127–142.

Liddle, W. (1965). *An investigation of the Wood Reading Dynamics method.* Ann Arbor: University Microfilms, No. 60–5559.

Lima, S. D. (1987). Morphological analysis in sentence reading. *Journal of Memory and Language, 26,* 84–99.

Lima, S. D., & Inhoff, A. W. (1985). Lexical access during eye fixations in reading: Effects of word-initial letter sequence. *Journal of Experimental Psychology: Human Perception and Performance, 11,* 272–285.

Lima, S. D., & Pollatsek, A. (1983). Lexical access via an orthographic code? The Basic Orthographic Syllable Structure (BOSS) reconsidered. *Journal of Verbal Learning and Verbal Behavior, 22,* 310–332.

Lin, D., McBride-Chang, C., Shu, H., Zhang, Y., Li, H., Zhang, J., et al. (2010). Small wins big: Analytic pinyin skills promote Chinese word reading. *Psychological Science, 21,* 1117–1122.

Lindamood, P., & Lindamood, P. (1998). *The Lindamood phoneme sequencing program for reading, spelling, and speech* (3rd ed.). Austin, TX: Pro-Ed.

Liu, W., Inhoff, A. W., Ye, Y., & Wu, C. (2002). Use of parafoveally visible characters during the reading of Chinese sentences. *Journal of Experimental Psychology: Human Perception and Performance, 28*, 1213–1227.

Liversedge, S. P., Paterson, K. B., & Clayes, E. L. (2002). The influence of only on syntactic processing of 'long' relative clause sentences. *Quarterly Journal of Experimental Psychology, 55A*, 225–240.

Liversedge, S. P., Pickering, M. J., Branigan, H., & van Gompel, R. P. G. (1998). Processing arguments and adjuncts in isolation and context: The case of by-phrase ambiguities in passives. *Journal of Experimental Psychology: Learning, Memory, and Cognition, 24*(2), 461–475.

Liversedge, S. P., Rayner, K., White, S. J., Findlay, J. M., & McSorley, E. (2006). Binocular coordination of the eyes during reading. *Current Biology, 16*, 1726–1729.

Liversedge, S. P., Rayner, K., White, S. J., Vergilino–Perez, D., Findlay, J. M., & Kentridge, R. W. (2004). Eye movements while reading disappearing text: Is there a gap effect in reading? *Vision Research, 44*, 1013–1024.

Liversedge, S. P., White, S. J., Findlay, J. M., & Rayner, K. (2006). Binocular coordination of eye movements during reading. *Vision Research, 46*, 2363–2374.

Livingstone, M., Rosen, G., Drislane, F., & Galaburda, A. (1991). Physiological and anatomical evidence for a magnocellular deficit in developmental dyslexia. *Proceedings of the National Academy of Sciences, 88*, 7943–7947.

Llewellyn-Thomas, E. (1962). Eye movements in speed reading. In R. G. Stauffer (Ed.), *Speed reading: Practices and procedures.* Newark, DE: University of Delaware Reading Center.

Locke, J. L. (1971). Phonemic processing in silent reading. *Perceptual and Motor Skills, 32*, 905–906.

Locke, J. L. (1978). Phonemic effects in the silent reading of hearing and deaf children. *Cognition, 6*, 173–187.

Locke, J. L., Hodgson, J., Macaruso, P., Roberts, J., Lambrecht-Smith, S., & Guttentag, C. (1997). The development of developmental dyslexia. In C. Hulme & M. Snowling (Eds.), *Dyslexia: Biology, cognition and intervention* (pp. 72–96). London: Whurr.

Loftus, G. R. (1983). Eye fixations on text and scenes. In K. Rayner (Ed.), *Eye movements in reading: Perceptual and language processes.* New York: Academic Press.

Loftus, G. R., & Mackworth, N. H. (1978). Cognitive determinants of fixation location during picture viewing. *Journal of Experimental Psychology: Human Perception and Performance, 4*, 565–572.

Lonigan, C. J., Burgess, S. R., & Anthony, J. L. (2000). Development of emergent literacy and early reading skills in preschool children: Evidence from a latent-variable longitudinal study. *Developmental Psychology, 36*, 596–613.

Lonigan, C. J., Burgess, S. R., Anthony, J. L., & Barker, T. A. (1998). Development of phonological sensitivity in 2- to 5-year-old children. *Journal of Educational Psychology, 90*, 294–311.

Lovegrove, W. J., Bowling, A., Badcock, D., & Blackwood, M. (1980). Specific reading disability: Differences in contrast sensitivity as a function of spatial frequency. *Science, 210*(4468), 439–440.

Lovett, M. W. (1984). The search for subtypes of specific reading disability: Reflections from a cognitive perspective. *Annals of Dyslexia, 34*, 155–178.

Lukatela, G., Popadic, D., Ognjenovic, P., & Turvey, M. T. (1980). Lexical decision in a phonologically shallow orthography. *Memory & Cognition, 8*, 124–132.

Lukatela, G., Savic, M., Gligorijevic, B., Ognjenovic, P., & Turvey, M. T. (1978). Bi-alphabetical lexical decision. *Language and Speech, 21*, 142–165.

Lundberg, I., Olofsson, A., & Wall, S. (1980). Reading and spelling skills in the first school years predicted from phonemic awareness skills in kindergarten. *Scandinavian Journal of Psychology, 21*, 159–173.

Lupker, S. J., Perea, M., & Davis, C. J. (2008). Transposed letter priming effects: Consonants, vowels and letter frequency. *Language and Cognitive Processes, 23*, 93–116.

Luttenberg, J. (1965). Contribution to the fetal ontogenesis of the corpus callosum in man. II. *Folio Morphologica, 13*, 136–144.

Lyle, J. G. (1979). Reading retardation and reversal tendency: A factorial study. *Child Development, 40*, 832–843.

Lyle, J. G., & Goyen, J. (1968). Visual recognition, developmental lag, and strephosymbolia in reading retardation. *Journal of Abnormal Psychology, 73*, 25–29.

Lyon, G. R., Fletcher, J. M., Shaywitz, S. E., Shaywitz, B. A., Torgesen, J. K., Wood, F. B., et al. (2001). Rethinking learning disabilities. In C. E. Finn, A. J. Rotherham, & C. R. Hokanson (Eds.), *Rethinking special education for a new century.* Washington, DC: Fordham Foundation.

Lyon, G. R., Shaywitz, S. E., & Shaywitz, B. A. (2003). A definition of dyslexia. *Annals of Dyslexia, 53*, 1–14.

MacDonald, M. C., Pearlmutter, N. J., & Seidenberg, M. S. (1994). The lexical nature of syntactic ambiguity resolution. *Psychological Review, 101*, 676–703.

MacDonald, M. C., & Seidenberg, M. S. (2006). Constraint satisfaction accounts of lexical and sentence comprehension. In M. J. Traxler & M. A. Gernsbacher (Eds.), *Handbook of psycholinguistics* (2nd ed., pp. 581–611). London: Academic Press.

Mackworth, J. F. (1972). Some models of the reading process: Learners and skilled readers. *Reading Research Quarterly, 7*, 701–733.

Mackworth, N. H. (1965). Visual noise causes tunnel vision. *Psychonomic Science, 3*, 67–68.

Mackworth, N. H., & Morandi, A. J. (1967). The gaze selects informative details within pictures. *Perception & Psychophysics, 2*, 547–552.

MacLeod, C. M. (1991). Half a century of research on the Stroop effect: An integrative review. *Psychological Bulletin, 109*, 163–203.

MacWhinney, B., & Bates, E. (Eds). (1990). *The crosslinguistic study of sentence processing*. New York: Cambridge University Press.

Mandler, J. M. (1986). On the comprehension of temporal order. *Language and Cognitive Processes, 1*, 309–320.

Manis, F. R., & Keating, P. (2005). Speech perception in dyslexic children with and without language impairments. In H. W. Catts & A. G. Kamhi (Eds.), *The connections between language and reading disabilities* (pp. 77–99). Mahwah, NJ: Lawrence Erlbaum.

Manis, F. R., Seidenberg, M. S., Doi, L. M., & McBride-Chang, C. (1996). On the bases of two subtypes of development dyslexia. *Cognition, 58*(2), 157–195.

Mann, V. A., Liberman, I. Y., & Shankweiler, D. (1980). Children's memory for sentences and word strings in relation to reading ability. *Memory & Cognition, 8*, 329–335.

Mannhaupt, G., Jansen, H., & Marx, H. (1997). Cultural influences on literacy development. In C. K. Leong & R. M. Joshi (Eds.), *Cross-language studies of learning to read and spell: Phonologic and orthographic processing* (pp. 161–174). Dordrecht: Kluwer.

Marcel, A. J. (1978). Unconscious reading: Experiments on people who do not know they are reading. *Visible Language, 12*, 391–404.

Marcel, A. J. (1983). Conscious and unconscious perception: Experiments on visual masking. *Cognitive Psychology, 15*, 197–237.

Marcel, T. (1974). The effective visual field and the use of context in fast and slow readers of two ages. *British Journal of Psychology, 65*, 479–492.

Marchbanks, G., & Levin, H. (1965). Cues by which children recognize words. *Journal of Educational Psychology, 56*, 57–61.

Margolin, C. M., Griebel, B., & Wolford, G. (1982). Effect of distraction on reading versus listening. *Journal of Experimental Psychology: Learning, Memory, and Cognition, 8*, 613–618.

Mark, L. S., Shankweiler, D., Liberman, I. Y., & Fowler, C. A. (1977). Phonetic recoding and reading difficulty in beginning readers. *Memory & Cognition, 5*, 623–629.

Markman, E. M. (1979). Realizing that you don't understand: Elementary school children's awareness of inconsistencies. *Child Development, 50*, 643–655.

Markman, E. M. (1981). Conprehension monitoring. In W. P. Dickson (Ed.), *Children's oral communication skills*. New York: Academic Press.

Marks, C. B., Doctorow, M. J., & Wittrock, M. C. (1974). Word frequency and reading comprehension. *Journal of Education Research, 67*, 259–262.

Marsh, G., Friedman, M., Welch, V., & Desberg, P. (1981). A cognitive–developmental approach to reading acquisition. In T. G. Waller & G. E. MacKinnon (Eds.), *Reading research: Advances in theory and practice, Vol. 3*. New York: Academic Press.

Marshall, C. M., Snowling, M. J., & Bailey, P. J. (2001). Rapid auditory processing and phonological ability in normal readers and readers with dyslexia. *Journal of Speech, Language, and Hearing Research, 44*(4), 925–940.

Marshall, J. C., & Newcombe, F. (1966). Syntactic and semantic errors in paralexia. *Neuropsychologia, 4*, 169–176.

Marshall, J. C., & Newcombe, F. (1973). Patterns of paralexia: A psycholinguistic approach. *Journal of Psycholinguistic Research, 2*, 175–200.

Marslen-Wilson, W. D. (1973). Linguistic structure and speech shadowing at very short latencies. *Nature, 244,* 522–523.

Marslen-Wilson, W. D., & Tyler, L. K. (1987). Against modularity. In J. Garfield (Ed.), *Modularity in knowledge representation and natural language understanding.* Cambridge, MA: MIT Press.

Martin, A., & McElree, B. (2008). A content-addressable pointer mechanism underlies comprehension of verb phrase ellipsis. *Journal of Memory and Language, 58,* 879–906.

Martin, M. (1978). Speech recoding in silent reading. *Memory & Cognition, 6,* 108–114.

Martin, S. E. (1972). Nonalphabetic writing systems: Some observations. In J. F. Kavanagh & I. G. Mattingly (Eds.), *Language by ear and by eye.* Cambridge, MA: MIT Press.

Mason, J. M. (1980). When do children begin to read: An exploration of four year old children's letter and word reading competencies. *Reading Research Quarterly, 15,* 203–227.

Masonheimer, P. E., Drum, P. A., & Ehri, L. C. (1984). Does environmental print identification lead children into word reading? *Journal of Reading Behavior, 16*(4), 257–271.

Massaro, D. W. (1975). *Understanding language: An information-processing analysis of speech perception, reading, and psycholinguistics.* New York: Academic Press.

Masserang, K. M., Pollatsek, A., & Rayner, K. (2009). *No morphological decomposition with parafoveal previews.* Presented at ECEM 15, 23.8–27.8, Southampton, UK.

Masson, M. E. J., & Isaak, M. I. (1999). Masked priming of words and nonwords in a naming task: Further evidence for a nonlexical basis for priming. *Memory & Cognition, 27,* 399–412.

Masson, M. E. J., & Miller, J. (1983). Working memory and individual differences in comprehension and memory of text. *Journal of Educational Psychology, 75,* 314–318.

Matin, E. (1974). Saccadic suppression: A review and an analysis. *Psychological Bulletin, 81,* 899–917.

Mattingly, I. G. (1972). Reading, the linguistic process, and linguistic awareness. In J. F. Kavanaugh & I. G. Mattingly (Eds.), *Language by ear and by eye: The relationship between speech and reading.* Cambridge, MA: MIT Press.

Mayberry, R. (2007). When timing is everything: Age of first-language acquisition effects on second-language learning. *Applied Psycholinguistics, 28,* 537–549.

Mayberry, R. I., Chamberlain, C., Waters, G., & Hwang, P. (2005). *Word recognition in children who are deaf and sign.* Poster presented at the Society for Research in Child Development, Atlanta.

Mayer, P., Crowley, K., & Kaminska, Z. (2007). Reading and spelling processes in Welsh–English bilinguals: Differential effects of concurrent vocalisation tasks. *Reading and Writing, 20*(7), 671–690.

McBride-Chang, C. (1996). Models of speech perception and phonological processing in reading. *Child Development, 67*(4), 1836–1856.

McBride-Chang, C., & Kail, R. V. (2002). Cross-cultural similarities in the predictors of reading acquisition. *Child Development, 73*(5), 1392–1407.

McCardle, P., & Chhabra, V. (2004). *The voice of evidence in reading research.* Baltimore, MD: Paul Brookes.

McCaughey, M., Juola, J., Schadler, M., & Ward, N. (1980). Whole-word units are used before orthographic knowledge in perceptual development. *Journal of Experimental Child Psychology, 30,* 411–421.

McClelland, J. L. (1986). The programmable blackboard model of reading. In J. L. McClelland, D. E. Rumelhart, & the PDP research group (Eds.), *Parallel distributed processing: Explorations in the microstructure of cognition. Vol. II.* Cambridge, MA: Bradford Books.

McClelland, J. L., & O'Regan, J. K. (1981). Expectations increase the benefit derived from parafoveal visual information in reading words aloud. *Journal of Experimental Psychology: Human Perception and Performance, 7,* 634–644.

McClelland, J. L., & Rumelhart, D. E. (1981). An interactive activation model of context effects in letter perception: Part 1. An account of basic findings. *Psychological Review, 88,* 375–407.

McClelland, J. L., & Rumelhart, D. E. (Eds.). (1986). *Parallel distributed processing: Explorations in the microstructure of cognition* (Vol. 2). Cambridge, MA: MIT Press.

McConkie, G. W., & Hogaboam, T. W. (1985). Eye position and word identification in reading. In R. Groner, G. W. McConkie, & C. Menz (Eds.), *Eye movements and human information processing.* Amsterdam: North-Holland Press.

McConkie, G. W., Kerr, P. W., Reddix, M. D., & Zola, D. (1988). Eye movement control during reading: I. The location of initial eye fixations in words. *Vision Research, 28,* 1107–1118.

McConkie, G. W., & Rayner, K. (1975). The span of the effective stimulus during a fixation in reading. *Perception & Psychophysics, 17,* 578–586.

McConkie, G. W., & Rayner, K. (1976a). Asymmetry of the perceptual span in reading. *Bulletin of the Psychonomic Society, 8,* 365–368.

McConkie, G. W., & Rayner, K. (1976b). Identifying the span of the effective stimulus in reading: Literature review and theories of reading. In H. Singer & R.B. Ruddell (Eds.), *Theoretical models and processes in reading.* Newark, DE: International Reading Association.

McConkie, G. W., Rayner, K., & Wilson, S.J. (1973). Experimental manipulation of reading strategies. *Journal of Educational Psychology, 65,* 1–8.

McConkie, G. W., Underwood, N. R., Zola, D., & Wolverton, G. S. (1985). Some temporal characteristics of processing during reading. *Journal of Experimental Psychology: Human Perception and Performance, 11,* 168–186.

McConkie, G. W., & Zola, D. (1979). Is visual information integrated across successive fixations in reading? *Perception & Psychophysics, 25,* 221–224.

McConkie, G. W., & Zola, D. (1981). Language constraints and the functional stimulus in reading. In A. M. Lesgold & C. A. Perfetti (Eds.), *Interactive process in reading.* Hillsdale, NJ: Erlbaum.

McConkie, G. W., & Zola, D. (1984). Eye movement control during reading: The effects of word units. In W. Prinz & A. F. Sanders (Eds.), *Cognition and motor processes.* Berlin: Springer-Verlag.

McConkie, G. W., Zola, D., Grimes, J., Kerr, P. W., Bryant, R. B., & Wolff, P. M. (1991). Children's eye movements during reading. In J. F. Stein (Ed.), Vision and visual dyslexia (pp 251–262). Oxford: Macmillan.

McConkie, G. W., Zola, D., & Wolverton, G. S. (1980). *How precise is eye guidance?* Paper presented at the annual meeting of the American Educational Research Association, Boston, MA, April.

McCusker, L. X., Bias, R. G., & Hillinger, M. L. (1981). Phonological recoding and reading. *Psychological Bulletin, 89,* 217–245.

McCutchen, D., & Berninger, V. W. (1999). Those who know, teach well: Helping teachers master literacy-related subject-matter knowledge. *Learning Disabilities Research & Practice, [Special Issue, Moving from research to practice: Professional development to promote effective teaching of early reading], 14*(4), 215–226.

McCutchen, D., & Perfetti, C.A. (1982). The visual tongue-twister effect: Phonological activation in silent reading. *Journal of Verbal Learning and Verbal Behavior, 21,* 672–687.

McDonald, S. A. (2006). Parafoveal preview benefit in reading is only obtained from the saccade goal. *Vision Research, 46,* 4416–4424.

McDonald, S. A., & Shillcock, R. C. (2003a). Eye movements reveal the on-line computation of lexical probabilities during reading. *Psychological Science, 14,* 648–652.

McDonald, S. A., & Shillcock, R. C. (2003b). Low-level predictive inference in reading: The influence of transitional probabilities on eye movements. *Vision Research, 43,* 1735–1751.

McElree, B., Traxler, M., Pickering, M. J., Seely, R. E., & Jackendoff, R. (2001). Reading time evidence for enriched composition. *Cognition, 78,* B17–B25.

McGee, L. M., Lomax, R. G., & Head, M. H. (1988). Young children's written language knowledge: What environmental and functional print reading reveals. *Journal of Reading Behavior, 20*(2), 99–118.

McGuigan, F. J. (1967). Feedback of speech muscle activity during silent reading: Two comments. *Science, 157,* 579–580.

McGuigan, F. J. (1970). Covert oral behavior during the silent performance of language tasks. *Psychological Bulletin, 74,* 309–326.

McGuigan, F. J. (1971). External auditory feedback from covert oral behavior during silent reading. *Psychonomic Science, 25,* 212–214.

McGuigan, F. J., & Bailey, S. C. (1969). Longitudinal study of covert oral behavior during silent reading. *Perceptual and Motor Skills, 28,* 170.

McGuigan, F. J., Keller, B., & Stanton, E. (1964). Covert language responses during silent reading. *Journal of Educational Psychology, 55,* 339–343.

McGuinness, D., McGuinness, C., & Donohue, J. (1995). Phonological training and the alphabet principle: Evidence for reciprocal causality. *Reading Research Quarterly, 30*(4), 830–852.

McGurk, H., & MacDonald, J. (1976). Hearing eyes and seeing voices. *Nature, 264,* 746–748.

McKague, M., Pratt, C., & Johnston, M. B. (2001). The effect of oral vocabulary on reading visually novel words: A comparison of the dual-route-cascaded and triangle frameworks. *Cognition, 80*(3), 231–262.

McKeown, M. G., Beck, I. L., Omanson, R. C., & Perfetti, C. A. (1983). The effects of long-term vocabulary instruction on reading comprehension: A replication. *Journal of Reading Behavior, 15*(1), 3–18.

McKoon, G., Gerrig, R. J., & Greene, S. B. (1996). Pronoun resolution without pronouns: Some consequences of memory based text processing. *Journal of Experimental Psychology: Learning, Memory, and Cognition, 22*, 919–932.

McKoon, G., & Macfarland, T. (2002). Event templates in the lexical representation of verbs. *Cognitive Psychology, 45*, 1–44.

McKoon, G., & Ratcliff, R. (1980). Priming in item recognition: The organization of propositions in memory for text. *Journal of Verbal Learning and Verbal Behavior, 19*, 369–386.

McKoon, G., & Ratcliff, R. (1986). Inferences about predictable events. *Journal of Experimental Psychology: Learning, Memory, and Cognition, 12*, 82–91.

McKoon, G., & Ratcliff, R. (2003). Meaning through syntax: Language comprehension and the reduced relative clause construction. *Psychological Review, 110*, 490–525.

McLaughlin, G. H. (1969). Reading at "impossible" speeds. *Journal of Reading, 12*, 449–454, 502–510.

McMahon, M. L. (1976). *Phonic processing in reading printed words: Effects of phonemic relationships between words on time.* Unpublished Master's thesis, University of Massachusetts, Amherst.

McNamara, D. S., Louwerse, M. M., McCarthy, P. M., & Graesser, A. C. (2010). Coh-Metrix: Capturing linguistic features of cohesion. *Discourse Processes, 47*, 292–330.

McRae, K., Ferretti, T. R., & Amyote, L. (1997). Thematic roles as verb-specific concepts. *Language and Cognitive Processes, 12*, 137–176.

McRae, K., Spivey-Knowlton, M. J., & Tanenhaus, M. K. (1998). Modeling the influence of thematic fit (and other constraints) in on-line sentence comprehension. *Journal of Memory and Language, 38*, 283–312.

Mehegan, C., & Dreifuss, F. (1972). Hyperlexia. *Neurology, 22*, 1105–111.

Mehler, J. (1963). Some effects of grammatical transformations on the recall of English sentences. *Journal of Verbal Learning and Verbal Behavior, 2*, 346–351.

Mehler, J., Bever, T. G., & Carey, P. (1967). What we look at when we read. *Perception & Psychophysics, 2*, 213–218.

Meltzer, H. S., & Herse, R. (1969). The boundaries of written words as seen by first graders. *Journal of Reading Behavior, 1*, 3–14.

Metsala, J. L., & Wally, A. C. (1998). Spoken vocabulary growth and the segmental restructuring of lexical representations: Precursors to phonemic awareness and early reading ability. In J. Metsala & L. Ehri (Eds.), *Word recognition in beginning reading* (pp. 89–120). Hillsdale, NJ: Lawrence Erlbaum Associates Inc.

Meyer, B. J. F. (1975). *The organization of prose and its effect on recall.* Amsterdam: North Holland.

Meyer, D. E., & Gutschera, K. (1975). *Orthographic versus phonemic processing of printed words.* Paper presented at the annual meeting of the Psychonomic Society, Denver, CO, November.

Meyer, D. E., & Schvaneveldt, R. W. (1971). Facilitation in recognizing pairs of words: Evidence of a dependence between retrieval operations. *Journal of Experimental Psychology, 90*, 227–234.

Meyer, D. E., Schvaneveldt, R. W., & Ruddy, M. G. (1974). Functions of graphemic and phonemic codes in visual word-recognition. *Memory & Cognition, 2*, 309–321.

Meyer, M. S., & Felton, R. H. (1999). Repeated reading to enhance fluency: Old approaches and new direction. *Annals of Dyslexia, 49*, 283–306.

Meyer, M. S., Wood, F. B., Hart, L. A., & Felton, R. H. (1998). Selective predictive value of rapid automatized naming in poor readers. *Journal of Learning Disabilities, 31*(2), 106–117.

Mezrich, J. J. (1973). The word superiority effect in brief visual displays: Elimination by vocalization. *Perception & Psychophysics, 13*, 45–48.

Mickish, V. (1974). Children's perceptions of written word boundaries. *Journal of Reading Behavior, 6*, 19–22.

Miellet, S., O'Donnell, P. J., & Sereno, S. C. (2009). Parafoveal magnification: Visual acuity does not modulate the perceptual span in reading. *Psychological Science, 20*, 721–728.

Miellet, S., Sparrow, L., & Sereno, S. C. (2007). Word frequency and predictability effects in reading French: An evaluation of the E–Z Reader model. *Psychonomic Bulletin & Review, 14*, 762–769.

Miller, G. A. (1956). The magical number seven, plus or minus two: Some limits on our capacity for processing information. *Psychological Review, 63*, 81–89.

Miller, G. A. (1962). Some psychological studies of grammar. *American Psychologist, 17*, 748–762.

Milne, E., Swettenham, J., Hansen, P., Campbell, R., Jeffries, H., & Plaisted, K. (2002). High motion coherence thresholds in children with autism. *Journal of Child Psychology and Psychiatry, 43*(2), 255–263.

Miozzo, M., & Caramazza, A. (1998). Varieties of pure alexia: The case of failure to access graphemic representations. *Cognitive Neuropsychology [Special Issue: Pure alexia (letter-by-letter reading], 15*(1–2), 203–238.

Mitchell, D. C. (1982). *The process of reading.* Chichester, UK: Wiley.

Mitchell, D. C. (2004). On-line methods in language processing: Introduction and historical review. In M. Carreiras & C. J. Clifton (Eds.), *The on-line study of sentence comprehension: Eyetracking, ERPs, and beyond.* Hove, UK: Psychology Press.

Mitchell, D. C., & Holmes, V. M. (1985). The role of specific information about the verb in parsing sentences with local structural ambiguity. *Journal of Memory and Language, 24,* 542–559.

Moats, L. C. (1994). Assessment of spelling in learning disabilities research. In G. R. Lyon (Ed.), *Frames of reference for the assessment of learning disabilities: New views on measurement issues* (pp. 333–350). Baltimore, MD: Paul Brookes.

Moats, L. C. (2010). *Speech to print: Language essentials for teachers* (2nd ed.). Baltimore, MD: Paul Brookes.

Moats, L. C., & Foorman, B. R. (2003). Measuring teachers' content knowledge of language and reading. *Annals of Dyslexia, 53,* 23–45.

Mohan, P. J. (1978). Acoustic factors in letter cancellation: Developmental considerations. *Developmental Psychology, 14,* 117–118.

Morais, J., Cary, L., Alegria, J., & Bertelson, P. (1979). Does awareness of speech as a sequence of phones arise spontaneously? *Cognition, 7,* 323–331.

Morgan, W. P. (1896). A case of congenital word blindness. *British Medical Journal, 1871,* 1378–1379.

Morris, R. D., Stuebing, K. K., Fletcher, J. M., Shaywitz, S. E., Lyon, G. R., Shankweiler, D. P., et al. (1998). Subtypes of reading disability: Variability around a phonological core. *Journal of Educational Psychology, 90*(3), 347–373.

Morris, R. K. (1994). Lexical and message-level sentence context effects on fixation times in reading. *Journal of Experimental Psychology: Learning, Memory, and Cognition, 20,* 92–103.

Morris, R. K., Rayner, K., & Pollatsek, A. (1990). Eye movement guidance in reading: The role of parafoveal letter and space information. *Journal of Experimental Psychology: Human Perception and Performance, 16,* 268–281.

Morrison, R. E. (1984). Manipulation of stimulus onset delay in reading: Evidence for parallel programming of saccades. *Journal of Experimental Psychology: Human Perception and Performance, 10,* 667–682.

Morrison, R. E., & Inhoff, A. W. (1981). Visual factors and eye movements in reading. *Visible Language, 15,* 129–146.

Morrison, R. E., & Rayner, K. (1981). Saccade size in reading depends upon character spaces and not visual angle. *Perception & Psychophysics, 30,* 395–396.

Morton, J. (1964). The effects of context upon speed of reading, eye movement and eye–voice span. *Quarterly Journal of Experimental Psychology, 16,* 340–354.

Morton, J., & Frith, U. (1995). Causal modeling: A structural approach to developmental psychopathology. In D. Cicchetti, & D. J. Cohen (Eds.), *Developmental psychopathology, Vol. 1: Theory and method* (pp. 357–390). Oxford, UK: John Wiley & Sons.

Morton, J., & Sasanuma, S. (1984). Lexical access in Japanese. In L. Henderson (Ed.), *Orthographies and reading.* Hove, UK: Lawrence Erlbaum Associates Ltd.

Mousty, P., & Bertelson, P. (1985). A study of Braille reading: Reading speed as a function of hand usage and context. *Quarterly Journal of Experimental Psychology, 37A,* 217–233.

Mozer, M. C. (1983). Letter migration in word perception. *Journal of Experimental Psychology: Human Perception and Performance, 9,* 531–546.

Murphy, L. A., Pollatsek, A., & Well, A. D. (1988). Developmental dyslexia and word retrieval deficits. *Brain and Language, 35*(1), 1–23.

Muter, V., Hulme, C., Snowling, M., & Taylor, S. (1997). Segmentation, not rhyming, predicts early progress in learning to read. *Journal of Experimental Child Psychology, 65,* 370–396.

Myers, J. L., & O'Brien, E. J. (1998). Accessing the discourse representation while reading. *Discourse Processes, 26,* 131–157.

Myers, J. L., Shinjo, M., & Duffy, S. A. (1987). Degree of causal relatedness and memory. *Journal of Memory and Language, 26,* 453–465.

Myers, M., & Paris, S. G. (1978). Children's metacognitive knowledge about reading. *Journal of Educational Psychology, 70,* 680–690.

Nation, K. (2005). Children's reading comprehension difficulties. In M. J. Snowling & C. Hulme (Eds.), *The science of reading: A handbook* (pp. 248–265). Malden, MA: Blackwell Publishing.

Nation, K., Angell, P., & Castles, A. (2007). Orthographic learning via self-teaching in children learning to read: Effects of exposure, durability, and context. *Journal of Experimental Child Psychology, 96*, 71–84.

Nation, K., Clarke, P., Marshall, C. M., & Durand, M. (2004). Hidden language impairments in children: Parallels between poor reading comprehension and specific language impairment? *Journal of Speech, Language and Hearing Research, 47*, 199–211.

Nation, K., & Cocksey, J. (2009). The relationship between knowing a word and reading it aloud in children's word reading development. *Journal of Experimental Child Psychology, 103*, 296–308.

Nation, K., & Hulme, C. (1998). Phonemic segmentation, not onset–rime segmentation, predicts early reading and spelling skills: Response. *Reading Research Quarterly, 33*(3), 264–265.

Nation, K., Marshall, C. M., & Snowling, M. J. (2001). Phonological and semantic contributions to children's picture naming skill: Evidence from children with developmental reading disorders. *Language and Cognitive Processes [Special Issue: Language and Cognitive Processes in Developmental Disorders], 16*(2–3), 241–259.

Nation, K., & Snowling, M. J. (1998). Semantic processing and the development of word-recognition skills: Evidence from children with reading comprehension difficulties. *Journal of Memory and Language, 39*, 85–101.

Nation, K., & Snowling, M. J. (1999). Developmental differences in sensitivity to semantic relations among good and poor comprehenders: Evidence from semantic priming. *Cognition, 70*(1), B1–B13.

Nation, K., & Snowling, M.J. (2004). Beyond phonological skills: Broader language skills contribute to the development of reading. *Journal of Research in Reading, 27*(4), 342–356.

National Institute of Child Health and Human Development, National Reading Panel. (2000). *Teaching children to read: An evidence-based assessment of the scientific research literature on reading and its implications for reading instruction (NIH Publication No. 00–4769)*. Washington, DC: U.S. Government Printing Office.

Navon, D., & Shimron, J. (1981). Does word meaning involve grapheme-to-phoneme translation? Evidence from Hebrew. *Journal of Verbal Learning and Verbal Behavior, 20*, 97–109.

Neely, J. H. (1977). Semantic priming and retrieval from lexical memory: The roles of inhibitionless spreading activation and limited-capacity attention. *Journal of Experimental Psychology: General, 106*, 1–66.

Neisser, U. (1967). *Cognitive psychology*. New York: Appleton, Century Crofts.

Newman, E. B. (1966). Speed of reading when the span of letters is restricted. *American Journal of Psychology, 79*, 272–278.

Newman, T. M., Macomber, D., Naples, A. J., Babitz, T., Volkmar, F., & Grigorenko, E. L. (2007). Hyperlexia in children with autism spectrum disorders. *Journal of Autism and Developmental Disorders, 37*(4), 760–774.

Nicolson, R. I., & Fawcett, A. J. (1994). Comparison of deficits in cognitive and motor skills among children with dyslexia. *Annals of Dyslexia, 44*, 147–164.

Nicolson, R. I., Fawcett, A. J., & Dean, P. (2001). Developmental dyslexia: The cerebellar deficit hypothesis. *Trends in Neurosciences, 24*(9), 508–511.

Niensted, S. M. (1968). Hyperlexia: An educational disease? *Exceptional Children, 35*(2), 162–163.

Nikolopoulos, D., Goulandris, N., & Snowling, M. J. (2003). Developmental dyslexia in Greek. In N. Goulandris (Ed.), *Dyslexia in different languages: Cross-linguistic comparisons* (pp. 53–67). Philadelphia, PA: Whurr Publishers.

Niswander, E., Pollatsek, A., & Rayner K. (2000). The processing of derived and inflected suffixed words during reading. *Language and Cognitive Processes, 15*, 389–420.

Niswander-Klement, E., & Pollatsek, A. (2006). The effects of root frequency, word frequency, and length on the processing of prefixed English words during reading. *Memory & Cognition, 34*, 685–702.

Nodine, C. F., & Evans, D. (1969). Eye movements of prereaders to pseudowords containing letters of high and low confusability. *Perception & Psychophysics, 6*, 39–41.

Nodine, C. F., & Lang, N. J. (1971). Development of visual scanning strategies for differentiating words. *Developmental Psychology, 5*, 221–232.

Nodine, C. F., & Simmons, F. G. (1974). Processing distinctive features in the differentiation of letterlike symbols. *Journal of Experimental Psychology, 103*, 21–28.

Nodine, C. F., & Steurele, N.L. (1973). Development of perceptual and cognitive strategies for differentiating graphemes. *Journal of Experimental Psychology, 8*, 158–166.

Noordman, L. G. M., Vonk, W., & Kempff, H. J. (1992). Causal inferences during the reading of expository texts. *Journal of Memory and Language, 31*, 573–590.

Norris, D. (2006). The Bayesian reader: Explaining word recognition as an optimal Bayesian decision process. *Psychological Review, 113*, 327–357.

Oakhill, J. V. (1984). Inferential and memory skills in children's comprehension of stories. *British Journal of Educational Psychology, 54*, 31–39.

Oakhill, J. V., Cain, K., & Bryant, P. E. (2003). The dissociation of word reading and text comprehension: evidence from component skills. *Language and Cognitive Processes, 18*, 443–468.

Oakhill, J. V., & Yuill, N. (1996). Higher order factors in comprehension disability: Processes and remediation. In C. Cornoldi, & J. Oakhill (Eds.), *Reading comprehension difficulties: Processes and intervention* (pp. 69–92). Mahwah, NJ: Lawrence Erlbaum Associates Inc.

O'Brien, E. J., & Albrecht, J. E. (1992). Comprehension strategies in the development of a mental model. *Journal of Experimental Psychology: Learning, Memory, and Cognition, 18*, 777–784.

O'Brien, E. J., Cook, A. E., & Guéraud, S. (2010). Accessibility of outdated information. *Journal of Experimental Psychology: Learning, Memory, and Cognition, 36*, 979–991.

O'Brien, E. J., Rizzella, M. L., Albrecht, J. E., & Halleran, J. G. (1998). Updating a situation model: A memory-based text processing view. *Journal of Experimental Psychology: Learning, Memory, and Cognition, 24*, 1200–1210.

O'Brien, E. J., Shank, D. M., Myers, J. L., & Rayner, K. (1988). Elaborative inferences during reading: Do they occur on-line? *Journal of Experimental Psychology: Learning, Memory, and Cognition, 14*, 410–420.

O'Connor, R. E., & Forster, K. I. (1981). Criterion bias and search sequence bias in word recognition. *Memory & Cognition, 9*, 78–92.

Olson, R. K., & Datta, H. (2002). Visual-temporal processing in reading-disabled and normal twins. *Reading and Writing, 15*(1–2), 127–149.

Olson, R. K., Forsberg, H., Wise, B., & Rack, J. (1994). Measurement of word recognition, orthographic, and phonological skills. In G. R. Lyon (Ed.), *Frames of reference for the assessment of learning disabilities: New views on measurement issues* (pp. 243–277). Baltimore, MD: Paul Brookes.

Olson, R. K., Kliegl, R., & Davidson, B. J. (1983). Dyslexic and normal children's tracking eye movements. *Journal of Experimental Psychology: Human Perception and Performance, 9*, 816–825.

Olson, R. K., Wise, B., Conners, F., & Rack, J. (1989). Specific deficits in component reading and language skills: Genetic and environmental influences. *Journal of Learning Disabilities, 22*(6), 339–348.

Omanson, R. C. (1985). Knowing words and understanding texts. In T. H. Carr (Ed.), *The development of reading skills*. San Francisco: Jossey-Bass.

Omanson, R. C., Beck, I. L., McKeown, M. G., & Perfetti, C. A. (1984). Comprehension of texts with unfamiliar versus recently taught words: Assessment of alternative models. *Journal of Educational Psychology, 76*, 1253–1268.

Oppenheim, G. M., & Dell, G. S. (2008). Inner speech slips exhibit lexical bias, but not the phonemic similarity effect. *Cognition, 106*, 527–537.

O'Regan, J. K. (1975). *Structural and contextual constraints on eye movements in reading*. Unpublished doctoral dissertation, University of Cambridge, UK.

O'Regan, J. K. (1979). Eye guidance in reading: Evidence for linguistic control hypothesis. *Perception & Psychophysics, 25*, 501–509.

O'Regan, J. K. (1980). The control of saccade size and fixation duration in reading: The limits of linguistic control. *Perception & Psychophysics, 28*, 112–117.

O'Regan, J. K. (1981). The convenient viewing position hypothesis. In D. F. Fisher, R. A. Monty, & J. W. Senders (Eds.), *Eye movements: Cognition and visual perception*. Hillsdale, NJ: Lawrence Erlbaum Associates Inc.

O'Regan, J. K. (1983). Elementary perception and eye movement control processes in reading. In K. Rayner (Ed.), *Eye movements in reading: Perceptual and language processes*. New York: Academic Press.

O'Regan, J. K., & Levy-Schoen, A. (1983). Integrating visual information from successive fixations: Does transsaccadic fusion exist? *Vision Research, 23*, 765–768.

Orton, S. T. (1928). Specific reading disability – strephsymbolia. *Journal of the American Medical Association, 90*, 1095–1099.

Osaka, N. (1987). Effect of peripheral visual field size upon eye movements during Japanese text processing. In J. K. O'Regan & A. Levy-Schoen (Eds.), *Eye movements: From physiology to cognition*. Amsterdam: Elsevier.

Ouellette, G. P. (2006). What's meaning got to do with it: The role of vocabulary in word reading and reading comprehension. *Journal of Educational Psychology, 98*, 554–566.

Paap, K. R., Newsome, S. L., McDonald, J. E., & Schvaneveldt, R. W. (1982). An activation-verification model for letter and word recognition: The word superiority effect. *Psychological Review, 89*, 573–594.

Paap, K. R., Newsome, S. L., & Noel, R.W. (1984). Word shape's in poor shape for the race to the lexicon. *Journal of Experimental Psychology: Human Perception and Performance, 10*, 413–428.

Palinscar, A. S., & Brown, A. L. (1984). Reciprocal teaching of comprehension fostering and monitoring activities. *Cognition and Instruction, 1*, 117–175.

Palmer, J., MacLeod, C. M., Hunt, E., & Davidson, J. E. (1985). Information processing correlates of reading. *Journal of Memory and Language, 24*, 59–88.

Pammer, K., Hansen, P. C., Kringelback, M. L., Holliday, I., Barnes, G., Hillebrand, A., et al. (2004).Visual word recognition: The first half second. *NeuroImage, 22*, 1819–1825.

Paris, S. G., Cross, D. R., & Lipson, M.Y. (1984). Informed strategies for learning: A program to improve children's reading awareness and comprehension. *Journal of Educational Psychology, 76*, 1239–1252.

Paris, S. G., & Jacobs, J. E. (1984). The benefits of informed instruction for children's reading awareness and comprehension skills. *Child Development, 55*, 2083–2093.

Parker, S. W. (1919). Pseudo-talent for words. *Psychology Clinics, 11*, 1–7.

Parkin, A. J. (1982). Phonological recoding in lexical decision: Effects of spelling-to-sound regularity depend on how regularity is defined. *Memory & Cognition, 10*, 43–53.

Pastizzo, M. J., & Feldman, L. B. (2002). Discrepancies between orthographic and unrelated baselines in masked priming undermine a decompositional account of morphological facilitation. *Journal of Experimental Psychology: Learning, Memory, and Cognition, 28*, 244–249.

Patterson, K. E. (1982). The relation between reading and phonological coding: Further neuropsychological observations. In A. W. Ellis (Ed.), *Normality and pathology in cognitive functions.* London: Academic Press.

Patterson, K. E., & Kay, J. (1982). Letter-by-letter reading: Psychological descriptions of a neurological syndrome. *Quarterly Journal of Experimental Psychology, 34A*, 411–422.

Patterson, K. E., & Marcel, A. (1977). Aphasia, dyslexia, and the phonological code of written words. *Quarterly Journal of Experimental Psychology, 29*, 307–318.

Patterson, K. E., Marshall, J. C., & Coltheart, M. (1985). *Surface dyslexia: Neuropsychological and cognitive studies of phonological reading.* Hillsdale, NJ: Lawrence Erlbaum Associates Inc.

Patti, P. J., & Lupinetti, L. (1993). Brief report: Implications of hyperlexia in an autistic savant. *Journal of Autism and Developmental Disorders, 23*(2), 397–405.

Pavlidis, G. T. (1981). Do eye movements hold the key to dyslexia? *Neuropsychologia, 19*, 57–64.

Pavlidis, G. T. (1985). Eye movement differences between dyslexics, normal, and retarded readers while sequentially fixating digits. *American Journal of Optometry & Physiological Optics, 62*, 820–832.

Pearlmutter, N. J., & MacDonald, M. C. (1995). Individual differences and probabilistic constraints in syntactic ambiguity resolution. *Journal of Memory and Language, 34*, 521–542.

Pearson, D. (1976). A psycholinguistic model of reading. *Language Arts, 53*, 309–314.

Penfield, W., & Roberts, L. (1959). *Speech and brain mechanisms.* Princeton, NJ: Princeton University Press.

Pennington, B. F., Filipek, P. A., Lefly, D., Churchwell, J., Kennedy, D. N., Simon, J. H., et al. (1999). Brain morphometry in reading-disabled twins. *Neurology, 53*, 723–729.

Pennington, B. F.,Van Orden, G. C., Smith, S. D., Green, P. A., & Haith, M. M. (1990). Phonological processing skills and deficits in adult dyslexics. *Child Development, 61*(6), 1753–1778.

Perea, M., Abu Mallouh, R., & Carreiras, M. (2010). The search of an input coding scheme: Transposed-letter priming in Arabic. *Psychonomic Bulletin & Review, 17*, 375–380.

Perea, M., & Acha, J. (2009). Space information is important for reading. *Vision Research, 49*, 1994–2000.

Perea, M., & Carreiras, M. (2007). Do transposed-letter similarity effects occur at a prelexical phonological level? *Quarterly Journal of Experimental Psychology, 59*, 1600–1613.

Perea, M., & Lupker, S. J. (2003). Does jugde activate COURT? Transposed-letter confusability effects in masked associative priming. *Memory & Cognition, 31*, 829–841.

Perea, M., & Lupker, S. J. (2004). Can CANISO activate CASINO? Transposed-letter similarity effects with nonadjacent letter positions. *Journal of Memory and Language, 51*, 231–246.

Perea, M., & Pollatsek, A. (1998). The effects of neighborhood frequency in reading and lexical decision. *Journal of Experimental Psychology: Human Perception and Performance, 24*, 767–779.

Perea, M., & Rosa, E. (2002). Does 'whole word shape' play a role in visual word recognition? *Perception & Psychophysics, 64*, 785–794.

Perea, M., Rosa, E., & Gómez, C. (2005). The frequency effect for pseudowords in the lexical decision task. *Perception & Psychophysics, 67*, 301–314.

Perfetti, C. A. (1985). *Reading ability*. New York: Oxford University Press.

Perfetti, C. A. (1988). Verbal efficiency in reading ability. In M. Daneman, G. E. Mackinnon, & T. G. Waller (Eds.), *Reading research: Advances in theory and practice, Vol. 6* (pp. 109–143). San Diego, CA: Academic Press.

Perfetti, C. A. (1992). The representation problem in reading acquisition. In P. B. Gough, L. C. Ehri, & R. Treiman (Eds.), *Reading acquisition* (pp. 145–174). Hillsdale, NJ: Lawrence Erlbaum Associates Inc.

Perfetti, C. A. (1994). Psycholinguistics and reading ability. In M. A. Gernsbacher (Ed.), *Handbook of psycholinguistics* (pp. 849–894). San Diego, CA: Academic Press.

Perfetti, C. A. (1998). Two basic questions about reading and learning to read. In P. Reitsma & L. Verhoeven (Eds.), *Problems and interventions in literacy development* (pp. 15–47). Dordrecht, The Netherlands: Kluwer Academic.

Perfetti, C. A. (2003). The universal grammar of reading. *Scientific Studies of Reading*, 7(3), 3–24.

Perfetti, C. A. (2007). Reading ability: Lexical quality to comprehension. *Scientific Studies of Reading [Special Issue: What should the scientific study of reading be now and in the near future?]*, *11*(4), 357–383.

Perfetti, C. A., Beck, I., Bell, L., & Hughes, C. (1988). Phonemic knowledge and learning to read are reciprocal: A longitudinal study of first grade children. In K. Stanovich (Ed.), *Children's reading and the development of phonological awareness* (pp. 39–75). Detroit, MI: Wayne State University Press.

Perfetti, C. A., Bell, L. C., & Delaney, C. (1988). Automatic phonetic activation in silent word reading: Evidence from backward masking. *Journal of Memory and Language, 27*, 59–70.

Perfetti, C. A., Beverly, S., Bell, L. C., & Hughes, C. (1987). Phonemic knowledge and learning to read: A longitudinal study of first grade children. *Merrill-Palmer Quarterly, 33*, 283–319.

Perfetti, C. A., & Goldman, S. R. (1976). Discourse memory and reading comprehension skill. *Journal of Verbal Learning and Verbal Behavior, 14*, 33–42.

Perfetti, C. A., Goldman, S. R., & Hogaboam, T. W. (1979). Reading skill and the identification of words in discourse context. *Memory & Cognition, 7*, 273–282.

Perfetti, C. A., & Hart, L. (2001). The lexical basis of comprehension skill. In D. S. Gorfein (Ed.), *On the consequences of meaning selection: Perspectives on resolving lexical ambiguity* (pp. 67–86). Washington, DC: American Psychological Association.

Perfetti, C. A., & Hart, L. (2002). The lexical quality hypothesis. In L. Vehoeven. C. Elbro, & P. Reitsma (Eds.), *Precursors of functional literacy* (pp. 189–213). Amsterdam: John Benjamins.

Perfetti, C. A., & Hogaboam, T. W. (1975). The relationship between single word decoding and reading comprehension skill. *Journal of Educational Psychology, 67*, 461–469.

Perfetti, C. A., Marron, M. A., & Foltz, P. W. (1996). Sources of comprehension failure: Theoretical perspectives and case studies. In C. Cornoldi, & J. Oakhill (Eds.), *Reading comprehension difficulties: Processes and intervention* (pp. 137–165). Mahwah, NJ: Lawrence Erlbaum Associates Inc.

Perfetti, C. A., & McCutchen, D. (1982). Speech processes in reading. In N. Lass (Ed.), *Speech and language: Advances in basic research and practice* (Vol. 7, pp. 237–269). New York: Academic Press.

Perfetti, C. A., & Sandak, R. (2000). Reading optimally builds on spoken language: Implications for deaf readers. *Journal of Deaf Studies and Deaf Education, 5*(1), 32–50.

Perfetti, C. A., & Tan, L. H. (1998). The time course of graphic, phonological, and semantic activation in Chinese character identification. *Journal of Experimental Psychology: Learning, Memory, and Cognition, 24*, 101–118.

Perry, C., Ziegler, J. C., & Zorzi, M. (2007). Nested incremental modeling in the development of computational theories: The CDP+ model of reading aloud. *Psychological Review, 114*, 273–315.

Petersen, S. E., Fox, I. T., Posner, M. I., Mintun, M., & Raichle, M. E. (1988). Positron emission tomographic studies of the cortical anatomy of single-word processing, *Nature, 331*, 858–589.

Phillips, C., & Wagers, M. (2007). Relating structure and time in linguistics and psycholinguistics. In M. G. Gaskell (Ed.), *Oxford handbook of psycholinguistics* (pp. 739–756). Oxford, UK: Oxford University Press.

Phillips, G., & McNaughton, S. (1990). The practice of storybook reading to preschool children in mainstream New Zealand families. *Reading Research Quarterly, 25*(3), 196–212.

Phinney, E., Pennington, B. F., Olson, R., Filley, C. M., & Filipek, P. A. (2007). Brain structure correlates of component reading processes: Implications for reading disability. *Cortex, 43*(6), 777–791.

Piaget, J. (1952). *The origins of intelligence in children*. New York: International Universities Press.

Pichert, J. W., & Anderson, R. C. (1977). Taking different perspectives on a story. *Journal of Educational Psychology, 69*, 309–315.

Pick, A. D., Unze, M. G., Brownell, C. A., Drozdal, J. G., & Hopmann, M. R. (1978). Young children's knowledge of word structure. *Child Development, 49,* 669–680.

Pickering, M. J., & Frisson, S. (2001). Processing ambiguous verbs: Evidence from eye movements. *Journal of Experimental Psychology: Learning, Memory, and Cognition, 27,* 556–573.

Pickering, M. J., McElree, B., Frisson, S., Chen, L., & Traxler, M. (2006). Underspecification and aspectual coercion. *Discourse Processes, 42,* 131–155.

Pickering, M. J., Traxler, M. J., & Crocker, M. W. (2000). Ambiguity resolution in sentence processing: Evidence against frequency-based accounts. *Journal of Memory and Language, 43,* 447–475.

Pickering, M. J., & van Gompel, R. P. G. (2006). Syntactic parsing. In M. J. Traxler & M. A. Gernsbacher (Eds.), *Handbook of psycholinguistics* (2nd ed., pp. 455–503). London: Academic Press.

Piñango, M. M., Zurif, E., & Jackendoff, R. (1999). Real-time processing implications of enriched composition at the syntax–semantics interface. *Journal of Psycholinguistic Research, 28,* 395–414.

Pinnell, G. S., & Fountas, I. C. (2000). *Guided reading: Research base for guided reading as an instructional approach.* Retrieved from the Scholastic website: http://teacher.scholastic.com/products/guidedreading/pdfs/GR_Research Base.pdf

Pintner, R. (1913). Inner speech silent reading. *Psychological Review, 20,* 129–153.

Pirozzola, F. J., & Rayner, K. (1977). Hemispheric specialization in reading and word recognition. *Brain and Language, 4,* 248–261.

Pirozzola, F. J., & Rayner, K. (1978). The normal control of eye movements in acquired and developmental reading disorders. In H. Avakian-Whitaker and H. A. Whitaker (Eds.), *Advances in neurolinguistics and psycholinguistics.* New York: Academic Press.

Plaut, D. C., McClelland, J. L., Seidenberg, M. S., & Patterson, K. E. (1996). Understanding normal and impaired word reading: Computational principles in quasi-regular domains. *Psychological Review, 103,* 56–115.

Plomin, R., & Kovas, Y. (2005). Generalist genes and learning disabilities. *Psychological Bulletin, 131*(4), 592–617.

Poldrack, R. A., & Gabrieli, J. D. E. (2001). Characterizing the neural mechanisms of skill learning and repetition priming. Evidence from mirror-reading. *Brain: A Journal of Neurology, 124,* 67–82.

Pollatsek, A., Bolozky, S., Well, A. D., & Rayner, K. (1981). Asymmetries in the perceptual span for Israeli readers. *Brain and Language, 14,* 174–180.

Pollatsek, A., Drieghe, D., Stockall, L., & de Almeida, R. G. (2010). The interpretation of ambiguous trimorphemic words in sentence context. *Psychonomic Bulletin & Review, 17,* 88–94.

Pollatsek, A., & Hyönä, J. (2005). The role of semantic transparency in the processing of Finnish compound words. *Language and Cognitive Processes, 20,* 261–290.

Pollatsek, A., Hyönä, J., & Bertram, R. (2000). The role of morphological constituents in reading Finnish compound words. *Journal of Experimental Psychology: Human Perception and Performance, 26,* 820–833.

Pollatsek, A., Lesch, M., Morris, R. K., & Rayner, K. (1992). Phonological codes are used in integrating information across saccades in word identification and reading. *Journal of Experimental Psychology: Human Perception and Performance, 18,* 148–162.

Pollatsek, A., Perea, M., & Binder, K. (1999). The effects of neighborhood size in reading and lexical decision. *Journal of Experimental Psychology: Human Perception and Performance, 25,* 1142–1158.

Pollatsek, A., Perea, M., & Carreiras, M. (2005). Does conal prime CANAL more than cinal? Masked phonological priming effects with the lexical decision task. *Memory & Cognition, 33,* 557–565.

Pollatsek, A., Raney, G. E., LaGasse, L., & Rayner, K. (1993). The use of information below fixation in reading and in visual search. *Canadian Journal of Experimental Psychology, 47,* 179–200.

Pollatsek, A., & Rayner, K. (1982). Eye movement control in reading: The role of word boundaries. *Journal of Experimental Psychology: Human Perception and Performance, 8,* 817–833.

Pollatsek, A., Rayner, K., & Balota, D. A. (1986). Inferences about eye movement control from the perceptual span in reading. *Perception & Psychophysics, 40,* 123–130.

Pollatsek, A., Reichle, E. D., & Rayner, K. (2003). Modeling eye movements in reading. In J. Hyönä, R., Radach, & H. Deubel (Eds.). *The mind's eyes: Cognitive and applied aspects of eye movement research* (pp. 361–390). Amsterdam: Elsevier.

Pollatsek, A., Reichle, E. D., & Rayner, K. (2006). Tests of the E-Z Reader model: Exploring the interface between cognition and eye-movement control. *Cognitive Psychology, 52,* 1–52.

Pollatsek, A., Slattery, T. J., & Juhasz, B. J. (2008). The processing of novel and lexicalized prefixed words in reading. *Language and Cognitive Processes, 23,* 1133–1158.

Pollatsek, A., Tan, L-H., & Rayner, K. (2000). The role of phonological codes in integrating information across saccadic eye movements in Chinese character identification. *Journal of Experimental Psychology: Human Perception and Performance, 26*, 607–633.

Porpodas, C. D. (2006). Literacy acquisition in Greek: Research review of the role of phonological and cognitive factors. In R. M. Joshi & P. G. Aaron (Eds.), *Handbook of orthography and literacy* (pp. 189–199). Mahwah, NJ: Lawrence Erlbaum Associates Inc.

Posnansky, C. J., & Rayner, K. (1977). Visual-feature and response components in a picture–word interference task with begining and skilled readers. *Journal of Experimental Child Psychology, 24*, 440–460.

Posner, M. I. (1980). Orienting of attention. *Quarterly Journal of Experimental Psychology, 32*, 3–25.

Posner, M. I., & Boies, S. W. (1971). Components of attention. *Psychological Review, 78*, 391–408.

Posner, M. I., & Snyder, C. R. R. (1975). Attention and cognitive control. In R. Solso (Ed.), *Information processing and cognition: The Loyola symposium*. Hillsdale, NJ: Lawrence Erlbaum Associates Inc.

Potter, M. C., Kroll, J. F., & Harris, C. (1980). Comprehension and memory in rapid, sequential reading. In R. S. Nickerson (Ed.), *Attention and performance* (Vol. 8). Hillsdale, NJ: Lawrence Erlbaum Associates Inc.

Poulton, E. C. (1962). Peripheral vision, refractoriness and eye movements in fast oral reading. *British Journal of Psychology, 53*, 409–419.

Preis, S., Jänke, L., Schmitz-Hillebrecht, J., & Steinmetz, H. (1999). Child age and planum temporale asymmetry. *Brain and Cognition, 40*, 441–452.

Pritchard, R. M. (1961). Stabilized images on the retina. *Scientific American, 204*, 72–78.

Pugh, K. R., Mencl, W. E., Jenner, A. R., Katz, L., Frost, S. J., Lee, J. R., et al. (2000). Functional neuroimaging studies of reading and reading disability (developmental dyslexia). *Mental Retardation and Developmental Disabilities Research Reviews [Special Issue: Pediatric Neuroimaging], 6*(3), 207–213.

Pugh, K. R., Mencl, W. E., Jenner, A. R., Katz, L., Frost, S. J., Lee, J. R., et al. (2001a). Neurobiological studies of reading and reading disability. *Journal of Communication Disorders, 34*(6), 479–492.

Pugh, K. R., Mencl, W. E., Jenner, A. R., Lee, J. R., Katz, L., Frost, S. J., et al. (2001b). Neuroimaging studies of reading development and reading disability. *Learning Disabilities Research & Practice [Special Issue: Emergent and Early Literacy: Current Status and Research Directions], 16*(4), 240–249.

Pugh, K., Shaywitz, B., Constable, T., Shaywitz, S., Skudlarski, P., Fulbright, R., et al. (1996). Cerebral organization of component processes in reading. *Brain, 119*, 1221–1238.

Pylkkänen, L., & McElree, B. (2006). The syntax–semantic interface: On-line composition of sentence meaning. In M. Traxler & M. A. Gernsbacher (Eds.), *Handbook of psycholinguistics* (2nd ed., pp. 539–580). New York: Elsevier.

Quinn, L. (1981). Reading skills of hearing and congenitally deaf children. *Journal of Experimental Child Psychology, 32*, 139–161.

Rack, J. P., Snowling, M. J., & Olson, R. K. (1992). The nonword reading deficit in developmental dyslexia: A review. *Reading Research Quarterly, 27*(1), 28–53.

Radach, R. (1996). *Blickbewegungen beim Lesen: Psychologisshe Aspekte der Determination von Fixationspositionen. (Eye movements in reading: Psychological factors that determine fixation locations)*. Munster, Germany: Waxmann.

Rader, N. (1975). *From written words to meaning: A developmental study*. Unpublished doctoral dissertation, Cornell University.

Ramus, F. (2003). Developmental dyslexia: Specific phonological deficit or general sensorimotor dysfunction? *Current Opinion in Neurobiology, 13*(2), 212–218.

Ramus, F. (2004a). Neurobiology of dyslexia: A reinterpretation of the data. *Trends in Neurosciences, 27*(12), 720–726.

Ramus, F. (2004b). The neural basis of reading acquisition. In M. S. Gazzaniga (Ed.), *The cognitive neurosciences* (3rd ed., pp. 815–824). Cambridge, MA: MIT Press.

Rankin, E. F. (1970). How flexibly do we read? *Journal of Reading Behavior, 3*, 34–38.

Rastle, K., Davis, M. H., Marslen-Wilson, W. D., & Tyler, L. K. (2000). Morphological and semantic effects in visual word recognition: A time course study. *Language and Cognitive Processes, 15*, 507–538.

Rastle, K., Davis, M. H., & New, B. (2004). The broth in my brother's brothel: Morpho-orthographic segmentation in visual word recognition. *Psychonomic Bulletin & Review, 11*, 1090–1098.

Rastle, K., Tyler, L. K., & Marslen-Wilson, W. (2006). New evidence for morphological errors in deep dyslexia. *Brain and Language, 97*(2), 189–199.

Ratcliff, R., Gomez, P., McKoon, G. (2004). A diffusion model account of the lexical decision task. *Psychological Review, 111*, 159–182.

Rawson, M. B. (1995). *Dyslexia over the lifespan: A fifty-five year longitudinal study*. Cambridge, MA: Educator's Publishing Service.

Rayner, K. (1975a). The perceptual span and peripheral cues in reading. *Cognitive Psychology, 7*, 65–81.

Rayner, K. (1975b). Parafoveal identification during a fixation in reading. *Acta Psychologica, 39*, 271–282.

Rayner, K. (1976). Developmental changes in word recognition strategies. *Journal of Educational Psychology, 68*, 323–329

Rayner, K. (1978a). Eye movements in reading and information processing. *Psychological Bulletin, 85*, 618–660.

Rayner, K. (1978b). Foveal and parafoveal cues in reading. In J. Requin (Ed.), *Attention and performance VII*. Hillsdale, NJ: Lawrence Erlbaum Associates Inc.

Rayner, K. (1979). Eye guidance in reading: Fixation locations within words. *Perception, 8*, 21–30.

Rayner, K. (1983). *Eye movements in reading: Perceptual and language processes*. New York: Academic Press.

Rayner, K. (1984). Visual selection in reading, picture perception, and visual search: A tutorial review. In H. Bouma & D. Bouwhuis (Eds.), *Attention and performance X*. Hillsdale, NJ: Erlbaum.

Rayner, K. (1985). Do faulty eye movements cause dyslexia? *Developmental Neuropsychology, 1*, 3–15.

Rayner, K. (1986). Eye movements and the perceptual span in beginning and skilled readers. *Journal of Experimental Child Psychology, 41*, 211–236.

Rayner, K. (1988). Word recognition cues in children: The relative use of graphemic cues, orthographic cues and grapheme–phoneme correspondence rules. *Journal of Educational Psychology, 80*, 473–479.

Rayner, K. (1998). Eye movements in reading and information processing: Twenty years of research. *Psychological Bulletin, 124*, 372–422.

Rayner, K. (2009). The Thirty-Fifth Sir Frederick Bartlett Lecture: Eye movements and attention during reading, scene perception, and visual search. *Quarterly Journal of Experimental Psychology, 62*, 1457–1506.

Rayner, K., Ashby, J., Pollatsek, A., & Reichle, E. D. (2004). The effects of frequency and predictability on eye fixations in reading: Implications for the E-Z reader model. *Journal of Experimental Psychology: Human Perception and Performance, 30*, 720–732.

Rayner, K., Balota, D. A., & Pollatsek, A. (1986). Against parafoveal semantic preprocessing during eye fixations in reading. *Canadian Journal of Psychology, 40*, 473–483.

Rayner, K., & Bertera, J. H. (1979). Reading without a fovea. *Science, 206*, 468–469.

Rayner, K., Carlson, M., & Frazier, L. (1983). The interaction of syntax and semantics during sentence processing: Eye movements in the analysis of semantically biased sentences, *Journal of Verbal Learning and Verbal Behavior, 22*, 358–374.

Rayner, K., Castelhano, M. S., & Yang, J. (2009a). Eye movements and the perceptual span in older and younger readers. *Psychology and Aging, 24*, 755–760.

Rayner, K., Castelhano, M. S., & Yang, J. (2009b). Eye movements when looking at unusual/weird scenes: Are there cultural differences? *Journal of Experimental Psychology: Learning, Memory, and Cognition, 35*, 254–259.

Rayner, K., Castelhano, M. S., & Yang, J. (2010). Eye movements and preview benefit in older and younger readers. *Psychology and Aging, 25*, 714–718.

Rayner, K., & Clifton, C., Jr. (2002). Language comprehension. In D. L. Medin (Ed.), *Stevens' Handbook of Experimental Psychology: Volume X* (pp. 261–316). New York: Wiley.

Rayner, K., & Clifton, C. Jr. (2009). Language processing in reading and speech perception is fast and incremental: Implications for event-related potential research. *Biological Psychology, 80*, 4–9.

Rayner, K., Cook, A. E., Juhasz, B. J., & Frazier, L. (2006). Immediate disambiguation of lexically ambiguous words during reading: Evidence from eye movements. *British Journal of Psychology, 97*, 467–482.

Rayner, K., & Duffy, S. A. (1986). Lexical complexity and fixation times in reading: Effects of word frequency, verb complexity, and lexical ambiguity. *Memory & Cognition, 14*, 191–201.

Rayner, K., & Fischer, M. H. (1996). Mindless reading revisited: Eye movements during reading and scanning are different. *Perception & Psychophysics, 58*, 734–747.

Rayner, K., Fischer, M. H., & Pollatsek, A. (1998). Unspaced text interferes with both word identification and eye movement control. *Vision Research, 38*, 1129–1144.

Rayner, K., & Fisher, D. L. (1987). Letter processing during eye fixations in visual search. *Perception & Psychophysics, 42*, 87–100.

Rayner, K., Foorman, B. R., Perfetti, C. A., Pesetsky, D., & Seidenberg, M. S. (2001). How psychological science informs the teaching of reading. *Psychological Science in the Public Interest, 2*, 31–74.

Rayner, K., Foorman, B. F., Perfetti, C. A., Pesetsky, D., & Seidenberg, M. S. (2002). How should reading be taught? *Scientific American, 286*(3), 84–91.

Rayner, K., & Frazier, L. (1987). Parsing temporarily ambiguous complements. *Quarterly Journal of Experimental Psychology, 39A*, 657–673.

Rayner, K., & Frazier, L. (1989). Selection mechanisms in reading lexically ambiguous words. *Journal of Experimental Psychology: Learning, Memory, and Cognition, 15*, 779–790.

Rayner, K., & Hagelberg, E. M. (1975). Word recognition cues for beginning and skilled readers. *Journal of Experimental Child Psychology, 20*, 444–455.

Rayner, K., Inhoff, A. W., Morrison, R., Slowiaczek, M. L., & Bertera, J. H. (1981). Masking of foveal and parafoveal vision during eye fixations in reading. *Journal of Experimental Psychology: Human Perception and Performance, 7*, 167–179.

Rayner, K., & Johnson, R. L. (2005). Letter-by-letter acquired dyslexia is due to the serial encoding of letters. *Psychological Science, 16*(7), 530–534.

Rayner, K., Juhasz, B. J., & Brown, S. (2007). Do readers acquire preview benefit from word n+2? A test of serial attention shift versus distributed lexical processing models of eye movement control in reading. *Journal of Experimental Psychology: Human Perception and Performance, 33*, 230–245.

Rayner, K., Kambe, G., & Duffy, S. (2000). The effect of clause wrap-up on eye movements during reading. *Quarterly Journal of Experimental Psychology, 53A*, 1061–1080.

Rayner, K., Li, X., & Pollatsek, A. (2007). Extending the E-Z Reader model of eye movement control to Chinese readers. *Cognitive Science, 31*, 1021–1034.

Rayner, K., Li, X., Juhasz, B. J., & Yan, G. (2005). The effect of predictability on the eye movements of Chinese readers. *Psychonomic Bulletin & Review, 12*, 1089–1093.

Rayner, K., Li, X., Williams, C. C., Cave, K. R., & Well, A. D. (2007). Eye movements during information processing tasks: Individual differences and cultural effects. *Vision Research, 47*, 2714–2726.

Rayner, K., Liversedge, S. P., & White, S. J. (2006). Eye movements when reading disappearing text: The importance of the word to the right of fixation. *Vision Research, 46*, 310–323.

Rayner, K., Liversedge, S. P., White, S. J., & Vergilino-Perez, D. (2003). Reading disappearing text: Cognitive control on eye movements. *Psychological Science, 14*, 383–389.

Rayner, K., & McConkie, G. W. (1976). What guides a reader's eye movements? *Vision Research, 16*, 829–837.

Rayner, K., McConkie, G. W., & Ehrlich, S. F. (1978). Eye movements and integrating information across fixations. *Journal of Experimental Psychology: Human Perception and Performance, 4*, 529–544.

Rayner, K., McConkie, G. W., & Zola, D. (1980). Integrating information across eye movements. *Cognitive Psychology, 12*, 206–226.

Rayner, K., & Morris, R. K. (1992). Eye movement control in reading: Evidence against semantic preprocessing. *Journal of Experimental Psychology: Human Perception and Performance, 18*, 163–172.

Rayner, K., Murphy, L., Henderson, J. M., & Pollatsek, A. (1989). Selective attentional dyslexia. *Cognitive Neuropsychology, 6*, 357–378.

Rayner, K., Pacht, J. M., & Duffy, S. A. (1994). Effects of prior encounter and global discourse bias on the processing of lexically ambiguous words: Evidence from eye fixations. *Journal of Memory and Language, 33*, 527–544.

Rayner, K., & Pollatsek, A. (1981). Eye movement control during reading: Evidence for direct control. *Quarterly Journal of Experimental Psychology, 33A*, 351–373.

Rayner, K., & Pollatsek, A. (1989). *The psychology of reading*. Englewood Cliffs, NJ: Prentice-Hall.

Rayner, K., Pollatsek, A., Liversedge, S. P., & Reichle, E. D. (2009). Eye movements and non-canonical reading: Comments on Kennedy and Pynte (2008). *Vision Research, 49*, 2232–2236.

Rayner, K., & Posnansky, C. (1978). Stages of processing in word identification. *Journal of Experimental Psychology: General, 107*, 64–80.

Rayner, K., & Raney, G. E. (1996). Eye movement control in reading and visual search: Effects of word frequency. *Psychonomic Bulletin & Review, 3*, 245–248.

Rayner, K., & Reichle, E. D. (2010). Models of the reading process. *WIRES Cognitive Science, 1*, 787–799.

Rayner, K., Reichle, E. D., Stroud, M. D., Williams, C. W., & Pollatsek, A. (2006). The effect of word frequency, word predictability, and font difficulty on the eye movements of young and older readers. *Psychology and Aging, 21*, 448–465.

Rayner, K., Sereno, S. C., Lesch, M. F., & Pollatsek, A. (1995). Phonological codes are automatically activated during reading: Evidence from an eye movement priming paradigm. *Psychological Science, 6*, 26–32.

Rayner, K., Sereno, S. C., Morris, R. K., Schmauder, A. R., & Clifton, C. (1989). Eye movements and on-line comprehension processes. *Language and Cognitive Processes, 4*, 21–49.

Rayner, K., Sereno, S. C., & Raney, G. E. (1996). Eye movement control in reading: A comparison of two types of models. *Journal of Experimental Psychology: Human Perception and Performance, 22*, 1188–1200.

Rayner, K., Slattery, T. J., & Bélanger, N. (2010). Eye movements, the perceptual span, and reading speed. *Psychonomic Bulletin & Review, 17*, 834–839.

Rayner, K., Slattery, T. J., Drieghe, D., & Liversedge, S. P. (2011). Eye movements and word skipping during reading: Effects of word length and predictability. *Journal of Experimental Psychology: Human Perception and Performance, 37*, 514–528.

Rayner, K., Slowiaczek, M. L., Clifton, C. Jr., & Bertera, J. H. (1983). Latency of sequential eye movements: Implications for reading. *Journal of Experimental Psychology: Human Perception and Performance, 9*, 912–922.

Rayner, K., Warren, T., Juhasz, B. J., & Liversedge, S. P. (2004). The effects of plausibility on eye movements in reading. *Journal of Experimental Psychology: Learning, Memory, and Cognition, 30*, 1290–1301.

Rayner, K., & Well, A. D. (1996). Effects of contextual constraint on eye movements in reading: A further examination. *Psychonomic Bulletin & Review, 3*, 504–509.

Rayner, K., Well, A. D., & Pollatsek, A. (1980). Asymmetry of the effective visual field in reading. *Perception & Psychophysics, 27*, 537–544.

Rayner, K., Well, A. D., Pollatsek, A., & Bertera, J. H. (1982). The availability of useful information to the right of fixation in reading. *Perception & Psychophysics, 31*, 537–550.

Rayner, K., White, S. J., Johnson, R. L., & Liversedge, S. P. (2006). Raeding wrods with jubmled lettres: There's a cost. *Psychological Science, 17*, 192–193.

Rayner, K., Yang, J., Castelhano, M. S., & Liversedge, S. P. (2011). Eye movements of older and younger readers when reading disappearing text. *Psychology and Aging, 26*, 214–223.

Reicher, G. M. (1969). Perceptual recognition as a function of meaningfulness of stimulus material. *Journal of Experimental Psychology, 81*, 275–280.

Reichle, E. D. (2011). Serial attention models of reading. In S. P. Liversedge, I. D. Gilchrist, & S. Everling (Eds.), *Oxford handbook on eye movements* (pp. 767–780). Oxford, UK: Oxford University Press.

Reichle, E. D. (2012). *Computational models of reading.* Oxford, UK: Oxford University Press.

Reichle, E. D., & Laurent, P. A. (2006). Using reinforcement learning to understand the emergence of 'intelligent' eye-movement behavior during reading. *Psychological Review, 113*, 390–408.

Reichle, E. D., Liversedge, S. P., Pollatsek, A., & Rayner, K. (2009). Encoding multiple words simultaneously in reading is implausible. *Trends in Cognitive Science, 13*, 115–119.

Reichle, E. D., Pollatsek, A., Fisher, D. L., & Rayner, K. (1998). Towards a model of eye movement control in reading. *Psychological Review, 105*, 125–157.

Reichle, E. D., Rayner, K., & Pollatsek, A. (2003). The E-Z Reader model of eye movement control in reading: Comparison to other models. *Brain and Behavioral Sciences, 26*, 445–476.

Reichle, E. D., Rayner, K., & Pollatsek, A. (2007). Modeling the effects of lexical ambiguity on eye movements during reading. In R. P. G. Van Gompel, M. F. Fischer, W. S. Murray, & R. L. Hill (Eds.), *Eye movements: A window on mind and brain* (pp. 271–292). Oxford, UK: Elsevier.

Reichle, E. D., Reineberg, A. E., & Schooler, J. W. (2010). Eye movements during mindless reading. *Psychological Science, 21*, 1300–1310.

Reichle, E. D., Vanyukov, P. M., Laurent, P. A., & Warren, T. (2008). Serial or parallel? Using depth-of-processing to examine attention allocation during reading. *Vision Research, 48*, 1831–1836.

Reichle, E. D., Warren, T., & McConnell, K. (2009). Using E-Z Reader to model the effects of higher-level language processing on eye movements during reading. *Psychonomic Bulletin & Review, 16*, 1–21.

Reilly, R., & Radach, R. (2006). Some empirical tests of an interactive activation model of eye movement control in reading. *Cognitive Systems Research, 7*, 34–55.

Reingold, E. M. (2003). Eye movement control in reading: Models and predictions. *Behaviorial and Brain Sciences, 26*, 500–501.

Reingold, E. M., & Rayner, K. (2006). Examining the word identification stages hypothesized by the E–Z Reader model. *Psychological Science, 17*, 742–746.

Reitsma, P. (1983a). Printed word learning in beginning readers. *Journal of Experimental Child Psychology*, *36*, 321–339.

Reitsma, P. (1983b). Word-specific knowledge in beginning reading. *Journal of Research in Reading*, *6*, 41–56.

Richman, L. C., & Wood, K. M. (2002). Learning disability subtypes: Classification of high functioning hyperlexia. *Brain and Language*, *82*(1), 10–21.

Ricketts, J., Nation, K., & Bishop, D. V. M. (2007). Vocabulary is important for some, but not all reading skills. *Scientific Studies of Reading*, *11*(3), 235–257.

Robertson, E. K., Joanisse, M. F., Desroches, A. S., & Ng, S. (2009). Categorical speech perception deficits distinguish language and reading impairments in children. *Developmental Science*, *12*(5), 753–767.

Robichon, F., & Habib, M. (1998). Abnormal callosal morphology in male adult dyslexics: Relationships to handedness and phonological abilities. *Brain and Language*, *62*(1), 127–146.

Rochelle, K. S. H., & Talcott, J. B. (2006). Impaired balance in developmental dyslexia? A meta-analysis of the contending evidence. *Journal of Child Psychology and Psychiatry*, *47*(11), 1159–1166.

Rosen, S., & Manganari, E. (2001). Is there a relationship between speech and nonspeech auditory processing in children with dyslexia? *Journal of Speech, Language, and Hearing Research*, *44*, 720–736.

Rosinski, R. R. (1977). Picture–word interference is semantically based. *Child Development*, *48*, 643–647.

Rosinski, R. R., Golinkoff, R. M., & Kukish, K. (1975). Automatic semantic processing in a picture–word interference task. *Child Development*, *46*, 243–253.

Rothkopf, E. Z. (1978). Analyzing eye movements to infer processing styles during learning from text. In J. W. Senders, D. F. Fisher, & R. A. Monty (Eds.), *Eye movements and the higher psychological functions*. Hillsdale, NJ: Lawrence Erlbaum Associates Inc.

Rothkopf, E. Z., & Billington, M. Z. (1979). Goal-guided learning from text: Inferring a descriptive processing model from inspection times and eye movements. *Journal of Educational Psychology*, *71*, 310–327.

Routman, R. (1988). *Transitions: From learning to literacy*. Portsmouth, NH: Heinemann.

Routman, R. (1991). *Invitations: Changing as teachers and learners K-12*. Portsmouth, NH: Heinemann.

Rozin, P., Bressman, B., & Taft, M. (1974). Do children understand the basic relationship between speech and writing? The Mow–Motorcycle test. *Journal of Reading Behavior*, *6*, 327–334.

Rozin, P., & Gleitman, L. R. (1977). The structure and acquisition of reading II: The reading process and the acquisition of the alphabetic principle. In A. S. Reber & D. L. Scarborough (Eds.), *Toward a psychology of reading*. Hillsdale, NJ: Lawrence Erlbaum Associates Inc.

Rubenstein, H., Lewis, S. S., & Rubenstein, M. H. (1971). Evidence for phonemic recoding in visual word recognition. *Journal of Verbal Learning and Verbal Behavior*, *10*, 645–647.

Rueckl, J. G., & Seidenberg, M. S. (2009). Computational modeling and the neural bases of reading and reading disorders. In K. Pugh & P. McCardle (Eds.), *How children learn to read: Current issues and new directions in the integration of cognition, neurobiology and genetics of reading and dyslexia research and practice* (pp. 101–134). New York: Psychology Press.

Rugel, R. P. (1974). WISC subtest scores of disabled readers: A review with respect to Bannatyne's recategorization. *Journal of Learning Disabilities*, *7*, 48–55.

Rumelhart, D. E. (1975). Notes on a schema for stories. In D. G. Bobrow & A. M. Collins (Eds.), *Representations and understanding: Studies in cognitive science*. New York: Academic Press.

Rumelhart, D. E. (1977). Toward an interactive model of reading. In S. Dornic (Ed.), *Attention and performance VI*. Hillsdale, NJ: Lawrence Erlbaum Associates Inc.

Rumelhart, D. E., & McClelland, J. L. (1982). An interactive activation model of context effects in letter perception: Part 2. *Psychological Review*, *89*, 60–94.

Rumelhart, D. E., & McClelland, J. L. (Eds.). (1986). *Parallel distributed processing: Explorations in the microstructure of cognition (Vol. 1)*. Cambridge, MA: MIT Press.

Rumsey, J. M., Andreason, P., Zametkin, A. J., & Aquino, T. (1992). Failure to activate the left temporoparietal cortex in dyslexia: An oxygen 15 positron emission tomographic study. *Archives of Neurology*, *49*(5), 527–534.

Rumsey, J. M., Donohue, B. C., Brady, D. R., Nace, K., Giedd, J. N., & Andreason, P. (1997). A magnetic resonance imaging study of planum temporale asymmetry in men with developmental dyslexia. *Archives of Neurology*, *54*(12), 1481–1489.

Rumsey, J. M., Dorwart, R., Vermess, M., Denckla, M. B., Kuesi, M. J. P., & Rappaport, J. L. (1986). Magnetic resonance imaging of brain anatomy in severe developmental dyslexia. *Archives of Neurology*, *43*(10), 1045–1046.

Rutter, M., Caspi, A., Fergusson, D., Horwood, L. J., Goodman, R., Maughan, B., et al. (2004). Sex differences in developmental reading disability: New findings from 4 epidemiological studies. *JAMA: Journal of the American Medical Association, 291*(16), 2007–2012.

Ryan, E. B. (1982). Identifying and remediating failures in reading comprehension: Toward an instructional approach for poor comprehenders. In G. E. MacKinnon & T. G. Waller (Eds.), *Advances in reading research* (Vol 3). New York: Academic Press.

Sailor, A. L., & Ball, S. E. (1975). Peripheral vision training in reading speed and comprehension. *Perceptual and Motor Skills, 41,* 761–762.

Saint-Aubin, J., Kenny, S., & Roy-Charland, A. (2010). The role of eye movements in the missing-letter effect revisited with the rapid serial visual presentation procedure. *Canadian Journal of Experimental Psychology, 64,* 47–52.

Saldaña, D., Carreiras, M., & Frith, U. (2009). Orthographic and phonological pathways in hyperlexic readers with autism spectrum disorders. *Developmental Neuropsychology, 34*(3), 240–253.

Samuels, S. J., & Flor, R. F. (1997). The importance of automaticity for developing expertise in reading. *Reading and Writing Quarterly: Overcoming Learning Difficulties, 13,* 107–121.

Samuels, S. J., LaBerge, D., & Bremer, C. D. (1978). Units of word recognition: Evidence of developmental change. *Journal of Verbal Learning and Verbal Behavior, 17,* 715–720.

Sandak, R., Mencl, W. E., Frost, S. J., Rueckl, J. G., Katz, L., Moore, D. L., et al. (2004). The neurobiology of adaptive learning in reading: A contrast of different training conditions. *Cognitive, Affective & Behavioral Neuroscience, 4*(1), 67–88.

Sanford, A. J., & Garrod, S. C. (1998). The role of scenario mapping in text comprehension. *Discourse Processes, 26,* 159–190.

Sanford, A. J., & Garrod, S. C. (2005). Memory-based approaches and beyond. *Discourse Processes, 39,* 205–224.

Sanford, A. J., Moar, K., & Garrod, S. C. (1988). Proper names as controllers of discourse focus. *Language and Speech, 31,* 43–56.

Savin, H. B. (1972). What the child knows about speech when he starts to learn to read. In J. F. Kavanagh & I. G. Mattingly (Eds.), *Language by ear and by eye.* Cambridge, MA: MIT Press.

Scanlon, D. M., Boudah, D., Elksnin, L. K., Gersten, R., & Klingner, J. (2003). Important publications in the field of LD in light of imminent topics. *Learning Disability Quarterly, 26*(3), 215–224.

Scanlon, D. M., & Vellutino, F. R. (1996). Prerequisite skills, early instruction, and success in first-grade reading: Selected results from a longitudinal study. *Mental Retardation and Developmental Disabilities Research Reviews, 2,* 54–63.

Scarborough, H. S. (1990). Very early language deficits in dyslexic children. *Child Development, 61*(6), 1728–1743.

Scarborough, H. S. (1991). Early syntactic development of dyslexic children. *Annals of Dyslexia, 41,* 207–220.

Scarborough, H. S., & Dobrich, W. (1994). On the efficacy of reading to preschoolers. *Developmental Review, 14*(3), 245–302.

Schank, R. C., & Abelson, R. P. (1977). *Scripts, plans, goals, and understanding: An inquiry into human knowledge structures.* Hillsdale, NJ: Lawrence Erlbaum Associates Inc.

Schatschneider, C., Fletcher, J. M., Francis, D. J., Carlson, C. D., & Foorman, B. R. (2004). Kindergarten prediction of reading skills: A longitudinal comparative analysis. *Journal of Educational Psychology, 96,* 265–282.

Schatschneider, C., Francis, D. J., Fletcher, J. M., Foorman, B. R., & Mehta, P. (1999). The dimensionality of phonological awareness: An application of item response theory. *Journal of Educational Psychology, 91,* 439–449.

Schilling, H. E. H., Rayner, K., & Chumbley, J. (1998). Comparing naming, lexical decision, and eye fixation times: Word frequency effects and individual differences. *Memory & Cognition, 26,* 1270–1281.

Schindler, R. M. (1978). The effect of prose context on visual search for letters. *Memory & Cognition, 6,* 124–130.

Schneider, D., & Phillips, C. (2001). Grammatical search and reanalysis. *Journal of Memory and Language, 45,* 308–336.

Schneider, W., & Shiffrin, R. M. (1977). Controlled and automatic human information processing: I. Detection, search, and attention. *Psychological Review, 84,* 1–66.

Schoonbaert, S., & Grainger, J. (2004). Letter position coding in printed word perception: effects of repeated and transposed letters. *Language and Cognitive Processes, 19,* 333–367.

Schuberth, R. E. & Eimas, P. D. (1977). Effects of context on the classification of words and nonwords. *Journal of Experimental Psychology: Human Perception and Performance*, *3*, 27–36.

Schultz, R. T., Cho, N. K., Staib, L. H., & Kier, L. E. (1994). Brain morphology in normal and dyslexic children: The influence of sex and age. *Annals of Neurology*, *35*(6), 732–742.

Schustack, M. W., Ehrlich, S. F., & Rayner, K. (1987). The complexity of contextual facilitation in reading: Local and global influences. *Journal of Memory and Language*, *26*, 322–340.

Schütze, C. T., & Gibson, E. (1999). Argumenthood and English prepositional phrase attachment. *Journal of Memory and Language*, *40*, 409–431.

Schwantes, F. M. (1981). Effect of story context on children's ongoing word recognition. *Journal of Reading Behavior*, *13*, 305–311.

Scott, J. A., & Ehri, L. C. (1990). Sight word reading in prereaders: Use of logographic vs. alphabetic access routes. *Journal of Reading Behavior*, *22*(2), 149–166. Retrieved from www.csa.com

Sears, C. R., Campbell, C. R., & Lupker, S. J. (2006). Is there a neighborhood frequency effect in English? Evidence from reading and lexical decision. *Journal of Experimental Psychology: Human Perception and Performance*, *32*, 1040–1062.

Segal, D., & Wolf, M. (1993). Automaticity, word retrieval, and vocabulary development in children with reading disabilities. In L. J. Meltzer (Ed.), *Strategy assessment and instruction for students with learning disabilities: From theory to practice* (pp. 141–165). Austin, TX: Pro-Ed.

Seidenberg, M. S. (1985). Constraining models of word recognition. *Cognition*, *20*, 169-190.

Seidenberg, M. S. (2011). Reading in different writing systems: One architecture, multiple solutions. In P. McCardle, J. Ren, & O. Tzeng, & B. Miller (Eds.), *Dyslexia across languages: Orthography and the brain–gene–behavior link* (pp. 151–168). Baltimore, MD: Brookes Publishing.

Seidenberg, M. S., & McClelland, J. L. (1989). A distributed, developmental model of visual word recognition and naming. *Psychological Review*, *96*, 523–568.

Seidenberg, M. S., & Vidanovic, S. (1985). *Word recognition in Serbo-Croatian and English: Do they differ?* Paper presented at Psychonomic Society Meeting, Boston.

Seidenberg, M. S., Waters, G. S., Barnes, M. A., & Tanenhaus, M. K. (1984a). When does irregular spelling or pronunciation influence word recognition? *Journal of Verbal Learning and Verbal Behavior*, *23*, 383–404.

Seidenberg, M. S., Waters, G. S., Sanders, M., & Langer, P. (1984b). Pre- and post-lexical loci of contextual effects on word recognition. *Memory & Cognition*, *12*, 315–328.

Seigneuric, A., Ehrlich, M. F., Oakhill, J. V., & Yuill, N. M. (2000). Working memory resources and children's reading comprehension. *Reading and Writing*, *13*, 81–103.

Selkirk, E. (1982). *The syntax of words*. Cambridge, MA: MIT Press.

Selkirk, E. (2003). Sentence phonology. In *International encyclopedia of linguistics* (2nd ed.). Oxford, UK: Oxford University Press.

Sénéchal, M., LeFevre, J., Thomas, E. M., & Daley, K. E. (1998). Differential effects of home literacy experiences on the development of oral and written language. *Reading Research Quarterly*, *33*(1), 96–116.

Sereno, S. C., O'Donnell, P. J., & Rayner, K. (2006). Eye movements and lexical ambiguity resolution: Investigating the subordinate bias effect. *Journal of Experimental Psychology: Human Perception and Performance*, *32*, 335–350.

Sereno, S. C., & Rayner, K. (1992). Fast priming during eye fixations in reading. *Journal of Experimental Psychology: Human Perception and Performance*, *18*, 173–184

Sereno, S. C., & Rayner, K. (2000). Spelling–sound regularity effects on eye fixations in reading. *Perception & Psychophysics*, *62*(2), 402–409.

Sereno, S. C., & Rayner, K. (2003). Measuring word recognition in reading: Eye movements and event-related potentials. *Trends in Cognitive Sciences*, 7, 489–493.

Sereno, S. C., Rayner, K., & Posner, M. I. (1998). Establishing a time-line of word recognition: Evidence from eye movements and event-related potentials. *Neuroreport*, *9*, 2195–2200.

Seymour, P. H., Aro, M., & Erskine, J. M. (2003). Foundation literacy acquisition in European orthographies. *British Journal of Psychology*, *94*(2), 143–174.

Seymour, P. H. K., & Evans, H. M. (1994). Levels of phonological awareness and learning to read. *Reading and Writing*, *6*(3), 221–250.

Shallice, T., & Warrington, E. K. (1980). Single and multiple component central dyslexic syndromes. In M. Coltheart, K. Patterson, & J. C. Marshall (Eds.), *Deep dyslexia*. London: Routledge & Kegan Paul.

Shankweiler, D., Liberman, I. Y., Mark, L. S., Fowler, C. A., & Fischer, F. W. (1979). The speech code and learning to read. *Journal of Experimental Psychology: Human Learning and Memory, 5*, 531–545.

Shankweiler, D., Lundquist, E., Katz, L., Stuebing, K. K., Fletcher, J. M., Brady, S., et al. (1999). Comprehension and decoding: Patterns of association in children with reading difficulties. *Scientific Studies of Reading, 3*(1), 69–94.

Share, D. L. (1995). Phonological recoding and self-teaching: Sine qua non of reading acquisition. *Cognition, 55*(2), 151–218.

Share, D. L. (1999). Phonological recording and orthographic learning: A direct test of the self-teaching hypothesis. *Journal of Experimental Child Psychology, 72*, 95–129.

Share, D. L. (2008). On the anglocentricities of current reading research and practice: The perils of overreliance on an outlier orthography. *Psychological Bulletin, 134*, 584–615.

Share, D. L., & Gur, T. (1999). How reading begins: A study of preschoolers' print identification strategies. *Cognition and Instruction, 17*(2), 177–213.

Share, D. L., Jorm, A. F., Maclean, R., & Matthews, R. (1984). Sources of individual differences in reading acquisition. *Journal of Educational Psychology, 76*(6), 1309–1324.

Share, D. L., Jorm, A. F., Maclean, R., & Matthews, R. (2002). Temporal processing and reading disability. *Reading and Writing, 15*(1–2), 151–178.

Share, D. L., & Stanovich, K. E. (1995). Cognitive processes in early reading development: A model of acquisition and individual differences. *Issues in Education: Contributions from Educational Psychology, 1*, 1–57.

Shaywitz, B. A., Fletcher, J. M., Holahan, J. M., & Shaywitz, S. E. (1992). Discrepancy compared to low achievement definitions of reading disability: Results from the Connecticut Longitudinal Study. *Journal of Learning Disabilities, 25*(10), 639–648.

Shaywitz, B. A., Holford, T. R., Holahan, J. M., & Fletcher, J. M. (1995). A Matthew effect for IQ but not for reading: Results from a longitudinal study. *Reading Research Quarterly, 30*(4), 894–906.

Shaywitz, B. A., Shaywitz, S. E., Blachman, B., Pugh, K. R., Fulbright, R.K., Skudlarski, P., et al. (2004). Development of left occipito-temporal systems for skilled reading following phonologically based reading intervention in children. *Biological Psychiatry, 55*, 926–933.

Shaywitz, B. A., Shaywitz, S. E., Pugh, K. R., Mencl, W. E., Fulbright, R. K., Skudlarksi, P., et al. (2002). Disruption of posterior brain systems for reading in children with developmental dyslexia. *Biological Psychiatry, 52*(2), 101–110.

Shaywitz, B. A., Skudlarksi, P., Holahan, J. M., Marchione, K. E., Constable, R. T., Fulbright, R. K., et al. (2007). Age-related changes in readings systems of dyslexic children. *Annals of Neurology, 61*(4), 363–370.

Shaywitz, S. E. (1998). Current concepts: Dyslexia. *The New England Journal of Medicine, 338*(5), 307–312.

Shaywitz, S. E., Fletcher, J. M., Holahan, J. M., Shneider, A. E., Marchione, K. E., Stuebing, K. K., et al. (1999). Persistence of dyslexia: The Connecticut Longitudinal Study at adolescence. *Pediatrics, 104*(6), 1351–1359.

Shaywitz, S. E., & Shaywitz, B. A. (2004). Neurobiologic basis for reading and reading disability. In P. McCardle & V. Chhabra (Eds.), *The voice of evidence in reading research* (pp. 417–442). Baltimore, MD: Paul Brookes.

Shaywitz, S. E., & Shaywitz, B. A. (2005). Dyslexia (specific reading disability). *Biological Psychiatry, 57*(11), 1301–1309.

Shaywitz, S. E., Shaywitz, B. A., Fletcher, J. M., & Escobar, M. D. (1990). Prevalence of reading disability in boys and girls: Results of the Connecticut Longitudinal Study. *Journal of the American Medical Association, 264*(8), 998–1002.

Shen, E. (1927). An analysis of eye movements in the reading of Chinese. *Journal of Experimental Psychology, 10*, 158–183.

Shiffrin, R. M., & Schneider, W. (1977). Controlled and automatic human information processing: II. Perceptual learning, automatic attending and a general theory. *Psychological Review, 84*, 127–190.

Siegel, L. S. (1984). A longitudinal study of a hyperlexic child: Hyperlexia as a language disorder. *Neuropsychologia, 22*(5), 577–585.

Siegel, L. S. (1992). An evaluation of the discrepancy definition of dyslexia. *Journal of Learning Disabilities, 25*, 618–629.

Simos, P. G., Breier, J. I., Fletcher, J. M., Bergman, E., & Papanicolaou, A. C. (2000). Cerebral mechanisms involved in word reading in dyslexic children: A magnetic source imaging approach. *Cerebral Cortex, 10*(8), 809–816.

Singer, M. (1979). Processes of inference in sentence encoding. *Memory & Cognition, 7*, 192–200.

Singer, M. (2007). Inference processing in discourse comprehension. In M. G. Gaskell (Ed.), *The Oxford handbook of psycholinguistics* (pp. 343–360). Oxford, UK: Oxford University Press.

Singer, M., & Ferreira, F. (1983). Inferring consequences in story comprehension. *Journal of Verbal Learning and Verbal Behavior, 22*, 437–448.

Singer, M., & Halldorson, M. (1996). Constructing and verifying motive bridging inferences. *Cognitive Psychology, 30*, 1–38

Slattery, T. J. (2009). Word misperception, the neighbor frequency effect, and the role of sentence context: Evidence from eye movements. *Journal of Experimental Psychology: Human Perception and Performance, 35*, 1969–1975.

Slattery, T. J., Angele, B., & Rayner, K. (2011). Eye movements and display change detection during reading. *Journal of Experimental Psychology: Human Perception and Performance*, in press.

Slattery, T. J., Pollatsek, A., & Rayner, K. (2007). The effect of the frequencies of three consecutive content words on eye movements during reading. *Memory & Cognition, 35*, 1283–1292.

Slattery, T. J., & Rayner, K. (2010). The influence of text legibility on eye movements during reading. *Applied Cognitive Psychology, 24*, 1129–1148.

Slowiaczek, M. L., & Clifton, C. Jr. (1980). Subvocalization and reading for meaning. *Journal of Verbal Learning and Verbal Behavior, 19*, 573–582.

Smith, F. (1971). *Understanding reading: A psycholinguistic analysis of reading and learning to read.* New York: Holt, Rinehart & Winston.

Smith, F. (1973). *Psycholinguistics and reading.* New York: Holt, Rinehart & Winston.

Smith, F. (2004). *Understanding reading* (6th ed.). Mahwah, NJ: Lawrence Lawrence Erlbaum Associates Inc.

Smith, F., & Goodman, K. S. (1971). On the psycholinguistic method of teaching reading. *Elementary School Journal*, 177–181.

Smith, P. T., & Groat, A. (1979). Spelling patterns: Letter cancellation and the processing of text. In P. A. Kolers, M. E. Wrolstad, & H. Bouma (Eds.), *Processing of visible language.* New York: Plenum.

Smith, F., Lott, D., & Cronnell, B. (1969). The effect of type size and case alternation on word identification. *American Journal of Psychology, 82*, 248–253.

Snedeker, J., & Trueswell, J. C. (2004). The developing constraints on parsing decisions: The role of lexical-biases and referential scenes in child and adult sentence processing. *Cognitive Psychology, 49*, 238–299.

Snowling, M. J. (1980). The development of grapheme–phoneme correspondence in normal and dyslexic children. *Journal of Experimental Child Psychology, 29*, 294–305.

Snowling, M. J. (2000a). *Dyslexia.* Malden, MA: Blackwell Publishing.

Snowling, M. J. (2000b). Language and literacy skills: Who is at risk and why? In D. V. M. Bishop & L. B. Leonard (Eds.), *Speech and language impairments in children: Causes, characteristics, intervention and outcome* (pp. 245–259). New York: Psychology Press.

Snowling, M. J. (2001). From language to reading and dyslexia. *Dyslexia, 7*, 37–46.

Snowling, M. J., Bryant, P. E., & Hulme, C. (1996). Theoretical and methodological pitfalls in making comparisons between developmental and acquired dyslexia: Some comments on A. Castles & M. Coltheart (1993). *Reading and Writing, 8*(5), 443–451.

Snowling, M. J., & Frith, U. (1986). Comprehension in "hyperlexic" readers. *Journal of Experimental Child Psychology, 42*(3), 392–415.

Snowling, M. J., Gallagher, A., & Frith, U. (2003). Family risk of dyslexia is continuous: Individual differences in the precursors of reading skill. *Child Development, 74*(2), 358–373.

Snowling, M. J., & Hulme, C. (2005). Learning to read with a language impairment. In M. J. Snowling & C. Hulme (Eds.), *The science of reading: A handbook* (pp. 397–412). Malden, UK: Blackwell Publishing.

Snowling, M. J., Nation, K., Moxham, P., Gallagher, A., & Frith, U. (1997). Phonological processing skills of dyslexic students in higher education: A preliminary report. *Journal of Research in Reading, 20*(1), 31–41.

Sokolov, A. N. (1972). *Inner speech and thought.* New York: Plenum.

Sparks, R. L. (2001). Phonemic awareness and reading skill in hyperlexic children: A longitudinal study. *Reading and Writing, 14*(3–4), 333–360.

Spear-Swerling, L., & Brucker, P. O. (2003). Teachers' acquisition of knowledge about English word structure. *Annals of Dyslexia, 53*, 72–96.

Speer, O. B., & Lamb, G. S. (1976). First grade reading ability and fluency in naming verbal symbols. *The Reading Teacher, 29*, 572–576.

Speer, S., & Clifton, C. Jr. (1998). Plausibility and argument structure in sentence comprehension. *Memory & Cognition, 26,* 965–979.

Sperling, A. J., Lu, Z., Manis, F. R., & Seidenberg, M. S. (2005). Deficits in perceptual noise exclusion in developmental dyslexia. *Nature Neuroscience, 8*(7), 862–863.

Sperling, A. J., Lu, Z., Manis, F. R., & Seidenberg, M. S. (2006). Motion-perception deficits and reading impairment: It's the noise, not the motion. *Psychological Science, 17*(12), 1047–1053.

Sperling, G. (1960). The information available in brief visual presentations. *Psychological Monographs, 74* (No. 498).

Sperling, G. (1963). A model for visual memory tasks. *Human Factors, 5,* 19–31.

Spragins, A. B., Lefton, L. A., & Fisher, D. F. (1976). Eye movements while reading and searching spatially transformed text: A developmental examination. *Memory & Cognition, 4,* 36–42.

Sprenger-Charolles, L., & Bonnet, P. (1996). New doubts on the significance of the logographic stage. *Current Psychology of Cognition, 15,* 173–208.

Sprenger-Charolles, L., Colle, P., Lacert, P., & Serniclaes, W. (2000). On subtypes of developmental dyslexia: Evidence from processing time and accuracy scores. *Canadian Journal of Experimental Psychology, 54*(2), 87–104.

Stahl, S. A., & Kuhn, M. R. (1995). Does whole language or instruction matched to learning styles help children learn to read? *School Psychology Review, 24*(3), 393–404.

Stahl, S. A., McKenna, M. C., & Pagnucco, J. R. (1994). The effects of whole-language instruction: An update and a reappraisal. *Educational Psychologist, 29*(4), 175–185.

Stanley, G., Smith, G. A., & Howell, E. A. (1983). Eye movements and sequential tracking in dyslexic and control children. *British Journal of Psychology, 74,* 181–187.

Stanovich, K. E. (1980). Toward an interactive-compensatory model of individual differences in the development of reading fluency. *Reading Research Quarterly, 16,* 32–71.

Stanovich, K. E. (1986). Matthew effects in reading: Some consequences of individual differences in the acquisition of literacy. *Reading Research Quarterly, 4,* 360–406.

Stanovich, K. E. (1988). Explaining the differences between the dyslexic and the garden-variety poor reader: The phonological-core variable-difference model. *Journal of Learning Disabilities, 21*(10), 590–604, 612.

Stanovich, K. E. (1992). Developmental reading disorder. In S. R. Hooper, G. W. Hynd, & R. E. Mattison (Eds.), *Developmental disorders: Diagnostic criteria and clinical assessment* (pp. 173–208). Hillsdale, NJ: Lawrence Erlbaum Associates Inc.

Stanovich, K. E. (2005). The future of a mistake: Will discrepancy measurement continue to make the learning disabilities field a pseudoscience? *Learning Disability Quarterly, 28*(2), 103–106.

Stanovich, K. E., Cunningham, A. E., & Cramer, B. (1984). Assessing phonological awareness in kindergarten children: Issues of task comparability. *Journal of Experimental Child Psychology, 38,* 175–190.

Stanovich, K. E., & Siegel, L. S. (1994). Phenotypic performance profile of children with reading disabilities: A regression-based test of the phonological-core variable-difference model. *Journal of Educational Psychology, 86*(1), 24–53.

Stanovich, K. E., Siegel, L. S., & Gottardo, A. (1997). Converging evidence for phonological and surface subtypes of reading disability. *Journal of Educational Psychology, 89*(1), 114–127.

Stanovich, K. E., Siegel, L. S., Gottardo, A., Chiappe, P., & Sidhu, R. (1997). Subtypes of developmental dyslexia: Differences in phonological and orthographic coding. In B. A. Blachman (Ed.), *Foundations of reading acquisition and dyslexia: Implications for early intervention* (pp. 115–141). Mahwah, NJ: Lawrence Lawrence Erlbaum Associates Inc.

Stanovich, K. E. & West, R. F. (1979). Mechanisms of sentence context effects in reading: Automatic activation and conscious attention. *Memory & Cognition, 7,* 77–85.

Stanovich, K. E. & West, R. F. (1983). On priming by a sentence context. *Journal of Experimental Psychology: General, 112,* 1–36.

Stanovich, K. E., & West, R. F. (1989). Exposure to print and orthographic processing. *Reading Research Quarterly, 24*(4), 402–433.

Stanovich, K. E., West, R. F., & Freeman, D. J. (1981). A longitudinal study of sentence context effects on second-grade children: Tests of an interactive-compensatory model. *Journal of Experimental Child Psychology, 32,* 185–199.

Staub, A. (2007a). The parser doesn't ignore intransitivity, after all. *Journal of Experimental Psychology: Learning, Memory, and Cognition*, *33*, 550–569.

Staub, A. (2007b). The return of the repressed: Abandoned parses facilitate syntactic reanalysis. *Journal of Memory and Language*, *57*, 299–323.

Staub, A., Clifton, C. Jr., & Frazier, L. (2006). Heavy NP shift is the parser's last resort: Evidence from eye movements. *Journal of Memory and Language*, *54*, 389–406.

Stein, J. (2001). The sensory basis of reading problems. *Developmental Neuropsychology*, *20*(2), 509–534.

Stein, J. F., & Fowler, S. (1982). Ocular motor dyslexia. *Dyslexia Review*, *5*, 25–28.

Stein, J. F., & Fowler, S. (1984). Ocular motor problems of learning to read. In A.G. Gale & F. Johnson (Eds.), *Theoretical and applied aspects of eye movement research*. Amsterdam: North Holland Press.

Stein, N. L., & Glenn, C. G. (1979). An analysis of story comprehension in elementary school children. In P. O. Freedle (Ed.), *New directions in discourse processing*. Norwood, NJ: Ablex.

Stephenson, K., Parrila, R., Georgiou, G., & Kirby, R. (2008). Effects of home literacy, parents' beliefs, and children's task-focused behaviour on emergent literacy and word reading skills. *Scientific Studies of Reading*, *12*, 24–50.

Stern, J. A. (1978). Eye movements, reading, and cognition. In J. W. Senders, D. F. Fisher, & R. A. Monty (Eds.), *Eye movements and higher psychological functions* (Vol. 2). Hillsdale, NJ: Lawrence Erlbaum Associates Inc.

Sternberg, S. (1969). The discovery of processing stages: Extensions of Donder's method. In W. G. Koster (Ed.), Attention and performance II. *Acta Psychologica*, *30*, 276–315.

Sternberg, S., Monsell, S., Knoll, R. L., & Wright, C. E. (1978). The latency and duration of rapid movement sequences: Comparison of speech and typewriting. In G. E. Stelmach (Ed.), *Information processing in motor control and learning* (pp. 117–152). San Diego, CA: Academic Press.

Stevenson, H. W., Parker, T., Wilkinson, A., Hegion, A., & Fish, E. (1976). Longitudinal study of individual differences in cognitive development and scholastic achievement. *Journal of Educational Psychology*, *68*, 377–400.

Sticht, T. G., & James, J. H. (1984). Listening and reading. In P. D. Pearson, R. Barr, M. L. Kamil, & P. Mosenthal (Eds.), *Handbook of reading research: Volume I* (pp. 293–317). White Plains, NY: Longman.

Storch, S. A., & Whitehurst, G. J. (2002). Oral language and code-related precursors to reading: Evidence from a longitudinal structural model. *Developmental Psychology*, *38*, 934–947.

Stowe, L. (1986). Parsing wh-constructions: Evidence for on-line gap location. *Language and Cognitive Processes*, *1*, 227–246.

Stringer, R., & Stanovich, K. E. (2000). The connection between reaction time and variation in reading ability: Unraveling covariance relationships with cognitive ability and phonological sensitivity. *Scientific Studies of Reading*, *4*(1), 41–53.

Stroop, J. R. (1935). Studies of interference in serial verbal reactions. *Journal of Experimental Psychology*, *18*, 643–662.

Stuart, M., & Coltheart, M. (1988). Does reading develop in a sequence of stages? *Cognition*, *30*(2), 139–181.

Stuebing, K. K., Fletcher, J. M., LeDoux, J. M., Lyon, G. R., Shaywitz, S. E., & Shaywitz, B. A. (2002). Validity of IQ-discrepancy classifications of reading disabilities: A meta-analysis. *American Educational Research Journal*, *39*(2), 469–518.

Sturt, P. (2007). Semantic re-interpretation and garden path recovery. *Cognition*, *105*, 477–488.

Sturt, P., Pickering, M. J., Scheepers, C., & Crocker, M. W. (2001). The preservation of structure in language comprehension: Is reanalysis the last resort? *Journal of Memory and Language*, *45*, 283–207.

Sturt, P., Sanford, A., Stewart, A., & Dawydiak, E. J. (2004). Linguistic focus and good-enough representations: An application of the change-detection paradigm. *Psychonomic Bulletin & Review*, *11*, 882–888.

Suh, S., & Trabasso, T. (1993). Inferences during reading: Converging evidence from discourse analysis, talk-aloud protocols, and recognition priming. *Journal of Memory and Language*, *32*, 279–300.

Sun, F., Morita, M., & Stark, L. W. (1985). Comparative patterns of reading eye movement in Chinese and English. *Perception & Psychophysics*, *37*, 502–506.

Swan, D., & Goswami, U. (1997). Phonological awareness deficits in developmental dyslexia and the phonological representations hypothesis. *Journal of Experimental Child Psychology*, *66*(1), 18–41.

Swets, B., DeSmet, T., Clifton, C. Jr., & Ferreira, F. (2008). Underspecification of syntactic ambiguities: Evidence from self–paced reading. *Memory & Cognition*, *36*, 201–217.

Swinney, D. (1982). The structure and time course of information during speech comprehension: Lexical segmentation, access, and interpretation. In J. Mehler, E. Walker, & M. Garrett (Eds.), *Perspectives on mental representation: Experimental and theoretical studies of cognitive processes and capacities* (pp. 151–167). Hillsdale, NJ: Lawrence Erlbaum Associates Inc.

Tabor, W., Galantucci, B., & Richardson, D. (2004). Effects of merely local syntactic coherence on sentence processing. *Journal of Memory and Language, 50*, 355–370.

Taft, M. (1979). Lexical access via an othographic code: The Basic Orthographic Syllable Structure (BOSS). *Journal of Verbal Learning and Verbal Behavior, 18*, 21–39.

Taft, M. (1981). Prefix stripping revisited. *Journal of Verbal Learning and Verbal Behavior, 20*, 284–297.

Taft, M. (1985). The decoding of words in lexical access: A review of the morphological approach. In D. Besner, T. G. Waller, & G. E. MacKinnon (Eds.), *Reading research: Advances in theory and practice* (Vol. 5). New York: Academic Press.

Taft, M. (1986). Lexical access codes in visual and auditory word recognition. *Language and Cognitive Processes, 4*, 297–308.

Taft, M. (2006). A localist-cum-distributed (LCD) framework for lexical processing. In S. M. Andrews (Ed.), *From inkmarks to ideas: Current issues in lexical processing*. Hove, UK: Psychology Press.

Taft, M., & Forster, K. I. (1975). Lexical storage and retrieval of prefixed words. *Journal of Verbal Learning and Verbal Behavior, 14*, 638–647.

Taft, M., & Forster, K. I. (1976). Lexical storage and retrieval of polymorphemic and polysyllabic words. *Journal of Verbal Learning and Verbal Behavior, 15*, 607–620.

Tallal, P. (1980a). Auditory temporal perception, phonics, and reading disabilities in children. *Brain and Language, 9*, 182–198.

Tallal, P. (1980b). Language disabilities in children: A perceptual or linguistic deficit? *Journal of Pediatric Psychology, 5*(2), 127–140

Tanenhaus, M., & Trueswell, J. C. (2006). Eye movements and spoken language comprehension. In M. J. Traxler & M. A. Gernsbacher (Eds.), *Handbook of psycholinguistics* (2nd ed., pp. 863–900). London: Academic Press.

Tangel, D. M., & Blachman, B. A. (1992). Effect of phoneme awareness instruction on kindergarten children's invented spelling. *Journal of Reading Behavior, 24*(2), 233–261.

Tarkiainen, A., Helenius, P., Hansen, P. C., Cornelissen, P. L., & Salmelin, R. (1999). Dynamics of letter string perception in the human occipitotemporal cortex. *Brain: A Journal of Neurology, 122*(11), 2119–2132.

Taylor, I. (1981). Writing systems and reading. In G. E. MacKinnon & T. G. Waller (Eds.), *Reading research: Advances in theory and practice* (Vol. 2). New York: Academic Press.

Taylor, I., & Taylor, M. M. (1983). *The psychology of reading*. New York: Academic Press.

Taylor, S. E. (1962). An evaluation of forty-one trainees who had recently completed the "Reading Dynamics" program. In E. P. Bliesmer & R. C. Staiger (Eds.), *Problems, programs, and projects in college adult reading. Eleventh yearbook of the National Reading Conference*. Milwaukee, WI: National Reading Conference.

Taylor, S. E. (1965). Eye movements while reading: Facts and fallacies. *American Educational Research Journal, 2*, 187–202.

Temple, C. M., & Carney, R. (1996). Reading skills in children with Turner's syndrome: An analysis of hyperlexia. *Cortex, 32*(2), 335–345.

Temple, E., Deutsch, G. K., Poldrack, R. A., Miller, S. L., Tallal, P., Merzenich, M. M., et al. (2003). Neural deficits in children with dyslexia ameliorated by behavioral remediation: Evidence from functional MRI. *Proceedings of the National Academy of Sciences, 100*(5), 2860–2865.

Thorndyke, P. W. (1977). Cognitive structures in comprehension and memory of narrative discourse. *Cognitive Psychology, 9*, 135–147.

Tinker, M. A. (1939). Reliability and validity of eye-movement measures of reading. *Journal of Experimental Psychology, 19*, 732–746.

Tinker, M. A. (1955). Perceptual and oculomotor efficiency in reading materials in vertical and horizontal arrangement. *American Journal of Psychology, 68*, 444–449.

Tinker, M. A. (1958). Recent studies of eye movements in reading. *Psychological Bulletin, 55*, 215–231.

Tinker, M. A. (1963). *Legibility of print*. Ames, IA: Iowa State University Press.

Tinker, M. A. (1965). *Bases for effective reading*. Minneapolis: University of Minnesota Press.

Torgesen, J. K. (2004). Lessons learned from research on interventions for students who have difficulty learning to read. In P. McCardle & V. Chhabra (Eds.), *The voice of evidence in reading research* (pp. 355–382). Baltimore, MD: Paul Brookes.

Torgesen, J. K., Alexander, A. W., Wagner, R. K., Rashotte, C. A., Voeller, K. K. S., & Conway, T. (2001). Intensive remedial instruction for children with severe reading disabilities: Immediate and long-term outcomes from two instructional approaches. *Journal of Learning Disabilities*, *34*(1), 33–58.

Torgesen, J. K., & Hudson, R. (2006). Reading fluency: Critical issues for struggling readers. In S. J. Samuels & A. Farstrup (Eds.), *Reading fluency: The forgotten dimension of reading success*. Newark, DE: International Reading Association Monograph of the British Journal of Educational Psychology.

Torgesen, J. K., Rashotte, C. A., & Alexander, A. (2001). Principles of fluency instruction in reading: Relationships with established empirical outcomes. In M. Wolf (Ed.), *Dyslexia, fluency, and the brain* (pp. 333–355). Timonium, MD: York Press.

Torgesen, J. K., Wagner, R. K., & Rashotte, C. A. (1994). Longitudinal studies of phonological processing and reading. *Journal of Learning Disabilities*, *27*(5), 276–286.

Torgesen, J. K., Wagner, R. K., Rashotte, C. A., Burgess, S., & Hecht, S. (1997). Contributions of phonological awareness and rapid automatic naming ability to the growth of word-reading skills in second- to fifth-grade children. *Scientific Studies of Reading*, *1*(2), 161–185.

Torgesen, J. K., Wagner, R. K., Rashotte, C. A., Rose, E., Lindamood, P., Conway, T., et al. (1999). Preventing reading failure in young children with phonological processing disabilities: Group and individual responses to instruction. *Journal of Educational Psychology*, *91*(4), 579–593.

Torneus, M. (1984). Phonological awareness and reading: A chicken and egg problem? *Journal of Educational Psychology*, *76*, 1346–1348.

Townsend, D. J. (1978). Interclause relations and clausal processing. *Journal of Verbal Learning and Verbal Behavior*, *17*, 509–521.

Townsend, D. T., & Bever, T. (1982). Natural units of representation interact during sentence comprehension. *Journal of Verbal Learning and Verbal Behavior*, *21*, 688–703.

Townsend, D. J., & Bever, T. (2001). *Sentence comprehension: The integration of habits and rules*. Cambridge, MA: MIT Press.

Townsend, J. (1976). Serial and within-stage independent parallel model equivalence on the minimum completion time. *Journal of Mathematical Psychology*, *14*, 219–238.

Transler, C., Gombert, J. E., & Leybaert, J. (2001). Phonological decoding in severely and profoundly deaf children: Similarity judgment between written pseudowords. *Applied Psycholinguistics*, *22*, 61–82.

Transler, C., & Reitsma, P. (2005). Phonological coding in reading of deaf children: Pseudohomophone effects in lexical decision. *British Journal of Developmental Psychology*, *23*, 525–542.

Traxler, M. J. (2007). Working memory contributions to relative clause attachment processing: A hierarchical linear modeling analysis. *Memory & Cognition*, *35*, 1107–1121.

Traxler, M. J., & Gernsbacher, M. A. (Eds.). (2006). *Handbook of psycholinguistics (2nd ed.)*. Amsterdam: Elsevier.

Traxler, M. J., Long, D. L., Johns, C. L., Tooley, K. M., Zirnstein, M., & Jonathan, E. (in press). Modeling individual differences in eye-movements during reading: Working memory and speed-of-processing effects. *Journal of Eye Movement Research*.

Traxler, M. J., Pickering, M., & Clifton, C. Jr. (1998). Adjunct attachment is not a form of lexical ambiguity resolution. *Journal of Memory and Language*, *39*, 558–592.

Traxler, M. J., Pickering, M. J., & McElree, B. (2002). Coercion in sentence processing: Evidence from eye movements and self-paced reading. *Journal of Memory and Language*, *47*, 530–548.

Traxler, M. J., Williams, R. S., Blozis, S. A., & Morris, R. K. (2005). Working memory, animacy, and verb class in the processing of relative clauses. *Journal of Memory and Language*, *53*, 204–224.

Treiman, R. A. (1984). Individual differences among children in reading and spelling styles. *Journal of Experimental Child Psychology*, *37*, 463–477.

Treiman, R. A., & Baron, J. (1983a). Phonemic analysis training helps children benefit from spelling–sound rules. *Memory & Cognition*, *11*, 382–389.

Treiman, R. A., & Baron, J. (1983b). Individual differences in spelling: The Phoenician–Chinese distinction. *Topics in Learning & Learning Disabilities*, *3*(3), 33–40.

Treiman, R. A., Baron, J., & Luk, K. (1981). Speech recoding in silent reading: A comparison of Chinese and English. *Journal of Chinese Linguistics*, *9*, 116–124.

Treiman, R. A., Freyd, J. J., & Baron, J. (1983). Phonological recoding and use of spelling sound rules in reading of sentences. *Journal of Verbal Learning and Verbal Behavior, 22*, 682–700.

Treiman, R. A., & Hirsh-Pasek, K. (1983). Silent reading: Insights from second-generation deaf readers. *Cognitive Psychology, 15*, 39–65.

Treiman, R. A., Kessler, B., & Bick, S. (2003). Influence of consonantal context on the pronunciation of vowels: A comparison of human readers and computational models. *Cognition, 88*(1), 49–78.

Treiman, R. A., Kessler, B., Zevin, J. D., Bick, S., & Davis, M. (2006). Influence of consonantal context on the reading of vowels: Evidence from children. *Journal of Experimental Child Psychology, 93*(1), 1–24.

Treiman, R. A., Mullennix, J., Bijeljac–Babic, R., & Richmond-Welty, E. D. (1995). The special role of rimes in the description, use, and acquisition of English orthography. *Journal of Experimental Psychology: General, 124*, 107–136.

Treiman, R. A., & Rodriguez, K. (1999). Young children use letter names in learning to read words. *Psychological Science, 10*(4), 334–338.

Treisman, A. (1988). Features and objects: The 14th Bartlett Memorial Lecture. *Quarterly Journal of Experimental Psychology, 40A*, 201–237.

Treisman, A., & Gelade, G. (1980). A feature integration theory of attention. *Cognitive Psychology, 12*, 97–136.

Trueswell, J. C. (1996). The role of lexical frequency in syntactic ambiguity resolution. *Journal of Memory and Language, 35*, 566–585.

Trueswell, J. C., & Tanenhaus, M. K. (1994). Toward a lexicalist framework of constraint-based syntactic ambiguity resolution. In C. Clifton, K. Rayner, & L. Frazier (Eds.), *Perspectives on sentence processing* (pp. 155–179). Hillsdale, NJ: Lawrence Erlbaum Associates Inc.

Trueswell, J. C., Tanenhaus, M. K., & Garnsey, S. M. (1994). Semantic influences on parsing: Use of thematic role information in syntactic disambiguation. *Journal of Memory and Language, 33*, 285–318.

Trueswell, J. C., Tanenhaus, M. K., & Kello, C. (1993). Verb-specific constraints in sentence processing: Separating effects of lexical preference from garden-paths. *Journal of Experimental Psychology: Learning, Memory, and Cognition, 19*, 528–553.

Tsai, J., Lee, C., Tzeng, O. J. L., Hung, D. L., & Yen, N. (2004). Use of phonological codes for Chinese characters: Evidence from processing of parafoveal preview when reading sentences. *Brain and Language, 91*, 235–244.

Tulving, E. (1972). Episodic and semantic memory. In E. Tulving & W. Donaldson (Eds.), *Organization and memory*. New York: Academic Press.

Tulving, E., & Gold, C. (1963). Stimulus information and contextual information as determinants of tachisto-scopic recognition of words. *Journal of Experimental Psychology, 66*, 319–327.

Tulving, E., Mandler, G., & Baumal, R. (1964). Interaction of two sources of information in tachistoscopic word recognition. *Canadian Journal of Psychology, 18*, 62–71.

Tunmer, W. E., Herriman, M. L., & Nesdale, A. R. (1988). Metalinguistic abilities and beginning reading. *Reading Research Quarterly, 23*(2), 134–158.

Turvey, M. T. (1977). Contrasting orientations to a theory of visual information processing. *Psychological Review, 84*, 67–88.

Turvey, M. T., Feldman, L. B., & Lukatela, G. (1984). The Serbo-Croatian orthography constrains the reader to a phonologically analytic strategy. In L. Henderson (Ed.), *Orthographies and reading*. Hove, UK: Lawrence Erlbaum Associates Ltd.

Tzeng, O. J. L., & Hung, D. L. (1980). Reading in a nonalphabetic writing system. In J. G. Kavanagh & R. L. Venezky (Eds.), *Orthography, reading and dyslexia. Baltimore: University Park Press*.

Tzeng, O. J. L., Hung, D. L., & Wang W. S-Y. (1977). Speech recoding in reading Chinese characters. *Journal of Experimental Psychology: Human Learning and Memory, 3*, 621–630.

Underwood, G. (1980). Attention and the non-selective lexical access of ambiguous words. *Canadian Journal of Psychology, 34*, 72–76.

Underwood, G. (1981). Lexical recognition of embedded unattended words: Some implictions for reading processes. *Acta Psychologica, 47*, 267–283.

Underwood, N. R., & McConkie, G. W. (1985). Perceptual span for letter distinctions during reading. *Reading Research Quarterly, 20*, 153–162.

Underwood, N. R., & Zola, D. (1986). The span of letter recognition of good and poor readers. *Reading Research Quarterly, 21*, 6–19.

Ungerleider, L. G., Doyon, J., & Karni, A. (2002). Imaging brain plasticity during motor skill learning. *Neurobiology of Learning and Memory*, 78(3), 553–564.

Unsworth, S. J., & Pexman, P. M. (2003). The impact of reader skill on phonological processing in visual word recognition. *Quarterly Journal of Experimental Psychology Section A: Human Experimental Psychology*, 56, 63–81.

Uttal, W. R., & Smith, P. (1968). Recognition of alphabetic characters during voluntary eye movement. *Perception & Psychophysics*, 3, 257–264.

Vaessen, A., Bertrand, D., Tóth, D., Csépe, V., Faisca, L., Reis, A., et al. (2010). Cognitive development of fluent word reading does not qualitatively differ between transparent and opaque orthographies. *Journal of Educational Psychology*, 102(4), 827–842.

Vallduvi, E., & Engdahl, E. (1996). The linguistic realization of information packaging. *Linguistics*, 34, 459–519.

Van den Bussche, E., Van den Noortgate W., & Reynvoet, B. (2009). Mechanisms of masked priming: A meta-analysis. *Psychological Bulletin*, 135, 452–477.

van Dijk, T. A., & Kintsch, W. (1983). *Strategies of discourse comprehension*. New York: Academic Press.

van Gompel, R. P. G., & Pickering, M. (2007). Sentence parsing. In G. Gaskell (Ed.), *Oxford handbook of psycholinguistics*. Oxford, UK: Oxford University Press.

van Gompel, R. P. G., Pickering, M., Pearson, J., & Liversedge, S. P. (2005). Evidence against competition during syntactic ambiguity resolution. *Journal of Memory and Language*, 52, 284–307.

Van Orden, G. C. (1987). A rows is a rose: Spelling, sound, and reading. *Memory & Cognition*, 15, 181–198.

Van Orden, G. C., Johnston, J. C., & Hale, B. L. (1987). Word identification in reading proceeds from spelling to sound to meaning. *Journal of Experimental Psychology: Learning, Memory, and Cognition*, 14, 371–386.

Van Petten, C., & Kutas, M. (1987). Ambiguous words in context: An event-related potential analysis of the time course of meaning activation. *Journal of Memory and Language*, 26, 188–208.

Velan, H., & Frost, R. (2009). Letter-transposition effects are not universal: The impact of transposing letters in Hebrew. *Journal of Memory and Language*, 61, 285–302.

Vellutino, F. R. (1979). The validity of perceptual deficit explanations of reading disability: A reply to Fletcher and Katz. *Journal of Learning Disabilities*, 12(3), 160–167.

Vellutino, F. R., & Fletcher, J. M. (2005). Developmental dyslexia. In M. J. Snowling & C. Hulme (Eds.), *The science of reading: A handbook* (pp. 362–378). Malden, MA: Blackwell Publishing.

Vellutino, F. R., Fletcher, J. M., Snowling, M. J., & Scanlon, D. M. (2004). Specific reading disability (dyslexia): What have we learned in the past four decades? *Journal of Child Psychology and Psychiatry*, 45, 2–40.

Vellutino, F. R., & Scanlon, D. M. (1987). Phonological coding, phonological awareness, and reading ability: Evidence from longitudinal and experimental study. *Merrill Palmer Quarterly*, 33, 321–363.

Vellutino, F. R., & Scanlon, D. M. (1991). The effects of instructional bias on word identification. In I. L. Rieben & C. A. Perfetti (Eds.), *Learning to read: Basic research and its implications* (pp. 189–204). Hillsdale, NJ: Lawrence Erlbaum Associates Inc.

Vellutino, F. R., Scanlon, D. M., Sipay, E. R., Small, S. G., Pratt, A., Chen, R., et al. (1996). Cognitive profiles of difficult-to-remediate and readily remediated poor readers: Early intervention as a vehicle for distinguishing between cognitive and experiential deficits as basic causes of specific reading disability. *Journal of Educational Psychology*, 88(4), 601–638.

Vellutino, F. R., Scanlon, D. M., & Spearing, D. (1995). Semantic and phonological coding in poor and normal readers. *Journal of Experimental Child Psychology*, 59, 76–123.

Vellutino, F. R., Scanlon, D. M., & Tanzman, M. S. (1994). Components of reading ability: Issues and problems in operationalizing word identification, phonological coding, and orthographic coding. In G. R. Lyon (Ed.), *Frames of reference for the assessment of learning disabilities: New views on measurement issues* (pp. 279–332). Baltimore, MD: Paul Brookes.

Venezky, R. L., & Massaro, D. W. (1979). The role of orthographic regularity in word recognition. In L. Resnick & P. Weaver (Eds.), *Theory and practice of early reading*. Hillsdale, NJ: Lawrence Erlbaum Associates Inc.

Vitu, F., McConkie, G. W., Kerr, P., & O'Regan, J. K. (2001). Fixation location effects on fixation durations during reading: An inverted optimal viewing position effect. *Vision Research*, 41, 3513–3533.

von Plessen, K., Lundervold, A., Duta, N., Heiervang, E., Klauschen, F., Smievoll, A. I., et al. (2002). Less developed corpus callosum in dyslexic subjects: A structural MRI study. *Neuropsychologia*, 40(7), 1035–1044.

Vonk, W. (1984). Eye movements during comprehension of pronouns. In A. G. Gale & F. Johnson (Eds.), *Theoretical and applied aspects of eye movement research*. Amsterdam: North-Holland.

Vurpoillot, E. (1968). The development of scanning strategies and their relation to visual differentiation. *Journal of Experimental Child Psychology, 6,* 632–650.

Wagner, R. K., & Torgesen, J. K. (1987). The nature of phonological processing and its causal role in the acquisition of reading skills. *Psychological Bulletin, 101,* 192–212.

Wagner, R. K., Torgesen, J. K., & Rashotte, C. A. (1994). Development of reading-related phonological processing abilities: New evidence of bidirectional causality from a latent variable longitudinal study. *Developmental Psychology, 30,* 73–87.

Wagner, R. K., Torgesen, J. K., Rashotte, C. A., Hecht, S. A., Barker, T. A., Burgess, S. R., et al. (1997). Changing relations between phonological processing abilities and word-level reading as children develop from beginning to skilled readers: A 5-year longitudinal study. *Developmental Psychology, 33*(3), 468–479.

Walker, R.Y. (1938). A qualitative study of the eye movements of good readers. *American Journal of Psychology, 51,* 472–481.

Walley, A. C. (1993). The role of vocabulary development in children's spoken word recognition and segmentation ability. *Developmental Review. Special Issue: Phonological Processes and Learning Disability, 13*(3), 286–350.

Walther, M., Frazier, L., Clifton, C. Jr., Hemforth, B., Konieczny, L., & Seelig, H. (1999). *Prosodic and syntactic effects on relative clause attachments in German and English.* Poster presented at AMLaP 99, Edinburgh, Scotland, September.

Walton, H. N. (1957).Vision and rapid reading. *American Journal of Optometry and Archives of American Academy of Optometry, 34,* 73–82.

Walton, P. D. (1995). Rhyming ability, phoneme identity, letter–sound knowledge, and the use of orthographic analogy by prereaders. *Journal of Educational Psychology, 87,* 587–597.

Wang, F. C. (1935). An experimental study of eye movements in the reading of Chinese. *Elementary School Journal, 35,* 527–539.

Wang, Y., Sereno, J. A., Jongman, A., & Hirsch, J. (2003). fMRI evidence for cortical modification during learning of mandarin lexical tone. *Journal of Cognitive Neuroscience, 15*(7), 1019–1027.

Warren, S., & Morris, R. K. (2009). *Phonological similarity effects in reading.* Paper presented at the European Conference on Eye Movements, Southampton, UK, August.

Warren, T., & McConnell, K. (2007). Investigating effects of selectional restriction violations and plausibility violation severity on eye-movements in reading. *Psychonomic Bulletin & Review, 14,* 770–775.

Warren, T., McConnell, K., & Rayner, K. (2008). Effects of context on eye movements when reading about possible and impossible events. *Journal of Experimental Psychology: Learning, Memory and Cognition, 34,* 1001–1007.

Wason, P. C. (1965). The contexts of plausible denial. *Journal of Verbal Learning and Verbal Behavior, 4,* 7–11.

Waters, G., & Caplan, D. (1999). Working memory and sentence comprehension. *Behavioral and Brain Sciences, 22,* 77–126.

Waters, G. S., Komoda, M. K., & Arbuckle, T.Y. (1985). The effects of concurrent tasks on reading: Implications for phonological recoding. *Journal of Memory and Language, 24,* 27–45.

Waters, G. S., Seidenberg, M. S., & Bruck, M. (1984). Children's and adult's use of spelling–sound information in three reading tasks. *Memory & Cognition, 12,* 293–305.

Weaver, C. (1994). Reconceptualizing reading and dyslexia. *Journal of Childhood Communication Disorders, 16,* 23–35.

Weber, R. (1970). A linguiistic analysis of first grade reading errors. *Reading Research Quarterly, 5,* 427–451.

Weekes, B. S. (1997). Differential effects of number of letters on word and nonword naming latency. *Quarterly Journal of Experimental Psychology, 50A*(2), 439–456.

Wheat, K. L., Cornelissen, P. L., Frost, S. J., & Hansen, P. C. (2010). During visual word recognition, phonology is accessed within 100 ms and may be mediated by a speech production code: Evidence from magnetoencephalography. *Journal of Neuroscience, 30,* 5229–5233.

Wheeler, D. D. (1970). Processes in word recognition. *Cognitive Psychology, 1,* 59–85.

White, S., Milne, E., Rosen, S., Hansen, P., Swettenham, J., Frith, U., & Ramus, F. (2006). The role of sensorimotor impairments in dyslexia: A multiple case study of dyslexic children. *Developmental Science, 9*(3), 237–255.

White, S. J., Rayner, K., & Liversedge, S. P. (2005a). Eye movements and the modulation of parafoveal processing by foveal processing difficulty. *Psychonomic Bulletin & Review, 12,* 891–896.

White, S. J., Rayner, K., & Liversedge, S. P. (2005b). The influence of parafoveal word length and contextual constraint on fixation durations and word skipping in reading. *Psychonomic Bulletin & Review, 12,* 466–471.

Whitehouse, D., & Harris, J. C. (1984). Hyperlexia in infantile autism. *Journal of Autism and Developmental Disorders, 14*(3), 281–289.

Whitehurst, G. J., & Lonigan, C. J. (1998). Child development and emergent literacy. *Child Development, 69,* 848–872.

Whitney, C. (2001). How the brain encodes the order of letters in a printed word: The SERIOL model and selective literature review. *Psychonomic Bulletin & Review, 8,* 221–243.

Whitney, C., & Cornelissen, P. (2008). SERIOL reading. *Language and Cognitive Processes, 23,* 143–164.

Wiley, J., & Myers, J. (2002). Availability and accessibility of causal inferences from scientific text. *Discourse Processes, 36,* 109–129.

Williams, C. C., Perea, M., Pollatsek, A., & Rayner, K. (2006). Previewing the neighborhood: The role of orthographic neighbors as parafoveal previews in reading. *Journal of Experimental Psychology: Human Perception and Performance, 32,* 1072–1082.

Williams, J. P. (1979). Reading instruction today. *American Psychologist, 34,* 917–922.

Williams, J. P. (1980). Teaching decoding with an emphasis on phoneme analysis and phoneme blending. *Journal of Educational Psychology, 72,* 1–15.

Williams, J. P., Blumberg, E. L., & Williams, D. V. (1970). Cues used in visual word recognition. *Journal of Educational Psychology, 61,* 310–315.

Williams, J. P., Taylor, M. B., & DeCani, J. S. (1984). Constructing macrostructure for expository text. *Journal of Educational Psychology, 76,* 1065–1075.

Williams, R. S., & Morris, R. K. (2004). Eye movements, word familiarity, and vocabulary acquisition. *European Journal of Cognitive Psychology, 16,* 312–339.

Willows, D. M., Borwick, D., & Hayvren, M. (1981). The content of school readers. In G. E. MacKinnon & T. G. Waller (Eds.), *Reading research: Advances in theory and practice* (Vol. 2). New York: Academic Press.

Wimmer, H., & Goswami, U. (1994). The influence of orthographic consistency on reading development: Word recognition in English and German children. *Cognition, 51*(1), 91–103.

Wimmer, H., & Hummer, P. (1990). How German-speaking first graders read and spell: Doubts on the importance of the logographic stage. *Applied Psycholinguistics, 11*(4), 349–368.

Wimmer, H., & Mayringer, H. (2001). Is the reading-rate problem of German dyslexic children caused by slow visual processes? In M. Wolf (Ed.), *Dyslexia, fluency, and the brain* (pp. 333–355). Parkton, MD: York Press.

Wimmer, H., & Mayringer, H. (2002). Dysfluent reading in the absence of spelling difficulties: A specific disability in regular orthographies. *Journal of Educational Psychology, 94*(2), 272–277.

Wimmer, H., Mayringer, H., & Landerl, K. (2000). The double-deficit hypothesis and difficulties in learning to read a regular orthography. *Journal of Educational Psychology, 92,* 668–680.

Wise, B. W., Ring, J., & Olson, R. K. (1999). Training phonological awareness with and without explicit attention to articulation. *Journal of Experimental Child Psychology, 72,* 271–304.

Witton, C., Talcott, J. B., Hansen, P. C., Richardson, A. J., Griffiths, T. D., Rees, A., et al. (1998). Sensitivity to dynamic auditory and visual stimuli predicts nonword reading ability in both dyslexic and normal readers. *Current Biology, 8,* 791–797.

Wittrock, M.C., Marks, C., & Doctorow, M. (1975). Reading as a generative process. *Journal of Educational Psychology, 67,* 484–489.

Wolf, M., & Bowers, P. G. (1999). The double-deficit hypothesis for the developmental dyslexias. *Journal of Educational Psychology, 91*(3), 415–438.

Wolf, M., Bowers, P. G., & Biddle, K. (2000). Naming-speed processes, timing, and reading: A conceptual review. *Journal of Learning Disabilities, 33*(4), 387–407.

Wolf, M., & Obregón, M. (1992). Early naming deficits, developmental dyslexia, and a specific deficithypothesis. *Brain and Language, 42*(3), 219–247.

Wolverton, G. S., & Zola, D. (1983). The temporal characteristics of visual information extraction during reading. In K. Rayner (Ed.), *Eye movements in reading: Perceptual and language processes.* New York: Academic Press.

Wood, F. B., & Felton, R. H. (1994). Separate linguistic and attentional factors in the development of reading. *Topics in Language Disorders [Special Issue: ADD and its Relationship to Spoken and Written Language], 14*(4), 42–57.

Woodworth, R. S. (1938). *Experimental psychology.* New York: Holt.

Yaden, D. B., Smolkin, L. B., & Conlon, A. (1989). Preschoolers' questions about pictures, print conventions, and story text during reading aloud at home. *Reading Research Quarterly, 24*(2),188–214.

Yan, M., Kliegl, R., Richter, E. M., Nuthmann, A., & Shu, H. (2010). Flexible saccade-target selection in Chinese reading. *The Quarterly Journal of Experimental Psychology, 63,* 705–725.

Yan, M., Richter, E. M., Shu, H., & Kliegl, R. (2009). Readers of Chinese extract semantic information from parafoveal words. *Psychonomic Bulletin & Review, 16,* 561–566.

Yang, J., Wang, S., Tong, X, & Rayner, K. (2011). Semantic and plausibility effects on preview benefit during eye fixations in Chinese reading. *Reading and Writing,* in press.

Yang, J., Wang, S., Xu, Y., & Rayner, K. (2009). Do Chinese readers obtain preview benefit from word n+2? Evidence from eye movements. *Journal of Experimental Psychology: Human Perception and Peformance, 35,* 1192–1204.

Yekovich, F. R., & Walker, C. H. (1978). Identifying and using referents in sentence comprehension. *Journal of Verbal Learning and Verbal Behavior, 17,* 265–277.

Yeni-Komshian, G. H., Isenberg, D., & Goldberg, H. (1975). Cerebral dominance and reading disability: Left visual field deficit in poor readers. *Neuropsychologia, 13,* 83–94.

Yik, W. F. (1978). The effect of visual and acoustic similarity on short-term memory for Chinese words. *Quarterly Journal of Experimental Psychology, 30,* 487–494.

Yuill, N., & Oakhill, J. (1991). *Children's problems in text comprehension: An experimental investigation.* New York: Cambridge University Press.

Yuill, N., Oakhill, J., & Parkin, A. J. (1989). Working memory, comprehension ability and the resolution of text anomaly. *British Journal of Psychology, 80*(3), 351–361.

Yule, W. (1973). Differential prognosis of reading backwardness and specific reading retardation. *British Journal of Educational Psychology, 43,* 244–8.

Yule, W., Rutter, M., Berger, M., & Thompson, J. (1974). Over and under achievement in reading: Distribution in the general population. *British Journal of Educational Psychology, 44,* 1–12.

Zangwill, O. L., & Blakemore, C. (1972). Dyslexia: Reversal of eye movements during reading. *Neuropsychologia, 10,* 371–373.

Zechmeister, E. B., & McKillip, J. (1972). Recall of place on the page. *Journal of Educational Psychology, 63,* 446–453.

Zetzsche, T., Meisenzahl, E. M., Preuss, U. W., Holder, J. J., Kathmann, N., Leinsinger, G., et al. (2001). In-vivo analysis of the human planum temporale (PT): Does the definition of PT borders influence the results with regard to cerebral asymmetry and correlation with handedness? *Psychiatry Research: Neuroimaging, 107*(2), 99–115.

Ziegler, J. C., & Goswami, U. (2005). Reading acquisition, developmental dyslexia, and skilled reading across languages: A psycholinguistic grain size theory. *Psychological Bulletin, 131,* 3–29.

Ziegler, J. C., Pech-Georgel, C., George, F., & Lorenzi, C. (2009). Speech-perception-in-noise deficits in dyslexia. *Developmental Science, 12*(5), 732–745.

Ziegler, J. C., Stone, G. O., & Jacobs, A. M. (1997). What's the pronunciation for _OUGH and the spelling for /u/? A database for computing feedforward and feedback inconsistency in English. *Behavior Research Methods, Instruments, & Computers, 29,* 600–618.

Zifcak, M. (1981). Phonological awareness and reading acquisition. *Contemporary Educational Psychology, 6,* 117–126.

Zola, D. (1984). Redundancy and word perception during reading. *Perception & Psychophysics, 36,* 277–284.

Zwaan, R. A. (1996). Processing narrative time shifts. *Journal of Experimental Psychology: Learning, Memory, and Cognition, 22,* 1196–1207.

Zwaan, R. A., & Radvansky, G. A. (1998). Situation models in language comprehension and memory. *Psychological Bulletin, 123*(2), 162–185.

AUTHOR INDEX

SUBJECT INDEX